MEDICAL ETHICS

A Guide for Health Professionals

Edited by

John F. Monagle, M.A., Ph.D.
President
American Institute of Medical Ethics
Davis, California

Adjunct Professor of Bioethics
Division of Professional Studies
University of San Francisco
San Francisco, California

Quality Assurance, Risk Management,
and Bioethical Education
Sullivan, Kelly & Associates, Inc.
Los Angeles, California

David C. Thomasma, Ph.D.
Fr. Michael I. English, S.J., Professor of Medical Ethics
Stritch School of Medicine
Loyola University Medical Center
Maywood, Illinois

AN ASPEN PUBLICATION®
Aspen Publishers, Inc.
1988

Rockville, Maryland
Royal Tunbridge Wells

Library of Congress Cataloging-in-Publication Data

Medical ethics.

"An Aspen publication."
Includes bibliographies and index.
1. Medical ethics. I. Monagle, John F.
II. Thomasma, David C., 1939-   . [DNLM: 1. Ethics,
Medical. W 50 M483]
R724.M29283 1988   174'.2   87-19511
ISBN: 0-87189-886-1

Editorial Services: Jane Coyle

Library of Congress Catalog Card Number: 87-19511
ISBN: 0-87189-886-1

Printed in the United States of America

1 2 3 4 5

To our teachers, instructors, and professors for instilling in us a love of the humanities and for encouraging our interest in the pursuit of medical ethics as a profession.

> For their worth cannot be measured against money, and they get no honor which will balance their services, but still it is perhaps enough, as it is with the gods and with one's parents, to give them what one can.

> —Aristotle, *Nicomachean Ethics* 1164b3–5

Table of Contents

PART VI—INSTITUTIONAL AND NATIONAL ISSUES

Contributors

Frederick R. Abrams, M.D.
Director, Center for Applied Medical
Ethics
Biomedical Ethics at Rose Medical
Center
Denver, Colorado

George J. Agich, Ph.D.
Associate Professor
Department of Medical Humanities
and Psychiatry
Director, Ethics and Philosophy of
Medicine Program
Southern Illinois University School of
Medicine
Springfield, Illinois

Susan S. Braithwaite, M.D.
Associate Professor
Department of Medicine, Section of
Endocrinology
Stritch School of Medicine
Loyola University Medical Center
Maywood, Illinois

Howard Brody, M.D., Ph.D.
Associate Professor and Coordinator
Medical Humanities Program
Department of Family Practice
Michigan State University Clinical
Center
East Lansing, Michigan

Jan S. Bruckner, P.T., M.S.
Assistant Professor
Physical Therapy Program
Division of Allied Health Sciences
Indiana University Medical Center
Indianapolis, Indiana

**Joel Brumlik, M.D., Ph.D. and
Stephanie A. Brumlik**
Professor
Department of Neurology
Stritch School of Medicine
Loyola University Medical Center
Maywood, Illinois

Sidney Callahan, Ph.D.
Associate Professor of Psychology
Consultant to Hastings Center
Mercy College
Dobbs Ferry, New York

Byron Chell, J.D.
General Counsel California Medical
Assistance Commission
Sacramento, California
Visiting Lecturer in Bioethics School
of Medicine
University of California
Davis, California

**David B. Clarke, Jr., D.Mn.,
J.D., M.P.H.**
Member of Bar
Commonwealth of Pennsylvania
Legislative Advocate for Hemlock
    Society
Sacramento, California

Gene Cleaver, M.D.
President
Siskiyou County Medical Society
Member
Committee on Evolving Trends in
    Society Affecting Life (Bioethics)
California Medical Association
Vice Chief of Staff
Mercy Medical Center Mt. Shasta
Mt. Shasta, California

Elena N. Cohen, J.D.
Staff Attorney
Society for the Right to Die
New York, New York

Maynard M. Cohen, M.D., Ph.D.
Professor of Neurology
Rush Medical Center
Chicago, Illinois

John A. Eaddy, M.D.
Associate Professor
Family Practice
University of Tennessee Memorial
    Research Center and Hospital
Knoxville, Tennessee

William J. Ellos, S.J., Ph.D.
Associate Professor of Philosophy
Adjunct Associate Professor, Medical
    Humanities
Stritch School of Medicine
Loyola University Medical Center
Maywood, Illinois

Edmund L. Erde, Ph.D.
Professor
Department of Family Practice
UMDNJ/SOM
Camden, New Jersey

Joseph Fletcher, S.T.D.
Visiting Scholar in Medical Ethics
School of Medicine
University of Virginia
Charlottesville, Virginia

Glenn C. Graber, Ph.D.
Director
University Studies
Professor of Philosophy
Clinical Medical Ethics Associate
University of Tennessee
Knoxville, Tennessee

Ruth Greenblatt, M.D.
University of California Medical
    Center
San Francisco, California

Arlene Gruber, M.A., M.S.W.
Department of Social Work
Foster G. McGaw Hospital
Loyola University Medical Center
Maywood, Illinois

**R. Morrison Hurley, M.D.,
M.Sc., F.R.C.P.(c)**
Professor and Chairman
Department of Pediatrics
Stritch School of Medicine
Loyola University Medical Center
Maywood, Illinois

Harold J. Jensen, M.D.
Clinical Assistant Professor of
    Medicine
University of Illinois College of
    Medicine

Immediate Past President, Chicago
  Medical Society
Vice-President of Medical Affairs
Ingalls Memorial Hospital
Harvey, Illinois

Eric T. Juengst, Ph.D.
Adjunct Assistant Professor
Division of Medical Ethics
School of Medicine
Department of Medicine
University of California
San Francisco, California

Bernard Lo, M.D.
Assistant Professor
Division of General Internal Medicine
University of California Medical
  Center
San Francisco, California

Erich H. Loewy, M.D., F.A.C.P.
Assistant Professor of Medicine
University of Illinois College of
  Medicine at Peoria
Adjunct Professor of Humanities
  (Ethics)
University of Illinois at Chicago
Chicago, Illinois

**Richard A. McCormick, S.J.,
S.T.D.**
John A. O'Brien Professor of
  Christian Ethics
Department of Theology
University of Notre Dame
Notre Dame, Indiana

Kenneth C. Micetich, M.D.
Associate Professor
Department of Medicine
Section of Hematology and Oncology
Stritch School of Medicine
Loyola University Medical Center
Maywood, Illinois

Nancy Milliken, M.D.
Robert Wood Johnson Scholar
Fellow
University of California Medical
  Center
San Francisco, California

John F. Monagle, M.A., Ph.D.
President
American Institute of Medical
  Ethics
Davis, California
Adjunct Professor of Bioethics
Division of Professional Studies
University of San Francisco
San Francisco, California
Quality Assurance, Risk
  Management and Bioethical
  Education
Sullivan, Kelly & Associates, Inc.
Los Angeles, California

**Laurence J. O'Connell, Ph.D.,
S.T.D.**
Vice President
Theology and Ethics
The Catholic Health Association of
  the United States
St. Louis, Missouri

David T. Ozar, Ph.D.
Associate Professor of Philosophy
Adjunct Associate Professor
Medical Humanities
Stritch School of Medicine
Loyola University Medical Center
Maywood, Illinois

Edmund D. Pellegrino, M.D.
John Carroll Professor of Medicine
  and Medical Humanities
Director
Kennedy Institute for Ethics
Georgetown University Medical
  Center
Washington, D.C.

Paul J. Reitemeier, M.A.
Michigan State University
Medical Humanities Program
East Lansing, Michigan

Domeena C. Renshaw, M.D.
Professor and Associate Chairperson
of Psychiatry
Director: Sexual Dysfunction Clinic
Stritch School of Medicine
Loyola University Medical Center
Maywood, Illinois

Donnie J. Self, Ph.D.
Professor
Department of Humanities in
Medicine
Texas A&M University College of
Medicine
College Station, Texas

Mark Sheldon, Ph.D.
Associate Professor of Philosophy and
Adjunct Associate Professor of
Medicine
Indiana University
Gary, Indiana
Senior Policy Analyst
American Medical Association
Chicago, Illinois

**Bonita Bergman Sheldon, Ph.D.,
M.P.H.**
Coordinator of Children and
Families in Transition
Department of Pediatrics
Department of Psychiatry
Evanston Hospital
Evanston, Illinois
Associate Faculty
Department of Psychiatry
Northwestern University Medical
School
Adjunct Assistant Professor
Graduate School

Department of Psychology
Northwestern University
Evanston, Illinois

D. Alan Shewmon, M.D.
Assistant Professor
Division Pediatric Neurology
University of California, Los Angeles
Center for Health Sciences
Los Angeles, California

Jack C. Siebe, M.D.
Medical Director, Consultant Medical
Staff Credentials and Quality
Assurance
Merrillville, Indiana

Joy D. Skeel, R.N., Mn.Div.
Director
Program in Medical Humanities
Departments of Psychiatry and
Medicine
Medical College of Ohio
Toledo, Ohio

**John H. Sorenson, D.Min.,
M.S.W.**
Chief
Division of Medical Humanities
The Medical College of Pennsylvania
Philadelphia, Pennsylvania

Patricia H. Steinecker, M.D.
Assistant Professor of Medicine
Section of Oncology
Rush Medical College
Chicago, Illinois

David C. Thomasma, Ph.D.
Fr. Michael I. English, S.J.,
Professor of Medical Ethics
Stritch School of Medicine

Loyola University Medical Center
Maywood, Illinois

Jo Ann Wegmann, R.N., Ph.D.
Associate Director of Nursing
Foster G. McGaw Hospital
Loyola University Medical Center
Maywood, Illinois

Charles H. White, Ph.D.
Executive Assistant to the Chief of
Staff
Grossmont District Hospital
Le Mesa, California
Formerly Senior Vice President
California Hospital Association
Sacramento, California

Preface

This book is for practicing health professionals who wish to become better informed about current and emerging ethical issues. Members of hospital ethics committees will find it especially helpful. Rather than cover well-examined ethical issues in health care, we encouraged the authors of our chapters (all authorities in their fields) to consider problems at the "cutting edge" of health care today.

Thus, the book can be considered a compendium of contemporary medical ethics, but importantly different from other such texts. Abortion receives only peripheral mention, while issues are thoroughly explored in geriatrics, competency, medical care for the poor, death and dying, advance directives, justice and economics, clinical ethics consults, medical gatekeeping, rehabilitation medicine, critical care nursing, computerized medical ethics, and sexual and elder abuse, to name only a few.

As a consequence of these far-reaching discussions, the book can also be used as a text in medical ethics courses. The chapters are authored by professionals in health care, health law, health administration, and health ethics. This variety demonstrates our conviction that bioethics embraces not only the patient's own perspective but those of all disciplines involved in the delivery of care. No single professional stance is adequate. An interdisciplinary approach is required by the complexity of the issues.

The chapters fall into two categories. Some present a current summary of positions on an issue in an unsettled territory of ethics in health care (e.g., genetic control, reproductive technologies). Others offer a sustained argument for one or another position (e.g., withdrawing care from comatose patients).

Within the limitations of space, we tried to balance such positions by an opposing point of view. Our readers should not assume that the authors or editors agree with one another. Nonetheless themes do emerge. All of our authors either explicitly assert or implicitly assume that resolutions to ethical dilemmas require exploring shared values in health care, that there is a hierarchy of human values in medicine, and that the patient's own values should most often prevail.

The book progresses from birth to death issues, and then from these to institutional and social ones. The final section contains chapters on ethical theories and a methodology for resolving ethical issues. Appendix A is a glossary of terms. If a chapter does not define its terms, it can be assumed that the glossary will do so.

Finally, certain central ideas, such as autonomy, patient rights, living wills, and euthanasia, are discussed from various perspectives in two or more different chapters. While such chapters overlap, each presents a specific point of view not found in the other or others. References and annotated bibliographies are usually provided for further study.

We hope that everyone reading this book will find a wealth of material to stimulate individual thinking and group discussion and provide a basis for resolving the clinical and institutional problems that face us now and that will arise in the foreseeable future.

John F. Monagle
David C. Thomasma

Acknowledgments

We wish to thank our professional colleagues, who labored under difficult deadlines, for so graciously believing in the potential of this book. Also Marjorie Monagle deserves our gratitude for her help in coordinating and editing the project, Lyn Thomasma for her insightful discussions and encouragement, and John P. McNulty, our research assistant. Finally we are in debt to our secretaries, Jo Ann Immekus, Kay Cahill Scarano, and Rebecca Norris, for their tireless assistance in preparing this manuscript.

Part I

Conception, Birth, and Adolescence

Chapter 1

Ethics and Genetic Control

Joseph Fletcher

Too often professional people in the health field fail to appreciate that modern medicine has created a strain on conventional wisdom. At both the clinical and research levels, medical advances have brought innovations which, at least initially, cut across traditional *mores* and sentiments, setting up tensions in both the patient population and the general public and leading to "intracultural shock."

Innovations of this kind might include delivering babies weeks or even months after the mother was pronounced "brain dead" (but artificially kept "going" by respirators and tube feeding) or having babies conceived in a dish in a medical laboratory, not in a mother's womb. We could draw up a long list of such new wrinkles in modern medicine. People often view them with distaste, if not with horror.

In the past half century, such discomforting innovations have been occurring wave after wave, with almost exponential frequency—not because of medicine's failure but because of its successes. It is the business of biomedical ethics to investigate the resulting shocks. It is these shocks or tensions that have fueled biomedical ethics and changed it into a significant discipline in the health services. When we find we *can* do something, the next question is whether we *ought* to (and with what limiting principles).

These science-related shocks have been particularly frequent in the field of genetics. In the nineteenth century—getting its start with the Austrian monk Gregor Mendel's selective reproduction of peas—genetics was only a matter of mathematics and empirical inferences. But in the present century, with the emergence of molecular genetics and with direct microscopic knowledge rather than inference, genetics has furnished one startling innovation or discovery after another. To put it fashionably, we have begun to "tinker" with or change the very building blocks of life (human and nonhuman).

We have all heard of families threatened with the risk of genetically diseased or defective children because of the biological mechanisms of inheritance. Such frightful disorders as cystic fibrosis, Huntington's disease, hemophilia, retinoblastoma, and polycystic kidney disease can be detected by testing before birth. Out of the 1500 such conditions already identified, about 200 can now be tested for, with more and more tests to come as genetic medicine progresses. However, a new test often means a heartrending decision to terminate some pregnancies, and for some in the patient population abortion is believed to be at least as wrong as bringing such unfortunates into the world. The tension and conflict cries aloud for sympathy.

One patient once said to this writer, after she had been informed of the options the new knowledge heaps upon expectant mothers, "I wish to God it was still as simple to have a baby as it was when my mother had me." The irony is that medicine's successes lead to an increase of anxieties, adding sometimes almost unbearably to the patient's decision-making burden. Biomedical ethics is by no means mere "fooling around" with far-fetched questions that are of only academic interest.

One more observation needs to be made here before we look at the ethical problems posed by our fast-growing control over the building blocks of life. Science, let it be said, does not and cannot work behind walls and fences. The affect of one discipline on others, as well as their interplay with practice or practical use, is such that credit for genetic advances should not go to genetics alone, but to a coalition or array of biological sciences, including micrometry, virology, molecular chemistry, bacteriology, and physical chemistry.

RECENT INNOVATIONS

We could plunge at once into the ethics of controlling ("manipulating") life and health through genetics, but for at least some it may be helpful to consider a few recent innovations in genetic engineering or control to help provide a realistic context for purposes of discussion. The "what" of our subject needs some preliminary attention, even though the "why" will be our main focus.

We might start where the tension between culture and science is perhaps slightest, with plant genetics. Until quite recently, genetics in agriculture and horticulture was based on the old Mendelian principles. If a desirable vegetable or flower was wanted, it was aimed at by selective reproduction. New and improved strains of corn, for example, were achieved by selecting the ones that came closest to what was wanted, then germinating and crossbreeding them.

The Russian Maliutka tomato is a case in point. Botanists grew the tomatoes in one place, moved them a hundred miles north, and did this again and still again, each time selecting the hardiest ones, until at last by grafting and crossbreeding they got the famous subarctic variety. Now, however, plant genetics can produce a totally new "breed" in a single generation and in a single setting by such techniques as gene insertion, deletion, and splicing.

For example, a genetics team at Stanford recently found out how to alter plant genes by micrometric splicing to get plants not only hardier but yielding heavier crops. They can put cactus genes into soybeans, corn, and wheat, getting less thirsty strains that need less water and less irrigation and therefore cost less to grow. At about the same time, in San Diego, firefly genes were inserted into tobacco plants, not only giving them a telltale glow but letting the scientists tag or mark the genes, thus learning more about how and when genes switch their functions on and off. Here, then, is a tobacco plant totally without any precedent in nature, a mutation by design rather than by accident, a rational or controlled innovation.

In a word, biotechnology is here. One of the issues of "social ethics" raised by this development is whether the creation of new forms of reproducible life should be considered private enterprise, with patents and protected monopolies of the sort that typify general commerce. A more fundamental question is whether biologists and geneticists should ever create such new forms of life to begin with, irrespective of who would profit by it or how the profits would be distributed.

Similar questions arise in animal husbandry. To be specific, genetic manipulation has produced a new growth hormone for cattle called bgH (bovine growth hormone). It increases milk production by a good 20 percent. In this particular case, the genetic innovation is fiercely opposed by a coalition of antigenetics ideologues (who disapprove of genetic control on ethical and religious grounds) and milk and dairy agribusiness investors (who stand to lose their profit margin because of how the genetic change will affect supply and demand).

With a little imagination, we can appreciate how genetics has the potential to invade a wide range of areas of interest, not only health, but custom and tradition, markets, money, law, and public policy. For example, on the international scene, the U.S. delegation is vetoing attempts by the United Nations' Food and Agricultural Organization to make new genetic strains of plants available to the underdeveloped nations, whether the strains have been developed either by biotechnology or more primitive methods. The availability of such strains is opposed because helping to counteract the threat of famine in such countries as Chad or Upper Volta or Ethiopia would weaken the profitable monopolies enjoyed by the Western interests that researched the better strains. Since the wild strains came largely from the undeveloped countries in the first place, Third World spokesmen call this Western policy "genetic imperialism." Such monopolization is legally protected in America by the federal Plant Variety Protection Act.

The attention of moral philosophers or ethicists has been mostly focused, however, on human or medical genetics. They have found it helpful to distinguish between two kinds of human genetic control. First, there is *therapeutic genetics*, that is, genetics used to cure or palliate genetic defects and diseases in patients. Second, there is *orthogenic genetics*, that is, genetics used to eliminate genes or repair chromosomes in the germline of people carrying unwanted inheritable traits. The first kind of genetics deal with the somatic or body cells of persons already born with genetic troubles; it tries to correct ills due to faults in the nonreproductive cells. The second kind deals with faults and errors in the reproductive or sexual cells *ab initio*. Both kinds of human genetics are on the drawing board.

Of the three leading techniques of genetic control (some antipathetic writers use the loaded term *manipulation*), it is gene splicing or cloning which is the most advanced. (The other two techniques are gene insertion and gene deletion.) A good example of the benefits of gene splicing is *humulin*, a new genetically designed form of human insulin. A major American pharmaceutical company has been licensed recently by the Food and Drug Administration to develop it by recombining selected cloned genes. This process creates a hormone which is something totally new in medicine's armamentarium; it makes it possible at last to produce the insulin which a diabetic's body simply cannot produce in big enough quantities. In consequence, life can be made easier for hundreds of thousands of patients.

Genetic engineering is not all smooth sailing. Far from it. Yet even a false trail can prove to be profitable. Take the work on Down's syndrome, for example. The latest stratagem is to try to develop models of this inherited disease using mice. Mice are research models for a lot of medical inquiry because biological phenomena in humans and mice are remarkably alike, strange as it may seem.

Neuroscientists have managed to develop models of genetic makeup for this purpose (an extra chromosome 21 in mice results in the same traits or physiological expressions). Thu , investigators now have sophisticated tools for learning how they can treat not only the mental retardation of Down's syndrome, but also the heart disease, facial distortion, premature senility, and early death that go with it—treat it by one or more of the methods of gene splicing, insertion, or deletion.

Finally, we might look at one more medical innovation which illustrates how science and conventional ethics are brought into tension, if not actual conflict. In this case we have a classic instance of the combined forces of microbiology, including genetics and other disciplines such as virology, bacteriology, embryology, and chemistry. A French pharmaceutical company has produced RU-486, a form of chemical abortion or "contragestation." American scientists are speeding down a parallel track. RU-486 is a substance of unprecedented molecular structure, altogether new in the pharmacology of reproductive medicine. It prevents the lining of the uterus (the endometrium) from getting progesterone. Therefore, a fertilized ovum either cannot implant or is turned loose quickly after implantation. Some would call it a cross between a contraceptive and an abortifacient. Incidentally, it has no steroid in it and thus escapes the unwelcome side effects experienced with the Pill. In the U.S., it is still held off the market by the National Institutes of Health and the F.D.A. for further study, including "lab" work and test runs, but the World Health Organization has announced it will be available this year.

It is easy to imagine the impact of RU-486 on antiabortionists in our society. Here is a new little pill which the user can take without knowing whether she is aborting an implanted or unimplanted early embryo—without knowing whether it is abortion or not. Abortion will thus become a private matter, as private as taking the Pill. The line between abortion and prevention of conception will be blurred, even for those with the most finely drawn distinctions.

In a sense, all of this is leading up to orthogenic genetic control, which involves changing the genetic constitution of a person. It goes beyond treating people with deadly or disfiguring defects by body or somatic genetics. It is a matter of controlling the germline by changing the reproductive cells—the cells in the sperm and ova—so that inheritable diseases and defects will be eliminated and not passed on to descendants. Sooner or later orthogenic genetics could eliminate or obviate muscular dystrophy, sickle cell anemia, Tay-Sachs disease, pyloric stenosis, and a long list of other genetic diseases and defects.

Eugenics, which was investigated earlier in this century, tried to reach its goals by increasing the frequency of desirable genes and decreasing the frequency of undesirable genes. It is now the case that new genes can be either synthesized or modified or normal genes substituted for abnormal ones.

Eugenics was felt to be unfair, because, like plant and animal husbandry at that time, it was proceeded by selective reproduction. This required that the genetically unfortunate had to be denied their natural desire to have children. But molecular genetics has eliminated such discrimination. Individuals with a questionable genetic makeup can now act on their desire for children, that is, they can improve their germline and reproduce without having their offspring suffer from genetic problems. Furthermore, they may get genetic help for their own defective condition by therapeutic genetic controls.

DOUBTS AND RESISTANCE

Here, then, are some practical modalities which might help to illustrate the ethical issues posed by genetic influences on human life and well-being. In prescientific times, breeding "supermen" or making humans by other than the natural sexual process was a favorite theme of mythmakers. But the mythmakers were always ambivalent about it. Faustus tried it by the philosopher's stone—in Goethe's version with the Homunculus in the phial. Icelandic sagas used androids, half human and half nonhuman. Prometheus came a cropper by trying to make men like gods. Golem were treated in the Talmud and by the cabalists very ambivalently. Paracelsus got good marks and bad. Mary Shelley's Frankenstein started good and ended bad.

The general public is more apt to have doubts about genetic control than those closer to the biological frontiers. Physicians and scientists often have technical doubts about the discoverability or workability of some genetic designs, but they seldom object on moral grounds. Their test is consequentialist: Does it or would it cure illness or promote health? If the answer is affirmative, with both remote and immediate effects taken into account, they find no fault.

Perhaps the most common ground of resistance (except for religious or authoritarian prohibitions) is what we call the *wedge* or *slippery slope* objection. One form of the objection is the claim that although one or a few uses of genetic control may result in good consequences, using it again or often would end in disaster. A second form is the claim that the immediate consequences of an innovation are acceptable, but the ultimate consequences would be disastrous. In both forms, the objection comes down to "Don't do it or you'll be sorry." Moral philosophers tend to regard slippery slope arguments with reservation. They have always been a feature of discussions in bars and bridge clubs, but they are also simplistic and often based on fear more than insight. There is hardly anything of use which is not misused or abused. An ancient principle in ethical reasoning is *abusus non tollit usum*—the possible abuse of a thing does not bar its constructive use. This seems to be the cast of thinking in medical and scientific circles.

We might add here, that the slippery slope objections to genetic engineering should not be confused with the cardinal virtue of prudence. Prudence tells us that if a course of action is one in which the foreseeably good consequences are, on balance, *probably* outweighed by bad consequences, we should forego it. Only a moment's reflection is needed to see that this differs from the slippery slope objections which hold that if a course of action might *possibly* weigh more heavily on the bad side, it ought to be foregone. This could, of course, apply to everything that is new and innovative. All human foresight is at best limited and we cannot exclude risk and error in any human deed or enterprise. In short, the slippery slope objections are at best uncreative timidity and at worst inanition, leading to moral lethargy.

People in science and medicine march to a different drum. They are accustomed to count benefits in terms of human health and comfort and their experience with our finite abilities leads them to give up any hope of simple or utter success at anything we try. Instead, they are familiar with making tradeoffs concerning the ends they seek. Almost always, the good they seek is seen as proportionate good—seldom, if ever, as perfect good. They are not idealists, either metaphysically or ethically; neither are they perfectionists.

How are we to cope, then, with the belief of many people that relativity in ethics is a false doctrine and subversive of moral standards? Even if we can fairly clearly identify and define our values, when we face "quality control" questions we soon discover that (1) we do not always agree on what is or is not a value (i.e., what is valuable or desirable) and (2) we do not all rank our values in the same order of priority. In other words, there seems little doubt that values *are* relative—relative, first, to the wants and wishes of individuals. Secondly, we do not all prize the same things, and even when we do, some will assign the highest value to things that others regard as only second or third in importance.

We have still another issue in ethical discourse, one which is of the highest importance for examining the value of genetics in itself, as well as for attempting to evaluate specific goals and purposes in genetics. Scientists tend to think in terms of *true* or *false* and they focus on facts; ethicists deal with *right* or *wrong* and they focus on values. People in general probably have a little of both focuses in the way they look at and discuss problems. If this is the case, it may mean that scientists need to strike a better balance between true-false and right-wrong.

Whatever the reason, scientifically oriented people such as geneticists seem somewhat out of synch with a large part of the public. The public's visceral reaction to innovations is usually mixed with fear of the unknown or the new. For many morally concerned people, the bird in the hand is worth more than the two in the bush. Among them are a minority that feel so opposed to genetics they condemn basic research—even of the most tentative kind. This radical posture raises the question, "If you don't know about something, how can you know whether you ought to know about it or not?"

This was seen in the seventies in the highly vocal opposition to research on gene splicing (recombinant DNA). Opponents aroused a fear that it was hazardous and might result in a decimating worldwide epidemic of strange diseases about which we would know nothing and against which we would have no defense. The handful of scientists who lent credibility to this fear have pretty much retreated into the background. One such scientist had been among the first to isolate a gene; he quit the whole field in 1970, afraid he was part of a threat against the human species.

This radical opposition to genetics has had some limited play in theological ethics, where it found a certain amount of support in the pseudoconsequentialist language of the slippery slope. Nonetheless, the opposition reflects a deep-seated uneasiness, and even if the resistance is more visceral than rational, it is typically human and deserves to be heard and seriously discussed. This is precisely the role of biomedical ethics.

Moral philosophy has a real stake in finding out what is true in the popular critique of genetics. Ethicists should not fall into the fallacy that because we can do something, we therefore ought to do it; nor into another fallacy, that because we can do something, we will be sure to do it. It is the proper business of ethics to find and formulate sound limiting principles on all human initiatives, whether they be in genetic research, birth technologies, the management of terminal illness, or any other area of medicine.

Another doubt about the liceity of genetic control is tied to respect for life. If we exercise radical control over the source of life (the "stuff" of life), will it not encourage a kind of arrogance? (This appears to be a part of the wedge objection.) Does it not cheapen life—the objection runs—to tailor life genetically, whether plant, animal, or human, by changing its makeup at will? Are we not degrading life if we conceive it in laboratory petri dishes or nurture it in glass containers rather than in human tissue wombs? Is it not disrespectful of life itself to "manufacture" lives by intervening in the gene structure and heredity of people?

It is not easy to take hold of a doubt like this, being so subjective and so untied to any specific course of reasoning. It is indeed more visceral than rational. Yet there it is, lurking in the cultural ambience, causing people to look with moral doubt or fear at how biology and medicine function. The idea that life as such is sacrosanct, that it is not only the highest good but somehow sacred and not to be tampered with, is obviously untenable in actual practice. On such an ethical basis, there could be no heroism or martyrdom, nor even any killing in self-defense.

All absolutes and universals are constantly contradicted by the very people who preach them (however sincerely). If they make persons the highest good, the *summum bonum*, their moral inconsistencies might be somewhat less obvious, but to hold that life as such is untouchable runs into too many exceptions to stand up as a moral rule.

Doubts based on respect for life remind us of the constant tension between a sanctity-of-life ethics and a quality-of-life ethics, which are two ethical positions that are often opposed to each other in the making of many clinical decisions and many policies. (Here, by the way, may well be the most fundamental and far-reaching philosophical issue running through biomedical ethics.)

The respect-for-life objection is tied psychologically to the feeling that genetic mastery of life will destroy life's mystery and that its mystery is essential for generating respect for it. This would appear to reinforce the "stop meddling" attitude favoring blissful ignorance—which would undermine or at least hobble not only genetics but the biology and chemistry which underlie it. However, most people seem inclined to agree that whatever favors ignorance is itself disrespectful of humankind and, as Aristotle explained long ago, is doomed to go down before one of the distinctive traits of humans: curiosity. Ethics has a ripe field here for analysis and explication.

Since religious beliefs are so widely (and often almost unconsciously) held, one of the most striking objections to genetic engineering and control concerns what the Greeks called *hubris*, that is, the overweening pride or presumptuousness of humans trying to "play God" and usurping what is proper to God alone. In this view, genetic control seems to be not humble enough; it seems to invite disaster, as in the myth of Icarus, who made himself wings to fly but tumbled to his death as a result, or of Adam and Eve, who ate the fruit of the tree of the knowledge of good and evil and were exiled from the Garden of Eden as punishment. (Ethics, let it be noted, is precisely the attempt of human thinkers to understand right and wrong, good and evil, and to choose between them—to eat the apple and to chew it well.)

There was a time, not so long ago, when many, if not most, human communities looked to God as the final moral court of appeal. They shared the same beliefs about God and for the most part accepted the same revelations of what God wills. But all of this is changed. People now live in communities which are religiously pluralistic and moral philosophers are no longer authoritarian. Jet travel moves us in a day from one distant culture to another, making it impossible to go on thinking about religious sanctions in the simple way we did when we lived in isolated, immutable, separate worlds.

Those who believe in God realize for the most part that they cannot draw universal norms or rules of conduct for daily decision making from what they themselves happen to believe about God or the supernatural. Perhaps most religionists—not all—agree that we can claim at best that God would have us live in love and peace; how to do so is no longer "set in stone" or in codes but is open-ended and up to responsible human moral agents to determine.

It is against some such religious backdrop as this that biomedical ethicists are trying to respond to the charge that genetic control is hubristic and impious. One thing is fairly certain: Nothing is to be gained and much might be lost if the problem is ignored or only dealt with superficially. Among the questions which we must consider when confronting the complaint that genetics (like medicine itself) is "playing God" are (1) whether genetics is indeed playing a role which religion would once have condemned as impious and dangerous (because it "invites God's wrath") and (2) which God exactly is genetics playing at being. How do we describe this God in relation to human initiatives and innovations?

Here, surely, is a point of tension between geneticists and the public, and biomedical ethics has here a well-defined task. The probability that it may make many scientists and philosophers uncomfortable is not a good reason for leaving this task to be accomplished using semantic bandaids. We owe it to sincere religious believers to deal with it straightforwardly and constructively.

Closely related to the complaint that geneticists play God is the common notion that genetic manipulation is somehow against nature, that genetics is unnatural or antinatural. The feeling that this is so is apparently tied to the idea that God is the creator—the author or constructor of the world—and has endowed human beings with their proper makeup. Therefore, to cause changes at such an elemental level is to defy the divine purpose and prerogative. Is this belief perhaps a religious form of determinism and thus not in keeping with the equally popular notion that man is a free creature? Does it, as some critics of religion have contended, entail fatalism—the idea that what is is what ought to be and that therefore whatever happens to be the constitution of an individual or a germline of individuals is right and good? Is it a question of an ethics of control versus a fatalistic ethics or an ethics of choice versus an ethics of chance?

As we have already remarked, medicine, by definition, clashes with fatalism and with any idea that what is natural is *ipso facto* good. If human beings are to be moral agents, choice makers, which is what ethics presupposes they are, can they be supine before any existing state of affairs, be it natural, political, or personal? Is there a balance between human freedom and the sovereignty of nature, and can biomedical ethics establish what it is?

A major difficulty is that the word *natural* has more than a dozen different definitions and connotations; it is a veritable semantic swamp. Awareness of this difficulty is usually more implicit than explicit in scientific discourse. Medicine is patently an interference with nature and natural processes (what theologians often speak of as "the created order"). We might even say medicine uses nature to outwit itself—to outwit such natural phenomena as deformity and disease. Medical genetics extends our medical capabilities.

Art, artifice, artifacts, the artificial—these each involve creative manipulations of "nature." Manipulation occurs when a sculptor reshapes a piece of marble, a surgeon reshapes a body of flesh and bone, or a geneticist reshapes a plant, animal, or human being. Is there any convincing reason for saying that the natural is morally superior to the artificial? If an event happens or if any object exists, it is therefore natural. Thus runs the thinking of people in medicine and genetics.

There is still another line of objection to genetic control, one that might at first sight appear to be more scientifically oriented. This is the objection that since geneticists tinker with the basic building blocks of life, they are in effect rejecting the wisdom of evolutionary biology. Evolution, to be sure, is a long-term, hunt-and-peck process of biological change, whereas genetics can bring about changes instantly—by deleting, inserting, or splicing genes.

As remarked above, several quite distinguished scientists have argued that today's genetic engineering attempts may be too hasty and thus may result in a worldwide disaster. It was this attitude which led them to support an attempt in the seventies to put a stop to even the most primitive research on gene splicing or cloning, on the grounds that lethal artificial bacteria might escape from laboratories and spread through a world unable to save itself from the unknown killer.

This is, to be sure, a slippery slope objection, but nevertheless it is, arguably, a morally motivated objection and therefore deserves to be fully explored. It should not be dismissed out of hand just because it expresses a mood rather than a reasoned line of argument. The fact is that the objection strikes a chord of concern among the general public, as real as the concern about a nuclear holocaust, and therefore we have substantial cause to explore the issue of ethical principles limiting both research and practice.

The attempt in this chapter to be impartial and to look clearsightedly at genetics and the moral problems it poses may for some readers be a failure. Therefore, the author closes with a quotation from a paper he published ten years ago in *The New England Journal of Medicine* (volume 285, pp. 776–783). This is a frank and candid statement of the bias running through this chapter. (If we agree with another's bias, we call it a conviction; if we do not agree, we call it a prejudice.)

> Man is a maker and a selector and a designer, and the more rationally contrived and deliberate anything is, the more human it is. Any attempt to set up an antinomy between natural and biologic reproduction, on the one hand, and artificial or designed reproduction, on the other, is absurd. The real difference is between accidental or random reproduction and rationally willed and chosen reproduction.
>
> In either case it will be biologic—i.e., according to the nature of the biological process. If it is "unnatural" it can be so only in the sense that all medicine is.
>
> It seems to me that laboratory reproduction is radically human compared to conception by ordinary heterosexual intercourse. It is willed, chosen, purposed and controlled, and surely these are among the traits that distinguish *Homo sapiens* from others in the animal genus, from the primates down. Coital reproduction is, therefore, less human than laboratory reproduction—more fun to be sure, but with our separation of babymaking from lovemaking, both become more human because they are matters of choice and not chance.
>
> This is, of course, essentially the case for planned parenthood. I cannot see how either humanity or morality are served by genetic roulette.

Chapter 2

Prenatal Diagnosis and the Ethics of Uncertainty

Eric T. Juengst

The practice of prenatal diagnosis has come of age with the twenty-first anniversary of the first chromosomal analysis of human amniocytes.[1] The discussion of the moral problems that the practice of chromosomal analysis can pose is almost as old.[2] This chapter reviews that discussion with an eye towards the issues that are particularly important for the practitioner. Many of the ethical issues that were raised during the infancy of prenatal diagnosis still influence clinical policies about its use. Some of these issues have been resolved with the accumulation of experience. The first part of the chapter surveys the points on which consensus has been reached. The second part examines the new questions that practitioners should prepare for as the practice of prenatal diagnosis matures.

There are now a number of techniques relevant to the diagnosis of diseases and defects *in utero*.[3] Some, like fetal biopsy techniques, are informative, but relatively invasive.[4] Others, like maternal serum screening for fetal proteins, are less risky, but also less revealing.[5] This chapter concentrates on two techniques that occupy the middle ground: amniocentesis and chorionic villi sampling. In amniocentesis, a needle is inserted through the mother's abdominal and uterine walls into the amniotic sac to withdraw fluid containing fetal amniocytes.[6] Chorionic villi sampling involves passing a catheter vaginally into the uterus to aspirate a sample of fetal tissue from the developing placenta.[7] Both kinds of fetal tissue are then available for analysis by a growing number of cytological, biochemical, and molecular tests.[8]

Amniocentesis is the oldest of the prenatal diagnostic techniques and has received the most ethical attention. The discussion has focused on four sets of questions, more or less in succession: (1) questions about how amniocentesis should be introduced into practice, given the initial uncertainties that surrounded it; (2) questions about the purpose of amniocentesis and the appropriate indications for its use; (3) questions about the moral dynamics of the practitioner-patient relationship in light of the problems in identifying patients that amniocentesis would benefit; and (4) questions about the future of prenatal diagnosis as a medical practice and the consequences of such diagnosis for our cultural and professional values.

Note: The research and writing of this chapter was supported in part by a grant from the Ethics and Values Studies program of the National Science Foundation.

This chapter surveys the current debate on these questions for amniocentesis and uses the review to highlight some issues raised by chorionic villi sampling. Chorionic villi sampling is still an experimental procedure, but its promise as a clinical alternative to amniocentesis is great. Its rapidly increasing use suggests that the ethical issues it raises will be the most prominent ones regarding prenatal diagnosis during its maturity.

Notice that all four sets of questions about amniocentesis involve forms of uncertainty: empirical uncertainty about the utility and safety of the technique, moral uncertainty about the justifications for its use, conceptual uncertainty about the "patient" it serves, and social uncertainty about its long-term effects. The ethics of uncertainty has provided a constant background to the discussion of amniocentesis. This background is emphasized in what follows to suggest some of its more important implications for the clinical practice of prenatal diagnosis.

RISK, BENEFITS, AND ELIGIBILITY CRITERIA

Two kinds of ethical questions almost always accompany the introduction of a new biomedical technology: questions about its unknown hazards and questions about its distribution. A novel technology, by definition, lacks the clinical record that usually supports medical assessments of risk. This raises concerns about how best to compile that record without placing patients in undue danger. A new technology is also usually scarce, if only because there are few clinicians experienced in its use. This raises concerns about how best to allocate the new resource among the patients whom it might benefit.

Amniocentesis was no exception on either score. The earliest discussions focused on the procedure's unmeasured potential for infection, hemorrhage, spontaneous abortion, and developmental damages to the fetus.[9] The uncertainty that provoked these discussions was empirical: It was simply not known how safe the new technique might be. At the same time, there were only about ten centers in the U.S. capable of offering amniocentesis to patients.[10] In this situation, the question who should be eligible to undergo this uncertain procedure was an important one.

This initial concern remains important for practitioners because of the ways it has been addressed in the intervening years. The responses reflected a strategy for dealing with empirical uncertainty that is rooted in the traditional medical obligation to prevent harm in the process of providing benefit. The first step was to circumscribe the potential dangers of the technique until the relevant uncertainties could be substantially diminished. This had two implications for the clinical introduction of the technique. First, it suggested that the first patients undergoing the procedure should be known to have a risk of carrying a fetus affected with a diagnosable condition. For these patients, the relative burden of the procedure's unknown dangers would be minimized and the relative benefits of its uncertain efficacy enhanced. Second, it suggested that, within this class of potential patients, the procedure should be used in cases that could help generate the missing knowledge.

The second step was to undertake the systematic clinical assessments of amniocentesis that these preliminary risk-buffered eligibility criteria made possible. Those assessments yielded the relatively low-risk figures—less than 1 percent morbidity and mortality—that have come to be associated with the procedure.[11]

The strategy used is familiar to anyone acquainted with designing research on human subjects. In effect, its aim was to select the initial recipients of amniocentesis as if they were research subjects. The emphasis was on structuring the distribution of the service in ways that would protect the more vulnerable potential recipients and also yield the information required for assessing the procedure's actual clinical utility.

One might say that these preliminary access policies served as the apron strings of the technique's youth. They protected it from its own unpredictability by keeping it within the cautious research setting that gave it birth. There comes a time, however, when apron strings should be cut. Eligibility criteria based on the original uncertainties continue to influence the use of amniocentesis. Now that the safety and efficacy of the technique has been established, the ethical justification of some of those policies is being reassessed.

For example, some early commentators argued that only parents who were willing to undergo an abortion in the case of a positive diagnosis should be considered candidates for amniocentesis. On this view, running the unknown risks of the procedure could only be justified if all the benefits it could offer were actually going to be realized. In the face of the gravity of the potential hazards, being unwilling to carry through with an abortion when the procedure provided an opportunity to prevent harm was thought to tip its risk-benefit balance enough to make rejecting the intervention the only reasonable choice.[12]

Today, there is a broad consensus that parental commitment to abortion is an ethically inappropriate criterion for selecting candidates for amniocentesis.[13] As we shall see below, there are powerful arguments against it that stem from the nature of the prenatal diagnostician's professional role and the place of abortion among the "benefits" of amniocentesis. The main point here is that, as the procedure's risk potential has now been determined, the argument in favor of the policy has lost its foundation. Not only do we know the risks (so that reasonable risk comparisons are possible), we also know them to be relatively low. Now that the dangers they would protect against have been dispelled, the paternalistic constraints of this particular apron string are no longer justifiable, even on their own terms.

Another eligibility policy that has roots in the initial uncertainties is the more common one of restricting amniocentesis—among candidates with no known family histories of diagnosable conditions—to women over the age of thirty-five. Early studies indicated that the incidence of Down's syndrome increased dramatically in children born to mothers older than thirty-five.[14] This meant that tests performed on those patients were likely to yield more positive diagnoses of the disease than tests performed on younger women. Thus, in the absence of known genetic risks, restricting amniocentesis to candidates over thirty-five would increase the procedure's effectiveness in preventing the disease and decrease the chances that a normal pregnancy would be endangered by its risks. Since the birthrate also declined steeply after age thirty-five, using maternal age as a selection criterion also produced a set of candidates the extant resources could accommodate.[15]

This policy was a justifiable way to introduce the technique, given the uncertainties that surrounded it. However, as the risks of amniocentesis have become established, and our knowledge of the incidence of Down's syndrome has improved, the rationale for this policy is beginning to be re-examined. Studies have shown that the incidence of Down's syndrome increases more gradually with maternal age than the earlier work indicated.[16] Meanwhile, the number of other age-independent disorders diagnosable through amniocentesis, many of which are far more devastating than Down's syndrome, continues to increase. As a result, providing amniocentesis to younger mothers now appears less risky and more likely to benefit than it did early on.

This new information raises questions about the fairness of access policies that still use age thirty-five as a cutoff for candidates who are not known to be at genetic risk for specific diagnosable conditions. Questions of fairness arise in considering the relevancy of the interpersonal differences we use to distribute our resources. Here, the concern is whether being thirty-five or younger is still a relevant difference for the purposes of allocating access to amniocentesis now that the original justification has been undermined.[17]

The maternal age criterion illustrates a general point about the risk-limiting strategy for dealing with empirical uncertainty. The logic of the strategy suggests that initial criteria for the use of innovative techniques will remain justifiable only if the worst-case risk scenarios are actually borne out by experience. In most situations, the strategy will include eventually loosening the apron strings and allowing the technology to benefit a broader range of patients.

Finally, it is important to note that eligibility criteria for newer prenatal diagnostic techniques may legitimately still be used cautiously. The systematic clinical assessments of the safety and efficacy of chorionic villi sampling have only recently begun.[18] Thus, experts advise that ''meanwhile, it is judicious to exercise every caution in view of potential hazards to both mother and child.''[19] For the moment, as we shall see, the apron strings that provide protections against such hazards also protect practitioners of chorionic villi sampling from having to deal with ethical issues quite unrelated to risk. As that technique matures, it will be important to make sure that outmoded constraints on the technique's use are not maintained simply to avoid dealing with those other issues.

Of course, even after the apron strings of a new technology have been cut, its use must still be governed by some criteria. If the initial criteria are now less defensible, how *should* the service of amniocentesis be delivered? Questions about how to deploy biomedical technologies are intimately connected with questions about the goals they help to achieve. In principle, the best way to use a technology is the way that best meets the needs the technology was designed to address. For any specific technology, like amniocentesis, there will be issues about the proportion of our general medical resources that should go into alleviating the scarcity of the technology in order to meet such needs.[20] However, there are also issues at the clinical level having do with the definition of the needs that amniocentesis is intended to meet. These are the issues discussed in the next two sections.

SELECTIVE ABORTION AND THE THERAPEUTIC IMPERATIVE

In most discussions about allocating a medical technology, the purpose of the technology is unproblematic. Most technologies provide some preventive or therapeutic benefit for patients with particular needs, and the problem is deciding how to distribute that benefit. One of the interesting features of the discussion of amniocentesis, however, has been the persistence of the question as to its purpose. Given that the risks of the procedure are low, what are the benefits it offers and are they legitimate ones for health care professionals to provide?

Implicit in the early use of amniocentesis prior to abortion seemed to be a belief that the prevention of harm by the selective abortion of diseased fetuses was the primary benefit to be gained from amniocentesis. Much of the ethical discussion has centered on the merits of this view and its implications for the appropriateness of amniocentesis as a medical practice.

Concern over the legitimacy of the practice is usually based in the recognition that, in the absence of more effective uses for the knowledge it produces, selective abortion is the primary practical intention behind performing an amniocentesis.[21] Critics find the practice unacceptable because they claim that selective abortion is an ethically inappropriate medical response to the diagnosis of fetal disease. Many of the arguments for this position reflect particular philosophical and theological views on the status of the fetus as a person and the moral rights to life and equal protection that it might possess.[22] As such, they are arguments against selective abortion as a general social practice and, to the extent that they are persuasive, indict amniocentesis indirectly.

However, there are also concerns about selective abortion as a *medical* practice, quite aside from the question of its social acceptability. Some argue that for health care professionals, it is irrelevant whether the fetal subject of an amniocentesis is a person or possesses rights. As long as the fetus is a legitimate *patient*, it falls within the scope of the practitioners' professional obligations and enjoys the benefits of their protection.[23]

One of the practices that the professional ethics of medicine has traditionally prohibited is the killing of patients, either for their own benefit or for the benefit of others.[24] Commentators point out that if the fetus is the patient in prenatal diagnosis, it is misleading to call the sequelae of positive diagnoses "therapeutic abortions" or to justify them in terms of the "prevention of harm." Fetal patients are selectively aborted precisely because they have been diagnosed as already suffering from incurable harms. Selective abortion on these grounds is neither therapeutic nor preventive; they say: it is simply a form of euthanasia.[25] As a result, some wonder whether amniocentesis might be an unacceptable practice for health care practitioners simply by the internal moral standards for their profession.

These concerns have been addressed in several ways. Some agree that selective abortion is not an ethically attractive response to the diagnosis of fetal disease, but they assert that it is also not the only possible response. They claim that in fact the intended purpose of amniocentesis is "the treatment and eventual cure of disease in the fetus or infant."[26] It is only because prenatal treatment has not yet caught up to diagnosis that selective abortion is a "sad, negative alternative."[27] An NIH consensus conference task force on antenatal diagnosis summarized this approach when it wrote,

> Thus, the techniques of prenatal diagnosis are not, except in very few instances, associated with any medical therapies for the alleviation of the diagnosed disorder. Many leaders in the development of this technology recognize this is unsatisfactory. They affirm that studies of the etiology of genetic and hereditary disorders are of the greatest importance and that, based on knowledge of etiology, therapeutic measures must be developed. Thus, prenatal diagnosis, while presently most often associated with the choice of abortion, is not inextricably linked to abortion: it may provide information leading to the planning for the birth of a defective infant and it has the potential for the better understanding of, and therapeutic interventions in, the disease state.[28]

In trying to establish an appropriate therapeutic purpose for amniocentesis, this argument looks both toward the past and the future. It points to the rationale behind the technology's development and to the promise of its eventual uses. These appeals are persuasive as far as they go. But even if the original intentions were laudably therapeutic, the proponents recognize that "realistically, for generations to come, the power to diagnose fetal disease will outstrip the power to treat with effective therapies.''[29] While the prospects of future treatments might justify the use of prenatal diagnosis in *research* efforts designed to shorten that lag, how do they help in addressing the critics' concerns about turning to the ''sad, negative alternative'' as a regular practice in the clinical setting?

A second response to these concerns is to agree that (for the time being) selective abortion is the principal clinical option after amniocentesis, but then to argue that abortion is sometimes morally justified. Again, the consensus of the NIH task force:

> In addition, there is something profoundly troubling about allowing the birth of an infant who is known in advance to suffer from some serious disease or defect. While the prevention of that suffering is attained in this case by eliminating the potential sufferer rather than the cause of the suffering, many would consider it an act of mercy. Because the fetus holds so uncertain a place in the moral community, many (among them many who are deeply devoted to fetal wellbeing) consider that ''act of mercy'' to fall in quite a different moral category than a similar act performed on an already born human being of whatever age.[30]

As this quotation indicates, those who argue this way must distinguish the merciful killing of fetal patients, which they support, from active euthanasia in the clinical setting, which they condemn. Again, an array of philosophical views about the ontological status of the fetus and its membership in ''the moral community'' can be drawn upon to make this distinction.[31] But the hallmark of those views, as of their counterparts among critics' of abortion, is the extent and intensity of scholarly disagreement over their merits. By contrast, the resources of traditional professional medical ethics are fairly sparse on these matters and cannot provide much guidance on the relevant distinction without appealing to one or another of these background views.

For the practitioner trying to decide how best to use amniocentesis, this dispute over the purpose of prenatal diagnosis creates a genuine problem of moral uncertainty. Is selective abortion an ethically appropriate response to fetal disease or not? Our cultural resources on the question are almost too rich, offering a perplexing variety of moral guidance, all of it equally controversial. The specific ethical resources of the profession, on the other hand, do not seem to provide enough guidance to definitively respond to the concerns. There are approaches to dealing with moral uncertainty, however, and in the next section one is outlined that allows practitioners to get beyond the moral quandary of selective abortion to the clinical business of prenatal diagnosis.

Before turning to that approach, there are two points about the moral quandary that are important to make. First, note that one of the primary clinical advantages of chorionic villi sampling is its capacity for circumventing some of that uncertainty. Unlike amniocentesis, chorionic villi sampling is performed during the first trimester of pregnancy, and the tissue samples it yields are immediately ready for laboratory analysis.[32] By allowing a diagnosis to be made much earlier in gestation, this technique allows the question of abortion to arise during a period in which the spontaneous abortion rate for defective fetuses is high and the philosophical status of the fetus, both as person and patient, is more tenuous than later.

It is also important to notice the source of the uncertainty over prenatal diagnosis as a medical practice. Both the concerns and their responses were framed against the basic clinical imperative to treat and cure disease. All the arguments so far have assumed that, for a diagnostic tool to have a legitimate medical purpose, it should be used to help benefit the victim of the diseases it uncovers. When prenatal diagnosis is understood in terms of this therapeutic imperative, the discussion naturally focuses on how the information it yields can help alleviate the suffering of the afflicted fetus. This perspective makes the asymmetry between our abilities to diagnose and treat the fetus morally troubling and prompts the discussion of whether selective abortion is an acceptable way to balance the therapeutic scales. Our uncertainty on that score is what creates most of the moral tension that accompanies the practice of prenatal diagnosis.

As strong as that tension is, however, it has not paralyzed the conscientious medical use of prenatal diagnosis. That is largely because the practice of prenatal diagnosis is also informed by another moral point of view, one which *does* provide the practitioner with a way to address this problem of uncertainty.

UNCERTAINTY AND THE ETHICS OF REPRODUCTIVE COUNSELING

There is important argument in defense of amniocentesis that was not mentioned with the others above, even though all are usually raised together. Proponents almost always stress that, in addition to its therapeutic goals, "we regard the provision of information as an important and legitimate purpose of prenatal diagnosis" independent of whether that information is used on behalf of the fetus.[33] One statement of this position is as follows:

> The desired and intended result of prenatal diagnosis is information about the presence or absence of a possible disease or defect in the fetus. In practice, the test results are negative in more than 96 percent of amniocentesis cases, providing these families with many months of relief from anxiety. . . . When diagnosis of the presence of disease or defect is made, parents and physicians use that information to make choices about subsequent action. . . . Ethical considerations make it imperative to separate the fact of a positive diagnosis from the choice about subsequent action. What parents and physicians decide to do is not automatically dictated by the diagnosis, but ought to be shaped by their ethical and social views. . . . These guidelines were developed in a moral framework favoring the protection of individual choice and the autonomy of parents, even when we disagree with their course of action.[34]

Notice that this approach defines the aim of performing an amniocentesis in terms of the parents' problems, not the fetus's. Prenatal diagnosis is, in essence, an adjunct to a form of psychological counseling: It provides information that practitioners can use to alleviate their parents' anxieties during pregnancy and to help them work through difficult reproductive decisions.[35]

This obviously reflects an important shift in the orientation of the discussion. Again, the discussion thus far has been informed, and limited, by the traditional ethics of clinical medicine. This shift reflects the influence of another professional tradition relevant to the practice of prenatal diagnosis: that of the genetic counselor. As the last lines of the passage above suggest, the ethical resources this tradition can contribute to the discussion have some important implications for the practitioner's response to the moral uncertainties of the practice.

The first important feature of this tradition is its relocation of the practitioner's primary professional obligations. As the purpose of amniocentesis shifts from helping the fetus to helping its parents, the latter become the practitioner's primary focus. The ethics of genetic counseling has traditionally been clear about the implications of this therapeutic shift for a counselor's professional commitments: "Counselors may find themselves pulled by an allegiance to the unborn child—whose well-being is, after all, the ultimate object of their concern as well as the motivating interest of the parents. As understandable as this concern may be, in the end it must give way to the duty owed to the counselee—the parents."[36]

The second important feature of this tradition is its substantive vision of the duties that the practitioner owes to the counselee. Along with duties to benefit and protect their patients, the ethics of clinical medicine commits physicians to the ideal of a physician-patient relationship marked by shared decision making.[37] In genetic counseling, the key to that relationship has been taken to be the practitioner's duty to respect patients' reproductive choices. Modern genetic counselors are especially careful not to impose their own values on their clients in the decision-making process. The goal of their practice is to improve their patients' abilities to cope with their reproductive experiences in their own terms. Thus, while counselors provide information, facilitate decision making, and make recommendations, they fully accept the obligation not to interfere with the reproductive decisions their clients make after counseling.[38]

In part, this ethical orientation has historical roots in the reaction of postwar clinical geneticists to the excesses of their eugenic predecessors. However, it also reflects an important strategy for dealing with the moral uncertainties of the reproductive decisions that genetic counselors help their clients make.[39] This strategy assumes that where moral uncertainty is high—either because of a paucity of ethical guidance or a variety of equally defensible views—practitioners may accept conscientious decisions favoring either side of an issue. Moreover, since reproductive issues in general and abortion issues in particular are among the most highly controverted and culturally colored moral issues, professionals engaged in helping people make reproductive decisions have a special obligation to respect their patients' considered judgments about these issues.[40]

This strategy seems to stand behind defenses of prenatal diagnosis like the one mounted in last passage quoted above. References to the "ethical considerations" that allow practitioners to divorce the propriety of their diagnostic interventions from what happens as a result and to the "moral framework" favoring parental autonomy "even when we disagree with their course of action" allude to the view that, in the face of a plurality of moral positions on abortion, practitioners should bracket their own uncertainties and focus on enhancing the parents' ability to make autonomous and conscientious reproductive decisions. Prenatal diagnosis is an acceptable medical practice, then, as a tool for helping parents to make those choices.

In the practice of prenatal diagnosis, this counseling model usually operates simultaneously with a therapeutic concern for the fetus. This is an effective combination in most cases, since the practitioner's respect for parental choice coincides with his or her obligations to the fetus. However, some of the more vivid ethical problems the practitioner faces are created in the rare cases in which these points of view diverge. Then questions arise again about which patients should be eligible for prenatal diagnosis. Once the apron strings of the practice have been cut and its purposes have been clarified, how should it be used? In particular, what is the range of reproductive choices the practitioner may facilitate through prenatal diagnosis when those choices conflict with his or her therapeutic obligations to the fetus?

Two kinds of cases that are especially important for today's practitioner are requests for prenatal diagnosis for sex selection and curable diseases. These kinds of cases pose limited, though real, problems for the practice of amniocentesis. The ease and efficacy of techniques like chorionic villi sampling, however, suggests that they will become increasingly common in the future.

PRENATAL DIAGNOSIS FOR SEX SELECTION

Is prenatal diagnosis performed in order to determine the gender of the fetus an acceptable practice in the absence of sex-linked genetic risks? Although this question has been faced by practitioners of amniocentesis, the maternal risks of late abortions and the experience of pregnancy past quickening have often been enough to dissuade candidates from the practice without having to deny them access to amniocentesis.[41] The main clinical promise of chorionic villi sampling, however, is precisely that it avoids those barriers to selective abortion by allowing diagnosis early in gestation.[42] This makes it physically and emotionally easier for the mother to have an abortion, and there is also greater uncertainty about the moral status of the fetus early in gestation, making an abortion easier to justify. At present, the practitioners of chorionic villi sampling are depending on the apron strings of the technique's youth to convince people that using it for sex selection is an inappropriate way to allocate a scarce and experimental resource.[43] As time passes, however, practitioners will have to face the issue squarely—and when there is likely to be an increased demand.

Most commentators have been critical of sex selection, even if they would not ban it. For example, in an important report on social issues in genetic screening, the President's Commission for the Study of Ethical Problems in Medicine and Biomedical and Behavioral Research states,

> Despite the strong reasons for not precluding individuals from having access to genetic services on the basis of what they may do with the information, society may sometimes be warranted in discouraging certain uses. A striking example would be the use of prenatal diagnosis solely to determine the sex of the fetus and to abort a fetus of the unwanted sex.[44]

The commission summarized the four most prominent arguments why, beyond the question of scarce resources, prenatal diagnosis for sex selection is an inappropriate use of the technology. The first three arguments impugn the motives of parents who would make such a request. First, such a request is often likely to be based on sexist thinking. Unlike selective abortion for defective fetuses, discrimination based on sheer prejudice against one gender is something that can be fairly confidently condemned as immoral. Second, the fact that parents are concerned enough to abort a child of the ''wrong'' sex raises questions about whether they are approaching the enterprise of having children responsibly or whether they are laboring under expectations that will end up working to the detriment of their children. Finally, the commission noted that ''taken to an extreme, this attitude treats a child as an artifact and the reproductive process as a chance to design and produce human beings according to parental standards of excellence.''[45]

Of course, these arguments rest on factual claims that may not be true for all parents who request prenatal diagnosis for sex selection. Thus, we cannot be sure, from the outset, that every request is a case of irrational sexism, nor can we determine how successfully prospective parents will raise their children or even what the final consequences of the practice would be on our cultural attitudes towards reproduction.[46] A thirty-year-old mother of three boys who would like a girl may have quite good reasons for her choice. In the face of uncertainty about the parents' motives, some argue, the practitioner should not deny them the benefit of the doubt.

These uncertainties do suggest that blanket policies against releasing sex information on request might be unjustified. But the commission also presented a fourth argument that is based less on uncertain empirical facts. The commission argued that

> although every reproductive decision based on information gained from genetic screening involves the conscious acceptance of certain characteristics and the rejection of others, a distinction can be made between seeking genetic information in order to correct or avoid unambiguous disabilities, or to improve the well-being of the fetus, and seeking such information merely to satisfy parental preferences that are not only idiosyncratic but also unrelated to the good of the fetus. Although in some cases it will be difficult to draw a clear line between these two types of interventions, sex selection appears to fall in the latter class.[47]

This argument returns to the issue of using the prenatal diagnosis for guidance, and in the process it integrates the two moral contexts of the practice—the genetic counselor's and the fetal therapist's—in an interesting way. In essence, it says that the purpose of the practice is to provide information relevant to making a *special subset* of reproductive decisions: decisions that revolve around the health of the fetus. Although the counselor's stress on the importance of parental autonomy would keep those decisions in the parents' hands, the therapist's focus on the medical problems of the fetus tends to limit the range of decisions the practice can serve to ones made in response to those problems. Since gender is not a pathological problem, requests for assistance in making gender-based reproductive decisions can be appropriately denied.

This response goes beyond simply combining the two ethical frameworks for prenatal diagnosis and using one or the other as the need arises. Its effect is to integrate the perspectives, so that prenatal diagnosis remains recognizably a medical practice (addressing the health problems of the fetus), but a practice that focuses primarily on helping parents make reproductive decisions in the light of those problems. This integrated framework allows practitioners to show why women at risk for fetal defects are appropriate candidates for prenatal diagnosis even in the absence of effective treatment and women at risk for carrying a fetus of a certain gender are not.

PRENATAL DIAGNOSIS FOR A TREATABLE DEFECT

The second kind of access question raises problems even within the context of the integrated approach of the President's Commission. The clinical advantages of chorionic villi sampling, together with the expanding ability to diagnosis genetic disorders at the molecular level, will mean increasing numbers of genetic diseases will be detectable *in utero*. Geneticists promise that with chorionic villi sampling, "prodigious opportunities exist for the first-trimester diagnosis of many different genetic disorders as long as the safety and accuracy are first assured. It is expected that all chromosomal abnormalities, biochemical genetic disorders whose enzymatic deficiencies have been characterized in cell culture, and all disorders in which the gene defect has been delineated will be detectable."[48] Of course, this will increase the *range* of detectable health-related fetal conditions as well as the number. As this happens, questions will become more frequent about the diagnosis of relatively minor conditions or of conditions like Huntington's disease or Alzheimer's disease that will not affect the fetus until much later in life.[49] Similarly, as more correlations are drawn between specific genetic markers and dispositions toward psychiatric conditions like depression, practitioners may face requests for testing for these markers. All of these questions will create tension between the practitioner's commitment to parental autonomy and his or her concern for fetal welfare. Perhaps most difficult will be requests for prenatal diagnosis for diseases for which there is effective therapy. Once the appropriate techniques are available, how should the practitioner respond to requests for prenatal diagnosis for a disease (e.g., phenylketonuria [PKU]) that is eminently treatable after birth?[50]

Here the two moral traditions that guide the practitioner seem at loggerheads. On one hand, the practitioner is committed to using chorionic villi sampling to provide the parents with the information they need in order to make reproductive decisions that concern fetal health. On the other hand, from the purely therapeutic point of view, the important benefits the practitioner can provide to the fetus make the obligation to do so in this case seem very strong. The conflict between the two perspectives generates conceptual uncertainty over who should be understood to be the primary patient. Usually, it is enough simply to accept, or reject, both parties as one's patients. Cases of treatable fetal problems, however, raise the necessity of arriving at some conclusion about the relative priority of the patients, even within the context of an integrated moral perspective that identifies them.[51]

A case can be made for placing the parents first, even in these hard cases. The argument starts with the merits of the genetic counselor's approach to the cultural and ethical complexities of reproductive decision making. Fetuses are patients only within the context of their parents' reproductive plans. These plans will be the starting point in all the cases a practitioner faces, as long as the presenting parents are not brain dead, comatose, or otherwise incapable of making reproductive choices. And parents' reproductive choices, as genetic counselors recognize, will be influenced by serious considerations that go well beyond the practitioner's ability to assess. Moreover, there are also significant risks in giving priority to the welfare of the fetus when it can be enhanced. These are primarily social risks, concerned with the consequences of such a move for the "right of privacy" by which reproductive choices have been traditionally protected.

To give priority to the therapeutic imperative in these cases would be to assume that it is an unacceptable medical practice to selectively abort a fetus that can be successfully treated for its condition. On this view, for example, requests for prenatal diagnosis for PKU may be legitimately denied if they are made with the intent to abort affected fetuses. However, to subordinate parental autonomy to fetal welfare in the way required to deny prenatal diagnosis for PKU would also provide justification for an unacceptably large range of other limitations on parental decision making.

For example, practitioners might withhold the information that a fetus had PKU if they knew the parents would use that information to abort the fetus. Agreeing to treatment of the disease could be made a condition for the prenatal diagnosis. Moreover, if it is the fetal PKU victim's status as a *treatable patient* that justifies the restriction on parental access to prenatal diagnosis, would not a fetus which is a prenatally treatable for other diseases merit similar protections? That is, might not clinics be justified in giving access only to parents committed to proceeding with prenatal therapies where they are available? In effect, limiting access to prenatal diagnosis would be a mirror image of the required-abortion policy. As the number of fetal treatments increased, the range of disorders for which selective abortion would no longer be held appropriate would grow, effectively limiting parental reproductive choice.[52]

Whether these developments would actually occur, of course, is uncertain. The point of the argument is not that giving priority to the therapeutic imperative would place us on some inevitable "slippery slope." The point is that doing so would by itself place us at the bottom of the slope—by providing the justification for all these coercive practices. On the other hand, giving priority to the parents' autonomy respects the context of the diagnostic intervention in the parents' reproductive decision making and protects the traditional moral privacy of those decisions. As the President's Commission stated,

> Nowhere is the need for freedom to pursue divergent conceptions of the good more deeply felt than in decisions concerning reproduction. It would be a cruel irony if technological advances undertaken in the name of providing information to expand the range of individual choices resulted in unanticipated social pressures to pursue a particular course of action."[53]

CONCLUSIONS

The moral framework that will guide the practice of prenatal diagnosis as a mature medical technology is still emerging. Its foundations are in the ethical traditions of clinical medicine and genetic counseling, with their complementary imperatives to enhance fetal welfare and facilitate parental choice. During the discussions of the safety and purpose of amniocentesis that shaped the youth of prenatal diagnosis, these two traditions could often be used interchangeably in establishing the legitimate boundaries of the practice. As the next generation of diagnostic techniques raises new moral, conceptual, and social uncertainties, the relationship between these two traditions will become increasingly crucial to the moral stability of the practice. Different approaches to integrating the professional obligations that each tradition stresses will produce divergent responses to the hard questions of access and eligibility that practitioners of prenatal diagnosis will increasingly face. One approach, designed with the new uncertainties in view, would try to improve the fit between these traditions in two steps. First, it would rely on medicine's therapeutic imperative to limit the range of appropriately diagnosed conditions to those relevant to the medical welfare of the fetus. But within that clinical sphere, it would reaffirm the commitment of the practitioner, as counselor, to enhance the parent's autonomy to make reproductive and therapeutic decisions in light of the information prenatal diagnosis can provide.

NOTES

1. M. Steele and W. Breg, "Chromosome Analysis of Human Amniotic Fluid Cells," *Lancet* 1 (1966): 383.

2. Maureen Harris, ed., *Early Diagnosis of Human Genetic Defects: Scientific and Ethical Considerations*, NIH Publication no. 72-25 (Bethesda, Md.: National Institutes of Health, 1971).

3. Michael Harrison, Mitchell Golbus, and Roy Filly, eds., *The Unborn Patient: Prenatal Diagnosis and Treatment* (New York: Grune & Stratton, 1984); National Institute of Child Health and Human Development, *Antenatal Diagnosis: Report of a Consensus Development Conference*, NIH Publication no. 79-1973 (Bethesda, Md.: National Institutes of Health, 1979).

4. Harrison, Golbus, and Filly, *The Unborn Patient*, 125–39.

5. National Institute of Child Health and Human Development, *Antenatal Diagnosis*, 118–28.

6. Ibid., 33.

7. G. Simoni, et al., "Diagnostic Application of First Trimester Trophoblast Sampling in 100 Pregnancies," *Human Genetics* 66 (1984): 252–259; C.H. Rodeck and J.M. Morsman, "First Trimester Chorion Biopsy," *British Medical Bulletin* 39 (1983): 338.

8. Frank Chervenak, Glenn Isaacson, and Maurice Mahoney, "Advances in the Diagnosis of Fetal Defects," *NEJM* 315 (1986): 305–7.

9. H. Nadler, "Prenatal Detection of Hereditary Disorders," *Pediatrics* 42 (1968): 912; John Littlefield, "The Pregnancy at Risk for a Genetic Disorder," *New England Journal of Medicine* 282 (1970): 627–28.

10. National Institute of Child Health and Human Development, *Antenatal Diagnosis*, I-61.

11. Ibid., I-60–I-67.

12. Littlefield, "The Pregnancy at Risk," 627–28.

13. National Institute of Child Health and Human Development, *Antenatal Diagnosis*, I-185; Tabitha Powledge and John Fletcher, "Guidelines for the Ethical, Social and Legal Issues in Prenatal Diagnosis," *New England Journal of Medicine* 300 (1979): 170–71.

14. The President's Commission for the Study of Ethical Problems in Medicine and Biomedical and Behavioral Research, *Screening and Counseling for Genetic Conditions* (Washington, D.C.: GPO, 1982), 77.

15. Ibid., 78.

16. Lewis Holmes, "Genetic Counseling for the Older Pregnant Woman: New Data and Questions," *New England Journal of Medicine* 298 (1978): 419.

17. E.W. Hook, "Genetic Triage and Genetic Counseling," *American Journal of Medical Genetics* 17 (1984): 531; M. Vekemans and A. Lippman, "Eligibility Criteria for Amniocentesis," *American Journal of Medical Genetics* 17 (1984): 531.

18. G. Pescia and H. Nguyen The, eds., *Chorionic Villi Sampling (CVS)* (Basel, Switzerland: Karger Publishers, 1985).

19. Aubrey Milunsky, "Prenatal Diagnosis: New Tools, New Problems," in *Genetics and Law III*, ed. A. Milunsky and G. Annas (New York: Plenum Press, 1985).

20. Gilbert Omenn, "Prenatal Diagnosis and Public Policy," in *Genetic Disorders and the Fetus*, 2d ed., edited by A. Milunsky (New York: Plenum Press, 1986), 869–77.

21. Jerome Lejeune, "On the Nature of Man," *American Journal of Human Genetics* 22 (1970): 121–28.

22. Leon Kass, "Implications of Prenatal Diagnosis for the Human Right to Life," in *Ethical Issues in Human Genetics*, ed. Bruce Hilton et al. (New York: Plenum Press, 1973), 185–99; Karen Lebacqz, "Prenatal Diagnosis and Selective Abortion," *Linacre Quarterly* 40 (1973): 109–27; Carol Tauer, "Personhood and Human Embryos and Fetuses," *Journal of Medicine and Philosophy* 10 (1985): 253–66.

23. Cf. Harrison, Golbus, and Filly, *The Unborn Patient*, 1–9; Roger Shinn, "The Fetus as Patient," in *Genetics and the Law III*.

24. George Gruman, Sissela Bok, and Robert Veatch, "Death, Dying and Euthanasia," *The Encyclopedia of Bioethics*, ed. Warren Reich (New York: Macmillan, 1978).

25. Paul Ramsey, "Reference Points in Deciding About Abortion," in *The Morality of Abortion*, ed. John Noonan (Cambridge, Mass.: Harvard University Press, 1970).

26. Powledge and Fletcher, "Guidelines," 170.

27. John Fletcher and Albert Jonsen, "Ethical Considerations," in *The Unborn Patient.*

28. National Institute of Child Health and Human Development, *Antenatal Diagnosis,* I-182,3.

29. Fletcher and Jonsen, "Ethical Considerations," 166.

30. National Institute of Child Health and Human Development, *Antenatal Diagnosis,* I-192.

31. Cf. William Bondeson et al., eds., *Abortion and the Status of the Fetus* (Boston: D. Reidel, 1983).

32. Milunsky, "Prenatal Diagnosis," 336–37.

33. Powledge and Fletcher, "Guidelines," 171.

34. Ibid., 170.

35. Thus, genetic counselors write that, far from simply "diagnosing" medical problems: "When the genetic counselor attempts to help the counselees reach appropriate health and reproductive decisions, he/she will probably use the same techniques that many psychotherapists would use under similar circumstances—clarification of motivations and beliefs, an examination of alternatives, with their pros and cons, a presentation of options not considered in the counselee's thinking, an identification and labeling of facts and fantasies, challenges to unrealistic beliefs, and so on. In other words, assisting counselees to make realistic personal decisions, a major goal of genetic counseling, perhaps more than any other function, requires that the counselor employ the skills of the psychotherapist" (Seymour Kessler, "The Psychological Paradigm Shift in Genetic Counseling," *Social Biology* 27 ([1980]: 167–85).

36. Alexander Capron, "Autonomy, Confidentiality and Quality Care in Genetic Counseling," in *Genetic Counseling: Facts, Values, and Norms*, Birth Defects: Original Article Series, vol. 15, no. 2, ed. Alexander Capron et al. (New York: Alan R. Liss, 1979), 334.

37. Cf. President's Commission for the Study of Ethics in Medicine and Biomedical and Behavioral Research, *Making Health Care Decisions: The Ethical and Legal Implications of Informed Consent in the Patient-Practitioner Relationship* (Washington, D.C.: GPO, 1982), 36.

38. Cf. Alex Capron et al., eds. *Genetic Counseling: Facts, Values and Norms* Birth Defects Original Article Series, vol. 15, no. 2 (New York: Alan R. Liss, 1979).

39. James R. Sorenson, "Biomedical Innovation, Uncertainty, and Doctor-Patient Interaction," *Journal of Health and Social Behavior* 15 (1974): 366–74.

40. Thus, writers sensitive to the moral nuances of language have begun saying "intrauterine" instead of "prenatal" diagnosis to accommodate the focus on the parent and the possibility that the intervention may not precede a birth at all. Cf. LeRoy Walters, "Ethical Issues in Intrauterine Diagnosis and Therapy," *Fetal Therapy* 1 (1986): 32–37.

41. Haig Kazazian, "Prenatal Diagnosis for Sex Choice: A Medical View," *Hastings Center Report* 10 (1980): 17–18.

42. Milunsky, "Prenatal Diagnosis," 337.

43. Karen Copeland, cited in "Gender Tests Leading to Abortions," *San Jose Mercury News* February 11, 1987, p. 13.

44. President's Commission, *Screening and Counseling*, 56.

45. Ibid., 57.

46. John Fletcher, "Ethics and Amniocentesis for Fetal Sex Identification," *New England Journal of Medicine* 301 (1979): 550–53; Mary Ann Warren, "The Ethics of Sex Preselection," in *Biomedical Ethics Reviews 1985*, ed. James Humbar and Robert Almeder (Clifton, N.J.: Humana Press, 1985), 73–93.

47. President's Commission, *Screening and Counseling*, 58.

48. Milunsky "Prenatal Diagnosis," 338.

49. John Fletcher, "Ethical Issues in Genetic Screening and Antenatal Diagnosis," *Clinical Obstetrics and Gynecology* 24 (1981): 1156.

50. Neil Holtzman, "Ethical Issues in the Prenatal Diagnosis of Phenylketonuria," *Pediatrics* 74 (1984): 424–27.

51. Frederick Schauer, "Slippery Slopes," *Harvard Law Review* 50 (1985): 361–383.

52. As is currently happening in other places: Cf. Lawrence J. Nelson, Brian Buggy, and Carol Weil, "Forced Medical Treatment of Pregnant Women," *Hastings Law Journal* 37 (1986): 703–65; Richard Hull, James Nelson, and L.A. Gartner, "Ethical Issues in Prenatal Therapies," in *Biomedical Ethics Reviews: 1984*, ed. J. Humbar and R. Almeder (Clifton, N.J.: Humana Press, 1984).

53. President's Commission, *Screening and Counseling*, 56.

Chapter 3

The Ethical Challenge of the New Reproductive Technology

Sidney Callahan

How should we ethically evaluate the new reproductive technologies developed to treat the increasing problem of human infertility? Our national debate over this troubling issue is just beginning. At this point, there are lacunae in law and regulatory procedures, while medical technological innovation and practice proceed without ethical consensus. This situation is due in part to the speed of recent developments, but we also find ourselves ethically perplexed because we, as a society, did not arrive at a consensus on the ethics of reproduction and responsible parenthood *before* the newest technologies appeared on the scene.

One obvious sign of the society's unresolved conflicts over the morality of reproduction can be found in the bitter debates over abortion and, to a lesser extent, contraception and contraceptive education in the schools. With no societal consensus on the ethical use of medical technology to plan, limit, or interrupt pregnancies, we are unprepared to evaluate the newest alternative reproductive technologies, which *promote* conception and pregnancies. At the same time as we have seen rapid advances in regulating fertility, we have experienced an evolution in attitudes toward women, children, sexuality, and the family. These intersecting social developments have produced the pressing need to develop a new ethic of parenthood and responsible reproduction.[1] My focus here, however, is on the most recent challenge. How should we ethically assess the innovative array of techniques developed to overcome infertility—egg and sperm donations, surrogate mothers, in vitro fertilization, and embryo transplants?

TWO INADEQUATE APPROACHES TO ALTERNATIVE REPRODUCTIVE TECHNOLOGY

Two inadequate approaches to the ethical assessment of the new alternative reproductive technologies are mirror images of each other in the narrowness of their focus and the limitations of their analysis. On the one hand, a conservative approach adopts as a moral standard the biological integrity of the marital sexual act. The married couple's marital sexual and reproductive acts must not be tampered with for any reason, and sexual intercourse and procreation must remain united in each marital act so that 'lovemaking and baby-making' are never separated. In this "act analysis," no technological intervention in the sexual act is countenanced or approved for any reason. Older arguments employed against artificial contraception are reiterated and applied to condemn any procedure separating functions which naturally occur together, and thus all reproduction by in vitro fertilization, artificial insemination, or third party surrogacy is deemed immoral. The only ethical stance toward new reproductive technologies would be to absolutely cease and desist; such procedures should come to a full stop.

At the other end of the ideological spectrum, another form of act analysis narrows its own focus to a person's desire for a child and the individual acts the person might perform in carrying out private arrangements for reproduction. As long as due process and informed consent by competent adults is guarded by proper contracts, any adult should be able to engage in any alternative reproductive procedure that technology can provide or that persons will sell or procure. This permissive stance is held to be justified on the basis of individual liberty, autonomy, reproductive privacy, and reproductive right. The burden of proof supposedly lies with those who would limit alternative reproductive technology, and in the name of liberty and individual autonomy, potential regulators are enjoined to show that concrete harmful consequences will result from a particular practice (if it is to be rejected). Of course, when there are as yet no existing consequences, it is impossible to *prove* harm will result. Indeed, even when there have been relevant cases (e.g., the AID children conceived by artificial insemination by donor), no long-term in-depth studies have been done. Therefore, the ethical response to alternative reproductive technologies is to proceed full steam ahead (with consideration given to due process and informed consent).

The premature ethical foreclosure implied in either of the above approaches to reproductive technologies is not adequate. An ethic based solely on the natural biological integrity of marital acts will not serve, because the mastery of nature through technological problem solving is also completely natural to us—indeed, it is the glory of *homo sapiens*. Yet, because we are rational, we can also see that a fully permissive attitude toward reproductive technology presents serious problems as well. We are reminded that in the past, innovative uses of technology have resulted in ecological and ethical disasters. Abuses have been either fully intended, as with the Nazis, or inadvertent and accidental, as in countless innovative interventions, such as the use of diethylstilbestrol (DES) or thaliomide, which had bad side effects far outweighing the supposed advantages. There is a grain of truth in the warning that "control of nature" often ends up producing increased control (or oppression) of some people by other more powerful people. Technology itself has to be ethically assessed and rationally controlled. Faced with new reproductive technologies, we should not let the technological imperative (what can be done should be done), fueled in this case by people's desires, decide the question whether a course of action is right or good.

THE BASIS FOR DEVELOPING AN ETHICAL POSITION

In the case of reproductive technology, ethical positions should emerge from a consideration of what will further the good of the potential child and the family, as well as provide appropriate social conditions for childrearing and strengthening our commitment to moral principles concerning individual responsibility in reproduction. We should move beyond a narrow focus on either biology or people's desires for children. In this serious matter, which involves children's lives and the social structure of our society, it is more prudent to consider first the values and goods safeguarded and protected at present by the operating norms of reproduction and childrearing before countenancing radical alterations. In matters of such serious collective import, the burden of proof should rightly be upon those who wish to experiment with the lives of others. (An ethical problem also arises concerning the justice of allocating medical resources to increase individual fertility in an overpopulated, impoverished world. However, since the main issue here concerns the use of reproductive technology, I think the correct statement of the ethical question is whether, or how far, present norms should be altered.)

One troubling tactic used by those urging the permissive acceptance of all new reproductive technologies is to base their arguments upon analogies from adoption or other childrearing arrangements that arise from divorce, death, desertion, or parental inadequacy. Much is made of the cases in which persons cope with single parenthood or successfully adapt to other less-than-ideal situations. But the adequacy of "after the fact" crisis management does not justify planning beforehand to voluntarily replicate similar childrearing situations. Emergency solutions make poor operating norms. Even a child conceived through rape or incest might adapt and be glad to have been born, but surely it would be wrong to plan such conceptions beforehand on the grounds that the future child would rather exist than not or that the sexual abuser had no other means to reproduce. Similarly, and more to the point, heretofore we have not ethically or legally countenanced the practice of deliberately conceiving a child in order to give it to others for adoption, with or without payment. We have forbidden the selling of babies or, for that matter, the purchasing of brides, sexual intercourse, or bodily organs. Certain cultural goods, safeguards, and values have been preserved by these existing norms. How can ethical guidelines for employing alternative reproductive methods strengthen rather than threaten our basic cultural values?

A PROPOSED ETHICAL STANDARD

It is ethically appropriate to use an alternative reproductive technology if, and only if, it makes it possible for a normal, socially well-adjusted heterosexual married couple to have a child that they could not otherwise have owing to infertility. Infertility does not seem strictly classifiable as a disease, but for a married couple it is clearly an unfortunate dysfunction or handicap, one which medicine may sometimes remedy. It seems wonderful, almost miraculous, that medical technology can often overcome a couple's infertility to restore normal function with techniques such as artificial insemination by husband (AIH), in vitro fertilization (IVF), or tubal ovum transfer methods. But holding to a proposed ethical standard of medical remediation and restoration of a married couple's average expectable fertility implies that medical professionals should not aim to alter or contravene what would otherwise exist as the normal conditions for procreation and childrearing.

A remedial standard based upon operating cultural norms requires that the genetic parents, the gestational parents, and the rearing parents be identical and that the parents be presently alive and well, in an appropriate time in their lifecycle, and possess average or adequate psychological and social resources for childrearing. Helping the severely retarded, the mentally ill, the genetically diseased, the destitute, the aged, or a widow with a dead spouse's sperm to have children they otherwise could not would be ethically unacceptable by this standard. It would also be unacceptable to alter average expectable conditions by efforts to produce multiple births or to select routinely for sex (the latter practice producing a whole host of other ethical problems which cannot be dealt with here). The power to intervene in such a crucial matter as the procreation of a new life makes the medical professionals or medical institutions involved into ethically responsible trustees of a potential child's future. As trustees, medical professionals would seem to have an ethical duty not to take risks on behalf of unconsenting others.

Medical professionals should be guided by a form of communal judgment influenced by cultural values and norms. What would most responsible would-be parents deem ethically appropriate reproductive behavior in a particular case? Physicians or other health care personnel can hardly, in good conscience, agree to and make possible irresponsible or ethically inappropriate reproductive acts affecting innocent new lives. Socially informed ethical judgments on behalf of the society are unavoidable. The fact that medical professionals and medical resources must be employed for remedial infertility treatments, which will produce direct social consequences, justifies using standards of judgment that take into account the general social good. Ethical standards which protect and strengthen positive outcomes for children, childrearing conditions, and cultural norms of responsible parenthood should be used to judge the appropriateness of a particular request for treatment of infertility.

The claim that an individual's right to reproduce would be violated if fertility treatments are not made available to any individual who requests them seems wrongheaded. A negative right not to be interfered with (e.g., the right to marry, which itself is not absolute) does not entail a positive right (e.g., that society is obligated to provide spouses). Moreover, as a society, we have already decided that when adequate childrearing conditions and the well-being of children are in the balance, social and professional intervention is justified. Adoption procedures, custodial decisions, and the child abuse laws involve rights and duties of professionals to make judgments on the fitness of parents. And as child abuse and resulting deaths regularly attest, it is far better to err on the side of safety than take risks. Should not medical professionals be similarly responsible in carrying out the interventions which will in essence give to a couple a baby to rear? If a couple seems within the normal range of average expectable parents, then remedial techniques that maintain the identicalness of genetic, gestational, and rearing parentage, techniques such as AIH or IVF or tubal ovum transfer, would be ethically acceptable.

Employing third party donors or surrogate mothers is not, in my opinion, ever an ethically acceptable use of reproductive technologies. Procedures using donors or surrogates separate and variously recombine the source of sperm, eggs, embryos, gestational womb, and rearing parents. Such a separation—whether through artificial insemination by donor (AID), embryo transplants, or surrogate mothers—poses too many ethical and social risks to the dignity and well-being of the future child, the donor, individual spouses, the family as a whole, and our cultural ethos. To argue the case against third party donors, even for acceptable couples, we need to consider what values, goods, and safeguards have been inherent in the cultural norm: two heterosexual parents who are the genetic, gestational, and rearing parents of their child.

Many proponents of third party donors in alternative reproduction—for single men and women, homosexual couples, or infertile couples—ignore what happens *after* a baby is conceived, produced, or procured. Focusing on an individual or on individual couples, the psychological and social dimensions of childrearing are separated from conception, gestation, and birth. Little account is taken of the fact that individuals live out their lifespan intergenerationally and in complex ecological and social systems.[2] No account is taken of the newest developments in family therapy and family systems analysis. The assumption seems to be that why and how one gets a baby makes no difference in what happens afterwards. This may be true of hens or cows, but it is hardly true of complex, thinking, emoting, imaginative human beings functioning within social systems.

Another equally invalid line of argument cites the current trends toward the breakdown of the traditional family unit and jumps to the conclusion that since the nuclear family seems to be disintegrating anyway, and the society survives, why try to preserve the norms heretofore valued? Ominous cultural effects on children and women that correlate with the breakdown of the family are dismissed as having no application to individual cases.[3] But a growing body of psychological literature points to a less sanguine judgment. Having *two* rearing parents provides important advantages, and fathers play more of a role in the moral, social, and sexual-identity development of the child than has been recognized.[4]

Legitimizing and morally sanctioning third party or collaborative reproduction or assisting single or homosexual conceptions can contribute directly to the specific negative childrearing conditions in the culture which *do* harm individuals and the larger community. The culture's operating norms concerning the family provide irreplaceable goods and safeguards—particularly for women and their children—which we come to truly value as we see them attenuated. Arguments for limiting reproductive interventions to remediation with no third party interventions can best be made by considering what is at stake if we alter our norms. We put at risk the good of the family, the parents, the child, and the donor(s), as well as our sexual morality, with its focus on sexual responsibility.

THE FAMILY

The advantages and safeguards of having two heterosexual parents who are the genetic, gestational, and rearing parents are manifold and basic; this type of family was not accidentally selected for in biological and cultural evolution. Mammalian "in vivo" reproduction and primate parent-child bonding provide adaptive means for the protection, defense, and complex socialization of offspring. They far outperform reproduction by laying eggs that are then left floating in the sea or buried in the sand to take their chances with passing predators.[5] With the advent of long-living rational animals such as human beings, the basic primate models are broadened and deepened, which results in family units that include fathers and encompass additional kinship bonds.[6] Two heterosexual parents supported by kin and clan can engage in even more arduous parenting, including nurturing the young over an extended period. The nuclear family is founded on biology and may have originally evolved through natural selection, but it is as a cultural phenomenon, with its psychological and social effectiveness in generating responsibility, socialization, and deep altruistic bonds, that the family has achieved stability and universality.

Why has the nuclear family worked for so long and held first place in the cultural competition?[7] The Western cultural ideal, gradually becoming less patriarchic as it comes to recognize the equality of women and children, has ensured far more than law, order, and social continuity. As the heterosexual members of a couple freely choose each other, they make a loving commitment to share the vicissitudes of life. Bonded in love and legal contract, they mutually exchange exclusive rights, giving each other emotional and economic priority. Love and sexuality often result in procreation, and the children then have a claim to equal parental care from both their father and mother. In addition, the extended families of both parents are important as supplemental supports for the couple, especially in cases of death or disaster.

No act analysis of one procreative period of time in a marriage can do justice to the fact that the reproductive couple exists as a unit within a family extended in time and kinship. Grandparents, grandchildren, aunts, cousins, and other relatives are important in family life for both pragmatic and psychological reasons. Individual identity is rooted in biologically based kinship and in small cooperating social units. The family is one remaining institution where status is given by birth, not earned or achieved. The irreversible bonds of kinship over time and through space produce rootedness and a sense of identity. Psychologically and socially the family provides emotional connections, social purpose, and meaning to life. Those individuals who do not marry and found families or who achieve membership in larger communities are still strongly connected to others through their families.[8] Each human being exists within a social envelope and must do so to flourish; the family is one of the most important elements in a human life. But as a cultural invention, why must a family be based upon biological kinship? Cannot any persons who declare themselves a family be a family?

While the internalized psychological image of a family and the intention to belong to a family are part of the foundations of a family, there is no denying the bond created by genetic kinship. One definition of the family is that a family consists of people who share genes. Sociobiologists have not exaggerated the importance of gene-sharing in human bonding.[9] In fact, the unwillingness of infertile couples to adopt and their struggles to have their own baby is testimony to the existence of what appears to be a strong innate urge to reproduce oneself. Culturally this is understood as the fusion of two genetic heritages, with the child situated within two lineages. Members of both lineages may be supportive, or one set of kin may by choice or chance be more important than the other, but having both sets provides important social resources. The child is heir to more than money or property when situated in a rooted kinship community.

The search by adopted children for their biological parents and possible siblings reveals the psychological need of humans to be situated and to know their origins.[10] When there is one or more third party donors—of sperm, eggs, or embryo—the child is cut off from either half or all of its genetic heritage. If deception is practiced concerning the child's origins, then both the child and the extended family will be wronged. Since family secrets are rarely kept completely, the delayed revelations produce disillusionment and distrust among those deceived. When a child and relatives are not lied to, the identity of the donor (or donors) becomes an issue for all concerned.

Parents and Spouses

Psychology has come to see genetic factors as more and more important in parent-child interactions and childrearing outcomes.[11] When rearing parents and genetic parents differ and the donor is unknown, there is a provocative void. If the donor is known and part of the rearing parents' family or social circle, there are other psychological problems and potential conflicts over who is the real parent and who has the primary rights and responsibilities. When the third party donor is also the surrogate mother, combining genetic and gestational parenthood, the social and legal problems can be profound. The much discussed Whitehead-Stern court struggle indicates the divisive chaos, struggle, and suffering that is possible in surrogate arrangements.

In the average expectable situation, two parents with equal genetic investment in the child are unified by their mutual relationship to the child. They are irreversibly connected and made kin to each other through the biological child they have procreated. Their love, commitment, and sexual bond has been made manifest in a new life. Their genetic link with the child, shared with their own family, produces a sense of family likeness and personal identification, leading to empathy and affective attunement. The child's genetic link to each spouse and his or her kin strengthens the marital bond. But the fact that the child is also a new and unique creation and a random fusion of the couple's genetic heritage gives enough distance to allow the child also to be seen as a separate other, with what has been called its "alien dignity as a human being" intact.[12] (Cloning oneself would be wrong for its egotistic intent and for the dehumanizing effects of trying to deny the uniqueness of identity.) The marital developments that occur during pregnancy also unite the couple and prepare them for the parental enterprise.[13] Since we are embodied creatures, the psychological bonds of caring and empathy are built upon the firm foundation of biological ties and bodily self-identity.

When technological intervention without donors, such as AIH or IVP or tubal ovum transfer, is used to correct infertility, the time, money, stress, and cooperative effort required serve to test the unity of the couple and focus them upon their marital relationship and their mutual contribution to childbearing. The psychological bonding between them can transcend the stress caused by the less-than-ideal technological interventions in their sexual lives. The result of their joint effort will, as in natural pregnancy, be a baby they are equally invested in and equally related to. (In adoption, both parents also have an equal relationship to the child they are jointly rescuing.) Given the equal investment in their child, both parents are equally responsible for childrearing and support.

With third party genetic or gestational donors, however, the marital and biological unity is broken asunder. One parent will be related biologically to the child and the other parent will not. True, the nonrelated parent may give consent, but the consent, even if truly informed and uncoerced, can hardly equalize the imbalance. While there is certainly no real question of adultery in such a situation, nevertheless, the intruding third party donor, as in adultery, will inevitably have a psychological effect on the couple's life. Even if there is no jealousy or envy, the reproductive inadequacy of one partner has been made definite and reliance has been placed on an outsider's potency, genetic heritage, and superior reproductive capacity.[14]

Asymmetry in biological parental relationships within a family or household has always been problematic, from Cinderella to today's stepparents and reconstituted families. The most frequently cited cause of divorce in second marriages is the difficulty of dealing with another person's children.[15] Empathy, identification, a sense of kinship, and assurance of parental authority arise from family likeness and biological ties. In disturbed families under stress, one finds more incest, child abuse, and scapegoating when biological kinship is absent.[16] Biological ties become psychologically potent, because human beings fantasize in their intersubjective emotional interactions with one another and with their children. Parents' fantasies about a child's past and future do make a difference, as all students of child development or family dynamics will attest. Identical twins may even be treated very differently because parents project different fantasies upon them.[17] Third party donors and surrogates cannot be counted on to disappear from family consciousness, even if legal contracts could control other ramifications or forbid actual interventions.

The Child

The most serious ethical problems in using third party donors in alternative reproduction concern the well-being of the potential child. A child conceived by new forms of collaborative reproduction is being made party to a social experiment without its consent. While no child is conceived by its own consent, a child not artifically produced is at least born in the same way as its parents and other persons normally have been. A child who has a donor or donors among its parents will be cut off from at least part of its genetic heritage and its kin in new ways. Even if there is no danger of transmitting unknown genetic disease or causing physiological harm to the child, the psychological relationship of the child to its parents is endangered, whether or not there is deception or secrecy about its origins.

It should be clear that adoption (which rescues a child already in existence) is very different ethically from planning to involve third party donors in procuring a child. An adopted child, while perhaps harboring resentment against its birth parents, must look at its rescuing adopters differently than a child would look at parents who have had it made to order. Treating the child like a commodity—something to be created for the pleasure of the parents—infringes the child's dignity. When one is begotten (not made), then one shares equally with one's parents in the ongoing transmission of the gift of life from generation to generation. The child procreated in the expectable way is a subsidiary gift arising from the prior marital relationship, not a product or project of the parental will.

Alternative reproductive techniques made available to single men and women or to homosexual couples will further endanger the child's status. Why should a child, at its creation, be treated as a property, a product, or a means to satisfy the wishes of adults? Even in natural reproduction, we now consider it ethically suspect to attempt to have a child not for its own sake, but because an adult wants to satisfy some personal need or desire.

Unfortunately, we are still saddled with residual ideologies that view children as a kind of personal property. Only gradually have we welcomed children as gifts—new lives given in trusteeship—and treated them as equal to adult persons in human dignity despite their dependency and their powerlessness.[18] Having a child for some extrinsic reason is now as generally unacceptable as marrying for money or some motive besides love and a desire for mutual happiness. Unfortunately, in the past some persons have wanted children to secure an inheritance, to prove sexual prowess, to procure a scapegoat, to gain revenge, to increase marital power, to secure social prestige, or to have someone of their own to love. The motives for conception influence the future relationship of the child to the parents. A couple absolutely and obsessively driven to have a child (as some couples become when faced with infertility) may not be prepared to rear the actual child once it is born. Being wanted and being well reared are not identical. Parental overinvestment in "gourmet children" can be psychologically difficult for a child.[19] Every child must achieve independence and a separate identity. Adolescent problems of anorexia, depression, and suicide have been seen as related to the dynamics of parental control.[20] Growing up and leaving home becomes a problem for children who have been used to fulfill parents.[21] The child who was wanted for all the wrong reasons is pressured to live up to parental dreams of the optimal baby or perfect child. Outright rejection of imperfect or nonoptimal babies contracted for by alternative reproductive technology is possible and should be a matter of grave concern.

In the course of a child's development, psychologists note that thinking and fantasizing about one's origins seems to be inevitable. A child with a "clouded genetic heritage" has a more difficult time achieving a secure personal identity.[22] Yet a secure identity, self-esteem, and a sense of autonomy and self-control are crucial in children's growth.[23] Parental control is overwhelming to children. If they know or believe their parents contracted to fabricate them rather than merely received them, they feel more reduced in power.

In alternative reproduction, the question "Whose baby am I?" becomes inevitable.[24] "Why was my biological parent not more concerned with what would happen to the new life he or she helped to create?" The need to know about possible half-siblings and other kin may become urgent at some point in later development. From the child's point of view, the asymmetry of the relationship with the rearing parents is also a factor. Even if the Freudian psychoanalytic account of Oedipal family relationships is not correct in all its details, there still exist extremely complex fantasies and psychological currents that arise in the family triangle of mother, father, and child. Having two parents with whom one can safely identify, love, and leave behind is a great advantage. One's sexual origins and one's kin are important psychological realities to a child.

DONORS AND THE CULTURAL ETHOS

Procuring donors of sperm, eggs, embryos, or wombs is an essential component of collaborative reproduction. Yet encouraging persons to give, or worse to sell, their genetic or gestational capacity attacks a basic foundation of morality—that is, the taking of responsibility for the consequences of one's actions. Adult persons are held morally responsible for their words and deeds. In serious matters, such as sex and reproduction, which have irreversible lifetime consequences, we rightly hold persons to high standards of moral and legal responsibility. To counter the tendency or temptation toward sexual irresponsibility or parental neglect, Western culture has insisted that men and women be held accountable for their contribution to the creation of new life.

A donor, whether male or female, who takes part in collaborative reproduction does not assume personal responsibility for his or her momentous personal action engendering new life. In fact, the donor contracts (possibly with payment) to abdicate present and future personal responsibility. The donor is specifically enjoined not to carry through on what he or she initiates, but instead to hand over to physicians or others, often unknown others, the result of his or her reproductive capacity. The generative power to create a new life is by design ejected from consideration. This genetic generative capacity is not like a kidney (or any other organ), but is part of the basic identity that is received from one's own parents. When a person treats this capacity as trivial or sells the use of it, he or she breaks an implicit compact. Parental responsibility is an essential form of the natural responsibility human beings have to help each other, and it gives rise to moral claims not governed by specific contracts or commitments.[25]

Persons who abdicate parental responsibility also deprive their own parents of grand-parenthood and any other of their descendants of knowledge of their kin. Future children of the donor, or other children of a surrogate mother, will never know their half brother or sister. To so disregard the reality of the biological integrity of our identity and allow donors to engage in contractual reproduction is to have a mistaken view of how human beings actually function—or should function.

If we succeed in isolating sexual and reproductive acts from long-term personal responsibility, this moral abdication will increase existing problems within the culture. Do we want to encourage women to be able to emotionally distance themselves from the child in their womb enough to give it up? Do we wish to sanction male detachment from their biological offspring? Already epidemics of divorce, illegitimate conceptions, and parental irresponsibility and failures are straining the family bonds and the firm commitment that are necessary for successful childrearing and the full development of individuals. If we legitimize the isolation of genetic, gestational, and social parentage and regularly allow reproduction to be governed by contract and purchase, our culture will become even more fragmented, rootless, and alienated.

One of the foundations of a responsible ethic concerning sexuality is to see sexual acts as personal acts involving the whole person. Lust is wrong because it disregards the whole person and his or her human dignity. Another person is reduced to a means of selfish pleasure, and if money is involved, exploitation of the needy can occur. So, too, it seems wrong to isolate and use a person's reproductive capacity apart from his or her personal life. When it is a woman donating her egg and gestational capacity, there is a grave danger of exploitation, as feminists have warned.[26] The physiological risks attending the drastic intervention in a woman's reproductive system needed for surrogacy or embryo transplants are considerable. But perhaps more important is that pregnancy is not simply a neutral organic experience, but a time of bonding of the mother to her child.

If a great deal of money is offered for surrogacy, needy women will be tempted to sell their bodies and suffer the emotional consequences—and the experience of prostitution leads one to expect that many of these women will then hand over the money to males. Feminists rightly protest that allowing women to be surrogates will in fact turn women into baby machines bought and regulated by those rich enough to pay.[27] From another perspective, a surrogate mother could also be seen as deliberately producing and selling her baby. What will these practices do to other children of the surrogate or, for that matter, other children in the society? Can children comprehend, without anxiety, the fact that mothers make babies and give them away for money? The great primordial reality of interdependency and mutual bonding represented by mother and child is attacked. Contracts and regulations can hardly stem the psychological and social harm alternative reproductive technologies make possible.

CONCLUSION

Our society faces a challenge to its traditional ethics of reproduction and family norms. The cultural norms, based upon biological predispositions, is for the genetic, gestational, and rearing parents to be identical and for the nuclear family to exist within an extended family kinship system. The family should be seen as an intergenerational institution having an ecological relationship with the larger society.

As the range of ethics has broadened to include a concern for the dignity, worth, and rights of women and children, so has our understanding of morally responsible parenthood been refined and developed. The parental enterprise is rightly seen as basically an altruistic one—children should not be viewed as a form of personal property or as a means to satisfy adult desires or fulfill adult needs. When making reproductive decisions, the good of the potential child, along with the general cultural conditions which further childrearing and family support systems, should take precedence over other considerations, such as biologically integral acts or individual desires.

I have argued for an ethical position that limits alternative reproductive techniques to remedying infertility in expectable parental conditions that preserve the cultural norm, which includes the identity of genetic, gestational, and rearing parents. Collaborative reproduction will not serve the good of the potential child or the family, nor will it meet the need of the culture for morally responsible reproductive behavior.

It seems a sign of cultural progress that children are highly valued and infertility is acknowledged as a misfortune. It is also wonderful that medical reproductive technology can remedy the handicap of infertility. But as medical professionals and people in general confront these innovative interventions, the ethical, psychological, and cultural dimensions of technological procedures cannot be discounted. For the good of the child, the donors, the family, and our society, certain ethical limits must be set. Not everything that can be done to satisfy individual reproductive desires should be done. As Ghandi said, "Means are ends in the making."[28] Collaborative reproduction using third parties comes at too high a price.

NOTES

1. See Sidney Callahan, "An Ethical Analysis of Responsible Parenthood," in *Genetic Counseling: Facts, Values, and Norms,* Birth Defects: Original Article Series, vol. 15, no. 22 (New York: Alan R. Liss, 1979).

2. Barbara M. Newman and Philip R. Newman, *Development through Life: A Psychosocial Approach* (Homewood, Ill.: The Dorsey Press, 1979); Lynn Hoffman, *Foundations of Family Therapy: A Conceptual Framework for Systems Change* (New York: Basic Books, 1981).

3. Daniel P. Moynihan, *Family and Nation* (New York: Harcourt Brace Jovanovich, 1986); Lenore J. Weitzman, *The Divorce Revolution* (New York: The Free Press, 1986).

4. The role of the father has been seen as critically important in both the female and male child's intellectual development, moral development, sex role identity, and future parenting; for a summary of relevant research, see Ross D. Parke, *Fathers* (Cambridge, Mass.: Harvard University Press, 1981) and Shirley M.H. Hanson and Frederick W. Bonett, *Dimensions of Fatherhood* (Beverly Hills, Calif.: Sage Publications, 1985).

5. See Jeanne Altman, "Sociobiological Perspectives on Parenthood," *Parenthood: A Psychodynamic Perspective* (New York: Guilford Press, 1984).

6. Kathleen Gough, "The Origin of the Family," *Journal of Marriage and the Family,* November 1971: 760–68. Peter J. Wilson, *Man the Promising Primate: The Conditions of Human Evolution* (New Haven, Conn.: Yale University Press, 1980).

7. George Peter Murdock, "The Universality of the Nuclear Family," in *A Modern Introduction to the Family,* ed. Norman W. Bell and Ezra F. Vogel (New York: The Free Press, 1968); Mary Jo Bane, *Here to Stay: American Families in the Twentieth Century* (New York: Basic Books, 1976).

8. Stephen P. Bank and Michael D. Kahn, *The Sibling Bond* (New York: Basic Books, 1982); Gunhild O. Hagestad, "The Aging Society as a Context for Family Life," *Daedalus: The Aging Society,* Winter 1986:119–39.

9. E.O. Wilson, *Sociobiology.* (Cambridge, Mass.: Harvard University Press, 1975).

10. Carol Nadelson, "The Absent Parent, Emotional Sequelae," in *Infertility: Medical, Emotional and Social Considerations,* ed. Miriam D. Mazor and Harriet F. Simons (New York: Human Sciences Press, 1984); Arthur D. Sorsky, Annette Baron, and Reuben Pannor, "Identity Conflicts in Adoptees," in *New Directions in Childhood Psychopathology,* vol. 1 (New York: International Universities Press, 1982).

11. Twin studies and the recognition of inherited temperamental traits have followed studies showing a genetic component to alcoholism, manic-depression, schizophrenia, antisocial behavior, and I.Q. For a popular discussion of the findings in regard to schizophrenia and criminal behavior, see Sarnoff Mednick, "Crime in the Family Tree,"

Psychology Today, 19 (March 1985): 58–61. For a more general discussion by an anthropologist, see Melvin Konner, *The Tangled Wing: Biological Constraints on the Human Spirit* (New York: Holt, Rinehart & Winston, 1982).

12. Helmut Thielicke, *The Ethics of Sex* (New York: Harper & Row, 1964), 32 ff.

13. Aidan Macfarlane, *The Psychology of Childbirth* (Cambridge, Mass.: Harvard University Press, 1977); M. Greenberg, *The Birth of a Father* (New York: Continuum, 1985).

14. The difficulties of undergoing AID are described in Sharon Gibbons Collotta, "The Role of the Nurse in AID," in *Infertility*; see also R. Snowden, G.D. Mitchel, and E.M. Snowden, "Stigma and Stress in AID," in *Artificial Reproduction: A Social Investigation.* (London: George Allen & Unwin, 1983).

15. Brenda Maddox, *The Half Parent: Living with Other People's Children* (New York: M. Evans and Company, 1975); Renato Espinoza and Yvonne Newman, *Stepparenting: With Annotated Bibliography* (Rockville, Md.: National Institute of Mental Health, Center for Studies of Child and Family Mental Health, 1979).

16. See "Explaining the Differences between Biological Father and Stepfather Incest," and "Social Factors in the Occurrence of Incestuous Abuse," in Diana E.H. Russell, *The Secret Trauma: Incest in the Lives of Girls and Women* (New York: Basic Books, 1986).

17. Daniel N. Stern, *The Interpersonal World of the Infant: A View from Psychoanalysis and Developmental Psychology* (New York: Basic Books, 1985).

18. There is the beginning of a philosophical reassessment of the status of children in Jeffrey Blustein, *Parents & Children: The Ethics of the Family* (Oxford: Oxford University Press, 1982), and in Onoroa O'Neill and William Ruddick, eds., *Having Children: Philosophical and Legal Reflections on Parenthood* (New York: Oxford University Press, 1979).

19. See "The Child as Surrogate Self" and "The Child as Status Symbol," in David Elkind, *The Hurried Child* (Reading, Mass.: Addison-Wesley, 1981).

20. Salvador Minuchin, Bernice L. Rosman, and Walter Baker, *Psychosomatic Families: Anorexia Nervosa in Context* (Cambridge, Mass.: Harvard University Press, 1978).

21. Jay Haley, *Leaving Home: The Therapy of Disturbed Young People* (New York: McGraw-Hill, 1980).

22. Betty J. Lifton, *Lost and Found: The Adoption Experience* (New York: Dial Press, 1979).

23. See "The Sense of Self," in Eleanor E. Maccoby, *Social Development: Psychological Growth and the Parent-Child Relationship* (New York: Harcourt Brace Jovanovich, 1980).

24. Lori Andrews, "Yours, Mine and Theirs," *Psychology Today* 18 (December 1984): 20–29.

25. Hans Jonas, *The Imperative of Responsibility: In Search of an Ethics for the Technological Age* (Chicago: University of Chicago Press, 1984).

26. Barbara Rothman, *The Tentative Pregnancy* (New York: Viking Press, 1986); H. Holmes, B. Hoskins, and M. Gross, *The Custom Made Child* (Clifton, N.J.: Humana Press, 1981).

27. Angela R. Holder, "Surrogate Motherhood: Babies for Fun and Profit," *Law, Medicine, and Health Care* 11 (June 1984): 115–17.

28. Mahatma Gandhi, *The Essential Gandhi* (New York: Random House, 1962).

Chapter 4

Caution in the Definition and Diagnosis of Infant Brain Death

D. Alan Shewmon

Of all the acts of doctors, a declaration of death has perhaps the most irreversible and profound consequences, so that accuracy in diagnosis is of the utmost importance. Now that the diagnosis of brain death in adults and older chidren has become more or less standardized, it is being made with increasing frequency in young children and even infants, a trend that has been accelerated by recent advances in organ transplantation. In this chapter the medical and philosophical aspects of brain death will be reviewed, followed by an analysis of the degree of certainty inherent in various types of diagnostic criteria. Some unique aspects of the infant brain will then be discussed, with emphasis on the errors that may result from an application of the type of criteria used for adults. After reviewing the difficulties of establishing valid criteria for infant brain death in the near future, some practical consequences will be considered in light of the increasing pressure on neurologists to diagnose it.

NEUROPATHOLOGICAL ASPECTS

There are two basic ways in which the brain can selectively die in the absence of serious damage to other organs. The most obvious is through severe open head trauma, with direct and total destruction of the brain. The other way, less obvious but far more common, begins with a cerebral insult that leads to a vicious cycle of brain swelling and decreased cerebral blood flow, which mutually exacerbate each other until blood flow ceases. In the process, the brain becomes so swollen that it herniates through the various cranial compartments and out through the opening into the spinal canal, destroying itself in the process. This can happen selectively to the brain even after such a systemic insult as cardiac arrest or drowning, because the brain is the organ most sensitive to lack of blood flow or oxygen and therefore is the first to become damaged. If the insult is not so severe as to damage all the other organs irreparably, but severe enough to initiate the above sequence of events in the brain, selective destruction of the entire brain can result.

Ordinarily, as soon as the brainstem becomes affected, either directly from the initial insult or from the process of brain herniation, the person stops breathing. The resultant lack of oxygen leads quickly to cardiac arrest and soon thereafter to disintegration of all bodily tissues. If, however, breathing is supported mechanically, the heart can continue beating on its own, in spite of the total brain destruction. This is the state known as *brain death*. The remainder of the body's cells can be kept alive for some time, even up to several months,[1] if ventilation, fluids, nutrition, and intensive nursing care are provided (the record is 201 days[2]). Meanwhile, the dead brain tissue first becomes soft, then liquefies, and eventually disappears entirely, leaving a bag of scar tissue full of watery fluid. Almost always, however, patients are disconnected from artificial life support long before this stage is reached. *Respirator brain* is the pathological term used to describe the early stages of this liquefactive necrosis. The challenge for the diagnostician is to distinguish early on and with certainty such total brain destruction (initially on a submicroscopic level) from a less severe insult producing only transient suppression of function. As we shall see, this distinction is often easy to make in the clinical setting, but at other times, especially with young infants, it is not.

PHILOSOPHICAL ASPECTS

Brain death became a philosophical problem as soon as it became a medical possibility, with the advent of improved mechanical ventilators in the 1950s. During the next two decades there was much confusion as to the nature of this state, as revealed by the various terms used to describe it. For example, *coma dépassé*[3] and *irreversible coma*[4] implied that there was a live patient in a permanent sleeplike state. Even the contemporary term *brain death* is ambiguous, in that it can be understood to mean either death of a particular organ (the brain) in an otherwise live body or death of the person by virtue of death of that organ. The well-intentioned attempts of some state legislatures to formulate brain death statutes often only aggravated the confusion by poor wording that implied that brain death was a mere legal fiction. For this and other more philosophical reasons, some respectable thinkers continue to object to the concept.[5]

It would be far beyond the scope of this chapter to attempt to cover all aspects of the debate, and the interested reader should refer to a recent review by Lamb.[6] Objections notwithstanding, the past decade or so has witnessed a general acceptance of the position that brain death is true personal death and not merely a legal status. Nevertheless, I would like to dwell on this point somewhat more than would otherwise be warranted, because of an emerging campaign (to be described shortly) to expand the legal definition of *brain death* for infants, a campaign based on a failure to comprehend fully the concepts involved.

One of the best ways to understand the true nature of brain death is through the following macabre example. Suppose that a ghoulish surgeon were to sever some victim's head from his body and connect the major vessels to a cardiopulmonary bypass machine. (This is actually not so far-fetched as it may seem; it has been done in Finland to living human fetuses for research purposes.)[7] If the nerves to the vocal cords were preserved and a flow of air passed through the trachea, the person could continue to communicate with us. Suppose also that the rest of the body were attached to a mechanical ventilator, so that the heart could continue to beat and the blood to circulate.

Imagine now that the dissection of the head is extended even further, so as to leave only the brain, mouth, and vocal apparatus connected to the life-support system. The person is now blind and deaf, but can still communicate with us. The parts of the head that had been removed are now reattached to the rest of the body on the ventilator (or one could more simply imagine that initially the brain, mouth, and vocal apparatus had been removed from the original body and attached to the life-support system). In one part of the room, then, is a person so severely mutilated that he hardly looks human, but he himself will tell us that he is indeed the same person as before. In the other part of the room is something that looks very similar to the person's former body, but it is clearly not the person's present body.

We now carry the experiment a step further. Realizing that the mouth and vocal apparatus are essential, not for consciousness or life, but only for communication, we imagine they are surgically disconnected from the person's brain and reattached to the "cadaver" on the ventilator in the other corner of the room. (Equivalently, the brain alone could initially have been removed from the intact body and placed on the life-support system.) There is now a human person cut off from communication with the rest of the world, but nonetheless conscious, thinking, remembering, imagining, and experiencing profound emotions. In the other corner is something that now looks *exactly* like the person's former body, but is clearly not the person's present body.

The cadaver on the mechanical ventilator is nearly identical to a brain-dead body. It is *not* a deeply comatose person, because the person, whose body it used to be, is in the other corner of the room and quite conscious. The person does not die if we remove the ventilator from the cadaver and the heart stops; rather, the person dies if we disconnect his brain from the life-support system or destroy it in some other way—and it is no mere legal fiction to declare him dead at that moment. If we put the dead brain tissue back into the skull of the cadaver on the ventilator, then we have something identical in every way to the kind of brain dead body encountered in modern intensive care units.

Because wound healing and other "vital" functions can still take place in such a brain dead body, many people have great conceptual difficulty calling such a body *dead*. But one should bear in mind that *life* is not a univocal term; therefore, to insist that either the original person is alive or there is no life at all is an oversimplification. For example, if a human body was entirely destroyed except for a single cell (e.g., a fibroblast), no one would say that the person was still alive, but neither would anyone claim that the cell was not alive. In fact, if placed in a proper culture medium, it would multiply into a whole colony of living cells similar to itself. The transition from human being to fibroblast is not a transition from life to death, but from human life to a lower form of life (of course, this does not invalidate the concept of the death of the person). The same would apply even if there was a residual group of cells rather than a single cell. The brain dead body is precisely such a group of cells, which happens to have the external appearance of a human body (because it once was one); however, it lacks the complexity and type of integration requisite for human nature. In summary, brain death and traditional cardiopulmonary death are not two different kinds of death, but simply two different medical contexts for one and the same good old-fashioned personal death.

NEW PROPOSALS TO EXPAND THE LEGAL DEFINITION OF
BRAIN DEATH

As clear as this may seem, much of the general public and not a few physicians (generally non-neurologists) have still not grasped the basic concept of brain death, in spite of their familiarity with the medical aspects of it. Their practice implies an equation of brain death with personal death, but their words betray an inner lack of conviction of that equivalence. For example, one article relates the results of research done on a child diagnosed, in effect, as brain dead (although the term was not explicitly used).[8] Neither the authors nor the journal editors saw any ethical problem with the research, since the child was presumably dead. Nevertheless, the following curious statement slipped out: "The study could not be continued because the child died from a mechanical ventilation problem."

News stories in the lay press frequently reveal an even deeper confusion on the part of reporters regarding the concepts of death, brain death, vegetative state, coma, termination of inappropriate life support, and active euthanasia, as though these were interchangeable or at least vaguely overlapped.

It is disturbing that such confusion exists even in the minds of legislators who have recently taken it upon themselves to expand the legal definition of brain death to include anencephalic infants for purposes of organ transplantation (California Senate Bill 2018). (Anencephaly is a severe congenital malformation with absent cerebral hemispheres, skull, and scalp, but a present and functioning brainstem. Because anencephalic infants live up to several weeks at the most, they are considered by some transplant specialists as a valuable source of organs. Nevertheless, these to-be-defined-as-dead infants breathe, move spontaneously, cry, and often can suck.) In one piece of promotional literature, for example, we are told that Karen Ann Quinlan was "brain dead" and that "her parents fought for the right to 'turn off' life support systems that kept [her]. . . '*technically alive.*'"[9] (The emphasis is added. In fact, she was in a persistent vegetative state, and her parents fought to discontinue ventilatory support because of its inappropriateness.) Later in the same article, we are told that the concept of brain death came about "only after much controversy, undue hardship and trauma to friends and relatives of *surviving brain dead* or *comatose* individuals" (emphasis added).

Neither does the notion of brain death as true personal death seem to be understood by those physicians who support such a redefinition (the most vocal so far have been pediatric transplant surgeons). In an article by one such physician, we read in one paragraph that these children should be considered legally dead by virtue of being "brain absent" (already misleading; they are really "cerebral hemisphere absent"). But in the next few paragraphs, we are told that the anencephalic should be treated "as a person" and that the removal of organs should be carried out "in a way that would not conceivably cause suffering . . . with compassion, sensitivity, and respect."[10]

Such inconsistencies betray a fundamental misconception that brain death in general is nothing more than a legalism to provide a facade of legitimacy for the removal of organs from living patients. This is implied in the author's statement that "the 'whole brain' definition of death was adopted to *protect* the comatose patient whose injured brain might conceivably recover function" (emphasis added)—as though the old cardiopulmonary definition of death were insufficient "protection" for such patients! Is not such a statement a kind of Freudian slip, revealing a latent concern that comatose patients might be in danger from a tendency to overzealousness on the part of some transplant surgeons? On the one hand, the author believes that anencephalics should be legally defined as dead; on the other hand, he maintains that one should "not detract from the dignity of [their] *dying* or abridge [their] *right to die*" (emphasis added). Do not the perceived need for protection and the self-contradictory assertion that someone can be legally dead while simultaneously having a "right to die" stem from an implicit belief that brain death in a patient derives more from the transplantation needs of someone else than from the intrinsic medical condition of the patient himself?

The press, with its characteristic tendency to sensationalism and oversimplification of complex issues, has also begun to take up the cause, obscuring the issue in a profusion of rhetoric and emotional appeals.[11] Only time will tell to what extent the general public and the legislatures will be convinced. Nevertheless, such a notion of brain death as a mere legal construct has no relevance to the concept of personhood, and if it ever becomes enshrined in law, it will only lead to confusion between legitimate organ donation and active *involuntary* euthanasia for the benefit of others.

Some thinkers have argued that *whole-brain death* is too restrictive a concept and that the absence (either congenital or due to postnatal destruction) of the cerebral hemispheres alone, inspite of an intact brainstem (i.e., *neocortical death*) is sufficient to constitute personal death.[12] This is clearly *not* the line of reasoning taken by the current promoters of an expanded legal definition to include anencephaly, as evidenced by the aforesaid and by the fact that they insist on excluding all other cases where there is an absence of cerebral hemispheres but with the brainstem intact (e.g., hydranencephaly, persistent vegetative state).

Even though I myself have some sympathy for the notion of neocortical death from a strictly theoretical standpoint, I believe that society would be gravely harmed by any attempt to implement a policy on neocortial death in the foreseeable future. Given the prevailing failure (at all levels of society, including the medical profession, legislatures, and the general public) to comprehend even the basic concepts involved in whole brain death, as well as the propensity of many physicians to make definitive diagnoses of persistent vegetative state or irreversible coma in the absence of any reliable criteria whatsoever, the gullibility of the courts in accepting such diagnoses, and the increasing pressure to obtain organs for transplantation, any expansion of the legal definition of death to include this condition would seem to spell nothing but social and medical disaster. (For a more complete development of arguments against a higher-cortical function definition of death, see Lamb.)[13]

Another important example of confusion of these fundamental concepts is the British approach, which considers brain*stem* death as equivalent to personal death because it renders the rest of the brain permanently nonfunctional and invariably leads to somatic death.[14] This position involves two mistakes. The first derives from the fact that the ''permanence'' of nonfunction of the rest of the brain is not *intrinsic*, but merely *occasioned* by the lack of input from the brainstem. It is theoretically possible that electrical stimulation of the cerebral hemispheres just above the level of the brainstem lesion could restore consciousness—and in fact this has actually been accomplished in a few human cases.[15] The second fallacy is to equate the inevitability of death with death itself. With respect to the concept of personal death, therefore, brainstem death is not so much a diagnosis as a prognosis (albeit a very reliable and useful one).

DIAGNOSTIC ASPECTS

Because of the definitiveness and far-reaching legal, social, religious, and emotional implications of a declaration of death, diagnostic criteria for brain death are unlike criteria for any other medical condition, in that they must leave no room whatsoever for false positive error. That is, the physician must be absolutely certain that no live person will ever be mistakenly diagnosed as dead; otherwise, he would merely be making a prognosis, not a diagnosis. In a sense, a prognosis is a statement about the physician's state of mind (his degree of certainty), whereas a diagnosis is a statement about the patient's state of health.

One of the most important ramifications of this distinction is that although very poor prognoses may justify termination of burdensome or otherwise inappropriate life-sustaining treatments, they do *not* justify hastening death by the removal of organs for transplantation. Intellectual honesty demands admission of the least uncertainty and postponement of a definitive pronouncement until certainty is achieved. Someone else's need for organs is insufficient reason for putting forward as certain what is in reality only an educated guess.

The Establishment of Diagnostic Certitude

Before we consider some of the unique problems surrounding brain death in infants, let us consider how diagnostic certitude is currently achieved in adults and older children. That this is not at all straightforward is evidenced by the fact that there continues to be a wide diversity of opinion and practice from one country to the next—and even within our own country in spite of the 1981 publication of a set of diagnostic guidelines recommended by the medical consultants to the President's Commission for the Study of Ethical Problems in Medicine and Biomedical and Behavioral Research (hereinafter referred to as the *President's Commission*).[16]

In a very small minority of cases, certainty of brain death derives from immediate evidence of total brain destruction, as in severe open head trauma with much of the skull and brain visibly missing. Even in the case of an intact skull, brain herniation from whatever cause is often diagnosable by a characteristic rostral-caudal ("head-to-tail") progression of signs and symptoms corresponding to the level of the brain affected.[17] Once that level has reached the lower end of the brainstem, there can be absolute certainty that the entire brain has been destroyed. This rostral-caudal progression is easily recognized by anyone trained in neurologic diagnosis, and no other condition mimics it. Demonstration of sustained absence of intracranial blood flow, beyond the limit of viability for nerve cells, is still another means to achieve certainty of destruction of the entire brain.

Curiously, even though the rostral-caudal sequence provides diagnostic certainty and is frequently utilized (especially by neurosurgeons), it is not mentioned explicitly in any of the standard sets of diagnostic criteria. This is undoubtedly because it simply does not occur in many cases of brain death. In order to be more generally applicable, therefore, essentially all brain death criteria are based on an absence of brain function that persists for some critical length of time, beyond which there is supposedly no possibility for even minimal recovery. Thus, the Uniform Determination of Death Act (UDDA) was formulated by the President's Commission in terms of brain nonfunction rather than brain destruction: "An individual who has sustained . . . irreversible cessation of all functions of the entire brain, including the brain stem, is dead. A determination of death must be made in accordance with accepted medical standards."[18] (See Byrne et al. for a discussion of some of the problems with a functional as opposed to structural definition of brain death.)[19] The various versions of "accepted medical standards" (of which over 30 had already been proposed prior to the Commission's report)[20] differ mainly in terms of the minimum observation time and the set of functions that must be tested. All recommend that the cause of the brain death be sought if it is not already known, and many make provisions for various "confirmatory" tests which can shorten the requisite observation period without loss of reliability.

The fact that there are so many variations among brain death criteria and that certain optional tests are called "confirmatory" suggests that some of the criteria may not have the perfect reliability that is assumed. Proponents of a given criterion usually try to prove its validity by collecting a large series of cases showing that the criterion did not result in a single misdiagnosis. The larger the database, the more certain the criterion. Thus, the President's Commission declared that "the published criteria for determining cessation of brain functions have been uniformly successful in diagnosing death," for which reason "medical experts testified to the Commission that the risk of mistake in a competently performed examination was infinitesimal."[21]

But is the mere uniformity of diagnostic success *to date* a theoretically valid way to guarantee that the risk of mistake is "infinitesimal"? Such a method of validation involves statistical sampling, which contains an element of intrinsic uncertainty. All that can be stated with absolute certainty is that no exception to the rule has occurred *yet* and that there has been no evidence so far to *in*validate a criterion. But how large must the sample size be in order for the probability of false positive error to be truly "infinitesimal," so that the criterion legitimately can be regarded as one of diagnosis and not merely of prognosis?

It may come as a surprise to many people, but such a calculation has never been carried out for any of the currently used brain death criteria. One reason is that the problem is not amenable to the usual methods of biostatistics. Nevertheless, by means of Bayesian probability theory, the theoretical probability of false positive error can be calculated quantitatively with no information other than that N out of N patients meeting some criterion experienced a uniform outcome.[22] That probability is on the order of $1/(N+2)$. As a corollary, the chance of making at least one false positive error among the next $(N+1)$ patients who meet the criterion is 50 percent. Of course, if the rate of drop-off of recoverers as a function of duration of criteria were also taken into account, the theoretical risk of false positive error could potentially be reduced considerably. That would require, however, a knowledge of the mathematical characteristics of the drop-off curve in the region of its asymptotic tail, which in turn would require a very large database, at least several orders of magnitude larger than what is currently available. A rigorous calculation of the risk of false positive error has therefore never been carried out for any of the standard criteria, and if the above methodology were applied to present databases, the theoretical risk would hardly turn out to be negligible, let alone infinitesimal, as the medical consultants to the President's Commission so gratuitously asserted.

This does not mean that brain death cannot be diagnosed with certainty. Examples of self-evidently valid criteria have already been given: the rostral-caudal sequence indicative of complete brain herniation, the persistent absence of intracranial blood flow, etc. But any criterion based on the mere cessation of some subset of brain functions for some arbitrary period of time is not at all valid self-evidently and, is therefore inherently unvalidatable as a diagnostic criterion by means of any realistic clinical study, although it could very well be proven to be a highly reliable prognostic criterion.

The Collaborative Study

As a case in point, consider the largest and most important U.S. study to date, the nine-hospital Collaborative Study sponsored by the National Institute of Neurological Diseases and Stroke (as it was then called) in 1971–73.[23] I dwell on this here because it illustrates many of the difficulties that will be inherent in any future analogous undertaking with respect to infants (plans for which are already being tentatively discussed). Although it was originally intended as a pilot project to investigate the suitability of various methodologies for a larger subsequent study, its results have been interpreted as themselves having validated a set of diagnostic criteria and the intended larger study has never materialized. Patient entry criteria consisted of ''cerebral unresponsiveness'' and apnea (manifested by lack of effort to override the ventilator, which is now recognized as an inadequate test for apnea), regardless of cause, with age over one year. Of the 844 patients entered, 503 still had these signs after at least 15 minutes. These constituted the main study group, and they were followed prospectively at frequent intervals until recovery or somatic death. Evidence of brain death was taken to be eventual cardiopulmonary death within three months (which occurred in 462 of the patients), although autopsy information was also available in 226 cases.

If the electroencephalogram (EEG) remained isoelectric (flat) for 24 hours, the attending physician had the prerogative to discontinue support at that time. This option (which accounted for as many as 140 out of the 185 who met the eventually arrived-at criteria),[24] while humane and ethically appropriate, introduced a major methodologic flaw. Those deaths could hardly be taken as evidence of the power of the criteria to predict death, except insofar as the criteria were self-fulfilling. As Masland succinctly put it, ''The study has a deficiency in that the determination of death was partly established on the criteria which the study was supposed to establish.''[25]

Putting this issue aside for the moment, let us see how a set of diagnostic criteria was derived. If cerebral unresponsiveness and apnea, both lasting 15 minutes, were taken together as a putative criterion, then this criterion would have been predictive of eventual death in 462/503 (92 percent) of the cases. If electrocerebral silence (ECS) on EEG was added to the above, then 187 patients would have met those criteria, of whom 185 died within a week (99 percent accuracy). In both of the two survivors, the etiology was drug overdose (both recovered completely). If, therefore, lack of drug intoxication was incorporated into the set of criteria, then all 185 out of 185 patients who met the criteria died.

But what if, through random sampling, those two had not been among the patients in the database prior to closure of the study? Or worse yet, what if toxicology screening had not been performed and the minimum duration for discontinuing treatment had arbitrarily been set at 12 rather than 24 hours? In either case, the process of criterion refinement would have stopped at the penultimate step, and we would have been told that all of the 185 (or 187) patients meeting the triple criteria of cerebral unresponsiveness, apnea, and ECS had died (100 percent accuracy). In spite of the uniformity of outcome, however, the true rate of false positive error for that set of criteria would have been around 1 percent, which is surprisingly close to the theoretical risk of $1/(N+2)$.

In a summary statement, the investigators qualified their reference to the 185 deaths with the clause ''all presumably with dead brains.''[26] The adverb ''presumably'' implies that the autopsy data were insufficient to confirm many of the diagnoses. In fact, only 81 of the cases that met the clinical and EEG criteria for brain death were autopsied, excluding those with less than 24 hours on the respirator after onset of those signs (insufficient time to develop the pathological changes of respirator brain). Of these, 12 (15 percent) did not have respirator brain,[27] indicating either that autopsy examination after 24 hours on the respirator was too insensitive a method of verification or that a disturbing proportion of those who met the diagnostic criteria and ''died'' within a week were actually not brain dead at the time the criteria were met (i.e., perhaps they might have experienced some degree of neurologic recovery if they had not died from cardiopulmonary arrest). Of course, the inevitability of somatic death was a spurious endpoint to begin with, hardly proving that the patient was already dead prior to that.

Thus, this monumental study did not in any way validate a set of diagnostic criteria for brain death. Its design rendered it intrinsically incapable of distinguishing dead from dying patients, the criteria were partially self-fulfilling, and the autopsies were partially nonconfirmatory. But perhaps most importantly, the number of patients was far too small to justify any claim concerning reliability. In spite of the fact that nine major medical centers joined in this herculean effort and as many as 844 patients were enrolled, only 69 who met the eventual criteria showed proof of total brain destruction. Nevertheless, the Collaborative Study still remains the best available source of information concerning the correlations of the major clinical and laboratory parameters relevant to coma prognosis and brain death in adults and older children.

That non-self-evident criteria cannot be validated by a clinical study was perhaps acknowledged obliquely by the investigators when they stated, "Perhaps at this time, an overlap of criteria is advisable in view of the difficulties in the determination of drug intoxications, the fallacies in clinical and laboratory tests, and the inevitable observer errors. However, the chance of even temporary survival if the proposed clinical and EEG criteria are met for 30 minutes is small, and are [sic] infinitesimal if the confirmatory test [absent cerebral blood flow] is also met."[28] In other words, if a declaration of death requires a truly infinitesimal, not just a small, chance of error (otherwise it should be called a *prognostication*), then the diagnosis must be based, not on the proposed clinical and EEG criteria, but on the "confirmatory test," so-called because of its self-evident validity. Nevertheless, it is still widely believed that this study has somehow validated a set of criteria.[29]

The President's Commission Criteria

Based on the information bank of the Collaborative Study, the remainder of the medical literature, two additional studies (retrospective and prognostic in nature, comprising a total of 316 patients, of whom 48 met criteria for brain death),[30] and their own combined personal experience, the medical consultants for the President's Commission proposed the following diagnostic guidelines,[31] which represent merely "one statement of currently accepted medical standards."[32]

   I. Cessation of *all* brain functions, including the following:
     A. Cerebral functions (assessed clinically)
     B. Brainstem functions (based on apnea and absence of brainstem reflexes)
  II. *Irreversibility* of such cessation, as demonstrated by all of the following:
     A. The cause of coma is established and is sufficient to account for the loss of brain functions
     B. Various conditions that can mimic brain death have been ruled out
     C. The cessation of all brain functions persists for an appropriate period of observation:
        1. If confirmatory EEG or blood flow test is used—6 hours
        2. If confirmatory EEG and blood flow test are not used and
           a) Irreversible condition is well established—12 hours
           b) Etiology is anoxia—24 hours

The guidelines also listed several complicating conditions (drug and metabolic intoxications, hypothermia, young age, and shock) that require special caution.

It should be pointed out that an EEG is not really as "confirmatory" as absence of blood flow. The critical duration of ECS required for certainty of irreversibility is as inherently unvalidatable as any other non-self-evident criterion. Upon close scrutiny of the evidence for waiting the magic six hours (cf. II.C.1. above), one realizes that out of the extensive cumulative experience with ECS, the number of patients with EEGs actually recorded at six hours after the onset of coma, followed by autopsy-documented total brain destruction (and not merely eventual somatic death), is unknown but probably relatively small.[33] The only truly confirmatory test for brain death (in the sense of being self-evidently valid) is sustained absence of intracranial blood flow.

Because there has not been a single case in the medical literature of anyone meeting these criteria and even partially recovering, the claim that the criteria carry only an "infinitesimal" chance of error is generally accepted by the medical community. Nevertheless, patients diagnosed as brain dead are not usually supported long enough for any rare potential (full or partial) recoverers to manifest themselves. The lack of documented exceptions to the rule proves nothing other than that the criteria are very successful at being self-fulfilling. This is not to say that the criteria are therefore unreliable, but merely that the reliability of every item under II.C. above, apart from the confirmatory blood flow test, has not yet been (and inherently cannot be) proven. The same applies for all other brain death criteria that have ever been proposed, particularly the British criteria, which base the diagnosis on clinical signs of brainstem function alone.[34] When the supporting data are carefully scrutinized, it becomes clear that the infallibility of current brain death criteria is more an article of faith than a scientifically proven fact.

Exceptions to the Rule?

It is not quite true that there have been no documented recoverers after a competently made diagnosis of brain death; it is simply that these stories have not passed from the lay press into the medical literature. As Walker recently stated, "Even in the 1980's, accounts of persons prematurely declared dead awakening in a morgue may be found in the press. . . . These modern Lazaruses usually suffered from hypothermia or drug intoxication."[35] They therefore represent failures to apply the criteria rather than failures of the criteria.

Note, however, his choice of the word "usually," as opposed to "always." Although Walker did not cite any examples not involving drugs or hypothermia, such cases *have* occurred, for example, that of a 46-year-old man who suffered a massive heart attack and became immediately unconscious. Five and one-half hours later, a neurologist determined that he had "no brain activity," and his wife gave permission for organ donation. Around 12 hours after the onset of coma, and literally on the verge of the incision for organ retrieval, his eyes blinked, whereupon he was immediately returned to the intensive care unit and ultimately recovered.[36] The newspaper account does not mention whether an EEG had been performed; if so, he conceivably could have met the President's Commission criteria (only one-half hour short of the magic six-hour mark); if not, he might at least have met some of the British criteria (no clinical signs of brainstem activity for 12 hours). Another case is that of a 19-year-old victim of an automobile accident, who was diagnosed as brain dead later that same day. The diagnosis was confirmed by EEG. Permission for organ donation was granted, but by the following day, while a suitable recipient was being sought, he began to show signs of neurologic recovery.[37] There is also the case of a 41-year-old man who was diagnosed as brain dead after having hanged himself in a jail four days earlier. The day after the declaration of brain death, a memorial service was held and his obituary published. He was then found to have regained spontaneous respiration and was returned to intensive care.[38]

We cannot tell from the press stories whether or not the above cases satisfied the President's Commission criteria for brain death, but one or two very well might have. They all certainly satisfied *someone's* criteria, and that is all the law requires. Such cases obviously warrant a conscientious investigation by those who are engaged in the development of brain death criteria. Nevertheless, they seem to have been brushed under the professional rug. They are an embarrassment; they give the lie to our collective delusion of diagnostic infallibility; publicizing them might diminish people's willingness to sign organ donor cards. It is much easier to dismiss them as undocumented and continue to preach, ostrichlike, that "the published criteria for determining cessation of brain functions have been uniformly successful in diagnosing death"[39] or that "there have been no documented reports of survivors when these guidelines have been followed."[40]

I am not the first to point out that criteria based on the mere absence of some subset of functions for some arbitrary period of time cannot be validated. In 1975, Masland stated (referring to the Collaborative Study), "I think it would be most unfortunate if, from studies such as the two we have just heard, there should develop a set of rigid guidelines. . . . A precise knowledge of the disease of which the patient is suffering and of the extent of the pathology is probably a far more crucial determinant in establishing the termination of life than any arbitrary criteria we could establish."[41]

Unique Aspects of Infants

If the above is true concerning the diagnosis of brain death in adults and older children, what can be said about infants? The President's Commission specifically excluded this age group from consideration because "the brains of infants and young children have increased resistance to damage and may recover substantial functions even after exhibiting unresponsiveness on neurological examination for longer periods than do adults. Physicians should be particularly cautious in applying neurologic criteria to determine death in children younger than five years."[42]

I would hasten to add another important reason for such caution: Very little information relevant to this age group is available. Perhaps the main reason for this is that, until very recently, there was simply no need for the diagnosis. Pediatricians and neonatologists have always practiced the discontinuation of ventilatory support with hopelessly ill infants; such decisions have not been based on brain death, but rather on the appropriateness of support.[43] The reason that infant brain death has suddenly become a major issue is that the technological advances in organ transplantation have recently created a need for infant donors. It is as though everyone, for some strange reason, expects the state of the art of neurologic diagnosis necessarily to advance in phase with that of transplant surgery. There are many reasons, however, why the two might not advance in tandem.

Particularly among neonates and very young infants, brain death is a relatively rare event. To begin with, their brains are more resistant to hypoxia than those of adults. Moreover, their expansile skulls make the vicious cycle leading to brain herniation less likely; even in those cases where it does occur, the classical rostral-caudal sequence of brain herniation is not usually seen. Babies with the most severe anoxic or infectious insults tend either to die (somatically) or to survive in a vegetative state; few suffer total brain death.

Not only is there an extreme lack of clinical information for this age group, but part of that information is disturbingly counterintuitive. Many people who claim to diagnose infant brain death overlook the fact that infants, especially neonates, are not miniature adults, even if this concept is given lip service. This is particularly true with respect to the neurodevelopmental phenomenon known as *encephalization*. This is the process by which the cerebral hemispheres (which are very underdeveloped at birth) gradually assume an increasingly prominent role in the dynamic hierarchy of the brain, suppressing and overriding the primitive automatic behaviors programmed into the brainstem (which is relatively mature even before birth). Encephalization is nowise better illustrated than by the fact that babies born without cerebral hemispheres but with intact brainstems (hydranencephalics) behave almost identically to normal newborns. Their parents may not suspect that anything is wrong until after a couple of months, when developmental milestones dependent upon the cerebral hemispheres do not appear.

One of the three pillars of adult brain death criteria, "cerebral unresponsiveness," is therefore utterly meaningless for this age group, because the responsiveness of newborns is entirely mediated by the brainstem. This is not to say that the cerebral hemispheres are without function; they are only without *clinically testable* function. Their function is primarily at the level of cellular development: branching and extension of axons and dendrites, formation of synaptic connections, etc. None of this development becomes clinically manifest until weeks, months, or even years later.

The only way to examine cerebral function in newborns is therefore through nonclinical tests, such as the EEG. The waves seen on EEG reflect the summed electrical activity of cortical neurons located approximately within a centimeter below the skull. Deeper brain structures modulate, but do not generate, the EEG patterns. Thus, the EEG and the clinical examination are much more complementary in newborns than in adults, the EEG revealing primarily cerebral function and the clinical examination revealing primarily brainstem function. In fact, it would not be an exaggeration to state that in infants the EEG should be considered an integral part of the neurologic examination itself, if one really intends to demonstrate absence of function of the *entire brain*. This is poorly appreciated by some neonatologists who still believe that neonatal EEGs are superfluous, even for the diagnosis of brain death.

But what is the critical duration of ECS in an infant beyond which there is no possibility of any degree of recovery? No one knows. All that is known is that it is considerably longer than in adults and older children. Moreover, there will not be a single critical duration valid for infants in general; rather, it will necessarily be a function of conceptional age: The younger, the longer. There are cases of return of electrical activity after ECS lasting more than two days (a term infant) or even ten days (a premature).[44] Of course, prolonged ECS, even in infants, correlates with a very poor long-term neurologic outcome (if not due to sedative intoxication, etc.), but there is insufficient information to measure accurately even the prognostic reliability of ECS with respect to various durations at various conceptional ages. I am aware of one case of a premature infant (around 30 weeks conceptional age) who had an isoelectric EEG for at least two days (not due to extrinsic factors such as drugs, etc.) but who has developed into a normal child.[45]

To confound things even further, EEG activity may sometimes be present in spite of autopsy evidence of total brain necrosis (the electrical activity presumably deriving from a few tiny, overlooked, isolated patches of surface neurons supplied by blood vessel collaterals from the meninges).[46] Thus, inclusion of ECS in the criteria, although necessary if false positive errors are to be avoided, will result in a higher rate of false negative errors than in older patients.

The critical duration beyond which brainstem nonfunction is irreversible is equally unknown, and even the prognostic value of brainstem failure for various durations in infants of various conceptional ages has not been worked out. There is a case of an infant of conceptional age 35 weeks who had total brainstem failure lasting 48 hours (and nearly total failure, with apnea and no brainstem function except for some tongue thrusting movements, for 80 hours) but who recovered completely.[47] The EEG was only mildly abnormal, which was one reason that life support was continued intensely.

Nevertheless, there are still those who believe that infant brain death can be diagnosed on purely clinical evidence. Pitts, for example, who adheres to the British school, which equates brainstem failure with brain death, maintains that "there are no special precautions for pronouncing brain death in infants and children."[48] According to his criteria, the above-mentioned infant would easily have qualified as brain dead and been removed from the ventilator. Oblivious to the child's potential for recovery, he could continue in all truth to state "there have been no documented reports of survivors when these guidelines have been followed."[49]

Laboratory indicators of brainstem dysfunction, such as heart rate variability[50] or evoked potentials,[51] provide no more certainty of irreversibility than clinical signs do, for there is simply no information relevant to critical duration. Additionally, one may think a function is being tested when in fact it is not. For example, the current sophistication of apnea testing was motivated by a study by Schafer and Caronna involving ten "apparently brain-dead subjects," all of whom seemed to be "apneic."[52] However, when the subjects were left off the ventilator long enough for carbon dioxide (CO_2) to build up in the blood, three of them began to breathe. Since then, several studies have addressed the issue of what level of CO_2 for what duration is necessary to document apnea in suspected brain death, and the critical level supported by evidence has ranged from 38 to 56 mm Hg.[53] Obviously, if the patients from one series who required a level of 56 to stimulate breathing had been at an institution where 38 was considered adequate, they could have been diagnosed as "apneic" and therefore "brain dead." The minimum level and duration of CO_2 for the ascertainment of apnea are as unknown as the minimum durations of ECS and brainstem failure for the ascertainment of irreversibility, and uniform results based on a mere handful of cases cannot validate the reliability of any proposed cutoff value.

Even blood flow studies are not necessarily as definitive in infants as in adults. What duration of absent flow guarantees destruction of brain tissue in an infant? The President's Commission suggested ten minutes as a reliable duration in normothermic adults[54] and considered absence of cerebral flow to be diagnostic of brain death even in the context of sedative overdose. Nevertheless, there is a documented case of total circulatory arrest (normothermic) for as long as 22 minutes, with complete neurologic recovery following treatment with thiopental.[55] Infants are able to tolerate total circulatory arrest longer than adults. In the context of deep hypothermia during open heart surgery, infants have been known to tolerate absent blood flow for as long as 90 minutes without neurologic deficit (although the safe upper limit is generally regarded as 45–60 minutes). The critical duration for irreversible brain destruction in normothermic, nonsedated infants at various conceptional ages has not been worked out.

Of course, absence of flow lasting several hours in a normothermic infant would intuitively seem to leave a generous enough safety margin to be considered a clearly valid indicator of irreversibility. Granting that, it still must be remembered that the most commonly utilized methods for determining intracranial blood flow in pediatrics—radionuclide bolus angiography,[56] doppler flow velocity,[57] or visualization of arterial pulsations by ultrasound[58]—all measure flow to the cerebral hemispheres only, not to the brainstem. Therefore, sustained absence of flow as revealed by these methods provides confirmatory evidence only for neocortical death, not for whole-brain death.

The only tests presently capable of demonstrating absence of blood flow to the entire brain, including brainstem, are standard three-vessel angiography, digital venous angiography, and positron emission tomography. Unfortunately, standard angiography is extremely impractical for very sick infants and position tomography is available only as a research tool in very few major medical centers. Digital venous angiography holds the most promise, but there is still relatively little experience with it,[59] and its accuracy in diagnosing infant brain death remains to be proven.

To confound matters further, although sustained absence of blood flow to the entire brain would result in its total destruction, such absence does not necessarily occur in all cases of brain death. In infants especially, there may even be increased flow in spite of autopsy evidence of total brain necrosis.[60] Thus, almost every clinical and laboratory parameter is associated with both false positive and false negative error when applied to infants, and the minimum duration of each that is needed to guarantee irreversibility remains totally unknown.

Infant Brain Death Criteria

The medical literature on infant brain death is extremely fragmented. Engel, in his 1975 monograph on neonatal EEG, declared that the clinical diagnosis of brain death was the same in neonates as in older patients, and that 12 hours of ECS was sufficient to confirm the diagnosis even in that age group, although he gave no data to support that contention.[61] Aside from some of the above-cited articles about specific confirmatory tests (each involving few patients), only two studies so far have addressed the overall issue of formulating pediatric brain death criteria, one based on 15 patients and the other on 61. Rowland et al. found total brain necrosis in 11 of the 15 patients who were autopsied and who had at least three days of unresponsiveness, apnea, and absent brainstem reflexes (complicating factors such as hypothermia, etc., were determined to be absent).[62] For Drake et al., ECS was a *sine qua non* for the diagnosis, along with the usual clinical signs, and cerebral blood flow study was an important determinant of the minimum duration of observation (which could range from less than 24 hours up to several days, depending on circumstances).[63] Autopsies showed a variety of neuropathological lesions, and it is not clear from the report whether the proposed criteria correlated with total, as opposed to partial, brain destruction in every case. It is important to bear in mind that both studies spanned nearly the entire pediatric age range, so that the cumulative experience with young infants is still very little. Rowland et al. had no infants under two months of age; Drake et al. had seven under two months and none under two weeks.[64] Drake et al. are to be credited for avoiding a pretense of unwarranted finality, carefully choosing phrases such as "*suspected* brain death" or, if the criteria were met, "the child *is believed* to have irreversible brain death" (emphasis added). They also did not claim to have established or validated their suggested criteria, but merely expressed the hope that their findings "will help to establish criteria" for the pediatric age group.

But progress in infant organ transplantation marches on, creating an inexorably growing need for infant donors and pressure upon pediatric neurologists to diagnose infant brain death. Some sort of diagnostic guidelines are sorely needed, even if they be merely prudential cautions acknowledging our current state of ignorance. To this end, the Ethics Committee of the Child Neurology Society, after a review of all the relevant information, proposed in 1984 (and reiterated in 1985) that an adapted version of the set of criteria of the President's Commission was probably applicable, with 'extreme caution,' to children down to the age of around two months, with proportionately longer periods of observation for those younger in age. Moreover, the so-called confirmatory tests, which are optional for older children and adults, should be mandatory for young children. The committee was of the opinion that brain death could not be reliably diagnosed at present below the age of two months. It also recommended that a multicenter collaborative study be undertaken, on the supposition that enough information could thereby be obtained to validate some set of criteria. In 1985 a joint task force on brain death in children was formed, with representatives from the Child Neurology Society, American Academy of Neurology, American Neurological Association, American Academy of Pediatrics, and American Medical Association. A subcommittee of the American Electroencephalographic Society has also been studying the issue. At the time of this writing, no formal statement from either of these groups has *yet* been issued.

If a multicenter collaborative study of infant brain death, analogous in scope to the National Institute of Neurological Diseases and Stroke (NINDS) Collaborative Study, is to be undertaken, serious consideration should first be given to the kinds of inferences that could be drawn from even the most ideal study. One should not forget that out of the 844 patients initially entered into the NINDS study, only 69 ended up both meeting the diagnostic criteria and having autopsy-proven total brain destruction (that ultimate fatality is a spurious endpoint for validating criteria for *present* death has already been emphasized). Given that brain death is much less common in infants than in older children and adults and that the study population would have to be broken down by neurologically homogeneous age brackets, then one might anticipate collecting at most 20 or so subjects in each age bracket who both met the diagnostic criteria for that age bracket and had autopsy-proven total brain necrosis. Even if the criteria were uniformly predictive of outcome, there would still be a theoretical risk of false positive error on the order of $1/(N+2)$, which for such small Ns would be totally unacceptable for a declaration of death. Any attempt to validate infant brain death criteria in the manner of the various adult criteria should be recognized from the outset as an extravagant exercise in futility.

This is not to say that such a study would not provide valuable information and should not be done, but rather that the information would be of a *prognostic* nature only. (As such, the results could be very helpful for making decisions about termination of treatment, but they would be inherently incapable of establishing criteria for brain death.) Also, the claim is not that infant brain death is inherently undiagnosable, but rather that the validity of the diagnostic criteria must be self-evident (e.g., sustained absence of blood flow to the entire brain) and not based on mere absence of function for some arbitrary duration or on the mere fact that the criteria have not failed yet. If the criteria are seen as being in need of validation by a clinical study, then, ironically, they are inherently incapable of being validated by any clinical study.

By what criteria, then, is infant brain death currently being diagnosed in actual practice? To answer this question, the Ethics Committee of the Child Neurology Society recently conducted a survey of some of the society's members, focusing on academicians, who presumably are the pacesetters in the field. The following results are provided through the courtesy of Edwin Myer, M.D., chairman of the committee. Of the 100 questionnaires mailed, there were 48 returns, of which 44 were complete. All responders agreed that brain death can be accurately diagnosed in infants older than three months. For progressively lower age brackets, fewer and fewer responders believed that brain death could be diagnosed, but even for the lowest age bracket (prematures younger than a conceptional age of 36 weeks), there were still as many as 57 percent who believed the diagnosis could be reliably made. All but one of the responders included clinical findings and history among the criteria, the one exception relying on doppler blood flow as a sole criterion. What is especially disturbing, in light of the striking case of the infant who made a complete recovery following 48 hours of total brainstem failure,[65] was that 5 of the 44 believed that the diagnosis could be made on the basis of clinical findings alone. Concerning the minimum duration for which criteria must be met, 8 required less than 12 hours, 5 at least 12 hours, 18 at least 24 hours, and 7 at least 48 hours. Twenty-one believed that the presently available ancillary tests (EEG, blood flow, etc.) were reliable, and 9 did not. Perhaps the most disturbing aspect of the entire survey (indicative of future trends?) was the high proportion (48 percent) who did not ''distinguish brain death from neocortical death.''

CONCLUSION

Given the startling confusion within the ranks of the experts, it is as if the UDDA requirement that ''a determination of death must be made in accordance with accepted medical standards''[66] is in reality being read thus: ''A determination of death may be made even in the complete absence of any accepted medical standards.'' To the question, ''By what criteria are these diagnoses currently being made?'' the honest answer—perhaps in the majority of cases—would seem to be ''gut feelings'' or ''educated guessing.'' The only certainty about infant brain death diagnosis seems to be that there is hardly ever any certainty, at least given the current state of the art.

It must be re-emphasized that brain death is not a prerequisite for the discontinuation of extraordinary life support. However, certainty of death *is* a prerequisite for the removal of organs for transplantation. The concerns raised here are not merely theoretical. I am aware of at least one case in which a supposedly brain dead baby (with death certificate issued) was transferred to a major medical center as an organ donor but was discovered by neurologists there to have some brain functions still present—resulting in immediate cancellation of the surgery.

It is frequently said (and enshrined in many state laws) that the diagnosis of death must be made independently of any transplant considerations. Are we content to pay mere lip service to this noble ideal, or are we prepared to implement it with full professional integrity, even if it means going against certain contemporary trends? In spite of the pressure from transplant teams, a moratorium should be called on all infant transplantation until valid (not merely ''accepted'') diagnostic criteria are available. This will necessarily put a temporary damper on the progress of transplantation technology for this age group and will result in the continued loss of life of potential recipients through their natural disease processes. Nevertheless, we are not morally obliged to be God and to cure everyone with terminal diseases, regardless of the means. We *are* morally obliged to respect the autonomy of every living patient and to do nothing directly harmful. To base a declaration of death on criteria that are at best probabilistic and prognostic in nature is morally equivalent to a hunter shooting at something moving in the bushes because it is *probably* a deer. Society cannot long survive a state of affairs in which there is tacit official willingness to have an unknown proportion of "poor prognosis" patients anonymously sacrificed for the benefit of others.

NOTES

1. J.E. Parisi et al., "Brain Death with Prolonged Somatic Survival," *New England Journal of Medicine* 306 (1982): 14–16.

2. T.W. Rowland et al., "Brain Death in the Pediatric Intensive Care Unit: A Clinical Definition," *American Journal of Diseases of Children* 137 (1983): 547–50.

3. P. Mollaret, M. Goulon, "Le coma dépassé," *Revue Neurologique* 101 (1959): 3–15.

4. H.K. Beecher et al., "A Definition of Irreversible Coma: Report of the Ad Hoc Committee of the Harvard Medical School to Examine the Definition of Brain Death," *Journal of the American Medical Association* 205 (1968): 337–40.

5. H. Jonas, "Against the Stream: Comments on the Definition and Redefinition of Death," in *Philosophical Essays: From Ancient Creed to Technological Man*, ed. H. Jonas (Englewood Cliffs, N.J.: Prentice-Hall, 1974), 132–40; B.S. Currie, "The Redefinition of Death," in *Organism, Medicine, and Metaphysics*, ed. S.F. Spicker (Boston: D. Reidel, 1978), 177–97; P.A.Byrne, S. O'Reilly, and P.M.Quay, "Brain Death—An Opposing Viewpoint," *Journal of the American Medical Association* 242 (1979): 1985–90; N. Fost, "Research on the Brain Dead," *Journal of Pediatrics* 96 (1980): 54–56; M. Siegler and D. Wikler, "Brain Death and Live Birth," *Journal of the American Medical Association* 248 (1982): 1101–2; A. Browne, "Whole-Brain Death Reconsidered," *Journal of Medical Ethics* 9 (1983): 28–31.

6. D. Lamb, *Death, Brain Death and Ethics* (Albany N.Y.: State University of New York Press, 1985).

7. P.A.J. Adam et al., "Oxidation of Glucose and D-B-OH-butyrate by the Early Human Fetal Brain," *Acta Paediatrica Scandinavica* 64 (1975): 17–42.

8. E. Casado de Frias et al., "Inappropriate Secretion of Antidiuretic Hormone and the Effect of Lithium in Its Treatment," *Journal of Pediatrics* 96 (1980): 153–55.

9. From the office of California Senator Milton Marks, "The Anencephalic as a Source for Pediatric Organ Transplants: A Question of Medical Ethics," October 29, 1986.

10. M.R. Harrison, "The Anencephalic Newborn as Organ Donor," *Hastings Center Report* 16 (April 1986): 21–22. See also M.R. Harrison, "Organ Procurement for Children: The Anencephalic Fetus as Donor," *Lancet* 2 (December 13, 1986): 1383–86.

11. D. Perlman, "Law Gets in the Way: Why a Baby's Death Was in Vain," *San Francisco Chronicle*, May 5, 1986, p. 1; D. Perlman, "Why Transplant Offers Have to Be Refused," *San Francisco Chronicle*, May 5, 1986, p. 4; S. Blakeslee, "Law Thwarts Effort to Donate Infants' Organs: Attempts to Transplant the Organs of Babies Born without Brains Are Turned Away," *New York Times*, September 9, 1986, p. C1.

12. R.M. Veatch, "The Whole-Brain-Oriented Concept of Death: An Outmoded Philosophical Formulation," *Journal of Thanatology* 3 (1975): 13–30; H.R.Beresford, "The Quinlan Decision: Problems and Legislative Alternatives," *Annals of Neurology* 2 (1977): 74–81; R. Pucetti, "The Conquest of Death," *The Monist* 59 (1976): 249–63; S.J. Youngner and E.T. Bartlett, "Human Death and High Technology: The Failure of the Whole Brain Formulations," *Annals of Internal Medicine* 99 (1983): 252–58.

13. Lamb, *Death, Brain Death and Ethics.*

14. C. Pallis, "ABC of Brain Stem Death: From Brain Death to Brain Stem Death," *British Medical Journal* 285 (1982): 1487–90.

15. R. Hassler, "Basal Ganglia Systems Regulating Mental Activity," *International Journal of Neurology* 12 (1977): 53–72.

16. President's Commission for the Study of Ethical Problems in Medicine and Biomedical and Behavioral Research, *Defining Death: Medical, Legal and Ethical Issues in the Determination of Death.* (Washington, D.C.: GPO, 1981).

17. F. Plum and J.B. Posner, *The Diagnosis of Stupor and Coma*, 3rd ed., (Philadelphia: Davis, 1980), 101–12.

18. President's Commission, *Defining Death*, 160.

19. Byrne, O'Reilly, and Quay, "Brain Death."

20. P.M. Black, "Brain Death," *New England Journal of Medicine* 299 (1978): 338–44, 393–401.

21. President's Commission, *Defining Death*, 27, 29.

22. D.A. Shewmon, "The Probability of Inevitability: The Inherent Impossibility of Validating Criteria for Brain Death or 'Irreversibility' through Clinical Studies," *Statistics in Medicine* 6 (1987):535–54. D.A. Shewmon, "The critical duration beyond which electrocerebral silence may be considered 'irreversible'." *Journal of Clinical Neurophysiology* 4 (1987): 266–67.

23. A.E. Walker et al., "An Appraisal of the Criteria of Cerebral Death. A Summary Statement. A Collaborative Study," *Journal of the American Medical Association* 237 (1977): 982–86; A.E. Walker, *Cerebral Death*, 3rd ed. (Baltimore, Md.: Urban & Schwarzenberg, 1985).

24. R. Masland, "Discussion," *Transactions of the American Neurological Association* 100 (1975): 33–34.

25. Ibid.

26. Walker et al., "An Appraisal," 984.

27. Walker, *Cerebral Death*, 124–25.

28. Walker et al., "An Appraisal," 985.

29. Plum and Posner, "Diagnosis of Stupor and Coma," 316.

30. President's Commission, *Defining Death*, Appendix B, 89–107.

31. See President's Commission, *Defining Death*, Appendix F, 159–66; reproduced in *Journal of the American Medical Association* 246 (1981): 2184–86; and in *Neurology* 32 (1982): 395–99.

32. Ibid., 161.

33. D. Silverman et al., "Irreversible Coma Associated with Electrocerebral Silence," *Neurology* 20 (1970): 525–33; G.E. Chatrian, "Electrophysiologic Evaluation of Brain Death: A Critical Appraisal," in *Electrodiagnosis in Clinical Neurology*, ed. M.J. Aminoff (New York: Churchill Livingstone, 1980), 525–88.

34. Pallis, "ABC of Brain Stem Death"; Conference of Medical Royal Colleges and Faculties in the United Kingdom, "Diagnosis of Brain Death," *Lancet* 2 (1976): 1069–70; B. Jennett, J. Gleave, and P. Wilson, "Brain Death in Three Neurosurgical Units," *British Medical Journal* 282 (1981): 533–39.

35. Walker, *Cerebral Death*, 9. Walker cites the following accounts: "Man Escapes Burial Alive," *Albuquerque Tribune*, May 23, 1980, p. C6; "Timely Cough Saves Life," *Albuquerque Tribune*, February 9, 1982, p. 1; "Woman Believed to Be Dead 'resurrected' on autopsy table," *Albuquerque Tribune*, April 19, 1983, p. B5.

36. "Heart Attack Victim Returns from 'Dead,'" *Rochester Democrat and Chronicle* (Rochester, Minn.), March 19, 1975, p. 19A; "Wink Saves Man Believed Dead," *Kansas City Times*, February 13, 1975, p. 3A.

37. "Crash Victim Alive despite 'Brain Death,'" *Kansas City Times*, September 30, 1978, p. 12A.

38. "Cincinnatian Reported Dead Still Clings to Life," *The Courier-Journal* (Louisville, Ky.), September 28, 1985, p. B4; "'Brain Dead' Man Survives," *The Burlington Free Press* (Burlington, Vt.) September 28, 1985, p. 2A.

39. President's Commission, *Defining Death*, 27.

40. L.H. Pitts, "Determination of Brain Death," *Western Journal of Medicine* 140 (1984): 628–31.

41. Masland, "Discussion."

42. President's Commission, *Defining Death*, 166.

43. S.C. Ragatz and P.H. Ellison, "Decisions to Withdraw Life Support in the Neonatal Intensive Care Unit," *Clinical Pediatrics* 22 (1983): 729–36.

44. S. Ashwal et al. "Radionuclide Bolus Angiography: A Technique for Verification of Brain Death in Infants and Children," *Journal of Pediatrics* 91 (1977): 722–27; A.C.C. Juguilon and E.L. Reilly, "Development of EEG

Activity after Ten Days of Electrocerebral Inactivity: A Case Report in a Premature Neonate—Hydranencephaly or Massive Ventricular Enlargement,'' *Clinical Electroencephalography* 13 (1982): 233–40.

45. Paul Byrne, M.D., personal communication, 1986.

46. S. Ashwal and S. Schneider, ''Failure of Electroencephalography to Diagnose Brain Death in Comatose Children,'' *Annals of Neurology* 6 (1979): 512–17; B. Drake, S. Ashwal, and S. Schneider, ''Determination of Cerebral Death in the Pediatric Intensive Care Unit,'' *Pediatrics* 78 (1986): 107–12.

47. J.F. Pasternak and J.J. Volpe, ''Full Recovery from Prolonged Brain Stem Failure following Intraventricular Hemorrhage,'' *Journal of Pediatrics* 95 (1979): 1046–49.

48. Juguilon and Reilly, ''Development of EEG Activity.''

49. Ibid.

50. P. Kero et al., ''Decreased Heart Rate Variation in Decerebration Syndrome: Quantitative Clinical Criterion of Brain Death?'' *Pediatrics* 62 (1978): 307–11.

51. P.R.F. Dear and D.J. Godfrey, ''Neonatal Auditory Brainstem Response Cannot Reliably Diagnose Brainstem Death,'' *Archives of Diseases of Children* 60 (1985): 17–19; M.J. Aminoff, ''The Clinical Role of Somatosensory Evoked Potential Studies: A Critical Appraisal,'' *Muscle & Nerve* 7 (1984): 345–54.

52. J.A. Schafer and J.J. Caronna, ''Duration of Apnea Needed to Confirm Brain Death,'' *Neurology* 28 (1978): 661–66.

53. Conference of Medical Royal Colleges, ''Diagnosis of Brain Death''; Schafer and Caronna, ''Duration of Apnea''; J.J. Riviello, Jr., et al., ''The Hypercarbia Stimulation Test (HST) for Pediatric Brain Death,'' *Annals of Neurology* 20 (1986): 442; M.P. Earnest, H.R. Beresford, and H.B. McIntyre, ''Testing for Apnea in Suspected Brain Death: Methods Used by 129 Clinicians,'' *Neurology* 36 (1986): 542–44; T.W. Rowland, J.H. Donnelly, and A.H. Jackson, ''Apnea Documentation for Determination of Brain Death in Children,'' *Pediatrics* 74 (1984): 505–8.

54. President's Commission, *Defining Death*, 164.

55. H. Breivik et al., ''Clinical Feasibility Trials of Barbiturate Therapy after Cardiac Arrest,'' *Critical Care Medicine* 6 (1978): 228–44.

56. Ashwal et al., ''Radionuclide Failure''; J.A. Schwartz, J. Baxter, and D.R. Brill, ''Diagnosis of Brain Death in Children by Radionuclide Cerebral Imaging,'' *Pediatrics* 73 (1984): 14–18; B.H. Holzman et al., ''Radionuclide Cerebral Perfusion Scintigraphy in the Determination of Brain Death in Children,'' *Neurology* 33 (1983): 1027–31.

57. J.B. McMenamin and J.J. Volpe, ''Doppler Ultrasonography in the Determination of Neonatal Brain Death,'' *Annals of Neurology* 14 (1983): 302–7.

58. T.L. Furgiuele et al., ''Prediction of Cerebral Death by Cranial Sector Scan,'' *Critical Care Medicine* 12 (1984): 1–3.

59. K. Vatne, P. Nakstad, and T. Lundar, ''Digital Subtraction Angiography (DSA) in the Evaluation of Brain Death: A Comparison of Conventional Cerebral Angiography with Intravenous and Intraarterial DSA,'' *Neuroradiology* 27 (1985): 155–57; B.C.P. Lee et al., ''Digital Intravenous Cerebral Angiography in Neonates,'' *American Journal of Neuroradiology* 5 (1984): 281–86.

60. D.I. Altman et al., ''Exuberant Brainstem Blood Flow and Intact Cerebral Blood Flow Despite Clinical and Pathological Evidence for Brainstem and Cerebral Necrosis in an Asphyxiated Newborn Infant,'' *Annals of Neurology* 20 (1986): 409; D.I. Altman et al., ''Elevated Brainstem Blood Flow in Newborn Infants: A Positron Emission Tomography Study,'' *Annals of Neurology* 20 (1986): 436.

61. R.C.H. Engel, *Abnormal Electroencephalograms in the Neonatal Period*, (Springfield, Ill.: Thomas, 1975), 4–10.

62. Rowland et.al., ''Brain Death.''

63. Drake, Ashwal, and Schneider, ''Determination of Cerebral Death.''

64. Dr. S. Schneider, personal communication, 1986.

65. Pasternak and Volpe, ''Full Recovery.''

66. President's Commission, *Defining Death*, 160.

BIBLIOGRAPHY

Byrne, P.A., S. O'Reilly, P.M. Quay, and P.W. Salsich, Jr. ''Brain Death—The Patient, the Physician, and Society.'' *Gonzaga Law Review* 18 (1982–83): 429–516. A comprehensive critique of current brain death formulations, from medical, legal, and philosophical perspectives.

Korein, J., ed. *Brain Death: Interrelated Medical and Social Issues.* Annals of the New York Academy of Science, vol. 315. New York: New York Academy of Science, 1978. A compendium of philosophical considerations and pre–President's Commission clinical data, especially those derived from the National Institute of Neurological Diseases and Stroke Collaborative Study.

Lamb, D. *Death, Brain Death and Ethics.* Albany, N.Y.: State University of New York Press, 1985. A recent review of the various philosophical debates surrounding the issue of brain death.

President's Commission for the Study of Ethical Problems in Medicine and Biomedical and Behavioral Research. *Defining Death: Medical, Legal and Ethical Issues in the Determination of Death.* Washington, D.C.: GPO, 1981. An important review of the philosophical and diagnostic issues surrounding brain death, with appendixes containing the brain death statutes of all states and the diagnostic criteria recommended by the commission's medical consultants.

Walker, A.E. *Cerebral Death.* 3rd ed. Baltimore, Md.: Urban & Schwartzenberg, 1985. The most recent thorough review of all medical aspects of brain death, focusing on data from the National Institute of Neurological Diseases and Stroke Collaborative Study, of which the author was project coordinator.

ADDENDUM

Since the time of writing of this chapter, the joint Task Force for the Determination of Brain Death in Children, mentioned on page 52, published its eagerly awaited diagnostic guidelines simultaneously in three major neurological journals.* At the heart of the guidelines is the contention that "irreversible cessation of all functions of the entire brain, including the brainstem, can be confidently determined by mere absence of function throughout the following observation periods at various ages (confirmation by absent blood flow being optional): 48 hours of clinical and EEG findings for children between 7 days and 2 months of age, 24 hours of clinical and EEG findings for children between 2 months and 1 year of age, and 12 hours of plain "observation" for children older than 1 year "when an irreversible cause exists." If an "irreversible cause" does not exist (particularly with hypoxic-ischemic encephalopathy), then 24 hours of purely clinical observation suffices for children older than 1 year. This observation time may be reduced by the demonstration of a flat EEG or absence of cerebral blood flow by radionuclide angiography (neither of which implies irreversibility of brainstem nonfunction). Given the considerations made in this chapter, particularly the nonexistence of a database for infants, I view the promulgation of these guidelines as premature and unfounded.

---

*Task Force for the Determination of Brain Death in Children. "Guidelines for the Determination of Brain Death in Children." *Annals of Neurology* 21(1987):616–17; *Archives of Neurology* 44(1987): 587–88; *Neurology* 37 (1987): 1077–78.

Chapter 5

Child Abuse: The Role of Health Care Professionals and the State

Domeena C. Renshaw and David C. Thomasma

According to a nationwide study released by the National Committee for the Prevention of Child Abuse on January 26, 1987, the number of deaths of children resulting from physical abuse and neglect jumped 29 percent in one year among a major cross section of states that contributed to the study. The incidence of child abuse itself, abuse that did not lead to death, also increased dramatically. One alleged expert on the dangerous sequelae to abuse reports that "workers have more cases to handle and fewer resources, and cases over time get worse."[1] The nation is clearly in a crisis involving its children.

Yet is society's commitment to children open-ended? It certainly seems so lately. Protection of children has become an important part of the role of health professionals in our society. Many physicians, nurses, social workers, and teachers define their roles as including the protection of children from the often tragic harms caused by abusive parents, elders, and society itself.

The papers have almost daily reports about health professionals and the state acting to protect children. Examples from the Chicago area include the following.

A young child in a divorce suit was bounced between his father and grandparents in Costa Rica and his mother in Illinois. After the divorce, the child was placed in joint parental custody. The mother, however, returned to court to get sole custody; consequently the father, with his own parents, fled the country and set up a farm in Costa Rica. The mother, in turn, placed a lien on property held by the grandparents in the U.S. When the grandfather came up to defend his property, he was put in jail. The father had to make an awful choice between his father and his son. Eventually he relinquished his son in order to get his father out of jail. The boy did not know his mother well after the several years he spent living with his father and grandparents. The law and society have not begun to address psychological abuse of children.

To curb abuse of children in foster homes, the state of Illinois will send to over 13,000 children in foster homes a brochure entitled "Your Rights in Foster Care and Shelters." Mentioned are rights to proper food, shelter, medical care, and even spending money. During fiscal years 1985–86, the Department of Children and Family Services (DCFS) of Illinois found that 296 children were abused or neglected by their foster parents. Of those, 90 were victims of sexual abuse, 125 were physically abused, and 80 were living in homes classified as neglectful, according to DCFS records.[2] Designated "protectors" are now themselves in need of evaluation.

Meanwhile, the state of Illinois itself has received warnings from the federal government that some of its facilities housing retarded children are environments of neglect, and federal funding will be stopped until the institutions come into compliance with federal standards. Thus, while one state agency seeks to improve the conditions of children, another is accused of neglecting the charge to protect them.

More disturbing is the result of a study done in 1982, which is that children often suffer a more subtle form of neglect in the very act of shuffling them from one home to another in order to achieve what is in their best interests. The study was done by the Center for Preventive Psychiatry. This national project found that children who were transferred among foster homes were two to three times more likely to experience problems as adults than children in stable living conditions. The problems cited in the study ranged from mental illness to higher incidences of substance and alcohol abuse. A lower level of intellectual achievement was also noted.[3] According to Illinois records, 44 percent of 13,000 children had been rotated among more than six foster homes. This raises the disturbing question of which is the lesser evil. Is the evil of removing a child from the birth family and then again from a foster home that is defined by the department as unsuitable greater or less than the evil of leaving the child in the initial environment?

On September 15, 1986, the *Chicago Tribune* headlined the following: "Child Abuse Deaths Soar in Illinois." Among the tragic details was that in one-fourth of the families investigated for child abuse, a child eventually died. In Illinois alone, 82 children died from physical abuse in a 12-month period, an increase of 49 percent over the previous year, despite statistical vagaries.[4] There was a pre-election political response. The Democratic candidate for governor, Adlai Stevenson III, immediately blamed the Republican governor, James Thompson, for these deaths, claiming that the governor had appointed political cronies rather than real professionals to deliver social services.[5] The state government immediately responded by plans for reform[6] which included mandatory prison terms for repeat child abuse offenders, jail for mothers who expose their children to abusive boyfriends, and involvement of state police in gathering evidence in serious cases of child abuse to "augment" investigations by the DCFS and the local police.[7] However, careful studies reveal that prevention is the only successful way to correct child abuse. Intervention, unfortunately, rarely works.[8]

CASE STUDY

Consider this complex case illustrating the difficulty of social intervention to protect children.

Welfare housing is provided by a religious health care corporation in the West (by Federal contract through Housing and Urban Development) to help those on welfare and those who are dispossessed by society to find a decent, caring environment, plus healing and hope.

A young divorcee has a son aged seven and a daughter aged ten. The mother has a history of seizures, is a known diabetic and heavy drinker, and lives in public housing. Neighbors and other residents of the complex report that there are frequent male visitors at the house. Home administrators are concerned for the safety of the children. Further, one of the mother's "boyfriends" was seen holding hands with the daughter on a number of occasions; once he kissed her.

After a considerable number of discussions with the mother by the administrators and some friends, she agreed to join Alcoholics Anonymous. She was encouraged by the housing staff and a social worker to improve her life, and she was also warned that if she did not continue to get help, she would lose custody of her two children. At first, the mother cooperated, but then she objected to this kind of coercion and failed to attend a couple of AA meetings.

One afternoon, she was roaring drunk. The neighbors complained about the noise. The housing administration and social worker took her to a detoxification center, while the children were placed temporarily with a neighbor who was a friend of the mother's and had initially reported the drinking problem out of concern for her friend and for the possibility of sexual abuse of the girl.

Against medical advice, the mother discharged herself from the detoxification center and took the children back to her own apartment, once again raising strong objections to the intrusion by others. Her friend became convinced that the ten-year-old daughter was being abused by a boyfriend, because of the stories she was told while she took care of the child. This friend called the Child Abuse Hotline.

All abuse causes ethical dilemmas. These dilemmas arise from questions regarding the rights of children, the breakdown of family structure and control, and the increasing role of the state and of health professionals acting *in loco parentis*, as happened in this case. Sexual abuse of children is one of many kinds of abuse engaged in by adults. Special problems are created by accusations or suspicions of such abuse.

In this chapter, we will first discuss the rights of children, then the incidence and causes of sexual abuse of children. Next we will examine clinical ethical issues created by suspicions or accusations of sexual abuse. Finally, we will discuss the ethical issues raised by the clinical problem and the role of the state.

THE RIGHTS OF CHILDREN

No doubt children have been abused sexually for centuries. This is a reasonable assumption given that children, like women, were often seen as chattel or property "owned" by the father. Recall also that ancient civilizations sacrificed children annually to the gods of the harvest. Children were exchanged in marriage agreements so that families could strengthen their economic and social position. Arranged weddings persisted in most of the world until this century and they still exist in many cultures.

The rights of children have only been recognized in the law in the past two centuries. The tendency of the state to set standards in child care and to intervene when those standards are not upheld is of much more recent origin. In the past, children were governed by the *patria potestas* of Roman law, under which wide powers of life and death were given to the head of the family. Since this legal view was generally carried over into feudal law in the Middle Ages, the notion that children deserved protection evolved slowly. Instead, there was an assumption in favor of strong familial control over children. Yet by the early Middle Ages, children were able to receive property in a will and to have guardians appointed to administer their affairs.

Only with the rise of child labor did laws emerge protecting children from cruelty, baby farming, and the like.[9] Some child protection laws appeared in England as early as 1832, but only in the late 1800s in England and the United States were there laws with "real teeth.'' Paralleling the child labor laws were laws governing the education of children. In England, in 1908, the ''Children Act'' consolidated all the piecemeal legislation governing children. It was the first such act anywhere. The stated rights for children were the right to a decent upbringing, the right not to be abused,the right to be given a chance for a healthy life, and the right to be protected from tobacco, prostitution, and begging. In probation and later reform, children also were given the right to a decent minimum level of child care, which was important because social conditions resulting from the Industrial Revolution were appalling in all ''advanced'' countries. Recall the novels of Charles Dickens about the abuse of children. These first appeared serialized in the newspapers, where they helped create a commitment among the public to alleviate the cruelty of conditions.

Perhaps it will be the next century before the rights of children become recognized within international law and the constitutions of countries. Until then, efforts to protect children will result in formal intervention in those families or child care settings judged inadequate by the standards set by society, by professionals, and by state law. Conflicting standards of care and the opportunities for misusing well-intentioned protective laws create additional ethical dilemmas.

CHILD SEXUAL ABUSE

In 1974 the Federal Child Abuse Prevention and Treatment Act mandated that failure to report ''any sex act'' between adult and child, even suspected acts, was criminal. There was protection for anonymous reporting.

In the early 1980s, newspapers headlined ''A U.S. Child Is Sexually Abused Every Two Minutes'' and ''Sex Abuse Up 600%.'' A clinician should ask whether these headlines are true. The answer is no. The National Study of Child Abuse and Neglect in 1982 revealed that nationwide 62 percent of those abused suffered neglect, 24 percent suffered physical abuse, 10 percent suffered emotional abuse, 7 percent (65,000 children) suffered sexual abuse, and 9 percent suffered other forms of abuse.[10] In the state of Illinois, figures paralleled those nationally. Allegations of sex abuse rose by 38 percent (from 5,170 reports in 1983 to 7,134 reports in 1984) and totaled 6.7 percent of the child abuse allegations for that year. Of the reports, 60 percent were eventually classified as ''Indicated'' and 40 percent were dropped for undisclosed reasons.[11] These figures should be of true concern, but there is *not* the pandemic loosely reported in the media. However, sex sells and is also a popular political issue.

Current knowledge about why adults sexually abuse children has not improved over the last 50 years.[12] Pedophiles, child rapists, and various types of incestuous adults are not new to our time, nor has one specific cause or cure yet been established. The range of adult-child sex behaviors is wide, including everything from fondling to rape killings.

Even in the absence of physical harm, adult-child sex is pathological, because of the inequality of the partners physically, cognitively, and experientially. Therefore, it can be regarded as a form of psychological coercion, which is the basis of the presumption that such a relationship is evil or morally wrong.[13] It is exploitation to use a less powerful human being for the pleasure of a more powerful one. Saying no is more difficult for the child because of normal curiosity, sexual ignorance, a possible unawareness of the consequences (pregnancy, infections), a general regard for adults as authorities, the enjoyment of having the special attention of the adult (with or without material or other enticements), and sometimes intimidation or physical force or injury.[14]

An interesting socio-legal blindspot in child protection concerns boy and girl prostitutes, aged 9 to 17 years, who are estimated to number 200,000 to 400,000. Some have been forced out of their homes without being reported as missing by their parents (throwaway children); others have left their homes without parental consent (runaways). They form a tragic group, selling sex to survive, often hooked on drugs, and lost in the cracks in the bureaucracy, since child prostitutes are much more likely to be arrested and jailed for soliciting than their adult consorts. The buyer is rarely charged with sexually abusing a child, although participation in this form of prostitution surely must be regarded as unethical exploitation. Although child prostitutes solicit money for sex, most of them are neglected minors deserving more social attention and outreach than occurs as a result of the few almost heroic privately sponsored shelters now available.

It comes as a shock to discover that there are only imprecise legal distinctions between what is and what is not to count as sexual child abuse. At present the definitions seem to be based on what each court hearing decides sexual abuse shall be.[15]

The literature on sexual abuse of children presents much pseudoscience and small, nonrandomized, noncomparative sample studies. One large study of 501 white and black women from Georgia and Florida is worth reading as a model to those who wish to do careful further study of early childhood sexual experiences.[16] As a rule of thumb, ''hard'' signs of child sexual abuse are confession by the teenage or adult partner, pregnancy, child genital injuries, the presence of semen on the child, and childhood V.D. ''Soft'' signs are controversial, because at times they occur as symptoms of family conflict, divorce, and personal distress. Withdrawal, nightmares, masturbation, and school difficulties are not always caused by sexual molestation, nor are genital abrasions, which may be from self-scratching, underwear, etc. These signs have been cited so often they seem to have acquired a presumed infallibility. Painting a child's genitals with toludine blue dye is newly suggested for searching for scratch marks. But might not the exposure and humiliation of such an invasion of privacy be a new kind of sexual abuse itself? How does the doctor obtain informed consent from a child to expose, paint, slitlamp, and photograph the genitals for such a nonspecific, inconclusive sign? Might not this procedure be more traumatic than the sex abuse? And how may the humiliation and trauma to child and adult be justified and rectified if no abuse occurred?

Well-meaning, uninformed reporters cite numerous signals as conclusive evidence of sexual abuse and use predictive and condemnatory terminology such as *perpetrator* and *victim* long before an allegation reaches the courts or has even been investigated. Using *alleged* before the word *perpetrator* does little to decrease the damage to an individual's reputation. Public outrage can be vicious and destructive.

CLINICAL ETHICAL DILEMMAS

Clinicians must not ignore signs of abuse, yet they must be aware of the potential for harm in inaugurating a criminal investigation. Most argue that no real harm can come to the accused if he or she is innocent and that one must act to protect the child. Although being more concerned for the child is to a large extent justified, such situations are unfortunately not as straightforward as they may appear.

The stress of postaccusation family rupture may trigger intense trauma. A manipulative mother-in-law or a suspicious neighbor may make an anonymous hotline report about supposed abuse during visitation. Each report must be followed by intrusive and sometimes destructive home investigations. The harm and stigma may endure long after the agency "closed the case" as unfounded. The accusation has gone into a computer for resurrection at any time (see Chapter 13 on elder abuse).

"Treatment" of sexual abuse may include removal of a child or accused parent from the home, thereby disrupting the family and causing trauma for all concerned. Foster home placement may do more to assuage the moral outrage of the professional than actually protect the allegedly molested child. There are cases where a child has been abused for the very first time in foster care.[17] This is a concern of foster parents and others who work with children.

Medical, psychiatric, and social work or counseling texts provide few guidelines for the clinician confronted with a case of suspected child abuse. However, with a federal mandate to report such situations for further investigation by legally constituted authorities, a role shift occurs. A health professional offering confidential assistance becomes a forensic evaluator who must report the sexual abuse. A possible criminal charge can be filed against the professional who does not report suspected child abuse.

It should be clear by now that medical literature must take care to use terminology accurately, avoiding prejudicial legal language such as *victim* and *perpetrator* and including such words as *alleged* when recording a verbatim statement—unless a criminal trial has already occurred and handed down a guilty verdict. This is one imperfect but important way to preclude observer bias (a bias that might lead to outright condemnation by the clinician rather than to an objective examination). Physicians in the past have been accused of underreporting suspected child abuse, most likely because of these legal and ethical concerns. The AMA has gradually educated physicians and allied health professionals about the presence of child abuse and the mandate to report.

National campaigns also have alerted persons to the dangers of child sexual abuse. Teachers, nurses, social workers, and parents now listen attentively to children who mention sexual abuse, who use precocious sexual language, or display sexually inappropriate behavior. However, it should not be forgotten that we live in an era where sex is pervasively explicit and sexual attitudes are permissive. Explicit sexual materials, old magazines in garages, X-rated cable television and videos, and nationally televised sex abuse education programs together have provided a sexual vocabulary to 9-year-olds well beyond that of 39-year-olds in the 1930s! We should remember this and not jump to conclusions. A child's words or actions may simply mimic what was viewed on a TV screen. Standard questions ought to include "Do you have cable or video TV at home?" "What programs do you watch?" "Where did you learn that?"

Numerous popular articles, unfortunately, list general symptoms of child distress—for example, bedwetting, withdrawal, daydreaming, sleeping in class, gym refusal, aggression, reading pornographic literature, being seductive, using obscene language, and poor grades—as specific to child sex abuse. If some of these occur, referral from a school for evaluation of potential child sexual abuse then follows. Concerned parents may also present their child for a checkup after hearing an education campaign about sex abuse or a lurid news story of sex with a teacher or principal.

More often, one divorced parent accuses the other of sexually abusing a child, who is then presented for evaluation. Judges and lawyers concerned about custody hearings have learned to be cautious about unscrupulous charges of child sexual abuse leveled against a former partner in an effort to gain custody.[18] Parents divorce one another; children do not divorce either parent. They suffer prolonged distress at the life changes occasioned by the divorce and desperately try to please each parent in order to restore the marriage. Some children will lie if told to do so by one parent, unaware of the destructive consequences.

Neither deductions nor assumptions are appropriate for the examining physician. The physician must maintain objectivity in the midst of the often highly complex and emotional situation. All adults claim they wish to protect the child. The physician's task is twofold: to do a physical examination and to obtain a history of what allegedly occurred (see Exhibit 5-1). The child's age, development, intellectual understanding of the words used and questions asked, information recall ability, and emotional state must all be described. The results of investigating both physical and psychogenic elements must be carefully and objectively recorded. Without opinions or unfounded statements, the facts must be presented straightforwardly, e.g., "The examination today revealed no genital injury," "The child denied any sexual contact," "The child states uncle had her place her mouth on his penis," etc.

Unfortunately, what sometimes happens is that the physician may be eager to protect the child and, after a normal examination, might be tempted to add "Normal physical exam compatible with sexual abuse." Such an ambiguous, subjective, and unfounded statement may later become extraordinarily destructive. The child's home may immediately be regarded as unsafe and a father or mother named as a perpetrator by the authorities and arrested. Family life may be disrupted. The child (or all children in the family) may be placed temporarily for days, weeks, or months in foster homes through to the end of the trial and perhaps even after. Separation anxiety results, which may then wrongly be attributed to supposed sexual abuse when in fact it is caused by separation from family, parents, school, and friends. Traumata can also be caused by sexually explicit questions, genital exams, magnifying glass scrutiny, etc. Standard medical "rape kits" are used to collect sperm, do cultures for venereal disease, and provide evidence for determining a suspected rapist's identity. In all of the bureaucratic flurry, the physician may neglect to report that the child's hymen is intact. This may negate a false claim of coital incest. Both positive and negative physical findings are to be recorded. Repeated questioning by many and different strangers and fear of a new placement may cause shame, a great and overriding sense of helplessness, a feeling of not being believed, of longing for kin, comfort, and home, and demoralization and depression. The child's best interests will hardly have been served by the intervention.[19]

In some cases there may be suspected sex abuse that led to this ambiguous evaluation, but in such a multiproblem family, the suspected sexual abuse is only one of a long list of family problems, such as alcohol abuse, wife abuse, poverty, etc. All of these will need subsequent interventions. Yet only the likelihood of sexual abuse (and not of other kinds of abuse) will be recorded. It alone will receive the most immediate and dramatic attention from the community agency involved.[20] Again, the child's best interests may not have been served by this exclusive focus.

If a sex abuse allegation is indeed accurate, most citizens and professionals believe that the family disruptions described above are justified to protect the child, because short-term life changes are needed to bring about long-term growth and adjustment. The doctor's evaluation is crucial.[21] History taking can be assisted by understanding some key elements involved in sexual exploitation. In a disturbed or fragmented family, there may have been

Exhibit 5-1 Child Sex History Form

RENSHAW CHILD SEX HISTORY
(Supplemental to Routine Medical/Psychosocial History)

Take history from child alone and adjust words for his age and ability to understand[1]

Patient name: _____ Age: _____ Date: _____
Birthday: _____ Address: _____ Phone: _____

*Dad:** Age? _____ Occupation? _____ Health? _____ Is he your real Dad, or is
he your stepfather or mother's boyfriend? _____ What kind of person is he? _____
What's best about him? _____
How do you get along with him? _____ What do you do together? _____
What's your biggest problem with Dad? _____ Does Dad drink alcohol? _____
Does he smoke/do drugs/use pot? _____ Is it a problem? _____
Does Mom know? _____ Does Dad give you special treats or money? _____
What do you do to earn it? _____
If you misbehave, how does Dad punish you? _____ Does he spank? _____
What do you do that makes you get spanked? _____ Does it hurt? _____
How does Dad show his love/affection for you? Kisses, hugs, etc. _____
Does he touch you in a way you like? _____ In a way you don't like? _____
Why? _____ How? _____
Does he do the same with anyone else? _____ Who? _____ When? _____
How does he get along with Mom? _____ Do they fight? _____ Does he hit Mom? _____
Do you worry about losing Dad? _____ Who's Dad's favorite (best person) at home? _____
How do you know that? _____ Who is Dad's worst person? _____
How do you know? _____
Is there anything that bothers you or that you don't like about you and Dad? _____
How often is Dad at home? _____ or away from home? _____
When he's away, does he call you? _____

*Same series of questions for stepfather, mother's boyfriend, grandfather, mother/stepmother, father's
girlfriend, grandmother, babysitter, etc., as appropriate.

Do you have brothers and sisters? _____ Names? _____
Ages? _____ Real/Step? _____
How do you get along? _____
Any special problems/secrets? _____
Do you have your own bedroom? _____ If not, who shares it? _____
Do you have your own bed? _____ Do you have privacy? _____
Do you play doctor? _____ What do you do? _____
Is it scary? _____ How does it feel? _____ Who plays? _____
Do you have pets? _____ Hobbies? _____
Do you feel like part of the family? _____ Why? _____ Why not? _____
What do you like best about your family? _____ Least? _____
Is there anything you'd change about your family? _____
Who else lives at home? _____
Details from first section, if significant: _____
Who's your very favorite person? _____
What makes him/her your favorite (best person)? _____
How do you show love/affection for your brothers and sisters? _____ Do you have fights? _____
Do you ever feel like you hate them? _____ Why? _____
What does hate mean? _____
When is bedtime? _____ How do you go to sleep, i.e., do you say prayers;
get a kiss from Mom or Dad; get tucked in? _____
How well do you sleep? _____ Do you wet the bed? _____

Exhibit 5-1 continued

Do you have dreams? _____ Do you ever repeat the same dream? _____ Are they happy dreams? _____
Scary dreams? _____ Do they wake you? _____ Then what happens? _____
Have you had a sexy dream? _____ Or a "wet dream" that normally happens to boys? _____
Do you have questions about it? _____ Do you have sexy daydreams or fantasies? _____
Does anyone come into your bed at night? _____ Who? _____ How many times? _____
What do they do? _____ How did it feel? _____
Details: _____
(*If child describes sex contact ask next batch of questions*):
Did you tell Mom? _____ Did she believe you? _____ Who else did you tell? _____
Details: _____
Can you tell someone else you trust? _____ Who? _____
Would he or she believe you? _____ Do you understand why it happened? _____
Do you have questions about it? _____
Has anyone else touched you in a way you don't like? _____
Where on your body? (*Show child explicit paper dolls.*) _____
Boys and girls wonder about private sex parts. Do you? _____ Has anyone helped you learn? _____
When? _____ How? _____
Has anyone shown you or scared you about private sex parts—theirs or yours? _____
Has anyone forced you to touch or do something you didn't like? Have they told you not to tell? _____
What did you do about that? _____
How does it make you feel to talk about it now? _____
What worries do you have in talking about it now? _____
If you could change it, how would you? _____
Do you think about it in school or at play? _____ Can you talk about it to anyone? _____
When did it begin? _____ How long has it gone on? _____

Who are your friends at school? _____
Who are your friends in the neighborhood? _____
Best friends: _____ Boyfriend/Girlfriend: _____
Details from first section, if significant.
Do you date? _____ What are your favorite TV programs? _____
Do you watch X-rated cable TV or videos? _____ Do you read sexy books? _____
Do you have sex feelings? _____ What types? _____
How do you handle these? _____
How do you feel about sex thoughts/feelings/touching/masturbation/intercourse/pregnancy? _____
Have you had problems (discharge, itch, pain, etc.) related to your penis/vagina? _____
Did you need to see a doctor? _____ Details: _____

Girls: Have you had a menstrual period? _____ Date of first one? _____ Date of last one? _____
What does it mean to you? _____
How does a baby come about? _____
Boys: Have you awakened with an erection? _____ Did you understand this? _____
Do you have questions about it? _____
Do you understand how babies come about? _____

Do you have questions about intercourse? _____ Have you learned about it? _____
Details: _____
Have you experienced it? _____ Do you want to talk about it? _____
Did you worry you may get hurt or get pregnant? _____
Is there anything else I should have asked you? _____
Is there anything you want to ask me? _____
With sex feelings it's normal to be private and rub yourself. Does this happen with you? _____
Has this caused you a problem? _____ Do you worry about it? _____
The grownup word for it is masturbation—both girls and boys normally do this in private. Some families and
religions teach about masturbation; has anyone at home talked to you about this? _____
Does anyone at school or home tease you? _____ About what? _____

Exhibit 5-1 continued

Do they ever tease you about sex? _____

Has there been any sex problem with a grownup or a bigger child in the family/at the school playground/on the bus/in the street/in a parking lot/in a toilet/at the movies/next door/elsewhere, etc.? _____
What sort of person? _____ Name: _____
What kind of problem? _____ Details: _____
What did you do/say? _____ How did you feel? _____
Did you tell anyone? _____ Who? _____ Details: _____
Did the police get involved? _____ Details: _____
How was that? _____ Did you have to tell the story to anyone? _____
Was it in the newspapers/radio? _____ How was that? _____
What did the family say? _____ Dad? _____ Mom? _____
Grandpa? _____ Grandma? _____ Brothers? _____ Sisters? _____
Friends? _____
Have you ever had a problem with telling lies? _____ Details: _____
Why do people lie? _____
Is lying ever O.K.? _____ Details: _____
Does anyone at home lie? _____ Details: _____
Why do people tell the truth? _____
Do you know about Pinnochio/Cry Wolf? _____
Has anyone taught you about truth/lies? _____ Details: _____
What else should we talk about? _____

[1]Confidentiality cannot be promised if sexual abuse is established.

Source: Reprinted from *Medical Aspects of Human Sexuality*, Vol. 20, No. 6, pp. 27–28, with permission of Hospital Publications Inc., © June 1986.

little or no education about sexuality and therefore little protection for children from sexual advances from any adult, even those in authority. For various reasons, learned sexual controls are not operative when an adult exploits an unequal, uninformed, nonresistive partner. Therefore, in the process of evaluating the child partner, the evaluator's task is to understand the child's general and sexual knowledge, values, and resistance level (self-protection) and to note physical problems (e.g., genital infection, genital injury, and pregnancy) and emotional distress. At times the child may experience quite natural sexual arousal and orgasmic responses from the sexual contact, which may be pleasing, confusing, or upsetting. If such feelings are elicited, the clinician must explain to the child that these feelings are quite normal reactions but that the partner was not appropriate, should have controlled himself or herself, and broke the law by such behavior.

Also to be explored is how the child views other family members (see Exhibit 5-1). Who was approached by the child after the abuse? What was the reason for approaching them: confusion, symptoms of pregnancy, anxiety? Details of divorce and stepfamily arrangements are also very important to prevent a charge of sexual abuse erroneously leveled toward a stepfather (particularly in familial disputes) when the actual sexual contact occurred between siblings or other peers. Special care is therefore needed when taking a sexual history, both from the parent who presents and from the child. In the main, objectivity should not be clouded by an assumption that a child's sexual knowledge or experience necessarily entails that sexual abuse occurred.

Taking a child's sexual history deserves special caution. Many videos presented in court show inexperienced child workers going "straight for the groin." This is a mistake. Leading questions will perhaps wrongly confirm the observer's assumptions or bias and may even mislead or confuse the child. The "official stranger" is perceived as a protective authority. A suggestible or frightened child may say yes or nod affirmatively to *all* questions to please this authority. A defensive child often will say "I don't know" to all questions. A child who wants to protect himself or herself or another person may, on the other hand, deny any sexual activity even when the evidence (e.g., pregnancy) is overwhelming. This denial may, in fact, be due to a threat from family members "not to say anything." Some children cover up well and are incredibly resistant. They will certainly need much more time to learn to trust the questioner or even to understand *why* the questions are being asked (which might simply be to get the child to cooperate). Comforting statements such as "It is not your fault" or promises that "No one at school will know" may be made to disarm a child, yet they are highly unethical and dishonest, especially if the story hits the newspapers and everyone finds out.

For those who work with children, a sexual history is now obligatory in doing a medical or psychiatric exam to rule out sexual abuse and is reportable by law in all U.S. states. Some pitfalls in history taking should be remembered by all who work in this difficult field. Since children try to please adults and their cognition is related to age and development, child witnesses may be unreliable.[22] In Illinois, children 13 and under are not considered criminally responsible for that reason. Children can easily be misled by rehearsal, coercive questions, or pointing to the genitals of a doll and asking, "Did daddy touch you here?" This is how *not* to take a sexual history. Curiosity about the genitals of these special "anatomically correct" dolls is quite normal in nonmolested children. Open-ended questions about where the child was touched or what happened next (or requests to show what happened) are neither leading nor misleading.

A child's interest in the genitals of the doll or drawings are not necessarily abnormal nor "clear evidence" of sexual abuse. A recent study was done with anatomically correct dolls in Canada using 17 day care center children from ages 2.4 to 5.2 years.[23] These were not abused children, but were volunteered by their parents. Eight types of behavior were noted in response to the dolls. Some children fled, too shy to look further at the dolls. Many actively handled the dolls and either concealed the sexual parts or had unusual and overt interest in the dolls' genitals, identifying the anatomy correctly, and so on. These dolls have recently been regarded as stock in trade for almost every emergency room and child agency in the country, yet there are lingering problems with relying on the dolls.

First, of course, the children's responses may not be interpreted correctly. Second, some of the dolls are not anatomically correct (e.g., the genitals may be disproportionately large, a doll may lack an anus, etc.). When a two-year-old child pointed to the only opening on a doll, it was misinterpreted by child authorities as vaginal penetration; in fact, her grandfather only wiped her anus when changing her diaper. Human genitals have been sewn on to a bunny or teddy bear, which can be dehumanizing and confusing to the child.[24] Some 1986 boy dolls come with velcro detachable penises in two models, circumcised and uncircumcised. What this will do to little boys with castration anxiety awaits further study!

A child may at times honestly confuse toilet help or medical care with sexual touch. For example, a principal who helped a five-year-old girl who had soiled her panties at school was accused of sex abuse, and a physical examination required for sports, with hernia check and a stethoscope across the chest, was reported as physician sexual abuse. Any statement that not all sexual contact is necessarily dangerous or harmful may be met with irrational anger and accusations from professionals or the public as being pro–child abuse! This is simply not true. Not every sexual experience a child has is abusive.

ETHICAL CONSIDERATIONS

Some of the ethical issues raised by taking a sexual history are covered in this section.

Is it possible to obtain informed assent from a child who is to give the abuse history? For children who have not reached the age of 18, the consent of a parent or guardian who assumes full responsibility for the child's actions and care must be gotten. When dealing with a child, the assent may not be obtained by a general statement (e.g., "We want to protect you/your father/your mother . . ."), because it could not begin to describe the kinds of life changes that the child and his or her family might undergo as a result of the abuse history. It also seems grossly inadequate to state, "We have a law that says I have to ask you some sexually explicit questions to protect you if you need it." We suggest this: "I am going to ask you some family and sexual questions that are part of this examination. Will you try to answer them?" Even this is inadequate, but it does open the opportunity for a child's assent. Keep in mind that the child is not considered legally competent to give total consent to the process; parental or guardian consent is the first step.

Most states have provisions dealing with juveniles. Illinois Revised Statute 38/6-1 states, "No person shall be convicted of any offense unless he has attained his 13th birthday at the time the offense was committed." Therefore, a developmentally immature child is not criminally liable. Any witness may lie for malice or for reward (actual or emotional) or out of fear when told to do so by a significant other. Before perjury charges may be brought, minimal mental capacity and moral reasoning must be established.[25] Due to flagrant taunting of police by young minors who commit well-planned crimes, the competency of juvenile offenders is an issue in regard to contracts, financial affairs, criminal responsibility, consensual sexual relations, obtaining contraceptive aids, medical treatment, and confidentiality from parents.[26] Judgement and perspective have been arbitrarily claimed to exist at 16 or 18 or 21 years of age in various states. Yet the myth that children do not lie has increasingly allowed the evidence of two- or three- or six-year-olds to be regarded as competent (at face value without cross-examination) and to incriminate accused persons who plead both innocence and discriminatory barriers to their individual rights to due process of U.S. law.

A third ethical issue regards confidentiality. How can confidentiality be promised to the child? Eliciting sexual abuse history turns physicians and other health care givers from healers into criminal investigators. Hence confidentiality should never be promised or implied. Sexual abuse is regarded as a reportable criminal offense and "evidence" evoked from the child must be reviewed by police and the law courts. A therapeutic alliance is, therefore, extraordinarily difficult to achieve. As soon as physical or sexual abuse is reported during a medical, family, or school history, a series of questions must be pursued (see Exhibit 5-1). The professional should inform the child, "The law requires me to report the sexual problem you have described so that we can protect you." To go further and promise help or treatment for the child or adult sex partner or family member may be misleading. There may be no funds for such therapy or no treatment resources other than foster placement, which often means the loss of home, friends, and parents. This may not be perceived by the child as help. The investigator cannot keep silent about the potential for family disruption and hide under a cloak of therapeutic assistance. Nobody wins in child sexual abuse cases. A never ending chain of grief may follow. Sometimes there is a reprieve from harassment, but this is not the same as healing.

A fourth issue concerns the wrongful "rescue" from a suspected child abuse situation. Suppose that despite all we have cautioned about, a therapist and child abuse team intervene destructively after a false sex accusation by a child. (In the recent years psychiatric and law literature has begun to reflect particular concern about false allegations of sexual abuse brought in child custody divorce disputes. Warring parents discovered this weapon some time ago—to the dismay of therapists and judges.) One ethical problem is how to provide recompense for a lost good name, a ruptured family life, and the total destruction by the state of familial trust (or in the case of professionals falsely accused, professional trust). It seems impossible to provide adequate recompense. Even a lawsuit for wrongful accusation would not repair the damage. Thus, it is extremely important, both clinically and ethically, that the professional understand the consequences of a child's physical and sexual abuse examination and evaluation, especially the consequences of calling the Child Abuse Hotline.[27] It is a matter not only of professional expertise, but also of justice to be trained in the proper taking of a sexual history and sex abuse evaluation. Persons untrained in this technique, even if they are charged by the state to protect children, should not presume guilt simply as a way to deal with their own uncertainty. They must request consultation for further evaluation.

CONCLUSION

Is there such a thing as a social imperative, paralleling the technological imperative? The technological imperative commands us to act to intervene using the technology at hand without stopping to reflect critically on its usefulness or humaneness. It leads to the "the button is there, push it" syndrome. Especially in medicine, its impact overrides the wishes of patients and, to some extent, the wishes of those who employ the technology. The reason for the technological imperative is that, as Martin Heidegger observed, modern technology, unlike its earlier cultural cousins, is all-pervasive.[28] Technology moved from being one of a number of options available for human use to being the unquestioned option. Because technology is there, ready and waiting to be employed, its impact on human values, especially on the human values of those on whom it is exercised, is left unexamined. This constitutes a failure to take responsibility for one's actions.[29]

Similarly, the social imperative may unconsciously compel intervention (as in the case cited at the beginning of this chapter) without critical reflection on the values of the persons who will be affected.

Today there is a child sex abuse industry that has a vested interest in "case finding" and in selling related materials and roadshows to schools. Some school plays intended to provide sex abuse education promote the stereotyped image of father as dangerous, mother as nonbelieving, and neighbors and agencies as protective. This viewpoint, often false, can threaten family integrity and confuse suggestible children, parents, and professionals. In the marketing of these expensive "education aids," a sex abuse hysteria occurs that precludes careful screening of the "products" purchased. Thoughtful child experts are truly concerned about these potentially harmful products. In well-meaning attempts to curb child pornography, parents and grandparents have been arrested for making nude photographs of a two-year-old for the family album!

It has been said that in child protection, truly destructive investigations may be those that do "too much too soon or too little too late."[30]

An accused's 6th Amendment right to confront witnesses and 14th Amendment right to due process may be waived as the court tries to protect the child witness from "courtroom trauma." Some courts have even allowed a surrogate witness (the mother or social worker) to speak for the child. This may make convictions easier, but at times an innocent ex-husband, ex-wife, stepfather, or stepbrother may be condemned. Plea bargaining to make a false confession to end a sex abuse hearing is a new evil. Undoing the resulting damage is endlessly expensive, prolonged, and emotionally draining. If witnesses lied, an innocent person may be legally coerced to have "therapy" or may develop despair, commit suicide, or be jailed for many years (in one case, 158 years). Further, the process is a tremendous drain on professional time, the legal system, and public funds (which may be used to pay as much as one million dollars for each long prison term).

The burgeoning field of child protection represents a sensitive interface of medicine, family life, society, the law, and ethics. Intense and immediate attention is required to properly protect children and, at the same time, protect the family and the community from misapplication of child abuse powers.

NOTES:

1. Anne H. Cohn, executive director of the National Committee for the Prevention of Child Abuse, as quoted in R. Bruce Bold, "Child Abuse Deaths Up 29%, Study Says," *Chicago Tribune*, January 26, 1987, sect. 1, p. 1.

2. Hanke Gratteau, "Foster Children Will Read Their Rights," *Chicago Tribune*, August 25, 1986, sect. 2, p. 1.

3. Ibid.

4. "Child Abuse Deaths Soar in Illinois," *Chicago Tribune*, September 14, 1986, sect. 1, p. 1.

5. K. Siegenthaler and W. Recktenwald, "Stevenson Attacks on Child Abuse Issue," *Chicago Tribune*, September 15, 1986, sect. 2, p. 3.

6. R.B. Dold, "New State Drive on Child Care," *Chicago Tribune*, October 20, 1986.

7. "Child Abuse Deaths Soar in Illinois," *Chicago Tribune*, September 14, 1986.

8. Anne H. Cohn, "Prevention Is the Key in Child Abuse," Letter to the Editor, *Chicago Tribune*, September 26, 1986, sect. 1, p. 26.

9. G. Abbott, *The Child and the State* 2 vols. (Chicago: University of Chicago Press, 1938); E.L. Johnson, *Family Law* (Chicago: University of Chicago Press, 1958).

10. Department of Health and Human Services, *National Study of Incidence and Severity of Child Abuse and Neglect*, DHHS Publication 81-03-325 (Washington, D.C.: U.S. Government Printing Office, 1981), 11.

11. D.J. Besharov, "'Doing Something' about Child Abuse: The Need to Narrow the Grounds for State Intervention," *Harvard Journal of Law and Public Policy* 8 (1985): 539–89.

12. D.C. Renshaw, "Sexual Exploitation: When and How Does It Begin?" *Proceedings of the Institute of Medicine of Chicago* 37 (October 1984): 146–49.

13. D.C. Renshaw, *Sex Talk for a Safe Child* (Chicago: American Medical Association, 1986).

14. Besharov, "'Doing Something' about Child Abuse."

15. Besharov, "'Doing Something' about Child Abuse."

16. A. Kilpatrick, "Childhood Sexual Experiences (501 Women)," *Journal of Sex Research* 22 (May 1986): 221–42.

17. R.B. Dold and H. Gratteau, "Strapped Agency Puts Kids Back in Harm's Way," *Chicago Tribune*, October 5, 1986, sect. 1, p. 1.

18. D.C. Renshaw, "When You Suspect Child Sex Abuse: Take the Child's Sexual History," *Medical Aspects of Human Sexuality* 20 (June 1986): 19–28.

19. Besharov, "'Doing Something' about Child Abuse."

20. M. Pride, *The Child Abuse Industry* (Westchester, Ill.: Crossway Books, 1986).

21. Renshaw, "When You Suspect Child Sex Abuse."

22. J. Varendock, "Les teroignages d'enfants dan un proces retenissant," *Archives of Psychology* 11 (1911): 129.

23. F. Gabriel, "Anatomically Correct Dolls in the Diagnosis of Sex Abuse of Children," *Journal of the Melamie Klein Society* (December 1985): 40–51

24. D.C. Renshaw, "When Sex Abuse is Falsely Charged," *Medical Aspects of Human Sexuality* 19 (July 1985): 116–24.

25. K. Quinn, "Competency to Be a Witness: A Major Child Forensic Issue," *Bulletin of the American Academy of Psychiatry and the Law* 14(1986): 311–21.

26. S.B. Billick, "Developmental Competency," *Bulletin of the American Academy of Psychiatry and the Law* 14 (1986): 301–9.

27. Renshaw, "When Sex Abuse Is Falsely Charged."

28. Martin Heidegger, "Only a God Can Save Us," in *The Question Concerning Technology and Other Essays* (New York: Harper & Row, 1977).

29. Hans Jonas, *Philosophical Essays: From Ancient Creed to Technological Man* (Englewood Cliffs, N.J.: Prentice-Hall, 1974).

30. Besharov, "'Doing Something' about Child Abuse."

Chapter 6

Teens and Birth Control

John A. Eaddy and Glenn C. Graber

Our goal in this chapter is to examine the ethical issues that arise in certain clinical practice situations. Consider what you would do if you were presented with each of the following cases. (It will be helpful to keep these and other similar situations in mind as you read the discussion which follows.)

Aileen is a 17-year-old whom you have known for some time and consider to be an unusually thoughtful and mature young woman. She comes to you requesting a prescription for birth control pills, volunteering a carefully reasoned explanation as to why she has chosen to become sexually active and why she prefers this form of contraception. Should you grant her request? Should you inform her parents of the request?

Brenda is a 14-year-old who is brought to your office by her 17-year-old boyfriend. (He stays in the car outside, however.) She nervously and haltingly requests a prescription for birth control pills. When you gently ask her to explain her reasons for wanting contraceptives, she merely looks at you sullenly and frightened. Should you grant her request? Should you inform her parents of the request? (Would it make a difference here whether you had an ongoing relationship with her parents?) Should you take another follow-up action instead of or in addition to notifying the parents? In particular, should you ask Brenda to have her boyfriend come in to talk with you?

Colleen is a 16-year-old who has been your patient since she was an infant. As she is halfway across the examining room towards the door following a camp physical, she shyly says, "Could I ask you some questions about birth control?" How should you respond? Should you notify her parents of her question?

Dora is a 16-year-old whose mother calls you the day before she is to come in for a camp physical and asks if you would talk with her about birth control. "Given all I have heard about teens and sex, I think she should be protected—but I could not possibly bring myself to suggest it to her." How should you respond to this request? Should you tell Dora of her mother's request?

In addition to these case examples, we offer some fallacies (or perhaps they should be called *phallicsies*) and several tables of facts relevant to the discussion. We recommend that you read these carefully and give some thought to their implications *before* you read the discussion of the issues that follows. We will be drawing on this data throughout this chapter.

Fallacies

- You cannot get pregnant unless you love him.
- You cannot get pregnant unless you want to get pregnant while you are having sex.
- Pregnancy is not something that can happen to me.
- You cannot get pregnant unless you are older than I am now.
- I have escaped pregnancy so far, so I am safe in the future.[1]

- Only a few teen-agers are sexually active.
- Those who are sexually active know enough to use birth control.
- In the U.S., sexual initiation most often takes place in the family car.
- Sex education will only encourage sexual activity by "giving kids the idea."
- For parents to talk to kids about birth control won't accomplish anything. If they are going to be responsible, they will be anyway; and if they are not, parental cooperation won't help.
- The only reason teenage girls do have sex is that their boyfriends pressure them into it.

Viewpoint

A major concern of some is that sex education will lead to promiscuity and moral decay. There is evidence that the opposite is true. The most sexually active adolescents have been found to have the least information about sex. Keeping sexual information from adolescents does not prevent them from sexual activity, nor does giving information promote sexual activity. Thus the physician need not worry that talking about sexual topics will "suggest" activities to adolescents.[2]

NORMAL SEXUAL DEVELOPMENT

Growing into and out of adolescence is a complex process of biologic, psychologic, and sociologic maturation. Before reaching age 20, the majority of adolescents have engaged in

Table 6-1 Sexually Active Adolescents by Age and Sex

Age	Sexually Active	
	Males (%)	Females (%)
13–14	18	6
15–17	50	33
19	80	66

Source: Adapted from *Teenage Pregnancy: The Problem That Hasn't Gone Away*, with permission of Alan Guttmacher Institute, © 1981.

sexual activity (Table 6-1). According to females, 60–85 percent of the time sexual intercourse is engaged in by mutual consent (Table 6-2). First intercourse is usually accomplished in someone's home (Table 6-3). Adolescents' emotional reaction to their first sexual intercourse involves a wide spectrum of feelings, which reflects the complexity of biologic, psychologic, and sociologic components of intimate sexual interaction (Table 6-4).

Although the adolescent birth rate has been going down since 1973, the pregnancy rate has continued to increase. More than one in ten teenagers gets pregnant each year. There are 1.3 million children living with teenage mothers, about half of whom are unmarried. Another 1.6 million children are under age five and live with mothers who were teenagers when they gave birth. Abortions and infants given up for adoption add significantly to the number of teenage pregnancies.

Pregnancy prevention by use of contraception usually reflects mature, responsible behavior and thinking on the part of the male and/or female adolescent. As Table 6-5 indicates, compliance in contraceptive use can be enhanced by parent involvement, adequate information sharing, and communication between adolescents and health care providers.

METHODS OF CONTRACEPTION

Choosing a contraceptive method can be a confusing ordeal for the teenager. Careful counseling regarding the spectrum of methods and the effectiveness of each is an integral part of effective health maintenance with this age group. Abstinence from sexual intercourse will provide protection from pregnancy. Permission-giving to delay sexual intercourse should not be neglected. Teenagers may seek cautionary adult advice as a counterweight to peer pressures to engage in sex. However, when sexual activity is already occurring or is anticipated, then full counseling regarding contraceptive methods is needed. Table 6-6 shows the relative effectiveness of various contraceptive methods. Tubal ligation, vasectomy, and injectable progestin are usually unacceptable methods for teenagers. At the present time, use of IUDs should be reserved for women who can accept the possibility of future sterility.

Both males and females have a "need to know" regarding the relative ineffectiveness of such methods as coitus interruptus, fertility awareness techniques, douche, and chance. Ta-

Table 6-2 Reason for Having Intercourse, According to Females

Reason for Having Intercourse	%
Mutual consent	60–85
Go along with boyfriend	13–28
Boyfriend couldn't say no	5–12
Boyfriend will leave for another girl	2–6
Other girls doing "it"	2–3

Source: Adapted from *Adolescent Sexuality in Contemporary America* by R.C. Sorensen, World Publishing, © 1973.

Table 6-3 Place of First Intercourse Among Adolescents

Place of First Intercourse	All (%)	Females (%)	Males (%)
In the teenager's home	19	21	18
In a friend's home	10	9	10
In an automobile	20	16	24
In the girl/boy's home	20	19	21
In a motel	2	0	5
Outdoors	20	26	13
Other	9	9	9
TOTAL	100	100	100

Source: Adapted from *Adolescent Sexuality in Contemporary America* by R.C. Sorensen, World Publishing, © 1973.

ble 6-7 documents the actual use of contraceptives by adolescent females aged 15 to 19. Healthy teenagers are at little risk of major side effects from use of oral contraceptives, especially when low-dose estrogen pills are used. Positive effects such as alleviation of menstrual cramps and of irregular, unpredictable menses may be seen as a major benefit for

Table 6-4 Adolescents' Reaction to Their First Intercourse

Reaction to First Intercourse	All (%)	Boys (%)	Girls (%)
Excited	37	46	26
Afraid	37	17	63
Happy	35	42	26
Satisfied	33	43	20
Thrilled	30	43	13
Curious	26	23	30
Joyful	23	31	12
Mature	23	29	14
Fulfilled	20	29	8
Worried	20	9	35
Guilty	17	3	36
Embarrassed	17	7	31
Tired	15	15	14
Relieved	14	19	8
Sorry	12	1	25
Hurt	11	0	25
Powerful	9	15	1
Foolish	8	7	9
Used	7	0	16
Disappointed	6	3	10
Felt raped	3	0	6

Source: Adapted from *Adolescent Sexuality in Contemporary America* by R.C. Sorensen, World Publishing, © 1973.

Table 6-5 Factors Related to Contraceptive Compliance

Factor	Reporting Factor (%)	Compliant (%)
Side effects on pill		
YES	15	55
NO	24	88
Parent made appointment for visit		
YES	15	87
NO	85	58
Parent accompanied patient to clinic		
YES	31	81
NO	69	54
Career goals: college bound		
YES	35	80
NO	65	53
Satisfied with pill as method of contraception		
YES	64	72
NO	36	44
Age at oral contraceptive prescription		
13–14	18	72
15–16	48	53
17–19	34	71
Physician considered helpful		
YES	80	69
NO	20	35
Satisfied with clinic		
YES	87	68
NO	13	23
Abortion before oral contraception		
YES	27	54
NO	73	66

Source: Journal of Adolescent Health Care, Vol. 3, pp. 120–123, Elsevier Science Publishing Company, Inc., © September 1982.

many adolescent women. A careful medical-social history and a physical examination are essential in helping an adolescent choose his or her own method of contraception.

LEGAL ISSUES

The legal warrant for counseling adolescents about contraception is far from clearly established. On the one hand, it is perhaps comforting to hear that "no case has been discovered where a doctor was found liable for damages resulting from the prescription of contraceptives to a minor of any age without parental consent."[3] On the other hand, statutes and court opinions provide little explicit warrant for such confidence. To properly ascertain the legal situation here, some history is necessary.

Table 6-6 Contraceptive Effectiveness Rates

Method	Lowest Observed Failure Rate[a]	Failure Rate in Typical Users[b]
Tubal ligation	0.04	0.04
Vasectomy	0.15	0.15
Injectable progestin	0.25	0.25
Combined birth control pills	0.5	2
Progestin-only pill	1	2.5
IUD	1.5	4
Condom	2	10
Diaphragm (with spermicide)	2	10
Cervical cap	2	13
Foam, creams, jellies, and vaginal suppositories	3–5	15
Coitus interruptus	16	23
Fertility awareness techniques (basal body temperature, mucus method, calendar, & rhythm)	2–20	20–30
Douche	——	40
Chance (no method of birth control)	90	90

[a]Designed to complete the sentence: "Of 100 women who start out the year using a given method, and who use it correctly and consistently, the lowest observed failure rate has been _____."
[b]Designed to complete the sentence: "Of 100 typical users who start out the year employing a given method, the number who will be pregnant by the end of the year will be _____."

Source: Adapted from *Contraceptive Technology, 1982-1983,* 11th rev. ed. by R.A. Hatcher et al., p. 5, with permission of Irvington Publishers, © 1982.

Table 6-7 Actual Use of Contraceptives by Adolescent Females 15–19 Years Old

Methods of Contraception	Use by Adolescents	
	First Intercourse (%)	Last Intercourse (%)
None	50	30
Pill	10	31
Condom	20	14
Withdrawal	18	12
Rhythm	1.7	3.2
Foam	1.2	3
IUD	0.4	2.2
Douche	0.4	1.1
Diaphragm	0.3	2.5

Source: Adapted from *Teenage Pregnancy: The Problem That Hasn't Gone Away,* with permission of Alan Guttmacher Institute, © 1981.

In a landmark case in 1965, the U.S. Supreme Court ruled that the use of contraceptive devices was protected *for married couples* under a constitutional right to privacy.[4] This also protected counseling, education, and prescriptions relating to birth control—but only for married couples. In 1972, recognition of this right was extended to unmarried adults.[5] A 1977 opinion struck down as unconstitutional a state statute that prohibited the distribution of any form of contraceptive device to minors under the age of sixteen.[6] However, this outcome should not be taken as recognizing an independent right to privacy for adolescents regarding reproduction, since one of the chief arguments given for striking down this law was that it denied *parents* of adolescents the right to provide birth control for their children if they choose to do so.[7]

It is somewhat ironic that a minor's right to abortion is more firmly established than the right to prevent pregnancy. In *Planned Parenthood of Central Missouri v. Danforth*, the Supreme Court ruled that states could not require parental consent as a *sine qua non* for a minor to have an abortion.[8] However, this does *not* leave the choice about abortion as a private matter between the minor and her physician (as it is for an adult patient, at least during the first trimester of pregnancy). There are two important qualifications to this right as applied to minors: (1) The Court left open the possibility that states might require a formal procedure (such as a judicial competency hearing) as the alternative to parental consent; (2) An opening was also left for states to require *notification* of parents that their daughter has had an abortion, even if their consent before the fact was unnecessary. This latter qualification was further reinforced in a 1981 ruling upholding a Utah notification requirement[9]—although this applied only to "unemancipated minors who have made no showing of maturity (and who have not shown the abortion to be in their best interests)."[10]

In 1982, the Department of Health and Human Services proposed a regulation that would require any clinic receiving federal funds to inform parents or guardians within ten days after issuing any prescription for a birth control measure to a girl under 18. This regulation, popularly known as "the squeal rule," was immediately challenged in court and struck down before it took effect.

Much of the legal regulation of adolescent reproductive rights, then, is left up to the states, and state statutes and court rulings vary widely, as can be seen in Table 6-8.

ETHICAL ISSUES

We would deny that the ethical issues relating to sexuality are wholly *sui generis*. There is not a "sexual ethics" which is discontinuous from the moral principles governing other human relationships. Seduction furnishes a good example. The wrongfulness of such an act is based, we would contend, not especially on its sexual nature, but rather on the fact that it involves deceiving, manipulating, and "using" another person. To manipulate someone by similar means into doing some nonsexual act against his or her fundamental wishes would be wrong *in exactly the same way* that seduction is wrong. Consider, for example, the "pigeon drop scam" (generally practiced on elderly persons), in which a person entices another to trust him or her with a large amount of money and then absconds with it. The intimacy of the sexual act and the momentous possible consequence (pregnancy) may heighten the degree of the wrongness of seduction, but it does not make it qualitatively different from nonsexual examples of manipulation such as the pigeon drop.

Table 6-8 Age of Consent for Medical and Sex-Related Health Care

Ages at which state legislation or court decisions have specifically affirmed the right of individuals to give consent for their own medical treatment as of January 1983.[a]

State	May Consent for Medical Care in General			May Consent For:		
	No Limitation	Special Status	In Emergency	Contraception	Pregnancy	VD Care
Alabama	14	E[i], M	X	14	X	X
Alaska	18	E[e], M	X	X	X	X
Arizona	18	E, M	X[j]	E, M	E, M	X
Arkansas	X[b,d]	E, M	X	X[b,l]	X[m]	X
California	18	15 E[f], M	X	X	X	12
Colorado	18	15 E[f], M	18	X	E, M	X
Connecticut	18	E, M	18	E	E, M	X[q]
Delaware	18	E, M	18	12	12	12
D.C.	18	E, M	X	X[c]	X[c]	X
Florida	18	E, M	X	X[r]	X[f]	X
Georgia	18	M	X	XF	X	X
Hawaii	18	18	18	14	14	14
Idaho	18	18	18	X[d]	18	14
Illinois	18	M[f]	X	X[h]	X	12
Indiana	18	E, M	X	18	18	X
Iowa	18	E, M	X	18[l]	18	X
Kansas	18	18	16	16	X	X
Kentucky	18	M, E, P	X	X	X	X
Louisiana	18[s]	M	X	F	X	X
Maine	18[r]	E	X	X[r]	18	X
Maryland	18	M, P	X	X	X	X
Mass.	18	M, E, P	X	X[d]	X	X
Michigan	18	18	18	18[l]	18	X
Minnesota	18	M, E, P[e]	X	X	X	X
Mississippi	18	M, E, P	X	X[o]	X	X
Missouri	18	M, E, P	X	X[f]	X	X
Montana	E, 18[i]	M, E, P	X	F[h]	X	X
Nebraska	19	M		19[k]	19	X
Nevada	X[e,r]	E, M, P	18	X[d]	X[d]	X
N. Hampshire	18	E, M	X	18	18	14
N. Jersey	18	E, M	18	18	X	X
N. Mexico	18	E, M	X[j]	18[l]	X[p]	X
New York	18	E, M, P	X	X	X[d]	X
N. Carolina	18	E, M	X	X	X	X
N. Dakota	18	E, M	18	18	18	14
Ohio	X[d]	18	X[d]	X[d,l]	X[d]	X
Oklahoma	18	E, M	X	M, P, E[e]	X	X
Oregon	15	M	X	X[m]	15[m]	X
Pa.	18	E[i], M	X	X[r]	X	X
R.I.	16	M	16, M	18	18	X
S. Carolina	16[t]	E, M	X	X[g]	X[g]	X[g]
S. Dakota	18	E, M	18	18[k]	18	X
Tennessee	18	18	18	X[o]	18	X
Texas	18	16 E, M	X	16	X[m]	X
Utah	18	M	X	18	X	X
Vermont	18	E, M	18	18	18	X
Virginia	18	E, M	14	X[c]	X	X

Table 6-8 continued

| State | May Consent for Medical Care in General | | | May Consent For: | | |
	No Limitation	Special Status	In Emergency	Contraception	Pregnancy	VD Care
Washington	18	E	18	18	18	14
W. Va.	18	16, E	X	18[l]	18	X
Wisconsin	18	E, M	18	18	18	X
Wyoming	19	19	19	19[l]	19	X

CODES: X = any age   E = emancipated   F = female   M = married   P = parent

[a]The fact that no affirmative legislation, court decision, or attorney general's opinion has been found in a particular state does not mean that some or even all categories of minors below the ages shown in the table do not have the right to obtain some or all medical services on their own consent.
[b]Excluding voluntary sterilization if under 18 and unmarried.
[c]Excluding voluntary sterilization.
[d]If mature enough to understand the nature and consequences of the treatment.
[e]*Emancipated* defined as living apart from parents and managing own financial affairs.
[f]And/or pregnant.
[g]Whenever such services are deemed "necessary" by the physician.
[h]If "professes" to be pregnant.
[i]*Emancipated* defined as a high school graduate, a parent, or pregnant.
[j]If no parent available, other may consent *in loco parentis*.
[k]Only for treatment of venereal disease.
[l]Comprehensive family planning law permits (or does not exclude) services to minors without parental consent.
[m]Excluding abortion.
[n]If referred by clergyman, physician, or Planned Parenthood or if "failure to provide such services would create a serious health hazard."
[o]If referred by clergyman, physician, family planning clinic, school or institution of higher learning, or any state or local government agency.
[p]Examination only.
[q]In public health agencies, public or private hospitals, or clinics.
[r]If married or pregnant or "may suffer, in the opinion of the physician, probable health hazards if such services are not provided."
[s]If minor "is or believes himself to be afflicted with an illness or disease."
[t]Except for operation essential to health or life.

Source: Reprinted from *The Rights of Young People* by M. Guggenheim and A. Sussman, pp. 294–297, Bantam Books, with permission of American Civil Liberties Union, © 1985.

Furthermore, we would contend that the status of being a teenager does not, in and of itself, alter rights and duties. Unless the capacity of the teenager, the effects on the teenager, or the like warrants a different moral verdict on a particular action, our duties toward the teenager are no different from our duties toward adults. Telling a lie to a teenager, for example, is no less wrong than lying to an adult. Both are equally capable of distinguishing truth from falsehood, of feeling deceived, and of angry reactions. Miss Manners is (as always) quite correct when she observes: "Rudeness to children counts as rudeness."[11]

Thus, in order to discern the rights and wrongs of professional dealings with adolescent sexuality, we must first examine the values (and disvalues) and general ethical principles that relate to sexuality. Then we must consider if anything in the condition of adolescence makes a difference in the rights and duties which apply to dealing with teenagers.

Values in Sexuality

To articulate the doubly obvious, (1) sex is a source of physical pleasure and (2) pleasure is a value. However, it should be equally obvious and uncontroversial that pleasurable sensations are not the sole source of value in sexual activity. Even the pleasure-oriented *Playboy* philosophy acknowledges that the chief erogenous organ is the brain. The pleasures of sex are found as much in the interpretations we apply to the experience as to the physical "feel" of the sexual response. Attempted descriptions of these additional elements are generally vague in the extreme. People commonly speak of sexual activities as "establishing intimacy" or "maintaining relationships" or "opening up communication."

There is no reason to believe that teenagers are any less capable of experiencing the physical sensations of orgasm than adults. There might be reason, however, to question whether teenagers are equally capable of understanding the "deeper meaning" of sexual activity. Perhaps this deeper meaning is a sophisticated intellectual matter which can only be mastered through reflection on considerable life experience and thus is unavailable to adolescents. Or perhaps it represents an advanced developmental stage.

The difficulty with this line of argument is that, as with many capacities, it is questionable whether it varies systematically with chronological age. Some teenagers, for example, are far more capable of understanding political issues than many adults. [12] It is only to save ourselves the trouble of administering comprehension tests as a condition for voting (plus the very real danger that any such program could be distorted to serve the ends of prejudice and partisan politics) that we make the initiation of voting privileges conditional on reaching a certain age. To a large degree, this condition is arbitrary. By denying the opportunity to vote to a teenager who is capable of voting intelligently and takes the trouble to comprehend political issues, we deprive the teenager of the personal benefits of political participation— and we also deny our society the benefit of the teenagers' thoughtful contribution to the political process.

It may be similarly true that some teenagers are at least as capable of comprehending the deeper meaning of sex as many adults. If so, then to deny all teenagers the opportunity to participate in sexual activity is arbitrarily to rob the capable ones of valuable experiences (and to fail to restrict sexual activity among adults who fail to comprehend the deeper meaning is to foster a cheapening of sex). Furthermore, the argument against individual determination of capacity which was cited in connection with the political franchise is not as plausible here. It might be possible to determine case by case whether teenagers (or adults) have the requisite capacities. Then we might issue a "sex license" like the currently prized driver's license. Actually, the doctrine of the "mature minor," which often entails permission of the state for an underaged person to marry, is not unlike this suggestion. Furthermore, the physician may be the proper professional to administer the qualifying test, since knowledge of sexual physiology and the medical consequences of sexual practices would be a central part of the qualifications.

Disvalues

In addition to the positive values experienced in sexual activity, there are also disvalues. Sex can be physically pleasant, but it can also be physically painful. Sex can have a deeper meaning that is positive and exhilarating, but it can also be a source of extraordinary anguish. (See Table 6-4, to be discussed further below.) There might be a reason to differentiate sexual opportunities for adolescents if we found that they were especially susceptible to the negative effects and ''more likely to be hurt.''

But can a chronological distinction be defended here? It is not obvious that it can. Furthermore, sexual frustration can also be a source of anguish, so we are not necessarily protecting teenagers from all disvalues associated with sex by enforcing sexual abstinence. Indeed, it might be argued that the prevailing sexual attitudes within our society—the heavy emphasis on sex in advertising and entertainment combined with the doctrine of adolescent abstinence and with educational and social patterns which prolong the period of adolescence (and thus of enforced abstinence)—contribute to a good deal of harm.

Sexual Rights and Wrongs

Some ethical rights and wrongs are not readily reduced to a calculus of values and disvalues, including justice, which involves fairness in the distribution of values and disvalues. On this source, it is disturbing to find in Table 6-4 that only one-half as many females as males reported feeling ''happy,'' ''satisfied,'' ''mature,'' or ''relieved'' from sexual intercourse and only one-third as many reported being ''thrilled,'' ''joyful,'' or ''fulfilled.'' On the other hand, four times as many females as males report being ''afraid'' or ''worried,'' twelve times as many reported feeling ''guilty,'' and five times as many reported being ''embarrassed.'' Even more serious cause for concern is that one-quarter of the females reported that they felt ''sorry'' or ''hurt'' as a result of their first sexual experience and some reported that they felt ''used,'' ''disappointed,'' or even ''raped.'' These results suggest that serious injustice can result from premature sexual initiation. But, here again, it is not clear that this problem is restricted to teenagers. Many young adults (or even middle-aged adults) might report similar reactions to recent sexual experiences. And to deny sexual expression to those teenagers who would neither experience these adverse reactions nor cause them in their partners would be an injustice to them.

Some argue that sex is morally wrong without the mutual commitment that occurs in marriage. But this merely pushes the issue back a step and raises questions about the legal and social prohibition on teenage marriage. If the response to this is that adolescents are incapable of supporting a family, the association of economic independence with personal commitment can be called into question. If the response is rather that adolescents are incapable of the level of personal commitment required for marriage, the question whether a chronological distinction can be defended is raised once again. Statistics show that teenage marriages have a higher failure rate than marriages later in life, but this is not sufficient basis for a chronological barrier applying to every person under a certain age. Developmental literature does not support a rigid age barrier, for all responsible developmental chronologies are acknowledged to be probabilistic generalizations. There may be teenagers who have progressed to the stage of being able to handle the intimacy that makes serious long-term commitment possible; there may be chronological adults who have not developed this capacity.

Similarly, for other moralistic sexual rules, reasons must be given for applying them especially to adolescents and not regulating the behavior of adults in the same ways. Unless such reasons can be given, special sexual restrictions on adolescents are unjustified.

Rights to Sexual Activity?

The arguments we have developed to this point might be taken to imply a *right* to sex for teenagers. However, this would be at most a "negative" right, i.e., a right not to have their actions interfered with. Even if no special harm or wrong were found in adolescent sexual experiences, it does not follow that teenagers possess a right to have others assist them in satisfying their sexual desires. Just as the teenage boy is unjustified when he insists to his girlfriend that she has an obligation to relieve his sexual frustration, adolescents of either sex are unjustified in insisting to their physicians that they ought to facilitate their sex life by providing contraception. And we will see below, there are other reasons to question the extent of the negative right not to be interfered with.

Rights to Contraception?

There is no valid basis for a claim of a right to contraception. If a physician decides it is morally appropriate to provide contraception to adolescent patients, the only sound basis would be to protect them or their sexual partners from harm.

The chief harm to be feared, of course, is from pregnancy, which causes significant physical, emotional, and social risks for teenagers. One key question is whether the disvalues of teenage pregnancy are sufficiently great to warrant the encouragement to sexual activity that might stem from making contraception available. It is clearly unfair to say that birth control information and assistance *causes* teenage sexual experimentation. As Table 6-7 demonstrates, one-half of teenagers do not use any method of contraception during their first intercourse and nearly one-third engage in sex later without protection. However, it does seem likely that the ready availability of contraception will tip the scales in *some* cases for adolescents who are debating whether to initiate sexual activity.

Furthermore, aside from the issue of the amount of harm that might follow, it matters greatly on some moral theories what an individual's relationship is to the harm. Thus the judgment that "teenagers are going to engage in intercourse anyway and making contraception available at least reduces the risk" overlooks one's special responsibility for the results that stem from one's own actions. The teenager is responsible for the risks of intercourse, but the physician bears moral responsibility (and legal liability as well) for the risks of forms of birth control he or she has prescribed.

Responsibilities of the Family

Thus far in the discussion, we have focused on the teenager as an individual, assessing personal capabilities, the personal values and disvalues of sexual intimacy, and individual ethical principles. In this, we follow the pattern of most discussions of these issues, which is also an accepted general pattern of inquiry, i.e., to isolate the phenomenon to be studied in order to focus attention more rigorously upon it.

But one result of this focus is that it pays inadequate attention to the social and cultural context in which the individual develops. One way of putting this point is to say that our discussion so far directly yields advice only for teenagers in the situation of the couple in the film *The Blue Lagoon*. But most teenagers are not isolated on a tropical island. Rather, they face these decisions in a social and cultural context, and one notable element of this context is the family in which the adolescent has been raised. In a case on a different matter, the U.S. Supreme Court characterized the role of the family in this way:

> The law's concept of the family rests on a presumption that parents possess what a child lacks in maturity, experience, and capacity for judgment required for making life's difficult decisions. More important, historically it has recognized that natural bonds of affection lead parents to act in the best interests of their children.[13]

This statement is unfortunately questionable, since far too many parents are both less wise and less caring than it suggests. However, it serves as a fine normative statement of the moral responsibility of the family. This is only part of the importance of the family, however. The Court stresses the *instrumental* value of family, i.e., how parents may serve to guide the adolescent toward correct choices—choices which the adolescent will find intrinsically satisfying. But we must also acknowledge the *intrinsic* value of the family. Independent of the correctness of parental guidance, the fact of belonging to a caring unit such as the family is itself important, especially for adolescents who have not yet established an independent identity (i.e., most adolescents). Thus parents have an obligation to provide thoughtful guidance to teenagers and also to provide an atmosphere of acceptance and affection even if the teenagers do not seek this guidance or wholly accept and follow it.

Responsibilities to the Family

The physician has a responsibility to support the above role for the family. However, this obligation has two components to it. It is not enough to notify parents of a teenager's request for contraception and to assume that helpful advice and greater family unity will result. The physician also owes it to the teenage patient to facilitate a healthy reaction within the family to such news. This can best be accomplished, we would argue, through a long-term plan of open discussions about sexuality with both the parents and the developing child, as well as by careful assessment of the strengths and weaknesses of the family system.

Smilkstein defines a family as "a psychological group consisting of the patient and one or more persons, children or adults, in which there is a commitment for members to nurture each other."[14] Family crises, defined as "life events, present and past, that have produced change in the functional state of family members," are classified into the four categories shown in Exhibit 6-1.

Note that all four of these types of crisis are called into play in connection with adolescent sexuality. The sexual partner represents a short-term *addition* to the family structure, and the possibility of pregnancy raises the possibility of a long-term addition. To the degree that the adolescent transfers affection, loyalty, etc., from the family to the partner, a kind of *abandonment* takes place. Initiation of sexual activity is likely to be a sort of activity that goes against the mores of the family, and hence *demoralization* takes place. And, finally, the onset of sexual activity itself causes a *status change* within the family structure and a new relationship to others outside the family structure.

The family's functional health can be measured in terms of the five basic components shown in Exhibit 6-2, which together make up a family APGAR scale. Based on this

Exhibit 6-1 Hill's Taxonomy of Family Crises

1. *Addition* is a crisis identified with the short- or long-term addition of one or more members to the family structure.
2. *Abandonment* is associated with the threat of loss or actual departure of a family member.
3. *Demoralization* is a crisis that occurs when a family member initiates a change in the previously ordained family moral code.
4. *Status change* is a crisis involving gain or loss of wealth, power, or position in the family or extrafamilial society.

Source: Family Medicine: Principles and Practice by R.B. Taylor et al. (Eds.), p. 235, Springer-Verlag, © 1978.

assessment, the physician can develop resources to provide counseling and aid to the family as they face the crisis of adolescent sexual activity.

Adolescents also have responsibilities within their family, though these are even more difficult to define. A teenager who critically evaluates parental teachings and develops his or her own values is exhibiting mature independence. But to reject parental values without thoughtful critical analysis or to act without any consideration for family values is immature rebellion—and this amounts to a form of ingratitude. In counseling the teenager, the physician may have to point out that discipline may be forthcoming (whether justly or unjustly) as a response to this crisis of demoralization within the family. The adolescent may be helped in coming to grips with this in several ways: (1) by asking the adolescent to try to wear the parents' shoes and to understand how the adolescent's actions might be perceived by the parents, or (2) by enlisting the adolescent in assessing the family's APGAR measure and in designing strategies to build on the areas of strength in a way that shores up the weaker areas. Counseling the entire family may be necessary in cases of severe functional disability.

Exhibit 6-2 Definitions of the Five Components of Family Function (Family APGAR)

Adaptation—the utilization of intra- and extra-familial resources for problem solving in times of crisis.

Partnership—the sharing of decision making and nurturing responsibilities by family members.

Growth—the physical and emotional maturation and self-fulfillment that is achieved by family members through mutual support and guidance.

Affection—the caring or loving relationship that exists among family members.

Resolve—the commitment to devote time to other members of the family for physical and emotional nurturing. It also involves a decision to share wealth and space.

Source: Reprinted from *Family Medicine: Principles and Practice* by R.B. Taylor et al. (Eds.), p. 236, with permission of Springer-Verlag, © 1978.

Confidentiality

Confidentiality between the physician and the adolescent regarding sexual issues is crucial. This can be facilitated by discussing with the parents of young teenagers the need for confidential communication as adolescents begin to mature. Most parents welcome the assistance of other mature, responsible, informed adults who are willing to share information giving and discussion of sexual issues with the adolescent. If the physician judges in a specific case that parental guidance would be helpful, the best approach is to guide the teenager to recognize this fact, perhaps by offering to take the role of facilitator in initiating a discussion of this topic between the teenager and the parents. To approach the parents directly—especially without giving prior notice of such a plan to the teenage patient—would destroy the trust vital to maintaining a professional relationship. If the physician is uncomfortable with having a confidential relationship with the teenage patient that the parents might not approve of, the best option may be to help the adolescent patient to select another care giver who would not face this conflict.[15]

Initiating the Discussion

Many adolescents who are sexually active do not discuss their need for contraception spontaneously. Many do not recognize the need for contraception. Health care givers most often need to initiate the discussion of issues of sexuality and contraception in a nonjudgmental way. This can be facilitated by including open discussion of sexual development throughout childhood care. One might begin with the very young child by asking questions like "Are you a boy or a girl? How do you know?" The physician can help the adolescent choose between available resources for sexual counseling and information, including family, public health clinics, planned parenthood agencies, and public school programs. And of course the physician can remain available to provide counseling and information himself or herself.

Paternalistic Responsibilities of Physicians

Would a physician be irresponsible to grant an adolescent patient's request for contraception? The position developed in this chapter implies that it would be appropriate to grant such a request if the physician judges that the patient is sufficiently mature to understand the nature of sexual activity and the risks of contraception (e.g., the case of Aileen presented at the beginning of this chapter). Confidentiality should be maintained if the patient insists on it, although it would certainly be appropriate to encourage him or her to seek the guidance of the parents—unless the physician has reason to believe that they would not be capable of offering helpful guidance.

As for the other cases cited at the beginning of the chapter, the response should hinge on the preparatory education and assessment that has been carried out with the patient, the physician's determination of the patient's maturity and comprehension of the issues, the physician's perception of the parents' acceptance of an independent adolescent-physician relationship, and an assessment of the parents' capabilities in providing constructive guidance to the patient.

Physicians and the Adolescent Male's Contraceptive Responsibility

Unsurprisingly, discussions of the issue of contraception focus primarily on females. What responsibility does the physician have to broach the issue of contraceptive responsibility with male adolescent patients?

Consider this case. Egmont is a 16-year-old boy who has been your patient since he was an infant. You are now giving him a camp physical. Should you bring up issues of sexual activity and contraceptive responsibility? If not now, when? If not ever, why not?

Health care providers have the same general obligations toward males as toward females. Granted, females bear the risk of the most momentous consequence of unprotected sexual activity. However, there can be significant effects for males, both physical and mental, and the responsibility of the male partner for ensuring the maturity and voluntariness of the relationship is no less than that of the female. The issues raised above dealing with development and family role apply to males and females equally. Thus the health professional has the same responsibility to assess sexual maturity and awareness for male patients as for females.

CONCLUSION

We have argued that although there is no separate sexual ethic, sexuality emphatically does involve ethical and value issues. Indeed, particularly for teenagers, decisions about sexuality involve ethical principles that concern more than just the two parties immediately involved. Issues of commitment to family values and the family structure of the teenagers' family systems are also raised in trying to decide whether to become sexually active and whether to use birth control. The duty of the physician in this context goes beyond technical assessment and prescribing contraceptives to include a responsibility to clarify, facilitate, and help resolve the family value issues, as well as the interpersonal issues that arise between the sexually active adolescent and his or her sexual partner.

NOTES

1. Walter R. Anyan, Jr., *Adolescent Medicine in Primary Care* (New York: Wiley, 1978), 265.

2. A. Karen Kessler Kreutner and Dorothy Reycroft Hollingsworth, *Adolescent Obstetrics and Gynecology* (Chicago: Year Book Medical Publishers, 1978), 17.

3. Martin Guggenheim and Alan Sussman, *The Rights of Young People* (New York: Bantam Books, 1985), 204.

4. *Griswold v. Connecticut*, 381 U.S. 479 (1965).

5. *Eisenstadt v. Baird*, 405 U.S. 438 (1972).

6. *Carey v. Population Services International*, 431 U.S. 678 (1977).

7. See Elizabeth Scott, ''Adolescents' Reproductive Rights: Abortion, Contraception, and Sterilization,'' in *Children, Mental Health and the Law*, ed. N. Dickon Reppucci et al. (Beverly Hills: Sage Publications, 1984), 132.

8. *Planned Parenthood of Central Missouri v. Danforth*, 428 U.S. 52 (1976).

9. *H.L. v. Matheson* 450 U.S. 398 (1981).

10. Hyman Rodman, Susan H. Lewis, and Saralyn B. Griffith, *The Sexual Rights of Adolescents: Competence, Vulnerability, and Parental Control* (New York: Columbia University Press, 1984), 119.

11. Judith Martin, *Miss Manners' Guide to Excruciatingly Correct Behavior* (New York: Warner Books, 1982), 49.

12. See J. Adelson, ''The Political Imagination of the Young Adolescent,'' in *Twelve to Sixteen: Early Adolescence*, ed. J. Kagan and R. Cole (New York: Norton, 1972).

13. U.S. Supreme Court, *Parham v. J.R. and J.L., Minors*, 442 U.S. 584, June (1979). Quoted in Rodman, Lewis, and Griffith, *The Sexual Rights of Adolescents*, 48.

14. Gabriel Smilkstein, "The Family in Crisis," in *Family Medicine: Principles and Practice* (New York: Springer-Verlag, 1978), 235.

15. For further discussion of these options, see John A. Eaddy and Glenn C. Graber, "Confidentiality and the Family Physician," *American Family Physician* (January 1982): 141–45.

BIBLIOGRAPHY

Alan Guttmacher Institute. *Teenage Pregnancy: The Problem That Hasn't Gone Away*. New York: Alan Guttmacher Institute, 1981. A thorough empirical study of current adolescent sexuality, with a discussion of policy implications.

Anyan, Walter R., Jr. *Adolescent Medicine in Primary Care*. New York: Wiley, 1978. An adolescent medicine text which includes a careful discussion of teenagers and birth control.

Eaddy, John A. and Glenn C. Graber. "Confidentiality and the Family Physician." *American Family Physician* (January 1982): 141–45. Discussion of a case somewhat parallel to those at the start of this article, with special attention to the role definition of the family physician.

Guggenheim, Martin and Alan Sussman. *The Rights of Young People*. New York: Bantam Books, 1985, pp. 200–209. A guide to legal rights, with some ethical discussion included, prepared under the auspices of the American Civil Liberties Union.

Hemphill, Anita M. and Charles F. Hemphill, Jr. *Womanlaw: A Guide to Legal Matters Vital to Women*. Englewood Cliffs, N.J.: Prentice-Hall, 1981. A survey of statutory law and court opinions on a variety of topics of special interest to women, including contraception. Not especially focused on teenagers.

Neinstein, Lawrence S., with contributions by Deborah C. Stewart. *Adolescent Health Care: A Practical Guide*. Baltimore: Urban, 1984. An adolescent medicine text which contains extensive factual data and discussions of implications for clinical decisions.

Rodman, Hyman, Susan H. Lewis, and Saralyn B. Griffith. *The Sexual Rights of Adolescents: Competence, Vulnerability, and Parental Control*. New York: Columbia University Press, 1984. Analysis of the present state of law and social policy and presentation of general guidelines for a future social policy.

Scott, Elizabeth. "Adolescents' Reproductive Rights: Abortion, Contraception, and Sterilization." In *Children, Mental Health and the Law*, edited by N. Dickon Reppucci, et al. Beverly Hills: Sage Publications, 1984. Careful summary and analysis of current case law.

Smilkstein, Gabriel. "The Family in Crisis." In *Family Medicine: Principles and Practice*. New York: Springer-Verlag, 1978. Resources for analysis of family situation and family counseling for the primary care physician.

Sorensen, R.C. *Adolescent Sexuality in Contemporary America*. New York: World Publishing, 1973. Extensive empirical study of sexual attitudes and practices among teenagers.

Chapter 7

Adolescents and Informed Consent

Mark Sheldon and Bonita Bergman Sheldon

Consideration of the issue of informed consent in relation to the treatment of adults raises difficult problems. Still, the problems are fairly clearly defined. For instance, what sorts of information should a person have who is about to undergo a particular procedure? What, beyond the possibilities of death or the burdens of rehabilitation, would a patient want to be told? What should be done if informing a patient of risks leads him or her to reject a procedure that would have ameliorated a horribly burdensome condition? What standard ought to be used for determining whether an adequate informed consent has been obtained?[1] What weight should the expertise of the doctors be given in determining the extent to which they should decide what a particular patient should know? Should the doctors be able to think about other patients whom they have encountered in their practice and be free to judge what information ought to be available to a patient presently under treatment? Does this expertise extend to justification of actions that are essentially paternalistic or does it issue only in what ought to be primarily a pedogogical posture, where the physician's expertise contributes primarily to his or her ability and obligation to educate the patient and to encourage an active participation by the patient in treatment decisions?

These are all very difficult to answer, but at least we know what questions to ask and, to some extent, how to begin to answer them. Also, we have an historical background that offers a perspective based on our assumptions about basic human rights, the responsibilities and privileges of professionals, and expectations concerning scientific progress. We also have our shared experience as adults that we can bring to questions about informed consent, enabling us to project what a reasonable or rational person would want or expect (the so-called ideal observer).

With adolescents, the situation is very different. How do we know what questions to ask, what perspectives to use to articulate assumptions, and what history to refer to in order to develop a framework for a rational analysis?

There is no question that one dimension of the informed consent issue is political. Human rights concerns are central. However, these issues are not new when related to adults, and it is more a matter of interpretation in relation to a new context than of new ideas. With adolescents, to the contrary, the ideas are new. Childhood and adolescence have been transformed.[2] Not only are children no longer viewed as property, but adolescence is increasingly viewed as a period of emancipated autonomy. At the same time, the family has been transformed as familial relationships have been subjected to rigorous analysis.[3] The difficulty involved in formulating questions stems, it appears, from our being of several minds on how to characterize and evaluate this transformation and on whether we ought to contribute towards a furtherance or a reversal of this process.

The point is that the physician is not a disinterested observer in relation to the dynamic described. He or she is in a position to have fundamental and direct impact on the process of family and adolescent transformation as basic social institutions and relationships undergo the most profound change. How should the physician respond to this situation and with what conceptual framework should he or she formulate a response?

When the topic of informed consent and the medical treatment of adolescents is considered, the usual issues addressed are questions concerning confidentiality and privacy and whether within a medical context it is appropriate for an adolescent, on his or her own, to consent to treatment. The kinds of cases that are most often examined involve young girls seeking contraceptives or abortions or teenagers requiring emergency intervention for drug overdoses. Society, in response to these cases, seems to recognize that where adolescents are concerned, certain conditions automatically qualify one as eligible to receive care just on the basis of one's own consent. No permission from parents is required. One concern is that forced parental involvement might discourage some adolescents from seeking treatment altogether.

On the other hand, there are cases in which it is clear that parental permission is, and should be, required. Society, in these cases, recognizes extensive parental discretion with which it will not interfere. Still, there are other cases where the nature of the treatment and a positive assessment of the maturity level of the adolescent would lead a physician to conclude that it is appropriate to seek the adolescent's consent before treatment proceeds. Finally, there are cases where permitting an adolescent to give informed consent contributes directly to the maturation process itself (though there are cases where the opposite occurs— regression or psychological turmoil). It is the intention of this chapter to deal with questions that tend to surface when the issue of adolescents and informed consent is raised.

CHILDREN AND FAMILIES

Various articles have appeared in the last several years examining different perspectives on the relationships between children, families, and society as they pertain to medicine and the treatment of children.[4] Some writers have stressed the importance of the family and warned against adversarial approaches that would threaten basic familial structures.[5] Others have distinguished between "consent" and "assent," arguing that while knowledge on the part of the child may not be possible or necessary, some sort of essential willingness to cooperate is.[6] They also stress the central significance of parental guidance and involvement to insure the psychologically healthy participation of the patient.

Other writers have vigorously defended the position that the child has an absolute right to informed consent. Among these is John Holt, who writes, "I believe informed consent implies a situation in which the people involved explain to the patient as honestly and fully as they can what is involved, what are the options, and what is the risk. What the patient makes of that information, none of us can know. . . . I do not believe that we have the power or the right to make a lot of judgments about how capable the patient is of understanding what we are saying."[7] Holt makes it very clear that he does not think age by itself should be a criterion. Even some eight-year-olds, he claims, are capable of as much understanding as adults.

Another approach involves emphasizing the importance of viewing each child individually to determine his or her level of competence. For instance, Adele Hofmann, pointing to broad differences among adolescents, writes, "Maturity, the most difficult element to measure, is best determined by such behavioral evidence as the following: An adolescent initiates his own health care contact . . . indicates that his medical affairs are to be confidential and gives good reasons . . . asks valid questions about his affairs."[8] Hofmann advocates flexibility in response to adolescents, as opposed to strict legal requirements, since "flexibility is precisely what is required in responding appropriately to the variable and diverse nature of adolescence and in enhancing the ultimate emergence of responsible, autonomous young adults."[9] Unlike Holt, Hofmann does view it as appropriate to assess the level of maturity of an adolescent, recognizing that children have various and diverse capacities to understand and to appreciate the consequences of certain decisions.

DOCUMENTS OF ORGANIZATIONS

Organizations and associations have also expressed different views. The American Academy of Pediatrics Committee on Youth published "A Model Act Providing for Consent of Minors for Health Care Services."[10] It was drafted to encourage all states to review their laws concerning the consent of minors to health care and to bring the states into agreement with the academy's recommendations. In the Prefatory Note, the following statement appears:

> In a democratic nation such as ours, individual rights are paramount. In order for everyone, including minors, to have the right of obtaining health services, the balance of this right against others becomes of the utmost importance. This Model Act accepts the concept that getting health services is a basic right. Also, it accepts that parents have their basic right of protecting and promoting the health and welfare of their minors. Therefore, this Act is a compromise and a balance of these two basic rights in the conditions specified. . . . Reasonable safeguards and limitations are stipulated in this Act to protect the minor's safety and the right of the parent. This Act also emphasizes the promotion of family harmony and minor's maturity.[11]

The language of the act is interesting since, on the one hand, it begins with what appears to be a very strong emphasis placed on individual rights. However, it becomes clear that as much significance is being ascribed to certain social institutions (families) and to those who have positions of influence within those institutions (parents). The concern of the academy is that quality health care be accessible to minors by making their consent sufficient in situations where requiring parental consent would discourage minors from seeking care. One can conclude that although concern is expressed for individual rights in the beginning of the document, those rights are clearly limited by the interests society appears to have in protecting the family. In fact, what is finally available to adolescents in terms of self-consent is based on practical considerations, in particular, that adolescents would otherwise avoid treatment altogether. It seems that concern for the rights of adolescents has, for practical purposes, been attenuated to the point of nonexistence.

Even in situations where consent by minors is viewed as acceptable, its consequences regarding other issues that might be of concern to the adolescent patient are not clear. For instance, Section 3 of the act identifies minors who can give consent for health services, and in item (4) of Section 3 the document indicates that any minor "who has physical or emotional problems and is capable of making rational decisions" and whose relationship with parents or legal guardian is such that the minor would otherwise avoid treatment may give consent for treatment.[12] So far, the document is consistent with its previous statements. The next statement, however, raises a troublesome issue: "After the professional establishes his rapport with the minor, then he may inform the parent, parents, or legal guardian unless such action will jeopardize the life of the patient or the favorable result of the treatment." This statement raises questions about the violation of confidentiality, but in terms of the informed consent issue it raises more central questions about the nature and extent of the consent that the minor gave. What sort of "rapport" was established? An *informed* consent, it seems, does not have to be obtained, since all consequences of consenting apparently do not have to be explained to the minor.

A very different document, produced but never published by the National Association of Children's Hospitals and Related Institutions, Inc., is the "Pediatric Bill of Rights."[13] Article 8 states, "Any person, regardless of age, who is of sufficient intelligence to appreciate the nature and the consequences of the proposed medical care, and if such medical care is for his own benefit, may effectively consent to such medical care in doctor-patient confidentiality."[14] The confidentiality requirement appears to be absolute, with no suggestion of any sort of qualification. It also ascribes to qualifying adolescent patients the ability to make judgments about what ought to be withheld from the family.

LEGAL CATEGORIES

The two legal categories that are particularly significant are the *emancipated minor* and the *mature minor*.[15] The emancipated minor is "usually one who is not living at home and is self-supporting, is responsible for himself economically and otherwise, and whose parents (voluntarily or involuntarily) have surrendered their parental duties and rights."[16] The category includes married minors, minors in the military, and, in almost all states, teenage unmarried mothers. College students living away from home, even those financially dependent on their parents, are considered emancipated. Runaways present a problem, but most courts view those that are unwilling to divulge the identity of their parents as emancipated.

The other category is that of the mature minor. State statutes vary, but a survey of various rules concerning permissible medical treatment of mature minors indicates agreement on the following points: (1) the treatment will benefit the minor, (2) the minor is near majority (at least fifteen) and displays sufficient understanding of the medical procedure in question, and (3) the medical procedures can be characterized as less than "major."[17]

Obviously, a great deal is left to the judgment of the physician in determining what, from a legal point of view, ought to be his or her response to a particular request for treatment from an individual adolescent. Mature minor rules, especially, raise difficulties, and one can think of a variety of cases which are very complicated and about which it would be hard to make a judgment.

DISCUSSION AND RECOMMENDATIONS

First, it is important to reiterate a point made earlier: Health care providers do not play a neutral role in relation to the question of the proper nature of adolescent consent to health care. Their response to the different perspectives described in this paper clearly commits them to certain positions concerning this controversy.

Second, it is reasonable to conclude that adolescents as a class should not be regarded as incompetent. Adolescents clearly exhibit different levels of dependability, awareness, and forethought. Therefore, it is important to determine what the issue of choice is and what the competence of the adolescent is in relation to the topic; only then should a judgment be made about the adolescent's qualifications to choose. Care should be taken, however, not to confuse issues. It should not be a question whether one agrees with the adolescent or whether the adolescent thinks in a way that one would want one's child to think. Also, there is a danger that one might idealize the adolescent's parents and deny the negative image portrayed by the adolescent, wishing to imagine that all parents are similar to one's own. In evaluating a particular person's ability to consent, a central consideration is the educational capacity of the adolescent regarding the particular procedure and his or her intellectual and emotional capacity to achieve competency as a result of being permitted to consent either partially or entirely alone. In fact, one right that adolescents ought to have is the right to grow and to develop the capacity for dealing satisfactorily with the world.

Third, Holt's belief in the capacity of the child to understand and consent may be faulted for being too romantic.[18] Yet, to take the opposite view is to make a greater and more grievous mistake. It is to confuse the difficulty of communication with the impossibility of communication and to lessen the capacity of a person—already limited by the conditions that would bring him or her to a physician—to have control over matters so totally affecting a life outcome.

Fourth, the recommendations presented thus far constitute a plea for a significant and active role for the health care professional. Yet there are no clear legal guidelines that appear satisfactory and that truly encourage a response to adolescents as individuals rather than as members of defined groups with specific conditions warranting treatment from health care professionals. Some argue that it is inappropriate to apply ''rights language'' to the family and that the family should not be conceptualized as a contractual society of individuals.[19] Children, it is argued, do not need rights, but trust, love, and care. Goldstein, Freud, and Solnit write, ''So long as a child is a member of a functioning family, his paramount interest lies in the preservation of his family.''[20] One point to keep in mind, however, is that the family is not always functioning and love and care are not always present. (See Chapter 5 on child abuse and Chapter 13 on elder abuse.)

The assessment of the state of the family must be left largely up to the adolescent. He or she must be able to judge, without interference, whether trust, love, and care are available. If they are not, the adolescent must be able to form a relationship with the health care professional that does involve, at the very least, trust and care. Access to this relationship, it might be proposed, is a right of the adolescent. The health care professional, as the only individual in the appropriate position, has an obligation to provide this relationship. It is not something which should be available only as a result of practical considerations, which is in effect the proposal in the document from the American Academy of Pediatrics.[21] The idea that access to this relationship is a right puts the health care professional in the position of having to accede to the adolescent's judgment of what would be in his or her best interest when that judgment is maturely expressed. This is a relationship which may be in conflict with the community's view of what the traditional limits of adolescent autonomy are, but the health care professional has responsibilities that exist independent of community perspectives.

Fifth, it ought to be stated that ideally families provide sperelationship is a right puts the health care professional in the position of having to accede to the adolescent's judgment of what would be in his or her best interest when that judgment is maturely expressed. This is a relationship which may be in conflict with the community's view of what the traditional limits of adolescent autonomy are, but the health care professional has responsibilities that exist independent of community perspectives.

Fifth, it ought to be stated that ideally families provide speither abusing nor neglecting one's child. Should society, as much as it values parenthood and the family, place even greater value on the passage of adolescents towards adulthood? To what extent, through its institutions and its courts, should it encourage this passage? These are questions to which health care professionals, with their experience of adolescents in private and protected circumstances, can contribute answers.

NOTES

1. Eugene G. Laforet, "The Fiction of Informed Consent," *Journal of the American Medical Association* 235 (April 12, 1976): 1579–85.

2. Jerome Kagan, "The Child in the Family," *Daedalus* (Spring 1977): 33–56.

3. Tamara K. Hareven, "Family Time and Historical Time," *Daedalus* (Spring 1977): 57–70.

4. T.F. Ackerman, "Fooling Ourselves with Child Autonomy and Assent in Nontherapeutic Clinical Research," *Clinical Research* 27(1979): 345–48; F. Schoeman, "Children's Competence and Children's Rights," *IRB* 4(1982): 1–6.

5. D.J. Rothman and S.R. Rothman, "The Conflict over Children's Rights," *Hastings Center Report* 10, no. 3(1980): 7–10. F. Schoeman, "Children's Competence and Children's Rights," *IRB* 4(1982): 1–6.

6. G.E. Pence, "Children's Dissent to Research—A Minor Matter?" *IRB* 2(1980): 1–4.

7. John Holt, "The Right of Children to Informed Consent," in *Research On Children*, ed. Jan van Eyes (Baltimore: University Park Press, 1978).

8. A.D. Hofmann, "The Right to Consent and Confidentiality in Adolescent Health Care: An Evolutionary Dilemma," in *Bioethics and Human Rights*, ed. E.L. Bandman and B. Bandman (Boston: Little, Brown, 1978), 187.

9. Ibid., 188.

10. Committee on Youth, American Academy of Pediatrics, "A Model Act Providing for Consent of Minors for Health Services," *Pediatrics* 51 (February 1973): 293–96.

11. Ibid., 293.

12. Ibid., 294.

13. A copy of "The Pediatric Bill of Rights" may be obtained from the National Association of Children's Hospitals and Related Institutions, Inc., 401 Wythe Street, Alexandria, Virginia 22314.

14. "The Pediatric Bill of Rights," 1.

15. Angela Roddey Holder, *Legal Issues in Pediatric and Adolescent Medicine*. (New Haven: Yale University Press, 1985).

16. Ibid., 128.

17. Ibid., 134.

18. Holt, "Right of Children to Informed Consent."

19. See Mark Sheldon, "Some General Problems Related to Informed Consent and the Psychiatric Treatment of Children," in *Ethics in Mental Health Practice*, ed. D. Kentsmith, S. Salladay, and P. Miya (Orlando, Fla.: Grune & Stratton, 1986), 111–22.

20. Joseph Goldstein, Anna Freud, and Albert J. Solnit, *Before the Best Interests of the Child* (New York: The Free Press, 1979), 5.

21. Committee on Youth, "A Model Act," 293–96.

BIBLIOGRAPHY

Bandman, Elsie L., and Bertram Bandman, eds. *Bioethics and Human Rights*. Boston: Little, Brown, 1978. This book contains an especially good section consisting of papers devoted to children's issues.

Elkind, David. *The Hurried Child*. Massachusetts: Addison-Wesley, 1981. This book is a recent analysis of society's changing attitudes towards children.

Eyes, Jan van, ed. *Research on Children*. Baltimore: University Park Press, 1978. While most of the papers in this book deal with the issue of children's consent to research, John Holt's paper focuses, for the most part, on the consent by children to therapeutic treatment; his view is quite unique.

Goldstein, Joseph, Anna Freud, and Albert J. Solnit. *Before the Best Interests of the Child*. New York: The Free Press, 1979. This book contains a very extensive analysis of the child-parent relationship and the basis for state intervention.

O'Neill, Onora, and William Ruddick, eds. *Having Children*. New York: Oxford University Press, 1979. The papers in this book are concerned with fundamental questions about children's and parents' rights, the right to parenthood, the relationship between the family as a social institution and the state, and the obligations that exist in the parent-child relationship.

Part II

Adult Medicine: Crises and Competence

Chapter 8

Competency: What It Is, What It Isn't, and Why It Matters

Byron Chell

A competent adult has the absolute right to refuse medical treatment—even lifesaving medical treatment! Can there be any doubt that this is a correct statement of principle, medical ethics, and law?[1]

In spite of this clear and seemingly straightforward declaration, however, when a patient refuses to accept needed medical care, we yet find much concern and confusion. This is especially true when the treatment is lifesaving.

The rule that a competent adult has the right to refuse any and all medical treatment emphasizes the importance of the concept of *competency*. In fact, if we are uneasy about a decision to refuse treatment, we immediately retreat to the thicket of competency.[2] Such a retreat is appropriate, however, because when confronted with a refusal of needed medical care, the first and key question we should ask is whether the patient is competent to make the required decision.

Yet difficulties regarding competency remain, because the concept is confusing. What is a competent adult? What is the definition of *competency*? Are those who refuse lifesaving treatment on religious grounds really competent? How do we find the proper answers to these questions when evaluating patients? Anyone involved in bioethics and medical decision making regularly confronts such questions.

This chapter discusses what competency is and is not. It also discusses what we should and should not be doing in making determinations of competency for the purpose of deciding whether to allow a patient to refuse medical treatment. If we have a clear understanding of what competency is, why we seek it, and why it matters, we will know how to approach and complete the task of determining competency without unnecessary anxiety and confusion.

WHAT COMPETENCY IS AND IS NOT

Competency is not a thing or a fact. It is not something we can look for and find if only we know how. Determinations of competency are not medical judgments. Clinical training is not required. Competency does not necessarily mean rational. We find many persons competent to make medical care decisions even though their refusal of treatment is based upon irrational beliefs. When we make determinations of ''competency'' we are not seeking truth or facts. We are not assessing the patient in light of a clear and neutral standard upon which we can make a definitive finding. It is not that easy.

Competent is simply a label we apply to persons after we examine various aspects of their physical and mental condition. Decisions relating to competency are legal and social decisions. They are legal decisions in that they are determinations of an individual's legal capacity to exercise the right to self-determination. No legal education is required, however. They are social decisions in that the statutory definitions we apply in the search are societal decisions. Additionally, when we make determinations of competency, we are doing so with imprecise criteria, vague notions, and personal beliefs and prejudices, all of which affect the outcome.

Considering the importance of the concept of competency in making determinations relating to, respecting, or overriding the patient's refusal, it would at first appear necessary that we fix upon *the* definition of the term "competency." But despite our attempt as a society to define it, we have failed to find an adequate definition.

THE SEARCH FOR THE DEFINITION OF "COMPETENCY"

Fortunately, we do not need to find the definition of "competency" to fulfill our task. This is fortunate because there is no pre-existing single definition of the term. We can only create a definition—or various definitions.

No standard definition of "competency" is to be found. No statutory consistency or line of cases can be uncovered which would allow the simple discovery of the meaning of the terms "competent" or "incompetent." Definitions of "competency" can be found in a number of different and specific situations where society and the law have always had to deal with the concept. We generally recognize that people can be competent to do one thing and not another or can be competent to some extent and not another. For example, we have laws regulating a person's competency to make a will, to enter into contracts, or to stand trial.

Definitions of "incompetency" have generally fallen into two categories: definitions which emphasize end results and definitions which emphasize thought processes. Both types of definition, however, are intimately and necessarily related in light of what we actually do in making determinations of competency.

Definitions in terms of end results essentially ask us to look at how persons live. What is their condition? What are the consequences or the end results of their thinking? For example, a former definition of the term "incompetent" for mental health commitment purposes is as follows:

> As used in this chapter the word incompetent shall . . . be construed to mean or refer to any adult person who . . . is unable properly to provide for his own personal needs for physical health, food, clothing or shelter, (or who) is substantially unable to manage, his own financial resources.[3]

A definition emphasizing end results tells us to look at what is happening to persons as a result of their thinking. Examine the physical consequences which follow from their mental status. An incompetent person is one whose mental processes lead to bad or serious consequences. A competent person simply would not live like that or be in that situation.

While such definitions work adequately in the context of mental health civil commitment proceedings, they are not very helpful in many cases of refusals of medical care. We question the competency of many persons who refuse medical treatment even though they are quite capable of providing for their own food, clothing, and shelter and can manage their daily affairs very well.

Because definitions in terms of living conditions or end results are not always adequate to the task, we also use definitions of "competency" which emphasize thought processes. A definition of "incompetency" in terms of thought processes involves determining if someone is competent by looking at how he relates to and decide things. One essentially tests the person's comprehension of reality, understanding, and ability to make rational judgments. One example of this type of incompetency definition is as follows:

> Several tests of competency might be applied, e.g., patients may be considered competent if 1) they evidence a choice concerning treatment, 2) this choice is "reasonable," 3) this choice is based on "rational" reasons, 4) the patient has a generalized ability to understand, or 5) the patient actually understands the information that has been disclosed. . . . [T]he courts have not settled on any single test of competency; in practice, doctors seem to apply an amalgam of some or all of these tests.[4]

A definition emphasizing thought processes involves listening to the patient and judging whether what is said "makes sense." Is the patient rational? The point is not to examine the physical consequences which follow from the patient's mental state but rather to examine the mental state itself.

There are currently many competing definitions of "competency," and this is simply a reflection of the fact that "competency" can be properly defined in many different ways.

> The search for a single test of competency is a search for the Holy Grail. Unless it is recognized that there is not a magical definition of competency to make decisions about treatment, the search for an acceptable test will never end. 'Getting the words just right' is only part of the problem. In practice, judgments of competency go beyond semantics or straightforward applications of legal rules; such judgments reflect social considerations and societal biases as much as they reflect matters of law and medicine.[5]

Competency is, of course, whatever we define it to be. The trick is to define it so that it best helps us to do the job which needs to be done. The job in this context is to make decisions involving decision making. We must decide whether or not we will allow the patient to decide. Thus, what are the proper considerations we must keep in mind in making our decisions? What is the essence of competency? What criteria should be reflected in a proper definition?

THE ESSENCE OF COMPETENCY

Competency is essentially the ability to make a decision. Regardless of the particular definition used, determining competency in a given situation basically involves answering one question: Should we allow this person to make this decision under these circumstances?

Generally, but not always, the answer to this question is yes and a person is labeled competent if (1) he or she has an understanding of the situation and the consequences of the decision, and (2) the decision is based upon rational reasons.

Determining whether the person does or does not understand his or her condition is usually not the troublesome part. Sometimes it is difficult to determine the seriousness of the patient's condition and sometimes physicians will disagree. But if the medical conclusion is that intervention is required to prevent death or serious harm, it is normally not too difficult to determine whether the patient understands what the doctors are saying and whether the patient appreciates the consequences of his choice. This aspect of determining competency does not create philosophical and conceptual confusion. It can do so, however, in some cases of religious refusals, which are discussed below.

Determining whether or not the patient's decision to refuse treatment is based upon rational reasons can cause us much concern. While "rational" may appear redundant, its meaning in this context is "sensible," "sound," "reasonable," or "lucid." The term "reasons" is used in the sense of "reasons why," "motive," or "explanation." Thus, the reason why or the explanation of the decision to refuse treatment is to be considered rational if it is sensible or sound, lucid and not deranged, and it conforms to reason. In other words— it makes sense! In lieu of rational reasons, we might require sound explanations, sensible motives, or even reasonable reasons why.

There is no way to specifically define terms such as "rational reasons," "sound explanations," or "sensible motives" or to definitively measure what is rational or reasonable. These determinations will necessarily vary from person to person. We can set out cases where most persons would conclude that the reasons for the refusal are rational or sensible under the circumstances and such examples can be instructive.

Suppose, for example, that an older patient is informed that her leg is gangrenous and that an amputation is necessary to save her life. Understanding the situation, she replies, "I refuse the amputation. I am not afraid of death. It is the natural end to life. I am 86 and I have lived a good and full life. I do not want a further operation, nor do I want to live legless. I understand that the consequence of refusing the amputation is death and I accept that consequence."

This woman understands both her situation and the consequences of her choice. Additionally, her decision is understandable. It is based on facts and logic. Although we might wish her to choose otherwise (or we might choose otherwise), her reasons and reasoning are sane, sound and sensible. She is competent.[6]

If she were to say, however, "I understand the consequences but I refuse the operation because the moon is full," it is not likely she would be considered competent. Although she understands her situation and chooses death to medical treatment, her decision is not understandable. Her decision does not rationally or reasonably follow from her premise. Her explanation doesn't make sense. She would be labeled incompetent.[7]

A thousand reasons for refusing treatment could be set out. Regarding each, we could ask the question, "Is this a rational or sensible reason?" On some we might all agree. On others, there would be great disagreement. It is simply important to recognize that it can be no other way. Understanding this fact relieves the anxiety which accompanies the attempt to find out what competency is or to apply the proper definition of "competency" or "rationality."

The fact that there can be neither a "true" finding of reasonableness nor a single test which will lead to uniform results should not, however, lead us to abandon our responsibility to make these judgments. Yet, when we weigh the reasons for the patient's choice, we many times discard the requirement of reasonableness and label persons competent even though their refusal is founded upon irrational beliefs. Patients who refuse necessary medical care based upon religious beliefs are often labeled competent even though their beliefs may be quite "irrational."

COMPETENCY IS COMPATIBLE WITH "IRRATIONALITY"— RELIGIOUS REFUSALS

We face many difficult questions when we confront a person who is refusing lifesaving medical care on the basis of religious belief.[8] If the patient is going to die because he or she is refusing a readily available medical procedure, we are puzzled and we necessarily question the patient's competency. We find it difficult to accept that a rational and competent person would die when a simple act would save his or her life.

In considering competency and making judgments regarding those who refuse necessary medical treatment on the basis of religious belief, we can apply the above general definition of competency with a slight modification.

In cases of religious refusals, a person is competent if (1) he or she has a proper understanding of the situation and the consequences of the decision, and (2) the decision is based upon religious beliefs ("irrational" beliefs) which are within our common religious experience or common notions of religion and do not appear to us "crazy" or "non-religious." If this definition seems vague, it is because it *is* vague.

To demonstrate how to apply this definition of competency, consider the following four examples of religious refusals. In each of these cases, suppose that the patient is refusing a lifesaving blood transfusion. Suppose also that each patient expresses sincerely held beliefs.[9]

Patient A states, "I refuse the blood transfusion because I am a Jehovah's Witness and I believe it is a violation of God's law to accept such blood. I understand that the consequence of my refusal is my death and I accept that result." Patient B states, "I refuse the blood transfusion because I am one of Yoda's Children and, based upon Luke Skywalker's teachings, I believe the acceptance of blood is a violation of Yoda's law and the work of the dark side of the Force. I understand that the consequence of my refusal is my death and I accept that result." Since we must make a determination relating to competency in these cases to decide if we are going to respect or override the patient's refusal, what will be the likely result?

The first patient will be judged competent and he will be allowed to refuse treatment and die. The second patient, while a more troubling case, will be labeled incompetent and some other person will be allowed to give substituted consent to the treatment necessary to prevent his death.

Now, why is this the case? If we ask what is the difference between the statement of patient A as opposed to the statement of patient B, the answer must be none. Both are identical as statements of "irrational" religious belief or faith.

Belief and faith *are* irrational in at least one sense. In the context of this discussion, the term "irrational" means not derived logically from facts, data, or circumstances—outside the scope of reason. Faith is essentially belief based upon that which is incapable of proof. It does not involve logic, facts, or proof; it is trust and belief in a matter empirically unknowable. If it were knowable through facts or proof, we would speak in terms of knowledge and truth and not faith and belief. Theologians should know this.

A discussion which would attempt to label patient A's belief in Jehovah a religious belief and patient B's belief in Yoda a religious delusion would go nowhere. A conclusion in this situation that A's faith is based upon a belief as opposed to a delusion would depend entirely on the beliefs, experiences, and prejudices of the person drawing that conclusion. In these cases the label applied to the belief and the determination of competency depends on the novelty of the belief and on whether we want to give priority to the individual's continued life or to respecting the individual's choice? If the former, we would conclude that the decision is "crazy" and label the individual incompetent. If the latter, we would conclude that his belief is "religious" and label him competent.

In these two cases, the only difference is that patient A has voiced a religious belief held by organized and recognized groups within our society while patient B has voiced a belief totally outside our common religious experience. The Jehovah's Witness's belief relating to the refusal of blood is now well within our society's general "religious belief experience." Because of our concurrent societal belief in the free exercise of religion, we "respect" the Jehovah's Witness's belief even though it is irrational.[10] We recognize the belief as religious and we label patient A competent. As far as patient B is concerned, sincere or not, religious or not, we conclude that his belief is too "crazy" to determine a life and death decision and we label him incompetent.

But what about the protections afforded by the First Amendment? If we do not accept patient B's belief, are we not unlawfully discriminating against this Yoda's Child and denying him his right to the free exercise of religion? While it is true that our constitution guarantees certain rights relating to the free exercise of religion, it is emphasized that only "religious beliefs" are protected.[11] And while it is often asserted that the courts will not assess or inquire into the truth or validity of individual religious beliefs,[12] the courts most certainly do decide what constitutes a "religion"[13] and what amounts to a "religious belief."[14] And in making such decisions, the courts also apply imprecise criteria and vague notions.

In determining whether a belief is a religious belief entitled to protection, the courts have at various times required that the belief be "truly held"[15] or that it be "sincere and meaningful,"[16] and judges have often emphasized the helpful test of orthodoxy.[17] The courts have also noted that some beliefs may simply be "too crazy" to qualify for protection.[18] In sum, the courts do judge the validity of religious beliefs and they do it in a manner similar to the method of determining competency described above. That is, if a belief is "too crazy," there is sufficient room within our law to conclude that the belief is "nonreligious," not "sincere and meaningful," not "truly held," or not sufficiently similar to orthodox religious beliefs. This is the conclusion that ought to be reached about patient B's belief in Yoda.[19] Because his belief is too crazy, we would label him incompetent, and the courts would label his belief as one not entitled to First Amendment protection. In doing so, both we and the courts would be acting properly.[20]

There may be objections to making such judgments, but, despite objections and difficulties, we ought and will continue to do so.[21] The only alternative to making such distinctions is to accept *any* statement of belief as consistent with competence and sufficient to support a life and death decision regardless of its apparent "craziness." Few would feel comfortable with such a rule.

Next, consider the following patients, who express slightly different reasons for refusing the life-saving medical care. Patient C states, "I refuse the blood transfusion because the full moon, properly understood, is the source of the human spirit and the key to human happiness and cures all disease. When the moon rises in full next week you shall see that it will cure me without the need of your medical procedure."

This is the easiest case. As with patient B, patient C has based her choice upon a belief quite outside our common religious experience. Additionally, she clearly does not appreciate either the nature of the situation or the consequence of her decision. She does not understand that her death is imminent. She fails both tests and is clearly incompetent. Is there any doubt that this patient's refusal would be overridden and action taken to provide the lifesaving care?

Patient D states, "I refuse the blood transfusion because I am a Jehovah's Witness and I believe it is a violation of God's law to accept such blood. God will heal me without the need of your medical procedures." This is a more difficult case. Would you allow this patient to refuse the lifesaving care?

This Jehovah's Witness has based her refusal upon a belief within our common religious experience. However, it is also evident that she does not appreciate either the nature of her situation or the consequences of her decision. She does not understand that without the blood transfusion, her death is imminent. While we may accept this patient's belief relating to the prohibition of blood, her religious beliefs go too far. Her belief in a cure without medical intervention in this situation does amount to a religious delusion.

Patient D is similar to the patient in a recent Ohio case where treatment was allowed in spite of the patient's "religious refusal." The patient refused to consent to treatment because she believed that she was the wife of an evangelist who would arrive to heal her. The court noted the rule that a patient's honestly held religious belief must be respected, but it decided that when those beliefs amount to a religious delusion, they may be disregarded.[22]

This may at first appear to be a subtle distinction, but it is a very important one. Carefully consider the difference between patient A and patient D. Patient A states, "I believe accepting blood is against God's will and I will not accept blood even though I will die because of my belief." Patient D states, "I believe accepting blood is against God's will and I will not accept blood. I also believe God will cure me and I will not die."

In failing to understand and recognize the consequences of her decision, patient D is *not* making the life and death decision required here. She is not deciding between the two, because she does not recognize one as being a consequence of her decision. The decision here is not simply to either accept blood or refuse blood. The decision which needs to be made involves the choice of either accepting blood *and living* or refusing blood *and dying*. In patient D's mind, she is simply choosing between life with treatment as opposed to life without treatment. One cannot freely decide between two choices if one does not understand what the choices actually are. If one cannot freely decide, one is not competent to decide.[23]

Since patient D is in fact not making the required decision between the two alternatives of life and death, in failing to respect her "nonchoice" we are neither denying the principle of personal autonomy nor freedom of religious expression. We are obligated only to respect a decision. In refusing treatment, patient D is not making the required decision based upon a religious belief. Rather, her religious belief prevents her from understanding that her death is imminent and what the decision is that we require her to make. Her belief in this situation is a delusion—religious or not—in that it has adversely affected her ability to understand.

In summary, in religious refusal cases and following the general definition of "competency" set out above, we ought only label a patient competent and respect a refusal of medical treatment when (1) the patient is not deluded and he or she understands the situation and appreciates the consequences of the decision, and (2) the patient's refusal is founded upon a religious belief which is within our common religious experience or our common notions of religion and is not perceived as extremely unreasonable, crazy, or nonreligious.

Some concepts involved in the issue of competency, the manner in which we should evaluate competency, and the conclusions which should be reached concerning patients A–D can be set out as in Table 8-1.

CONCLUSIONS RELATING TO COMPETENCY

The above view of how to determine competency in cases involving understanding, appreciation, rationality, and religious belief can be summarized in another fashion. As with the cards used by police officers to assist in giving *Miranda* warnings, a medical decision-making card might state the following:

Process for Determining Competency
of Patients Who Refuse Medical Treatment

Answer the following questions concerning the patient:

1. Does the patient understand his or her medical condition?
2. Does the patient understand the options and the consequences of his or her decision?

Table 8-1 Competency among Patients A–D

	Proper Understanding	Acceptable Belief	Competent
Patient A (Jehovah's Witness)	Yes	Yes	Yes
Patient B (Yoda's Child)	Yes	No	No
Patient C (Moon Child)	No	No	No
Patient D (Jehovah's Witness)	No	Yes	No

Proper Understanding: The patient understands his or her condition and the consequences of the decision. In these cases, the patient understands he or she is going to die without medical intervention. His or her understanding is not "deluded" by religious belief.

Acceptable Belief: The person's decision is based upon a belief which is within our common religious experience. It is a belief which has been held by a sufficient number of persons for a sufficient period of time or is sufficiently similar to other orthodox beliefs so that we label it a religious belief and not nonreligious, unsound, or insane.

Competent: The label we apply in the various situations.

3. Is the patient's refusal based upon rational reasons?
4. If the refusal is based upon religious beliefs, are the religious beliefs acceptable and entitled to First Amendment protection, i.e., beliefs held by a sufficient number of persons for a sufficient period of time or sufficiently similar to other orthodox beliefs such that we do not label the beliefs crazy or nonreligious?

If the answers to (1), (2), (3), and (4) are all yes, then the patient's refusal will be respected. He or she should be labeled "competent." If the answer to either (1), (2), (3), or (4) is no, then the patient's refusal should not be respected and action should be taken to obtain substitute consent. He or she is incompetent.

Using this procedure, one will reach a proper result in all cases, no matter who makes the determination, be it physician or judge, or what the particular statutory definition might be. If the answer to all four questions is yes, any proper statutory definition of competency will be fulfilled. If the answer to any of the four is no, any proper definition of incompetency will be met.[24] This is not to say that in any given case there is a proper conclusion or that different persons asking these same questions will not reach different conclusions. This is also not to say that such questions can be easily answered in all cases. Sometimes it is easy to answer these questions and we feel quite confident in our conclusions. Sometimes it is terribly difficult. Nevertheless, following this type of procedure will give a proper result simply because these questions are based on the essence of the concept of competency. They contain the necessary considerations, vague and slippery as they may be, to make the required decision. Such a procedure simply allows us to reach a conclusion in a straightforward manner and this is all we can hope to do.

WHY IT MATTERS

It is always important to emphasize the significant ethical and moral issues involved in labeling a person incompetent. Such emphasis underscores our need to work hard at making proper determinations.

Consider just what it is we are saying when we exercise the power of the state to override a patient's specific refusal of medical care because the patient is incompetent. We are, most assuredly, judging the validity of the patient's reasoning and the truth of the patient's beliefs. We do so without precise criteria or objective standards. We decide which reasons expressed by the patient are acceptable and which are proper religious beliefs entitled to protection.

As a society, we simply think that some persons, for one reason or another, should not be allowed to make certain decisions. We reach this conclusion for the same reason that we think certain defendants should not be held responsible for otherwise criminal actions. Based on our experience, some persons just do not appear to be rational, responsible, or competent human beings.

In medical decision making, we must distinguish between rational and irrational reasons and between acceptable religious beliefs and craziness (or whatever one wishes to call it). If we do not make such distinctions, then we must allow the refusal of any patient no matter what the basis, even though the patient's beliefs are such that they delude the patient's understanding of the situation and prevent him or her from making the required decision.

What if the patient's beliefs seems clearly senseless and unacceptable, as nonsensical as the beliefs of an acutely psychotic person who chooses death based on "commands" from the television set.

As a further matter, consider this aspect of judging a person to be incompetent. In spite of the person's stated choice, we make a different choice and force our choice upon the person. We do so claiming that we have the right (and the duty) to force our decision on the person— we do so for his or her "own good." We do so because, in spite of the person's choice (an incompetent choice), the person has a right to the benefits of our decision (a competent choice). We reason the person has a right to the benefits of the choice which he or she would have made if competent. If the person were competent to decide and had reached a different conclusion, he or she would be, in effect, a different person. When you change a person's understanding, beliefs, thoughts, conclusions, and choices, you have changed the person. In forcing our choice upon the patient, we are claiming that the patient has a right to the benefits of being a different person. Indeed, we are insisting that he or she be a different person. It is not difficult to understand and appreciate the ethical and moral problems involved in negating personal autonomy under such circumstances and in using power and force, if necessary, to insist that a person be another person.

Of course, most persons are aware that good intentions and the exercise of power for another person's own good can bring about horrendous results. Controversial decisions and disagreements have always and will always result from determinations of competency. Such is our condition, however, and the nature and consequences of these decisions simply underscores the weight of our obligations.

SUMMARY AND CONCLUSION

While more needs to be said, this discussion has attempted to explain what competency is and to set out a fairly straightforward process for making determinations of competency.

The patient's competency is the first and foremost question which must be resolved in deciding whether or not we will respect or override the patient's refusal. There is no single definition of "competency" and many different ways of stating the concepts involved in that term.

The term "competent" is nothing more than a label we place on a person when we conclude that we should allow him or her to make the decision at issue. Generally, we apply the label to the person who understands his or her condition and the consequences of the choices and whose reasons make sense to us. Sometimes, however, especially in cases of religious refusals and First Amendment considerations, we apply the term "competent" to persons who base their refusal upon irrational beliefs as long as those beliefs are within our common religious experience and do not seem too strange.

In making determinations of competency and in forcing treatment on others, we are engaged in serious matters. These are decisions which should not be avoided, however. We must use our experience of the human condition and our best judgment in the attempt to make proper decisions. As long as they are made with proper motives and a proper understanding of the task, they are properly made. And although these decisions may yet be difficult in individual cases, they should be made without unnecessary concern or doubt because in doing so we are doing all that can properly be done. We are, after all, simply human beings attempting to make very difficult decisions relating to other human beings.

NOTES

1. Judge Cardoza stated it this way: "Every human being of adult years and sound mind has a right to determine what shall be done with his own body . . ." Schloendorff v. Society of New York Hospital (1914) 105 N.E. 92,93. See also Matter of Spring (1980) 405 N.E.2d 115; Superintendent of Belchertown v. Saikewicz (1977) 370 N.E.2d 417; Bartling v. Superior Court (1984) 163 Cal.App.3d 186; Barber v. Superior Court (1983) 147 Cal.App.3d 1006.

2. "On balance, the right to self-determination ordinarily outweighs any countervailing state interests and competent persons generally are permitted to refuse medical treatment, even at the risk of death. Most of the cases that have held otherwise . . . have concerned the patient's competency to make a rational and considered choice of treatment." Matter of Conroy (1985) 486 A.2d 1209,1225.

3. Cal. Welf. & Inst. Code Sec. 1435.2 (repealed Jan. 1, 1981).

4. Roth Meisel and Lidz Meisel, *Toward a Model of the Legal Doctrine of Informed Consent*, American Journal of Psychiatry 134 (March 1977): 285, 287.

5. Roth Meisel and Lidz Meisel, *Tests of Competency to Consent to Treatment*, American Journal of Psychiatry 134 (March 1977): 279, 283.

6. See Lane v. Candura (1978) 376 N.E.2d 1232 for a decision respecting a patient's refusal of an amputation under similar circumstances.

7. Matter of Schiller (1977) 372A.2d 360 is another case where the court struggled with the refusal of an amputation. In the Matter of Schiller, the patient was found incompetent and a guardian was appointed primarily because Mr. Schiller failed to properly evidence an understanding of his medical condition and the reality of death, the more likely situation in such cases.

8. Our additional concern is occasioned, of course, by the First Amendment to the Constitution of the United States. "Congress shall make no law respecting an establishment of religion, or prohibiting the free exercise thereof . . ."

9. Of course, in making determinations of competency one would always want to know more and would question the patient carefully and thoroughly.

10. It should be emphasized that the beliefs of Jehovah's Witnesses are not used to single out those beliefs as being less rational than or deserving of less respect than any other religious beliefs. The Jehovah's Witness examples are used solely because the beliefs of Jehovah's Witnesses form the most widely known religious basis for the refusal of medical care in this country.

11. "Only beliefs rooted in religion are protected by the Free Exercise Clause, which, by its terms, gives special protection to the exercise of religion." Thomas v. Review Board (1981) 450 U.S. 707,715.

12. "Men may believe what they cannot prove. They may not be put to the proof of their religious doctrines or beliefs. Religious experiences which are as real as life to some may be incomprehensible to others." United States v. Ballard (1944) 322 U.S. 78, 86. "[R]eligious beliefs need not be acceptable, logical, consistent, or comprehensible to others in order to merit First Amendment protection." Thomas v. Review Board (1981) 450 U.S. 707,714.

13. See Engel v. Vitale (1962) 370 U.S. 421 (school prayer); Loney v. Scurr (1979) 474 F.Supp. 1186,1194. "[T]he Church of the New Song qualifies as a 'religion.'" Theriault v. Silber (1978) 453 F.Supp. 254,260. "The Church of the New Song appears not to be a religion." Malnik v. Yogi (1977) 440 F.Supp. 1284 (transcendental meditation).

14. See Wisconsin v. Yoder (1972) 406 U.S. 205, which contrasted the "religious beliefs" of the Amish with the "philosophical and personal" beliefs of Thoreau; also, United States v. Seeger (1965) 380 U.S. 163, which determined whether or not the beliefs of a conscientious objector qualified as "religious beliefs" to allow an exemption.

15. "[W]hile the 'truth' of a belief is not open to question, there remains the significant question whether it is 'truly held.'" United States v. Seeger (1965) 380 U.S. 163,185.

16. "We believe that . . . the test of belief 'in a relation to a supreme being' is whether a given belief that is sincere and meaningful occupies a place in the life of its possessor parallel to that filled by the orthodox belief in God of one who clearly qualifies for the exemption." United States v. Seeger (1965) 380 U.S. 163,166.

17. "[D]oes the claimed belief occupy the same place in the life of the objector as an orthodox belief in God holds in the life of one clearly qualified for exemption?" Seeger supra at 184. "[I]t is at least clear that if a group (or an individual) professes beliefs which are similar to and function like the beliefs of those groups which by societal consensus are recognized as a religion, the First Amendment guarantee of freedom of religion applies." Loney v. Scurr (1979) 474 F.Supp. 1186,1193 citing Welsh v. United States (1970) 398 U.S. 333,340. "While recently

acquired religious views are worthy of protection, the history of a religious belief and the length of time it has been held are factors to be utilized in assessing the sincerity with which it is held." In re Marriage of Gove (1977) 572 P.2d 458, 461, citing Wisconsin v. Yoder.

18. "One can, of course, imagine an asserted claim so bizarre, so clearly nonreligious in motivation, as not to be entitled to protection under the Free Exercise Clause . . ." Thomas v. Review Board (1981) 450 U.S. 707,715.

19. If a professed belief in "Star Wars" characters and making a life and death decision based upon faith in Yoda and Luke Skywalker is not sufficiently "crazy" for you, create your own patient. Consider, for example, a refusal by the patient who tells you he is "Serumzat, believer in the teachings of the Prince of Liquids and Tabletops; I believe that accepting blood is wrong and will prevent my passage to the afterlife, which I am destined to rule."

20. As a further example of how court's make these decisions, see Powell v. Columbian Presbyterian Medical Center (1966) 267 N.Y.S.2d 450. The facts presented the classic case of the Jehovah's Witness who did not want to die but who refused a life-saving blood transfusion. In a most candid decision that demonstrated the reality of the difficulty, vagueness, and room for legal discretion involved in these matters, the court stated in part: "This matter generated a barrage of legal niceties, misinformation and emotional feelings on the part of all concerned—including the Court personnel. . . . Never before had my judicial robe weighed so heavily on my shoulders. . . . I, almost by reflex action subjected the papers to the test of justiciability, jurisdiction and legality. . . . Yet, ultimately, my decision to act to save this woman's life was rooted in more fundamental precepts. . . . I was reminded of 'The Fall' by Camus, and I knew that no release—no legalistic absolution—would absolve me or the Court from responsibility if I, speaking for the Court, answered 'No' to the question 'Am I my brother's keeper?' This woman wanted to live. I could not let her die!" 267 N.Y.S.2d at 451,452.

21. It should be noted that in all cases of refusals of medical care, religious or not, as our certainty in the prognosis decreases, our willingness to allow the refusal increases. See, for example, Petition of Nemser (1966) 273 N.Y.S.2d 624, which contains an interesting discussion of these issues, although in some areas the court's analysis is incomplete or incorrect.

22. In re Milton, 505 N.E. 2d 255 (Ohio 1987). What would we do if this patient was Mrs. Oral Roberts?

23. Consider how terribly subtle these distinctions can be, however. Does it make a difference if the patient says "I leave my fate to Jehovah," as opposed to "I believe Jehovah will cure me"? Or if the patient states "God will save me" as opposed to "God may save me"? Again, we would explore this patient's understanding and beliefs carefully.

24. It should also be remembered that if the answer to any of these questions is no, the patient is also unable to *consent* to treatment.

Chapter 9

Behind the Curtain of Silence: Ethical Dilemmas in Rehabilitation

Jan Bruckner

Rehabilitation therapists offer an opportunity to their patients that no other branch of health care can. For the neonate with multiple congenital deformities, the young adult with a high spinal cord injury from a motorcycle accident, or the senior citizen who sustained a massive cerebral vascular accident, acute care offers survival but rehabilitation offers meaningful existence, independence, and self-fulfillment.

The American population is growing older. Improved medical technology means that more lives can be saved, but many of these people will survive with severe disabilities. If society is uncomfortable letting these people die, at what level of functioning will society support them? If these people have a right to life, do they also have a right to a minimal quality of life? Are they morally entitled to rehabilitation, maximal independence, and the least restrictive environment? Many rehabilitation patients and professionals are made to feel that their opinions are unimportant and unwanted. They learn that health care for the handicapped exists behind a shroud of powerlessness and a curtain of silence.

Before examining the issues, some terms must be clarified. *Allied health* is a term that can be applied to approximately two hundred health professions. These professions include diagnostic specialties such as nuclear medicine and cytotechnology, administrative specialties such as medical records administration, and rehabilitative specialties such as speech pathology and occupational therapy. This chapter will focus on the latter group and use the terms *rehabilitation specialist, rehabilitation professional,* and *therapist* interchangeably. A colleague of mine has pointed out that within the field of rehabilitation, there exist specialties in acute care, preventive health, and rehabilitation. I will argue that the interventions and philosophical approaches used by rehabilitation therapists doing acute care vary significantly from physicians doing acute care. Throughout this chapter, I will use the term *acute care medicine* to designate care provided by physicians and *rehabilitation services* to designate the care given by rehabilitation therapists. These distinctions are arbitrary, not quite accurate, but necessary if we are to examine the issues.

THE CURTAIN OF SILENCE

Case Study 1

Arlene is a 26 year old black female with a diagnosis of cerebral palsy, mental retardation, and developmental delay. She is hearing impaired and does not talk. She grew up in a state institution and has only recently begun receiving rehabilitative services. Arlene's speech pathologist has taught Arlene approximately fifteen words in American Sign Language and Arlene is using them to communicate. Arlene's occupational therapist has been teaching Arlene to dress herself, wash her face and hands, and transfer independently on and off the toilet. In physical therapy, Arlene has been working on gross motor skills. Arlene never learned to walk. In the institution, Arlene crawled on hands and knees using primitive reflexes and immature motor patterns. Both of Arlene's feet are fixed in equinovarus deformities and both tibial plateaus show large callous formations from years of crawling. To assist the rehabilitation program, a variety of adaptive equipment, including a wheelchair, was needed. Since Arlene received Medicaid, the institution staff decided to have her seen in an orthopedic clinic and have the attending physician prescribe the equipment.

Arlene and her physical therapist attended the clinic. An attending surgeon examined Arlene and x-ray films taken of both Arlene's lower limbs. The surgeon said that he could reduce the equinovarus deformities and bring Arlene's feet plantargrade so Arlene could stand. He recommended surgery. The therapist gave the physician the list of requested adaptive equipment and asked for a prescription order. The physician said that the wheelchair and the transfer board would not be necessary after the surgery and refused to prescribe them.

The therapist said that Arlene had the gross motor skills of someone 5 months old and that Arlene was using asymmetric tonic neck and other primitive reflexes to crawl around. To walk, a person must have the gross motor skills of someone developmentally 9–12 months old. Surgically bringing Arlene's feet plantargrade would not give Arlene the motor control required for walking. Arlene had been using her present motor plan for approximately twenty years so change would be slow, if possible at all.

The therapist thought that the surgery would be harmful instead of helpful. She had worked with other mentally retarded clients who had undergone surgery. She had observed her clients regress cognitively and had attributed their regressions to the anesthetic and to changes in their usual routine. Some clients had reacted to the unfamiliar people and the surgical pain by becoming aggressive or self-abusive and had to be heavily sedated. Under the effects of the heavy sedatives, the clients regressed further. The therapist knew that Arlene was doing well in her school program and feared that the surgery would interfere with Arlene's progress. She explained her concerns and again asked the surgeon to sign the Medicaid forms ordering the equipment.

The surgeon told the therapist that he disagreed with the treatment program and refused to be a "rubber stamp." He said that they had wasted enough of the clinic's time and he called for the next patient.

At the core of the conflict is a power struggle between two opposing philosophies. The physician comes from a background in orthopedic surgery. He knows that he can surgically correct Arlene's deformities and he believes that the patient will benefit from having her feet in a more normal alignment. The therapist comes from a background in rehabilitation. She studied the foundations of motor control and her evaluation of Arlene's gross motor development places Arlene below the stage where the foot deformities would interfere with function. Normal children five months of age do not walk. To the therapist, a short-term goal of walking is premature and the surgical correction of the deformities is an orthopedic solution to a neuro-developmental problem.

Acute care medicine differs from rehabilitation in treatment goals, the type of patient, the type of practitioner, and the fundamental issues of health care delivery. In acute care, the goals of treatment are to save the patient's life, cure the disease, and stabilize the condition. In rehabilitation, treatment goals focus on accommodating disabilities, maximizing functional capacities, and returning patients to society. Acute care patients may be passive participants, even comatose, while the health professionals do most of the care. In rehabilitation, the patients must be actively involved in the rehabilitative process and the health professionals act as consultants and advisors.

In acute care, the physician heading the team makes the diagnosis and sets the treatment protocols based on knowledge and experience from medical school and residency. In rehabilitation, the primary diagnosis has already been established and the emphasis is more on accommodation rather than cure. The physician oversees the medical management of the patient but the treatment goals are set by nursing and allied health personnel, and, sometimes, the patient. The physician may or may not have any formal training in rehabilitation.[1]

The curtain of silence allows only one-way communication—from the physician to the other members of the treatment team. Allied health professionals tend to express their opinions, but only some physicians will listen.

Strategies of Silence

Suffering in Silence

Some allied health professionals choose to yield responsibility for all decision making to the referring physicians.[2] The therapists say that the physicians are the leaders of the treatment teams and that all professional and ethical responsibilities fall on them. In the case study, such a therapist would have little problem going along with the physician's recommendation for surgery.

For therapists who choose yielding responsibility to the physicians, new problems may arise. Patients see these deferential allied health professionals as pawns of the physicians. Patients may lose respect for their therapists and in disgust seek other health care providers or alternative forms of care. For patients, like Arlene, who cannot speak for themselves, the silence of the allied health professionals deprives them of the very advocates who could help them the most. In abrogating their professional responsibilities, the allied health professionals help undermine the basic trust inherent in the patient-healer relationship.

Protesting by Silence

A second option for allied health professionals is withdrawal. If they disagree and do not want to go along with their physicians' recommendations, the allied health professionals can withdraw from the cases. This option allows the allied health professionals to preserve their professional integrity. In the case study, Arlene will receive the surgery if the therapist withdraws from the case. Withdrawing from the case may be the only way a therapist can express protest after an unsuccessful challenge.

Managing the Silence

Allied health professionals may have learned through clinical experience that direct assertion of their professional opinions may anger the powerful physicians. Angry physicians can cause problems for the allied health professionals. The problems vary from public humiliation to professional ostracism. For therapists dependent on physicians for patient referrals, angering a physician may severely affect their livelihood. Direct confrontations must be avoided, and so subtle strategies have been developed to "manage" difficult physicians. One of the strategies has been described by Stein as the "doctor-nurse game."[3]

In Stein's description, the object of the game is for the nurse to recommend types of patient treatment without challenging the authority of the physician. The nurses must be indirect and deferential while the physicians are positive and accepting. Skillful players of the doctor-nurse game uphold the occupational stereotypes while maintaining an effective working relationship.

Allied health professionals may play their own version of the doctor-nurse game. To avoid problems, the allied health professionals develop their own indirect approaches. One method is to broadly interpret the physicians' orders. A speech pathologist received an order for "speech therapy" for a profoundly retarded child who was having difficulty feeding. The therapist knew that the child really needed a feeding program. Functional speech given the child's mental condition did not seem likely. Since she had previous negative encounters with the referring physician, the speech pathologist decided "not to bother him" and implemented a "prespeech" program of oral-motor control and feeding. This treatment did succeed in helping the child eat more easily, which pleased the referring physician. How morally justifiable is this therapist's action? What about legal responsibilities if harm occurs?

Other "management" strategies take the form of public relations campaigns. In the staff room of one physical therapy department, the therapists joked about how they had "trained" their in-house physicians to write appropriate orders. They had provided massage and hot packs to the doctors and had discussed the real nature of therapy during the treatments. An occupational therapy department held an "open day." While the physicians were eating homemade baked goods, the therapists explained about daily living skills assessments, perceptual testing, and fine motor evaluations.

How morally justifiable are these management approaches? If the patient improves, we may be inclined to say that the therapist's actions were justified. What happens if a patient is injured while the therapist is using a broader approach? Now we may be inclined to criticize the therapist for being professionally irresponsible. Perhaps therapists should only broadly interpret physician orders if they can ensure a positive outcome, but how many therapists can do this?

A second problem with the managerial approach is that it ignores actions that appear inherently wrong. Broad interpretations of physician's orders are intentional misrepresentations of the truth. By failing in his or her duty to provide truthful, accurate information, the therapist may undermine the trust inherent in both the patient-healer relationship and the therapist-physician relationship.

THE RUBBER STAMP AND THE SILENT UNDERGROUND

In case study 1, the physician's comment about being a "rubber stamp" is appropriate. Physicians can graduate from medical school with little or no knowledge of rehabilitation, its philosophical approaches, its goals, and methods. For third party reimbursement, insurance companies require physicians to prescribe rehabilitation services and equipment.

Lacking the necessary background, physicians have two options. Some physicians are content to sign prescription orders written by rehabilitation therapists. Other physicians refuse to be a rubber stamp for the rehabilitation team and insist on their own plan of action. Physicians have the legal right to override the professional opinions of the rehabilitation team, but asserting this prerogative creates conflicts for the rehabilitation professionals and their patients.

When physicians ignore team input, they create ethical dilemmas for the allied health professionals. The allied health professionals must choose between their duty to provide the best quality care to their patients and their duty to follow the orders of their referring physicians. The patients get caught in the middle of the conflict and their experiences tend to erode their trust in their health care providers.

Case Study 2

Franklin is a 15-month-old white male with a diagnosis of microcephaly, spina bifida, and mental retardation. He has an Arnold-Chiari malformation, mitral valve defect, and bilateral pes cavus. At 8 months of age, Franklin had bilateral Achilles tendon lengthenings and was given bilateral ankle foot orthoses and high-topped shoes with Thomas heels. At 15 months of age, Franklin had minimal head control and could not roll, crawl, or tolerate being placed prone. He could sit in a highchair if given support.

Franklin's mother was a social worker. She was the president of the local spina bifida support group and determined to find the appropriate services for her child. She contacted a physical therapist in private practice and asked the therapist to evaluate Franklin. The therapist said that state law required a physician's referral and when such a referral was obtained she would be happy to see Franklin.

The mother called the orthopedic surgeon who lengthened Franklin's heelcords and requested the referral. The surgeon did not think that physical therapy was needed and urged the mother to "accept Franklin for what he was." Outraged at the physician's reply, the mother began calling the other physicians who followed Franklin. Franklin's pediatrician agreed to write the therapy referral.

Today's physicians are gatekeepers for health care. Physician's orders are required for third party reimbursement for services. No order means no insurance payment. Rehabilitation patients and their families are increasingly more knowledgeable about disorders, disabilities, and treatments. Franklin's mother had an opportunity to learn more about her son's disorder at the monthly meetings of the spina bifida support group. As a former social worker, the mother was familiar with the benefits of therapy, and as a knowledgeable health care consumer, she knew that she could shop around until she could find a physician willing to honor her request.

Many people with long-term disabilities or chronic problems are dissatisfied with the paternalistic "trust me" response that they get from some physicians. Instead, they are trying to help themselves. These people may find out about rehabilitation from their friends, other members of a particular support group, or through their own investigative research. They may ask a therapist for more information and respond, "Why didn't my doctor tell me about this?" Most probably, their doctors did not know.

Physician ignorance of allied health services undermines the trust people have in their physicians. The need for a physician's referral serves to restrict access to services that could help people with long-term disabilities. If the physicians are unaware of the benefits of rehabilitation, they will not refer for services. The process is especially painful if, like in Franklin's case, the patient or the patient's family must search for a cooperative physician. Franklin's mother was quite frustrated with the orthopedic surgeon. Seven months after the surgery, Franklin was still showing no progress in gross motor skills. After one month of physical therapy, Franklin began crawling independently. On seeing her son crawl, Franklin's mother was convinced that the orthopedic surgeon knew less about rehabilitation of developmental disabilities than the therapist. This may indeed have been the case.

Knowledgeable patients and families pose special dilemmas to allied health professionals. Inadvertently, these knowledgeable individuals ask the allied health professionals to help them undermine physician referrals. On learning that their physicians will not refer them for therapy, the patients may ask the allied health professionals to recommend another doctor who will. Such a request creates a conflict of duties for allied health professionals.

Therapists have professional duties to provide information about their professions to the public. These duties come from their professional codes of ethics. The foundation for these professional duties is the duty of beneficence, the obligation to "do good" and help people. Also included in their codes of ethics are duties to the referring physicians, duties such as fidelity, nonmaleficence (avoidance of harm), and loyalty.

Any direct resolution of conflicts of duties forces the allied health professionals to violate their duties to either their patients or their physicians. Most allied health professionals do not want to choose between their patients and their physicians, so they avoid any direct action. Instead, the curtain of silence forces the rehabilitation therapists underground into a realm of indirect and covert activities. Allied health professionals may provide indirect answers. If a concerned parent mentions that Dr. X refuses to refer for rehabilitation services, a therapist may respond, "If it were my child, I would get a second opinion." Therapists who have worked in a community for a while may suggest that an individual contact the local support group. The therapist knows that the support group members have already discovered the "good" physicians. The support group members do not have the same obligations that bind the allied health professionals, and thus they can give the inquiring person direct information.

When confronted by a particularly needy patient, some therapists actually provide "courtesy" treatments. These are services that the therapists provide on their own time and without charge. They may take the form of suggestions for work simplification, word recognition, or postural exercises. Franklin's therapist, for example, might tell the mother that she just learned a new therapy technique and then treat Franklin under the guise of practicing her new skill. Self-referral by patients may lead rehabilitation specialists to skirt the edges of the law.

How can the therapists resolve conflicts of duties? For example, should Arlene's therapist be silent and let Arlene have the surgery that she considers unwarranted? Should therapists advise their patients and surrogates to seek other medical opinions until they find a doctor who will rubber stamp the rehabilitation plan? Do patients have the right to hear both the therapist's and the physician's opinions if there is disagreement? How should the rehabilitation therapists answer their knowledgeable patients? How morally defensible is the "rehabilitation underground"? Why is the curtain of silence so strong that it forces the therapists into covert practice?

ENFORCING THE CURTAIN OF SILENCE

Many factors contribute to maintaining the curtain of silence. One factor can be found in the power structures of health care. Claus and Bailey identified three kinds of power and influence: organizational, social, and personal.[4] The first two kinds form the basis for the formal power structures of the administrative bureaucracy and the medical hierarchy described by Germain.[5] Allied health professionals have little access to the sources of these kinds of power and they exert little influence on the formal power structures of health care. The third kind of power is personal, which forms the basis of an informal power structure. Only in this informal structure do allied health professions have any power.

The first formal power structure, the administrative bureaucracy, manages the health care system. Responsibilities include fiscal management, personnel supervision, and administration of ancillary services, such as laundry and transportation. This structure has an organizational source of power. The health care organization is granted legal authority for patient care by a licensing or an accrediting agency. Few allied health professionals sit on health care managing boards as directors or trustees. The rehabilitation therapists have little influence in health care administration.

The second formal power structure, the medical hierarchy, provides patient care and derives its power from the social role of healer. As described by Pellegrino, the foundation for this relationship is trust.[6] The healer-physician professes to have the authentic knowledge and skills to help the patient in need. The patient trusts that the physician will help him, and in return for being healed, the patient lets the physician exercise some control, authority, and influence over him. Great healers are granted considerable power.

Allied health professionals enter into the healing relationship through physicians' referrals. The physicians decide that their patients could benefit from therapy and send them for treatment. At the conclusion of treatment, the therapists return the patients to the referring physicians. All of the formal authority rests in the hands of the doctors.

Modern American health care is seeing a blending of the two formal structures.[7] Groups of physicians are now practicing together. Health maintenance organizations and for-profit hospitals are employing physicians and applying business management techniques to health care. What effect these new health care structures will have on rehabilitation remains to be seen.

While allied health professionals struggle to influence the formal power structures of health care, they fare better in the informal network of personal interactions. The basis for power in this structure is personal attributes. Charm, charisma, and vitality are important qualities, but the major factor in professional relationships is competency. Allied health professionals can demonstrate their competency in helping their patients.

While individual therapists may develop reputations for being very skilled and knowledgeable, the authority to practice one's profession depends on personal contact. For therapists whose skills are well-known to the physicians, patient referrals will be easily obtained and few conflicts will arise. As personnel change, the direct contact will be lost. Therapist reputations for competency may no longer be recognized by the new physicians and patient referrals may be more difficult to get. The authority for rehabilitation therapists to practice their professions is dependent on the agreement and knowledge of individual physicians.

In addition to the health care power structures, a second factor enforcing the curtain of silence concerns socioculturally defined sex roles. Allied health professionals are predominantly female. Navarro pointed out that domestic chores and child care responsibilities are traditionally "female" activities and that working women retain these responsibilities in addition to their work outside the home.[8] This means that working women have double the workload and divided loyalties.

To implement change in the health care power structure, political activity is required. Laws and regulations will have to be changed to permit allied health professionals more professional authority and autonomy. Allied health professionals will have to present their side of the issues to legislators and health care administrators. Women professionals, who have dual responsibilities at work and at home, have less time and energy to devote to these additional professional activities. These women are less apt to be agents for change. If these women represent a high percentage of the profession, the curtain of silence will remain.[9]

Education helps maintain the curtain of silence. Both the level of education and the content of the professional curricula contribute to allied health powerlessness. Allied health professionals enter their fields with an Associate's or Bachelor's degree. The curricula of allied health programs emphasize treatment procedures and patient care. Little time or emphasis is placed on abstract reasoning, research, or the verbal expression of ideas. As a result, most allied health professionals have technical competence in the realm of patient care but are on uncertain ground when challenged to defend their opinions. Their uncertainty is reinforced by a genuine lack of scientific knowledge. Many of the therapy procedures are empirically developed and lack systematic validation. Scientific bases for treatment come from research. Only a minority of allied health professionals have the skills required to carry out clinically relevant investigations.

Even if they do research or develop new concepts, allied health professionals are slow to publish their ideas and share them with their colleagues. Johnson reported that nurses were reluctant to publish because they thought that their ideas were not good enough, that their writing skills were inferior, and that their colleagues would ridicule them.[10] Allied health professionals share similar feelings. Most allied health professionals find writing difficult and avoid it. Abstract issues such as those that arise in bioethics are especially difficult. One reason may be that allied health curricula lack sufficient humanities content. In her survey of ethics components in allied health curricula, Purtilo found a wide variation in time, approaches, and format.[11] Teachers of these components were described as "competent amateurs." The humanities foster the development of logical and critical thinking. Curricular deficits in the humanities may result in allied health authors being less productive, less articulate, and less persuasive. Thus, even if they try to verbalize their point of view, allied health professionals tend to reinforce their own inferiority and contribute to the maintenance of the curtain of silence.

A final contributing factor is professional exhaustion. After several years of battling physicians and hospital administrators to secure quality care for their patients, the allied health professionals get tired and frustrated. This situation reinforces the curtain of silence. It prevents them from getting the assistance they need. No one hears their problems. Some leave their profession to find more fulfillment elsewhere.

The curtain of silence prevents the allied health professionals from assistance with their ethical dilemmas. Few bioethicists realize the distinction between acute care and rehabilitation or the special dilemmas that confront allied health professionals. The bioethics literature rarely discusses allied health issues and gives little insight into strategies for resolving the dilemmas of rehabilitation. A notable exception is *Ethical Dimensions in the Health Professions* by Purtilo and Cassel.[12]

Unable to obtain appropriate referrals for their patients, effect changes necessary for successful rehabilitation, or resolve ethical dilemmas, therapists may not only withdraw from a patient's case, they may withdraw from the profession. Many therapists are choosing to withdraw. In 1982, for example, approximately 74 percent of the physical therapists were younger than 40.[13] The median number of years worked as a physical therapist was 8.61 years. While the trend appears to be slowly changing, the profession is still losing its most experienced and most knowledgeable practitioners. These people have the best understanding of how the health care system works and the best chance of promoting change. They are victims of the curtain of silence.

ISSUES OF SOCIAL JUSTICE AND DILEMMAS FOR SOCIETY

People in need of rehabilitation services and ultimately the general public are victims of the curtain of silence. Institutions that care for the multihandicapped or geriatric patient have the greatest difficulties attracting and retaining good quality rehabilitation professionals. Arguably, such patient populations can benefit most from the knowledge and skills of the allied health professionals. The patients have multiple and complicated problems; therefore, the allied health professionals must have a high level of knowledge and skill. An institution may employ a large number of staff and employee turnover may be quite high. The therapists may find the establishment of an effective informal network difficult. Ethical dilemmas arise with increased frequency among the frail and multidisabled populations. Few of these issues are examined in depth in the bioethics literature. If therapists have difficulties working in these institutions, who will treat the patients?

If short-term rehabilitation is more cost-effective than long-term maintenance, should society pay for rehabilitation? Who should allocate rehabilitation services? Physicians who head the treatment teams but know little about rehabilitation? Ethics boards or citizens groups? Patient support groups? Allied health professionals?

CAN THE CURTAIN BE LIFTED?

Within the health care community and throughout society in general, people need to ask how much they value rehabilitative care. If they see benefits in allied health, they ought to ensure the following. If physicians desire to retain their authority to prescribe rehabilitation services, then they should be required to learn more about it. If physicians refuse to learn about rehabilitation, they should relinquish their authority and let the rehabilitation therapists be independent practitioners. With independent therapist practitioners, people could look at the differences between the acute care medicine and rehabilitation and choose their own health care approaches.

Lifting the curtain of silence will entail a major revolution. The power structures of health care must be changed. Education of allied health professionals must be revised. Socioculturally defined sex roles must be challenged and the patient-health practitioner relationship must be re-examined. Bioethicists must be encouraged to consider the ethical dilemmas of allied health. Ultimately, society will have to confront two very difficult questions: Can society tolerate raising the curtain? Can society afford to leave it in place?

NOTES

1. F.K. Fox et al., "Resident Physicians' Perceived Knowledge of Physical Therapy," *Physical Therapy* 64 (May 1984): 720. The authors state that while 46 states require physician referrals for physical therapy, only half of the U.S. medical schools offer courses in rehabilitation care. Of the responding residents, 98 percent referred patients for physical therapy but only 53.6 percent felt adequately informed to do so.

2. Ruth B. Purtilo, "Ethics in Allied Health Education: State of the Art," *Journal of Allied Health* 12 (August 1983): 210–20. The first section of this paper considers the view that ethical decision making is more relevant for physicians than for other health professionals. Purtilo argues that the demands of future practice obligate allied health professionals to become their own decision makers and that educational programs must meet this challenge.

3. Leonard I. Stein, "The Doctor-Nurse Game," *Archives of General Psychiatry* 16 (June 1967): 699–703. The relationship of the doctor and the nurse are described from a social scientist's perspective. While the observations show signs of another age, the basic behaviors patterns remain current. Sex and occupational roles enforce inequalities and result in nurses using indirect and deferential strategies to promote better patient care.

4. Karen E. Claus and June T. Bailey, "Power Bases for Leadership," in *Power and Influence in Health Care: A New Approach to Leadership* (St. Louis, Mo.: Mosby, 1977). The authors are two nurses who have developed an intricate model for analyzing the power structures of health care and a series of strategies for developing power and influence. For people, especially nurses, interested in studying the power structures of health care, this book offers some intriguing insights.

5. Carol Germain, *The Cancer Unit: An Ethnography* (Wakefield, Mass.: Nursing Resources, 1979). The author is a nurse who got her doctorate in anthropology. This volume is her doctoral thesis and shows how the principles and methods of social science can be applied to health care. The author provides some astute observations which would interest both those considering a career in health care and seasoned health professionals who wish an analytic view of the field.

6. Edmund D. Pellegrino, "What is a Profession?" *Journal of Allied Health* 12 (August 1983): 168–76. Pellegrino describes his "virtue" theory of the healing professions with eloquence and simplicity. The patient-healer relationship is based on trust and Pellegrino explains the professional obligations inherent in that trust. This article reminds us of the ideals that initially lead us to choose a career in health.

7. Gregg Easterbrook, "The Revolution in Medicine," *Newsweek*, January 26, 1987, 40–74. An informative and comprehensive look at the development of our modern American health care system. It details and explains terminology, trends, and traumas. A nice synopsis in understandable English.

8. Vincente Navarro, "Women in Health Care," *New England Journal of Medicine* 292 (February 1979): 398–402. The author examines the health labor force in terms of occupational categories, social class, and sex. He found that the vast majority of medical professionals are upper middle class men while middle level, clerical, and service workers tend to be lower middle and working class women. This discrepancy is attributed to the role of women in their families and in the labor force.

9. *Active Member Profile—1982: A Summary Report* (Washington, D.C.: American Physical Therapy Association, 1983). This is a report of the 1978 and 1982 active membership profile survey results. The data include biographical information, professional information, gross earned income, and educational information. The physical therapy profession is 75 percent female. Higher percentages of female physical therapists than male physical therapists hold part-time salaried positions while higher percentages of male physical therapists hold full-time self-employed positions. Male physical therapists outnumber their female colleagues in administrative and management positions and supervisory and coordination positions. Male physical therapists have higher academic degrees and have higher annual gross earned incomes. People interested in similar information on the other allied health professions can contact the individual professional organizations.

10. Suzanne Hall Johnson, "Publishing as a Source of Power," in *Power and Influence: A Source Book for Nurses*, ed. Kathleen R. Stevens (New York: Wiley, 1983). The main thrust of this chapter is to convince nurses that they can and should publish. Johnson explores the reasons why nurses are reluctant to publish and then gives techniques in developing "publishing power."

11. Ruth B. Purtilo, "Ethics Teaching in Allied Health Fields," *Hastings Center Report* 8 (April 1978): 14–16. A report of a survey of 59 physical therapy programs and 48 occupational therapy programs detailing ethics teaching in the curricula and exposure to ethics outside the programs. Purtilo found that the programs varied widely in their approaches and she called for more research to establish allied health ethics and methods for teaching it.

12. Ruth Purtilo and Christine Cassel, *Ethical Dimensions in the Health Professions* (Philadelphia: W.B. Saunders, 1981). A nice, simple, straightforward book that explains the basics about bioethics for allied health professionals. The examples are easily identifiable and the principles are explained clearly. This is an excellent resource for the ethics component of allied health education programs. Clinicians will also find it helpful.

13. *Active Member Profile—1982.*

Chapter 10

"A Clean Heart Create for Me, O God": Impact Questions on the Artificial Heart

Richard A. McCormick

INTRODUCTION

On May 24, 1985, there appeared in the *New York Times*, under the byline of Dr. Lawrence Altman, the following statement: "[This is] probably the single most expensive medical procedure available . . . Yet in a report yesterday that would redirect national priorities on one of the boldest experiments in medical history, The Working Group called for a greatly expanded Federal research effort to develop a fully implantable, permanent heart."[1]

Altman was referring to a report of an advisory panel of the National Heart, Lung and Blood Institute of the National Institutes of Health. Albert R. Jonsen, a member of this panel (known as The Working Group on Mechanical Circulatory Support) disputes Altman's claim that the Working Group endorsed "a greatly expanded effort." It recommended, he states, only that the present effort continue.[2]

Whatever the case, there can be little doubt that the arrival of mechanical circulatory support (dating to the December 2, 1982, implantation of an artificial heart in Dr. Barney Clark at the University of Utah) will function as a symbol of the way this country faces its health challenges in the next decade or so.

A CONTROVERSIAL ISSUE

It is an easy prediction that we will relive the debate that surrounded dialysis for end stage renal disease. Medicare began to operate in 1967. At that time, kidney dialysis was provided by law for three groups: those eligible for veterans' benefits, Medicare beneficiaries aged sixty-five and over, and beneficiaries of Medicaid programs covering this expensive procedure. In 1972 Congress extended coverage for kidney dialysis to all who needed the treatment. Joseph Califano describes the discussions that preceded this congressional generosity.

> There was a spirited, sometimes angry, discussion around the conference table in my White House West Wing office. Some said it was immoral not to provide care to all who needed it. Others said even the Great Society at its peak could not provide every medical service to all who needed it. But this was a matter of life itself, another heatedly added, pointing out that just because of quirks in the law, some were eligible and others not; some had the money to pay for it, others did not. The discussion went on and on.[3]

Califano's brief cameo accurately identifies the two poles that also anchored the broader congressional discussion: life and money. Could the wealthiest nation in the world choose to withhold such a service from some citizens? Is it fair to let some people die when we have the means to give them added years of life? Obviously such questions are important to try to answer. But I have to wonder whether they should so dominate the policy discussion in the way they did. Many people have had long second thoughts about the end stage renal disease program. Many of these thoughts are probably stimulated by the fat $2 billion bill. But I believe that there may be more behind such second thoughts than the expense.

Virtually every technological advance has its costs. Benefits come with burdens. Therefore, it is essential to an ethical analysis that all of the possible impacts of our interventions be identified. With that in mind, I will list areas of possible impact in the future of the artificial heart, especially from the permanent use of such a devise as opposed to its use as a temporary assistive device. It should be emphasized that I am raising issues or questions rather than making assertions. Indeed, to stress this, each point will conclude with a question.

TEN CRUCIAL QUESTIONS

1. How We View Life and Death. How we preserve life manifests and reinforces what we think of life and death. In the Christian view, as I have stated already, life is a basic good, but not an absolute one. The Christian lives in faith that he or she is on a pilgrimmage, that death is a transition, not an end, that just as Christ conquered death, so will we. We organize our lives around this belief.

Question: How will this faith be affected by the artificial heart? In a sense, such faith is affected by all medical interventions *in principle*. But the artificial heart might be in a category by itself.

2. How We Evaluate People. In its 1972 study, the Artificial Heart Assessment Panel of the then National Heart and Lung Institute made repeated reference to a return to functionability as a possible benefit of the artificial heart. In a key paragraph it stated:

> If the artificial heart works well, the demand for it may be so great that society will find itself hard pressed to supply the devise to all who want it. Even assuming that an adequate supply would be forthcoming at some price so that rationing would not be necessitated by absolute scarcity, society might be unwilling to supply the device at public expense to all needful patients. Convicted criminals, drug addicts, and perhaps other persons viewed as non-contributing members of society might be seen as candidates for exclusion. But any such governmental process of rationing life on the basis of the value of individual members to society would take a heavy toll in public values.[4]

Question: Will the availability and use of this technology subtly affect our evaluation of human persons so that we increasingly perceive them in terms of their functionability or value to society?

3. How We Evaluate Other Health Care Needs. "Other health care needs" refers above all to preventive medicine and life style. The artificial heart is the "ultimate repair job." Short of such ultimate repair, we are societally deficient in attending to the causes of illness: high cholesterol, smoking, lack of exercise. As Thomas Preston, chief of cardiology at The Pacific Medical Center (Seattle), notes, "If the goal is to save lives, that can be done more quickly, more broadly and more surely by other means. Let us spend our resources instead on reducing our infant mortality rate, or treating hypertension in the inner cities, or taking care of the 25 million Americans who are without insurance or means of attaining adequate medical care."[5]

Joseph Califano makes the point I want to raise. "Heart disease is America's number-one killer. Daily newspapers and television dramas give the impression that coronary bypass surgery, modern cardiopulmonary techniques, miracle hypertension pills, human heart transplants, and in the future, animal and artificial heart transplants are the way to battle heart disease. Right? Couldn't be more wrong."[6]

Question: Will the artificial heart blind us to more basic health care needs and comfort us in a comfortable life style that is radically unhealthy? Will it comfort the afflicted in their unspoken heterodoxy: "If it can be fixed, why worry about the breakdown?"

4. How We Evaluate Other Societal Needs. The appropriate allocation of our resources to various societal needs is a major social issue. Roughly 11 percent of the G.N.P. goes to health care. But there are other pressing needs: education, the environment, housing, hunger, defense, etc.

Question: Will the introduction of this technology obscure or downplay other societal needs, some far more basic?

5. How We Deal with Our Elderly Population. The Artificial Heart Assessment Panel noted the following:

> A particularly important societal impact of the artificial heart will appear in the form of an expanding elderly population. Persons who would have died young will live longer and may be substantially more productive in their older years than they would have been without the artificial heart. Moreover, elderly patients who are otherwise in good health should surely not be denied the right to an artificial heart—at public expense if that is the way things go. The result of enlarging the older population will be to exacerbate the problems which our society is already experiencing in trying to provide a meaningful existence for its senior citizens. Many older people who are in all respects, both physical and mental, the equal of many younger people are treated as if their ability to make any useful contribution to society had long since ended. For those who are less well off, the need to supply decent and dignified living conditions is also not being met. The costs and human challenges are very great already, but the artificial heart will add to both.[7]

Add to these considerations the fact that some cardiac disease is genetic in origin. The artificial heart might enable carriers of cardiac disease to reproduce, thus increasing prevalence of genetic heart disease. Thus the artificial heart may generate additional candidates for its use in future generations.

Question: Will the artificial heart promote or undermine our society's efforts to deal with the elderly population? While extending lives, will it also exacerbate problems we have not yet solved?

6. How The Patient Views Herself/Himself. There are any number of possible reactions and combinations of reactions that might affect the attitudes of recipients. There might be anxieties due to dependence on an external source of power. There might be preoccupation about being "dehumanized" by an artificial heart. There might be worries about finances that could lead to guilt feelings and intrafamily tensions.

Question: What will be the overall quality of life available to patients with artificial hearts?

7. How the Question of Fairness is Faced. I believe it is highly probable that the government will not pay for clinical practice involving artificial hearts. We simply cannot afford it. Therefore artificial hearts will be available only to those who can afford them. Increasingly this kind of limited availability is seen as unacceptable in our egalitarian society.

It is this very unacceptability that leads others to a different view of public funding of clinic practice in this area. Thus Albert R. Jonsen writes,

> The possibility exists that a cry will be raised for federal subsidy of clinical implantation of artificial hearts. The sight of individuals doomed to die because they cannot afford an existing lifesaving treatment stimulates the demand for equality: in the face of death, the allocation of a lifesaving technology on the basis of an individual's ability to pay seems blatantly discriminatory.[8]

If public funds are allocated for clinical implantation of artificial hearts, there are likely to be other budgetary reallocations to accommodate this strain. As Jonsen notes, these reallocations are likely to be restrictions in already underfunded programs and this could have tragic effects on access to care. In this way, a new rescue technology ends up threatening the health of others.

Question: If the artificial heart becomes accepted clinical practice, how will its accessibility affect our notion of justice and fairness?

8. How We Evaluate Euthanasia and Suicide. Presently both mercy killing and suicide are rejected by our society, even though there are powerful forces at work to legitimize both. For a variety of reasons, we have experienced ethical confusion about the moral propriety of withholding or withdrawing respirators, nasal gastric tubes, and gastrostomy tubes. Repeatedly judges have stated that removal of such life-support systems would subject those removing them to the homicide laws. This happened early on in the Quinlan case (New Jersey) and the Clarence Herbert case (California). It also happened in the case of Michael Brophy (Massachusetts). Behind such confusion—and I believe it is precisely that—there probably lies a single fact: The more we survive by machines and artificial life-sustainers, the more turning them off or withdrawing them looks like euthanasia or suicide.

Question: Will the obviously optional character of artificial heart operations further erode our rejection of mercy killing?

9. How the Direction of Medicine Is to Be Charted and by Whom. The type of health care we get can be determined in any number of ways, for instance, by the public or by independent medical investigators and their entrepreneurial backers. Since what kind of medicine we get and what we spend on it affects many other aspects of social life, these determinations pertain to the common good. I take that to mean that they should be governed by the public.

Question: Does the independent character of a program like that of Humana constitute a further step away from public scrutiny and control of the direction and priorities of medicine?

10. How Medicine Perceives Its Role and Implements It. Everyone admits that the health care system in the United States is in the midst of a major structural revolution. Whether it is merely a symptom or a cause, a key feature of this transition is a move from medicine as a non-profit service to medicine as a business.

Question: If, *per impossibile*, news reportage of artificial heart implants was prohibited by law, would Humana be involved with them? In general terms, what is the impact of medicine's move to a business ethos on its self-concept, its practitioners, and its quality?

The ten questions I have raised may appear to some as answers looking for questions. I hope that they are not that. They were crafted out of the conviction that in dealing with the artificial heart we must consider more than life and money. Restriction of our deliberations to these twin factors could lead to a high-minded, warm-hearted, but short-sighted humanitarianism. If I am correct, an adequate discussion of the artificial heart plunges us deeply into social ethics.

NOTES

1. *New York Times*, May 24, 1985.

2. Albert R. Jonsen, "The Artificial Heart's Threat to Others," *Hastings Center Report* 16 (February 1986): 9.

3. Joseph A. Califano, Jr., *America's Health Care Revolution* (New York: Random House, 1986), 146.

4. Artificial Heart Assessment Panel, *The Totally Implantable Artificial Heart* (Bethesda, Md.: NIH, 1973), 74.

5. Thomas Preston, "Who Benefits from the Artificial Heart?" *Hastings Center Report* 15 (February 1985), 7.

6. Califano, *America's Health Care Revolution*, 187.

7. Cf. Artificial Heart Assessment Panel, *The Totally Implantable Artificial Heart*, 75.

8. Jonsen, "The Artificial Heart's Threat to Others," 10.

Chapter 11

Human Experimentation and Clinical Consent

George J. Agich

Informed consent is central to contemporary medical ethics to such an extent that there is a danger of becoming blasé about the significant theoretical and practical problems involving consent. In this chapter, I address some of these concerns by first considering some definitional aspects of clinical consent involving the distinction between research and therapy as well as the question of the place of experimentation in each. In so doing, I contrast the ethics and structure of the physician-patient relationship and the researcher-subject relationship as well as consider the social and legal definition and standards of informed consent in common law and federal regulations governing research with human subjects. Second, I consider some saliant practical problems associated with consent to experimentation in clinical settings against this definitional background. I argue that consent requirements vary with the relationship in question—whether it is research or therapy—and with risk-benefit considerations, patient competence, and the actual medical circumstances.

THE DEFINITIONAL PROBLEM

Informed consent is the cornerstone of contempory medical ethics. At least since the Nuremberg Tribunals, it has been widely acknowledged that the voluntary consent of a human subject is ethically required before that subject can participate in experiments. Since 1974, federal regulations have required institutions receiving federal funds to conduct prospective and continuing formal review of all biomedical and behavioral research involving human subjects.[1] These regulations accord informed consent a central, though not absolutely paramount, place in human subjects research (this point is discussed at the end of this chapter). A doctrine of informed consent has also developed separately in common law that makes it a duty of physicians to disclose relevant information prior to securing patients' permission to undertake diagnostic or therapeutic interventions. It is a matter of scholarly debate whether informed consent in clinical settings is a nineteenth or twentieth century phenomenon.[2] What is clear is that while examples of consent in medical practice can be found prior to the twentieth century, the doctrine of *informed* consent came to be recognized generally as a legal obligation of physicians in the relatively recent period between 1957 and 1972.[3]

In response to the Nazi medical experiments, the Nuremberg Code of 1947 was promulgated with an absolute commitment to informed consent: "The voluntary consent of the human subject is absolutely essential."[4] The duty and responsibility for ascertaining the quality of the consent, interestingly, was said to rest "upon each individual who initiates, directs, or engages in the experiment. It is a personal duty and responsibility which may not be delegated to another with impunity."[5] Presumably, the focus on the investigator's primary moral responsibility in conducting human experimentation was a response to one of the common defenses made before the Nuremberg tribunals, namely, that the accused was merely following orders or serving a subsidiary role in the research. The Nuremberg code properly stresses that moral responsibility is primarily a personal rather than a social phenomenon. This differs somewhat from the approach taken under federal regulations that require Institutional Review Board (IRB) review of biomedical and behavioral research involving human subjects. Although the regulations also assume that the principle investigator is primarily responsible for designing and conducting the research in a manner consistent with ethical standards and protective of the rights and welfare of subjects, formal review of proposed research is nonetheless required to provide assurance that research is conducted in an ethically acceptable fashion.

Federal regulations require that consent and consent forms generally involve the following: (1) the subject's involvement must be identified as research and a description of the research and its purposes must be provided; (2) the risks must be described; (3) the benefits must be described; (4) if the investigation is clinical, then diagnostic and therapeutic alternatives must be described; (5) a description must be given of the confidentiality of research records and data; (6) an explanation must be given of the availability or unavailability of compensation or treatment for injury; (7) identification must be made of whom to contact for answers regarding the conduct of the research and the subject's rights as well as whom to contact in the event of injury; (8) an explanation must be given of the subject's rights to refuse participation and to withdraw from the study.[6] Additional elements may be required by the IRB when appropriate, for example, information regarding currently unforeseeable risks, reasons why an investigator might expel a subject from a study, identification of additional costs to the subject incurred as a result of participation in the study, consequences of the subject's withdrawal from the study (e.g., risk of severe side effects if study medication is withdrawn precipitously), information about pertinent new findings, and information about the number of subjects participating in the research project.[7]

The required and additional elements of consent for human subjects involved in research point up a significant difference between consent in therapeutic and research settings. Under common law, informed consent is a positive duty of the physician, who is mandated to disclose information regarding the proposed course of treatment, alternatives, and the risks and benefits which are material to patient decision making.[8] As such, informed consent constitutes a standard of care which courts are willing to enforce; however, there is no prospective formal review of consent in physician-patient relationships, because such review would be intrusive in what is socially and legally regarded as a private and special professional relationship. Instead, informed consent standards are explicitly established retrospectively when a breach of duty proximally causing injury is decided in a malpractice proceedings to have occurred. The physician (and presumably any other health professional) in a therapeutic relationship is thus free from external scrutiny except after the fact (if a lawsuit is initiated). On the other hand, the researcher is subject to formal, prospective, and continuing review requirements, including explicit and detailed standards for the information disclosed.

This difference in the structure of review and the establishment of consent standards reflects an important difference between therapeutic and research relationships.[9] The physician-patient relationship has traditionally been regarded as a fiduciary relationship in which the physician is obligated to act as the agent of the patient and primarily in the patient's best interest. The research relationship, however, is a relationship designed to gather evidence or data for testing hypotheses, thus contributing to the advancement of scientific knowledge generally. Of course, in some instances subjects of research stand to benefit from participating in the study, but such benefit is not the primary goal of the research relationship as such and is not necessarily an intended outcome of the research endeavor.

The distinction between research and therapeutic relationships, then, is both social and intentional. Research is a formal activity supported in large part through public funds with the aim of advancing generalizable scientific knowledge. Therapeutic relationships, however, are fiduciary, professional, and private relationships which primarily aim at enhancing individual patient welfare. The practice of medicine, however, has come to combine research and therapeutic activities—in what Talcott Parsons has termed the "professional complex" of research, service, and teaching[10]—to such an extent that the distinction between research and therapy has proven troublesome. The troublesome aspects of this distinction can be expressed by reflecting on the confusions surrounding the term *therapeutic research* and the experimental nature of medical practice.

Although it is not clear how the term *therapeutic research* entered usage, it has certainly caused difficulty. The concept is at least implicit in the World Medical Association's Declaration of Helsinki, which distinguishes clinical research combined with professional care from "non-therapeutic clinical research."[11] Since it is not conducted for the benefit of the subjects involved, nontherapeutic research is often seen as suspect ethically and as requiring stronger justification than therapeutic research, which, it is often implied, is of benefit to the subject.[12] This assumption, however, is not clearly well-founded, because whether a treatment being researched will be therapeutic is precisely what is in question.

The objective of clinical research usually is to determine the safety or efficacy of a particular therapeutic method or procedure or to gain knowledge of basic physiological processes. Implicit in the need to ask the research question is a basic scientific uncertainty regarding which method or procedure provides the best outcome. This uncertainty means that the question of therapeutic benefits is unresolved and so cannot validly be assumed, even though the question is being investigated in the context of a relationship which aims at providing clinical benefits.

Karen Lebacqz and Robert J. Levine, both members of the National Commission for the Protection of Human Subjects of Biomedical and Behavioral Research, have separately criticized the National Commission's early definition of "therapeutic research," or "the spurious distinction between therapeutic and non-therapeutic experimentation" in its first report, *Research on the Fetus*.[13] Both argue for a view which was later articulated in the National Commission's *Belmont Report*:

> For the most part, the term "practice" refers to interventions that are designed soley to enhance the well-being of the individual patient or client and that have a

reasonable expectation of success. The purpose of medical or behavioral practices is to provide a diagnosis, preventive treatment or therapy to particular individuals. By contrast, the term ''research'' designates an activity designed to test a
hypothesis, permit conclusions to be drawn and thereby to develop or contribute
to generalizable knowledge (expressed, for example, in theories, principles, and
statements of relationships). [14]

On this view, research and practice (or therapy) are logically distinct activities. The term
research refers to a class of activities designed to produce generalizable knowledge,
whereas *therapy* or *practice* refers to a class of activities that is meant to benefit patients and
enhance patient welfare. The distinction is primarily predicated on the intention behind both
activities and is reflected in their planning, execution, and the structure of the attendant relationships. While research may be joined with therapy—as in research on the treatment of
individuals—the research itself does not thereby become therapeutic. [15] Confusion occurs
because research and therapy can occur together in the practice of clinical medicine—for
example, research designed to evaluate the safety and efficacy of a therapeutic method or
drug—and because notable departures from standard practice are often called experimental
when the terms *experimentation* and *research* are not carefully distinguished. [16]

Levine argues that the departures from standard practice, which the *Belmont Report*
terms ''innovations,'' should be thought of as a class of activities separate both from
research and from those therapies which have been scientifically validated and established.
He terms this class ''non-validated practices.'' He states, ''Novelty is not the attribute that
defines this class of practices, rather it is the lack of suitable validation of the safety or ethics
of the practice.''[17] In the *Belmont Report*, however, the National Commission focused on
innovation:

> When a clinician departs in a significant way from a standard or accepted practice,
> the innovation does not, in and of itself, constitute research. The fact that a
> procedure is ''experimental'' in the sense of new, untested or different, does not
> automatically place it in the category of in research. Radically new procedures of
> this description should, however, be made the object of formal research at an
> early stage in order to determine whether they are safe and effective. [18]

Requiring that innovations and nonvalidated practices be made the object of research and,
hence, subject to formal prospective and continuing review by IRBs raises the important
question: What is the proper function of ''experimentation'' in the practice of medicine and
how does this bear on the problem of clinical consent?

An experiment is not simply a formal test of something, but it is also a tentative procedure
adopted under conditions of uncertainty regarding whether it will achieve the desired
purposes or results. On this definition, much of the practice of medicine is experimental in
nature. As Herman L. Blumgart has argued:

> Every time a physician administers a drug to a patient, he is in a sense performing
> an experiment. It is done, however, with therapeutic intent and within the doctor-
> patient relationship since it involves a judgment that the expected benefit out-
> weighs the risk. . . . We can standardize drugs, but we cannot standardize

patients; medical care of the patient demands adjusting the drug to the individual's unique characteristics.[19]

Francis D. Moore has made a similar observation in the context of surgery: "Every new operation, for example, is an experiment; indeed every operation of any type contains certain aspects of experimental work."[20] The important point to note is that the experimentation in question is done on the basis of established knowledge and with the primary intention of enhancing the well-being of the patient. Experimentation in this sense is not only compatable with the therapeutic relationship, but seems essential to it.

When the treatment is innovative or experimental, things become more complicated ethically. Experimentation (in the sense of novel or new procedures) is probably a common feature of clinical medicine, especially in emergency care. It is essential that a physician respond quickly and sometimes creatively to unusual presentations of serious illness or trauma. Some responses will be routinized; others will of necessity be novel. Similarly, in the course of surgery, untoward events or unexpected occurrences require modifications of normal procedures. Sometimes, these modifications are due to individual, biological variation or because there is simply not sufficient time for standard approaches. This seems to indicate that such experimentation can be conducted without meeting formal requirements of informed consent when the situation presents no feasible alternatives and when the risk-benefit ratio for the particular subject is acceptable. However, this does not mean that consent can be waived *by the investigator* for experimentation designed to test a hypothesis, to permit conclusions to be drawn, or to develop generalizable knowledge.[21]

Any research that asks fundamental questions about the nature of an abnormality and the extent of the human body's response but has no immediate or long-range therapeutic potential for the individual patient would have to be regarded as nontherapeutic. Nontherapeutic clinical research has been regarded as morally suspect in some quarters unless a stringent standard of an informed consent is observed. For example, the Declaration of Helsinki requires that nontherapeutic clinical research meet the following requirements:

> Clinical research on a human being cannot be undertaken without his free consent, after he has been fully informed. . . . The subject of clinical research should be in such a mental, physical, and legal state as to be able to exercise fully his power of choice." Furthermore, "the doctor can combine clinical research with professional care, the objective being the acquisition of new medical knowledge, only to the extent that clinical research is justified by its therapeutic value for the patient.[22]

This view would seem to preclude clinical research as we know it, for example, research into basic physiological processes. The thrust of the Declaration of Helsinki is to prevent human subjects from being coerced by the trust they placed in physicians *qua* physicians. If the physician is also a researcher, the activities of research and practice should be strictly kept distinct. But this approach is problematic because it attempts to force the social role to reflect what is merely a logical distinction between research and practice. Modern medicine, however, has combined these activities. Rather than proscribe nontherapeutic clinical research, procedures have been developed under federal regulations that require that clinical research protocols be subject to IRB review, a review mandated to protect the welfare and rights of the subjects of research. This provides protection of subjects by socializing the ethical review of consent and thus avoids outright proscription of non-therapeutic clinical research.

The problem of consent to experimentation thus needs to be addressed by addressing at least three categories of experimentation. The first category includes experimentation conducted for the purpose of research, in which case the research-subject relationship is in force and the strict canons of research with human subjects apply. The second category includes experimentation conducted for the purpose of research but involving medical procedures performed on the subject with little or no prospect of immediate benefit to the subject. Examples might include Phase I drug studies and the study of basic physiological processes. Here, the relationship is primarily that of research-subject and research ethics applies, but the research may also be grafted onto or structured within therapeutic relationships. The third category includes experimentation conducted for the purpose of benefiting subjects within physician-patient relationships. The experimentation either is conducted as part of formal research (for example, Phase III drug studies, where formal IRB review and approval is necessary) or is simply the novel application of a technique or drug to new situations (for example, the use of a drug for a non-FDA-approved indication). This simple categorization is admittedly fuzzy, because it melds the distinctions between research and practice, research ethics and clinical ethics, and the intentional and social definitions of these activities. Nonetheless, such an ambiguous conceptual background does exist and it complicates the ethical problems associated with clinical consent to experimentation.

PRACTICAL ASPECTS

Consent is an essential ingredient of a morally acceptable medical practice. Without consent, medicine risks contributing to the destruction of important human values rather than to their enhancement or restoration. Consent is morally important, because it is a significant means for respecting persons. Competent individuals clearly deserve disclosure of relevant information regarding proposed diagnostic and treatment procedures, available alternatives, and risks and benefits reasonably to be expected from a proposed intervention. As Alan Donagan has forcefully expressed it, ''A physician is simply not competent if he is unable to describe, in words intelligible to his patients, everything that could matter to them as patients about the character of any course of treatment he proposes.''[23] However, even in an alert, communicative adult, there are potential problems of comprehension. The relevant information is often complex and complicated. The patient's own emotional state sometimes makes understanding and assessment of the information difficult. To suffer an illness or disability compromises one's autonomy; hence, consent to experimental procedures in clinical settings is made especially difficult. In order to address these difficulties, I discuss three related issues concerning consent to experimental procedures in clinical settings: what constitutes a valid consent, patient competence, and the contribution of cost-benefit considerations.

Informed consent generally involves adequate information, comprehension or understanding of the information, and voluntariness or absence of coercion. Adequate information would include everything that rational persons would want to know, including the benefits and costs involved in the various alternatives and the probabilities associated with each. In addition, each individual should know of anything else that might affect his personal decision, such as information that might bear on his cultural, personal, or religious beliefs or values. (See Chapter 32 on Quality Assurance, Risk Management, and Ethical Issues.) Individuals, however, do not need to know the technical details regarding the treatment.[24] Patients, of course, may refuse information. Such waivers of the right to obtain adequate information regarding a particular procedure, however, should never be *inferred*, but must be explicitly and unequivocally stated by the individual.

Ideally, comprehension of the information disclosed should allow the individual's personal beliefs and values to be reflected in any decision. That is, the highest level of comprehension will include a reflective consideration of the proposed course of treatment, available alternatives, and risks and benefits in light of an individual's personal beliefs.[25] Various tests for patient competence have been proposed in the literature. These tests focus variously on the evidence that a choice has been made, the reasonableness or rational basis of the choice, and the ability to understand or the actual understanding of the information provided. However, as Loren H. Roth et al. argue,

> In effect, the test that is actually applied combines elements of all the tests described above. However, the circumstances in which competency becomes an issue determine which elements of which tests are stressed and which are under-played. Although in theory competency is an independent variable that deter-mines whether or not the patient's decision to accept or refuse treatment is to be honored, in practice it seems to be dependent on the interplay of two other variables: the risk/benefit ratio of treatment and the valence of the patient's decision, i.e., whether he or she consents to or refuses treatment.[26]

Common law and medical ethics recognize the frequency of situations in which a patient is unable to grant consent (for a variety of reasons). Obvious examples are patients who are obtunded or comatose. Even more troublesome is the situation in which a patient is confused or simply too physically ill to comprehend the information and implications of the decision he or she is asked to make. In such circumstances, the patient's representative or proxy, usually a spouse or family member, is permitted to grant consent on the patient's behalf. Proxy consent is permitted, because the overriding value in situations of acute illness is patient welfare. The principle of respect for persons involves two essentials: that individuals should be treated as autonomous agents and that persons with diminished autonomy are entitled to protection.[27] Proxy consent is intended to satisfy the latter.

However, in a situation of acute illness such as cardiac arrest, it is naive to believe that a spouse or family member is able to grant *informed* consent for the patient. Even if the surrogate were immediately available, it is unlikely that many individuals could resist the natural urge to "do something" or be able to evaluate the subtler aspects of the therapeutic alternatives in a purely rational and an objective fashion. For these reasons, emergency treatment relies on a concept of *implied* consent. Thus, the fiduciary obligations which structure the relationship require that actions be taken to assure patient welfare.

Underlying this discussion is the belief that the requirements of consent vary not only with patient competence, but with the degree and kind of risks and benefits associated with the procedure for which consent is sought. This is clearest in the therapeutic relationship. The physician is not obligated to inform a patient of all aspects of treatment, but only of those aspects material to the patient's informed choice. Another way of expressing this point is that the physician is obligated to obtain patient consent for the proposed course of treatment, but not for every component of the actual treatment as it proceeds. As Donagan expresses it, "Advancing a claim to decide a course of treatment that one is to undergo in no way encroaches upon the physician's authority over how that course of treatment is to be carried out."[28]

Risk and benefit considerations and actual clinical circumstances are also relevant in the research-subject relationship, but they serve to constrain investigator authority rather than to enhance it, as in therapeutic relationships. Because advancing scientific knowledge is the primary goal of the research relationship, research ethics (as expressly stated in federal regulations) constrain the investigator to describe in detail the purposes of the research and the details of the subject's involvement. Even in cases where IRBs do not require that the consent forms include detailed discussion of every single aspect of the investigational procedure, the IRB is required to evaluate them in making an assessment of the risk-benefit ratio. Thus, the principal investigator is required to provide sufficient information in the protocol to permit the IRB to estimate the risk-benefit ratio even though the IRB may permit this information to be summarized and explained in lay language to prospective subjects in the consent form.

Unless subjects stand to benefit from the research in a substantial way—as is the case in some clinical research—the principle of respect for persons requires that autonomy be respected by according the individual maximal free choice. When free choice is problematic (e.g., with so-called captive subjects, namely, prisoners, the institutionalized mentally ill, and children), specific regulations apply which either proscribe or limit the involvement by placing burdens on the PI to justify involving these subjects and to develop additional methods for assuring that autonomy is respected. For example, in the case of the institutionalized mentally ill, an ombudsman or consent monitor might be used to assure that subjects are uncoerced by the principal investigator in securing consent. In the case of children, assent must be uncoerced (that is, agreement of a child to an experimental procedure is required in addition to informed consent from parents or guardians).

These requirements indicate that in the research relationship, consent is balanced by risk-benefit considerations and concern for subject welfare in such a way that the authority is located in the IRB primarily rather than the investigator. It is the IRB that has the authority to make the final judgment regarding the application of the required and additional elements of consent given the risk-benefit considerations of the particular protocol. In the therapeutic relationship, however, it is the physician who bears final responsibility for modifying consent requirements in order to enhance patient welfare. In both situations, however, the underlying principles are the same: respecting patient autonomy and protecting patient welfare. These goals serve as the touchstone for judging the ethical acceptability of a consent process, though their application can vary with the conditions just discussed.

In the case of clinical research, the standards of clinical medical ethics and research ethics overlay the problem of consent. Not surprisingly, then, consent in clinical experimentation is complex. One factor contributor to this complexity is that subjects are often under stress and naturally suffer from anxiety or other emotional reactions to illness. Consent to either experimentation with a therapeutic intention or nontherapeutic research under these circumstances, therefore, is problematic. Imposing a standard that simply demands consent ignores the subtleties associated with the actual competence of patients in clinical settings. In point of fact, there are degrees and qualities of consent that need to be distinguished.

As discussed earlier, consent itself must be seen in terms of patient competence, risk-benefit considerations, and the actual clinical circumstances surrounding the consent.

Along these lines, James F. Drane has proposed a "sliding-scale model" for determining competence.[29] The model involves three standards of consent which apply to different objective medical decisions. The first standard proposes the minimal requirements of *awareness* (orientation to one's medical situation) and *assent* (explicit or implicit acceptance or refusal). Such a standard would be appropriate for refusing, for example, an effective treatment or for consenting to effective treatment for acute illness or procedures involving high benefit and low risk where the alternatives are limited and where there is diagnostic certainty. Generally, emergency situations would meet these requirements.

The second standard involves the median requirements of *understanding* the medical situation and the proposed treatment and of *choice* based on medical outcomes. This standard would apply, for example, in the case of a chronic condition with a doubtful diagnosis or the case where the outcome of therapy for acute illness is uncertain, where risks and benefits of proposed interventions are balanced, or where a proposed treatment is possibly effective but burdensome.

The final standard involves the maximum requirements of *appreciation* (critical and reflective understanding of the illness and treatment) and *rational decision making* (making choices that reflect one's own articulated beliefs and values). This highest standard of competency is necessary for consent to ineffective treatment (i.e., experimental and unproven treatment) or for refusal of effective treatment for acute illness either where diagnostic certainty and benefit are high, risk is low, and there are limited alternatives or where the disorder is immediately life threatening. This approach is of particular interest because the standard of competency for *refusing* ineffective treatment is the minimal requirement of awareness and assent, whereas the competency standard for *consent* to ineffective treatment, including experimental treatment with a high risk to benefit ratio, is the maximum requirement of appreciation and rational decision making.

The threat of coercion is always present in clinical settings where patients suffer the stress of illness and disability and exhibit anxiety, grief, or psychological defense mechanisms.[30] There is a spectrum of cases to be sure. On the one side is the situation in which the physician is commonly perceived as "my doctor," who has "my interest" foremost; in such a case, a physician can often get a patient to agree to almost any procedure. The use of experimental procedures under such circumstances is problematic, because the possibility of subtle coercion is always present. However, if the procedure has minimal or low risk and the benefit is potentially great and no standard treatments are available, then consent that relies simply on patient assent and awareness might be justified. Alternatively, a device or drug might be justified for use if there is scientific evidence for its effectiveness but the drug or device has not yet received FDA approval. A minimal standard of consent could be justified, because the primary obligation of the physician in the clinical setting is the care of the patient. When experimental procedures have a relatively high degree of probability of enhancing patient welfare, consent that meets the minimal requirements set forth by Drane is adequate.

What might be an example of such a procedure or intervention? Consider the use of Cimetidine for duodenal ulcer. The drug was widely used abroad, with clinical results reported a number of years prior to its approval for use under FDA regulations. To be sure, the drug could not be used without conforming to FDA and IRB consent requirements, including the use of a detailed consent form. However, if the patient were to listen distractedly to the information, read the consent form perfunctorily, and sign it without evidence of complete understanding, would it be ethical for the physician to proceed to administer the medication? Here, the patient is compliant to such an extent that he would accept a *treatment* even if not fully informed. Of course, the physician is morally obligated to provide adequate information to his patient, but it does not seem that the physician is obligated to assure that the highest standard of comprehension is met in this circumstance if there are valid moral reasons for the patient's less-than-full understanding, because the investigational drug is so far along in the approval process that the therapy is more like a standard than an experimental one.

On the other side of the spectrum, patient defense mechanisms such as denial or regression, which might hinder a patient in assuming the necessary active role in therapy (consider the so-called cardiac cripple, who avoids even usual and desirable activities such as sexual relations for fear of inducing another attack), can lead to a patient's refusing the procedure. If the patient meets only the lowest standard of competence as described above, should the physician desist from offering an innovative or what Levine terms "a non-validated practice"? I think not. In this case, the obligation of the physician is to benefit his patient. He should work with the patient and family to attain a higher level of understanding. Of course, unless the situation is life threatening, the physician has to respect the patient's decision in the end no matter how minimal the standard of competence. The important point is that the initial refusal (based solely on the standard of assent and awareness) does not ethically justify the physician to go along with the patient and provide merely perfunctory care.

If a patient manifests denial of his illness, yet mistakenly—one might almost say, delusionally—believes that his participation in the research protocol would benefit others because it would provide normal control required by the experimental design, what standard of consent would need to be met? On the face of it, such a patient does not manifest sufficient understanding of his medical situation and the proposed experimental intervention to meet even median standards. Therefore, he could not validly consent to any experimental procedure that involved more than minimum risk. But would a minimal level of awareness and assent be adequate for experimentation involving minimal risk?

If one analyzes the situation from the point of view of the ethics of the physician-patient relationship, the answer must be that consent is not valid unless the patient were to benefit. Otherwise, one would simply *use* the patient for one's own end. Such an action would pervert the fiduciary and caring character of the physician-patient relationship. A researcher, however, is under no similar direct and overriding obligation to the subject. Therefore, the focus shifts from enhancing the patient's welfare in physician-patient relationships to respecting the subject's autonomy by providing full disclosure of information and by avoiding coercion in the process of recruitment.

In cases of experimentation with no or low benefits, meeting the highest standards of consent may not be achievable. For such cases, the authority for modifying consent requirements shifts from the investigator to the IRB, which is charged with balancing requirements of consent with considerations of risk and benefit in light of clinical circumstances. For example, the regulations governing human subjects research permit the waiver or alteration of informed consent requirements in cases in which the research involves minimal or no risk to the subject and in which the knowledge to be gained is significant. Specifically, federal regulations permit an IRB to approve a consent procedure which does not include, or which alters, some or all of the elements of informed consent or even to waive the requirements to obtain informed consent provided that the IRB finds and documents the following: (1) that the research involves no more than minimum risk to the patient; (2) that the waiver or alteration will not adversely effect the rights and welfare of the patient; (3) that the research could not practicably be carried out without the waiver or alteration; and (4) that patient will be provided, whenever appropriate, with additional pertinent information after participation.[31] The authority for determining whether these conditions apply in particular protocols rests with the IRB, not with the principal investigator. If the social good of advancing scientific knowledge is to compromise in any way the principle of informed consent, it is only the IRB, removed from the research itself, which can make such a determination.

The ethical justification of consent to experimentation in clinical settings involves consideration of the clinical circumstances, patient competence, and the risk-benefit ratio in the light of the intentions behind and the social objectives of the research and therapy. Underlying and justifying informed consent is the principle of respect for persons, which also requires that persons be protected—sometimes from their own choices, sometimes from their own or family members' intentions. The solution to the problem of consent, thus, inevitability depends on how one addresses the issue of paternalism. This latter question has not been addressed directly, but note that an answer to this question is implicit in the ways that consent requirements actually vary in therapeutic and research relationships. Whether these answers are paternalistic and whether they can be justified is another matter, one which requires further discussion.

NOTES

1. "Protection of Human Subjects," *Code of Federal Regulations* 45 CFR 46, revised March 8, 1983.

2. Martin S. Pernick, "The Patient's Role in Medical Decisionmaking: A Social History of Informed Consent in Medical Therapy," in President's Commission for the Study of Ethical Problems in Medicine and Biomedical and Behavioral Research, *Making Health Care Decisions*, vol. 3 (Washington, D.C.: GPO, 1982), 1–35; Jay Katz, *The Silent World of Doctor and Patient* (New York: Free Press; Macmillan, 1984).

3. Ruth R. Faden and Tom L. Beauchamp, *A History and Theory of Informed Consent* (New York: Oxford University Press, 1986), 125–132.

4. *Trials of War Criminals before the Nuremberg Military Tribunals under Control Council Law*, no. 10 (Washington, D.C.: GPO, 1949), 2.

5. Ibid.

6. "Protection of Human Subjects," sec. 46.116.

7. Ibid.

8. Faden and Beauchamp, *History and Theory*, 23–49, 114–50; Jay Katz, *Experimentation with Human Subjects* (New York: Russell Sage Foundation, 1972).

9. Larry R. Churchill, "Physician-Investigator/Patient-Subject: Exploring the Logic and Tension," *Journal of Medicine and Philosophy* 5 (1980): 215–24.

10. Talcott Parsons, "Research with Human Subjects and the 'Professional Complex,'" in *Experimentation with Human Subjects*, ed. Paul A. Freund (New York: George Braziller, 1970), 116–51.

11. World Medical Association, "Declaration of Helsinki," adopted by the 18th World Medical Assembly, Helsinki, Finland, 1964 and revised by the 29th World Medical Assembly, Tokyo, Japan, 1975.

12. A proposed but never implemented policy of HEW involved prohibiting entire categories of "non-beneficial research" without regard to consideration of risk involved. See Department of Health, Education and Welfare, "Proposed Policy," *Federal Register* 39 (August 23, 1974): 30648–57.

13. Karen Labacqz, "Reflections on the Report and Recommendations of the National Commission: Research on the Fetus," *Villanova Law Review* 22 (1977): 357–66; Robert J. Levine, "The Impact on Fetal Research of the Report of the National Commission for the Protection of Human Subjects of Biomedical and Behavioral Research," *Villanova Law Review* 22 (1977): 367–383; National Commission for the Protection of Subjects of Biomedical and Behavioral

Research," *Report and Recommendations: Research on the Fetus*, DHEW Publication no. (OS) 76-127 (Washington, D.C.: GPO, 1975).

14. National Commission for the Protection of Human Subjects of Biomedical and Behavioral Research, *The Belmont Report: Ethical Principles and Guidelines for the Protection of Human Subjects of Research*, DHEW Publication no. (OS) 78-0012 (Washington, D.C.: GPO, 1975).

15. Lebacqz, "Reflections," 362.

16. National Commission, *Belmont Report*, 2.

17. Robert J. Levine, "Clarifying the Concepts of Research Ethics," *Hastings Center Report* 9 (1979): 22.

18. National Commission, *Belmont Report*, 3.

19. Herman L. Blumgart, "The Medical Framework for Viewing the Problem of Human Experimentation," in *Experimentation with Human Subjects*, ed. Paul A. Freund (New York: George Braziller, 1970), 44.

20. Francis D. Moore, "Therapeutic Innovation: Ethical Boundaries in the Initial Clinical Trail of New Drugs and Surgical Procedures," in *Experimentation with Human Subjects*, ed. Paul A. Freund (New York: George Braziller, 1970), 358.

21. For discussion and analysis of a case that seems to meet these circumstances, see Stuart Frank and George J. Agich, "Non-therapeutic Research on Subjects Unable to Grant Consent," *Clinical Research* 33 (1985): 459–64.

22. World Medical Association, "Declaration of Helsinki."

23. Alan Donagan, "Informed Consent in Therapy and Experimentation," *Journal of Medicine and Philosophy* 2 (1977): 315.

24. The view of the adequacy of information in consent is developed by Charles M. Culver and Bernard Gert, *Philosophy in Medicine* (New York: Oxford University Press, 1982), 43–50.

25. Haavi Morreim, "Three Concepts of Patient Competence," *Theoretical Medicine* 4 (1983): 239–46.

26. Loren H. Roth et al., "Tests of Competency to Consent to Treatment," *American Journal of Psychiatry* 134 (1977): 274.

27. National Commission, *Belmont Report*, 4.

28. Donagan, "Informed Consent," 313.

29. James F. Drane, "Competency to Give an Informed Consent," JAMA 252 (1984): 925-927 and "The Many Faces of Competency," *Hastings Center Report* 15 (1985): 17–21.

30. For discussion of related concerns, see Stephen D. Mallary, *et al.,* "Family Coercion and Valid Consent," *Theoretical Medicine* 7 (1986): 123–26; Thomas Tomlinson, "The Physician's Influence on Patients' Choices," *Theoretical Medicine* 7 (1986): 105–21.

31. "Protection of Human Subjects," sec. 46.116–46.117.

BIBLIOGRAPHY

Faden, Ruth R., and Tom L. Beauchamp. *A History and Theory of Informed Consent*. New York: Oxford University Press, 1986. A comprehensive historical and theoretical discussion and analysis of informed consent in practice and research settings.

Katz, Jay. *Experimentation with Human Beings*. New York: Russell Sage Foundation, 1972. A comprehensive casebook with edited coverage of the principal documents pertaining to human subjects research and relevant secondary material; somewhat dated, but nonetheless an important work for consultation.

————. *Silent World of Doctor and Patient*. New York: The Free Press, 1986. Katz argues that disclosure and consent requirements, except the most rudimentary, are obligations which are alien to medical thinking and practice.

Levine, Robert J. *Ethics and Regulations of Clinical Research*, 2d ed. Baltimore, Md.: Urban, 1986. An overview of problems and present solutions regarding the ethics and regulation of clinical research; it is strongly orientated towards federal research guidelines.

National Commission for the Protection of Human Subjects of Biomedical and Behavioral Research. *The Belmont Report*. DHEW Publication no. (OS) 78-0012. Washington, D.C.: GPO, 1975. A summary of the ethical principles which guided the work of the National Commission. Importantly, this report came after the majority of the Commission's work was completed and is basically a reflection on the principles that guided its decision making rather than a justification of them.

Theoretical Medicine 7 (June 1986): 105–164; 181–194. An issue focusing on the physician's ways of influencing patient decision making, i.e., through persuasion, manipulation, and coercion.

Chapter 12

Quality of Life Judgments in the Care of the Elderly

Bernard Lo

Decisions about the care of incompetent patients commonly present ethical dilemmas. As discussed in Chapter 18, the recommended approach to decisions regarding an incompetent patient is to follow preferences that the patient previously expressed while competent. In many cases, however, such preferences are unclear or unknown; this chapter analyzes how to make decisions in this situation.

Writings on medical ethics and court rulings agree that when the incompetent patient's preferences are unknown or unclear, decisions should be based on the patient's *best interests*.[1] The patient's surrogate and the physician will need to weigh the benefits and burdens of the proposed treatments for that particular patient. In deciding what is best for a patient, the patient's functioning, emotional state, independence, privacy, dignity, and suffering are often assessed, as well as the duration of life. Such characteristics are often taken to constitute what is called the "quality of life." Competent patients may decline treatments that might prolong life, deciding that they would rather not be alive than endure the side effects, dependency, or indignity of treatment. Similarly, it seems reasonable that the length of survival should not be the only consideration in decisions regarding incompetent patients. Life-prolonging technology may not be considered appropriate, for example, in end stage dementia, when the patient might no longer be able to recognize relatives.

QUALITY OF LIFE

Different Definitions of Quality of Life

The term *quality of life* is ambiguous and is used in various ways, depending on who is making the assessment and what standards are applied. Some judgments of quality of life are based on patients' own values and preferences. Some patients may state that if they became severely demented, they would consider the quality of their life so unacceptable that they would not want pneumonia treated with antibiotics. Such patient preferences about quality of life should be respected.

Quality of life may also be judged by people other than the patient, using their own values rather than those of the patient. Because the quality of life is so subjective, such judgments by others must be interpreted cautiously. Observers may disagree over another person's quality of life.[2] Patients, families, physicians, and nurses may disagree in their assessments of a patient. When healthy people are asked how much they think life would be worth if they had a specific illness, they place less value on years of illness or disability than do the people who actually have the illness.[3] Life situations that would be intolerable to young, healthy people may be acceptable to older patients with chronic illness. Many elderly people have learned to cope with chronic illness, develop support systems, and continue to find substantial pleasure in life.

Problems in Judging Quality of Life

Assessments of quality of life made by someone other than the patient may be arbitrary, biased, and discriminatory. Observers may project their own values onto the patient, perhaps without even realizing it. Unconscious biases about quality of life are more likely to be recognized and compensated for if people with different viewpoints participate in decisions, including family members, nurses, and social workers.

Often it is unclear how a patient would assess the quality of his or her life in a particular clinical situation. Family members and health professionals then may try to infer what would be the patient's assessment from their knowledge about the patient. Although they are attempting to determine what judgment the patient would make, they may actually be imposing their own value judgments. For example, if a patient had been reluctant to see physicians, or loved to read or garden, care givers may conclude that the patient would not want life prolonged if severely demented. However, such inferences might go well beyond the evidence and mistake what actually would have been the patient's wishes.

Certain uses of the term *quality of life* should be avoided. Assessments of quality of life are sometimes based on economic value to society, social worth, or comparisons with other patients. Because the elderly have less income, less economic productivity, and higher medical costs than other groups, such considerations may lead to bias and discrimination against the elderly.[4] Therefore, such considerations are not appropriate in making bedside medical decisions.

Quality of life assessments sometimes consider burdens to the family, such as economic costs or psychosocial stress. While it is acceptable for the patient to consider these factors in assessing quality of life, it is less acceptable for others to do so. Families who infer, for example, that the patient would not want to live if their savings were depleted may be confounding their own interests with those of the patient.

Assessments of quality of life often are most needed in situations where they are most likely to be flawed. When the patient's own preferences and values are known, decisions can be based on those preferences without reference to quality of life. But if an incompetent patient's preferences are unclear or unknown, then quality of life becomes a more important consideration. (See Chapter 8 on competency.) For an incompetent, critically ill patient with poor prognosis, a caregiver might argue that the anticipated quality of life, even if treatment is successful, is so poor that life would not be worth living. However, as we have discussed, when the patient's quality of life is judged without clear evidence of the patient's own preferences, judgments can be arbitrary or biased.

Suggestions

To avoid the above mentioned problems, some have suggested that consideration of quality of life is justified only in strictly limited situations. Jonsen and colleagues propose that only when the patient falls below a minimal threshold of irreversible loss of cognition and communication (as in a persistent vegetative state) should quality of life be regarded as a *decisive* factor in decisions.[5] This precept, however, does not address the more general question of when and how quality of life factors may be given *some* weight by the surrogates and physicians of incompetent patients whose preferences are not known.

Another suggestion to overcome subjectivity and bias in judgments of quality of life is to adopt a "reasonable person standard": Would a reasonable person in this situation judge the quality of life to be acceptable enough to accept treatment?[6] This approach shifts attention from assessments of quality of life to judgments about what treatments are appropriate in particular clinical situations. This standard would not attempt to follow that individual patient's preferences, but instead would identify a range of acceptable decisions. Within this acceptable range, the surrogate and physician can make a mutual decision based on their own values. The reasonable person standard, however, may be impractical, because in America there is no consensus about what quality of life or treatments a reasonable person would consider acceptable. Suggestions have been made to poll elderly people with different illnesses to determine if there is agreement that certain conditions offer such poor quality of life that almost no one would choose life-sustaining treatment. But such polls have not been conducted, and there is no consensus on how much agreement would be needed before a policy of no treatment could be adopted. Hence, suggestions about a reasonable person standard are not clinically useful. At the present time, appeals to a reasonable person standard tend to be disguises for mere speculation or guesswork. In contrast, in Great Britain there is a social, political, and medical consensus that it is not reasonable for frail or severely demented elderly patients to be hospitalized or receive intensive care, even for such treatable diseases as pneumonia or myocardial infarction. It is considered reasonable, however, to provide extensive home care and geriatric day care.[7]

These problems with judgments about quality of life should motivate care givers to ask competent patients about their preferences in advance. Such advance discussions may be effective preventive medicine for ethical dilemmas about incompetent patients.

EXTERNAL CONSIDERATIONS

Although decisions about medical care should be based on the medical indications for treatment and on the patient's wishes or best interests, external considerations may also be important. It is important to recognize these external factors, because they may be confounded with assessments of the patient's quality of life. Reimbursement systems and the cost of care increasingly influence decisions.[8] Prospective payment under Medicare offers hospitals incentives to shorten acute care hospitalizations for elderly patients. Care givers may be placed in the role of financial watchdogs for the hospitals in addition to having their traditional role of serving patients. While limiting care that is superfluous or not beneficial poses no ethical dilemmas, physicians also face incentives to cut beneficial care. For patients and the public to maintain trust in physicians, there must be no suspicion that physicians withhold significantly beneficial treatments from patients in order to save money for hospitals.[9]

Pressures on physicians to contain costs are particularly difficult because the U.S. has no comprehensive health policy to guide restrictions in care. While no one would disagree that treatments that provide insignificant benefits but are inordinately expensive are not indicated, it is unclear in practice what proportion of benefits to costs is reasonable. Rather than setting priorities in health care and making tradeoffs among competing health care needs, the U.S. is trying to contain costs by financial and administrative restrictions. Medicare payments for diagnosis related groups (DRGs) are based on statistical averages. The categories do not comprise homogeneous groups of patients; some in each category will be much sicker than others. Moreover, the relative reimbursement for various DRG categories does not reflect health care needs or priorities. Patients may be harmed if doctors fail to appreciate that such reimbursements are averages and that the hospital should not expect to make a profit on every patient or on every diagnosis related group. In decisions regarding the care of individual patients, these economic considerations generally should not be decisive. For example, the financial costs to society should not be considered in assessing the patient's quality of life unless the patient himself or herself wanted this to be done.

Another external factor is fear of malpractice suits or criminal charges. Legal concerns sometimes may deter physicians from withholding life-sustaining treatment, even if the patient or surrogate does not want such treatment.[10]

Finally, danger to other people sometimes justifies overriding the patient's wishes or interests. For example, a patient may leave food on the kitchen stove and start fires. If less restrictive measures, such as taking the knobs off the stove or arranging for geriatric day care, are ineffective, then involuntary placement in supervised housing may be justified.

SPECIFIC CLINICAL DECISIONS

"Extraordinary" Care

Advanced technology like kidney dialysis or mechanical ventilation gives rise to dramatic ethical dilemmas. Such care is often termed "extraordinary" or "heroic" and distinguished from "ordinary" care. This distinction, however, is ambiguous and confusing.[11] All medical treatments have benefits and burdens. The appropriateness of a treatment depends not on the nature of the treatment, but on whether the patient judges that the benefits outweigh the burdens in a particular clinical situation. Thus a patient may not want "ordinary" treatments like antibiotics for pneumonia to be given if the patient had become severely demented.

Decisions to withhold one type of life-sustaining treatment do not preclude other treatments. Strictly speaking, a "Do Not Resuscitate" (DNR) order means only that cardiopulmonary resuscitation will not be initiated in case of cardiopulmonary arrest.[12] Decisions about other care need to be made separately. A patient with a DNR order might still receive antibiotics for infection. Supportive care to relieve symptoms like pain is always indicated, no matter what other treatment is withheld.

Tube feedings in severely demented patients who cannot take adequate nourishment by hand are a controversial and emotional issue.[13] Some people consider adequate nutrition ordinary care that must always be given, because feeding symbolizes caring and affection for the helpless. However, recent court decisions have ruled that artificial feedings must be considered in the same way as other medical treatments; they have burdens and benefits that must be weighed in each case. The benefits may be small when severely demented patients consistently refuse feedings by hand. It is unlikely such patients suffer from hunger or thirst. In addition, demented patients cannot appreciate why the artificial feedings are being given. The burdens may be particularly onerous when patients are sedated or physically restrained to keep them from repeatedly pulling out feeding tubes. Such measures, which compromise whatever dignity and independence these patients retain, are difficult to reconcile with the goal of humane care.[14]

Nursing home placement may be an agonizing decision, since the patient's wishes or interests may conflict with the family's interests or resources. The family may lack the finances, time, or patience to provide adequate care at home, even with home help or geriatric day care. Expectations of family responsibility for the elderly are changing. Nuclear families are smaller and geographically dispersed. Women, the traditional care givers for elderly parents, now often work outside the home. A minimum standard of care is required by laws on elder abuse. Most people would agree that families have a duty to make reasonable sacrifices to care for demented patients. However, there is no agreement on how much sacrifice is heroic rather than reasonable—and therefore admirable but not obligatory.[15]

Decisions are even more difficult if the patient had requested of the family never to be "put away" in a nursing home. One ethical problem is whether respecting the patient's wishes or keeping a promise is an absolute duty. Is the family morally required to do literally everything to fulfill a promise?[16] Or is the obligation to do what is reasonable? And how is this decided, since people will have different interpretations of what is reasonable? The dilemma also illustrates how unconditional statements by patients about future care may be inflexible and impractical.

For patients residing in nursing homes, special ethical problems may occur. Even simple tests like a chest x-ray may be difficult to obtain. For the patient who develops a fever or cough or has a worsening mental status, several options are available: transfer to an acute care hospital for evaluation and treatment, empirical treatment with antibiotics, or supportive care with oxygen and antipyretics.[17] In some cases, allowing the patient to die comfortably may seem the most humane course. Often such decisions are made unilaterally by physicians based on what they believe is best for the patient or on how reversible the disease appears to be. In other cases, decisions follow implicit agreements between physicians and families. It is possible that concern about discrimination against frail patients in nursing homes will lead to more explicit or more formal decision making procedures. For instance, in New Jersey the Office of the Ombudsman must investigate all cases of withholding life-sustaining treatment from nursing home patients as possible cases of elder abuse.[18] As discussed in Chapter 18, wider use of advance directives may be more effective than governmental review for safeguarding these vulnerable patients.

PRACTICAL SUGGESTIONS FOR CARE GIVERS

In making decisions about the care of incompetent patients whose preferences are unclear or unknown, care givers may find the following suggestions useful.

1. *Anticipate future problems by discussing patient preferences in advance, while patients are still competent.* Advance directives are the most satisfactory way to make decisions for incompetent patients.

2. *Clarify the medical facts about the patient's diagnosis and prognosis.* In geriatrics, reversible diseases are often overlooked or misdiagnosed. An elderly patient's condition may be too quickly judged to be irreversible. Sound ethical judgments presuppose that the medical facts are correct. For example, nursing home placement may be debated for a patient with dementia. If his recent deterioration in mental status is due to depression, drug effect, or superimposed acute illness, then dilemmas about placement can be avoided if the patient can return home after reversible factors are corrected.

3. *Determine the patient's wishes.* Asking family members to report the incompetent patient's previously stated wishes, rather than their own preferences, may reduce guilt. The physician might say, "We'd like to do what your mother would want. Did she ever talk about what care she would want in a situation like this?"

4. *Discuss emotional reactions explicitly.* Leading questions may be needed to initiate discussions: "Many families feel guilty thinking about nursing homes. Do you ever feel that way?" Ambivalence and frustration need to be recognized as normal reactions. Acknowledging such emotions may lessen their impact on decisions. Moreover, practical measures may be taken to decrease frustration, such as arranging for more home help or for respite care.

5. *Discuss the decision with all members of the health care team.* In geriatrics, care givers with different perspectives may contribute fresh information, point out unquestioned assumptions, or suggest alternative ways to resolve a dilemma. House officers and nurses carry out the orders of the attending physician and often have more direct contact with patients and families. They need to understand the reasoning behind the decision and to have their concerns addressed. Persistent disagreements are often a warning to rethink the decision. An institutional ethics committee may help resolve such disagreements.

6. *Pay attention to the practical details of care.* Imaginative practical solutions can often be arranged even when philosophical disagreements persist. For instance, if a patient leaves the stove on in the kitchen, there is a conflict between the duty to respect the patient's wish to manage his own house and the duty to prevent harm to others. This ethical conflict can often be resolved by removing the knobs from the stove, installing devices to turn off the gas automatically, or arranging for geriatric day care.

7. *Play an active role in decision making.* The physician should make a recommendation rather than merely present options and leave the family of an incompetent patient to choose.[19] The physician who assumes an active role helps relieve families of guilt. In some cases, there are no therapeutic alternatives or choices. For example, septic shock may persist despite appropriate antibiotics and pressor agents. In such a situation, where the patient will die in a few days no matter what treatment is given, further treatment is not medically indicated, regardless of the wishes of the family or patient. It is a mistake to give them the impression that a therapeutic choice exists.

CONCLUSION

Ethical dilemmas occur when elderly patients are incompetent to make decisions about their health care. When a patient's preferences are unknown or unclear, decisions based on assessments of the patient's quality of life may be controversial or biased. In weighing the best interests of such patients, care givers should pay attention to emotional reactions, communication, and the practical details of care and they should play an active role in decision making.

NOTES

1. President's Commission for the Study of Ethical Problems in Medicine and Biomedical and Behavioral Research, *Deciding to Forego Life-sustaining Treatment* (Washington, D.C.: GPO, 1983), 43–90; B. Lo and L. Dornbrand, "The Case of Claire Conroy: Will Administrative Review Safeguard Incompetent Patients?" *Annals of Internal Medicine* 104 (1986): 869–73.

2. T.J. Starr, R.A. Perlman, and R.F. Uhlmann, "Quality of Life and Resuscitation Decisions in Elderly Patients," *Journal of General Internal Medicine* 1 (1986): 373–79.

3. J. Avorn. "Benefit and Cost Analysis in Geriatric Care: Turning Age Discrimination into Health Policy," *New England Journal of Medicine* 310 (1984): 955–59.

4. Ibid.

5. A.R. Jonsen, M. Siegler, and W.J. Winslade, *Clinical Ethics* (New York: Macmillan, 1982), 109–24.

6. D.C. Thomasma, "Quality of Life Judgments, Treatment Decisions and Medical Ethics," *Clinics in Geriatric Medicine* 2 (1986): 17–27.

7. N. Daniels, "Why Saying No to Patients in the United States Is So Hard," *New England Journal of Medicine* 314 (1986): 1380–83.

8. S. McPhee, B. Lo, G. Charles, "Cost Containment Confronts Physicians," *Annals of Internal Medicine* 100 (1984): 604–5.

9. N.G. Levinsky, "The Doctor's Master," *New England Journal of Medicine* 311 (1984): 1573–75.

10. B. Lo, "The Death of Clarence Herbert: Withdrawing Care Is Not Murder," *Annals of Internal Medicine* 101 (1984): 248–51.

11. Ibid.

12. B. Lo and R.S. Steinbrook, "Deciding Whether to Resuscitate," *Archives of Internal Medicine* 143 (1983): 1561–63.

13. M. Siegler and A.J. Weisbart, "Against the Emerging Stream: Should Fluids and Nutritional Support be Discontinued?" *Archives of Internal Medicine* 145 (1985): 129–31; B. Lo and L. Dornbrand, "Guiding the Hand That Feeds: Caring for the Demented Elderly," *New England Journal of Medicine* 311 (1984): 402–4.

14. Lo and Dornbrand, "Guiding the Hand That Feeds."

15. C.K. Cassel and A.L. Jameton, "Dementia in the Elderly: An Analysis of Medical Responsibility," *Annals of Internal Medicine* 94 (1981): 802–7.

16. R.M. Veatch, *A Theory of Medical Ethics* (New York: Basic Books, 1981), 177–89.

17. D. Hilfiker, "Allowing the Debilitated to Die: Facing Our Ethical Choices," *New England Journal of Medicine* 308 (1983): 716–19.

18. Starr, Perlman and Uhlmann, "Quality of Life."

19. F.J. Ingelfinger, "Arrogance," *New England Journal of Medicine* 303 (1980): 1507–11.

BIBLIOGRAPHY

Avorn, J. "Benefit and Cost Analysis in Geriatric Care: Turning Age Discrimination into Health Policy." *New England Journal of Medicine* 310 (1984): 955–59. Avorn argues that cost-benefit analyses contain assumptions about quality of life that are biased against the elderly.

Jonsen, A.R., M. Siegler, and W.J. Winslade. *Clinical Ethics*. New York: Macmillan, 1982. A concise, clear review of concept of quality of life is given on pp. 109–24.

Lo, B., and L. Dornbrand. "The Case of Claire Conroy: Will Administrative Review Safeguard Incompetent Patients?" *Annals of Internal Medicine* 104 (1986): 869–73. Analysis of an important legal decision regarding decisions about life-sustaining treatment for an elderly incompetent patient.

Starr, T.J., R.A. Perlman, and R.F. Uhlmann. "Quality of Life and Resuscitation Decisions in Elderly Patients." *Journal of General Internal Medicine* 1 (1986): 373–79. Empirical study showing that patients and physicians disagree in assessments of quality of life.

Thomasma, D.C. "Quality of Life Judgments, Treatment Decisions and Medical Ethics." *Clinics in Geriatric Medicine* 2 (1986): 17–27. Analysis of which differences between elderly and younger patients are morally relevant for decisions about medical care.

Chapter 13

Elder Abuse: Mandatory Reporting

Joel Brumlik and
Stephanie A. Brumlik

You are called to the emergency room at 2 A.M. When you arrive, the nurse informs you that an elderly woman was found by her neighbor on the floor of her own home lying in a pool of blood. She was brought to the emergency room by paramedics. You examine her and find her to be unresponsive, with a two-inch laceration over her right forehead that is still oozing blood despite a pressure dressing. Her general appearance is unkempt; her teeth are in poor repair and her hair is matted. The neighbor who accompanied her says that the woman was found in the center of the living room floor and she could not see how the woman could have hit her head. She says that the woman lives with her husband, but he was not at home.

At 7 A.M., her husband arrives at the emergency room. He says that his wife has been drinking a case of beer a day for the past 30 years. Last night she got drunk again and fell asleep on the living room floor. He confides in you that he has been attending Al-Anon meetings, and on their suggestion he allowed her to sleep on the floor and he spent the night with a friend. She was "fine" when he left. His best guess is that their dog bit her, causing her forehead laceration. He substantiates this theory by relating that every time his wife got drunk, she would beat the dog. You learn that the blood alcohol level and drug screen are negative.

The patient is now awake, although confused. She tells you that she "takes only an occasional nip." She is not able to provide an explanation as to why she was found on the floor or why there is a cut on her forehead. The question now is, Do you suspect elder abuse? If so, by whom? And how can you best serve your patient?

Our population is aging. The elderly were 3 percent of the nation in 1900 and will be 11 percent in 1990. Only 6 percent of the elderly live in institutions and they are usually chronically ill or have no one to care for them. Most of our elderly live at home with their spouse (50 percent); one in seven live with a son or daughter.[1]

"One of the sad myths of our society is that old people are not looked after by relatives and friends as they should be."[2] It would be self-assuring to say that all elderly are well-cared for by family and friends, but some are not. Some are exploited financially, others are abused physically, and still others are neglected to the point of hurt. This general kind of social ill in its various forms and degrees has been labeled *elder abuse*. Some characterize a typical abused elder as older than average, middle class, white, frail, mentally or physically

148

impaired, highly dependent on others for daily needs and abused psychologically by relatives.[3] Others say that the most vulnerable to physical, psychological,and multiple abuse are white women who live with a spouse and are between 66 and 83 years old, not severely ill, and have incomes of $7000 or less.[4]

Statistics regarding the frequency of elder abuse can be misleading. They have been gathered from uncontrolled studies based on anecdotal cases and they contain no uniform definition of *elder*, let alone *elder abuse*.

In 1980, for instance, the estimated number of those suffering elder abuse was about 50,000 to 250,000, or 10 percent of the population over age 65.[5] The estimated incidence in 1986 was 200,000 to 500,000.[6] This latter figure can only be a projection at best, since it was reported before the end of 1986. Therefore, we believe the problem may be exaggerated. One of the few controlled studies available states "society has every reason to believe that the majority of frail elderly live comfortably at home, receiving care from family members who are willing and prepared to perform services."[7] What must be dealt with is that smaller group of frail elderly who live with relatives who are unable or unwilling to care for them in a humane manner. To this end, most states have now enacted mandatory reporting laws for elder abuse. Armed with new statutes from legislatures, an army of social workers has gone forth to help.

A discussion of mandatory reporting of elder abuse must be taken in context. It does little good to have a mandatory reporting law that ends with the investigation itself or does not result in an improved level of care for the individual. What constitutes elder abuse? Shall it be reported? If so, how shall the laws be written? What penalties, if any, shall attach to violation of these laws? Mandatory reporting of abuse in context is simply one step toward alleviating a social injustice and providing care and protection for a helpless family member who cannot protect him/herself. We must look at the entire picture of elder abuse and at the real nature of the "corrective" system into which mandatory reporting casts both the guilty and the innocent.[8]

HISTORICAL PERSPECTIVE

The current statutes regarding elder abuse trace their origins to the ancient concept of *parens patriae* (the parenthood of the state) drawn from English chancery laws justifying the English Crown's assumption of the parental role in order to protect the estates of orphaned minors. Although the original concept of *parens patriae* might have been formulated with the best intentions, it has developed over the centuries to mean that the state is the ultimate parent of all individuals and, therefore, has everyone's best interest in mind. This might seem acceptable to some, but it seriously limits the role of the family. It is now socially acceptable to assume that parents do not have the best interest of their children in mind if they make decisions with which the state disagrees. As the Illinois Supreme Court, in a sweeping judgement, ruled in 1882,

> It is the unquestioned right and imperative duty of every enlightened government, in its character of *parens patriae*, to protect and provide for the comfort and well-being of such of its citizens as, by reason of infancy, defective understanding, or other misfortune or infirmity, are unable to take care of themselves. The performance of this duty is justly regarded as one of the most important of governmental

functions, and all constitutional limitations must be so understood and construed so as not to interfere with its proper and legitimate exercise.[9]

Having circumvented parental and constitutional rights, this judgement set a tone that is still being heard a century later.

The first to feel the effect of this judgement were children. Since the problem of elder abuse has far less historical precedent, an overview of how protective policies concerning children came into being and how they function will help us understand what is now being advocated for our aged population.

The juvenile justice movement of the 1890s—the first overt application of social science and social work to the law—has been enshrined in liberal mythology as a radical break with the past and a progressive, humane advance in public policy. It was, in fact, none of these. The informality of the new juvenile courts—no formal charges, no trial, no rules of evidence, no right of counsel, no right to confront one's accusers, indeterminate sentencing—merely represented new codifications of Constitution-straddling systems existing since the mid-1800s.[10]

According to Miriam Van Waters, perhaps the most widely read defender of the juvenile court system, social workers held a clear view of the healthy family, where "the father is dominant but not cruel or mean," where the mother "is comfortable" and "not restlessly seeking her life gratification apart from mate and children," and where both parents "genuinely love and enjoy children."[11] In her book *Parents on Probation*, she argued that "hardly a family in America is not engaging in the same practices, falling into the same attitudes, committing the same blunders which . . . bring the court families to catastrophe." She looked forward to the day when children would be "severed from parents who violated the right of the child to sanity and integrity of mind and body." On that great day, the parent would throw himself into the therapeutic arms of social work, "willingly cooperate in a plan for his own welfare," and then face "the superparent, which is mankind [with a] face stained with tears [saying] 'Sure, I'll make good.'"[12]

That "great day" has arrived in the United States. Based upon nothing more than an anonymous phone call, individuals with no more education than a high school diploma can descend upon a family and remove the children to foster care. All of this can be done without benefit of a warrant; the parents are not allowed to know what the accusation is nor who made it. The accuser is presumed to be reporting in "good faith" and the parents are presumed guilty until proven innocent. A parent who "cooperates in a plan for his own welfare" generally has the children returned promptly. Parents who, through innocence and a basic trust in the American judicial system, choose to defend themselves will have no right to a trial by jury and will be faced with a separation from their children, perhaps for years. All of this is allegedly in the best interest of the child.

Some have remained calm in the face of "abuse hysteria" by the public. Justice Abe Fortas directly attacked *parens patriae*, noting that "its meaning is murky and its historic credentials are of dubious relevance. . . . [T]here is no trace of the doctrine in the history of criminal jurisprudence." He concluded. "Juvenile court history has again demonstrated that unbridled discretion, however benevolently motivated, is frequently a poor substitute for principle and procedure."[13]

Utah Supreme Court Justice Dallin Oaks stated, "This parental right [to rear one's children] transcends all property and economic rights. It is rooted not in state or federal statutory or constitutional law, to which it is logically and chronologically prior, but in nature and human instinct.'' There is no surer way to destroy authentic pluralism, Oaks added, than by terminating the rights of parents who violate the ''trendy'' definitions and ''officially approved values imposed by reformers empowered to determine what is in the 'best interest' of someone else's child.'' While not suggesting evil motives, he did quote James Madison: ''It is proper to take alarm at the first experiment on our liberties.''[14]

Although we can draw hope from the statements of both Justice Fortas and Justice Oaks, we cannot falsely conclude that all is well with the mandated child abuse reporting system. Before a family would be before the bench of either justice, there would literally be the expenditure of years, fortunes, and the childhoods of the children, (probably spent in foster care). Even if innocent families never were harmed by the present system, even if no child ever were wrongfully placed in foster care, and even if everyone agreed that the surrender of our civil liberties was not too high a price, our present child protection laws would suffer from one fundamental problem: They don't work. Of all the children in the United States believed to have died of child abuse or neglect, an estimated 25 percent were known to child protective agencies at the time of their deaths.[15]

In 1962, the ''battered child syndrome'' was identified by pediatric physicians. Since 1962, the ''battered wife syndrome'' and the ''battered elder syndrome'' have also been identified, in both cases by social workers. Social workers' livelihoods depend directly upon ''discovering'' social ills. Therapists can earn up to $1000 per day for treating and testifying on child abuse. As one psychologist admits, ''Therapists love child abuse because it makes more work for them. There hasn't been a lot done on the fact that the growth in statistics on child abuse comes from people in whose advantage it is to discover it.''[16] If therapists do indeed enjoy financial benefits from the existence of child abuse, it would seem reasonable that any other kind of abuse would be just as rewarding.

WHAT IS ELDER ABUSE?

Doctors, nurses, and other health professionals, indeed almost all who work with the elderly, have had personal experiences with individual cases such as the following.

In December of 1977, the Baltimore Sun reported the case of an 82-year-old woman who was starving to death in a slum. She was found curled up in bed, her emaciated body covered only by a nightgown, lying in a pool of her own feces. Her house was in disarray. A window was missing from the front door. Anyone could have entered, assaulted her, and taken her belongings. No one was able to help her, despite valiant efforts by visiting nurses and other agencies. Her daughter-in-law controlled and spent her money and refused agency requests to intervene.[17]

One study reported on a nefarious case of ''plant clipping.'' A resident in a nursing home noticed that her favorite plant seemed to be growing smaller. It was later discovered that staff members were clipping ''starts'' from the plant without permission. This case has been used to support the hypothesis that thievery in nursing homes is the most frequent and insidious crime against the aged.[18] It is also included in the statistics with physically abusive beatings.

There was a woman of unknown age who had forced her adult son to move from her home because of his drug abuse. He later returned and broke into her home, stealing to support his drug habit.[19] The woman was at work during the break-in, so this raises the question of whether she could legitimately be considered elderly. This case also appears in the statistics, which further illustrates how they are skewed.

Before *elder abuse* can be defined, there must be an adequate definition of *elder*. Out of 50 states, 9 do not have any law governing reports of in-home adult or elder abuse, 17 states have chosen to combine disabled adults with the elderly and have legislation that mandates reporting of abuse of anyone 18 or older, 12 states define "elder" legislatively as 60 or older, 1 state uses the arbitrary age of 55, 4 states do not include any age, and the remaining 7 states consider 65 to be the age at which one becomes an elder.[20]

Legislatively, there is no consistency on what constitutes abuse. For example, in Massachusetts the following definitions were placed into law (emphasis is added):

Warning signs that a relationship *may* be abusive include:
1. The elder *seems* unduly afraid of the care-giver or unduly compliant.
2. Untreated sores or decubitus ulcers, burns.
3. The *elder* says the injuries were due to improbable causes.
4. Evidence of overall poor care, poor hygiene, poor grooming.
5. Inappropriate food, drink, or medication.
6. Signs of malnutrition.
7. The caretaker *seems* unable to meet the elder's needs.
8. Lack of supervision.
9. Elder needs medical attention.
10. Home maintenance is poor, repairs needed, heating inadequate.[21]

In regard to warning signs 1 and 7, there are no guidelines as to how to arrive at the judgment called for. In regard to warning sign 3, there is no allowance for the credibility of the elder who might be impaired mentally by age or disease. Warning sign 10 requires nothing more than poverty to be met and warning signs 4 and 5 might only indicate a cultural difference.

At the other extreme, Delaware defines only *exploitation*. The fact that the definitions do not tally in the particulars is important: What may seem to be obvious abuse may not be so as defined by law. However, it would probably be generally accepted that there are six primary types of elder abuse:[22]

1. *Physical abuse:* the infliction of physical harm (beatings, burns, restraints)
2. *Physical neglect:* refusal to provide assistance with activities of daily living or required medications or physical therapy
3. *Psychological abuse:* verbal assaults, threats
4. *Psychological neglect:* isolation, lack of attention, deprivation of social contact
5. *Material abuse:* theft or misuse of money and/or property
6. *Violation of rights:* forcing placement in a nursing home against an elder's will or preventing free use of money

Even these categories do not answer the question, What is elder abuse? Are the restraints alluded to under category 1 always abusive or are they periodically necessary in the case of a demented or confused individual? Under category 6, there might be instances where an elder does not wish to leave his or her home and yet can no longer adequately care for himself or herself. If the family intervenes to ensure proper care, is that a violation of rights?

If the family does not intervene, is that physical neglect? What about the woman who "tied" her aged mother to a chair so she could finish the housework? Is this abuse or care? And what about the 70-year-old man with Alzheimer's disease who confusedly would take all the living room furniture and place it on the lawn every morning and then wander off? Should his wife lock the door and keep the key? Is this an infringement of her husband's rights? Or is she sincerely caring for him? What would constitute abuse in the case of one person might be in another individual's best interests.

Uncontrolled studies and anecdotal reports characterize physical abuse as "mild to moderate," psychological abuse as "moderate to severe," and economic abuse as "moderate."[23] Similar studies stereotype the abused elder as passive, socially isolated, and compliant. Abusers of the elderly are depicted as possessive, confused as to their roles in life, with a tendency to externalize blame and displace anger. They have poor impulse control, lack empathy with the elder, and come from a violent background.[24] Alleged external factors involved in producing abuse of the elderly include society's attitude towards the dependent elder (and indeed toward old age itself), the dependency of the elder, and stress experienced by the care giver.

Controlled studies are rare. One such study compared a group of the elderly whose relationships were characterized as "abusive, neglectful" with another whose relationships were characterized as "good."[25] Contrary to what one might expect on the basis of the above uncontrolled studies, there were no significant differences between the "good relationship" group and the "abused group" regarding vulnerability of the elders, physical functioning, and high stress levels. These factors seemed to be shared by families that grow old together, whether there is abuse or not. The only four parameters that were lower in the "abused" group were "friends who call on the phone," "people who correspond," "people who call in times of trouble," and "family members in the house available to help."

WILL LEGAL INTERVENTION HELP?

Many are the proponents of mandatory reporting. Block and Davidson drafted what they considered an ideal mandatory reporting law for elder abuse.[26] *Elder* was defined as over 60 years of age; *abuse* was characterized as physical, psychological, material, or violation of rights; reporting was to be made on the basis of *questionable suspicion* and a mandated reporter was to report *all* incidents where abuse was either known or suspected without having to identify either intent or the perpetrator. No complaint would have to be signed; the reporter was presumed to be acting in "good faith." Reporters included doctors, nurses, social workers, administrators of care centers for the aged, social security counselors, volunteers, and funeral directors. Though Block and Davidson would have us believe that departments of social services or their equivalents focus on a program of help rather than criminal procedure, it is best not to be deceived: the state attorney's office is a phone call away and the social workers are also mandated to report any possible criminal act.[27] Social service and criminal prosecution are not mutually exclusive.

Legal intervention includes temporary alternate shelter or guardianship.[28] The question of whether an elder may refuse services has been raised, and the answer, in general, is yes.[29] But in most cases, as Whitehead opines, "Legal intervention will help no one."[30] Help is temporary at best, and without correcting the fundamental problem, the elder cannot return home.

While out of the home, the problem is temporarily at bay but nothing has been done to help the abuser control his or her behavior. The abuse may simply be transferred to another family member, friend, or neighbor.[31]

Will counseling help? There are no controlled studies to show that it will. Will financial aid help? An unloving alcoholic may drink the money away. Will design of the home to make it safe for the elder be effective? There have been no studies done to verify this. What is logical is not often effective in real life.

Nursing home placement is not the answer either. Abuse can take place there as well as at home.[32] And it is not necessarily "third class" nursing homes that provide substandard care. Physical, psychological, and financial harm comes to elders in nursing homes where the person is maltreated and abandoned by nurses, doctors, and loved ones alike. The nursing home experience, like foster care for abused children, is not nirvana. There is every reason to believe that hideous acts are as often encountered in nursing homes as within the family.[33]

MANDATORY REPORTING OF ELDER ABUSE

> Someone must have been telling lies about Joseph K., for without having done anything wrong he was arrested one fine morning.
>
> —Franz Kafka, *The Trial*

One assumption that underlies mandatory reporting laws is that elder abuse is "under-reported." It is more common, it is said, than anyone suspects. It has been alleged that health professionals hesitate to report because of the fear of falsely accusing the family or invading its privacy. Further, symptoms of elder abuse resemble normal aging. Finally, abused elders are often reluctant to report abuse from loved ones, because of the embarrassment of such problems in their families and because of feared retaliation from the abuser and possible forced institutionalization.[34]

So, if elder abuse is under-reported (although we do not know that it is), it has seemed reasonable to many to require everyone who is potentially in contact with an elder to report suspected abuse under threat of penalty. "Elder abuse requires a certain amount of suspicion. Because the victim is unlikely to volunteer information, the health care worker must play detective."[35] It has been advocated that photographs be taken of suspected victims (possibly without their permission).[36] But writers on the topic admit that apparent signs and symptoms of abuse may in fact be due to the aging process itself. Increased capillary fragility leads to easy bruising. Poor vision, imbalance, and mental confusion lead to falls, which, coupled with osteoporosis, makes for easy fractures.

The mandate puts twofold pressure on the health professional: the wish to provide maximum care to the patient and the fear of getting into trouble him- or herself. It creates an atmosphere that tends to cause over-reporting, which is then taken as support for the measures for which the elder-savers are lobbying. Also, with *all* health professionals mandated to report abuse, while an emergency room doctor might not believe an elder has been abused, the floor nurse might think otherwise and make a report. The elder-savers would then have "caught" two culprits—the "abusing" family and the nonreporting emergency room doctor, who possibly would now have to face misdemeanor charges or suspension of licence. The environment becomes one of suspicion—suspicion of patients' families, colleagues, and other personnel. The attitude easily becomes one of report before *you* are reported. As in Kafka's famous novel, the atmosphere of a police state would be upon us.

By making the report, has the health professional fulfilled his or her obligation and thus, like Pontius Pilate, be able to wash his or her hands of it? If the case has merit, won't the victim be protected? And if not, the authorities will soon set things right, won't they? But herein lies the fallacy: The victim is *not* protected and may be returned to the same situation unchanged or be placed in a nursing home. Block and Sinnot found that 95 percent of the reported victims received no assistance![37] The alleged abuser may or may not accede to counseling. If the alleged abuser does, the results can be frightening. Guilty or not, the person is thrust into the state's system, which is not, as the naive believe, wise and benevolent. He is now in a situation where his constitutional right to jury trial, to there being a warrant for search and seizure, to see evidence, and to know one's accuser are set aside. Does the end justify the means? Those who believe that it does, might feel justified if the system worked. But it does not. At least half the reports are unfounded and families are disrupted. Many agency workers ''felt'' that their efforts led to a change in the situation. We must say that mere feelings constitute rather vague evidence of ''a change,'' and the nature and degree of change and its permanence were not specified.

Can we, as citizens, sanction totalitarian methods in America? We need more hard data before we can consent to having our civil liberties bypassed in the name of expediency and necessity. There are no national statistics on follow-up of reported cases, confirmation of suspected abuse, case management that ensued, or end result.[38]

But the proponents of mandatory reporting remain vocal: ''Police and the court . . . have largely ignored domestic assaults.'' This is partly due to the belief that family violence is a family matter and partly to the assumption that ''domestic calls can be very dangerous for the police.''[39] Therefore, ''normal criminal approaches are not recommended.'' Although the Federal Government has promulgated the need for easing the barriers to involuntary service and placement, others have disagreed. Faulkner calls mandatory reporting an ''inappropriate, ineffective and ageist response,'' and encourages the use of the criminal justice system.[40] Why should assault and battery be handled differently if it occurs between family members as opposed to strangers? For example, if I break my father's arm, should my constitutional rights be different than if I break yours? Should my father not have the same right to redress that he would have if we were not related? Do my parents not have the same right to protection from me as from a stranger? But what if my father fell and a malicious neighbor said I broke his arm? The standard of proof needed is the lowest— credible evidence—and suddenly I find myself in a situation where I have to prove my innocence instead of disproving my guilt. Am I not protected by the constitution in my own home? Is my parent to be taken from a warm, loving environment and forcibly placed within the cold confines of a nursing home while an already overburdened court deliberates on what is in his ''best interest''?

Although social service departments could arrange placement in long-term care facilities, elders usually preferred adult foster homes or congregate living facilities, even though these were rarely available.[41] Sadly, those responding in the Salend study concluded that the ''major intent of reporting laws was to extend statutory authority to social service departments providing adult protection.''[42]

Mandatory reporting may bring elder abuse into public awareness and generate needed funds, but it may also turn an allegedly under-reported problem into an over-reported crusade, especially if such categories as self-neglect are included (as they have been in some studies).[43] But is self-neglect a reportable matter? The elder-savers would have us think so. Self-neglect may be nothing more than poverty and why should there be punitive measures for being poor? Should these cases be grouped with physical violence for statistical and funding purposes? Self-neglect is really neither neglect nor abuse; it becomes a social problem only if the individual is mentally incompetent and in need of protection or funds; "otherwise one man's self-neglect is another man's exercise of free judgement."[44]

Salend et al. concluded that the rights and well-being of the elderly cannot be protected under the existing statutes, which infantilize them and stereotype them as helpless and incompetent.[45] Indeed this country is as stereotyped about the elderly as it is about other minority and disadvantaged groups.[46] "People classified as 'old' are seen as intellectually unfit, narrow-minded, ineffective, and ready to die momentarily. . . . Perhaps we should take a few steps backward in the advocacy of mandatory reporting for a thorough conceptualization of what should be reported and why."[47]

Katz, Regan, and Mitchell, each writing from the legal standpoint, urged that our legal mechanisms for involuntary intervention and guardianship be reviewed and restructured.[48] The question of paternalism versus individual liberty is now raised again. Regan points out that having "no better alternative" does not justify institutionalization, since this removes the elder's personal liberties in the name of "necessity." Instead of total guardianship or institutionalization, there should be a case-by-case process of matching guardianship to the needs of the elder.[49]

Gilbert cited three principles that mandatory reporting laws should serve: those of *beneficence, autonomy,* and *nonmaleficence.*[50] The principle of beneficence is that people should act in a manner which benefits others. This includes removing harm, preventing harm and providing benefits. Stopping abuse is removing harm. However, "there is little reason to believe that legislation has stopped abuse of elders." Does mandated reporting prevent harm? Comparison groups are few and statistics are scanty. Does mandatory reporting provide benefits? Again, the answer is not uniform from state to state; in some, services are not widely available, lack funding, and are of dubious quality.

Does mandatory reporting support the principle of autonomy, which is that individuals have a right to self-determination and should not infringe others' right to self-determination? Most statutes state that services are not to be provided without the consent of the elder. But because there is the coercion of shame, dread of reprisal, guilt, and fear of institutionalization, is either consent or refusal really voluntary? Recent decisions uphold the idea that mental incapacity must be total or nearly total before the principle of autonomy can be violated; but there is no agreement on what it means "to lack the capacity to consent." Moreover, 26 out of 32 statutes mentioned consent to services, but only 3 mentioned consent to the investigation and none mentioned consent to having the report filed with the agency in the first place.

Autonomy is further undermined by ageism, which insinuates that old age is automatically accompanied by incompetence. No data yet supports the idea that old age per se prevents a person from behaving autonomously, nor that physical disability alone is grounds for removing a person's right to decide his own fate. That an elder might make a choice different from what another "enlightened" person or agency might make for the elder should not be used to declare the elder of "unsound mind."

The third principle, nonmaleficence, is that people should act so as not to harm others. In short, *primum non nocere*, the first principle of the physician should be remembered when considering mandatory reporting: Do no harm intentionally or unintentionally by acting or failing to act. There is ample potential for the mandated reporter to cause harm: Records may be erroneous and only seven states provide recourse to correct or destroy erroneous records; elders may be wrongfully deprived of their rights (a guardianship hearing can be devastating); allegations may be false and precipitate chaos in the family; and the elder can be institutionalized to endure experiences similar to, if not worse than, those at home.[51] In Connecticut, placement in an institution was anticipated for 60 percent of those referred. It is thus the physician's responsibility, whether the report of suspected abuse is mandatory or voluntary, to consider the ramifications of such a report by understanding the entire system that purports to alleviate abuse. *Primum non nocere.* Reporting can cause harm and mandated reporting places an emphasis on reporting rather than solutions.

Gilbert points out conflicts between these principles: (1) the rule to stop elder abuse by mandatory reporting may conflict with the rule to obtain consent; (2) the rule to prevent harm may conflict with the rule to protect confidentiality; (3) the rule to promote benefits may conflict with the rule not to inflict harm. Any risk of harm from mandated reporting is unacceptable when benefits cannot be demonstrated.[52] Callahan believes that the well-being of the elderly will be undermined rather than improved, by current statutes.[53] By themselves, laws cannot make society free of the "root causes" of abuse and neglect.[54]

Now that the proposed system of mandatory reporting has been reviewed, it is time to return to the initial case of the elderly woman with a lacerated forehead. The case was resolved when the neighbor substantiated the husband's account of the drinking history and the plastic surgeon considered the wound compatible with a dog bite. The next day the patient confided that she did indeed drink a case of beer per day. She improved and was discharged home in her husband's care with appropriate medical and nursing followup.

This is an actual case that occurred in a state which currently allows for voluntary reporting for elder abuse. Because of this, the attending physician was given the time and opportunity not only to provide proper medical care but also to ensure the best interests of his patient and her husband. With mandatory reporting, the case would probably have been reported as suspected elder abuse at the time of initial examination in the emergency room, and a couple who had been married for 50 years might have been separated "for their own good."

CONCLUSIONS

1. Current statistics about elder abuse have been inflated by interest groups, such as psychologists and social workers, who have lobbied for increased funds, and the media. These groups have incited the public to over-reaction. The resulting bias prevents a rational approach to the problem.
2. Thus far, the only controlled study indicates that the difference between abusive and nonabusive environments is a problem of social isolation; the alleged stereotypes of abusive families have not stood up to critical review.

3. Mandated reporting has many drawbacks.

- There is no general agreement on what is meant by *elder*, and definitions of elder abuse are so general that what should be reported is vague. Frequently reports are made on suspicion only, and even "self-neglect" has been included.
- Reporters are coerced into over-reporting by penalties for not doing so.
- Reporters are most often unaware of the system into which persons are thrust by their report. They conceive their duty as making a report, and do not understand that the system involved in following up the report is not beneficent.
- Anonymous reporting can be malicious and fosters a police state atmosphere.
- The health professional must assume that the care giver does not have the best interests of the elder in mind. This creates an atmosphere of suspicion, which hinders the healing process.

4. The system that is involved in following up a report is ineffective, unconstitutional, and ageist.

- *Ineffective:* Investigations are often poorly done and done by unqualified personnel. Help is often not available, even in cases of definite abuse.
- *Unconstitutional:* The legal system deprives the elder of constitutional rights and self-determination. The alleged abuser is deprived of due process.
- *Ageist:* The entire system stereotypes and denigrates the elderly.

5. Mandated reporting tends to worsen the situation by forcing the elder into a nursing home or other institution.
6. There is no evidence that mandated reporting of suspected abuse works better than voluntary reporting.
7. By itself, mandated reporting of abuse is useless. It is not a solution. If it is not a solution, then mandated reporting is unnecessary. Indeed, it is actually harmful.

RECOMMENDATIONS

1. Statistical reports should be based on factual data, not allegations. Trivial problems and those germane only to social and financial poverty should be excluded.

- Services to remedy the problem should be readily available: Meals-on-Wheels, day care centers, "elder sitters," self-help groups, individual counseling, and, in rare cases, bona fide foster care or nursing homes.
- For abuse which is not related to social or financial poverty, police departments should be trained to deal with domestic violence. Family violence (of any kind) should not be decriminalized by setting up special family courts. The alleged abusers should be prosecuted under the criminal statutes, thereby ensuring the constitutional rights and due process for both elder and alleged abusers. This would also alleviate the problems of defining *elder* and *elder abuse* legislatively.

2. Personnel who are responsible for investigating reports of abuse should be accountable to the public and shed the cloak of secrecy and anonymous informants. These
individuals should be qualified to perform criminal or civil investigations and to make
referrals to appropriate services.

3. If competent elders are ethically entitled to refuse medical treatment in hospitals,
despite the fact that their decision may end in death, then they should be entitled to
make less onerous choices (e.g., about place of residence, food, dress, and life style)
despite what social workers or the state may want them to choose. A person has an
ethical right to live with a risk greater than what others would choose for the person or
for themselves.

4. Voluntary, rather than mandatory, reporting laws for elder abuse can provide ample
assistance to social agencies and police unless and until hard data show us otherwise.
First, do no harm. A report of suspected abuse should be a mature, informed
judgement on the part of the health professional. A mandate to report says ''report or
be punished,'' and it thereby encourages premature reports based on insufficient data.
Anyone who reports must be aware of the consequences and ramifications of that
report and of the system into which he or she thrusts the elder. It is not enough to report
and walk away.

FINAL THOUGHTS

The expectation that a mandatory reporting law will eradicate abuse of any kind is naive.
Mandatory reporting of gunshot wounds has not decreased the use of handguns in violent
situations. It has only enabled police to investigate instances where a crime *might* have been
committed.

What is needed is an underlying respect and honor for our elderly, a new role for them to
play in the lives of their children and in society, and a new attitude on the part of those of us
who care for them.

> When my 87-year-old father was dying, he felt embarrassed when I had to lift him
> from the bed to the commode. ''I am too much of a burden,'' he said. ''When I
> was a boy was I ever too much of a burden for you?'' ''No, I loved you,'' he said.
> ''Well, that answers the question,'' I replied, ''I love you, too.''
>
> Joel Brumlik, M.D.

> Children, obey your parents in the Lord: For this is right. Honor thy father and
> mother; which is the first commandment with promise; that it may be well with
> thee, and thou mayest live long on the earth. And, ye fathers, provoke not your
> children to wrath: But bring them up in the nurture and admonition of the Lord.
>
> Ephesians 6:1–4

NOTES

1. M. Eastman, ''Abusing the Elderly,'' *Nursing Mirror* 159 (1984): 19–20.

2. T. Whitehead, ''Battered Old People,'' *Nursing Times* 79 (1983): 32–33.

3. M.R. Block and J.D. Sinnott, *The Battered Elder Syndrome: An Exploratory Study* (College Park, Md.: University of Maryland, Center on Aging, 1979).

4. P. Ebersole and P. Hess, *Toward Healthy Aging: Human Needs and Nursing Response* (St. Louis, Mo.: Mosby 1985) 369–644.

5. C.B. Clark, "Geriatric Abuse—Out of the Closet," *Journal of the Tennessee Medical Association* 8 (1984): 470–71.

6. C. Mildenberger and H.C. Wessman, "Abuse and Neglect of Elderly Persons by Family Members," *Physical Therapy* 66 (1986): 537–39.

7. L.R. Phillips, "Abuse and Neglect of the Frail Elderly at Home: An Exploration of Theoretical Relationships," *Journal of Advances in Nursing* 8 (1983): 379–92.

8. K.D. Katz, "Elder Abuse," *Journal of Family Law* 18 (1979–80): 695–722.

9. A.C. Carlson, "The Child-Savers Ride Again" *Persuasion at Work* 8 (1985): 1–9.

10. Ibid.

11. M. Van Waters, *Youth In Conflict* (New York: New Republic, 1932), 65–66.

12. M. Van Waters, *Parents on Probation* (New York: New Republic, 1927), 3–6, 35, 167.

13. Carlson, "The Child-Savers."

14. Ibid.

15. R. Wexler, "Invasion of the Child Savers" documentary produced for WXXI-TV, Rochester, N.Y., 1985.

16. Carlson, "The Child-Savers."

17. J.J. Regan, "Intervention through Adult Protective Services Programs," *Gerontologist* 18 (1978): 250–54.

18. Ebersole and Hess, *Toward Healthy Aging*.

19. M.C. Sengstock and S. Barrett, *Domestic Abuse of the Elderly* (Reston, Va.: Reston Publishing Co., 1984), 146–88.

20. M. Thobaben and L. Anderson, "Reporting Elder Abuse: It's the Law," *American Journal of Nursing* 85 (1985): 371–74.

21. Ebersole and Hess, *Toward Healthy Aging*.

22. Mildenberger and Wessman, "Abuse and Neglect of Elderly Persons."

23. Block and Sinnott, *Battered Elder Syndrome*.

24. T.T. Fulmer and K. Carr, "Abuse of the Elderly: Screening and Detection," *Journal of Emergency Nursing* 10 (1984): 131–40; Sengstock and Barrett, *Domestic Abuse*.

25. Philips, "Abuse and Neglect of Frail Elderly."

26. Block and Sinnott, *Battered Elder Syndrome*.

27. E. Salend et al., "Elder Abuse Reporting: Limitation of Statutes," *Gerontologist* 24 (1984): 61–69.

28. T.T. Fulmer and V.M. Cahill, "Assessing Elder Abuse: A Study," *Journal of Gerontological Nursing* 10 (1984): 16–20; G. Taler and E.F. Anesello, "Elder Abuse," *American Family Practitioner* 32 (1985): 107–14.

29. Taler and Anesello, "Elder Abuse."

30. Whitehead, "Battered Old People."

31. Sengstock and Barrett, *Domestic Abuse*.

32. V.E.L. Harrington, "Nursing Home Abuse: The Tragedy Continues," *Nursing Forum* 3 (1984): 102–8.

33. A. Langslow, "Age Must Not Invite Harm or Hurt," *Australian Nursing Journal* 14 (1984): 20–21.

34. Mildenberger and Wessman, "Abuse and Neglect of Elderly Persons."

35. J. Riffer, "Elder Abuse Victims Estimated at One Million," *Hospitals*, March 1, 1985, p. 60.

36. Ibid.

37. Block and Sinnott, *Battered Elder Syndrome*.

38. T. Fulmer and T. Wetle, "Elder Abuse: Screening and Intervention," *Nursing Practitioner* 11 (1986): 33–38.

39. Sengstock and Barrett, *Domestic Abuse*.

40. L.R. Faulkner, "Mandating the Reporting of Suspected Cases of Elder Abuse: An Inappropriate, Ineffective and Ageist Response to the Abuse of the Older Adults," *Family Law Quarterly*, 16 (1984): 69–91.

41. A. Langley, "Identification of and Access to the Abused Elderly," *Human Services* 27 (1981)): 19–27.

42. Salend et al., "Elder Abuse Reporting."

43. Mildenberger and Wessman, "Abuse and Neglect of Elderly Persons."

44. Salend et al., "Elder Abuse Reporting."

45. Ibid.

46. Block and Sinnott, *Battered Elder Syndrome*.

47. Salend et al., "Elder Abuse Reporting."

48. Katz, "Elder Abuse"; Regan, "Adult Protective Services Programs"; A.M. Mitchell, "The Objects of Our Wisdom and Our Coercion: Involuntary Guardianship for Incompetants," *Southern California Law Review* 52 (1979): 1405–99.

49. Regan, "Adult Protective Services Programs."

50. D.A. Gilbert, "The Ethics of Mandatory Elder Abuse Reporting Statutes," *Advances in Nursing Science* 8 (1986): 51–62.

51. Katz, "Elder Abuse."

52. Gilbert, "Ethics of Mandatory Elder Abuse Reporting Statutes."

53. Callahan, J.J., Jr. Elder Abuse Programming. Will It Help the Elderly? Urban Social Change Review 15: 15–16, 1982.

54. Katz, "Elder Abuse." For a survey of the requirements for mandated reporting of elder abuse in various states, see Fulmer and Weltle, "Elder Abuse: Screening and Intervention"; Thobaben and Anderson, "Reporting Elder Abuse"; Salend et al., "Elder Abuse Reporting."

BIBLIOGRAPHY

Beck, C. and L. Philips. "The Unseen Abuse: Why Financial Treatment of the Elderly Goes Unrecognized." *Journal Gerontological Nursing* 10 (1984): 26–30.

Clark, C.B. "Geriatric Abuse Intervention Team in a Family Practice Setting." *Journal of the Tennessee Medical Association* 8 (1984): 535–36.

Clark, C.B. "Successfully Resolved Geriatric Abuse Cases by the Geriatric Abuse Intervention Team," *Journal of the Tennessee Medical Association* 8 (1984): 599–600.

O'Malley, T.A., H.C. O'Malley, D.E. Everitt, and D. Sarson. "Categories of Family Mediated Abuse and Neglect of Elderly Persons." *Journal American Gerontological Society* 32 (1984): 362–69.

Pedrick-Cornell, C., and R.J. Gelles. "Elder Abuse: The Status of Current Knowledge." *Family Relations* 31 (1982): 457–65.

Part III

Critically Ill and Dying Patients

Chapter 14

Ethical Issues in Critical Care Nursing

Jo Ann Wegmann

Delivery of health care has been and will continue to be influenced by several recent trends. Health care in general is highly technical and undergoes rapid and dramatic changes. Critically ill individuals with a variety of diseases survive longer and require advanced nursing care in more acute phases of illness than previously.[1] Conversely, individuals in poor health but not termed "critical" are experiencing shorter or no hospital stays, with an increasing amount of their health care delegated to family members within the home setting.

Bioethical dilemmas arise in all areas of health care delivery. The purpose of this chapter is to explore several types of ethical issues specific to critical care nursing. Philosophical issues in ethics are presented and definitions of common terminology are discussed. Variations within critical care settings are identified and potential influences regarding future critical care issues are explored. The reasons why the discipline of nursing needs an ethical framework are discussed and a model for ethical decision making is described.

DEFINITIONS OF TERMS

Philosophy consists of theories and analysis about conduct, thought, knowledge, and the nature of the universe.[2] A central task of philosophy is to aid a culture to clarify its view of reality and its values.[3] Helm identifies three components of philosophy: ethics, which consists of rules governing values and choices; metaphysics, which is the study of reality; and epistemology, which is concerned with distinguishing beliefs from knowledge.[4] Of importance here is ethics, especially the subdiscipline of bioethics. (See definitions in Appendix A).

As Englehardt states, the term *ethics* is ambiguous.[5] Clearly, ethics involves duty, responsibility, justice, conscience, and other societal concerns. Ethical viewpoints address the well-being of large groups (e.g., society), as well as the mores and values of specific interest groups (e.g., religion). Ethics also concerns rules and standards of conduct of special professional groups (e.g., health care providers).[6]

Bioethics is concerned with ethical problems and decisions that arise from medical care of the ill and from delivery of health care in general.[7] Concepts of bioethics are changing and emerging as a result of interactions between modern technology and the diverse cultures of today's world. In the delivery of care to critically ill individuals, bioethics represents a response to the rapid and remarkable advances in health care technology and related sciences.[8] In the presence of rapidly advancing technology, nurses are immediately and directly involved with the resolution of ethical dilemmas through judgment, interpretations, consideration of patient and family wishes, and a variety of other factors.[9]

CRITICAL CARE NURSING

The American health care system has evolved from being concerned exclusively with preventing death from infectious disease to being concerned with prolonging life through antibiotic use, advanced cardiac support, and advanced technology in many other areas of treatment.[10] A direct outcome of the discovery of antibiotics and the medical-surgical life-preserving techniques developed during World War II and the Korean War, as well as rapidly developing advanced cardiac support technology, was the development of the modern intensive care unit. The role of critical care nurse has evolved as a result of the rapidly changing and highly demanding skills required of nursing care delivery in intensive care units. Aspects of critical care nursing in a variety of critical care settings are explored here.

Other factors contributing to the growth of critical care include recent cost containment endeavors, such as prospective payment, utilization review, and diagnosis related groups (DRGs). A recent news column in the *American Journal of Nursing* argues that DRGs have resulted in more and sicker patients being treated in intensive care units (ICUs). Conversely, less ill patients, typically seen in acute hospital settings, now comprise only a small number of individuals needing inpatient care. The result is that many hospitals are increasing the number of ICU beds while decreasing the number of acute care beds.[11] This has had dramatic effects on nursing care in general, including an increase in the number of critical care nurses; i.e., registered nurses possessing specialized, highly technical skills in critical care.

It is only in the past two decades that ICUs became what they are today.[12] Indeed, between 1972 and 1982, 28.5 percent of the total hospital bed increase in this country was in critical care beds, and types of intensive care beds have proliferated. These factors, combined with advancing technology and dramatic reimbursement constraints in health care, have given rise to serious ethical issues in most parts of health care.

TECHNOLOGICAL ADVANCES

The past three decades have witnessed rapid developments worldwide in many areas of technology. Such advances are easily identified in communications, recreation, science, and the medical fields. Medical technological advances have made important contributions to the rapidly changing nature of health care in this country. Examples of such technology include allogeneic transplantation of organs and bone marrow, autologous transplantation of marrow, methods of advanced cardiac and respiratory life support, and the utilization of artificial organs, including artificial hearts. A direct result of such advances has been the growth in ICUs, where social and medical traditions generally support giving the best care that is technologically possible.[13]

Medical technological advances, however, may generate conflicts with traditional attitudes and practices toward both the living and the dead.[14] Three specific areas in which technology has had dramatic impact are explored here: prolongation of life and resulting prognosis, brain death, and organ transplantation.

Advances in technology have resulted in prolongation of life for some individuals who otherwise would not live through prolonged illnesses. An outcome of such survival has been the expansion of hospice programs. This chapter will not address hospice issues but will focus on issues of life prolongation and the resulting ethical dilemmas that have arisen as a result of hospice development.

Recent trends in health care allocation for patients who require care but need to receive such care outside of the acute care hospital have endorsed various hospice approaches. Yet, as with inpatient care, innovative forms of home or outpatient care have been scrutinized by third party payers in light of reimbursement policies. Hospice care, while desirable for the terminally ill individuals near death, has come under such scrutiny. This has forced physicians to make prognostications regarding expected time of death in order for such patients to qualify for reimbursement, usually Medicare, for hospice care.

Brody and Lynn[15] have questioned the accuracy of such prognostications. These authors question the value of judgments about length of remaining life in the face of imminent death. For example, current Medicare requirements for home hospice reimbursement demand a prognosis of death within six months of hospice program placement. Brody and Lynn assert that it is difficult, possibly dangerous, to precisely determine time of death (often months before the event is expected). These authors fear that such predetermination may destroy the essential feature of the hospice movement, the provision of palliative, humanistic care during the final months of life.

Likewise, nursing care of terminally ill often assumes characteristics of critical care in general (advanced life support mechanism), but may be limited by rigid adherence to a forecast of the expected time of death. To halt palliative or life-prolonging efforts because a patient survives beyond the predicted time of death poses serious ethical dilemmas for all involved. Specifically, a nurse might confront the question of euthanasia through withholding such treatments as blood component therapy, antibiotic therapy, and fluids and nutrition.

Advanced life-support technology permits maintenance of vital body functions (tissues oxygenation via a beating heart and artificially maintained respirations), which has resulted in the diagnosis of brain death. Indeed, death of the entire brain is widely accepted as constituting the death of the person.[16] Thus, criteria to determine brain death have been adopted by legislators and judges and are utilized by physicians for the organ donation process. Issues of brain death and organ transplantation are described together, since both kinds illustrate how technological advances give rise to ethical dilemmas.

The demand for organs and donors for transplantation has outpaced the supply.[17] According to Younger et al., brain death diagnoses (which largely occur in ICUs) have potentially destructive effects, with many coinciding ethical problems.[18] Such ethical problems discussed here include effects on health care workers and possible reactions of family members to the diagnosis of brain death and the request for organ donation.

Little attention has been given to the disturbing effects on staff members of organ retrieval surgery. The concern may exist that an organ donor is not truly dead and that the organ recovery process may thus kill the donor. The diagnosis of brain death has created a new group of dead patients who resemble living individuals in body temperature, color, and presence of vital functions.[19] Maintaining organs for transplantation necessitates treating dead patients as if they were alive and it creates serious questions regarding allocation of scarce funds, selection of organ recipients, and long-term effects on staff members involved in the organ retrieval process. Yet the existence of organ transplantation as a lifesaving measure cannot be denied, and brain death as a diagnosis should not be dispensed with.[20]

The diagnosis of brain death in a previously healthy individual prompts the physician to seek consent from the family for organ donation. Hosford has noted that the absence of traditional indicators of death often confuse family members, particularly during the vulnerable state of shock and grief over the death.[21] To enable family members to accept the fact of death in the presence of ongoing vital functions, critical care policies often require two separate testings for brain function, both with negative results, prior to declaring actual brain death.

Three specific ethical problems arise from the organ retrieval process. During organ retrieval, the donor's welfare is no longer at stake and therefore does not provide the rationale for the aggressive surgical procedures required to obtain the health organs. Furthermore, the organ recovery process seems to violate a more general respect for persons, forcing the treatment of human beings as mere means to the survival of other individuals. Finally, organ retrieval may be viewed as disrespectful to the dead in a culture that respects both the recently dead and the graves and memories of those who have been long dead. Such heroic, life-sustaining measures use diminishing health care resources and create serious ethical dilemmas. In such circumstances, questions arise regarding financial burden and responsibility and the appropriate determination of the organ recipient.

Although pursuing life-sustaining efforts on a brain dead victim provokes some ethical questions, few topics in medicine are more complicated or more controversial than with-holding life-sustaining efforts from hopelessly ill individuals. Wanzer et al. have addressed the patient's role in decision making.[22] While the patient remains competent, he or she must have an active voice in whether to continue to rely on life-sustaining methods. The physician also has a major role in the decision-making process. Of equal importance, although not discussed by these authors, is the role of the nurse in situations where long-term relationships with terminally ill patients have been established. In such situations, the nurse may be in the best position to know the patient's previously expressed desires. A nurse's input into decision making merits respect from members of the health care team and from family members. A framework for nursing participation in ethical decision making is presented later in this chapter.

Critical care areas within hospitals have been briefly described, and reference has been made to the high technology and nature of care issues which are typical of modern ICUs. However, intensive or critical care today encompasses various patient diagnoses and classifications of care. It is valuable to explore variations within critical care in order to identify multiple areas with the potential for giving rise to ethical dilemmas, both expected and unexpected.

Many factors have contributed to the explosive growth in ICUs in this country during the past several decades. Following the atrocities of World War II, institutional review boards were created. These swiftly developed policies regarding human experimentation and informed consent.[23] In this period of rapid financial growth, health care in America witnessed a proliferation of academic health centers heavily involved in biomedical research and often funded by federal grants. Furthermore, the growth in the health care system has occurred as a result of a larger supply of physicians and improved insurance coverage, encouraging widespread use of hospitalization and experimentation in curative procedures.[24]

Technological advances contributing to the development of early ICUs include cardiovascular life support, artificial respirators, dialysis for kidney failure, and antibiotic therapy. Academic medicine traditionally has demanded active biomedical research contributions from its practitioners, and advancing medical technology provided life-support methods in areas beyond cardiac impairment.

A typical ICU today will accept surgical patients immediately following a cardiac bypass procedure. The patient suffering a myocardial infarction will be hospitalized in a coronary care unit, with continuous availability of telemetry, intra-aortic balloon pump monitoring, and other types of sophisticated monitoring. Such patients generally are older adults with some form of cardiac impairment. Medical intensive care units usually receive patients experiencing multiple system failures. Trauma victims (who are of all ages) may be admitted to either surgical or medical intensive care units.

Other types of critical care units today include pediatric ICUs and neonatal ICUs. It is estimated that 250,000 low-birth-weight infants are born every year in this country.[25] Prematurity and low birth weight result in multiple problems for these infants, such as malnutrition, respiratory insufficiency, brain damage, and life-threatening infection. Other infants who may be admitted to neonatal ICUs include those suffering from severe birth defects, birth injury, or genetic disorders.[26] Two significant factors have contributed to many emergent ethical problems in the treatment of critically ill neonates: (1) the development and availability of neonatal ICUs and (2) recent government intervention in the protection of seriously impaired neonates. With the emergence of neonatal critical care, disagreement about the proper course of action regarding many of these cases of impairment has become evident. Shapiro and Frader note the need for a social policy regarding the treatment of impaired infants.[27]

Other specialty units have been developed which may be classified as critical care units. Several examples are offered, though these are by no means exhaustive. Victims of trauma were identified above as likely admissions to either medical or surgical ICUs. In today's competitive market, certain health centers are seeking government designation as trauma centers. Thus, trauma has emerged as a subspecialty of medicine, with victims of multiple or extreme traumas becoming recipients of critical nursing and medical care. Depending on the nature of the event that caused the injuries, trauma patients may require long episodes of critical care, and questions may arise regarding progressive treatment versus salvage of the patient. Also, victims of trauma frequently are children, adolescents, and young adults involved in automobile accidents and near drownings. Such patients often were in good health immediately prior to the traumatic event, and are viewed as likely organ donors if brain death occurs. (See Chapter 4 on caution in infant brain death.) As more critically ill trauma victims are successfully maintained, one expects to see the development of specialized trauma ICUs. Resulting ethical issues include next-of-kin consent for organ donation and equitable allocation of available organs.

Advances in medical care have resulted in development of other subspecialties, with segregation of patients into specialized areas of treatment. Several are briefly described here.

Bone marrow transplantation is one type of organ donation that has been used as a potentially curative treatment for some cancers, as well as other diseases, in the past several decades. This treatment is considered experimental, and recipients (in increasing numbers) usually receive the treatment in academic health centers within a specialty bone marrow transplantation unit. Unlike most other types of organ donation, bone marrow transplantation requires donation from a living donor. The donor may be a close relative or even the patient him- or herself (through harvesting of healthy marrow prior to intensive, marrow-destructive therapy).

While the benefits of successful bone marrow transplantation cannot be denied, this remains a procedure with high emotional and financial costs. The patient undergoing bone marrow transplantation generally develops serious side effects from the treatment and can expect a prolonged hospital stay. The success rate for bone marrow transplantation is improving, but remains troublingly low in view of the anticipated side effects and limitations imposed on the recipient's life. Another area of concern that has received little attention is the impact on family members who are identified as the matched donors. While the bone marrow recipient becomes critically ill as a result of the treatment designed to save his or her life, it is still worth considering the psychological consequences for the donor when, for example, the donated marrow fails to engraft or the recipient's immune system rejects the new marrow. Such consequences warrant more than the scant scientific attention they have received in view of the ever-increasing trend toward various organ donations, from both living donors and cadavers.

As in the case of trauma centers or bone marrow transplantation units, some health centers have created specialized areas for the treatment of patients sustaining burns. Indeed, because of the nature of some burns, their treatment is now recognized as another critical care area, and working in such a unit demands the critical care skills and compassion required in any other ICU. Patient care within a burn unit also involves engraftment of skin, a living tissue (although often retrieved from a cadaver). Thus, the nurse working within such a setting also must confront the issues of organ, or tissue, retrieval and transplantation.

Finally, within large medical centers, the emergency department has increasingly become another type of critical care unit. If the hospital is recognized as a designated trauma center, the emergency department often serves as point of entrance for the victims of trauma. Also, the nature of more acutely ill patients requiring hospitalization today may result in such patients using the emergency department to gain access to the health care system for care, particularly in view of economic constraints and issues concerning poor or underserved populations. Thus, we are witnessing uses of emergency departments that are far different from the originally intended use when such facilities were first designed.

EXAMPLES OF MAJOR ETHICAL ISSUES

Ethical issues which nurses confront in various critical care settings may be classified as treatment related, resource allocation related, or related to nurse-physician (and other) relationships. Treatment-related issues are numerous, and many are identified in this chapter.

A specific example involving nursing is found with the cancer patient about to undergo chemotherapy for the first time. Frequently such patients are unaware of the severity of likely side effects of treatment, because they have not been thoroughly informed or were unable to comprehend information given them. The nurse must often decide whether to disclose information that may prove unnecessary or even deleterious to the patient. Furthermore, nursing disclosure of such information may be deemed inappropriate by the physician, placing the nurse in an undesirable position with respect to both physician and patient.

Ethical issues related to resource allocation have been alluded to. Resources include available organs for transplantation and critical care. Nurses providing care to a bilateral amputee with a 30-year history of drug and alcohol abuse, as well as a prolonged history of unemployment, may have to assess their own value systems. If such a patient is using resources unavailable to others who may be considered more worthy or deserving, serious ethical questions must be addressed. Nurses can choose to not participate in health care settings where there are activities or policies that conflict with their personal value systems. Thus, a registered professional nurse may refuse employment in an obstetrics department that performs abortions.

Another potential source of conflict and resulting ethical dilemmas is when either the nurse or the physician disagrees with the other's professional practice. Many such situations exist that involve nurse-physician relationships as well as those between nurses and other hospital employees. The reader is directed specifically to the works by Muyskens and by Benjamin and Curtis described in the annotated bibliography at the end of this chapter. A recent event is described below to illustrate the nature of conflicts between nurses and physicians.

A nursing policy at a large teaching hospital is that nurses may take verbal orders from physicians via telephone only in emergencies. Based on laboratory results and her knowledge of a patient's cardiac status, a nurse believed the patient needed potassium supplements. The patient requested that he receive the potassium orally, as previous intravenous administration of potassium had been painful. Upon telephoning the resident, the nurse obtained an order for three separate oral doses of potassium to be given at two-hour intervals and to be completed at 6 A.M. Because it was after 1:30 A.M., the resident stated he would come to the unit later in the night to sign the order. Since the nurse believed that the patient needed the potassium, she repeated the order to the resident, obtained the medication, and carried out the order.

Shortly after the final dose, the patient suffered a cardiac arrest. Resuscitation was unsuccessful and an hour later the patient died. The resident was present during the resuscitation, and afterwards refused to sign the earlier order for the potassium, stating the nurse had made an error and given the patient too much potassium.

Subsequent investigation determined that the potassium order was appropriate and had not contributed to the cardiac arrest. Several hours after the event, the original order was signed by the resident. In the intervening hours, however, accusations were made, individual integrities were questioned, and much interpersonal trust was destroyed. Subsequently, the nurse was disciplined for breaking policy and taking a verbal order.

The outcome of this, like similar situations, was far-reaching but could have been avoided. Of importance is that an essential nurse-physician relationship was destroyed, with resulting distrust and animosity, the effects of which directly impacted the patient care unit and ultimately the patient care itself.

The few examples of major ethical issues presented above are representative of the continuing dilemmas that permeate nursing care today. In a recent editorial, E.C. Theis addresses the urgent need for physicians to consult and collaborate with nurses regarding ethically troublesome situations.[28] Decisions about ethical dilemmas cannot be made unilaterally. All health care professionals and other appropriate individuals, such as clergy, must share their knowledge of patient conditions and situations to determine the best possible course of action and avoid tragic consequences.

NURSING ETHICAL FRAMEWORK

Any discussion of ethical issues involved within a critical care setting must be open-ended. When applying components of ethical decision making to critical care issues, the nurse's considerations must be taken seriously and fully into account. As in any hospital setting, it is the nurse who remains at the patient's bedside the greatest amount of time. In critical care settings, the nursing staff typically are with the patient continuously. Therefore, the following nursing ethical framework is put forth, adapted largely from an earlier paper by the author.[29]

Until recently, nursing education and therefore practice were based largely on the medical model, an approach to health and illness focusing on disease process and life preservation. As nursing education has become more sophisticated and nursing staffed with a greater number of advance degree nurses, various components of nursing models have emerged and have been partially adopted.

Nurses functioning within the framework of a medical mode have shaped their practice to mimic or cohere with that of the physician, often overlooking perplexing nursing and patient care problems that would benefit from a purely nursing approach. They have also had to confront the ethical problems of patients involved in studies conducted by physicians.[30] For both nursing research and practice to best serve the patient and further the profession of nursing, nursing models or frameworks must be used.

A nursing framework also has value for dealing with ethical issues. The profession's growing efforts to develop a sound basis of knowledge for practice necessitates a commitment to a philosophical framework with which to address important ethical issues. Thus, working within such a framework can provide nurses with a sound method of decision making while serving the patient's best interest.

Simply stated, an ethical dilemma—such as those described in this chapter—occurs when all choices or options are equally unacceptable. None of the possible actions is unproblematic; all will result in some negative or unwanted outcome and may violate certain rights.[31]

Some ethical dilemmas are common, such as those involving informed consent, human experimentation, "Do Not Resuscitate" orders, the right to die, and brain death. Some not-so-common dilemmas involve organ transplantation (including the effect on family) and infants impaired as a result of fertility drug use.

As nurses become more involved in specialized care, such currently uncommon dilemmas can be expected to increase in type and incidence. The value of practicing within an ethical framework is that in the face of such dilemmas, situational ethics—where there is no sustaining underpinning to validate decisions—may be avoided. An ethical framework provides the basis for sound decision making and prevents emotive or intuitive decision making. For these reasons, it is valuable to discuss a model for ethical decision making.

Gadow discusses two philosophical ideals that are available to nursing.[32] One of these ideals is beneficence, that is, performing acts of kindness or charity. Beneficence defines the role of the nurse as one of cooperation with others—particularly the physician and the institution—concerned with benefiting patients. Underlying this cooperation is the assumption that the professional is better qualified than the patient to define benefit and harm. Professional judgment is generally medical rather than nursing, because benefit is defined by medical criteria, i.e., the reversing of pathology and the preventing of death.

The second philosophical ideal is autonomy. This ideal requires that one respect the patient's right to self-determination provided that the individual's decision is a free and considered one and that it does not endanger others. Acting under this ideal, the nurse tries to support patients in the development of autonomous health care decisions. Nurses are still obligated to act in a patient's best interest, but it is the patient and not the professional who decides what the patient's best interests are. Autonomy does not force patients to participate in treatment decisions; it only ensures the possibility of and the assistance needed for participating if they choose to do so. Some patients will not or cannot participate.

Nurses cannot practice with both a philosophy that endorses professional determination of what is in the patient's interest (paternalism) and a philosophy of patient autonomy. It is strongly recommended that nurses adopt the ideal of autonomy. Patients lose nothing but can gain significantly, because they still have the benefit of professional expertise and judgment and also the freedom to exercise their own personal judgment.

A nursing philosophy based on patient autonomy requires the nurse to be morally aligned with the patient rather than with the physician, family, or hospital. The patient is the person who is to have the principal voice, and thus the patient cannot remain the person of lowest standing in the health hierarchy. The nurse is in the hazardous position of mediating between the patient's right to self-determination and the well-meaning attempts of those who would override that right. This type of patient advocacy is a nursing, not a medical, process. Nurses support the attempt of the patient or family to understand fully the information brought to them. If the patient is incompetent, nurses must then respect the wishes of the family.

PATERNALISM VERSUS AUTONOMY

Paternalism is the practice of acting in ways that go against a person's wishes or desires in order to protect or advance the "true" interests of that person.[33] Paternalism is an old concept and viewed within health care as a means to legitimate the role of the physician as a kind of parent. The physician's intentions are presumed to be benevolent and directed toward the patient's welfare. Paternalism entails that the physician makes at least some decisions for the patient, rather than the patient assuming total responsibility for decision making. Thus, paternalism breeds dependency, undermines autonomy, and sometimes results in humiliation.

As nurses perfect their role as patient adovcate and learn to support patient autonomy, they also may enhance their own skills and talents. One area where this is possible (in autonomous nursing practice) is in dealing with ethical dilemmas. Helm suggests a four-step process:

1. Gather as much information as possible in a value-free effort.
2. Determine the precise nature of the ethical dilemma.
3. Decide what should be done and how best it can be done, using several people to gain scope.
4. Take action, and take responsibility for that action.[34]

RECOMMENDATIONS

The nature of contemporary health care results in many and various ethical dilemmas. Often no easy answers or methods are available, and health care providers must explore their own belief systems and collaborate to best facilitate ethical decision making. The following recommendations are offered as suggestions for those who must confront bioethical issues.

Ethical Awareness. Typically, health care professionals have no preparation to deal with ethical crises. When they occur, reactions usually include panic, stress, dread, and other inappropriate responses of helplessness. Until recently, little or no course content on ethics was offered in medical school curricula.[35] The same is true of nursing education. Such content must be developed and incorporated in both nursing and medical health care development curricula.

Documentation. Documentation is the key to dealing with ethical dilemmas as they emerge. Thorough, objective, immediate documentation can demonstrate many things, for example, that the patient received the same kind of treatment, or lack of it, that any other patient would receive in the same or similar circumstances. Documentation of ethical issues by nursing personnel is often inconsistent within institutions and certainly from one geographic region to another. (See Chapter 32 on quality assurance, risk management, and ethical issues.)

Education. Those now practicing in health care must be educated about the nature of ethical problems and methods of problem resolution. Medical staff must become cognizant of present and emerging situations, and nursing staff must assume an important role in ethical decision making, working within an ethical framework and adopting a model for such decision making.

Many nurses are not well prepared by background, education, or experience to function as ethically autonomous practitioners, nor has the social structure of our health care system been supportive of nursing as an autonomous profession. Education should address these deficits as well.

Ethics Committee. Health care facilities and institutions should form interdisciplinary advisory ethics committees. Access to such committees must be made available to physicians, nurses, and anyone else involved in an ethical dilemma. An ethics committee might replace a patient care committee or an institutional review board. The purposes of such committees are to develop policies and protocols and to establish parameters to deal with ethical dilemmas.[36] (See Part 6 on institutional and national issues.)

In 1984 the American Hospital Association established guidelines for the formation of ethics committees, including those limited to giving advice from a voluntary, educational perspective.[37] Ethics committees should be composed of, but not necessarily limited to, physicians, nurses, and clergy. The main purpose is mutual discussion and exploration of issues, with resulting decisions arrived at by many individuals instead of only a few.

Another purpose of an ethics committee is to focus on high-risk areas or units, to predict problems, and focus on specialized nursing care. Such anticipatory attention helps to prevent severe ethical dilemmas from arising suddenly and to prevent or allay the weariness or burnout associated with highly technological, advanced practice care settings.

Research. Prospective research has proved valuable. With the realization that times are changing in health care, individuals can identify potential areas of ethical challenge and design both nursing and interdisciplinary prospective studies. Data gathered through such studies may then be analyzed through techniques of multivariate analysis to identify trends and predict outcomes.

Nurses, physicians, and other professionals view work settings or institutions differently than in the past. Changes in society, education, attitudes, and values result in ethical issues arising from intraprofessional and interprofessional relationships. Many of these issues were not confronted in the past. As nursing has come of age, it has modeled itself on other professions. Given the urgency of the dilemmas posed by the changes occurring in the health care system today, nursing cannot wait to model itself on other professions in the matter of ethics. The situation demands that nursing be in the forefront in identifying and confronting the important ethical issues.

NOTES

1. J.A. Wegmann, "Ethical Issues in Advanced Nursing Practice," in *Patterns of Specialization: Challenge to the Curriculum* (New York: National League for Nursing, 1986).

2. A. Helm, "Ethical Dilemmas and Nursing," *Aviation, Space and Environmental Medicine* 55 (1984): 754–58.

3. H.T. Englehardt, *The Foundations of Bioethics* (New York: Oxford University Press, 1986), 17–104.

4. Helm, "Ethical Dilemmas and Nursing."

5. Englehardt, *Foundations of Bioethics.*

6. Ibid.; L. Curtin and M.J. Flaherty, *Nursing Ethics—Theories and Pragmatics* (Bowie, Md.: R.J. Brady, 1982).

7. Wegmann, "Ethical Issues in Advanced Nursing Practice"; Helm, "Ethical Dilemmas and Nursing."

8. H. Whitman, "Ethical Issues in Cancer Nursing: Defining The Issues," *Oncology Nursing Forum* 7, no. 4 (1980): 37–40.

9. Wegmann, "Ethical Issues in Advanced Nursing Practice"; Whitman, "Ethical Issues in Cancer Nursing."

10. A.R. Tarlov, "The Increasing Supply of Physicians, the Changing Structure of the Health Services System, and the Future Practice of Medicine," *New England Journal of Medicine* 308 (1983): 1235–44.

11. "ICU Nurse Shortage," *American Journal of Nursing* 86 (1986): 960–66.

12. J.R. Lave and W.A. Knaus, "The Economics of Intensive Care Units," in *Medicolegal Aspects of Critical Care,* ed. K. Benesch et al. (Rockville, Md.: Aspen, 1986).

13. Ibid.

14. Wegmann, "Ethical Issues in Advanced Nursing Practice."

15. H. Brody and J. Lynn, "The Physician's Responsibility under the New Medicare Reimbursement for Hospice Care," *New England Journal of Medicine* 14 (1984): 920–22.

16. B. Hosford, *Bioethics Committees* (Rockville, Md.: Aspen, 1986), 16, 91–103.

17. Wegmann, "Ethical Issues in Advanced Nursing Practice."

18. S.J. Younger et al., "Psychosocial and Ethical Implications of Organ Retrieval," *New England Journal of Medicine* 313 (1985): 321–24.

19. Ibid.

20. Wegmann, "Ethical Issues in Advanced Nursing Practice."

21. Hosford, *Bioethics Committees.*

22. S.H. Wanzer et al., "The Physician's Responsibility toward Hopelessly Ill Patients," *New England Journal of Medicine* 310 (1984): 955–59.

23. Hosford, *Bioethics Committees.*

24. E. Ginzberg, "The Destabilization of Health Care," *New England Journal of Medicine* 315 (1986): 757–61.

25. R.S. Shapiro and J.E. Frader, "Critically Ill Infants," *Medicolegal Aspects of Critical Care.*

26. Ibid.

27. Ibid.

28. E.C. Theis, "Ethical Issues: A Nursing Perspective," *New England Journal of Medicine* 315 (1986): 1222–24.

29. Wegmann, "Ethical Issues in Advanced Nursing Practice."

30. S. Kaempfer, "A Care Orientation to Clinical Nursing Research," *Oncology Nursing Forum* 9, no. 4 (1982): 36–38.

31. Helm, "Ethical Dilemmas and Nursing."

32. S. Gadow, "Ethical Issues in Cancer Nursing: A Model for Ethical Decision Making," *Oncology Nursing Forum* 7, no. 4 (1980): 44–47.

33. Ibid.

34. Helm, "Ethical Dilemmas and Nursing."

35. R. Sider, et al., "Basic Curricular Goals in Medical Ethics," *New England Journal of Medicine* 313 (1985): 456–57.

36. Hosford, *Bioethics Committees.*

37. American Hospital Association, *Guidelines: Hospital Committees on Biomedical Ethics* (Chicago: American Hospital Association, 1984).

BIBLIOGRAPHY

Benesch, K., N. Abramson, A. Grenvik, and A. Meisel, eds. *Medicolegal Aspects of Critical Care*. Rockville, Md.: Aspen, 1986. The editors of this book include a nurse, a lawyer, a physician, and a psychiatrist-lawyer. Nine chapters by various contributors cover topics such as informed consent, the right to refuse treatment, the impaired infant, determination of death, patients, families, and health professionals. Guidelines for foregoing life-sustaining treatment are discussed. This is an excellent book, with much useful information. Contributors include an economist and a sociologist, and the varied disciplines represented by the authors contribute to the value of this book.

Benjamin, M., and J. Curtis. *Ethics in Nursing*. 2d ed. New York: Oxford University Press, 1985. This book provides general information on the nature of moral dilemmas. Ethical issues which impact nurses are categorized. Application of ethical analysis and reasoning is illustrative through individual cases.

CA—A Cancer Journal for Clinicians 36, no. 2 (1986). This issue of *CA* presents seven articles exploring various ethical issues confronting clinicians and patients in regard to cancer. Topics such as disclosure of diagnosis, patient placement in clinical trials, suicide, and palliative care are discussed. This group of articles is timely and addresses sensitive issues in the care of cancer patients.

Chinn, P.L., ed. *Ethical Issues in Nursing*. Rockville, Md.: Aspen, 1986. This book is a compilation of essays written by nurses, philosophers, and others on the theoretical and philosophical dimensions of nursing ethics. Fundamental issues of ethics are addressed, followed by consideration of the specific issues of autonomy, privacy, and rights related to life and death. Specific teaching approaches to ethics and value choices are offered. This book also is a good general guide to nursing literature on ethics.

Englehardt, H.T., Jr. *The Foundations of Bioethics*. New York: Oxford University Press, 1986. The author of this comprehensive book is a physician and philosopher. The book explores the theoretical foundation of bioethics. The principles and intellectual foundations of bioethics are described, and issues pertinent to health care are discussed. This book offers a good basis for the understanding of ethical dilemmas and the discipline of bioethics.

Gorovitz, S. *Doctors' Dilemmas: Moral Conflict and Medical Care*. New York: Macmillan, 1982. This book offers an excellent theoretical discussion of philosophical and ethical issues in medicine. The relation of theory to practice is accomplished through the presentation of real cases. While realistic solutions to ethical problems in the practice of medicine are lacking, much needed information on medical error and uncertainty is offered, making this a valuable book.

Hosford, B. *Bioethics Committees*. Rockville, Md.: Aspen, 1986. This book explores the value of bioethics committees in health care decision making. Recent troublesome cases are used as examples of ethical dilemmas. Different sections of the book identify steps in establishing a bioethics committee, the functions of such a committee, and the special types of committees and legal issues involved. This book is helpful to groups seeking guidance in the management of bioethical issues.

Muyskens, J.L. *Moral Problems in Nursing*. Totawa, N.J.: Rowman & Littlefield, 1982. The foundation for ethical decision making is explored through the ethical codes of nursing and the Judeo-Christian moral tradition. Critical reasoning is encouraged through presentation of actual situations drawn from nursing literature and clinical examples. This book is directed specifically to registered nurses and is an important contribution to nursing ethics literature.

Thompson, J.E., and H.O. Thompson. *Bioethical Decision Making for Nurses*. Norwalk, Conn.: Appleton-Century-Crofts, 1985. The purpose of this book is to provide nurses and other health care professionals with a practical model for ethical decision making. Theoretical foundations for bioethics are discussed and the process of ethical decision making is explored.

Chapter 15

Intravenous Fluid and Nutritional Therapies and the Chronically Ill Patient

Kenneth C. Micetich, Arlene Gruber, and Patricia H. Steinecker

There are many levels or intensities of care. Physicians and health care professionals are constantly faced with questions regarding the appropriate degree of intervention that should be undertaken. Technology applied and care rendered may range from simple comfort measures to the administration of blood products and antibiotics or to cardiopulmonary resuscitation, advanced life support, and aggressive medical and surgical therapeutic strategies. It is to be recognized that there is always a basic level of care which is required, namely, those measures which are necessary for the comfort of the patient. What we do after that, however, is determined by a complex decision-making process. The factors influencing our decisions are: (1) the natural history of the patient's disease, (2) the patient's clinical course, and (3) the patient's wishes and preferences.

The natural history of a disease is of utmost importance in determining the level of care. Diseases are acute and chronic, reversible and irreversible. Acute, reversible illnesses are treated aggressively and with a high-level of intense care (if need be), because the expectation is that the patient will survive if treated appropriately. Likewise, a chronic, treatable illness will usually receive a high-level of aggressive medical care.

Chronic, untreatable illnesses pose the most problems for health care professionals when determining the level or intensity of care. In these cases, the level of care and support given to a patient and the level of technology used depends usually on where we judge the patient to be in the natural history or time course of the disease. Within the group of irreversibly and chronically ill patients, there are two important subgroups of patients on which we will focus in this chapter. First, there are those patients with advanced incurable cancer. Second, there are those patients with chronic progressive neurological disease (Alzhemier's disease, senile dementia, advanced Parkinsonism, etc.).

Both groups of patients have several features in common. First, each has a progressive, incurable illness. Second, at some point in their clinical course, the patients may be unable to take adequate oral fluids and calories to maintain hydration and nutrition. Third, at some point both groups of patients may be unable to care for themselves and may be confined to bed. Fourth, the clinical course of both groups of patients may, from time to time, be complicated by the development of an acute medical or surgical illness which is reversible if an appropriate level of care is rendered.

While the advanced incurable cancer patient and the patient with a chronic progressive neurological disease have features in common, there is an important distinction to be made.

The cancer patient will ultimately succumb to his or her disease because the cancer will, by virtue of space-occupying or infiltrative lesions, produce a profound alteration in the physiology of one or more organ systems which is incompatible with life. The patient with a chronic progressive neurological disease, on the other hand, usually does not have profound alterations in the physiology of one or more non-neurological organ systems induced directly by the disease process. Patients with these types of diseases are more likely to develop concomitant acute medical illnesses (such as urinary tract infections and orthostatic and aspiration pneumonia) than the patient with advanced cancer.

In other words, at some point in the clinical course of the patient with advanced cancer, physiological derangements become so profound that the death of the patient is imminent. As health care providers, we all have seen and cared for this type of patient. In contrast, patients with progressive neurological disease, although incurable, do not have concomitant physiologic alterations induced by the disease itself. Rather, they develop medical complications related to neurological impairment of voiding, swallowing, etc. These complications are generally treatable when they occur. Thus, death rarely becomes imminent due to the neurological disease process itself in the patient with chronic progressive neurological disease.

Although there are many questions which could be asked concerning the care of patients with advanced incurable cancer and the patient with a chronic progressive neurological disease, we will focus on what we consider to be three important issues. First, should these patients receive intravenous fluids if they are no longer able to take oral fluids? Second, should these patients receive enteral or parenteral alimentation if they can no longer eat? Third, should a patient with a chronic disease be treated if he or she develops an acute medical or surgical illness which is reversible?

In trying to answer these questions for the two groups of patients we wish to consider, we will proceed as follows. We will consider whether intravenous fluids and nutritional support are medical therapies and thus whether their use is governed by the same rules regarding the application of medical therapies in general. Second, we will consider whether the decision to stop or discontinue such therapies is a decision that must involve quality of life arguments. Third, we will discuss what we consider to be principles of management of the patients with advanced incurable cancer and chronic progressive neurological disease (what therapies are required and who decides). Finally, we will indicate that the intravenous fluid and nutrition debate must go beyond the medical profession and that it is society that must reach a consensus.

INTRAVENOUS FLUIDS AND ALIMENTATION ARE MEDICAL THERAPIES

Intravenous fluids and alimentation are clearly medical therapies. Their safe and effective administration requires the supervision of highly trained medical personnel. Fluid overload, electrolyte imbalance, aspiration pneumonia, osmotic diarrhea, thrombosis, and infections are but a few of the complications which can occur as a result of intravenous fluid administration and enteral or parenteral alimentation.

Therapies are considered efficacious if they can cure, palliate, or prolong the survival of the patient. Intravenous fluids and alimentation are rarely, if ever, curative in and of themselves. Rather, they support the patient until the underlying problem leading to dehydration and malnutrition is corrected, if possible. In the two groups of patients we are considering, we must ask if these therapies will palliate or prolong the survival of the patient. If we conclude yes, then institution of such therapies is judged to be meritorius and should be encouraged if the patient is in agreement with the proposed course of action. If not, then their institution is without benefit and therefore not indicated.

Intravenous hydration and fluids may palliate thirst. However, the sensation of thirst in conscious patients can be ameliorated by glycerin sticks and ice chips and, in fact, dehydration may allow the patient to be cared for by nursing personnel more easily.[1] Thus, the palliative role of intravenous fluid therapy must be seriously questioned. Additionally, intravenous fluids can prolong the survival of the patient. Whether it does or not depends upon the particular patient population under consideration. It is not likely to prolong survival in the patient whose death is imminent, but it will prolong survival in the patient whose death is not imminent.

Enteral or parenteral alimentation can be viewed in the same manner. Physicians feel that alimentation is beneficial in patients with acute, reversible illness. Here the purpose of alimentation is to support the patient who cannot ingest enough calories to prevent weight loss and concomitant loss of body protein and muscle mass. In the patient whose death is imminent, it has no useful purpose. Patients who are ill have no appetite and therefore we are not palliating the sensation of hunger. However, the patient who is chronically irreversibly ill, but whose death is not imminent, will have a shortened survival if alimentation is not instituted.

Therefore, in applying these two forms of therapy, two critical questions to ask in the decision-making process are these: (1) Will therapy effectively palliate the patient? (2) Will survival be prolonged? If the answer to either of these questions is in the affirmative and the patient has not expressed wishes to the contrary at some other time, then these therapies are mandatory.

QUALITY OF LIFE ARGUMENT

Is the decision to withdraw or to withhold intravenous fluid therapy or alimentation from a chronically ill patient a quality of life decision? This is most troublesome to health care providers, because all realize that quality of life decisions are relative and that one individual cannot make a quality of life decision reliably for another. Once we judge that the application of a medical therapy will *not* prolong the survival of, cure, or palliate the patient, then failure to recommend or to institute that therapy, even if it leads to the death of a patient, is good medical policy. To act thus is to rightly accept the inevitable progression of disease and refuse to apply technology for technology's sake.

If health care professionals fail to recommend or to institute a therapy for a patient whose life will be prolonged by that therapy and the patient has not expressed wishes to the contrary at some other time, then a quality of life decision is clearly being made.

PRINCIPLES OF MANAGEMENT OF THE PATIENT WITH INCURABLE CANCER

At the time that we judge the death of the patient with advanced incurable malignancy to be imminent (death will occur soon despite any therapeutic modality employed), our obligation is to not prolong the dying process.[2] We recommend to the patient only those measures which are essential for his or her comfort. Normally, intravenous fluids are not ordered unless there is a palliative goal for that therapy.[3] Intravenous fluids administered to this type of patient cannot usually reverse the profound physiologic derangements secondary to neoplastic infiltration of a major organ system or systems. Thus, fluid therapy has only a marginal impact (or no impact) on prolonging survival. Likewise, alimentation of any type for these patients is not indicated, because such therapy lacks curative, palliative, or life-prolonging effects.

The death of a patient is not imminent at the time of first diagnosis of the incurable malignancy. If death is not imminent, then temporary use of intravenous fluids may be appropriate. Treatment of intercurrent acute medical and surgical illnesses must also be considered if palliation by means of the therapy is to be realized. It would be unusual to ever have to consider enteral nutritional support at any time during the clinical course of the patient with advanced incurable malignancy.

In the real practice of medicine, patients who have advanced, incurable malignancy and whose death is imminent do not pose much of a management problem. Most die at home without intravenous fluids and without alimentation. If they are admitted for palliation and terminal care (to receive parenteral medications), the temptation to hydrate the patient should be resisted, since it is medically useless. On occasion, families and health care professionals may insist on useless therapies.[4] Each case must be handled individually, but in our experience such behavior on the part of families may constitute denial of the impending death. Empathic education and orientation to the goals and realistic expectations of therapies generally does much to relieve disquiet and concern.

We acknowledge the strong symbolism of food and water, but feel that health care professionals must view it in its proper perspective.[5] We recognize that spoon feeding small amounts of sustenance and offering sips of water by mouth are symbolic ways of showing our compassion and care to a patient—whether the patient is dying at home or in an institution such as a hospital or extended care facility. The strong symbolism attached to that caring gesture cannot be dismissed. However, once feeding cannot be done through these human gestures of concern and care, and medical interventions become necessary to accomplish it then the feeding becomes medical therapy, with its own inherent indications, contraindications, and associated risks and benefits. It is not appropriate to render a medical treatment whose sole value is symbolic.

PRINCIPLES OF MANAGEMENT OF PATIENTS WITH CHRONIC PROGRESSIVE NEUROLOGICAL DISEASE

The chronically ill patients whose deaths, although inevitable, are not imminent will at some point not be able to ingest enough fluids or food to maintain hydration or nutrition. Intravenous fluids and alimentation prolong survival. There is no reason from a medical point of view *not* to provide this therapy. Failure to recommend or to institute this therapy in the patient who has not expressed wishes to the contrary is a quality of life decision.

Quality-of-life modifications of the medical recommendation are proper when it is the patient who is making them. Those who provide care for these patients should speak with them frequently and work with them so that when a critical event occurs, a plan which is based on patient wishes and preferences has already been made. The concept of a living will helps remind all of us to do this. But in the absence of such prior directives, the patient must be treated. Thus, these patients should be nutritionally supported and hydrated. When these patients develop acute, reversible medical or surgical illnesses, in the absence of patient wishes to the contrary, there is no medical reason not to treat.

Although this follows logically from our definition as to what constitutes a useful medical therapy, it is a policy with which we are all inherently uncomfortable. When is enough enough? We are struck with the futility of prolonging the life of a patient with chronic progressive neurological disease. Additionally, from our own life experiences and from talking to our patients and their families, we know that most people would not want to be bedridden, be force-fed artificially, or be unable to care for themselves. Yet, we feel uncomfortable making a quality of life decision for others. It is proper that the medical profession should refrain from making these types of decisions. The technology to sustain these patients is here. The natural history of the underlying disease process cannot be reversed. Should these patients be treated? Who decides? Who judges that a life is no longer worth living?

WHO DECIDES?

In the case of the patient whose death is imminent, competency and incompetency are not critical issues when it comes to treatment of intercurrent illness, intravenous fluid, or nutritional support. These therapies are of no utility. No decision by the patient or a surrogate need be made, because one never recommends a useless therapy.

In the case of the patient with a chronic progressive neurological disease, however, competency and incompetency are critical issues, because failure to institute the types of therapies we are talking about will lead to the death of the patient. Most of these patients are competent early in the course of their illness, and we would suggest that it is the duty of medical professionals to formulate a treatment plan with a patient during the early stages of the disease which addresses, at the very least, the issues of hydration, alimentation, and treatment of complicating medical and surgical illness. The requisite conversations are difficult but must be held. Since quality of life decisions are being made, it must be the patient who makes them. The natural history of these types of patients is well known. It is reliably predictable what will occur to these patients over time. The question is not whether a progressive decline in neurological function and performance status will occur, but only when it will occur.

What should we do, however, when we find ourselves treating a patient with chronic progressive neurological disease whose wishes are unknown to us? For reasons outlined earlier, the presumption is to treat intercurrent medical problems, to hydrate, and to aliment. However, there is discomfort about the continued treatment of these patients. Who can make a quality of life decision for a patient when his wishes are unknown?

What are some of the factors which might lead society to accept continuing or discontinuing the support of these chronically ill patients? The right to life argument supports continued treatment. The life-not-worth-living argument supports discontinuation of treatment. Certain cultural and religious segments of society may support continued treatment, while others may not. Health care administrators may prefer not to support further care and treatment of these patients, because caring for them takes away financial resources which might better be applied elsewhere. Families, doctors, and hospitals might support continued treatment because not to do so may lead to legal reprisals. From a strict medical indications point of view, continued support and treatment is mandatory.

However, because of the conflicting values, we have turned to the courts, thinking that they would provide the answer.[6] In the case of a competent patient, for example, the California Superior Court stated that a patient's decision to forgo medical treatment or life support through mechanical means is a moral and philosophical decision belonging to the patient alone, not to physicians, lawyers, judges, or ethics committees.[7] Courts have found that competent patients have the right to refuse life-prolonging treatments.

In the case of an irreversibly comatose incompetent patient (irreversible coma being the most extreme manifestation of the patient with chronic progressive neurological disease), both the New Jersey and California courts have ruled that ventilatory and nutritional support could be discontinued.[8] In the case of a noncomatose incompetent patient, the New Jersey Supreme Court stated that even though a treatment may prolong life, if it does not benefit the patient's condition, the substitute decision maker must attempt to respect both the patient's right to life and his right to die of natural causes.[9]

It must be remembered, however, that the decisions handed down in favor of withdrawing treatment have been decisions reversing prior decisions reflecting the confusion of the courts. And in cases requiring the opinion of more than one jurist, the findings have not been unanimous. We therefore cannot assume at this time that there is a groundswell of legal support for the position of forgoing nutritional therapy. Case law exists in a limited number of states. But what if it existed in all fifty states? This would only tell us that a legal consensus existed that our termination of treatment was not a criminal or homicidal act. In other words, termination of treatment would be a permissible act but not a mandatory one.

In addition to legal findings, the March 1986 opinion of the AMA's Council on Ethical and Judicial Affairs must be considered.[10] It states that withholding of artificial nutrition from terminally ill patients or those in a permanent coma is not unethical when done in consultation with the family.

There are those who are relieved that a groundswell of legal and other kinds of support does not exist. Their relief is not because they disagree with the judgment that withholding nutritional support is correct, but because they fear too rapid a change could compromise professional and societal goals.[11]

Are the above mentioned court decisions consistent with medical ethics? At this point in time, it is extremely difficult to judge whether or not a legal ruling is consistent with medical ethics, since the individual members of the medical profession, despite the AMA's statement, are still debating the artificial nutrition issue. It may be that the legal profession assumes that medical professionals, individually as well as collectively, have a single position and that it will now consider this presumed unitary position when determining their findings. It may also be that some physicians look to these findings and interpret the legal position as an ethical position (when in fact no ethical position has been definitely determined). We, therefore, could be seeing two powerful professions looking to each other for guidance, believing that they are reading each other correctly, and moving society in a direction each believes the other sanctions—and doing all this before society has had the opportunity to fully examine, debate, and decide for itself.

Do these legal and medical statements represent a consensus that society has not yet endorsed? It should be pointed out that while society has not yet signaled its dissatisfaction with the discontinuation of care in the chronically neurologically ill patient, it would be premature to presume that society approves.

Callahan suggests a soft public policy regarding nutritional support.[12] He asks for government involvement in the form of encouragement of public discussion and the prodding of health care professionals and institutions to collect data, publicize the issues, and develop informal guidelines. His intention is to avoid a hard public policy encoded in laws and regulations. We would like to believe that the government would not have to prod but would only have to support an already existing effort by health care professionals to assist society in its debate and in the formulation of a nutritional therapy policy.

What if, after all of the discussions have taken place, we find that 55 percent of all adults in this society believe that forgoing nutritional support in the patient with chronic, irreversible neurological disease is acceptable. Would we then know that it is the right thing to do? Is it not possible for the majority to believe an act to be ethical when it is in fact unethical? It *is* possible. Therefore, when the act we are considering is the termination of human life, deliberation about policy must be done extraordinarily carefully. We would hope that then the chance of society's choosing an unethical policy would decrease. We must look honestly and critically at our options and their respective consequences, identify, examine, and weigh our duties, and be convinced that our choice is rational, not rationalized.

SUMMARY

In this chapter, we have argued that the principle of management of the patient whose death is imminent is to institute only those measures necessary for the comfort of the patient. Any therapies which do not have a palliative intent are unnecessary. The management of the patient with chronic progressive neurological disease is more complicated, since the death of these patients is not imminent. Here we reason that since intravenous fluid therapy, nutritional support, and the treatment of complicating acute but reversible medical and surgical illnesses will be either palliative or life prolonging, these patients should be treated.

From a medical point of view we realize—and are frustrated by—the progressiveness and irreversibility of the neurological condition despite best medical therapy. However, to withdraw or to withhold therapy is a quality of life decision which cannot be made other than by the patient. We sense that most people with chronic progressive neurological disease would not want their lives prolonged. We call for improved patient-physician discussions early in the course of the disease to ascertain how the patient wants to be treated as the disease progresses. We also call for a national debate for the purpose of reaching a consensus on how these patients should be managed.

NOTES

1. J.N. Zerwekh, "The Dehydration Issue," *Nursing* 13 (1983): 47–51.

2. P. Ramsey, *The Patient as Person* (New Haven, Conn.: Yale University Press, 1970), 113–129.

3. D.C. Thomasma, K.C. Micetich, and P.H. Steinecker, "Continuance of Nutritional Care in the Terminally Ill Patient," *Critical Care Clinics* 2 (1986): 61–71; K.C. Micetich, P.H. Steinecker, and D.C. Thomasma, "Are Intravenous Fluids Morally Required for a Dying Patient?" *Archives of Internal Medicine* 143 (1983): 975–78.

4. K. Micetich, P. Steinecker, and D. Thomasma, "An Empirical Study of Physician Attitudes," in *By No Extraordinary Means: The Choice to Forgo Life-sustaining Food and Water*, ed. Joanne Lynn (Bloomington, Ind.: Indiana University Press, 1986), 39–43.

5. G. Meilaender, "On Removing Food and Water: Against the Stream," *Hastings Center Report* 14 (December 1984): 11–13.

6. R.S. Dresser and E.V. Boisaubin, Jr., "Ethics, Law and Nutritional Support," *Archives of Internal Medicine* 145 (1985): 122–24; D.W. Meyers, "Legal Aspects of Withdrawing Nourishment from an Incurably Ill Patient," *Archives of Internal Medicine* 145 (1985): 125–28; A.M. Capron, "Historical Overview: Law and Public Perceptions," in *By No Extraordinary Means*.

7. Bouvia v. Superior Court, 225, Cal. Rptr. 297.

8. In re Quinlan, 70 N.J. 10, 355 A.2d 647, cert. denied, 429 U.S. 922 (1976); Barber v. Los Angeles County Superior Court, 147 Cal App. 3d 1006, 195, Cal. Rptr. 484, (Ct. App. 1983).

9. In re Conroy, 98 N.J. 321, 486 A.2d 1209 (1985).

10. American Medical Association, "Current Opinions of the Council on Ethical and Judicial Affairs of the American Medical Association" (Chicago: American Medical Association, 1986), secs. 2.18–2.19, pp. 12–13.

11. M. Siegler and A.J. Weisbard, "Against the Stream: Should Fluids and Nutritional Support Be Discontinued?" *Archives of Internal Medicine* 145 (1985): 129–31.

12. D. Callahan, "Public Policy and the Cessation of Nutrition," in *By No Extraordinary Means*.

Chapter 16

Making Treatment Decisions for Permanently Unconscious Patients

Maynard M. Cohen, Elena N. Cohen, and David C. Thomasma

THE MEDICAL PERSPECTIVE*

Six considerations are of paramount importance in relation to medical management of permanently unconscious patients beyond treatment of their physical condition: (1) employment of an adequate and universally recognized terminology, (2) recognition of the scope of medical treatment, (3) accurate delineation of the cause of death following withdrawal of food and liquids, (4) determination of the patient's ability to perceive pain, (5) costs of the medical treatment, and (6) responsibility of the physician.

Terminology

Confusion and inaccuracies in terminology by both medical personnel and the laity have frequently compounded the difficulties in management of patients being maintained on life-support systems or through artificially administered nutrition and hydration. The President's Commission for the Study of Ethical Problems in Medicine and Biomedical and Behavioral Research did much to clarify the problem in their 1983 report *Deciding to Forgo Life-Sustaining Treatment.*[1] It defined the unconscious patient as one in whom all components of mental life are absent—all thought, feeling, sensation, desire, emotion, and awareness of self or environment. In such patients all higher cerebral cortical functions are absent. The lower centers in the brain stem essential to the maintenance of life, however, may remain functional in certain varieties of permanent unconsciousness, as may the spinal cord. Simple reflex responses such as grimacing or withdrawing in reaction to painful stimuli, eye opening or closing, swallowing, or pupillary reaction to light may still be present, giving the uninformed an impression of purposeful movement.

The majority of catastrophic conditions such as severe head trauma, stroke, hypoglycemia, near drowning, asphyxia, carbon monoxide poisoning, and cardiac arrest soon result in either recovery of consciousness or death. About 12 percent of victims will remain permanently unconscious in a persistent vegetative state (PVS). Although apocryphal

_____

*This section of Chapter 16 is by Maynard M. Cohen.

186

statements have appeared claiming recovery from a persistent vegetative state of greater than one month duration, only three such instances have been reported in the medical literature.[2] Severe nervous system damage occurred in all three. Two "awoke" only to enter the locked-in state, in which they became aware of their surroundings but were incapable of speaking or making any movement other than with their eyes. They were able to answer yes or no questions by eyeblinks and could communicate further by indicating letters of the alphabet through blinking. In this manner, one of the survivors indicated he felt his condition worse than unconsciousness and even worse than death.[3]

One recently publicized patient was reported to have recovered consciousness after almost two months in "coma." It is uncertain, however, that she was indeed in a persistent vegetative state. Following awakening she continued to exhibit severe residuals in the form of amnesia, paresis, and balance and gait difficulties.[4]

In addition to PVS, four other categories of the permanently unconscious were defined by the President's Commission. The first includes those patients demonstrating progressive neural involvement from untreatable conditions such as neoplasms and vascular malformations. They are nonresponsive, and can be expected to remain in true coma for days, weeks, or occasionally months until succumbing to their disease.

Patients in the next group similarly have a short survival span and remain comatose until death. In these individuals, loss of consciousness is sudden following trauma, cardiac arrest, or stroke, and brain stem function fails to stabilize sufficiently to allow entry to a persistent vegetative state.

The last two groups defined by the President's Commission include patients in the end stages of severe dementia (Alzheimer's Disease and related conditions) and anencephalic infants. Because of the very special circumstances surrounding these latter groups, they are outside the scope of this chapter. (See Chapter 4 on caution regarding infants.)

Difficulties have arisen because of the imprecise use of terms, particularly *irreversible coma,* which refers to a condition in which the patient never awakens. The term applies most appropriately to those two groups in which unconsciousness is followed by death within a period of days, weeks, or months. Strictly speaking, PVS is distinct from irreversible coma, since patients in PVS stabilize and have sleep-awake cycles. They may respond reflexly to loud noises or painful stimuli. Their sensorium is nonreactive, however, and they fulfill the criteria of the permanently unconscious. As long as they are provided food and water, they may remain in such a state for extended periods unless threatened by infection or other destabilizing conditions. The longest recorded instance of survival in PVS was 37 years.[5]

Unfortunately even the American Medical Association has been imprecise in its terminology. The section in *Current Opinions of the Council on Ethical and Judicial Affairs* entitled "Withholding or Withdrawing Life-Prolonging Medical Treatment" uses the term *irreversible coma* where the intention clearly is to refer to the permanently unconscious, including those in PVS.[6]

Scope of Medical Treatment

The second consideration, what constitutes medical treatment, has been adequately dealt with by both medical and legal opinion. Any procedure requiring a physician's presence or supervision or needing a physician's order for implementation is medical treatment. This is of particular import in the case of artificially administered nutrition and hydration. The brief submitted by the American Academy of Neurology to the Massachusetts Supreme Court in the case of Paul Brophy[7] is in accord with the position of the American College of Physicians and the Massachusetts Medical Association in considering feeding and hydration through nasogastric or gastrostomy tube to be medical treatment. Further support is evidenced in legal opinion, such as that of Judge Thomas A. Fortkort, who refers to the nasogastric tube as "probably the simplest medical procedure."[8]

Cause of Death

Similarly the cause of death following withholding of food and liquids has been unequivocally settled. Medical opinion holds the underlying condition to be the cause of death. For example, brain tumors produce an increase in the intracranial pressure, which in turn compresses the brain stem and impairs respiration and circulation. It is the tumor that is the cause of death, for without it, life would have persisted. Likewise, if there is a spontaneous rupture of a major artery that produces blood loss and results in inadequate oxygen supply to the brain, the cause of death is the arterial rupture. In its Brophy brief, the American Academy of Neurology clearly stated the cause of death in the event of withdrawal of food and water would be the ruptured cerebral aneurysm.[9]

Perception of Pain

After observing patients withdraw a limb from a painful stimulus (often accompanied by facial grimaces), the uninformed have frequently concluded that individuals in a persistent vegetative state retain the ability to perceive pain. Indeed, even Peter Gubellini, the court-appointed lawyer for Paul Brophy, maintained that Mr. Brophy would experience intolerable pain if denied food and water. In their Brophy brief, the American Academy of Neurology recognized that no pain could be experienced in an individual in PVS.[10] The perception of pain requires a functioning cerebral cortex to receive pain signals and recognize them as such. In PVS, the cortex is nonfunctional and, as in deep anesthesia, the sensation of pain is absent.

Medical Costs

Our society is extremely loath to put a monetary value on any individual life. In an economy of abundance, this is a defensible position. However, we operate in an economy of scarcity. There is an ever-growing limitation on the costs that will be borne by government and other third party payers. Increase of funds in one area of medical service is inevitably counterbalanced by decreases in other health services. The cost of maintaining Paul Brophy, borne entirely by Blue Cross for over three years, exceeded $10,000 a month. Costs of $1,000 a day have been reported for a shorter period.[11] An estimated 5,000 to 10,000 patients in PVS at any one time in our country would thus result in a cost exceeding $1 billion a year. The issue of whether this expenditure is medically and ethically justified in the face of our present limited resources is one that must soon be faced by society.

Physician Responsibility

The final consideration is the responsibility of the physician in aiding decision makers in arriving at the most suitable choice. The law is becoming increasingly clear in delineating the boundaries of those choices. (This subject will be covered in the next section of this chapter.) It is thus an important responsibility of the physician to become familiar with the law and to be aware of all available options. At each stage, the physician must fully inform the patient's surrogate of the clinical condition, the treatment options available, and the consequences of each of those options. Two often choices have been based on unrealistic hopes and expectations. It is the physician's responsibility not to force a choice, but to bring realism into each clinical situation—tempered always with compassion.

THE LEGAL PERSPECTIVE*

The American legal system has long recognized that every person has a right to determine what is done to his or her own body.[12] In the wake of the Quinlan case and the nation's first "living will" statute, courts and legislatures have answered difficult questions concerning termination of medical treatment for a special category of patients: those who are no longer capable of making treatment decisions for themselves (the decisionally incapacitated).[13]

A consensus in the law has emerged that (1) a person able to make medical decisions, regardless of prognosis, has a right to refuse treatment (including artificially administered nutrition and hydration), and that the right is not lost if he or she becomes later incapable of exercising it (i.e., another must exercise it on the patient's behalf); (2) the *patient's* previously expressed wishes (not the wishes of the patient's family or physician) determine whether life support should be used; (3) there is no legal distinction between *withholding* and *withdrawing* treatment; (4) the view that "extraordinary," but not "ordinary," treatment can be forgone generally has been abandoned in favor of a benefits/burdens analysis (treatment can be forgone when, from the patient's perspective, burdens of treatment outweigh benefits); (5) forgoing treatment does not constitute murder, suicide, or assisted suicide; and (6) providing life-sustaining treatment against a patient's known wishes constitutes battery.[14]

These recent strides, however, have not resolved all the legal controversies, largely because of technological advances in sustaining biological life. Special questions have arisen concerning patients in a persistent vegetative state (PVS)—who by definition cannot make medical decisions—because some of these patients can live almost indefinitely with life-sustaining treatment. Courts and legislatures are continuing to clarify the legal issues concerning this group of patients.

The Courts

When determining the boundaries of the right to refuse treatment, courts traditionally have weighed this right against competing state interests (the preservation of life, maintain-

---

*This section of Chapter 17 is by Elena N. Cohen.

ing the ethical integrity of the medical profession, prevention of suicide, and protection of innocent third parties). In the seminal Quinlan case, in which the New Jersey Supreme Court authorized the ending of treatment for PVS patient Karen Quinlan, as her father requested, the court wrote that the state interest in preserving life weakens and the individual's right to privacy grows as "the degree of bodily invasion [during treatment] increases and the prognosis dims."[15] The state interest in preserving life, even in cases of positive prognosis with treatment, is usually not sufficient to outweigh a person's right to refuse treatment.[16] This state interest becomes even weaker in cases of permanent unconsciousness, since the prognosis is very dim, there being no potential (based on reasonable medical judgment) for return to cognitive life.

Nevertheless, concerns have been raised that artificial feeding should not be withheld from these patients, some parts of the medical and legal community claiming that the treatment is not sufficiently invasive (since it causes no physical discomfort) and that the prognosis is not sufficiently dim (since the PVS patient could live indefinitely if artificial feeding were continued). Appellate courts throughout the country, however, consistently have rejected these arguments.[17]

The Brophy decision involves many of the salient issues concerning permanently unconscious patients.[18] Paul Brophy had been in a persistent vegetative state for over three years before his gastrostomy tube was withdrawn and he died peacefully. In September of 1986, the Massachusetts Supreme Judicial Court (SJC) overturned a trial court's refusal to terminate treatment and held that the "substituted judgment" of a PVS patient to refuse artificially administered sustenance must be honored.[19] The SJC agreed with the trial court's factual finding that Brophy would have declined artificial feeding in this instance, even though he never expressed this preference in writing and never explicitly referred to artificial feeding. It rejected, however, the finding that Brophy might experience a "painful" death if his artificial feeding were withdrawn, citing several medical authorities in support of the proposition that a person in a persistent vegetative state does not experience pain or suffering.

The court also decided that Brophy's right to discontinue treatment overrode the state interest in preserving life, even though Brophy was not "terminally ill" in the traditional sense. It stressed that "the State's interest in life encompasses a broader interest than mere corporeal existence. In certain . . . circumstances the burden of maintaining the corporeal existence degrades the very humanity it was meant to serve. The law recognizes the individual's right to preserve his humanity, even if to preserve his humanity means to allow the natural processes of a disease or affliction to bring about a death with dignity." The SJC, disagreeing with the lower court, noted that, under this approach, the *individual,* not the state, determines quality of life. Turning to the ethical integrity of the medical profession, the court wrote that authorizing removal in this case is consistent with "sound medical practice."

This SJC decision, as the first written state supreme court opinion both issued while the patient was still alive and authorizing artificial feeding removal, is extremely significant. Especially important are its statements that (1) the trial court's finding that PVS patients may feel pain was incorrect because it was contrary to the weight of medical opinion; (2) therefore, a gastrostomy tube is no less invasive to a PVS patient than is a respirator, even though it could be less invasive for a conscious patient; (3) a feeding tube which the patient would not want and which does not cause pain can be "intrusive" and "extraordinary"; and (4) when a feeding tube is removed from a person in a persistent vegetative state, the cause of death is the underlying condition which prevents swallowing, not the tube removal.

Since the *Brophy* decision, several significant decisions in other states, including Arizona, New Jersey, and New York, have adopted and expanded upon the *Brophy* approach (see Bibliography at the end of the chapter). In summary, courts are protecting the right of permanently unconscious patients to forgo any medical treatment, including artificial feeding.

Legislation

Most of the 39 "natural death" statutes passed in the United States as of August 1987 allow a person's *living will* (also called an *advance directive*) to become effective when he or she is in a *terminal condition,* as the statutes define this.[20] Although some statutes clearly cover permanently unconscious patients,[21] others are ambiguous,[22] and still others exclude such PVS patients.[23] Some language which initially appears ambiguous does cover permanently unconscious patients when read in context.

For example, in the Uniform Rights of Terminally Ill Act, adopted in 1985 by the National Conference of Commissioners on Uniform State Laws, a declaration under the act becomes effective only when a person has a terminal condition, which the act defines as "an incurable or irreversible condition that, *without* the administration of *life-sustaining treatment,* will, in the opinion of the attending physician, result in death within a relatively short time" (emphasis added).[24] Under the act, *life-sustaining treatment* means "any medical procedure . . . that . . . will serve only to prolong the process of dying." The law commissioners write in their comments: "If nutrition and hydration are not necessary for comfort care or alleviation of pain, they may be withdrawn." Therefore, a person in a persistent vegetative state would have a terminal condition, since he or she would die within a relatively short time without artificially administered nutrition and hydration. This interpretation is not tautologous, nor mere semantics, but recognizes that people whose natural abilities have already been lost cannot be forced to have medical treatment provided against their wishes.

Since legislation concerning life-sustaining treatment is relatively recent (the first natural death act was passed in 1976), statutory language is being refined by judicial construction and legislative amendment. In response to uncertainty about whether certain patients were covered by the terms of a specific act and also in response to concerns about whether an act provided the exclusive method for a patient to refuse life-sustaining treatment, individual court decisions recently have clarified the following: (1) a person has a constitutional right to refuse artificial feeding even if this is not a treatment that can be withheld under a natural death act;[25] (2) a person's death is nonetheless imminent (part of the definition of *terminal condition* in some acts) when he or she could live for months with treatment;[26] and (3) *persistent vegetative state* does not automatically mean the same as *irreversible coma.*[27] Statutes have been amended to broaden their coverage to include hopelessly ill patients whose life expectancy with treatment may not be extremely limited, a move toward including permanently unconscious patients under the statutes.[28]

Issues for the Future

It is now generally well settled in ethics, law, and medicine that health-care providers must honor a permanently unconscious patient's wishes (expressed while able to make medical decisions) to reject any artificial life-sustaining procedure, including artificial feeding. Specific issues have emerged recently and undoubtedly will receive more attention in the future: (1) the obligations of an institution or physician to forgo treatment consistent with a patient's wishes, even when doing so violates the institution's or physician's policy (the trend is that such policies cannot be implemented if they restrict patient rights);[29] (2) the civil liability of health care providers who treat without consent;[30] (3) the appropriate procedure for determining patient wishes (e.g., the correct evidentiary standard and judicial intervention if necessary); (4) procedural safeguards to confirm the accuracy of prognosis; and (5) decision-making procedures for permanently unconscious patients who have never previously expressed their wishes.

THE ETHICAL PERSPECTIVE*

The most difficult problem in making decisions for permanently unconscious patients is that of determining the wishes of such patients. If there are no wishes that can be determined, the main problem then becomes making quality of life judgments for others. These problems are examined in four sections. First the moral meaning of a permanent coma (PC) and the persistent vegetative state (PVS) is discussed.[31] Second, the "right to die" is explored from the vantage point of a number of ethical principles. Third, current instruments for determining wishes are discussed, with special focus on their inadequacies. Finally, proposals are advanced that would improve our ability to make judgments about the treatment of patients in a permanent coma or persistent vegetative state.

This section of the chapter builds on the medical and legal considerations already advanced. As Dr. Maynard Cohen pointed out in the first section of this chapter, PC and PVS are entirely different states. But even though they are importantly different from a medical perspective, I will argue that they are identical from a moral perspective—indeed, both are morally identical to being in the process of dying.

The Moral Meaning of Coma and Vegetative State

It seems odd to speak of a "moral meaning" of a medical condition. Yet most medical conditions do involve questions of value.[32] PC or PVS involves an especially difficult question, because both assault the self-determining capacity of human beings, the very center of personhood. When a person can no longer make decisions for himself or herself, we turn our efforts toward making the best decisions for him or her. About this move there is both uncertainty and controversy. Let us look at the most straightforward objection to

---

*This section of Chapter 16 is by David C. Thomasma. The position taken by the author is entirely his own, and this section does not reflect the views of the Society of the Right to Die, even though he is on the board of directors.

withdrawing food and water from permanently unconscious patients in order to understand the logic of the uncertainty and the controversy.

It is agreed, the objection goes, that one can apply the moral rules to dying patients and conclude that their dying should not be prolonged. In short, we have a duty to not prolong dying.[33] Thus, withdrawal of extraordinary means is permissible to ensure that a person's dying is not prolonged. But a coma and a vegetative state are not the same as dying. They are medical conditions that are clearly distinct from death. Persons in such states who are properly maintained can live a very long time. Indeed, some persons spontaneously emerge from comas and some, though fewer, from vegetative states. Consequently, one cannot withhold or withdraw life-prolonging treatments from such patients. This is essentially the pro-life argument regarding the issue of withdrawing food and water.

The answers to this objection reveal the moral meaning of a permanent coma or persistent vegetative state. First, it must be acknowledged that there is a physiological difference between coma and the process of dying. But there is no life-enhancing difference for the person. The person is removed from the normal intercourse of human affairs. The person does not abide in the affective and cognitive realm. In fact, eventual removal from the biosphere through terminal illness can be less gruesome than permanent removal from the affective and cognitive realm.

In re Conroy, the court articulated this well, arguing that once a person no longer had the capacity to participate meaningfully in human life, one could in effect regard that person as dying and apply the rules about not prolonging dying.[34] According to this line of reasoning, although a coma or vegetative state is not physiologically the same as dying from a terminal disease, each is morally identical (or if not identical, even worse than dying). When one cannot enjoy those things that provide meaning to human life, then the quality of that life has suffered irreversible damage.[35] We might call this the "cognitive life rule."

If being in PC or PVS is worse than dying, then the rules about not prolonging dying can be applied to patients in such conditions. Treatments can be withheld and withdrawn in their best interests. The pro-life objection does not hold.

Further, the pro-life argument misses several other very important points. These points are adumbrated elsewhere and are merely listed here for emphasis:

1. All treatment decisions should be reviewed when patients face a grim prognosis, not just when they are certified as dying.
2. Treatment decisions are patient-driven: Patients should determine all medical treatment, not just that given during crises in their lives. When a patient is incompetent, the patient's proxy must defend the wishes of the patient. To date, the clearest expression of this right of self-determination is found in Conroy.[36] If patients predetermine that they do not wish to have their lives prolonged in a PC or PVS by the use of specified treatments, then no such treatments should be ordered. Whether the patients are clinically judged as dying is not germane.
3. Withdrawing treatments that prolong conditions which would normally lead to death without the treatments is a form of recognition that the death occurs as a result of a natural condition. (See the discussion of the Uniform Rights of the Terminally Ill Act in the section "The Legal Perspective.") Hence one does not "kill" such patients by terminating or withholding treatment. Rather, one organizes and directs life-prolonging technology to humane ends.

There is, however, a "zone of freedom" that admits of legitimate disagreements about treatment.[37] Therefore, it is best to limit the discussion about withdrawing or withholding treatment from permanently comatose patients to the question of the right to die and the inadequacies of current instruments for giving due respect to that right.

The Right to Die

Although the right to die is not now legally recognized, it appears that society is on the verge of giving it legal recognition. Below is a summary of some of the moral rules that bear on the right to die and the question whether to give such a right formal recognition.

Autonomy

Autonomy entails having a respect for the free choices people make. Allowing persons autonomy does not require respect for persons as much as respect for their wishes, whether we agree with them or not.[38] At the very least, autonomy buttresses the right of privacy, the right to determine medical treatment, and the proxy duty to act in accordance with the patient's previously expressed wishes or what the patient probably would have wished given the patient's values. Respecting the autonomy of persons means that patient wishes predominate in their care if the wishes can be reliably determined. When they cannot, we must turn to a different principle.

Beneficence

The principle of beneficence is that one should act in the best interests of others. It is often misunderstood to entail that one can act over the objections of a person or in the absence of that person's consent if the act is in the person's best interest. To act in this way is paternalism (although even paternalism is sometimes warranted under certain circumstances). Beneficence should be understood to be acting for the good of a person where the person defines the good.

Beneficence buttresses the right to die in cases when patients themselves understand that it is in their best interests to die. Often patients will clearly express their understanding of this during the dying process—when the pain and suffering of dying becomes too much for them. When patients cannot speak for themselves, making judgments about what is beneficent is far more difficult, especially if we do not know their values. In such cases, we turn to the benefits/burdens calculus and try to decide whether the burden of a contemplated intervention is less than the benefit to the patient. Here we can employ the "rule of the less well-off." If he or she would be less well-off, that intervention should not be introduced.

From time to time it is necessary to cease being a bystander and to become involved in deciding whether death would in fact be a relief for an incompetent patient who is suffering while dying. If such a determination is made, then a therapeutic plan should be put into place to effect that death (so-called death induction) without violating our own conscious or the known or presumed values of the patient. Most often this will mean withholding or withdrawing treatments that we now judge would make the patient less well-off while dying.

Maleficence

The principle of maleficence is in a sense a negative form of the principle of beneficence: We should do no harm. It also bears importantly on the right to die.

There are real dangers in prolonging life at all costs. Not the least of these dangers are personal and social. First, the personal dangers include, but are not limited to, a loss of control of one's own dying. In the remote past, persons were in control of their own dying process. But with the advent of major life-prolonging technologies, this control was lost. Second, being under the control of life-prolonging technologies, patients cannot make a final statement about their lives and their values. This is an important part of the ritual of dying that now is often lost in the technological setting of a modern hospital. Finally, there is the danger of adversely affecting all of what the patient desires and values. For example, a terminally ill farmer may be forced to sell one or two first-rate farms. These farms might have been in his family for generations, but they would have to be sold to pay for the respirator and other interventions during a comatose dying process.

There are also social values, and their neglect can rip apart our institutions as well. Patient dumping results when the high-technology interventions reach their appointed time—the time at which insurance runs out. When a hospital transfers such individuals, it is in danger of giving the lie to its commitment. In effect it says, "We love and will care for you, but only when you can pay for all we want to give you." As a partial consequence of this sort of reasoning, almost 40 percent of the Medicare and Medicaid annual budget is spent on the last three months of persons' lives, while over 20 million people in our society cannot get any kind of health care at all.[39] Thus, it is not too far-fetched to say that prolonging life at all costs not only denies personal values, it also tends to reduce civil liberties and health care for the poor.

An objection can be raised at this point. Granted that prolonging life at all costs can adversely affect individual persons and society at large, it is still not always easy to determine when we are prolonging life and when we are prolonging the dying process. Furthermore, in some religious traditions (e.g., the Orthodox Jewish tradition), life is seen as sacred and as having a value independent of the life lived. According to these traditions, to preserve life at all costs does *not* violate fundamental values; it rather respects the sacredness of life.

The answer to this objection is that this is really a theological matter. No one should be coerced into violating his or her religious convictions about the dying process. Nonetheless, the rest of society should not have to pay as a result of these convictions. The rest of society does become involved when it must make the tragic choice between prolonging the dying process of one person and the provision of health care for others.[40] Unfortunately, it is harmful to society to uncritically accept all bills tendered.

Justice

Considerations of justice also support a right to die. Patients often recognize their duties to their family and to society in the language they use about their impending death. We can easily spot this sense of justice in the phrases "I do not want to be a burden on my family" or "I do not want anything extraordinary done to prolong my life." In effect, the patient understands that his or her life is coming to an end and that to prolong it is meaningless. Not only is it meaningless, it is unjust to the welfare of the family.

There is also a duty to future generations that is sometimes recognized. One can easily imagine a comatose patient momentarily awakening, learning of his (or her) hopeless state, and saying, "I do not want my treatment to cost so much that my family loses the assets we have struggled to achieve and maintain. They deserve to share in whatever prosperity we have jointly created." In effect this is a soft form of what we might call Lammism, after former Governor Lamm of Colorado. Lamm purportedly said, "The aged have a duty to die and get out of the way."[41] The softer form is that elderly people, and dying people, have a duty to sacrifice what might conceivably be due them so that future generations can have at least some basic form of health care. There is a sort of maldistribution of health care that occurs because of our technology. Persons over 65 tend to spend twice as much as younger persons per hospitalization; for those over 85, the rate is three times as much. Couple this with the costs of dying and it is not difficult to argue that prolonging life is not always a reasonable medical or social goal.

The right to die can be defended by means of the four ethical principles we have just examined. Even if there is still no generally recognized right to die, the fact that dying ought to be patient-driven leads to an awareness of inadequacies in the current instruments that help us limit treatments while persons die and help us act on the wishes of persons during their coma or persistent vegetative state. Let us turn to these now.

Inadequacies

The inadequacies to be discussed are found in "Do Not Resuscitate" (DNR) orders, living will legislation, the AMA Judicial Council Opinion, and the Opinion of Scientists for the Vatican Ministry of Health Care.

DNR Orders

DNR orders are used in many hospitals and have been widely studied.[42] They usually apply to cardiopulmonary resuscitation technologies in the event that a patient suffers an arrest during the dying process. One problem with such orders is that patients are often not consulted about whether to institute such orders. One study found this lack of consideration for patient wishes in 70 percent of the cases examined.[43] Second, DNR orders restrict such decision making only to the use of cardiopulmonary resuscitation during a terminal process.[44] Third, the DNR orders restrict the discussion of appropriate interventions only to cardiopulmonary resuscitation technologies, neglecting other treatments such as food and water, antibiotics, and the like. The latter have the same or even greater potential for prolonging life unduly and for allowing the ignoring of a patient's wish to die.

Living Will Legislation

Living will legislation also is too restrictive.[45] It also limits the decision-making power of the patient only to the dying process rather than extending it to all health care decisions. Most laws recognize this restriction by noting that nothing in the act can abrogate other rights under common law.[46] Presumably included among these rights is the right to refuse any and all treatment, even if one is not dying. Often the legislation requires that one must be certified to be terminal by two physicians in writing.

The patient's autonomy is restricted by limiting the treatments to be covered. In a number of states, for example, food and water cannot be refused (see Chapter 19 on euthanasia and the law). This may change in the near future as the effect of the Florida case *Corbett v. D'Allesandro* comes into play. In the case in question, the Supreme Court of Florida determined that the right to refuse food and water could not be restricted by a statute.[47] (See Chapters 17 and 18 on living wills and advance directives for other models.)

The AMA Judicial Council Opinion

The Judicial Council of the AMA issued an opinion governing the care of the dying in March 1986. This statement is worthy of support. Yet, among other things, the opinion restricts patient refusal of food and water and other life-prolonging technology to the dying process only, and it suggests that the physician should never will the death of a patient.[48] Nonetheless, the statement does admit that an irreversible process can also lead to justifiable discontinuance of care by the physician: "Even if death is not imminent but a patient's coma is beyond doubt irreversible and there are adequate safeguards to confirm the accuracy of the diagnosis and with the concurrence of those who have responsibility for the care of the patient, it is not unethical to discontinue all means of life prolonging medical treatment."[49]

By contrast, the right to die approach entails that patients have a right to determine any and all care ahead of time and to have their expressed wishes apply at the time they do lapse into a permanent coma or vegetative state, rendering moot the issue whether such conditions are in fact terminal (as shown in the beginning of this section of the chapter).

Vatican Statement

Although it has no religious or legal force, a statement issued by what is effectively the Vatican ministry of health argued that food and water were essential components of care and that they could not be withheld or withdrawn from dying patients.[50] It did not, however, cover comatose and vegetative states. In essence this statement develops a moral argument on the basis of a medical definition: Care cannot be withdrawn from dying patients, even though specific treatments can and even must be. Food and water are then included in the definition of care that cannot be withdrawn. They must therefore be employed in every case, even if they prolong dying.

Clearly this statement is in conflict with the right to determine treatment. In the United States, if it were implemented by Catholic hospitals, it would lead to lawsuits on the grounds that the patient's right to determine treatment was abridged. Yet it makes an important point. While treatments may be withdrawn from dying patients, care should never be. It challenges us to think more creatively about what kind of care we could offer were we to stop technological interventions. In the case of comatose and vegetative patients, little could be done. They would die almost immediately.

Proposals

By way of summary, the following proposals are offered for the care of PC and PVS patients.

1. All treatment decisions should be patient-driven. By this is meant that the patient should determine treatment ahead of time and make his or her wishes known and that these wishes should be honored if the patient becomes comatose. For enhancing this aspect of health care, consider the following suggestions:

- Churches and civic groups should become involved in promoting advance directives among their members.
- Advance directives should be required at the time of retirement as a condition for receipt of retirement social security income.
- Upon reaching 18 years of age, all citizens should be required to make a declaration of a proxy for health care. This requirement could be enforced through the IRS or by making it a condition for receiving a driver's license.
- At any time a patient is in the hospital for more than 48 hours, an advance directive protocol would be instituted. This protocol would include a team visit to the patient (or family) to concretize the advance directive made earlier. Such concretization would include explicit discussion of possible side effects and the treatment decisions required if they occur. This expanded form of the DNR can be called TDS (for treatment decision status). (See Chapter 35 for hospital policy models).[51]

2. Physician-patient negotiations should occur regularly. It is too late to consider a discussion with the patient about values once a PC or PVS has occurred. Instead such negotiation should be an essential component of all doctor-patient encounters. The notion of "hold harmless" legislation should be supported. Such legislation gives civil and criminal immunity to physicians who act on the basis of the documented wishes and values of their patients. By passing such legislation, the inviolability of the patient-physician relationship can be protected. This is not the case when open discussions have not been recorded or when there is no living will legislation that covers the situation. Interestingly, this was the argument of an *amicus curiae* brief created by the Massachusetts Chapter of the American College of Physicians in the Brophy case decided in 1986.[52] The college argued that the values Paul Brophy carried with him into the doctor-patient relationship had to be respected because of the inviolability of that relationship (i.e., that no outside parties, like the hospital or a diocese, pro-life group, or union of disabled persons could petition the court for a change of those values).

Given the need for social and institutional values to be allowed a place in solving the difficult dilemmas we face, the legal brief as it stands probably overstates the case. Nonetheless, if documented values can be found, the argument that no outside values should supersede the patient's values becomes very important. Recall that the New Jersey Supreme Court noted in its final determination in the Quinlan case that her father's wishes on Karen Quinlan's behalf (based on her values) took precedence over the interests of the state in preserving life, given the poor prognosis.[53]

Thus, it is important to establish the values of patients, even more than their preferences. Values perdure, while preferences often change. It is true that patients who express wishes ahead of time while relatively healthy have no real grasp of what they might wish done when they do succumb to a coma or vegetative state. Yet if their wishes are based on values that perdure (frugality, a lifetime of working on the farm, care for future generations in the family), most likely the wish not to have one's life prolonged in a coma is value informed and should be protected by hold harmless legislation (as is often done in living will legislation).

3. Surrogates should be designated. When patients do become incompetent with life-threatening disorders such as comas, surrogates must then speak for them and defend their values. Following are some important recommendations relating to the use of surrogates.

Physicians ought to institute anticruelty therapy and make this a chart order.[54] By making it a positive chart order, the therapy of care for the patient can be more clearly distinguished from needless life-prolonging therapy. The surrogate's decisions in this regard must rest on the values of patient. When these cannot be determined, they must rest on what is "not cruel." (See Chapter 28 on protherapeutics.)

Substituted judgment can be used to determine the wishes of patients. The best data to have, naturally, are the documented values of the patients and the preferences based on those values. Second best are presumed wishes based on the values and lifestyle of the patient. Apparently these presumed wishes were what convinced the New Jersey Supreme Court not to act on Claire Conroy's behalf (though she had already died), because there was insufficient evidence of her wishes. Her nephew had argued that she would not have wanted her life prolonged given the senile, debilitated state she was in.[55]

The least good basis for making surrogate decisions is a constructed value history (a hierarchically arranged list of values). Even here, however, a defensible substituted judgment can be reached. For example, if we know that a woman had lived an independent life and that in the nursing home she often refused to let others even bathe and feed her, we can reasonably assume that her values did not change after suffering a stroke and its concomitant coma. When it becomes clear that nothing further can be done for her, her value history tells us that it would be foolish to prolong her life unduly.

4. The role of the family should be clarified. Perhaps no more difficult problem exists than determining what role the family should play in making health care decisions.[56] Suffice it to say here that family members must take into account the values of the patient and not their own in assisting physicians to act in the best interests of a comatose patient.[57] In other words, the family must try to be a good proxy.[58] The physician can then act in the best interests of the patient (which might not be identical to the best interests of the family). This would eliminate a common cause for unduly prolonging life: fear of litigation.

Conclusion

Once patients enter a permanent vegetative state or coma, little can reliably be done to determine their values and preferences. Without these in hand, withholding or withdrawing treatment must depend on substituted judgment and the family's efforts to honor the wishes of their loved one. This may take hours of discussion with physicians, or worse, hours, days, weeks, months, years, of court action. In place of such harrowing and wasteful activities, specific steps for establishing values and preferences ahead of time can be made in order that treatment not be unduly prolonged. These steps provide a way of respecting the right to die and ensuring that it is not infringed.

NOTES

1. President's Commission for the Study of Ethical Problems in Medicine and Biomedical Behavioral Research, *Deciding to Forgo Life-Sustaining Treatment* (Washington, D.C.: GPO, 1983).

2. Ronald Cranford, personal communication; G.A. Rosenberg, S.F. Johnson, and R.P. Brenner, "Recovery of Cognition after Prolonged Vegetative State," *Annals of Neurology* 2 (1983).

3. Ronald Cranford, personal communication.

4. T. Pula, personal communication.

5. President's Commission, *Deciding to Forgo Life-Sustaining Treatment*.

6. American Medical Association, *Current Opinions of the Council on Ethical and Judicial Affairs of the American Medical Association* (Chicago: American Medical Association, 1986).

7. Brief submitted by the American Academy of Neurology to the Massachusetts Supreme Court in Brophy v. New England Sinai Hospital, Inc., 398 Mass. 417, 497 N.E.2d 626 (1986).

8. T. Fortkort in Hazelton [sic] v. Powhatan Nursing Home, Inc., No. CH 98287 (Va. Cir. Ct. Fairfax Co., Aug. 29, 1986).

9. Brief submitted to the Massachusetts Supreme Court in Brophy v. New England Sinai Hospital, Inc.

10. Ibid.

11. President's Commission, *Deciding to Forgo Life-Sustaining Treatment*.

12. See Union Pacific Railway Co. v. Botsford, 141 U.S. 250, 251 (1891). For a summary of the legal basis for the right to refuse treatment (the constitutional right of privacy and the common law right of self-determination), see Society for the Right to Die, *The Physician and the Hopelessly Ill Patient: Legal, Medical and Ethical Guidelines* (New York: Society for the Right to Die, 1985), 19–20, 92.

13. The term *decisionally incapacitated* is used in this chapter instead of *incompetent* (even though courts often use *incompetent*), because *incompetent* usually is associated with a judicial determination that an individual lacks the ability to care for him- or herself. Decisional incapacity, however, is a narrower concept referring to a person's ability to understand the consequences of a particular medical decision and to communicate the decision made. A patient's ability to understand other unrelated concepts is not relevant.

14. See generally *The Physician and the Hopelessly Ill Patient* and the bibliography at the end of this chapter.

15. In re Quinlan, 70 N.J. 10, 41, 355 A.2d 647, 664, cert. denied sub nom. Garger v. New Jersey, 429 U.S. 922 (1976).

16. See, e.g., Lane v. Candura, 6 Mass. App. Ct. 377, 376 N.E.2d 1232 (1978); In re Quackenbush, 156 N.J. Super. 282, 383 A.2d 785 (Morris County Ct. 1978).

17. See, e.g., Rasmussen v. Fleming, No. CV-86-0450-PR (not reported at time of printing). Barber v. Superior Court, 147 Cal. App.3d 1006, 195 Cal. Rptr. 484 (Ct. App. 1983); Corbett v. D'Alessandro, 487 So.2d 368 (Fla. Dist. Ct. App. 1986), review denied, 492 So.2d 1331 (Fla. 1986); Brophy v. New England Sinai Hospital, Inc., 398 Mass. 417, 497 N.E.2d 626 (1986); In re Peter, 108 N.J. 365, 529 A.2d 419 (1987). In re Jobes, 108 N.J. 394, 529 A.2d 434 (1987). Delio v. Westchester County Medical Center, 129 A.D.2d 1, 516 N.Y.S.2d 677 (App. Div. 2d Dep't 1987); In re Bayer, No. 4131 (N.D. Burleigh County Ct. Feb. 5, 11, 1987) (Riskedahl, J.). For cases on artificial feeding which do not involve PVS patients, see also Bouvia v. Superior Court, 179 Cal. App. 3d 1127, 225 Cal. Rptr. 297 (Ct. App. 1986), review denied (Cal. June 5, 1986); In re Rodas, No. 86PR139 (Colo. Dist. Ct., Mesa County Jan. 22, 1987) (Buss, J.); In re Conroy, 98 N.J. 321, 486 A.2d 1209 (1985); In re Requena, 213 N.J. Super. 475, 517 A.2d 886 (Super. Ct. Ch. Div.), aff'd, 213 N.J. Super. 443, 517 A.2d 869 (Super. Ct. App. Div. 1986) (per curiam); In re Application of Brooks (Leguerrier) (N.Y. Sup. Ct. Albany County June 10, 1987) (Conway, J.). Hazelton [sic] v. Powhatan Nursing Home, Inc., No. CH 98287 (Va. Cir. Ct. Fairfax County Aug. 29, 1986) order signed (Sept. 2, 1986) (Fortkort, J.), appeal denied, Record No. 860814 (Va. Sept. 2, 1986).

18. Brophy v. New England Sinai Hospital, Inc., supra note 17.

19. The doctrine of substituted judgment permits another to apply a patient's previous values or choices to the present situation when the patient is unable to do so. The decision maker must then stand in the patient's shoes and try to make the decision the patient would have made under those circumstances. Under this doctrine, decision makers are not permitted to choose what they think is best for the patient if that is not what the patient would have chosen.

20. See generally, Society for the Right to Die, *Handbook of Living Will Laws: 1987 Edition.* (New York: Society for the Right to Die, 1987); Society for the Right to Die, *Checklist Chart of Living Will Laws* (New York: Society for the Right to Die, 1987).

21. In 1987, Arkansas replaced a 1977 statute with the Rights of the Terminally Ill or Permanently Unconscious Act, 1987 Ark. Acts 713; New Mexico's Right to Die Act applies when "brain stem functions remain but the major components of the cerebrum are irreversibly destroyed" (the act calls this "irreversible coma," but the definition covers all permanently unconscious patients.) N.M. Stat. Ann. §§ 24-7-2 to 24-7-11 (Supp. 1986).

22. See, e.g., Alabama's Natural Death Act, Ala. Code §§ 22-8A-1 to 22-8A-10 (1984).

23. See, e.g., Georgia's Living Wills Act, Ga. Code Ann. §§ 31-32-1 to 31-32-12 (1985 Supp. 1986), amended 1987 Ga. Laws 488; Maine's Living Wills Act, Me. Rev. Stat. Ann. tit. 22, §§ 2921 to 2931 (Supp. 1986).

24. Uniform Rights of Terminally Ill Act, 9A Uniform Laws Annotated 456-64 (Supp. 1986). Uniform Laws are not binding statutes, but rather statutory language endorsed by the National Conference of Commissioners on Uniform State Laws. This Act was also endorsed by the American Bar Association.

25. Corbett v. D'Alessandro, supra note 17; In re Rodas, supra note 17.

26. Hazelton v. Powhatan, supra note 17.

27. In re Lance Steinhaus (Minn. County Ct. Fam. Div. Redwood County, Sept. 11, 1986) (Harrelson, J.), *amended on other grounds* (Oct. 13, 1986). In Rasmussen v. Fleming, supra note 17, the Arizona Supreme Court noted that even though there is the difference between PVS and irreversible coma, as described in Part 1 of this chapter, there is no "material" difference between the two conditions.

28. See, e.g., Arkansas Rights of the Terminally Ill or Permanently Unconscious Act, 1987 Ark. Accts 713.

29. See, e.g., In re Jobes, supra note 17; In re Requena, supra note 17; In re Rodas, supra note 17. In two cases (Brophy and Delio, supra note 17) where the courts did not order the patient's original institution to stop treatment, instead of authorizing transfer, the parties requesting termination did not ask the court to force the original institutions to honor the patients' wishes; thus the failure to require compliance did not imply that institutions have the option to refuse compliance when the party requesting termination does ask for such relief.

30. See, e.g., Leach v. Shapiro, 13 Ohio App. 3d 393, 469 N.E.2d 1047 (Ct. App. 1984).

31. Whenever the text refers to PC, PVS, coma, or vegetative state, these references are to be taken as defined by Dr. Cohen in the first section of this Chapter. From time to time the text refers to a condition in shorthand, but the permanence of the condition is always assumed. Specifically ruled out is any reference to a temporary coma or remitting vegetative state.

32. A. Jonsen, M. Siegler, and W. Winslade. *Clinical Ethics,* 2d ed. (New York: Macmillan, 1986).

33. Paul Ramsey, *Ethics at the Edges of Life* (New Haven: Yale University Press, 1981).

34. In re Conroy, 98 N.J. 321, 486 A.2d 1209 (1985). See also N.L. Cantor, "Conroy, Best Interests, and the Handling of Dying Patients," *Rutgers Law Review* 37 (Spring 1985): 543–77.

35. See the suggestion of Joseph Fletcher in Chapter 1 that the fundamental moral conflict in medical ethics is between a person-centered morality and a quality of life morality. The argument being made here assumes a quality of life moral perspective.

36. In re Conroy. The decision went out of its way to insist that the rights determined for Ms. Conroy were based on common law rights, although it acknowledged that constitutional rights might be implicated.

37. In re Brophy.

38. H.T. Engelhardt, Jr., *The Foundations of Bioethics* (New York: Oxford University Press, 1986).

39. The figures in 1986 range from 20 million to 30 million, depending on the poverty cutoff point employed. The figure cited in the text is a conservative one, based on a personal communication with Sen. David Durenberger, R-Minn., at the time chairman of the Subcommittee on Health of the Senate Finance Committee.

40. Calabresi and Bobbitt, *Tragic Choices* (New York: Norton, 1978).

41. Lamm's more recent views are found in Richard Lamm, *Megatraumas: America at the Year 2000* (Boston: Houghton, Miflin, 1985), 35–50.

42. "Standards and Guidelines for Cardiopulmonary Resuscitation (CPR) and Emergency Cardiac Care (ECC)," *Journal of the American Medical Association* 244 (August 1, 1980): 453, 504–508; "Reports of the Judicial Council of the American Medical Association, December 1984—Terminal Illness: Patients' Preferences," *Journal of the American Medical Association* 253 (April 26, 1985): 2424; S.H. Wanzer et al., "The Physician's Responsibility to Hopelessly Ill Patients," *New England Journal of Medicine* 310 (1984): 955; A.L. Evans and B.A. Brody, "The Do-

Not-Resuscitate Order in Teaching Hospitals,'' *Journal of the American Medical Association* 253 (April 19, 1985): 2236–39; S.H. Miles and M.B. Ryden, ''Limited-Treatment Policies in Long-Term Care Facilities,'' *Journal of the American Geriatrics Society* 33 (1985): 707–11.

43. Evans and Brody, ''The Do-Not-Resuscitate Order.''

44. This point is not intended to be a profound criticism of DNR orders if their limitations are properly recognized. In fact, they are a tremendous advance over the previous lack of discussion about treatment options.

45. The use of the word *restrictive* here requires clarification. It is not intended to mean that living will legislation restricts the freedom of persons to determine treatments during the dying process. In this sense, it, like the DNR order, is a major advance. It is an easily recognizable and effective means for refusing treatment in more common situations. Thus, support for living will legislation has been widespread, including support by thé Society for the Right to Die. By *restrictive* is meant that the legislation does not go far enough, as the text argues.

46. Society for the Right to Die, *The Physician and the Hopelessly Ill: Legal, Medical and Ethical Guidelines* (New York: Society for the Right to Die, 1985).

47. Corbett v. D'Allesandro, 12th Circuit, Lee County, Florida, Case No. 84-5627 CA-JRT, Feb. 28, 1985.

48. American Medical Association, ''Withholding or Withdrawing Life-Prolonging Medical Treatment, statement of the Council on Ethical and Judicial Affairs, March 15, 1986: ''For humane reasons, with informed consent, a physician may do what is medically necessary to alleviate severe pain, or cease or omit treatment to permit a terminally ill patient whose death is imminent to die. *However, he should not intentionally cause death''* (emphasis added).

49. Ibid.

50. Opinion of the Scientists, *L''Observatore Romano*.

51. The New Jersey chapter of the American College of Physicians is also considering models for limiting treatment. These are contemplated for use in nursing homes. No publication of these models has occurred at the time of this writing. Contact Dr. Michael Nevins, governor of the chapter, for details.

52. Brief of the Massachusetts chapter of the American College of Physicians as reported in the *American College of Physicians Observer*.

53. In re Quinlan, 70 N.J. 10, 355 A.2d 647, cert. denied, 429 U.S. 922 (1976).

54. S. Braithwaite, and D. Thomasma, ''New Guidelines on Forgoing Life-sustaining Treatment in Incompetent Patients: An Anti-Cruelty Therapy,'' *Annals of Internal Medicine* 104 (1986): 711–15.

55. In re Conroy.

56. Erich Loewy, ''Patient, Family, Physician: Agreement, Disagreement, and Resolution,'' *Family Medicine* 18 (November-December 1986): 375–78. Also see the entire issue of *Theoretical Medicine* (forthcoming), guest editor H. Brody, on the role of the family in medical decisions.

57. E.D. Pellegrino and D.C. Thomasma, *For the Patient's Good: The Restoration of Beneficence in Medicine* (New York: Oxford University Press, forthcoming).

58. D.C. Thomasma and E.D. Pellegrino, ''The Role of the Family and Physicians in Decisions for Incompetent Patients,'' *Theoretical Medicine*, forthcoming.

BIBLIOGRAPHY—THE LEGAL PERSPECTIVE

Significant Court Cases

Barber v. Superior Court, 147 Cal. App. 3d 1006, 195 Cal. Rptr. 484 (Ct. App. 1983). Dismissed homicide charges against physicians who withdrew a respirator and artificial feeding from a patient in a vegetative state.

In re Bayer, No. 4131 (N.D. Burleigh County Ct. Feb. 5, 11, 1987) (Riskedahl, J.) (authorized removal of artificial feeding from a PVS patient).

Brophy v. New England Sinai Hospital, Inc., 398 Mass. 417, 497 N.E.2d 626 (1986). Authorized removal of artificial feeding from a PVS patient.

In re Colyer, 99 Wash. 2d 114, 660 P.2d 738 (1983), overruled in part, In re Guardianship of Hamlin, 102 Wash. 2d 810, 689 P.2d 1372 (1984). Authorized removal of respirator from a PVS patient.

Corbett v. D'Alessandro, 487 So. 2d 368 (Fla. Dist. Ct. App. 1986), review denied, 492 So. 2d 1331 (Fla. 1986). Held that PVS patients have a constitutional right to forgo artificial feeding, and Florida's natural death statute could not restrict that right.

Delio v. Westchester County Medical Center, 129 A.D.2d 1, 516 N.Y.S.2d 677 (App. Div. 2d Dep't 1987) (authorized removal of artificial feeding from a PVS patient).

In re Guardianship of Hamlin, 102 Wash. 2d 810, 689 P.2d 1372 (1984). Held that PVS patient's guardians had authority to consent to termination of patient's life support, which included respirator.

Hazelton [sic] v. Powhatan Nursing Home, Inc., No. CH 98287 (Va. Cir. Ct. Fairfax Co. Aug. 29, 1986) order signed (Sept. 2, 1986) (Fortkort, J.), appeal denied, Record. No. 860814 (Va. Sept. 2, 1986), 6 Va. Cir. Ct. Op. 414 (Aspen 1987). Authorized removal of artificial feeding tube under Virginia Natural Death Act from a permanently unconscious patient suffering from a brain tumor.

In re Jobes, 108 N.J. 394, 529 A.2d 434 (1987). Authorized stopping artificial feeding for PVS patient, holding that close family members or patient-appointed proxies can usually authorize such action without going to court.

Leach v. Akron General Medical Center, 68 Ohio Misc. 1, 426 N.E.2d 809 (Com. Pl. 1980). Authorized respirator removal from a PVS patient.

Leach v. Shapiro, 13 Ohio App. 3d 393, 469 N.E.2d 1047 (Ct. App. 1984). Held that providing life support against an incompetent patient's previously expressed and known wishes constitutes battery.

In re L.H.R., 253 Ga. 439, 321 S.E.2d 716 (1984). Authorized family or legal guardian of PVS patient to make treatment termination decisions without prior judicial approval or consultation with ethics committee.

In re Peter, 108 N.J. 365, 529 A.2d 419 (1987). (Authorized ending artificial feeding for PVS patient and set forth guidelines for similar decisions for nursing home patients age 60 and over).

In re Quinlan, 70 N.J. 10, 355 A.2d 647, cert. denied sub nom. Garger v. New Jersey, 429 U.S. 922 (1976), overruled in part, In re Conroy, 98 N.J. 321, 486 A.2d 1209 (1985). Authorized termination of life support for a PVS patient.

Rasmussen v. Fleming, No. CV-86-0450-PR, (not reported at time of printing). (Ariz. July 23, 1987) (authorized guardian in certain circumstances to refuse to consent to medical treatment, including do-not-resuscitate and do-not-hospitalize orders, for PVS patient who had never expressed treatment preferences, and provided decision-making procedures when a guardian requests forgoing treatment for his or her ward).

In re Storar (Eichner), 52 N.Y.2d 363, 420 N.E.2d 64, 438 N.Y.S.2d 266, cert. denied, 454 U.S. 858 (1981). Held that life support can be forgone for PVS patients when there is clear and convincing evidence that the patient would have wanted it forgone.

In re Torres, 357 N.W.2d 332 (Minn. 1984). Authorized removal of life support from a PVS patient.

Books

Lynn, J., ed. *By No Extraordinary Means: The Choice to Forgo Life-Sustaining Food and Water*. Bloomington, Ind.: Indiana University Press 1986. A collection of interdisciplinary essays concerning legal, medical, and ethical implications of forgoing artificial feeding.

Office of Technology Assessment. *Life-Sustaining Technologies and the Elderly*. Washington, D.C.: GPO 1987 OTA-BA-306. A comprehensive study of several technologies, including artificial feeding and antibiotics, for the elderly, many of whom are permanently unconscious).

President's Commission for the Study of Ethical Problems in Medicine and Biomedical Behavioral Research. *Deciding to Forgo Life-Sustaining Treatment*. Washington, D.C.: GPO, 1983. A comprehensive report of interdisciplinary presidential commission concerning existing and recommended law and practice in forgoing life support. See especially pp. 171–96, 459–66.

Society for the Right to Die. *Handbook of Living Will Laws: 1987 Edition*. New York: Society for the Right to Die, 1987. A comprehensive guide to developments in the right-to-die movement, including text and analysis of enacted statutes.

Society for the Right to Die. *Checklist Chart of Living Will Laws*. New York: Society for the Right to Die, 1987. A detailed comparison chart of major provisions in the 39 natural death statutes enacted before August 1987.

Society for the Right to Die. *The Physician and the Hopelessly Ill Patient: Legal, Medical and Ethical Guidelines.* New York: Society for the Right to Die, 1986. A booklet including articles by ten distinguished physicians recommending levels of care; questions and answers about the state of the right-to-refuse-treatment law; and a state-by-state summary of statutes and court cases.

Chapter 17

Advance Directives: When the Patient Cannot Communicate

Fredrick R. Abrams

Death is not the worst; rather in vain to wish for death and not to compass it.

Sophocles

Advance directives are devices designed to protect a patient's control over health care decisions in the event he or she becomes incompetent or otherwise unable to communicate his or her desires.

The underlying assumption for advance directives is that patient-centered decision making is proper, an assumption strengthened by our society's directions to the medical profession via the law, both statutory and common. The medical profession faces conflicts, wishing to do what is good for the patient as interpreted by physicians yet having to accept the patient's right to make decisions that are sometimes not in keeping with medical recommendations. The judiciary, with increasing consistency, has taken a position affirming patient autonomy and rejecting paternalism, despite its usually beneficent intent. The trend has been characterized in the words of various courts and is particularly well stated in the case of Natanson v. Kline: "Anglo American Law starts with the premise of thoroughgoing self-determination. It follows that each man is considered to be master of his own body, and he may if he be of sound mind, expressly prohibit the performance of live-saving surgery or other medical treatment."[1] It has been made clear that a competent person may refuse medical or surgical treatment even when it is life-saving.

The issue has been joined, however, on the question of competence. Mere disagreement with a physician's recommendation has been clearly held to be insufficient evidence for determining a patient is incompetent.[2] One court decision concerning when life may be shortened stated this well: "The value of life . . . is lessened not by a decision to refuse treatment, but by the failure to allow a competent human being the right of choice."[3]

Paradoxically, there may be less challenge to patients' directives made in advance in the case where patients become unconscious or otherwise incompetent. Written advance directives appear to be more readily accepted because they were made at a time when the patient was considered competent, and witnesses frequently attest to the patient's competence when the document is created. A person refusing life-saving treatment verbally appears more likely to have his or her competence questioned.

205

THE LIVING WILL

The best known type of document is the living will, which in its generic form constitutes a refusal to undergo medical interventions if a patient is in a terminal, irreversible state. It is designed to prevent prolongation of the dying process. No uniform law has been passed which is applicable in all states. Variations include (1) permitting or prohibiting minors from making a valid document, (2) invalidating a ''will'' in case of pregnancy, (3) including or excluding nutrition and hydration as a refusable option, (4) witness or notarization requirements, (5) periodic updating, (6) model formats or exact forms which must be used, and (7) restrictions or requirements which local political considerations impose. Laws by state are available in concise publications listing all current laws. Space need not be taken here to duplicate these valuable resources. [4]

The constitutionality of laws limiting the extent of refusal has been challenged. One court, in referring to a patient in a permanent vegetative state, repudiated a restriction barring refusal of parenteral nutrition in cases where the patient's wishes are clearly expressed. The court indicated that refusal of any undesired intervention is likely to be widely accepted as a constitutional right, but that although the Florida right to die law ''excludes the right to decline sustenance providing life-prolonging measures, that charter does not affect the otherwise existing Constitutional rights of persons . . . to forgo the use of artificial life-sustaining measures.''[5]

In the event a patient is incompetent and in a state where no treatment will bring about recovery of sapient consciousness, an optimal law would

- permit a patient to refuse any treatment under the predetermined circumstances
- place sanctions on a physician unwilling to comply with a patient's request or alternatively direct transfer of the patient to a physician willing to accede to the patient's request
- free from civil or criminal liability those institutions, physicians, or other persons complying with a patient's directive

DURABLE POWER OF ATTORNEY

Although such wills can stand alone as an expression of a patient's desires, they cover only a very narrow area of health care decision making, applying to terminal illness or irreversible illness decisions only. Patients may of course become incompetent in cases where health care decisions need to be made but the illness is not terminal or irreversible. A second type of advance directive is useful for this. It is called a *durable power of attorney*. Most people are aware that any person may legally authorize another to act in his or her behalf, enabling the attorney-in-fact (the name given to the person selected) to make any commitment which would be legal for the original party to make. It would be as binding as if the original party had acted him- or herself. This is a nondurable authority that ordinarily terminates if the original party becomes incompetent. In the case of durable power of attorney, the authority to act comes into existence only if and when the original party becomes incompetent. Many states have enacted such laws not only for ordinary transactions, but especially for health decisions, creating a durable power of attorney for health care.

A durable power of attorney for health care empowers a person selected by the original party to make health care decisions in the event that the original party becomes incompetent. The advantages include that such a person is chosen by the patient rather than appointed by a court and that such a person probably would accurately represent the patient's viewpoint. In most circumstances, it is helpful to the physician who desires to act in accord with a patient's wishes to have such a designee, but there can still be recourse to the courts if the decisions made by an attorney-in-fact are questionable.

As these devices become better known to both the public and the professionals, there will be more open and frank discussions of terminal illness and other severe incapacities. Taboos about discussing these subjects are gradually breaking down, leading to family discussions and more candid doctor-patient interchanges. Having an understanding of patient values is very important, since they vary so widely. Accommodating a patient's wishes in our overly litigious society requires that something more than verbal understanding be achieved and available for consideration.

Perhaps the best outcomes will result from a combination of the two types of instruments. First, a patient may designate in a written and witnessed statement what his or her desires would be under varying circumstances. How detailed this would be depends on how sophisticated the patient becomes regarding health-impairing possibilities. Discussions are best begun not in the shadow of a crisis but rather as a part of good physician-patient relationship, allowing understanding to be achieved when thinking is not impaired. The patient's desires should be documented, signed, and, made part of the patient's records (see Chapter 18 on advance directives).

Clearly it is possible that attitudes change with illness, and no doctor ought to refuse to provide care which is currently being sought despite a patient's earlier statement of refusal. Nevertheless, compatibility of attitudes between patient and physician is extremely important. Finding a disparity in the cool light of morning is a vastly better alternative than learning there are sincerely held value differences at a time when critical decisions are being made. A patient ought to express his or her attitude toward hydration and nutrition in the event of severe neurologic impairment of consciousness or cognition. Most patients will understand explanations which deal in terms of the prognosis for returning to a sapient state.

Second, precisely because each and every variable cannot be spelled out, the general written and witnessed statement of desires (with those particulars the patient prefers to include) could be combined with the designation of an attorney-in-fact (with durable power of attorney) who would press to see that the patient's desires, as best understood by such a designee, are fully met.

SUMMARY

It appears that society continues to approve increasing self-determination, recognizing that a person belongs to no king and that the state must limit its paternalism to legitimate state interests. The state considers that a competent person should be allowed to make health care decisions according to personal values, not official state values, even at the cost of life. Respect for sapient life is not diminished by a refusal to protect mere biologic life from a person's clear desires to end such a life. Various instruments have been devised to enable health care professionals to understand and respect an individual's values. Some give direct instructions that apply only in very narrow circumstances. Others designate a proxy decision maker most likely to uphold a patient's values. Use of these modalities and open discussion about the hitherto taboo subjects of death and severe mental and physical handicaps will help continue patient-centered decision making in an increasingly complex medical world.

NOTES

1. Natanson v. Kline 186 Kan. 393, 404, 350 p. 2d 1093, 1104, (1960).

2. Lane v. Candura, 6 Mass. App. Ct., 376 N.E.2d. 1232, (1978).

3. Superintendent of Belchertown State School et al. v. Saikewicz, Mass. 370 N.E.2d. 417, (1977).

4. See, for example, Society for the Right to Die, *The Physician and the Hopelessly Ill Patient: Legal, Medical and Ethical Guidelines* (New York: Society for the Right to Die, 1985).

5. Corbett v. D'Alessandro, 487 So.2d 368 (Fla. Dist. Court App. 1986).

Chapter 18

The Clinical Use of Advance Directives[*]

Bernard Lo

Life-sustaining treatment presents dilemmas because some goals of treatment, but not others, can be achieved. In a critically ill patient, an acute episode like pneumonia may be reversible, even though restoring function and reversing another underlying disease may not be. Dilemmas about which treatments are humane and appropriate are particularly difficult when patients are mentally incompetent. It would be inappropriate either to subject patients to treatments that they do not want or that provide little benefit or to withhold desired or beneficial treatments.

PRINCIPLES FOR MAKING MEDICAL DECISIONS

Shared Decision Making

Ideally decisions should be made jointly by physicians and informed, competent patients.[1] The doctor should define the benefits and burdens of treatment and the alternatives. Care givers are not obligated to provide medically futile treatments, even at the request of the patient or family. On the other hand, competent, informed patients may decline treatment. Recent court decisions have permitted patients to decline life-prolonging treatments—ranging from respirators to feeding tubes—even if they are not terminally ill. This active role for the patient is justified by the ethical principle to respect the autonomy of individuals and by the legal doctrine of informed consent.

Sometimes patients may make decisions that might shorten their lives or that others consider unwise. In such cases, care givers may educate, counsel, negotiate, and check that patients are informed. Such interventions are justified by the ethical principle of beneficence: Health care providers should act to benefit patients. However, care providers should not override the wishes of informed, competent patients to forgo treatments, even though they strongly disagree.[2]

---

*This work supported in part by a grant from the Commonwealth Fund.

Problems of Competency

Patients may not be mentally competent to give informed consent or refusal.[3] Often competency is questioned because a patient declines a treatment that is considered beneficial. Mere refusal of treatment, however, does not imply incompetency. Care givers often regard as incompetent those patients who perform poorly on mental status tests. A more valid standard, however, is whether the patient understands the nature of the treatment, the risks and benefits, and the alternatives. Even if patients are not capable of giving informed consent, their assent to treatment may still be needed. Uncooperative patients who thwart treatments (for example, by pulling out intravenous lines) may wind up being restrained or sedated. Insisting on treatment may not be justified if the patient is subjected to indignity and cannot comprehend the reasons for the treatment.

Decisions for Incompetent Patients

Patients frequently are incompetent to make decisions about medical care. In acute care hospitals, about one-half of the decisions about "Do Not Resuscitate" orders involve incompetent patients.[4] Patients with acquired immunodeficiency syndrome (AIDS) may be particularly at risk for becoming incompetent, since the human immunodeficiency virus (HIV) attacks the brain directly, and central nervous system infections are frequent. In nursing homes, there are estimated to be 800,000 patients with dementia, most of whom are incompetent to make decisions about their care. Decisions for incompetent nursing home patients may involve hospitalization, antibiotics and other medications, and feeding tubes. The challenge is to grant incompetent patients the same right to refuse treatments as competent patients, while giving them additional protection because they are vulnerable.

In decisions concerning incompetent patients, two questions must be answered: What standards should be used and who should make the decisions? A medical, ethical, and legal consensus recommends that decisions follow preferences that the incompetent patient previously expressed while competent.[5] Such prior wishes are called advance directives. Following patient preferences, even when patients are not able to express them directly, is consistent with the ethical principle to respect patient autonomy.

When advance directives are not available or are unclear, other methods of decision making must be considered. Substituted judgments are attempts to decide as the individual patient would decide if he or she were not incompetent. Such substituted judgments, however, may be no more reliable than guessing if there are no advance directives. Another method is to try to determine the best interests of the patient. Acting in accordance with the patient's best interests has been generally accepted as appropriate when the patient's own preferences are unknown or unclear. Determining a patient's best interests, however, is often speculative and controversial. (Chapter 12 discusses how assessments of the quality of life of incompetent patients may be biased or ambiguous.) Because of these problems with alternative standards, encouraging patients to give advance directives is essential.

The second question regarding incompetent patients is who should act as surrogate decision maker for the patient. Traditionally, the family fills this role and makes joint decisions with physicians, because relatives are presumed to act for the patient's benefit.[6] However, with the decline of the extended family, many incompetent patients have no relatives. Over one-third of patients in nursing homes have no surviving relatives. Alternatively, family members may decline to make a decision, may find decisions difficult because of ambivalence, guilt, or grief, or may disagree with each other. Moreover, a conflict of interest may occur because of an inheritance or pension or because of the stress of caring for an elderly patient. Family members may base decisions on what is best for themselves rather than on what is best for the patient.

Because of these problems with decisions by families, other approaches have been tried. Physicians sometimes make unilateral decisions about what is best for the patient. However, decisions not only require scientific expertise but also involve questions of value, and the preferences of physicians may differ from those of patients or families.[7] The judicial system may be an impartial forum to determine the patient's best interests. But decision making by the courts is too cumbersome to be used routinely, and the adversarial nature of the legal system may polarize families and physicians. In addition, guardianship procedures are often superficial, and guardians who are not relatives or friends may put little effort into a patient's affairs. Institutional ethics committees have been suggested to review cases and make recommendations.[8] However, it is not known if such committees actually improve decision making or can make decisions rapidly enough. Review by the state office of the ombudsman (mandated for nursing home patients in New Jersey)[9] may be time consuming and may impose intolerable bureaucratic requirements. To avoid these problems, it has been suggested that competent patients appoint surrogates (presumably trusted relatives or friends) to make decisions in case they become incompetent.

TYPES OF ADVANCE DIRECTIVES

Informal discussions with family members, friends, and health care providers are the most common type of advance directive. Several recent court decisions have accepted such informal discussions as evidence of a patient's preferences.[10] However, informal discussions may present problems. People who had discussions with the patient may not be available after the patient becomes incompetent and actual decisions must be made. Observers may disagree over what the patient previously said. Some health care providers who fear legal liability may be reluctant to follow such informal directives.

More formal directives include living wills and durable powers of attorney. By March 1986, 37 states had passed laws variously called *living will, natural death, death with dignity,* or *right to die laws.*[11] These laws allow patients to direct their physicians to withhold or withdraw life-sustaining treatment if they should become terminally ill. (Chapter 17 discusses living wills in more detail.)

Extensive legislation about living wills has not resolved several fundamental problems. First, many terms used in living wills are difficult to define operationally. Since people may interpret differently such phrases as "terminal illness," "life-sustaining treatment," and "only serve to prolong the process of dying," clinical confusion and controversy may occur.

Second, living wills apply only to terminal illness. They do not assist in decisions about incompetent patients who might survive for months or years, such as patients with severe dementia or in irreversible coma.

Third, only certain treatments may be refused. In some states, patients may forgo only treatments that would not prevent imminent death even if they were administered. Living will directives in these states are unlikely to have significant clinical impact, since it would not be sound medical practice to administer such futile treatments. Under the wording of some living will laws, it is not clear that terminally ill patients may refuse antibiotics or blood transfusions. Also, in some states, patients are not permitted to refuse artificial nutrition and hydration through living wills. Because of these problems with living wills, other forms of advance directives, particularly durable powers of attorney, may be more useful.

The durable power of attorney for health care (discussed in Chapter 17) is more flexible and comprehensive than the living will and applies to all situations in which the patient is incompetent.[12] Only a few states have passed laws specifically authorizing the durable power of attorney for health care. In other states, existing laws about durable powers of attorney may be interpreted to allow this device to be used for medical decisions. However, such use is not explicity authorized, and no test cases have been tried. There are several important advantages to specific legislation authorizing the durable power of attorney for health care. Such laws can establish forms and procedural safeguards. They can also require the proxy to follow the previously expressed preferences of the patient. Most important, statutes can guarantee legal immunity to care givers who follow the directives of surrogates.

THE IMPORTANCE OF DOCTOR-PATIENT COMMUNICATION

Despite the theoretical advantages of advance directives, particularly the durable power of attorney for health care, several practical problems have limited their clinical usefulness. Many of these problems can be resolved by improved communication between care givers and patients.

First, advance directives are infrequently used. In one study, only 6 percent of elderly or chronically ill patients had discussed their preferences for life-sustaining treatment with their physicians, even though over two-thirds wanted such discussions.[13] No patient in this study had completed a living will or durable power of attorney for health care. Second, advance directives may not be informed, since healthy patients may not fully understand treatments or appreciate the consequences of their choices.[14] Third, to be effective, directives must be both specific and flexible. Vague statements that a patient ''wouldn't want to live like a vegetable'' or wouldn't want ''heroic treatments'' do not help a physician make specific clinical decisions, such as whether to give antibiotics for pneumonia following a severe stroke. Conversely, very specific preferences may not be germane to a particular decision to be made. Since exhaustive plans for all future situations are impossible, some flexibility is needed. Fourth, people may change their minds after making advance directives, and circumstances may also change. Medical advances may improve prognosis, or a patient may develop a new disease. Fifth, disagreements can occur if patients desire care that care givers consider unreasonable.

Improved communication between physicians and patients can resolve these problems with advance directives. The search for the best legal format for advance directives may have the undesirable side effect of focusing attention on documents rather than on the physician-patient relationship. As in any instance of informed consent or refusal, physicians should educate patients, discuss issues, negotiate, and make recommendations. Such discussions help protect patients from unwise or ill-considered decisions. Because discussions are impossible after patients become incompetent, they are especially important when advance directives are made.

Physicians should invite elderly patients and patients who have severe chronic illness to discuss life-sustaining treatment. Such discussions might be included as part of routine evaluations. Straightforward questions may broach the topic: "Would you like to discuss how we should make decisions about your medical care in case you become too sick for me to talk with you directly?" Consistent reluctance to discuss such issues should be respected. Most patients, however, welcome such discussions and want physicians to initiate them.[15]

Doctors can encourage patients to give specific directives. Who should make decisions for them if they become incompetent? What care would they would want if their disease progressed? If they became severely demented, would they want cardiopulmonary resuscitation, admission to the hospital, antibiotics for infection, or tube feedings? Care givers can ask competent patients to clarify vague or ambiguous statements. "Can you tell me what you mean by 'no heroic treatment'?" Care givers can also ask patients to think about the issues and return for further discussions.

Although specific directives are important, advance directives also need to be flexible if they are to be helpful in new situations and after medical advances. Physicians can ask patients if their wishes would change if significant medical discoveries occurred. They also can ask how much discretion the surrogate should have in interpreting the patient's wishes.

Advance directives that differ from previous decisions or statements deserve further discussion. A patient's values may change because of progression of illness or new experiences. Care givers, however, should check that changes of mind are not caused by reversible medical, psychological, or social problems.[16]

Patients may have unrealistic expectations, as when they request mechanical ventilation for respiratory failure due to lung metastases. As with any disagreement, physicians should elicit the patient's concerns with open-ended questions.[17] "What do you think happens to patients whose cancer spreads like that?" In some cases, physicians may need to explain that the patient's goals are impossible. "I wish that were the case. Unfortunately when cancer spreads that much, even breathing machines don't help patients live longer." In such discussions, physicians need to reassure patients about supportive care, since patients often fear abandonment or pain more than death itself. "Of course, no matter what happens, we'll be with you and make sure that you're not in any pain."

Several barriers may hinder discussions between physicians and patients about advance directives. Deficiencies in medical education may cause problems. Physicians receive little formal training about conducting discussions about life-sustaining treatment.[18] Many physicians are troubled by a sense of personal failure or professional inadequacy when their patients are dying. Such feelings make discussions about advance directives difficult. More teaching in medical school and residency about interviewing skills and about medical ethics may improve such discussions.[19]

Another important barrier may be reimbursement. Raising the question of reimbursement for discussing advance directives may seem crass or even offensive. In an ideal system, physicians would carry out such discussions even if they were not reimbursed. However, the fact that few patients have given advance directives suggests that such altruism and idealism do not always occur in practice. At a time when the economic aspects of medicine are widely discussed, it may be appropriate to consider how economic incentives may discourage advance directives. Under fee-for-service reimbursement, performing technical procedures is reimbursed at a much higher hourly rate than educating and counseling patients.[20] While the concept of placing a dollar value on the doctor-patient relationship may seem repugnant, in fact the current reimbursement has already assigned a dollar value—and a relatively low one. Since economic incentives are effective in encouraging physicians to shorten hospital stays and reduce tests, it seems reasonable that they affect other physician behaviors as well. If society values discussions about advance directives, it may need to revise relative reimbursement incentives.

UNRESOLVED ISSUES

Several issues about advance directives need to be resolved. First, most states do not have statutes that explicitly authorize the durable power of attorney for health care. Will the courts allow existing laws about powers of attorney to apply to decisions about health care?

Second, statutory law about advance directives may conflict with case law about withholding care. For example, the Florida Life-Prolonging Procedures Act specifically excludes "sustenance" from treatments that may be withheld or withdrawn.[21] However, in Corbett v. D'Alessandro, a Florida court ruled that "the right to have a nasogastric tube removed is a constitutionally protected right" that could not be limited by the Florida statute.[22] Such apparent inconsistencies in the law may cause confusion and make care givers reluctant to withhold care.

Third, statutes about advance directives may conflict with administrative regulations. Nursing home administrators and workers may be reluctant to honor advance directives because they fear charges of elder abuse or citations from state regulatory agencies. Such fears might be assuaged if statutes about living wills and advance directives were amended to guarantee immunity from such charges for institutions and individuals who in good faith follow properly executed advance directives. Similarly, emergency medical services may be concerned about their legal liability if they withhold emergency resuscitation from a patient who has executed a living will or durable power of attorney.[23]

Fourth, a patient's advance directives may conflict with a physician's professional ethics or personal conscience. Care givers may refuse to comply with a patient's advance directives if they believe that the treatment requested is not medically appropriate. Under the durable power of attorney for health care, patients may give directives for maximal care as well as directives for withholding care. For example, the California Medical Association has printed forms for executing the durable power of attorney for health care on which patients may check the following directive. "I want my life to be prolonged to the greatest extent possible, without regard to my condition, the chances I have for recovery, or the cost of the procedures." Many physicians fear that this directive may request futile or unavailable treatment and may violate their professional duty to provide reasonable, high-quality care.[24]

Care givers also may have conscientious or religious objections to patient directives to withhold care, particularly directives to withhold artificial feeding. Physicians have no ethical obligation to honor all patient requests; they may terminate the doctor-patient relationship and transfer care to other providers who *will* honor them.[25] Many living will laws require physicians to inform patients when they cannot agree to their advance directives and to help arrange transfer of care. This approach, however, is not always feasible; transfer may not be possible or may impose severe burdens on patients.

Several recent court decisions suggest that a patient's right to refuse treatment ultimately takes precedence over the conscientious objections of care givers. In the Bartling case, the court ruled that physicians in an avowedly Christian, pro-life hospital should have honored a patient's request to discontinue a ventilator after efforts to transfer him had failed.[26]

Another court ruled that Beverly Requena, a woman with end stage amyotrophic lateral sclerosis, could not be transferred against her wishes after she decided to refuse artificial feedings. Although another hospital was willing to honor her refusal, the court gave considerable weight to the patient's emotional attachment to the hospital where she had been on a respirator for 17 months. The ruling declared, "It is fairer to ask [the hospital staff] to give than it is to ask Beverly Requena to give."[27]

Fifth, the duty of care givers to protect incompetent patients needs to be clarified. Physicians who do not know an incompetent patient before admission must rely on secondhand information about the patient's wishes. While it is clearly desirable to confirm such information through other sources, how much detective work by care givers is appropriate? Asking the patient's previous physician or another family member to confirm secondhand information seems prudent and practical. Sometimes care givers may suspect a conflict of interest between the surrogate and patient. Because the courts may be too cumbersome and slow, it would be useful to develop intrahospital mechanisms, such as institutional ethics committees, to resolve such cases.

In conclusion, when patients are mentally incompetent, following advance directives is the preferred approach to making decisions. The durable power of attorney for health care is more flexible and comprehensive than other types of advance directives, such as the living will. Discussions between physicians and patients can assure that advance directives are informed, specific, and consistent.

NOTES

1. President's Commission for the Study of Ethical Problems in Medicine and Biomedical and Behavioral Research, *Deciding to Forgo Life-Sustaining Treatment* (Washington: GPO, 1983); D.C. Thomasma, "Beyond Medical Paternalism and Patient Autonomy: A Model of Physician Conscience for the Physician-Patient Relationship," *Annals of Internal Medicine* 54 (1983): 243–48; B. Lo and A.R. Jonsen, "Clinical Decisions to Limit Treatment," *Annals of Internal Medicine* 93 (1980): 764–68.

2. J.F. Childress, *Who Should Decide? Paternalism in Health Care* (New York: Oxford University Press, 1982).

3. L.H. Roth, A. Meisel, and C.W. Lidz, "Tests of Competency to Consent to Treatment," *American Journal of Psychiatry* 134 (1977): 279–83; J.F. Drane, "Competency to Give an Informed Consent," *Journal of the American Medical Association* 252 (1984): 925–27.

4. B. Lo et al., "Do Not Resuscitate Decisions: A Prospective Study at Three Teaching Hospitals," *Archives of Internal Medicine* 145 (1985): 1115–17.

5. President's Commission, *Deciding to Forgo Life-Sustaining Treatment*; A. Buchanan, M. Gilfix and D.W. Brock, "Surrogate Decision Making for Elderly Individuals Who Are Incompetent or of Questionable Competence," *Milbank Memorial Quarterly*, in press.

6. R.M. Veatch, "An Ethical Framework for Terminal Care Decisions," *Journal of the American Geriatrics Society* 32 (1984): 665–69.

7. B.J. McNeil, R. Weichselbaum and S.G. Pauker, "Speech and Survival: Tradeoffs between Quality and Quantity of Life in Laryngeal Cancer," *New England Journal of Medicine* 305 (1981): 982–87.

8. N. Fost and R. Cranford, "Hospital Ethics Committees," *Journal of the American Medical Association* 253 (1985): 2687–92.

9. In re Conroy, 98 N.J. 321, 486 A.2d 1209 (1985); B. Lo and L. Dornbrand, "The Case of Claire Conroy: Will Administrative Review Safeguard Incompetent Patients?" *Annals of Internal Medicine* 104 (1986): 869–73.

10. B. Lo, "The Death of Clarence Herbert: Withdrawing Care Is Not Murder," *Annals of Internal Medicine* 101 (1984): 248–51; Brophy v. New England Sinai Hospital, Inc., 398 Mass. 497 N.E.2d 626 (1986).

11. Society for the Right to Die, *Handbook of 1985 Living Will Laws* (New York: Society for the Right to Die, 1986); idem, *Handbook of Living Will Laws 1981–1984*. (New York: Society for the Right to Die, 1984).

12. R. Steinbrook and B. Lo, "Decision Making for Incompetent Patients by Designated Proxy," *New England Journal of Medicine* 310 (1984): 1598–1601.

13. B. Lo, G. Mc Leod and G. Saika, "Patient Attitudes towards Discussing Life-Sustaining Treatment," *Archives of Internal Medicine* 146 (1986): 1613–15.

14. R. Steinbrook et al., "Preferences of Homosexual Men with the Acquired Immunodeficiency Syndrome for Life-Sustaining Treatment," *New England Journal of Medicine* 314 (1986): 457–60.

15. Lo, Mc Leod, and Saika, "Patient Attitudes."

16. D.L. Jackson and S. Youngner, "Patient Autonomy and 'Death with Dignity,'" *New England Journal of Medicine* 301 (1979): 404–8.

17. M. Lipkin et al., "The Medical Interview: A Core Curriculum for Residencies in Internal Medicine," *Annals of Internal Medicine* 100 (1984): 277–84.

18. A. Miller and B. Lo, "How Do Physicians Discuss Do Not Resuscitate Orders?" *Western Journal of Medicine* 143 (1985): 256–58.

19. C. Mangione, "How Medical School Did Not Prepare Me for Internship," *Journal of Medical Education* 61, part 2 (1986): 3–10.

20. T.P. Almy, "The Role of the Primary Care Physician in the Health Care Industry," *New England Journal of Medicine* 304 (1981): 325–29.

21. Florida, *Statutes* (1984), Chapter 84-58, sections 765.01-.15.

22. Corbett v. D'Alessandro. 487 So. 2d 368 (Fla. App. Ct. Dist. 1986).

23. S.H. Miles and T.J. Crimmins, "Orders to Limit Emergency Treatment for an Ambulance Service in a Large Metropolitan Area," *Journal of the American Medical Association* 254 (1985): 525–27.

24. R. Steinbrook et al., "Ethical Dilemmas in Caring for Patients with the Acquired Immunodeficiency Syndrome," *Annals of Internal Medicine* 103 (1985): 787–90.

25. Thomasma, "Beyond Medical Paternalism and Patient Autonomy."; T.E., Quill, "Partnerships in Patient Care: A Contractural Approach," *Annals of Internal Medicine* 98 (1983): 228–34.

26. Bartling v. Superior Court. 209 Cal. Rptr. (Cal. App. 2d Dist., 1984).

27. In re Requenna. No. A-442-86T5 (N.J. Super. Ct. App. Div. Oct 6, 1986).

BIBLIOGRAPHY

A. Buchanan, M. Gilfix, and D.W. Brock. "Surrogate Decision Making for Elderly Individuals Who Are Incompetent or of Questionable Competence." *Milbank Memorial Quarterly*, in press. This article contains a thoughtful, comprehensive discussion of advance directives.

B. Lo, G. Mc Leod, and G. Saika. "Patient Attitudes Towards Discussing Life-Sustaining Treatment." *Archives of Internal Medicine* 146 (1986): 1613–15. As described in the article, most patients who were elderly or had serious chronic illness had thought about advance directives and had specific preferences, but few had discussed advance directives with physicians and none had executed a living will or durable power of attorney for health care.

President's Commission for the Study of Ethical Problems in Medicine and Biomedical and Behavioral Research. *Deciding to Forgo Life-Sustaining Treatment*. Washington: GPO, 1983. A comprehensive discussion of advance directives is found on pp. 121–70.

Society for the Right to Die. *Handbook of Living Will Laws 1981–1984*. New York: Society for the Right to Die, 1984. This and the following reference contain texts of living will laws. R. Steinbrook, and B. Lo. "Decision Making for Incompetent Patients by Designated Proxy." *New England Journal of Medicine* 310 (1984): 1598–1601. An analysis of California's comprehensive statute authorizing the durable power of attorney for health care.

―――. *Handbook of 1985 Living Will Laws*. New York: Society for the Right to Die, 1986.

Chapter 19

Euthanasia and the Law

David B. Clarke, Jr.

A decade has past since California became the first of a current majority of states to enact "living will" legislation, but it remains difficult for a person to plan for and achieve the dignified death envisioned by supporters of such legislation.[1] While death with dignity remains a goal for many people contemplating a prolonged and painful dying process, there continue to be significant legal and institutional impediments to successful planning. The "right to die" has become a national concern not only for those people who seek to utilize available vehicles for self-determination, but also for courts, legislatures, health care facilities, and, especially, health care professionals.

This chapter will examine from a broad perspective the current status of euthanasia as a legal and ethical concept. Primary consideration will be given to legal options presently available, legal and practical problems associated with implementation, and emerging trends.

Health care professionals and legal representatives should note well that the focus is on areas of the law which are undergoing both substantive and procedural change. With few exceptions, these changes are occurring at the state level. A bibliography is provided at the end of the chapter to facilitate legal research in substantive areas such as determination of competence, forgoing of life-sustaining procedures, professional obligations, and advance directives. Sources of supporting data and information are also included.

CURRENT SITUATION

Recent polls indicate that there is overwhelming public support for the legal right to forgo life-sustaining procedures in cases of terminal illness. In June 1986, 73 percent of 1,510 respondents to a poll commissioned by the American Medical Association favored "withdrawing life support systems, including food and water, from hopelessly ill or irreversibly comatose patients if they or their family request it."[2] A similar poll sponsored by the Pacific Presbyterian Medical Center in San Francisco showed even broader support. Of 2,000 people sampled at the conclusion of a nationwide televised conference, 90 percent "agreed strongly with the proposition that adults who are competent to make their own decisions should have the right to refuse life-sustaining treatment even if their doctors and their families object."[3]

Nor is such sentiment limited to the lay public. In the past year, both medical and legal professional associations have made formal policy statements which support an individual's right to refuse life-sustaining procedures in cases of terminal illness. On March 15, 1986, the Council on Ethical and Judicial Affairs of the American Medical Association released the following policy statement:

> The social commitment of the physician is to sustain life and relieve suffering. Where the performance of one duty conflicts with the other, the choice of the patient, or his family or legal representative if the patient is incompetent to act in his own behalf, should prevail. . . . In treating a terminally ill or irreversibly comatose patient, the physician should determine whether the benefits of treatment outweigh its burdens. At all times, the dignity of the patient should be maintained.[4]

The Los Angeles County Bar Association and the Los Angeles County Medical Association approved ''Principles and Guidelines Concerning the Forgoing of Life-Sustaining Treatment for Adult Patients.''[5] Designed to help both physicians and lawyers deal with the important ethical and legal implications of life-support termination decisions, the document is a significant collaborative effort of the two professions guided by, but not limited to, current California law.

These public statements by professional associations are especially important in two respects. First, they are a clear indication that critical decision making is a process which may involve contributions from interested professions but in which the right of the competent adult person to decide his or her own medical care is paramount. Second, they address several questions which are currently at the heart of the right to die movement: Is there a constitutionally protected right to die such that even a non–terminally ill person can refuse treatment which would prolong life? Does medical treatment include not only medication, but also nutrition and hydration? Must life-sustaining treatment be continued solely because it was initiated? If the person has made no informed decision regarding medical treatment or is discontinuance, who decides and by what guidelines? Can human life be shortened or terminated on request of the patient?

Public opinion polls and professional policy statements give little indication, however, of the considerable controversy within law, medicine, philosophy and religion, and politics over the issue of euthanasia. At the present time, it is safe to say that there simply is no uniformity of thought or law regarding the practice of euthanasia.

What does exist are some independent state statutes regulating individual rights and professional practice, as well as a relatively small body of case law setting precedent in a handful of states, notably California, Massachusetts, and New Jersey. Official positions of various religious traditions range from strict opposition to both passive and active euthanasia to full support for individual decision making.[6] Physicians trained to bear sole decision-making responsibility for their patients' welfare are often bewildered, if not indignant, at seeing some of that responsibility being passed to patients and their families. State legislators are reluctant to support proposals which would jeopardize good constituent relations, even when the proposed legislation is shown to have overwhelming public favor. And while various state courts continue to make increasingly fine distinctions in matters of substantive and procedural law, they do so in the absence of relevant rulings from the United States Supreme Court.

At the center of all this change and indecision is a simple concept: euthanasia. (*Euthanasia* literally means a good or gentle death.) The questions prompting discussion are also relatively simple: Should an individual have a legally protected right to a good death, and what means should be available to him or her to achieve it?

As indicated, euthanasia is taken to mean a voluntary request by a person to be spared a lingering, painful, and undignified death. Voluntary euthanasia can be either passive (allowing a "natural" death by choosing to forgo artificial life-sustaining procedures such that death occurs from a terminal illness or condition, dehydration, or starvation) or active (where a patient acts or requests someone else to act in such a way as to cause death). Living will or natural death laws, for example, allow for voluntary passive euthanasia. A more comprehensive discussion of the legal aspects of both voluntary and involuntary euthanasia will be found later in this chapter.

BACKGROUND

Euthanasia is not a new concept. The ancient Greeks and Romans practiced euthanasia as a socially and legally acceptable way to avoid the sufferings and indignities of terminal illness. With the rise of Christianity, and its teaching that human life belonged to the deity alone, the practice was prohibited and socially disfavored for more than a thousand years in the West. (It is still practiced in the East, e.g., hari-kari in Japan.) The sixteenth century European Renaissance brought about an awakening of intellectual and scientific thought. Without abandoning Christian doctrine, the great teachers and writers were able to question people's capacity for personal autonomy and their obvious ability to improve life. The current geometric increase of scientific knowledge and technology has its roots in the universities, churches, and laboratories of more than four hundred years ago.[7] There, too, began our continuing concern for the rights of the individual and our passion for the privilege of self-determination.

More recently, four developments in particular have made the issue of euthanasia of current concern. First, modern medical practice and innovations in medical technology have raised, since the turn of the century, the average life expectancy by many years. Diseases once life-threatening have either been eradicated entirely, as was the case with smallpox, or are now easily treatable or preventable. And while certain afflictions of old age continue to plague us, despite intensive research efforts, the capacity to sustain health well into a person's eighties or nineties is now commonplace. Mechanical substitution of ordinary physiologic processes permits an otherwise dying person to be maintained almost indefinitely. Complex machines can be used to replace natural breathing, blood circulation, eating, and drinking, even for persons whose brain functioning is severely or totally impaired. Many persons have come to believe that there is no moral imperative to do all that can be done when there is no reasonable hope for recovery.

Second, while the medical technology may be impressive, so are the costs. The price tag for the current array of diagnostic and treatment procedures is staggering and presently accounts for a significant percentage of our gross national product. A large part of the cost is understandably associated with catastrophic illness, where life and death are at stake, not simply illness and wellness. Costs have also reflected increases in physician malpractice litigation, salaries in a labor intensive field, and drug and treatment research. In an effort to contain rising costs, the federal government recently altered its payment scheme under

Social Security from a total reimbursement system to one which pays fixed amounts based on diagnosis related groups (DRGs).

Late in 1986, several federal legislators suggested that federal insurance be made available specifically to cover catastrophic illness among Social Security recipients.[8] A 1985 report by the chairman of the House of Representatives Select Committee on Aging had made the following recommendation:

> Catastrophic out-of-pocket health cost burdens for the terminally ill should be limited so that they do not create undue financial pressure on the terminally ill or bankrupt the family. Currently, the out-of-pocket cost burden on the terminally ill and their families can be astronomical and can result in decisions to refuse medical treatment that are not in the best interest of the terminally ill person.[9]

Third, although two generations removed from current events, the Nazi genocide of European Jews remains fresh in the minds of survivors. Critics of any organized euthanasia movement are quick to point out that the horrors of the extermination camps had their origin in efforts to "euthanize" persons who were terminally ill or chronically insane. Only when both the public and the medical profession accepted the logic of such therapeutic "kindnesses" were other unfortunates targeted as socially undesirable.[10] Once euthanasia is accepted, critics argue, the "slippery slope" will lead us inevitably to a repeat performance.

Supporters of the voluntary euthanasia movement note that the Holocaust, which had as victims not only Jews, but also Gypsies, homosexuals, the developmentally disabled, and political dissidents, involved involuntary killing from the outset. The entire notion of voluntariness, evidenced by traditional forms of consent, was absent. Even a cursory reading of typical hospital admitting forms, medical malpractice complaints, or the most current right to die litigation arguments will indicate the stringent requirements concerning timely and informed consent under present law.

The last of the four significant developments has been the institutionalization of voluntary passive euthanasia through the legal recognition of living wills. Following publication of "Due Process of Euthanasia: The Living Will, A Proposal" by Louis Kutner in 1969, the Euthanasia Education Council in New York (now two distinct groups: Society for the Right to Die and Concern for Dying) began to circulate a unique document.[11] The living will, patterned after a revocable inter vivos trust, was a directive to one's physician and others by which a currently healthy and competent person could request that no heroic measures be taken to preserve life should there be no reasonable hope for recovery from a future illness or condition. Though signed and witnessed, the living will was not binding on physicians or family members. It did, however, provide a good indication of a person's own wishes in cases of subsequent incompetence. In 1976, California became the first state to recognize the legal validity of the living will concept through its Natural Death Act.[12]

Why are these developments important? For the average person who is sufficiently ill or old to give matters of life and death more than casual thought, consideration of these developments may have significant influence on the way that person sees his or her relationship to the health care system. Depending on the degree of awareness or ignorance, the person may faithfully follow a physician's advice and submit to treatment which only prolongs suffering. The person may forgo essential treatment out of concern for the family's financial well-being. Never having discussed preferences with a physician or family members, the person may find him- or herself suddenly unable to communicate and thus subject to the wishes of others. Ignorant of research protocols, the person may opt for untried or unproven experimental procedures.

Health care professionals should be fully aware that the average person has only a vague notion of the forces at work in the health care system. Infrequent experiences with other family members, television dramas, and the popular press are the chief means of information about the medical community for most people. Their own eventual confrontation with the prospect of dying is a poor time to learn about informed consent, advance directives, and the most recent case law. Medical staff whose personal value systems are substantially different from those of their patients may provide yet another element of confusion for patients needing to make crucial decisions.

Medical staff, especially those with direct patient contact, must be effective ''teachers'' in the broadest sense. While not charged with providing encyclopedic information, they must have at least a general awareness of the following: the major social events which have helped to form shared social values; the broad range of moral and ethical positions held by patients; and the general trends in appropriate areas of law. With a working knowledge of this information, a health care professional is not only better able to reduce the risks of liability, but better equipped to distinguish personal preferences from the true wishes of the patient.[13] One may not agree with a patient's choice, but the patient may desperately need to be understood in making the choice.

ETHICAL CONSIDERATIONS

The moral distinction between active and passive euthanasia has become less clear, largely because of our increased technical ability to sustain an otherwise dying or dead person. Many persons believe, for example, that removing a patient from a respirator upon request of the patient is active euthanasia. Both moral and legal norms now hold that where artificial means are the sole source of vitality, consensual removal does not constitute suicide by the patient, nor any moral or legal wrong by the person doing the removing. The California Natural Death Act codifies this view: ''No physician or health facility which, acting in accordance with the requirements of this chapter, causes the withholding or withdrawal of life-sustaining procedures from a qualified patient, shall be subject to civil liability therefrom . . . [or] shall be guilty of any criminal act or of unprofessional conduct.''[14]

Pope John Paul II, in a 1980 reaffirmation of earlier statement by the Roman Catholic Church, also affirmed this view:

> It is also permitted, with the patient's consent, to interrupt these means [the most advanced medical techniques], where the results fall short of expectations. . . . [Doctors] may judge that the techniques applied impose on the patient strain or suffering out of proportion with the benefits which he or she may gain from such techniques. . . . When inevitable, death is imminent in spite of the means used; it is permitted in conscience to make the decision to refuse forms of treatment that would only secure a precarious and burdensome prolongation of life, so long as the normal care due to the sick person in similar cases is not interrupted.[15]

In order to preserve the integrity of the medical profession, courts and legislatures have recognized the legal right of health care professionals and facilities to refuse to do acts considered medically unethical. Typical of many living will statutes, California's includes the following provision:

> No physician, and no licensed health professional acting under the direction of a physician, shall be criminally or civilly liable for failing to effectuate the directive of the qualified patient pursuant to this subdivision. A failure by a physician to effectuate the directive . . . shall constitute unprofessional conduct if the physician refuses to make the necessary arrangements, or fails to take the necessary steps, to effect the transfer of the qualified patient to another physician who will effectuate the directive of the qualified patient.[16]

Similarly, in Brophy vs. New England Sinai Hospital, Inc. (where the wife of a patient in a persistent vegetative state requested that the hospital discontinue artificial nutrition and hydration), the Massachusetts Supreme Judicial Court held, "It would be particularly inappropriate to force this hospital, which is willing to assist in a transfer of the patient, to take affirmative steps to end the provision of nutrition and hydration to him. A patient's right to refuse medical treatment does not warrant such an unnecessary intrusion upon the hospital's ethical integrity in this case."[17]

The morality of voluntary active euthanasia continues to prompt debate far from the forum of the courtroom. In the same "Declaration on Euthanasia" in which he allowed for active withdrawal from life supports, Pope John Paul II also warned that "nothing and no one can in any way permit the killing of an innocent person" and that "intentionally causing one's own death, or suicide, is therefore equally as wrong as murder." Advocates of the right to end life when it becomes terminally unbearable point out that it may be morally preferable (or morally equivalent) to take active steps rather than to suffer the pain and indignities of a passive "natural" death. Joseph Fletcher is one of the more articulate supporters of this position:

> What, then, is the real issue? In a few words, it is whether we can morally justify taking it into our own hands to hasten death for ourselves (suicide) or for others (mercy killing) out of reasons of compassion. The answer to this in my view is clearly Yes, on both sides of it. . . .
>
> The really searching question of conscience is, therefore, whether we are right in believing that *the well-being of persons* is the highest good. If so, then it follows that either suicide or mercy killing could be the right thing to do in some exigent and tragic circumstances.
>
> This position comes down to the belief that our moral acts, including suicide and mercy killing, are right or wrong depending on the consequences aimed at (we sometimes fail, of course, through ignorance or poor reasoning), and that the consequences are good or evil according to whether and how much they serve humane values. In the language of ethics this is called a "consequential" method of moral judgment.[18]

Remembering that legal considerations have been left aside for the moment (and that they may have a great deal of influence on choice of conduct), we will here focus on the fact that all persons make decisions based on some set of principles, regardless of whether they can actually put those principles into words. Medical decisions—made by professionals or patients—are similar. Beauchamp and Childress, in their now standard *Principles of Biomedical Ethics,* include the following principles:[19]

- the principle of autonomy, which entails that a person's chosen course of action should be respected by others
- the principle of beneficence, which entails that there is a duty or obligation to do good to others
- the principle of nonmaleficence, which entails that there is an affirmative duty to do no harm to others (this is different from the principle of beneficence)
- the principle of justice, which entails that the rightness (or wrongness) of an act is determined (at least in part) by issues of fairness, equality, and equity

It is not difficult to see that strict adherence to any one of these guiding principles, to the exclusion of the others, would lead to an inflexible dogmatism of little use in clinical settings. For instance, a patient who demanded his autonomy be respected in choosing to forgo necessary treatment might do so in disregard of real needs of his dependents. Take the case of a physician who has been requested by an end stage renal failure patient to terminate treatment. The Hippocratic Oath requires that the physician do no harm, though she is also compelled to be beneficent toward her patient, that is, to spare the patient useless suffering. This is a classic ethical dilemma where the decision maker must choose between two options neither of which is clearly better.

The most emotionally demanding situations arise when the health care professional and the patient are both seeking to make difficult decisions about the patient's welfare, but are basing their respective choices on differing, perhaps conflicting, ethical principles. Unless both people can be guided by an overarching principle, the situation must be resolved either by deference or compromise. In matters of euthanasia, it is precisely these interrelated dilemmas—pitting patients, families, and medical staff against each other as decision-making adversaries—which eventuate in the use of the legal arena for resolution.

AVAILABLE OPTIONS

Persons seeking an easier or more dignified death than the normal course of a terminal disease or condition might afford have several options under current law. At present, these options include palliative care, refusal of all treatment including nutrition and hydration, or the use of either of two kinds of advance directive (the living will or the durable power of attorney). Since suicide does not carry any criminal penalties and is frequently employed as a means of voluntary active euthanasia in cases of terminal illness, it must also be considered an option.

Hospice

Those for whom any active intervention would be unacceptable can opt for hospice care. Hospice is a modern palliative care treatment program for dying persons based loosely on the old European concept of hospitality—welcoming a traveler into one's home for the primary purpose of providing rest, food, and companionship. Developed in England by Dame Cicely Saunders, the hospice movement has blossomed in this country largely under the impetus and guidance of Dr. Elisabeth Kübler-Ross.

While most of the one thousand hospice programs are home-based rather than in inpatient hospital facilities, the hospice seeks to provide whatever services are necessary to ensure a dignified and virtually painless dying. Medical and nursing personnel not only make sure that there are sufficient analgesics to avoid the debilitating pain of some terminal illness, but also play an active role in training family members to cope with the distinctive needs of dying relatives. The thousands of trained hospice volunteers offer respite time for the family as well as a substantial degree of practical help during what is often a protracted "journey." With its conviction in the rightness of natural death, the Roman Catholic Church understandably sponsors many of the larger and more successful hospice programs nationwide.

There are problems with hospice care, as with any service, and it certainly isn't the answer for every terminally ill person. First, hospice programs provide palliative care, an abatement of pain, discomfort, and indignity, but they do not provide a cure. Second, even the most aggressive pain suppression regimen cannot guarantee absolute freedom from pain, nor from equally discomforting medication side effects. Third, there aren't enough programs for those who would use them, and only a fraction of applicants are served. Fourth, although there is a change for the better, some health care insurance still doesn't reimburse for hospice care. Finally, no matter how well trained the volunteers, no matter how accepting the family and gracious the hospitality, no matter how diminished the pain, some people would prefer to die on their own terms at a time of their choosing.

Treatment Refusal

Anyone seeking treatment in a modern health care facility has been confronted with consent forms, those small-type, preprinted pages which have a place to sign at the bottom. They are printed because they give the treatment facility a piece of written documentation, acknowledged by the patient, that the patient has been informed of the treatment about to be performed and has consented to it. Very few patients fully understand the legal right being exercised, and even fewer know its negative counterpart.

Since the beginning of this century, competent adults have had the common-law right to give their consent to any proposed medical treatment. In a landmark New York case, Schloendorff v. Society of New York Hospital, Justice Benjamin Cardozo stated the rule which has become the foundation of our modern doctrine of informed consent. He stated, "Every human being of adult years and sound mind has a right to determine what shall be done with his own body."[20] Without consent, argued Cardozo, the treatment would constitute battery of the patient, making the physician liable for civil damages.[21]

In order to have true consent, the patient must be sufficiently informed by the physician to make a cogent evaluation of the possibilities. How much must the physician tell the patient? The traditional "professional standard" was to provide whatever information a *typical* physician, similarly situated, would tell a patient. The modern trend clearly favors the patient: The patient is entitled to know whatever an average reasonable person in like circumstances would want to know to make an informed choice.[22]

The right to be allowed to give or withhold consent before being treated is virtually absolute. The four exceptions are emergencies, when consent of a patient will be implied until he or she regains the capacity to consent; cases of patient incompetence, though exercise of the right will usually be passed to a proxy; cases in which a physician determines that it would be more harmful to a patient's well-being to be told about a treatment; and cases in which a patient waives the right.

If one has an almost unqualified right to give consent, then it follows that one has a correlative right to withhold consent, that is, to refuse to be treated. Since the large majority of persons approach the health care system seeking treatment, the right to withhold consent is not a common issue. However, when patients confront life and death decisions, the exceptions listed above may engender considerable problems. For example, only three states specifically define the emergencies which would allow a physician to treat without the patient's consent. While imminent death might be welcomed by the patient, the attending physician may see the situation as requiring emergency intervention. A similar conflict might arise when a physician thinks it would be harmful to tell a patient about a prospective treatment. (Note that there is a growing body of evidence showing that patients are more frequently benefited by medical information than harmed by it.)[23]

As in other areas of the law, persons are presumed competent to perform legal acts, such as make contracts or execute wills, unless their competency is challenged and adjudged to be lacking. Problems may arise when a patient confronting his or her own dying is seen by others to be making a decision under circumstances too stressful or confusing to allow presumption of competency. Problems also may arise when a patient makes a decision apparently inconsistent with prior life style or convictions. It is important to note that the patient's right under consideration here is the right to choose, not the right to choose only from options favored by others. Nevertheless, the decision that is inconsistent may be the basis to challenge a patient's competency (see Chapter 8).

Also, the definition of competency is frequently obscure. It would make a great deal of difference if the threshold test was, for example, the mere physical ability to express consent to treatment as compared to a test requiring a showing that the patient understood the nature of the treatment, its risks, and its benefits. There is considerable variety among such tests (in the cases where there is any required test at all). Lastly, it should be noted that a patient may be incompetent (even adjudged incompetent) for some purposes (e.g., to manage personal business affairs), though perfectly competent to make health care treatment decisions.

By far the most frequent worry of families of patients approaching death is who will make decisions about the patient's treatment should he or she become incompetent. The right to consent to or refuse treatment belongs to a person whether competent or incompetent. In cases of incompetency, the only difficulty is determining who will exercise the right for the patient and upon what criteria. The trend in the courts is toward empowering a surrogate decision maker (usually a family member or someone appointed by the court) to determine the patient's care under the "substituted judgment" standard. Here, the decision maker must determine what the patient would want were the patient competent to make his or her own decision. The surrogate may rely on information such as advance directives made by the patient or any written or oral evidence of the patient's own wishes. Still in use is another standard which requires the surrogate to determine what would be in the "best interest" of the patient and to decide accordingly.[24] The surrogate may not substitute his own preference for that of the patient.

In general, courts have allowed persons (or their surrogates) to refuse life-saving and life-sustaining treatment, including nutrition and hydration, irrespective of whether the patient was competent or whether the illness was terminal—unless there was shown a compelling state interest to the contrary. In one case, the court ruled that the state had a responsibility not to allow a patient to abandon her infant child by refusing life-saving transfusions on religious grounds.[25] Countervailing state interests might include the preservation of life, the protection of interests of innocent third parties (e.g., the infant minor just mentioned), the prevention of suicide, and the maintenance of the ethical integrity of the medical profession.[26]

It is especially noteworthy that courts in at least three states have grounded treatment refusal decisions on an asserted constitutional right to privacy, citing both Roe v. Wade and Griswold v. Connecticut. Neither of these landmark United States Supreme Court cases, the first sanctioning a woman's right to abort a pregnancy and the second holding that married couples have a right to use contraceptives, have extended the unwritten right of privacy beyond relatively narrow boundaries. To date, the Supreme Court has made no ruling extending privacy to include the right to refuse medical treatment.[27]

Living Will Laws: The Legal Perspective

Living will or Natural Death Act provisions are the only legally valid directives concerned exclusively with voluntary passive euthanasia. In general, these advance directives to physicians and others permit a competent person to specify that in the event of terminal illness or condition and a concurrent inability to make decisions, no life-sustaining procedures or treatment should be used to prolong the dying process.

Most of the statutes also provide for legal recognition of acts which otherwise would be subject to case-by-case judicial determination. They relieve physicians and persons acting under their direction of civil and criminal liability for acceding to the request. And, despite growing criticism, most statutes fail to impose any substantial penalty on a physician who either fails to accede to the request or fails to transfer the patient to a physician who will. Typically, statutes affirm that the act of forgoing life-sustaining treatment does not constitute suicide. This entails that execution of the document alone cannot be the basis of a competency challenge or of mental health proceedings. It relieves any health professional assisting in the withholding or withdrawing of treatment of potential criminal liability. Finally, it limits conflicts arising from the issuance of or payment under a life insurance policy.

The major problem with living will laws is that there are now 39 of them, each slightly different in form, requirements, scope, complexity, and so on. It is imperative to know the particular statute that applies within one's jurisdiction. In 1985, the National Conference of Commissioners on Uniform State Laws approved a model Uniform Rights of the Terminally Ill Act. It is to be hoped that this flexible and comprehensive model, based on the best provisions from the various laws, will soon be adopted by all the states. The Society for the Right to Die regularly updates a thorough comparison chart listing all provisions of present statutes and the proposed Uniform Act.

Health care providers should be aware of just a few variations in living will laws. Only three states recognize documents from other states. Several states require that a provided form be followed precisely. In a handful of states, a directive must be renewed periodically.

All states have strict requirements for execution of the document, and most states place limitations on who may witness the signing. Three states specify that the patient must have signed the directive after having been certified terminally ill in order to make the directive binding; if executed before the patient becomes terminally ill, presumably the directed physician may, but need not, accede to the request.

Durable Power of Attorney: The Legal Perspective

The durable power of attorney is the more powerful of the two directives, but certainly the lesser known. Derived in form from a common legal device, this relatively recent variant has yet to be thoroughly tested in the courts. A traditional power of attorney allows an individual to authorize any other person (known as the *attorney-in-fact*, though the named agent need not be an attorney at all) to conduct business in the "principal's" behalf. For example, a husband might authorize his wife to sign the necessary escrow papers for their new home on his behalf while he was away on business. The wife's signature, undersigned with the phrase "attorney-in-fact for (husband's name)," is legally acceptable and binding as his act. In the power of attorney document, the husband probably would have added a specific instruction that this authorization to conduct business for him was limited to signing the escrow papers.

The law understands that the authorization granted by the principal is a continuing one but that the authority disappears if the principal dies or become incompetent, i.e., becomes physically or legally unable to continue the grant of authority. The stumbling block was the issue of incompetency. Many people wanted a way to authorize an agent to conduct business in their behalf when they themselves were legally unable to do so. Hence, the *durable* power of attorney, which becomes effective only when the principal becomes incompetent (or which continues to be effective despite the subsequent incompetency of the principal, depending on the desired date of effectiveness).

All states now have durable power of attorney statutes, some modeled on the Uniform Durable Power of Attorney Act suggested by the National Conference of Commissioners on Uniform State Laws.[28] For the purposes of this review, such a statute would allow a person to name an agent to conduct a specific kind of business in the person's behalf: the making of health care decisions on behalf of the person if and when the person becomes incompetent. The Uniform Act and most state acts provide a great deal of latitude in drafting such instruments and require only general language to distinguish the desired durable power from traditional nondurable power. In addition, the principal is encouraged to be as specific as possible about the extent and limits of authority, including conditions under which treatment would be desired or refused, threshholds of physical disability or illness which would trigger treatment refusal, and other relevant information to guide the attorney-in-fact.

The authorized power under a durable power of attorney is limited not only by specific instructions from the principal, but also by a significant body of agency law. The named agent cannot break the law, nor breach any fiduciary trust, nor exceed the authority granted to him or her. But as mentioned above, depending on the extent of the decision making authority given, the named agent would have the authority to refuse life-sustaining procedures on behalf of the principal, assuming that the principal could have done so if competent.

Though to a lesser extent, the same practical problems that attend the living will laws occur with respect to the various durable power of attorney statutes. Furthermore, since both directives are relatively recent legal innovations, there is no substantial body of case law for direction. For instance, while it is widely presumed that a directive for health care decision making made by means of a durable power of attorney would be valid, this has not been tested. At least one state (California) has two separate acts, one for uniform durable power of attorney and another for durable power of attorney for health care.

Both living wills and durable power of attorney documents may present problems in a clinical setting. Unless a directive (of either kind) is glued to the front of the patient's chart or is made a part of the standing orders, it may be overlooked in the medical record. Health care facilities would be well advised to inquire of the existence of a directive upon admission, either from the patient, family member, or attending physician. As both kinds of directives become more widely used, it is presumed that sanctions against health care professionals and facilities will become more severe for failing to ascertain the existence of a valid directive or for failing to heed it.

Suicide

While suicide still arouses strong moral opposition, especially from the more conservative religious denominations, it has become more common than previously for terminally ill persons who wish to avoid the anguish of a protracted dying. It is useful to distinguish suicide (as legally defined) from other forms of euthanasia. A suicide occurs when a person him- or herself puts into motion the mechanism which ultimately causes death. It is the self-produced act which has aroused moral opposition, not the death itself. In cases of terminal illness or condition, then, a person's refusal of life-sustaining procedures cannot be taken as suicide, since death results from the illness or condition, not the treatment refusal. Note that the legal and medical professions have held that artificial hydration and nutrition are treatments which can also be frequently withdrawn or withheld, like any other life-sustaining procedure.[29]

Even though the state may act to prevent a suicide, there are no criminal penalties for attempting suicide. However, in most states, evidence that a person is a clear danger to him- or herself, plus evidence of mental illness, is grounds for involuntary psychiatric commitment proceedings.

For terminally ill persons considering suicide, practical considerations, such as method, privacy, painlessness, and impact on others, are primary concerns. One of the voluntary euthanasia societies, the Hemlock Society of Los Angeles, publishes a book entitled *Let Me Die before I Wake*, which is described as "the only guide to self-deliverance for the dying person published in the United States."[30] First published in 1981, the slim volume has sold more than 70,000 copies and is commonly available in libraries and bookstores. A CBS "60 Minutes" feature on the Hemlock Society called the book "the bible" of the euthanasia movement.

Persons who assist others in a suicide risk criminal prosecution in many jurisdictions for felony "aiding and abetting," manslaughter, or murder. Under current law, motivation for the assistance is simply not a factor, though it may affect the severity of the penalty imposed. If the intent of the assistance was to help bring about the death of the suicidal person, it makes little difference whether the act was to encourage verbally, to plan, to provide the specific means, or to help in a physical way (as might be required with a terminally ill person who had lost mobility or dexterity). Nor does it matter that the entire process was planned, directed, and requested by the suicidal person. A lesser charge might be conspiracy (conspiracy occurs when two or more people agree to do an illegal act and at least one person takes an action in furtherance of the agreement).

As with any crime, the risk of criminal prosecution depends upon detection of the crime and identification of those involved. One might presume that there have been many assisted suicidal deaths which have gone unprosecuted because the death was not unexpected and secrecy between the suicidal person and any helper was maintained effectively.

Mercy Killing

Mercy killing, or taking the life of another for compassionate reasons with or without the victim's consent, is murder in all American jurisdictions. Traditional defenses, such as self-defense, crime prevention, or extreme provocation, are almost never available in mercy killing cases. Most true mercy killings are tragic cases in which one person is driven to do a desperate act by being intimately involved with the unbearable suffering of the victim, most often a spouse or family member.

The only recent study of mercy killings nationwide indicates that the number of publicized cases is rising dramatically: There were as many cases between 1980 and 1986 as there were from 1920 to 1980. What is most interesting is that in all but 3 of the 30 mercy killings since 1980, the defendant has not been imprisoned for the offense. Instead, courts have usually found defendants not guilty (on grounds of temporary insanity) or have imposed considerable periods of probation.[31] Of those sentenced to prison, two are currently serving life terms.

EMERGING TRENDS

There is a growing number of people who believe that there should be a legal and humane way to end life when death is imminent (though perhaps not immediate) and the quality of life has reached a personally unacceptable level. Under current law, a terminally ill person in such circumstances has only two legal options: to forgo life-sustaining or life-prolonging medical treatment and starve to death or to submit to palliative care until natural death occurs at some indefinite time in the future. Legally risky options include committing suicide with the assistance of another or requesting to be killed by another. In some few other countries, motivation is a factor considered in the prosecution of homicide, and compassionate killing or killing on request does not incur the same penalties as murder.[32]

Both supporters and critics of voluntary euthanasia have been watching closely events in the Netherlands, where voluntary active euthanasia has been legalized under narrow case law. In 1981, the Rotterdam Criminal Court developed guidelines under which a terminally ill person could receive direct aid in dying from a physician. Among the ten items used to determine appropriateness are the following:[33]

- There must be physical or mental suffering which the sufferer finds unbearable.
- The suffering and the desire to die must be lasting.
- The decision to die must be the voluntary decision of an informed patient.
- The person must have a correct and clear understanding of his or her condition and of other possibilities; the person must be capable of weighing these options and must have done so.
- There is no other reasonable solution to improve the situation.
- The time and manner of death will not cause avoidable misery to others.
- A medical doctor must be involved in the decision and prescribe the correct drugs.

According to Dr. Pieter Admiraal, senior anesthetist at the Delft General Hospital, approximately 5,000 persons annually request and are granted voluntary euthanasia under these guidelines.[34] Admiraal explained the practice from a physician's perspective: "Euthanasia as an act of respect to an incurable patient in such patient's interest and on his request is regarded in our hospital as a dignified last act of medical care for a patient in his terminal phase."[35]

In the United States, there is presently an effort to secure similar legislation. The Humane and Dignified Death Initiative, introduced by the Hemlock Society in 1986 and being actively advanced by the Glendale-based Americans Against Human Suffering, calls for a California voter initiative to amend the current Natural Death Act and the Durable Power of Attorney for Health Care. The two groups hope to place the measure on the November 1988 ballot. Briefly, the proposed legislation would permit a competent terminally ill person to request a physician to administer aid in dying. Under the proposal, "terminal" refers to any incurable condition leading to death within six months and "aid in dying" refers to any medical procedure that will terminate the life of the dying patient swiftly, painlessly, and humanely.

Supporters of such innovative legislation point to a 1986 Roper Poll which indicated that 62 percent of 2,000 American adults answered yes to the following question: When a person has a painful and distressing terminal disease, do you think doctors should be allowed by law to end the patient's life if there is no hope of recovery and the patient requests it?[36] Also cited is Justice Compton's concurring opinion in the California appellate decision granting Elizabeth Bouvia, a disabled but non–terminally ill person, the right to refuse nutrition and hydration:

> Elizabeth apparently has made a conscious and informed choice that she prefers death to continued existence in her helpless and, to her, intolerable condition. . . . This state and the medical profession instead of frustrating her desire, should be attempting to relieve her suffering by permitting and in fact assisting her to die with ease and dignity. The fact that she is forced to suffer the ordeal of self-starvation to achieve her objective is in itself inhumane.
> . . . The medical profession, freed of the threat of governmental or legal reprisal, would, I am sure, have no difficulty in accommodating an individual in Elizabeth's situation.

In the past decade, euthanasia as a moral and legal concept has prompted heated discussion. Representatives from the professions of law, medicine, and religion, as well as concerned advocates from various voluntary associations, have appeared in the media and testified in protracted judicial challenges. At issue are the exercise of fundamental individual liberties and the protection of persons unable to plead in their own behalf. It is to be hoped that the discussion will continue, providing further refinement of critical issues of law and health care but without yielding to absolutes which would effectively close the conversation to all.

NOTES

1. To date, 39 states and the District of Columbia have enacted so-called living will or natural death statutes allowing competent persons to forgo life-sustaining procedures in cases of terminal illness. The following states do *not* have similar statutes: Ky., Mass., Mich., Nebr., N. Dak., N.J., N.Y., Ohio, Pa., R.I., and S. Dak.

2. "Most Respondents Favor Ending Life Support," *American Medical News*, November 28, 1986.

3. "90% in Poll Back Patients' Right to Die," *New York Times*, December 2, 1986.

4. American Medical Association, Council on Ethical and Judicial Affairs. "Withholding or withdrawing Life-Prolonging Medical Treatment," policy statement, March 15, 1986.

5. "Principles and Guidelines Concerning the Foregoing of Life-Sustaining Treatment for Adult Patients," *LACMA NEWS*, Los Angeles County Medical Association, January 1986.

6. Gerald Larue, *Euthanasia and Religion* (Los Angeles: Hemlock Society, 1985).

7. Derek Humphry and Ann Wickett, *The Right to Die: Understanding Euthanasia* (New York: Harper & Row, 1986), 1–19.

8. "Insurance Program Proposed to Cover Catastrophic Illness," *New York Times*, November 21, 1986, p. 1.

9. House Select Committee on Aging, *Dying with Dignity: Difficult Times, Difficult Choices* (Washington, D.C.: GPO, 1985).

10. Leo Alexander, "Medical Science under Dictatorship," in *Death, Dying, and Euthanasia*, ed. Dennis J. Horan and David Mall (Frederick, Md.: University Publications of America, 1985). See also Frederic Wertham, "The Geranium in the Window: The 'Euthanasia' Murders," ibid., for a psychiatric perspective.

11. Louis Kutner, "Due Process of Euthanasia: The Living Will, A Proposal," *Indiana Law Journal* 44:539–554 (Summer 1969), cited in Humphry and Wickett, *The Right to Die*, 86–87.

12. California Health and Safety Code, Section 7185 et seq.

13. David B. Clarke, Jr., "Helping Patients Make Health Care Decisions," *Euthanasia Review* 1, no. 2 (1986): 85–96.

14. California Health and Safety Code, Section 7190.

15. Pope John Paul II, "Euthanasia—Declaration of the Sacred Congregation for the Doctrine of the Faith, Pope John Paul II (May 1980)," *Death Education II*, 422–28.

16. California Health and Safety Code, Section 7191.

17. Brophy v. New England Sinai Hospital, Inc., 398 Mass. 417, 441 (1986).

18. Joseph Fletcher, "Ethics and Euthanasia," in *Death, Dying, and Euthanasia*, ed. Horan and Mall.

19. Tom L. Beauchamp and James F. Childress, *Principles of Biomedical Ethics* (New York: Oxford University Press, 1979).

20. Schloendorff v. Society of New York Hospital, 211 N.Y. 125, 129, 105 N.E. 92 (1914).

21. Battery is any unconsented touching, no matter how slight. Nor does it matter that the touching was done by a health professional in a therapeutic manner for the sole benefit of the patient. The key word is *unconsented*.

22. Lori B. Andrews, "Informed Consent Statutes and the Decisionmaking Process," *Journal of Legal Medicine* 5, no. 2 (1984): 176–77.

23. President's Commission for the Study of Ethical Problems in Medicine and Biomedical and Behavioral Research, *Making Health Care Decisions: The Ethical and Legal Implications of Informed Consent in the Patient-Practitioner Relationship* (Washington D.C.: GPO, 1982), 99–102.

24. Fay A. Rozovsky, *Consent to Treatment: A Practical Guide* (Boston: Little, Brown & Co., 1984), 443–61.

25. Application of President and Directors of Georgetown College, Inc., 118 U.S.App.D.C. 80, 331 F.2d 1000 (D.C.Cir.), rehearing denied, 118 U.S.App.D.C. 90, 331 F.2d 1010, cert. denied, 337 U.S. 978, 84 S.Ct. 1883, 12 L.Ed.2d 746 (1964).

26. Brophy v. New England Sinai Hospital, Inc., p. 432.

27. See Bouvia v. Superior Court for Los Angeles County, 225 Cal. Rptr. 304 (Ct. App. 1986); Brophy v. New England Sinai Hospital, Inc., 398 Mass. 417 (1986); and In re Conroy, 98 N.J. 321 (1985).

28. Uniform Durable Power of Attorney Act, 8 U.L.A. 74 (1982).

29. See Brophy v. New England Sinai Hospital, Inc., pp. 433–40, for the most recent discussion of this issue. See also Bouvia v. Superior Court, which holds that even a non–terminally ill person has the right to refuse nutrition and hydration; also, the 1986 policy statement of the American Medical Association, which holds that "life prolonging medical treatment includes . . . nutrition or hydration."

30. Derek Humphry, *Let Me Die before I Wake* (Los Angeles: Hemlock Society, 1981).

31. Ann Wickett, "Most Mercy Killings in Living Will States," *Hemlock Quarterly*, 1986, no. 23:3.

32. Humphry and Wickett, *The Right to Die*, 218–28.

33. Adrienne Van Till, "Dutch Doctors Get Guidelines," *Hemlock Quarterly*, 1984, no. 17:1.

34. Pieter V. Admiraal, "Euthanasia in the Netherlands: A Dutch Perspective," address at the Third National Voluntary Euthanasia Conference, Washington, D.C., September 25–27, 1986.

35. Pieter V. Admiraal, "Active Voluntary Euthanasia," *Hemlock Quarterly*, 1985, no. 21:3.

36. "Most Americans Think There Should Be a Legal Right-to-Die," *Hemlock Quarterly*, 1986, no. 24:1.

BIBLIOGRAPHY

Americans against Human Suffering. "Humane and Dignified Death Initiative." Glendale, Calif.: Americans against Human Suffering, 1986.

Andrews, Lori B. "Informed Consent Statutes and the Decisionmaking Process." *Journal of Legal Medicine* 5, no. 2 (1984): 163–217.

Barber v. Superior Court, 147 Cal.App.3d 1006, 195 Cal. Rptr. 484 (1983).

Bartling v. Superior Court, 163 Cal.App.3d 186 (1984).

Beauchamp, Tom L., and F. James, Childress *Principles of Biomedical Ethics*. New York: Oxford University Press, 1979.

Bouvia v. Superior Court for Los Angeles County, 225 Cal. Rptr. 297 (Ct. App. 1986).

Brophy v. New England Sinai Hospital, Inc., 398 Mass. 417 (1986).

Canterbury v. Spence, 464 F.2d 772 (D.C. Cir.), cert. denied, 409 U.S. 1064 (1972).

Carmi, A., ed. *Euthanasia*. Medicolegal Library 2. Berlin: Springer-Verlag, 1984.

Clarke, David B., Jr. "Helping Patients Make Health Care Decisions," *Euthanasia Review* 1, no.2 (1986): 85–96.

Council on Ethical and Judicial Affairs, "Withholding or Withdrawing Life Prolonging Medical Treatment." Chicago: American Medical Association, 1986.

Engelhardt, H. Tristam, JR., and Michele Malloy. "Suicide and Assisting Suicide: A Critique of Legal Sanctions." *Southwestern Law Journal* 36 (1982): 1003–37.

Fletcher, Joseph. *Humanhood: Essays in Biomedical Ethics*. Buffalo, N.Y.: Prometheus Books, 1979.

Horan, Dennis J., and David Mall, eds. *Death, Dying, and Euthanasia*. Frederick, Md.: Aletheia Books, University Publications of America, 1980.

Humphry, Derek. *Let Me Die before I Wake*. Los Angeles: Hemlock Society, 1986.

Humphry, Derek, and Ann Wickett. *The Right To Die: Understanding Euthanasia*. New York: Harper & Row, 1986.

In re Conroy, 98 N.J. 321 (1984).

In re Quinlan, 70 N.J. 10 (1976).

Kohl, Marvin, ed. *Beneficent Euthanasia*. Buffalo, N.Y.: Prometheus Books, 1975.

Law Reform Commission of Canada. "Euthanasia, Aiding Suicide and Cessation of Treatment." Working Paper 28. Ottawa: Law Reform Commission of Canada, 1982.

Law Reform Commission of Canada. ''Report on Some Aspects of Medical Treatment and Criminal Law.'' Ottawa: Law Reform Commission of Canada, 1986.

Los Angeles County Medical Association and Los Angeles County Bar Association (Joint LACBA-LACMA Committee on Biomedical Ethics). ''Principles and Guidelines concerning the Forgoing of Life-Sustaining Treatment for Adult Patients.'' Los Angeles: 1986.

National Legal Center for the Medically Dependent and Disabled. Issues in Law and Medicine 2, no.2 (September 1986). This issue is entitled Ethical Symposium: The Ethical Standards for Withholding/Withdrawing Nutrition and Hydration.

Piccione, Joseph J. *Last Rights: Treatment and Care Issues in Medical Ethics*. Washington, D.C.: Free Congress Research and Education Foundation, 1984.

Pope John Paul II. ''Euthanasia—Declaration of the Sacred Congregation for the Doctrine of the Faith.'' In *Death Education II* edited by Wass et al. (New York: Hemisphere Publishing Corporation, 1985).

President's Commission for the Study of Ethical Problems in Medicine and Biomedical and Behavioral Research. *Making Health Care Decisions: The Ethical and Legal Implications of Informed Consent in the Patient-Practitioner Relationship*. Washington, D.C.: GPO, 1982.

——————. *Deciding to Forgo Life-Sustaining Treatment: Ethical, Medical, and Legal Issues in Treatment Decisions*. Washington, D.C.: GPO, 1983.

Rozovsky, Fay A. *Consent To Treatment: A Practical Guide*. Boston: Little, Brown & Co., 1984.

Solnick, Paul R. ''Proxy Consent for Incompetent Non–Terminally Ill Adult Patients.'' *Journal of Legal Medicine* 6, no.1 (1985): 1–49.

Superintendent of Belchertown State School v. Saikewicz, 373 Mass. 728 (1977).

United States Catholic Conference, *Ethical and Religious Directives for Catholic Health Facilities*. St. Louis, Mo.: The Catholic Health Association of the United States, 1971.

U.S. Congress. House. Select Committee on Aging. *Dying with Dignity: Difficult Times, Difficult Choices*. Washington, D.C.: GPO, 1985.

Williams, Glanville. *The Sanctity of Life and the Criminal Law*. New York: Alfred A. Knopf, 1957.

Winslade, William J., and Judith Wilson Ross. *Choosing Life or Death: A Guide for Patients, Families, and Professionals*. New York: The Free Press, 1986.

Wolhandler, Steven J. ''Voluntary Active Euthanasia for the Terminally Ill and the Constitutional Right to Privacy.'' *Cornell Law Review* 69, no.2 (1984): 363–83.

Chapter 20

The Determination of Death: The Need for a Higher-Brain Death Concept

John H. Sorenson

The Uniform Determination of Death Act (UDDA), devised in 1981, was a landmark.[1] It gave legal expression to a most remarkable consensus which had been developing over the past 30 years, namely, that the traditional heart-lung standards for determination of death were no longer adequate and that brain functioning needed somehow to be taken into account. The leadership of the President's Commission for the Study of Ethical Problems in Medicine and Biomedical and Behavioral Research provided the catalyst.

Since the early 1950s, it has become increasingly clear that mechanical ventilators were able to produce artifacts of respiration and heart beat. By 1959, the clinical entity *le coma depasse,* a totally unresponsive, irreversible state beyond coma, had been described by Mollaret and Goulon.[2] This state steadily gained acceptance in the neurological literature under the name *brain death.*[3]

For the presidential commissioners to propose an act which would solemnly and succinctly state who should be considered ''dead'' was probably politically irresistable. Rapidly the National Conference of Commissioners on Uniform State Laws gave their approval in 1980, along with the American Bar Association and the American Medical Association. An almost audible sigh of relief echoed through the state legislatures across the United States as the proposed act began to pass into law. (The initial rush to legislation appears, however, to have slowed down. At the end of 1986, 19 states and the District of Columbia had passed the UDDA into law. Two states have passed the Uniform Brain Death Act, previously proposed in 1978 by the National Conference of Commissioners on Uniform State Laws, but superseded by the Commissioners' subsequent approval of the UDDA.)[4] Finally, it seemed, there was a way out of the confusion surrounding the question of when someone was really dead.

Not so. Death has not been defined. When a person is dead has not been adequately specified. Instead, two independent standards of death, the cessation of heart-lung functioning and the cessation of whole brain functions (the newer standard), are described without any explanation of their interrelationship.[5] The practical consequences of this confusion, especially for health care professionals, are dealt with in this chapter. It is my contention that the irreversible loss of higher-brain capacity is the proper standard for determining personal death.

Whole brain death, ''irreversible cessation of all functions of the entire brain, including the brain stem,'' is an overdetermination of death.[6] The whole brain death concept lumps

234

together higher- and lower-brain capacities; it blurs the crucial distinction between essential personal capacity and vegetative functions. What subsequently occurred by using the whole brain concept of death within the UDDA was a basic confusion (correctly identified by Tomlinson) between "a *function* and the mechanism that performs it."[7] The whole brain, i.e., the mechanism, came to be regarded as the equivalent of its functions. In the words of the President's Commission, the whole brain has primacy "not merely as the sponsor of consciousness (since even unconscious persons may be alive), but also as the complex organizer and regulator of bodily functions."[8] Although all cases of personal death *eventually* become cases of whole brain death, using the whole brain death standard may include as "persons" those human bodies that only function biologically and are irreversibly unresponsive, unreceptive, and incapable of any recall. Consequently, some persons who are judged dead by the higher-brain capacity criterion are judged alive by the whole brain death criterion.

THE UNIFORM DETERMINATION OF DEATH ACT

The UDDA reads as follows:

> An individual who has sustained either (1) irreversible cessation of circulatory and respiratory functions or (2) irreversible cessation of all functions of the entire brain, including the brain stem, is dead. A determination of death must be made in accordance with accepted medical standards.[9]

The UDDA's most prominent feature is the introduction of a second standard for determining death: "irreversible cessation of all functions of the entire brain." Thus, whole brain death has become an option for determining death in addition to the traditional permanent stoppage of heartbeat and breathing. By law, either of these standards may be applied to determine death. It is noteworthy that no interrelationship between these two standards is stated.

Construction and Language of the UDDA

The President's Commission sought to define death in its proposed statute "at the level of general physiological standards rather than at the level of more abstract concepts or the level of more precise tests."[10] Since legislation requires sufficient agreement for its passage, the commissioners understandably opted for the middle ground. On the one hand, they wanted to avoid the philosophical and theological controversy surrounding the question of what occurs when a human being dies. In particular, they did not want to try to define *person* or *human being*. On the other hand, they wanted to avoid specifying particular clinical tests for determining death, because they did not want to build technological obsolescence into their proposed legislation.

It appears that in considering how to define who is dead, the notion of an integrated, functioning organism that could be tied to the ontological understanding of what constitutes an "individual" was highly influential. This notion was developed and presented by Green and Wikler.[11] Their report makes clear that the Commission felt that in the "vast majority of cases'' the traditional standard of heart lung stoppage would be sufficient to determine death.[12] They did not want to impose the "new" whole brain death standard when it would not be necessary to do so.

They gave a bow in the direction of law by taking into account the work of the Law Reform Commission of Canada, which defined death as irreversible cessation of brain functions. Canadian law thus clearly recognizes the brain as the primary organ integrating bodily functions. The Canadian legislative proposal permits the standard to be met not only by direct measurements of brain activity, but also by prolonged absence of spontaneous heart and lung functions.[13]

Critique of the UDDA

The UDDA makes cessation of functions of the *entire* brain one of its two standards for death. The practical result is that the patient may be considered alive even though the level of integrated functioning, spontaneous breathing, and heart beat may be so low, so primitive, that only vegetative, biologic life continues. While including this second standard is understandable given the commission is a politically sensitive body appointed by the President, it is not a very helpful move for public policy in the long run. What persists is the failure to recognize (by the lay public as well as by some health care professionals) that *until* heart and lungs cease to function spontaneously, death has not occurred. The inevitability of heart-lung cessation resulting from whole brain death, even when grasped at the intellectual level by trained medical professionals, may be difficult to grasp at the level of basic emotions.

By applying its criteria to so-called *individuals,* the Commission avoided the philosophically and theologically controversial designations *person* and *human being.* A person or human being is more than an organism with mere integrated functions. The UDDA sets the presence of life above independent cellular activity or viability (even temporary) of any separate organs. But this level is so low that it perpetuates support of the body at the biologic, vegetative level by confusing it with the person or human being who has ceased to exist.

By careful choice of its terminology, the Commission made clear that its definition of death does *not* include "any patient who had lost only 'higher' brain functions or, conversely, who maintains those functions but has suffered solely a direct injury to the brain stem which interferes with the vegetative functions of the body."[14] But it is precisely these higher functions which are necessary for the patient to be a human being, a person. The need to understand death as a unitary event (instead of dying as a process)[15] should not lead to disintegration as a criterion or a return to the putrefaction standard of two centuries past. Rather, the need is for death to be pronounced for those bodies which have ceased to be persons.

In sum, the UDDA, by the addition of a whole brain death standard, was an advance inasmuch as it allowed ventilator-supported heart-lung functioning to be shut down. However, by propounding a whole brain death standard, it perpetuated basic confusion about *human* life. Two steps forward, one step back.

HIGHER-BRAIN CONCEPT OF DEATH

Confusion surrounding the act of determining death can be reduced, if not eliminated, by clarification of the concept of death. The concept of death, for the purposes of this chapter, includes (1) the *definition* of who has died (a person or human being); (2) the standards or *criteria* that determine when death has occurred; and (3) the *tests* that indicate whether the criteria of death have been met. Each of these three components is distinct, but all are interrelated.

Definition of Person

Defining death requires defining *person* or *human being*. Without specification of what exactly it is that dies (or remains alive), the criteria of death are rendered arbitrary. The term *individual* is not adequate. A robot is an example of an individual, one whose bodily capacities are mechanical and electronic. But of course a robot is not a person. The crucial difference between a robot and a person is that a person has necessarily (or essentially) the capacity to regulate and coordinate bodily functions, even if those functions are artificial; a robot does not. This essential capacity of a person ought not to be confused with the integrated functioning that results; even a robot can have integrated functions. Youngner and Bartlett provisionally identify the capacities essential to persons as consciousness and cognition.[16]

In line with Youngner and Bartlett's provisional and overly concise identification of the essential capacities of human beings, Schmidt states, ''Consciousness is a state which, in all its subtle shadings, can only be appreciated introspectively but is surely the essential fact of human existence.''[17] While clearly acknowledging that the ''whole topic is still very much in a state of flux,'' he goes on to list observable aspects of human and animal behavior which can be taken as indications of the presence of consciousness:

1. Attentiveness and the ability to direct attention in a purposeful way.
2. The creation of and familiarity with abstract ideas, and the ability to express them by words or other symbols.
3. The ability to estimate the significance of an act in advance, and thus to have expectations and plans.
4. Self-recognition and the recognition of other individuals.
5. The presence of esthetic and ethical values.[18]

To be sure, this list is quite restrictive. It raises the question, for example, whether certain retardates would qualify as having consciousness. What is needed, in principle, is to take such a listing (or definition) and apply it to actual cases. In this way, the definition will assist in the refinement of criteria and the development of tests. In turn, feedback from these applications will contribute to a refinement of the definition. To reverse the process and begin with actual cases is likely to restrict the definition of a person to what we can readily count and measure.

For our purposes, cognition should be taken to include learning and memory. Again Schmidt is helpful: ''The receipt, storage, and retrieval of information are general properties of neuronal networks that serve to adapt individual behavior to the environment.

Without the ability to learn and to retain and retrieve items by way of memory it would be possible neither to repeat successes according to plan nor to avoid failure intentionally.''[19] Schmidt acknowledges that satisfactory theories about learning and memory have still to be formulated. Nevertheless, the identification of these components of cognition is sufficient for this discussion.

The distinction, then, can be clearly made between a human capacity (which is innate and spontaneous) and an artificial capacity (which is neither). For example, the capacity of a ''smart'' cardiac pacer to sponsor heart rhythms with sophisticated sensors and electronic chips for self-programming is not innate or spontaneous. The pacer itself still needs to be sponsored. It needs to be programmed, implanted, and checked. It can only run within its limits. These admittedly may be so wide as ordinarily to encompass the recipient's everyday lifestyle, but the pacer is never fully able to deal with the unexpected. The integration of essential functions which the pacer achieves can still be distinguished from the essential capacities—consciousness and cognition—which sponsor the pacer itself.

There is remarkably little agreement about how exactly to define what a person is. Defining personhood or humanness is difficult and controversial. Englehardt puts it thus: ''The controversies concerning definitions of death spring in great part from unclarities regarding the kind of life that is being declared at an end.''[20] He continues,

> Life as biological process has ceased to be a mystery requiring special soul-like catalysts. The systematic integration of the body can be understood without invoking the presence of either the soul or a moral agent. On the other hand, moral agency requires the presence of self-consciousness. Self-consciousness has a sense and meaning that contrast with mechanical, chemical, and biological structures. The life of minds, if it is to be understood adequately, must be captured, at least in part, in introspective psychological terms.[21]

Being a moral agent is what is critical to being a person in Englehardt's view. He concludes, ''To look at things this way requires a momentous conceptual step. It requires recognizing that mere human biological life is of little moral value in and of itself. It requires acknowledging that it is the life of human persons in the strict sense that is central to moral concerns.''[22]

Youngner and Bartlett point out that ''one must specify the type of living entity in question—a human. Otherwise, one runs the risk of identifying the life or death of the wrong kind of entity.''[23] They specifically reject, although acknowledging its initial appeal, the argument advanced by Wikler and Mayo to the effect that an adequate definition of death only needs to include those characteristics common to all living things. According to Youngner and Bartlett, this argument fails because it provides no standard for determining which systems are principal and how much breakdown is too much. They maintain that ''the concept of a person is the standard for identifying the principal systems. In this context, the principal systems are those that are proximately responsible for consciousness and cognition.''[24]

We ordinarily make judgments about the quality of life, with rankings from high to low. Presumably all life can be ranked thus, even life which is ranked as poor. An important moral issue concerns when (if ever) human life is of insufficiently good quality to prolong. The presence of life (whatever its quality) is different from the absence of all life. Determining the presence or absence of potential for essential human capacities does not involve values. On the other hand, judging that a certain quality of life is insufficiently good to justify maintaining a life does involve the values of the person making the judgment.

Various catalogues and definitions of humanness or personhood have been attempted.[25] Quite properly they include considerations beyond the moral, such as aesthetic and kinetic considerations, because these make life worth living for many. How one looks, whether one can move about independently, whether one can sing, dance, speak, see—these are the sort of considerations often taken to be important. None of the catalogues or definitions has gained broad acceptance because their inherent subjectivity and relativism render them arbitrary. Yet this is not to say that these definitions are useless. Indeed, they merit respect as expressions of the kind of consciousness and cognition which make us what we are— persons. From these definitions may come significant social policies with strong moral implications, such as procedures for withholding and withdrawing life support. But it is essential to keep separate the determination of human death from the judgment that a human life is of good or poor quality.[26]

Green and Wikler contribute an ontological (i.e., state of being) argument to the brain death controversy. They conclude,

> A given person ceases to exist with the destruction of psychological continuity and connectedness. We know these processes are essentially neurological, so that irreversible cessation of upper brain functioning constitutes the death of that person. Whole-brain death is also death for persons, but only because whole-brain death is partly comprised of upper-brain death. Tests for either will be tests for death.[27]

They go astray when they confuse minimal integration of bodily functions without upper brain capacities with being a person. Youngner and Bartlett correctly argue that essential capacities, that is, consciousness and cognition (which are spontaneous and innate), define a human being. Whether integrated functioning (or lack of it, as in the case of functions performed by artificial implants) constitutes personhood is what needs to be determined.

Criteria

Death is an event. We are dead when our essential human capacities cease.[28] Those capacities necessary and sufficient for human life are consciousness and cognition.[29] Death events, events terminating vitality of cells and organs in various parts of our bodies, may occur slowly or suddenly, catastrophically or sequentially. However, as persons, our death occurs when vitality has ceased in our brains and we are no longer capable of consciousness and cognition. For humans, this is the death event that is necessary and sufficient to distinguish a corpse from an existing person.

In a corpse, some organic functions and some cellular vitality may continue in some tissues. For example, hair and finger and toe nails may continue to grow. All the time that we are alive, there are cells in our bodies which die. In the normal course of events, most of these dead cells are replaced (although not all of them uniformly). We recognize that an arbitrary sum of these separate death events do not add up to human death. For example, we might say, "The left leg of this patient is dead and needs to be amputated." But we do not confuse this "leg-death" with human death.

At issue is not some minimal set of capacities which, if exercised in an integrated fashion, constitute a person. Rather, being a person requires the presence of any capacity for consciousness and cognition, whereas being dead requires the absence of all capacity for consciousness and cognition. This essential capacity for consciousness and cognition (which is spontaneous and innate) sponsors all other functions, regardless of their exercise by natural, transplanted, or artificial means. Stated this way, the capacity for consciousness and cognition is the criterion by which to determine human death as an event, drawing the line at the point when the capacity for consciousness and cognition ceases to exist.

Tests

Death is the absence of life. The importance of a clear definition of personhood and of clear criteria of death consistent with that definition becomes more apparent as the understanding of the temporality of death increases. The occurrence of death is an event. Tests of when death occurs need to determine the time when specific relevant vital processes cease. In complex organisms, dying is a series of death events. Determining when death of a particular living entity has occurred, therefore, involves choosing the particular death event that precludes the capacity or capacities essential for that entity's existence.

Two points should be noted. First, there is a distinction between actual and potential. Any of our personal capacities may be not yet be actualized. We may only have the potential to realize ourselves as persons. Perhaps the difference between potential and actual is most apparent when we observe infants, whose personhood is mostly potential. But it is also apparent that persons at any point in their lives actualize only a portion of their capacities. Thus, it is essential that tests to determine death, which require clinical tests for the absence of vital signs, be able to demonstrate presence or absence of potential rather than achievement. It must be emphasized that clinical tests do not yet exist that accurately measure presence versus absence of consciousness and cognition.

However, the tests for validating whole brain death also lack great reliability. Whole brain death determinations seem still to be a matter of clinical judgment corroborated by various tests. The number of false negatives and false positives given by tests of whole brain death, such as electroencephalograms and readings of electrocerebral silence, make these tests more predictors than validators of the absence of whole brain functions.[30] Currently, the determination of higher-brain death by clinical judgment supported by empirical tests does not achieve full validation. In contrast, determination of whole brain death—by receiving more apparent, although not necessarily conclusive, empirical support—is considered ''safer'' as a basis for clinical decisions, such as withdrawal of life support. The strictness of whole brain death tests, such as the Harvard criteria[31] and the guidelines for the determination of death given in a report by medical consultants to the President's Commission,[32] has, as I have argued, resulted in the overdetermination of death, so that bodies with mere vegetative vitality are treated as living persons. However, it seems most likely that validated testing to demonstrate potential for the essential capacity for consciousness and cognition will be forthcoming.

The second point concerns the relation of potentiality and actuality to moral agency. The presence of a demonstrated potential for consciousness and cognition does not entail these capacities will be exercised in morally good or bad ways. Determination of human life or death is, as Green and Wikler note, ''agnostic'' with respect to morality.[33]

CLINICAL APPLICATIONS

The higher-brain death definition espoused in this chapter needs to be applied to three major clinical problem areas in order to test its "real world" practicality. These major problem areas are indicated by the following questions:

1. How should determination of death guide withholding or withdrawal of treatment?
2. How should the determination of death guide humane efforts to relieve suffering for the survivors?
3. How should the determination of death guide just allocation of the biologic resources (e.g. body parts) of the dead?

Decisions to Withhold or Withdraw Treatment

Since the advent of the modern intensive care unit in the 1950s, patients have been pushed by modern life-support capabilities into the limbo which I call living death. The critical issue is whether the loss of higher-brain functions (consciousness and cognition) is irreversible. Only when this has been determined are those "human entities" legitimately considered among the living dead.[34]

Examples of such living dead are bodies that are irreversibly comatose, without necessary brain structure (congenitally absent or lost through disease or trauma), or irreversibly demented beyond cognition. (Cognition includes learning and memory. The patient so demented as to be without capacity to learn or remember lacks cognition.) Biologic vital signs persist, but a catastrophic event, such as cardiac arrest, is the inevitable outcome. There can be no return of the former patient to a conscious, cognitive state.

Patients in persistent vegetative state are more problematic.[35] Their survival, which may extend for years, encourages hopes for return to consciousness and cognition. Hansotia remarks, "Exactly how long such a state may persist before it can be confidently declared permanent is yet uncertain. It is clear that patients destined to make a reasonable recovery (including those who will have considerable disability) do not usually pass through the vegetative state as a phase of their recovery from coma."[36] They should receive humane care which will neither reduce nor prolong their survival.[37] (See Chapter 16 on Coma and PVS.)

For those at the bedside, including physicians, residents, nurses, and family, what death means under these circumstances is not an abstract philosophical question. What matters is whether this particular body in the bed in front of them is still the person whom those in attendance knew. This question is *not* the same as asking whether there is any hope. It is more fundamental. Whether it is a patient or instead a corpse that is present determines whether *any* treatment can affect personal life. Prognosis needs to be about the person's survival and to address both its duration and quality, so that there can be a rational basis for treatment and consideration can be given to moral obligations owed to persons (if applicable). Moral obligations owed to human bodies in which there is only continuing biologic, vegetative vitality are different. Withholding and withdrawing treatment from a dead person is appropriate. With proper consent (see below), maintaining biologic functions to support organs for eventual donation is appropriate. If the decedent willed his or her body to science, there would be no reason to continue treatment, since a dead body is what is involved, not a living one. However, to construe such a donation as license to hasten the demise of the patient would clearly be in violation of law.[38]

Respect due the memory of a dead person calls for humane care of the biologically functioning body. This translates into obligations to the living at two levels. First, the family should be able to choose the disposition for the body and should be given support in achieving a healthy resolution of their grief and mourning. Allowing the biologic functions of the decedent to cease without hastening or postponing the end constitutes humane treatment of the family. Second, at the societal level, it would be brutalizing to institute a general practice of terminating the functions of the living dead. Human life requires protection in a peaceable, civilized society. Respectful, humane treatment of the living dead, rather than terminating remaining vital functions, therefore promotes protection of human life generally.

Artifacts of ''natural'' cardiopulmonary functioning, for example, can be produced by ventilator functioning. Maintaining these artifacts when the person is dead is absurd. (Keeping the biologic functions of the body going for other reasons is another matter, which relates to the allocation issues raised by the third problem.)

As matters stand now, the higher-brain death (as defined) is *not* testable. The current state-of-the-art of testing does not mean that the higher-brain death definition is irrelevant. It is as relevant as the presence of a living person is necessary for rational medical treatment. How precisely whole brain death should be tested is also controversial. Higher-brain functions are supported by lower functions, but lower-brain functions are not dependent upon the higher. This conceptual framework helps provide a definition and criteria for higher-brain death. It can thus guide clinical judgment and the development of tests. Hence, when lower functions cease, since at present these can neither be resuscitated nor replaced, the essential higher-brain functions will be irretrievably lost.

This situation is not likely to persist over the long run. There will be a continued refinement of our understanding of the differentiation between structures which sponsor higher-brain functions and those which sponsor the lower. Also, it seems likely that with increased understanding of the interrelationships between the mechanisms of higher and lower functions will come therapeutic applications of medications and technologies which will produce possibilities for brain resuscitation.[39] As a result, it will become increasingly apparent that the preservation or maintenance of lower vegetative brain functioning when there is no evidence of higher-brain functioning can become an artifact of life just as much as ventilator support.

An immediate implication for clinical decision making is that brain death criteria should be regularly applied in the determination of death. It is no longer sufficient in all cases to apply the traditional criteria of irreversible cessation of heart-lung functions, because these are only predictors. Clinicians using brain death criteria now have the opportunity to be definitive. In clinical practice this opportunity already appears to be taken advantage of, since neurologists and neurosurgeons routinely start ''from the top down,'' applying clinical judgment and tests for the higher-brain functions of consciousness and cognition. It may be that this determination of brain death primarily rests upon clinical observation corroborated by observation of absence of heartbeat and breathing. However, starting with brain death criteria, whether involving whole brain functions or higher-brain functions, will contribute to the standard use of brain functions and will hasten development of the tests needed for validation. These developments will lead to the acceptance of the primacy of higher-brain capacities in determining what is a person. Additionally, clinicians should support those policies in their respective institutions which call for the determination and documentation of death by brain criteria.

A final note. Determination of death by clinicians ought not to be taken as identical to the determination of the quality of life. What is involved is determining whether there is a basis for any personal life at all, no matter what quality or duration. The question is not whether the specific person is desirable or undesirable, morally good or morally bad. These are important issues. However, if clinical decision making is based upon one standard of care for all persons (taking into account their particular medical needs), then these other significant issues are of lesser priority. Engelhardt expresses the matter more philosophically. His espousal of a higher-brain death concept rests upon his view that to be a person requires the capacity to be a moral agent.[40] Without higher-brain functions, this is not possible. But even though lacking the capacity for moral agency, these bodies with only vegetative, biologic functions may possibly, like animals, feel pain and fear. And like animals—neither less nor more (this is admittedly controversial)—these human entities deserve our humane consideration and care.

Humane Efforts to Relieve Suffering of Survivors

The death of a patient impacts upon all involved—family, friends, and health care professionals—though in variable degrees. Loss and bereavement, perhaps lessened by anticipatory grief or attenuated by denial, perhaps distorted by guilt and anger, exacts its toll on all. It is one of the most basic of human responsibilities (which we all have toward each other) to seek to relieve the pain and suffering occasioned by the death of a fellow person.

Discussion of effective bereavement support is, of course, beyond the scope of this chapter.[41] It is important to acknowledge, however, that health care professionals as well as family members suffer loss and grief when patients die. The stress is exacerbated when there is uncertainty whether the patient is living or dead. Continuing to care for a dead person's biologically functioning body, if it is not allowed to cease functioning humanely, becomes increasingly difficult as time passes.

The higher-brain determination of death addresses two aspects of bereavement which the whole brain definition does not. First, the overdetermination of death of the whole brain standard can result in some former persons being moved into a "no man's land" or "frontier between life and death."[42] As a result, suffering is increased for those who survive. The person is dead, but the continued existence of the biologic entity which was formerly the person evokes concern and other feelings which have no reasonable hope of ever being fulfilled or reciprocated. It is difficult to see how the perpetuation of false hope can ever lead to anything other than continued suffering. Properly speaking, the person is dead. Lacking in consciousness and cognition, the corpse which is left cannot suffer. However, I again emphasize, such biologically living bodies should *not* be actively killed.

Second, using a higher-brain death standard should prevent a harmful confusion. It is when the life status of biologically functioning, irreversibly decerebrate bodies is confused with the life status of live persons that humane treatment becomes problematic. Since these decerebrate bodies are dead and no longer persons, humane treatment must now consist in allowing the remaining vegetative, biologic functions to cease in a dignified manner. Since these human entities are no longer moral agents (because their capacity to make responsible choices is gone), regard for their autonomy is no longer morally relevant. The obligation that remains is to respect the choices made by the patient before death or by the survivors afterward. Without perpetuating the mistake that a human entity in a chronic vegetative state is still a person, respect for a former person can be exercised by supporting biologic, vegetative existence of the body at a level appropriate for allowing functioning to cease.[43] Clarification of the death status of the person will be helpful to those who mourn. Their adjustment to the realities of living without the person is facilitated by helping them to understand that the person to whom they were attached is in fact dead, although vegetative functioning may persist.

Just Allocation of Bodily Resources of the Dead

Human body parts and human bodily functions are now of use after the death of the person embodied in them. The successful transplantation of human organs is enhanced if the viability of those organs is maintained by the donor body until their removal. Maintaining the biologic functioning of brain dead pregnant women has successfully advanced the gestational age and hence improved the viability of the fetuses they were carrying.[44] These are further demonstrations of the special value to be placed on human bodies which are still alive but no longer persons.

A medical team needs to avoid conflicts of interest in these relatively novel situations. Those who transplant and those who maintain maternal bodily support for fetuses should have concern for the interests of the donors as well as the recipients. The body of the dead has no autonomy and cannot of its own volition donate an organ or choose to maintain its functions for the benefit of another. Such decisions can only be made by others. What matters is that authorization was properly made by the decedent prior to death or that consent for such procedures is properly obtained from the family after death. The Uniform Anatomical Gift Act specifies these requirements.[45] (See Chapter 21 on donation of organs.)

Overdetermination of death and confusion as to when a person is dead provide reasons why a higher-brain death standard is superior to both the whole brain death and the heart-lung criteria of the UDDA. Application of the whole brain death standard causes lower, vegetative functioning to render irrelevant the end of the higher-brain functioning that is essential to being a person. This override prevents removal of organs while they are still viable and can be most successfully transplanted to the recipient. Organs could be lost for transplant because the patient had specified no donation or because the family, following the patient's death, had refused. In either event, losing viable organs for transplant would be unfortunate but not unjust. The autonomy of patient and family ought to take precedence over the claims of potential recipients for the organs. It would be abhorrent to force such donation. Recent legislation for routine request for harvest makes this point. It remains to be seen whether in practice that legislation will be coercive.[46] But surely confusion about when a person is dead would needlessly compound problems for those who have authority to consent to organ donation. They can mistakenly remain tied to moral obligations which apply to persons but not to bodies in a vegetative state. Surely respect for the dead is different from respect for living persons, who have capacity for self-determination and whose choices should therefore be honored.

Research using biologically functioning bodies of the dead is another broad area of concern. The possibilities of such research loom large. Of particular interest are questions concerning brain functioning and therefore brain death. There are at present no reliable tests for higher-brain functioning, and the best that can be done by testing is the determination of death using the whole brain standard, which results in overdetermination. It is especially important to develop reliable tests for the absence of demonstrated potential for higher functions of consciousness and cognition. Differentiation between higher and lower mechanisms would eventually allow for the development of brain resuscitation and even for transplantation and implantation of organs, tissues, and devices that could regulate support for the higher brain. These are exciting possibilities. They are also ethically controversial.[47]

Biomedical research involving dead persons whose bodies maintain biologic vitality is analogous to nontherapeutic human subject research. The benefits of the research are for future patients. The object of the research is a body of a dead person with only biologic, vegetative functioning; it most likely is incapable of experiencing pain and suffering. (However, if pain responses were to be evoked, it would be incumbent upon the researchers to treat the body humanely.)

The usual calculus of burdens versus benefits does not apply to an object; it applies only to a subject who is a person. This is not to say that there should be indiscriminate treatment or disposition of a body which still maintains a level of biologic functioning. Such a human entity ought to be treated with respect for the former person it once embodied. I think that research, the quest for generalizable knowledge based on rational, scientific protocol, can justifiably be performed on bodies that still have lower vital functions, provided that voluntary, informed consent has been obtained from the patient prior to death or from the family. The results of investigations involving bodies with continuing biologic functions will most likely benefit others when they are validated by scientific research procedures. Mere explorations seem less ethically justifiable, because they would not have a clearly defined purpose, nor would specific benefits be likely to occur. In these circumstances, a dying patient or a decedent's family should not be asked for permission.

It seems most likely that these pressing needs—organs for transplantation, bodily functions for the biologic support of others, and nontherapeutic research—will continue to exist. For health care professionals to engage in these activities of potential benefit to others requires at least three things. First, they will need to know clearly that the person who was embodied in the object of their continuing care is truly dead. They will need to be clear about the definition and standards of death, as well as the tests for it which may develop. Second, they will need to be clear about the claims which are being made on behalf of others and who is making these claims, so that they can obtain voluntary, informed permission for such research from the deceased person's family. The potential for conflicts of interest is present. The person who is not yet dead ought not to be violated by an overzealous transplant team harvesting organs before death has been carefully determined. Neither should the family be coerced into making a donation of their relative's organs. Finally, health care providers who participate in procedures involving living bodies of dead persons need to be clear that their efforts can be scientifically validated or therapeutically assessed.

CONCLUSION

This chapter has discussed competing definitions, standards, and tests for the determination of death. Currently there are three rivals: (1) cessation of heart-lung functions (the traditional standard), (2) whole brain death, and (3) higher-brain death. I have advocated acceptance of a higher-brain death concept because of its conceptual accuracy and practical helpfulness. It defines the death of persons. It requires standards which are not reducible either to substitution by transplanted organs or by implanted artificial devices. The fact of the matter is that there are not yet valid tests which can measure the complete absence of essential higher-brain capacities, which I have provisionally identified as consciousness and cognition. But these tests will almost certainly be forthcoming. In the meantime, it is incumbent upon health care professionals to be forward-looking, yet not get ahead of themselves. The conceptual clarity of higher-brain death determination is useful even in the current situation where overdetermination of death results from the present tests for the absence of whole brain functions. For one thing, it will keep efforts for refinement focused. The restraint called for by the current state-of-the-art tests will require continued support of those persons we *think* are dead but cannot prove to be. It cannot be denied that care and the resources to support care require vast expenditures. Yet for now, such expenditures need to be made. Regaining of consciousness and cognition may sometimes occur given our present imperfect tests. Careful observation in cases where return to consciousness and cognition, though hoped for, does not occur will hasten the day when it will be possible to determine accurately when a person truly has died.

NOTES

1. President's Commission for the Study of Ethical Problems in Medicine and Biomedical Research, *Defining Death: A Report on the Medical, Legal and Ethical Issues in the Determination of Death* (Washington: GPO, 1981).

2. P. Mollaret and M. Goulon, "Le Coma Depasse," *Revue Neurologique* 101 (1959); 3–15.

3. President's Commission, *Defining Death*, 2; A. Earl Walker, *Cerebral Death*, 3rd ed. (Baltimore, Md.: Urban, 1985), 11–23.

4. *Uniform Laws Annotated* (St. Paul, Minn.: West Publishing, 1975), vol. 12, *Civil Procedural and Remedial Laws*, 1986 Annual Pocket, 270–73.

5. James L. Bernat, Charles M. Culver, and Bernard Gert, "Defining Death in Theory and Practice," *Hastings Center Report* 1 (1982): 5–9.

6. President's Commission, *Defining Death*, 31–41; Michael B. Green and Daniel Wikler, "Brain Death and Personal Identity," *Philosophy and Public Affairs* 9 (1980): 105–133.

7. Tom Tomlinson, "The Conservative Use of the Brain-Death Criterion—A Critique," *Journal of Medicine and Philosophy* 9 (1984): 380.

8. President's Commission, *Defining Death*, 34.

9. Ibid., 2.

10. Ibid., 73; Alexander Morgan Capron and Leon R. Kass, "A Statutory Definition of the Standards for Determining Human Death: An Appraisal and a Proposal," *University of Pennsylvania Law Review* 121 (1972): 87–118.

11. Green and Wikler, "Brain Death."

12. President's Commission, *Defining Death*," 73–74.

13. Ibid; Bernat, Culver, and Gert, "Defining Death in Theory and Practice," 7.

14. President's Commission, *Defining Death*, 75.

15. Ibid., 77; Bernat, Culver, and Gert, "Defining Death in Theory and Practice."

16. Stuart J. Youngner and Edward T. Bartlett, "Human Death and High Technology: The Failure of the Whole-Brain Formulations," *Annals of Internal Medicine* 99 (1983): 252–57.

17. Robert F. Schmidt, "Integrative Functions of the Central Nervous System," in *Fundamentals of Neurophysiology*, 2d ed., ed. Robert F. Schmidt, trans. M.A. Biederman-Thorson (New York: Springer-Verlag, 1978), 290.

18. Ibid., 290–91.

19. Ibid., 300.

20. H. Tristam Engelhardt, Jr., *The Foundations of Bioethics* (New York: Oxford University Press, 1986), 203.

21. Ibid., 205.

22. Ibid., 206.

23. Youngner and Bartlett, "Human Death and High Technology," 253.

24. Ibid., 257.

25. Joseph Fletcher, "Indicators of Humanhood," *Hastings Center Report* 2 (1972): 1–4; Richard A. McCormick, "To Save or Let Die: The Dilemma of Modern Medicine," *Journal of the American Medical Association* 229 (1974): 172–76.

26. Leon R. Kass, "Death as an Event: A Commentary on Robert Morison," *Science* 173 (1971): 698–702.

27. Green and Wikler, "Brain Death," 127.

28. Robert S. Morison, "Death: Process or Event?" *Science* 173 (1971): 694–98; Kass, "Death as an Event"; Robert M. Veatch, *Death, Dying and the Biological Revolution: Our Last Quest for Responsibility* (New Haven: Yale University Press, 1976), 21–54.

29. Youngner and Bartlett, "Human Death and High Technology," 257.

30. A. Earl Walker, project coordinator of collaborative study, "An Appraisal of the Criteria of Cerebral Death: A Summary Statement," *Journal of the American Medical Association* 237 (1977): 982–86; D. Alan Shewmon, "Caution in the Definition and Diagnosis of Infant Brain Death," Chapter 4 of this book.

31. Ad Hoc Committee of Harvard Medical School to Examine the Definition of Brain Death, "A Definition of Irreversible Coma: Report of the Ad Hoc Committee of the Harvard Medical School to Examine the Definition of Brain Death," *Journal of the American Medical Association* 205 (1968): 337–40.

32. President's Commission, *Defining Death*, Appendix F, pp. 159–166. "The preparation of this report was facilitated by the President's Commission but the guidelines have not been passed on by the Commission and are not intended as matters for governmental review or adoption" (p. 159).

33. Green and Wikler, "Brain Death," 128.

34. Englehardt uses the term "human entities" in *Foundations of Bioethics*, p. 213.

35. Joseph Fletcher, "Four Indicators of Humanhood—The Inquiry Matures," *Hastings Center Report* 4 (1974): 4–7.

36. Phiroze L. Hansotia, "Persistent Vegetative State: Review and Report of Electrodiagnostic Studies in Eight Cases," *Archives of Neurology* 42 (1985): 1049–52.

37. Sheldon Berrol, "Considerations for Management of the Persistent Vegetative State," *Archives of Physical Medicine and Rehabilitation* 67 (1986): 283–85; David C. Thomasma and Joel Brumlik, "Ethical Issues in the Treatment of Patients with a Remitting Vegetative State," *American Journal of Medicine* 77 (1984): 373–77; Thomas M. Walshe and Cheri Leonard, "Persistent Vegetative State: Extension of the Syndrome to Include Chronic Disorders," *Archives of Neurology* 42 (1985): 1045–47.

38. Uniform Anatomical Gift Act, 8 *Uniform Laws Annotated* 608 (1972).

39. Tomlinson, "Conservative Use of Brain-Death Criterion," 377–93.

40. Engelhardt, *Foundations of Bioethics*, 205–6.

41. Elisabeth Kübler-Ross, *On Death and Dying* (New York: Macmillan, 1969); Ernest Becker, *The Denial of Death* (New York: The Free Press, 1973); Robert S. Weiss and Colin Parkes, *Recovery from Bereavement* (New York: Basic Books, 1983).

42. C. Loeb, "Clinico-Electrographic Determination of Cessation of Cerebral Functions," in *Handbook of Electrocephalography and Clinical Neurophysiology*, ed. Richard Harner and R. Naquet, vol. 12 (Amsterdam: Elesvier, 1975), 114.

43. Anthony Preus, "Respect for the Dead and Dying," *Journal of Medicine and Philosophy* 9 (1984): 409–15; Gary E. Jones, "A Reply to Preus," *Journal of Medicine and Philosophy* 9 (1984): 417–18.

44. William P. Dillon et al., "Life Support and Maternal Brain Death During Pregnancy," *Journal of the American Medical Association* 248 (1982): 1089–91; Mark Siegler and Daniel Wikler, "Brain Death and Live Birth," *Journal of the American Medical Association* 248 (1982): 1101–2; Robert M. Veatch, "Maternal Brain Death: An Ethicist's Thoughts," *Journal of the American Medical Association* 248 (1982): 1102–3; Lyndon M. Hall, "Management of Maternal Vegetative State during Pregnancy," *Mayo Clinic Proceedings* 60 (1985): 469–72.

45. Uniform Anatomical Gift Act, supra note 38.

46. Act 141 (H.B. 90), amending Title 20 of Pa. C.S.A. [i.e., the Anatomical Gift Act]. In Pennsylvania, for example, 1986 legislation amending the Anatomical Gift Act requires routinely that when a patient has died in a hospital, the family be asked to donate the decedent's body or usable organs for transplant.

47. Shewmon, "Infant Brain Death."

BIBLIOGRAPHY

Ad Hoc Committee of Harvard Medical School to Examine the Definition of Brain Death. "A Definition of Irreversible Coma: Report of the Ad Hoc Committee of the Harvard Medical School to Examine the Definition of Brain Death." *Journal of the American Medical Association* 205 (1968): 337–40. In this landmark paper, very conservative whole brain death criteria were presented, and these continue to be highly influential. However, the committee presented criteria for irreversible coma; it did not define brain death.

Kass, Leon R. "Death as an Event: A Commentary on Robert Morison." *Science* 173 (1971): 698–702. Kass eloquently and sensitively defends his subtitle: "Attempts to blur the distinction between a man alive and a man dead are both unsound and dangerous." His arguments for death as an event (instead of a process) are important for public policy.

McCormick, Richard A. "To Save or Let Die: The Dilemma of Modern Medicine." *Journal of the American Medical Association* 229 (1974): 172–76. By drawing a careful distinction between "vitalism," which this ethicist rejects, and the sanctity of life, which he espouses, McCormick suggests a "truly human" life is determined by its "potentiality for human relationships." This is of use in making life-support decisions.

President's Commission for the Study of Ethical Problems in Medicine and Biomedical Research, *Defining Death: A Report on the Medical, Legal and Ethical Issues in the Determination of Death*. Washington, D.C.: GPO, 1981. Unlike most bureaucratic reports, this slim volume became a best seller. It is a concise, readable justification for the Uniform Determination of Death Act, which this chapter criticizes.

Schmidt, Robert F., ed. *Fundamentals of Neurophysiology*. 2d ed. Translated by M.A. Biederman-Thorson. New York: Springer-Verlag, 1978. This programmed text is clear, readable, and well organized. It is particularly helpful for the non-neurologist.

Veatch, Robert M. *Death, Dying and the Biological Revolution: Our Last Quest for Responsibility*. New Haven, Conn.: Yale University Press, 1976. This book ranges from philosophical discussions to policy considerations. Veatch carefully considers competing points of view. He defends his own stand, which is generally in accord with a higher-brain concept of death. One does not have to agree with Veatch to find this a useful book.

Youngner, Stuart J., and Edward T. Bartlett. "Human Death and High Technology: The Failure of the Whole-Brain Formulations." *Annals of Internal Medicine* 99 (1983): 252–58. This well-argued critique of the whole brain concept of death (in support of a higher-brain alternative) provides a concise, clear, and needed counterpoint to the report of the President's Commission, *Defining Death*.

Chapter 21

Waste Not, Want Not: Communities and Presumed Consent

Erich H. Loewy

When man dies he is disposed of by burial, by cremation, or by other means. His remains are kept but briefly, and only a memory of his days persists. As the reality of being yields its fruits to memory, symbolism, often expressed in private or public ritual, takes its place. It is a time to reflect, to take stock, to grieve for what might have been or to rejoice in what was; it is a time when men confront their own mortality and their own brief stay. Grief, if it is to be tempered by compassion instead of turned only inwards toward the self ("my loss," "my grief," "my mortality"), involves awareness of the mortality, suffering, and tenuous existence of others.

Burial and cremation, then, dispose of what only briefly remains and inevitably decays. Society does not bury, cremate, or dispose of memory but seeks to enhance and fortify remembrance by symbolism expressed in concrete ritual. Whatever act is chosen may be meaningful and fitting to that end. Burying, cremating, or otherwise disposing of the remains is hallowed in tradition and confirmed in fact. The methods of disposition evolve over time and differ in diverse cultures, serving the ends of the living rather than that which is beyond benefit or harm. Life, indeed, is for the living, and so are the rites and rituals which mark its passage.

The dead serve the living by providing a period of reflection, of realization, and ultimately of self-renewal. Dissection and autopsy of the remains, until recent times, were the only ways that the dead could make a contribution to the living. And as important as dissection and autopsy continue to be, they rarely involve an immediate life-saving measure needed by someone living in order to function or stay alive. However, things have changed today. The dead, rather than contributing to the living in a rather indirect manner, are able to make critical contributions to living persons. These contributions do not diminish the dead. In fact, they can indeed enhance the symbolism and symbolic value of transition for the living.

The dead, today, are often vitally needed by the living in more than a symbolic sense. They are needed both to increase our knowledge of life processes and disease through doing careful autopsies, and to enhance the life of the living in a very concrete manner by tissue and organ donation. To destroy a resource critically needed by a living person and entirely useless to another seems morally odd.

This chapter will examine the following topics involved in the issue of tissue waste: (1) the problem of tissue waste as it has developed through history and the problem today;

(2) community, justice, and mutual obligation; (3) scarce resources and organs donation; (4) objections to the customary salvage of organs; and (5) a possible resolution of this problem.

THE PROBLEM TODAY

The idea of using tissues and organs is not new; however, the reality is. The miraculous transplantation of organs was spoken of in medieval times and a sixteenth century picture by Fernando del Rincon hanging in the Prado shows a sacristan whose leg had become gangrenous receiving a new leg from a black man, presumably a slave. (The instrument of consent and the outcome of this venture are unfortunately not stated!) Despite the apocryphal stories (and the probably equally apocryphal story of Pope Innocent VIII's "transfusion" in 1492),[1] there is no evidence that tissue transfers took place prior to the seventeenth century, when Richard Lower, in England, first transfused blood from one animal to another.[2] In Paris shortly thereafter, Denys first transfused animal blood into humans. A failure of one such procedure and a suit brought by the patient's widow (who, it was later found, had murdered her husband and blamed the physician)[3] soured physicians and no further attempts occurred until 1818, when Blundell at Guy's Hospital first transfused blood from human to human. From then on, transfusions (tissue transplants in their own right) were carried out, some meeting with success, others unaccountably resulting in disaster. It was not until Landsteiner in 1900 described blood groups and he and Wiener made further refinements in 1940 that these disasters were understood and safe blood transfusions became a reality.[4] Successful skin grafting and early transplantation occurred in the late nineteenth and early twentieth century. Ullman in Vienna[5] and Alexis Carrel in New York[6] first successfully transplanted the kidney of one animal into another in 1902. Transplants of other organs, blood vessels, and limbs soon followed.[7]

Successful transplants from nontwins, or at least from nonrelated donors, awaited a better understanding of the immune process and, where needed, its relatively safe suppression. Tissue transplants, other than corneas (not usually subject to rejection) and blood (transfusable since the development of blood grouping), have become a reality only in very recent times. Now, however, the transplantation of kidneys, hearts (or hearts and lungs), livers, and corneas, as well as bones and sometimes skin, is an everyday event. Each newly dead could potentially restore sight to two sightless persons, renal function to two dialysis-dependent persons, liver function to one person in liver failure, and heart or heart-lung function to another on the brink of death—aside from serving as a possible donor of other tissues. Scarcity of organs, partly due to an archaic and inefficient retrieval system, is the limiting factor. Throughout this country only about 10 or 15 percent of suitable donors ever become actual ones, and even these rarely end up donating fully.[8]

There are three possible ways of looking at organ retrieval. We can (1) consider the use of cadaver organs immoral and forbid it altogether; (2) allow the donation of organs; (3) routinely salvage organs regardless of consent or dissent. The first possibility is neither a moral nor a legal option. It slams the door on life or function and permits needless death to occur. The second possibility, voluntarism, comes in two forms: Either we can make nongiving the norm and giving a supererogatory act or we can establish giving as the norm and allow dissent in unusual cases. The third possibility, taking useful cadaver organs under all circumstances, would require neither assent nor permit dissent.

In America today, voluntarism of the first kind described above is the established norm. A person declared brain dead (by a procedure which keeps the retrieval team distinct from the team caring for a donor) serves as a donor after valid instruments of donation have been executed and accepted. The process, criteria, and validity of declaring persons brain dead have been established in ethics and in law.[9] Premortem donation is legally accepted in all states.[10] In theory, such instruments when properly executed are the only vehicle of donation needed; in practice, partly because of the ever present fear of litigation, no team is willing to harvest organs in the face of objections by the next of kin.[11] When no instrument has been executed, donation can be made by the next of kin. However, the hospital staff is often loath to request donation. The newly dead who might be a suitable donor is generally a young person unexpectedly visited by disaster. As a result, the family is stunned.[12] It is a time when emotions run high and when rational deliberation is unlikely to occur. Hopes, fears, grief, guilt, superstition, and just plain fatigue mitigate against a dispassionate decision.[13] The process of organ donation will prolong the ordeal and will extend the time when family and staff are obliged to remain in a state of confusion, anguish, and fatigue.

Voluntarism of the second part, called *presumed consent,* shifts the burden. It allows physicians and hospitals to remove and transplant needed organs unless the decedent prior to death has objected or, when there is no express wish, the next of kin after death specifically objects. In case of conflict, the decedent's wishes have primacy over those of the family.[14] This kind of consent is extensively used and readily understood throughout much of the world. It still leaves much to be desired, because teams in hospitals not actively engaged in transplants have shown a tendency to place salvage low in their scale of priorities.[15] Salvaging potentially useful organs from all brain dead patients, regardless of assent or dissent, is enticing from a purely utilitarian perspective, but it smacks of autocracy. Its moral justifiability in a given community depends, as we shall see, largely on how that community conceives of itself.

COMMUNITY, JUSTICE, AND MUTUAL OBLIGATION

The way in which we view communities underlies our concept of justice, our sense of mutual obligation, and ultimately our laws and procedures.[16] The notion that members of communities are bound only by the duty to refrain from harming one another is critically different from the notion that they are united by far more than this. In communities where the sole duty is to refrain from harm, freedom is likely to be a condition of morality (a "side-constraint," as Nozick would have it)[17] rather than a value. It, therefore, cannot be negotiated or limited in any way. Freedom for any individual should be restricted only to the extent that it directly interferes with another's freedom. The sole legitimate power of the community is to enforce and defend individual freedom. Beyond the duty to refrain from harming one another, persons have the freedom, although not the duty, to help each other. Except when such help is freely and explicitly agreed upon by mutual contract, they have no obligation to respond to their neighbors' problems.[18]

A collection of individuals living together cannot long endure if it is not united by certain ways of behaving towards each other.[19] The duty to refrain from harming one another is essential for coexistence. Individuals must avoid killing or injuring each other and must refrain from other clearly injurious acts. But refraining from harm, by itself, is insufficient for maintaining what we ordinarily think of as a community. A community, in ordinary thinking, demands common goals toward which all members work (besides working toward their individual goals). A community is cemented by the inclination of its members to aid each other. A "minimalist ethic" is insufficient.[20] If a community is to endure, perfect duties (duties where no discretion is allowed, such as the duty to refrain from harming others) must be leavened by imperfect duties (duties where discretion or inclination is allowed, such as the duty of benevolence, which one can fulfill by helping this, that, or the other person).[21]

The two views of community described above entail starkly differing consequences. If one views freedom as the absolute condition of morality and community members as bound only by duties of noninterference, one will refuse to tax the affluent for the benefit of the poor, be unwilling to assure the safety (or free availability) of drugs, and be inclined to allow men to sell themselves freely into slavery. Freedom would no longer be a bargaining chip. Instead of being a fundamental communal value, one promulgated, secured, and safeguarded by the community, freedom becomes an untouchable absolute. As such, it too easily leads to the domination of the weak by the strong, the poor by the rich.[22] Communities in which freedom is an absolute have their moral views fixed; no room exists for development, where freedom is concerned.

If, on the other hand, one views freedom as a fundamental societal value (but a value nonetheless), other consequences follow. One can, for example, tax the rich, set standards of safety, and limit the term of subjugation of one person to another. In such communities, the principle that one can (or even should) ameliorate gross inequities will be generally held. Obligations to others are far more complex and more fruitful. Such a view permits and even facilitates experimentation, growth, and evolution.

Our notion of the nature of communities underlies our view of what is and what is not just. If by justice we mean giving each person his or her due, we are left with the question of what that due might be.[23]

The pure individualist, who holds freedom to be a side constraint and who therefore sees a community as united only by duties of noninterference, conceives justice to consist purely of allowing every member as much opportunity for achieving whatever desired as is consonant with everyone else having the same opportunity. For example, a neighbor in need must be allowed the opportunity to seek freely food or other goods as long as in so doing that opportunity for others is not diminished.

Those who see in community an association of people united by more than this will affirm that a neighbor's want creates certain positive obligations. They will readily acknowledge that discharging such obligations inevitably must diminish untrammeled freedom and attenuate individual liberty. Yet the obligation to help one's less fortunate neighbor becomes obvious for those who conceive of communities in this way.

Justice, as John Dewey has pointed out, is not an end in itself.[24] It is a means for facilitating communal life as well as individual opportunity, and its content will, therefore, vary with history. Justice, like all other human concepts and activities, is biologically grounded and must adapt and support survival and growth. If we affirm communities to be united by more than mere duties of noninterference, we allow adaptation and growth to occur and we see justice and the attendant obligations as dynamic and evolving. Obligations are not strictly bound or circumscribed. They vary with time, with circumstance, and with technical advances, as well as with a community's vision of the good life—which itself changes and will ever change.

SCARCE RESOURCES AND ORGAN DONATIONS

Scarcity is a relative matter. Medical resources are often scarce today because of an increase in costs and because society seems less willing to allocate more funds to health care. Whether this need be so is another matter. The availability of medical resources as ordinarily conceived is generally a societal construct, for it is ultimately society which allocates, or fails to allocate, necessary funds. Resources, for the most part, are renewable, obtainable, and limited in their availability only by our reluctance to allocate sufficient funds for them. Even the most expensive goods can be made available by the expenditure of more funds.

Goods which are unrenewable, however, are a different matter. Once used up, they cannot then be created. There is an unbridgeable gap between what is extremely expensive and hard to produce and what is priceless and not possible to make. The problem is similar to that of dealing with the infinite or eternal on human terms. No number, no matter how large, no length of time, however great, serves as a stepping stone to the infinite or the eternal. The difference between the eternal and the transitory, the infinite and the finite, the unrenewable and the renewable is like an impenetrable barrier.[25]

Intuitively, most people would hold that destroying resources useless to the one destroying them but critically needed by another is morally wrong. Our view on this, of course, depends upon our view of communities. Disposing of food down my disposal while my neighbor starves may not be nice, but it is not morally blameworthy if a community is only united by the duty to refrain from harm. (Taking food away from my neighbor, of course, would be morally wrong.) If, however, a community entails obligations beyond refraining from harm, destroying a meal while my neighbor goes hungry becomes morally problematic. If, furthermore, my neighbor would be certain to die without this food, its destruction would surely be a blameworthy act.

Cadaver organs differ radically from most other resources in a number of pertinent ways. First, organs cannot be renewed (although they could certainly be made far more readily available and be less wasted than they are today). Second, they are of vital use to the living persons whose organs they are, but aside from being potentially transplantable they are of use to others only under exceptional circumstances. Third, when organs are of use to other living persons, they are critical to the continuance of these persons' lives or functioning. Fourth, organs are not, once a person is dead, the property of any specific other person, except perhaps for purposes of burial (and then such property rights are hedged) or organ donation.[26] Finally, cadaver organs were (up to the time of death) organic parts of living, breathing, and thinking persons, members of a community sharing in their values, hopes, and aspirations and united with it by a social contract. As such, such organs are of symbolic value to others and to the community.

OBJECTIONS TO CUSTOMARY SALVAGE

The idea of transplanting the organs of the newly dead into the living makes some persons uncomfortable. This uneasiness is related to a not unreasonable fear of technocracy and an adversion to the philosophy so prevalent today which holds that what can be done ought to be done.[27] The fear of "mutilation" and notions of wholeness, as well as the fear that making body parts interchangeable between individuals will serve to make individuals be looked upon as themselves (complex) organs to be disposed of by others at will, are central to the issue of transplantation.[28] It has also been feared that diluting the respect for natural symbols (such as newly dead bodies) will weaken the important communal respect for symbols.[29] A long religious tradition which endows the physical remains with mystic qualities beyond the symbolic often helps to sustain such fears.[30]

The argument from wholeness essentially takes the following form. The first premise is that capriciously removing a part of an organism (say, hacking off an ear merely for the sake of doing this) is not only irrational but is mutilation and unacceptable.[31] Persons are their body's stewards and are compelled not to treat their body in injurious ways. (A hidden premise often is that this is offensive to God.) Second, persons are justified in removing a part of their body threatening the integrity of the whole.[32] Assuming the notion of stewardship is correct, such self-mutilation is not only permissible but perhaps mandatory. Third, mutilation of the body by removing a part is impermissible for any reason (even to help one's neighbor) other than to preserve the integrity of the whole body of which it is a part. Fourth, totality to be preserved persists intact when a person dies. (This harkens back to issues dealing with resurrection.) The conclusion is that donation of organs is impermissible.

The fear that allowing the invasion of one body for the sake of another will create a society less mindful of individual rights is connected with the argument from wholeness.[33] It can take the following argumentative form. First, a person's wholeness may be disrupted only for the sake of preserving the person's own integrity. Second, communities and their members relate to each other in ways substantially different from the relationship of individuals to their parts. Third, although one might hope for more, individuals are bound together within communities by the duty to refrain from harming others and not by any other duties. Fourth, if one allows people to be invaded for the sake of other people or of the community as a whole, one is apt to produce a state of affairs in which a person is perceived as merely another organ of the community and is disposable for the needs of the state. Since this state of affairs is undesirable, organ transplantation should not be allowed to be customary.

It can be added to the above argument that making organ retrieval customary, even if not mandatory, reduces property rights, dispels an opportunity for generosity, dilutes a laudatory communal urge, and unduly burdens families in their hour of grief.[34] Customarily salvaging tissues and organs (even when dissent is permitted and accepted) will lessen communal respect for other symbols and hence for the reality which they represent.[35] A society geared only to reality and unmindful of its symbols may, it is feared, become callous and uncaring.

Those who see community as a group of people united merely by duties of noninterference and who hold absolute freedom to be the necessary condition of morality and justice will look askance at a society in which tissues and organs are routinely taken, even if the possibility of dissent were to remain. They would argue that in a community where noninterference is the only moral principle, the only reasonable presumption is the members will refrain from harming each other, not that they will act to benefit each other. Since no act of beneficence should be presupposed or in any way mandated, to presume consent to organ donation would, they feel, violate the basic notion of respect for others.[36] Some, no doubt, would find it laudatory to donate organs. They would see such donation as a supererogatory instance of generosity rather than as a duty or as an instance of justice.

A POSSIBLE RESOLUTION

Failure to use the organs and tissues of the newly dead for persons whose future life or function is dependent upon them seems, at the very least, wasteful. And yet, the idea of affording persons no choice in the disposition of their own or their relatives remains seems almost as repugnant. We balance feeling against fact, symbol against reality, and ultimately we stand in danger of committing one grievous wrong to prevent another.[37] Objections to making organ donation customary basically rely on fears of violating symbols. The fear of destroying wholeness, the fear of mutilation, the equating of cadaver organs with those of living persons and the consequent fear for the security of the living, and finally the fear that allowing the invasion of one body for the sake of another will weaken individual rights all depend on a confusion of symbol with reality or on mistakenly holding that symbol and reality have equal value.

Symbols come into being as the epiphenomena of a reality which they come to represent. Symbols, wherever found, relate to reality. They may outlast it or become distorted and hard to recognize. Nevertheless, symbols must either represent reality or, as happens occasionally, be derived from yet another symbol that itself is ultimately grounded in reality. But symbols are not reality itself. Confounding a symbol with the reality it represents, or holding it to have the same value, ultimately distorts reality. When symbols rather than the thing they stand for assume primary value, the sentiment of benevolence is replaced by sentimentality.

Communities are cemented together by sentiments of mutual benevolence. Communities consist of individuals affected by each other's needs. Sentiments of benevolence are related to respect for such needs. Respect for the newly dead is symbolic of respect for the living. In respecting the grief of relatives, we respect the relatives as well as the object of their grief. But that respect may be increased, rather than lessened, by using newly dead as a bridge to continued life for the living. Symbols change and adapt with reality, not, it is hoped, the other way around. When we make refusal instead of assent the norm and forgo using the tissues of the newly dead to build these bridges because we fear violating a symbol, we create a new and distorted reality, a reality without substance. And, what is worse, we impair the reality of the sick out of respect for mere symbolism.

Symbols comfort the bereaved. They stand for the person that was as well as for ideals and aspirations. Symbols allow the abrupt transition from life to death to be softened, and in a sense they postpone the moment of loss. The newly dead, no longer really here, is honored in memory and through symbols. Many objects and acts can be symbols or be symbolic. What is symbolic at a given time or to a given individual may be meaningless at other times or to other persons. The type of symbols we use are an expression of the "education and discipline of the feelings."[38]

Communities consist of persons each with their own troubles. If just communities are conceived of as caring communities, then we must presume that caring will be expressed in meaningful ways by their individual members. Building bridges by using the newly dead to give life and function to the living creates new symbols of love and caring. Routinely taking the organs and tissues of the newly dead to serve the critical need of others is to presume the newly dead to have been members of the same caring community as the currently living. Presuming the newly dead not to have cared about their neighbors' needs, not to have wanted to serve as the bridge to life and function for others, is hardly to show respect for them. Instead of violating a symbol, presuming consent may allow symbols to evolve.

Seeing in the cadaver a holy object not to be "violated" for fear of violating a symbol neglects two important facts—that the cadaver has still viable organs and tissues and that the life of another member of the community depends on these very organs and tissues. Seeing in the cadaver a bridge to live for another changes the form of the symbolism but does not destroy it. Cadavers still can be seen as holy objects in their own right and with their own purpose. In so doing, respect for the newly dead is fully expressed.

Unless we are to resort to arguments involving mysticism or belief in an afterlife, arguments of which the premises can be neither refuted nor proven, no one can reasonably hold that the dead are diminished by anything done to them after death. Harm, if possible, is purely symbolic. Even when the reputation or "memory" of the dead is impaired, the dead are not injured in themselves. Gratuitous injuries done to reputation or memory or other forms of disrespect shown to the dead constitute harm done to the community (by dragging a role model into the dirt or by gratuitously violating a symbol and thereby blunting sensitivity) and to the nearest kin. But it is not harm done to the deceased in the sense that harm can be visited upon the living.[39] Symbols manifest the reality for which they stand. The bereaved tend to remember the deceased in positive ways: they remember intelligence, beauty, and generosity; they generally fail to dwell on stupidity, ugliness, and greed. They do this because the traits of intelligence, beauty, and generosity are valued in our peculiar community and the others are not. Respect for the dead, it seems, would be shown by presuming the dead to have shared fully in what the community considers to be positive traits.

When all is said and done, we are still confronted with the problem of wasting as little tissue from the newly dead as possible while meaningfully showing respect for the symbolism so dear to some members of our community. If one were to salvage all organs regardless of assent or dissent, a maximal supply could be obtained. This would be done at the price of seriously discomforting those members of community who belong to a moral enclave that considers the use of such organs to be reprehensible. (Their objections should probably preclude their receiving organs should the need arise, a rule which would be hard to implement!) But our larger community has no such strictures. Most members of a just community would, in the cold light of day, affirm their belief that it is just to give to living persons who critically need them the organs from cadavers, which have no use for them.[40] Presumed consent merely affirms this. To presume to be the case what is unlikely to be the case (i.e., refusal of consent) is not rational. And of course a policy of presumed consent would respect dissent if it were explicitly expressed.

Presumed consent as the instrument of donation has, furthermore, an educational effect. By affirming the values of the community, it tends to emphasize societal norms and to weave them more solidly into the fabric of community expectations while continuing to exhibit that respect for peculiar beliefs which a pluralistic community demands. Families, "heavily burdened in their hour of grief",[41] will be less likely to be afflicted by the fear of violating imagined communal symbols while still able, by dissenting, to apply standards peculiar to their own moral enclave or to their own moral conscience. Making the donation of organs a supererogatory act subtly suggests that nongiving rather than giving is the norm; it suggests the value of symbol over reality and lends a hand to the ascendency of sentimentality (which values the symbol more than what the symbol represents). Making the donation of organs a societal norm (while allowing dissent) suggests that the just community is a caring community in which sentiment inclines its members to build bridges for the living. It helps to educate, discipline, and channel feelings and thus to create new symbols of caring and respect.

NOTES

1. J.L. Joughin, "Blood Transfusion in 1492," *Journal of the American Medical Association* 62 (1914): 553–54.

2. F.H. Garrison, *An Introduction to the History of Medicine* (Philadelphia, Pa.: W.B. Saunders, 1929).

3. C. Singer and E.A. Underwood, *A Short History of Medicine* (New York: Oxford University Press, 1962).

4. Ibid.

5. E. Ullman, Experimentelle Nierentransplantation," *Wien Klin Wochenschr* 15 (1908): 281–82.

6. A. Carrell, "Results of the Transplantation of Blood Vessels, Organs and Limbs," *Journal of the American Medical Association* 51 (1908): 1662–67.

7. S.N. Chatterjee, ed, *Organ Transplantation* (London: John Wright PSG, 1982).

8. S.J. Youngner et al, "Psychosocial and Ethical Implications of Organ Retrieval," *New England Journal of Medicine* 313 (1985): 321–32; A.L. Caplan, "Organ Procurement: It's Not in the Cards," *Hastings Center Report* 14, no. 5 (1984): 9–12; Medical News, "The Organ Procurement Problem: Many Causes, No Easy Solutions," *Journal of the American Medical Association* 254 (1985): 3285–88.

9. Ad Hoc Committee of the Harvard Medical School to Examine the Definition of Brain Death, "A Definition of Irreversible Coma; Report of the Ad Hoc Committee of the Harvard Medical School to Examine the Definition of Brain Death." *Journal of the American Medical Association* 205 (1968): 337–40; B. Green and D. Winkler, "Brain Death and Personal Identity," *Philosophy and Public Affairs* 9, no. 2 (1980): 104–33; President's Commission for the Study of Ethical Problems in Medicine and Biomedical and Behavioral Research, *Defining Death: A Report on the Medical, Legal and Ethical Issues in the Determination of Death* (Washington, D.C.: GPO, 1981); F. Plum and J. Posner, *The Diagnosis of Stupor and Coma,* 3rd ed. (Philadelphia, Pa.: Davis Publishing, 1980); E.L. Pallis, "ABC of Brain Stem Death," *British Medical Journal* 285 (1982): 1409–12; F. Plum, "Prognosis in Severe Brain Damage and Diagnosis of Brain Death," in *Cecil's Textbook of Medicine,* 17th ed., ed. J.B. Wyngarden and L.H. Smith (Philadelphia, Pa.: W.B. Saunders, 1985).

10. A.M. Sadler, B.L. Sadler, and E.B. Stason, "The Uniform Anatomical Gift Act," *Journal of the American Medical Association* 206 (1968): 2501–6.

11. T.D. Overcast et al., "Problems in the Identification of Potential Organ Donors," *Journal of the American Medical Association* 251 (1984): 1559–62.

12. P. Ramsey, *The Patient as Person* (New Haven, Conn.: Yale University Press, 1970).

13. E.H. Loewy, "Presumed Consent in Organ Donation: An Almost Binding Duty," in *Covenants of Life: Essays in Honor of Paul Ramsey*, ed. K.E. Vaux (Urbana, I.L.: University of Illinois Press, in press).

14. C. Perry, "The Right of Public Access to Cadaver Organs," *Social Science and Medicine* 15 (1981): 163–66; J. Dukeminier and D. Sanders, "Organ Transplantation: A Proposal for Routine Salvage of Cadaver Organs," *New England Journal of Medicine* 269 (1968): 413–19; J.L. Muyskens, "An Alternative Policy for Obtaining Cadaver Organs for Transplantation," *Philosophy and Public Affairs* 8, no. 1 (1978): 88–99; E.H. Loewy, "Presumed Consent in Organ Donation: Values and Means in the Distribution of a Scarce Resource," in *Ethical Dilemmas in Modern Medicine: A Physician's Viewpoint* (Lewiston, N.Y.: Edwin Mellen Press, 1986).

15. F.P. Stuart, F.J. Veith, and R.E. Cranford, "Brain Death Laws and Patterns of Consent to Remove Organs from Cadavers in the United States and 28 Other Countries," *Transplantation* 31, no. 4 (1981): 238–44; Report of the Swedish Committee on Defining Death, *The Concept of Death* (Stockholm: Swedish Ministry of Health and Social Affairs, 1984).

16. E.H. Loewy, "Communities, Obligation and Health-Care," in press.

17. R. Nozick, *Anarchy, State and Utopia* (New York: Basic Books, 1974).

18. H.T. Engelhardt, *The Foundations of Bioethics* (New York: Oxford University Press, 1986).

19. J.P. Reeder, "Beneficence, Supererogation and Role Duty," in *Beneficence and Health Care*, ed. E.E. Shelp (Dordrecht, Holland: D. Reidel, 1982).

20. D. Callahan, "Minimalist Ethics," *Hastings Center Report* 11, no. 5 (1981): 19–25.

21. Kant I., *Foundations of the Metaphysics of Morals*, trans. L.W. Beck (Indianapolis, Ind.: Bobbs-Merrill, 1978).

22. R. Niebuhr, "Rationing and Democracy," in *Love and Justice*, ed D.R. Robertson (Philadelphia, Pa.: Westminster Press, 1957).

23. Aristotle, *Nicomachean Ethics*, trans. M. Ostwald (Indianapolis, Ind.: Bobbs-Merrill, 1962); W.K. Frankena, "The Concept of Social Justice," in *Social Justice*, ed. R.B. Brandt (Englewood Cliffs, N.J.: Prentice-Hall, 1962).

24. J. Dewey, *Theory of the Moral Life* (New York: Holt, Rinehart & Winston, 1960).

25. E.H. Loewy, "Drunks, Livers and Values: Should Social Value Judgments Enter into Transplant Decisions?" In preparation.

26. Perry, "Public Access to Cadaver Organs."

27. Loewy, "Presumed Consent in Organ Donation."

28. Ramsey, *Patient as Person*.

29. W. May, "Attitudes towards the Newly Dead," *Hastings Center Report* 1, no. 1 (1973): 3–13.

30. Ramsey, *Patient as Person*; Loewy, "Presumed Consent in Organ Donation"; May, "Attitudes towards the Newly Dead."

31. B. Gert, *The Moral Rules* (New York: Harper & Row, 1973).

32. G. Kelly, "The Morality of Mutilation: Towards a Revision of the Treatist," *Theological Studies* 17, no. 3 (1952): 332–48.

33. Ramsey, *Patient as Person*.

34. Ibid.

35. May, "Attitudes towards the Newly Dead."

36. Engelhardt, *Foundations of Bioethics*.

37. J. Feinberg, "The Mistreatment of Dead Bodies," *Hastings Center Report* 15, no. 1 (1985): 31–37.

38. M. Tanner, "Sentimentality," Proceedings of the Aristotelian Society 77 (1977): 127–47.

39. E. Partridge, "Posthumous Interests and Posthumous Respect," *Ethics* 91 (1981): 243–64.

40. C.E. Koop, "Increasing the Supply of Solid Organs for Transplantation," *Public Health Report* 98, no. 6 (1983): 566–72.

41. Ramsey, *Patient as Person*.

Part IV

Justice, Economics, and Health Care

Chapter 22

Rationing Health Care: The Ethics of Medical Gatekeeping*

Edmund D. Pellegrino

An ethically perilous line of reasoning is gaining wide currency in our country today. It starts with a legitimate concern for rising health care costs, finds them uncontrollable by any means except some form of rationing, and concludes that the physician must become the "gatekeeper," the designated guardian of society's resources. By negative and positive financial incentives, it is reasoned, the physician can be forced to conserve tests, treatments, operations, hospitalization, and referrals for consultation. In this way, costs will presumably be cut by the elimination of "unnecessary" medical care.

There are three ways in which the physician can function as gatekeeper: One is morally mandatory, one is morally questionable, and one is morally indefensible.

The first form of gatekeeping is the traditional function imposed by the responsibility to practice rational medicine, i.e., to use only those diagnostic and therapeutic modalities beneficial and effective for the patient. The proper exercise of traditional gatekeeping is not only morally imperative but economically sound.

The second form of gatekeeping, negative gatekeeping, usually occurs within some form of prepayment system in which the physician is expected to limit access to health care services. For a physician to take on this role is morally dubious, because it generates a conflict between the traditional responsibilities of the physician as a primary advocate of the patient and his new responsibilities as guardian of society's resources. Under certain carefully defined conditions of economic necessity and moral monitoring, a negative gatekeeping role might be morally justifiable.

The third form of gatekeeping is positive gatekeeping. In positive gatekeeping, the physician encourages the use of health care facilities and services for personal or corporate profit. This is an indefensible form of gatekeeping for which no moral justification can be mustered.

This chapter delineates the nature of the ethical dilemmas of gatekeeping from the viewpoint of the patient's interests. It concludes that it is in the interest of society to preserve the integrity of the physician's primary responsibility to his or her patient, that rationing may not be as inevitable as generally supposed, and that rationing is morally valid only if other means of cost containment have been exhausted.

---

*Adapted from *Journal of Contemporary Health Law and Policy*, Vol. 2, pp. 23–38, with permission of The Catholic University of America Press, Inc., © 1986.

THE DE FACTO CONFLICT OF INTEREST

When the first physician requested a fee for his services, economics and conflict of interest entered medicine.[1] Ever since, physicians' fees and the degree to which physicians could equate necessity for their services with maintaining their own income have been sources of suspicion and contention between physicians and patients.

This de facto conflict of interest is difficult or impossible to eliminate given the fact that physicians must earn a living to support their families and are entitled to the same access to material goods as others. What mitigates the conflict is the ethical commitment of the physician to the patient's good, which can be conceived of as a commitment to the principle of beneficence.[2] This principle has been the central one of medical ethics. It is implicit in the Hippocratic Oath, the ancient codes of India and China, and in the ethics of Thomas Percival (which inspired the AMA's first code and all subsequent ones). Beneficence means acting on behalf of, in the interest of, or as an advocate of the patient. It has always implied some degree of effacement of the physician's self-interest in favor of the interests of the patient. Indeed, this effacement is what distinguishes a true profession from a business or craft.[3] And it is the expectation that physicians will by and large practice some degree of self-effacement that warrants the trust that society and individual patients place in them. It is also the physician's public commitment to service beyond self-interest that constitutes the real entry of the medical graduate into the profession. The awarding of a medical degree only signifies successful completion of a course of study. But the oath the physician takes is a public act of commitment to the special way of life and the special obligations demanded by the nature of medicine.[4]

Ethical commitments can, and do, mitigate the conflicts of interest inherent in medical practice, but they do not eliminate them—except perhaps in the heroic examples of self-sacrifice we expect only of saints and martyrs. Even if the physician's financial incentives are reduced, other motives can conflict with the care owed the patient, i.e., prestige, power, professional advancement, self-indulgence, unionization, and family obligations. These can be just as detrimental to the patient's well-being as the physician's monetary interests.

While there has always been some irreducible quantum of self-interest in medicine, rarely, if ever, has self-interest been socially sanctioned, morally legitimated, or encouraged in the way it is in the rationing approach to cost containment. Today, the physician's self-interest is deliberately used by policy makers to restrict the availability, accessibility, and quality of services to the patient. It is against this background—that is, how they accentuate the de facto conflict of interest in medicine—that the several forms of gatekeeping, licit and illicit, must be examined.

THREE FORMS OF GATEKEEPING

Morally Obligatory Gatekeeping: The Traditional Role

There is in the nature of the medical transaction an unavoidable gatekeeping function which the physician has always exercised and, indeed, is under compulsion to exercise in a morally defensible way. The unavoidable fact is that the physician recommends what tests, treatments, medications, operations, consultations, periods of hospitalization, nursing home, etc., the patient needs. Today physicians are responsible for 75 percent of all our health and medical care expenditures.

This fact imposes a serious positive moral duty on the physician to use both the individual patient's and society's resources optimally. In the case of the individual patient, the physician has the obligation, inherent in his promise to act for the patients' welfare, to use only those measures appropriate to the cure of the patient or alleviation of the patient's suffering. What the physician recommends must be *effective* (i.e., it must materially modify the natural history of the disease) and it must also be beneficial (i.e., it must be to the patient's benefit). Some measures are highly effective—like treatments for pneumonia—but may not be always beneficial if they prolong unnecessarily the act of dying and thus impose the burden of futility and expense without benefit for the patient. There are also treatments that benefit the patient but are not effective in altering the ultimate course of the disease, e.g., pain relief, nursing or home care, artificial feedings, etc. The same applies to diagnostic procedures.

Physicians, therefore, have a legitimate and morally binding responsibility to function as gatekeepers. They must use their knowledge to practice competent, scientifically rational medicine. Their guidelines should be *diagnostic elegance* (i.e., using the right degree of economy of means in diagnosis) and *therapeutic parsimony* (i.e., providing just those treatments that are demonstrably beneficial and effective). In this way, the physician automatically fulfills economic and moral obligations. He simultaneously avoids unnecessary risk to the patient from dubious treatment and he conserves the patient's financial resources, and society's as well.

This form of gatekeeping entails no conflict with the patient's good. Economics and ethics, individual and social good, and doctors' and the patients' interests are congruent. In this morally obligatory and traditional gatekeeper role, physicians use their de facto position to advance the good of their patients. In contrast, two new forms of gatekeeping have been introduced, each open to serious ethical objection because their primary intent is economic benefit, not the well-being of patients.

The Negative Gatekeeper Role

In the "negative" version of the gatekeeper role, the physician is placed under constraints of self-interest to restrict the use of medical services of all kinds, but particularly those that are most expensive. A variety of measures is used, each of which interjects economic considerations into the physician's clinical decisions and limits his or her discretionary latitude in making decisions.

One way this occurs is through the diagnostic related group (DRG) program, which assigns to well over 400 disease categories a fixed sum or fixed number of days of hospitalization. If the actual number of days of hospitalization (or tests, etc.) exceeds the allotted sum or number, the institution or the physician "loses" the difference; if the number of days of hospitalization (or tests, etc.) is less than the allotted sum or number, the institution or physician makes a "profit." In other plans, the physician or institution contracts to provide care for some prescribed number of patients for a fixed annual sum. Again, if the total costs of care exceed the contracted amount, the provider bears the loss; if the costs are less, the provider makes a profit. Variations on these themes are several. They need not be detailed here. The essence of each plan is to motivate the provider to limit access to care by appealing to the provider's self-interest.[5]

With all these plans, the physician becomes the focus of incentives and disincentives in several ways—as a private practitioner when the physician hospitalizes a patient under the DRG system and as the employee or partner in a prepayment insurance plan, like a health maintenance organization (HMO), independent practice association (IPA), or primary care network (PCN). Increasingly in each case the physician's economic efficiency is monitored and deviations from the norm are rewarded or punished. The rewards may be in the form of profit sharing, bonuses, promotion in the organization, or other perquisites and preferments. The disincentives are loss of profit, limits on admitting privileges, or nonrenewal of co-employment contract. In some instances, productivity and efficiency schedules, "pass through" criteria, and other quantitative measures (not only of cost containment but of profit making) are used to evaluate the physician's performance.

The major pressure in these plans at present is upon the primary care physician, the first contact member of the health care system who makes the majority of decisions about entry into the system. The primary care physician may be a family practitioner, general internist, or pediatrician. The primary care physician has the greatest influence over access to expensive resources of hospitalization, testing, and consulting. For this reason, many prepayment plans insist that the patient must stay with one primary care physician within the system lest he or she shop around for one who might be more compliant. Gradually, as pressures for cost containment increase, the consultant and tertiary care specialists will very likely also be included as gatekeepers, with constraints and criteria suited to the nature of their specialties.

The Positive Gatekeeper Role

The "positive" form of gatekeeping is less well defined and not usually explicitly formalized. In this version, the physician is constrained to increase rather than decrease access to services. However, the purpose here is not containing costs but enhancing profits. For those who can pay, the latest and most expensive diagnostic or therapeutic services are made available; services are provided based on market "demand" rather than medical need. The aim is to "penetrate" or "dominate" the market and to eliminate services that are not profitable. Increasing the demand for services is an implicit goal, and the physician becomes virtually a salesman. We see this most blatantly expressed in the TV and newspaper advertisements soliciting clients for elective surgery and all sorts of other services, some beneficial and some quite useless.

As positive gatekeepers, physicians use their position of control over access to medical care for their own financial advantage or for that of their employers. They share in the profit directly if they are owners of or investors in the service provided or they are rewarded by pay increases, advancement, etc., if they are employees.

THE ETHICAL ISSUES IN MEDICAL GATEKEEPING

Ethical Issues in Negative Gatekeeping

Both the positive and negative forms of gatekeeping exploit the de facto position of the physician as the conduit through which patients gain access to services. The purposes to be served by such gatekeeping are not entirely consistent with the patient's interests. Ethical issues arise inasmuch as these purposes reduce the trust the patient places in the physician as the patient's primary agent, minister, and advocate.

Efforts at cost containment are not in themselves unethical, and, as noted above, they are morally mandatory when they are in the best interests of the patient. They violate those interests if, for whatever reason, they deny needed services or induce the patient to demand, or the physician to provide, unneeded services. The ethical dilemmas of gatekeeping therefore arise out of the way economic incentives and disincentives modify the physician's freedom to act in the patient's behalf. While in the past the physician was largely responsible for defining "necessary" and "unnecessary" care, those determinations are now formularized by policy. In applying the formulas, the physician becomes the agent of the hospital or the system rather than the patient. Furthermore, the medical criteria used to determine necessary treatment are subject to modification or veto by economic considerations.

Many of the ethical dilemmas are illustrated in the Medicare prospective payment system now in force in the majority of states. In this system, the cost-base per diem reimbursement system of the past is replaced by a prospective payment system (PPS) based in fixed prices for 471 diagnostic related groups. The initial motivation behind this transition was to improve quality of care by linking quality of care directly to reimbursement. It was reasoned that the DRG system would also cut costs by causing a closer scrutiny of care aimed especially at limiting "unnecessary" tests, drugs, procedures, and hospitalization. Besides being economically wasteful, unneeded care is also dangerous to patients.

These cost containment measures are not intrinsically unethical. Certainly we cannot consider them unethical simply because they limit the physician's latitude in decision making. Rather it is the effect of this limitation on the patient that is ethically crucial, and it is the moral responsibility of the physician operating within such a system to be concerned about this effect when it appears to be harmful to the patient.

The difficulty in the application of present DRG policies arise in the determination of what is necessary for quality care for a particular patient. In a system based on "average" lengths of stay for each disease, individual patients may suffer, since no disease manifests itself in the same way in every patient. As a result, disease entities are treated rather than individual patients, and the original goal (i.e., quality care) is compromised, sometimes dangerously.

Two tendencies deleterious to patients are already apparent in the way the DRG system is being administered in many hospitals. One is that patients are being discharged "quicker and sicker." The second is that extra funds are not being provided to those who need lengthier stays, etc., than the DRG allows. In both instances it is often the frail elderly patient who suffers—sent "home" with no adequate provision for posthospital care such as nursing home care, home care, etc. In fact, the trend of public policy at the moment is to curtail payment for nonhospital and long-term care, further aggravating the harm done by premature discharge.

In prospective payment systems, the physician is automatically a negative gatekeeper. To the extent that there is greater scrutiny of the quality of care rendered and that unnecessary care is avoided, the good of the patient is served. But when the system harms the patient, the question of the physician's primary duty arises. If the physician is primarily the patient's advocate, agent, and minister, then the physician must protect the patient's interests against the system, even with some risk or damage to the physician's own interests.

There is also pressure in prospective payment plans to disfavor or disenfranchise the sicker patients, those with chronic illness and those who need the more expensive kinds of care. Less admirable still is the way cost containment can be used consciously or unconsciously to justify the denial of services to those troublesome or obnoxious patients that physicians prefer not to see—the neurotics, the "complainers," or the "hypochondriacs."

Another deleterious effect of negative gatekeeping is to foster the wrong kind of competition among providers. Instead of competition to provide the highest quality care (as judged by the standards of rational medicine), there is competition to compile the best records in terms of savings, productivity, efficiency, short hospital stays, or least number of procedures done.

To be effective, many prospective payment plans insist that patients must be locked into care by one primary care physician. The choice of physicians and the freedom to change physicians is severely limited. The most sensitive aspect of the healing relationship, the confidence one must have in one's personal physician, is thus ignored or compromised. Especially in regard to chronic or recurrent illness, this confidence is essential to effective care.

All of these factors converge to drive the physician's interests into conflict with the patient's. Such conflicts are heightened by the rather drastic changes occurring in the economics of the medical profession, which are making the physician more vulnerable to economic pressure. There is today an oversupply of physicians in urban areas and in many specialties.[6] Many physicians now graduate with debts due to the cost of their education in the neighborhood of $100,000. On top of this, expensive malpractice premiums must be paid before any physician dares risk even a day of medical practice. Consequently, competition from corporately owned and operated clinics can force even conscientious physicians into "survival" tactics of questionable morality.

The result is that many young and even older physicians are being driven into salaried group practices and automatically become negative gatekeepers. The physician's independence, as Paul Starr has shown, is rapidly eroding, and with it the physician's ability to withstand the institutional and corporate strictures inconsistent with his or her judgment about what is good for the patient.[7] It is becoming ever more costly personally and financially for even the most morally sensitive physician to practice the effacement of self-interest that medical ethics requires.

Ethical Issues in Positive Gatekeeping

The ethical conflicts in the positive form of gatekeeping are less subtle and more explicit. Here the profit motive is primary. The transaction between physician and patient becomes a commodity transaction. The physician is an independent entrepreneur or the hired agent of entrepreneurs and investors who themselves have no connection with the traditions of medical ethics. The physician thus begins to practice the ethics of the marketplace, to think of his or her relationship with the patient not as a covenant or trust but as a business and contractual relationship. Ethics becomes, not a matter of obligations or virtue, but a matter of legality. The metaphors of business and law replace those of ethics. Medical knowledge becomes proprietary, the doctor's private property to be sold to whom the doctor chooses at whatever price and under whatever conditions the doctor chooses.

The dependence, anxiety, lack of knowledge, and vulnerability of the sick person are exploited for personal profit. It is easy to exploit this vulnerability to encourage unnecessary cosmetic surgeries, hysterectomies, CAT scans, sonograms, fiber optic endoscopies, etc. The patient is led to believe he or she is getting "the latest and the best." All of this is inconsistent with even the most primordial concept of stewardship of patient interests. The moral questionableness is more obvious than in the negative form of gatekeeping. The patient becomes primarily a source of income. The crasser financial motives that have motivated the most selfish physicians are legitimated and even given social sanction.

For the positive form of gatekeeping there is not, as there may be for the negative form, any plausible moral justification. Some argue the profit motive is necessary for medical progress, for maintaining quality of service, or even for funding charitable care. It would be unrealistic to deny that for some physicians these are the only effective motives and that some good can come of them. But ultimately the profit motive erodes the ethical sensitivities and standards of the profession. When a conflict occurs between profit and patient welfare, patient welfare is sure to suffer in the end. Unrestrained monetary instinct corrupts medicine as surely as does an unrestrained instinct for power or prestige.

SOME SOCIAL ETHICAL CONCOMITANTS OF RATIONING

The negative and the positive gatekeeper roles both involve ethical consequences for society. Both tolerate and indeed foster two or more levels of quality and availability of health care. Affluent persons can buy whatever they need or want. Affluent "outliers" can afford to supplement what a DRG plan allows. Prepayment plans and organizations seek eagerly to enroll such persons. The less affluent and the poor do not have such easy access to care. They may or may not be assured a so-called adequate level of care. "Adequacy" is always vaguely defined. On any definition, the gap between the health care provided to the rich and poor will widen. The poor and the lower economic strata of the middle class will be relegated to public hospitals. We have spent two decades trying to eliminate these institutions and the disparate levels of care they imply. Now it seems they must be re-established and financed.

The differences in the care provided in public and private hospitals extend beyond mere conveniences, plushness of accommodations, or frills. Anyone whose experience, like the author's, goes back to the large municipal hospitals of several decades ago will know that the differences are nontrivial. The efforts of the last two decades to undo the injustices of a multilevel system of health care are being reversed by the move toward rationing, cost containment, and gatekeeping.

A different kind of social-ethical issue arises if we ask whether it is defensible for society to transpose its responsibility for rationing onto the physician. Are not the criteria for when and how to ration the responsibility of all of us? In situations of extreme economic exigency, rationing could be justified. But the criteria for rationing and the principle of justice to be followed should rest with society, not with physicians. There is no assurance that a physician is any fairer or juster than others in deciding who shall receive so crucially important a resource as health care. Do we as a society really want to give this kind of power to physicians?

A very careful balance between the relative place of societally determined criteria for rationing and the latitude allowed physicians in making rationing decisions must be struck. Society may wish to use the DRG mechanism as a way of expressing its value choices. But can physicians accept the resulting criteria if they violate the physicians' prime duty to act as patient advocates?

Because of the conflicts of interests they generate and the social injustice they foster, both positive gatekeeping and negative gatekeeping erode the commitment to the patient welfare that is mandatory in medical care. This commitment flows from the nature of illness and the promise of service made by individual physicians and by the profession as a whole. It has its basis in the empirical nature of the healing relationship, in particular, the fact that a sick person—dependent, vulnerable, exploitable—must seek out the help of another who has the knowledge, skill, and facilities needed to effect a cure. It is inevitably an unequal relationship in terms of freedom and power and one in which the stronger is obliged to protect the interests of the weaker.[8]

IS RATIONING INEVITABLE?

The only plausible justification for rationing is economic necessity. Some people have a fear that rising health care costs will seriously compromise the availability and accessibility of other goods our society needs to thrive—nutrition, housing, jobs, national security, etc. This fear is cited as justification for efforts to put some arbitrary ceiling on the percentage of gross national product dedicated to health care. But is the assumption of an impending national bankruptcy due to health care costs empirically sound? If it is, rationing might be justified. Then the ethical question becomes, under what conditions? If it is not, then rationing has no ethical sanction.

The main question concerns the truth or falsity of the initial premise in the argument for rationing as inevitable. This is a difficult question to answer, because comparable figures on national expenditures for other things our society wants are hard to come by. Moreover, whether there is a crisis or not depends very much on the value we place on other expenditures. Some of the data on health care costs that policy makers find distressing are the following.

The nation's total health care bill now exceeds $1 billion per day in the U.S. The percentage of our gross national product going into health care is higher than for almost any other nation and it is increasing each year. Two and one-half billion dollars is spent on keeping 70,000 patients with chronic renal disease alive and $4.4 billion is spent on heart and liver transplants. Ten percent of all operating costs of a university hospital go into the last three to six months of life. Eighty percent of those who die do so in a hospital, as compared with 50 percent in 1949 and much lower percentages at the turn of the century. Each year 230,000 babies are born weighing less than 2,500 grams. Only half of them survive, and 15 percent of these end up with some residual defect. Two billion dollars per year are spent on neonatal intensive care units.

These and other figures have been cited by various advocates of rationing medical care for certain groups. Rationing for these groups is proposed on utilitarian, economic, and humanitarian grounds, i.e., to reduce the number of dependent, nonproductive members of society; to save money for other socially useful purposes or needs; or to prevent dooming the retarded and the disabled to lives of poor "quality." Some suggest that persons over a certain age should not be offered dialysis, that high-technology procedures like liver and heart transplants or even coronary bypasses should not be performed, that research in high-technology treatments like artificial hearts be halted, that babies under a certain cutoff weight should not be treated, that there should be a monetary limit on the expenditures for persons with terminal illnesses in the last few months of life, that those above a certain age should not be treated vigorously, etc.

These proposals deserve more critical examination than is possible here. They illustrate a range of policy options, all of which center on rationing expensive forms of care. Let it merely be noted that these expenditures should be compared with certain other expenditures which as a nation we make willingly, indeed sometimes avidly: $40 billion for alcohol, $30 billion for tobacco, $65 billion for cosmetics, $65 billion for advertising, $3.7 billion for potato chips, and unspecified billions for recreational hand guns, illicit drugs, gambling, and various types of luxuries.[9]

What decisions would we make if we consciously compared these expenditures with those for health care? Is $2.5 billion too much to spend on keeping 70,000 people with renal disease alive (many of them leading active lives) or $4 billion to return people to active life by means of cardiac, liver, or renal transplants, which are becoming more effective each year? What about the 50 percent of underweight babies who *do* survive and the 85 percent of those who are not disabled or retarded? Can we decide what is "quality" life for another person, especially for an infant, whose values cannot possibly be known? How do we distinguish between futile and burdensome treatments and effective, though expensive, life-saving treatments? How do we protect the vulnerable—the old, the very young, the poor, and the socially outcast—from being discriminated against in rationing decisions? How do we know when research into high technology may turn out to be beneficial for all rather than for just a few?

How would we answer these questions if we considered health a higher value than some of the other things for which we make great expenditures without questioning them at all? Would we have to ask these questions at all if we could cut out truly unnecessary care, reduce inefficiencies in the care we now give, and establish some priority among the categories of care based on need, benefit, and effectiveness as seen from the patient's point of view?

If we address these questions in an orderly way, identifying the underlying values and making conscious choices, we might decide that rationing and lifeboat ethics are not warranted in this country today. It would take more space than this chapter permits to establish a position on these issues. The questions have yet to be examined with sufficient attention to their underlying value desiderata. This is a sensitive operation and one whose conclusions might prove embarrassing. How we make the choices required by rationing could well reveal more about the kind of people we are, and want to be, than we might wish.

NOTES

1. Fees for service—in goods, preferments, or money—are as old as medicine. Fees, their level, problems in collection, and the like are found in many of the books of the Hippocratic Corpus.

2. E.D. Pellegrino and D. Thomasma, *For the Patient's Good* (forthcoming). In this book Thomasma and I unpack the notion of patient good: to examine its components and the order of their moral importance.

3. H. Cushing, *Consecratio Medici and Other Papers* (1929). See also, Pellegrino, "What is a Profession?" *Journal of Allied Health* 12 (1983): 168–76.

4. The Hippocratic Oath is still the most common public declaration of voluntary assumption of ethical obligations inherent in medicine. Other oaths like the so-called Oath of Maimonides, the Oath of Geneva, World Health Organization, etc., all carry the same message of commitment to the good of others.

5. Studies of the experiences with physician gatekeeping are beginning to appear. Samples of such studies are these: John M. Eisenberg, ''The Internist as Gatekeeper,'' *Annals of Internal Medicine*, 102, no. 1 (April 1985): 537–43; A.R. Somers, ''And Who Shall be the Gatekeeper? The Role of the Physician in the Health Care Delivery System,'' *Inquiry* 20 (1983): 301–313; J.K. Inglehart, ''Medicaid Turns to Prepaid Managed Care,'' *New England Journal of Medicine*, 308 (1983): 976–80; S.H. Moore, ''Cost Containment Through Risk Sharing by Primary Care Physicians,'' *New England Journal of Medicine* 300 (1979): 1359–62. Some of the ethical ramifications of prepayment plans are outlined in *AMA News*, January 2, 1987.

6. *Summary Report of the Graduate Medical Education National Advisory Committee to the Secretary*, Department of Health and Human Services (Washington: GPO, 1980).

7. Paul Starr, *The Social Transformation of American Medicine* (New York: Basic Books, 1982), 514.

8. E.D. Pellegrino, ''Toward a Reconstruction of Medical Morality: The Primacy of the Act of Profession and the Fact of Illness,'' *Journal of Medicine and Philosophy* , 4, no. 1 (March 1979): 32–56.

9. Figures for national expenditures for goods, commodities and services are difficult to evaluate. For our purposes the important point is the relative order of magnitude of specific health and medical care expenditures as compared with other expenditures. For current statistics see: United States Department of Commerce, Bureau of Economic Analysis: Survey of Current Business (July issue annually).

Chapter 23

The Social Obligations of Health Care Practitioners

David T. Ozar

Almost everyone would agree that when one makes a voluntary commitment to act in a certain way for a specific individual or group, one thereby comes to have an *obligation* to so act. Thus, health care practitioners certainly do have some social obligations, namely the obligations to specific individuals and groups that each has voluntarily undertaken. We can also speak meaningfully of a general, underlying social obligation that all humans, including health care practitioners, have to keep the commitments they make.

But are there other kinds of obligations that health care practitioners have toward others? Do they have any obligations toward others that are not dependent on their voluntary commitments to specific individuals and groups but are incumbent on them for other reasons? It is obligations of this sort (if there are any) that will be referred to as *social obligations* throughout the remainder of this chapter. The aim of the chapter is to inquire whether health care practitioners have any such obligations.

The first step will be to examine several answers to the following question: Do human beings in general have any obligations toward other humans that are not dependent on their voluntary commitments to specific individuals and groups but are incumbent on them for other reasons? If the answer to this question is yes, then health care practitioners will have some social obligations (in our sense of the term) simply because they are members of the human community. If the answer is no, then the only social obligations that health care practitioners could have would be obligations specifically due to their roles as health care practitioners. The first part of this chapter examines several important accounts of the foundations of social obligation.

In either case, whether the first question is answered yes or no, the second step will be to ask whether health care practitioners have any social obligations specifically due to their roles as health care practitioners. If the answer to either the first or the second question is yes, then a third question must be asked: When health care practitioners' social obligations come into conflict with one another or with the obligations toward specific individuals and groups that they have voluntarily undertaken (especially their obligations towards specific patients), how should such conflicts be resolved?

GENERAL SOCIAL OBLIGATIONS

Libertarianism

Do human beings in general have any obligations toward other humans that are not dependent on their voluntary commitments to specific individuals and groups but are incumbent on them for other reasons? One important answer to this question holds that we have obligations only to specific individuals with whom we deal and no obligations beyond those. The most frequent defense of this answer rests on the claim that there is, at bottom, only one fundamental rule of morality for all relations between persons. This rule: Respect people's liberty. That is, do not interfere with people's efforts to choose, act, and live in accord with their own values, goals, ideals, or principles provided only that their actions in turn respect the comparable liberty of others. (In practice, this view of our obligations towards others primarily concerns the interactions of competent adults. Other principles are taken to govern the dealings of competent adults with other humans who are not at the time competent. Other principles also govern the special circumstance in which someone is deliberately violating our own or another person's liberty.)

This approach to morality has several names, the most distinctive being *libertarianism*. Libertarianism does not recognize any obligations between persons beyond the original obligation to respect others' liberty and those obligations that have been voluntarily undertaken by the persons involved. Consequently, there is no general category of social obligations that are incumbent upon all human beings (or all competent human beings), but only such obligations as human beings actually undertake in their voluntary dealings with other human beings (plus the fundamental obligation to respect others' liberty).

But could it not be the case that people undertake obligations to "society"? From one perspective it is hard to see how this could be the case, because it is hard to see what "undertaking an obligation to society" could mean. When I agree to act in a certain way for someone's benefit, undertaking an obligation towards him or her, there is a "someone" who benefits and who, in most instances, undertakes to act in a certain way towards me in return. But both elements of this common relationship seem to be lacking in regard to "obligations towards society." *Who* is the beneficiary of the action that I commit myself to perform? *Who* is it who might act for my benefit in some way in return? "Society," one version of libertarianism would argue, is simply a word we use to refer generically to all the people in a given place who interact with each other, undertaking thousands of obligations to act for one another in thousands of different ways, but none of them undertaking to act in some way for the benefit of *all* the rest. From this point of view, there is nothing concrete enough in the idea of society to enable us to make good sense of "undertaking an obligation towards society."

So in this version of libertarianism, there are no general social obligations that all humans have beyond the fundamental rule to respect others' liberty. Nor is there something called "society" to which they might undertake obligations by their voluntary acts. Instead there are only the dealings of individual humans with other specific individuals and groups, dealings that tend to generate freely chosen commitments and their concomitant obligations. There are no social obligations (in our sense of the term).

But there is another way to look at the notion of society within the libertarian tradition. John Locke, a famous seventeenth century British political philosopher, claimed that when a group of people voluntarily place the use of force—for the punishment of wrongdoers among them (e.g., those who violate others' liberty) and for protection from external enemies—into the hands of a select few, then the whole group form themselves by doing so into a new kind of actor within the human community, a collective actor that Locke calls "civil society." They do this by each voluntarily contracting with all the others to be governed by the decisions of the majority; that is, they agree, in the "social contract" that establishes civil society, to be obligated to carry out these majority decisions.

There is much more to be said about all this, of course. For a civil society cannot function effectively without establishing a government that makes and enforces laws in the name of the whole group and that is supported from the property of the whole group. There are also some important limitations, Locke argues, on the range of decisions by the majority (or its government) that are obligatory for the citizens. In particular, citizens have no obligation under the original social contract to give up their property to the society or its government for the improvement, for example, of anyone's life or living conditions. In the original social contract they have committed their property only to the extent needed to prevent crime, to try, convict, and punish wrongdoers, and to protect the society from external enemies. Since taking a person's property is violating his or her liberty and other takings were not originally agreed to, all other takings of property must be specifically and voluntarily agreed to either directly or through the people's representatives in the government.

What is important for our purpose in that there *is* here a notion of society as a thing toward which an individual person can have obligations by reason of participation in the original social contract. Each member of the community participates in this contract either directly by choosing to participate in a society's political life or, Locke also holds, simply by living there and enjoying the benefits of the society's increased social and economic potential. Thus everyone who lives within a political community has obligations, which are clearly social obligations in our sense, to obey the laws of the land and to contribute from his or her property for the maintenance of the society's appropriate legislative, executive, judicial, and military activities. But beyond providing what the decisions of the majority properly require, no one in a Lockean civil society has any other obligations except the fundamental obligation to respect others' liberty and such obligations to specific individuals and groups as each one might voluntarily undertake.

There are many other traditions of moral reflection that, like the Lockean version of libertarianism, begin with an understanding of human obligations generally and draw out from it an understanding of significant obligations to society. Three of these are, like the two versions of libertarianism already discussed, important modes of moral and social reflection in contemporary American society. Unlike the Libertarian model, each of them holds that humans *do* have social obligations simply by reason of their membership in the human community. Each also claims that our social obligations are more fundamental and more inclusive than the social obligations acknowledged in Lockean libertarianism. The three traditions we shall examine are the golden rule tradition, the utilitarian or value-maximizing tradition, and the human rights tradition.

These three traditions differ from one another in many ways. But about one thing they agree, namely, that the picture of human beings that is found in both versions of libertarianism is seriously flawed because it omits something essential. All three of these views hold that libertarianism, in both its versions, is mistaken in presupposing that social relationships are something "added on" to already complete human beings. For all three of these traditions, a human being's relationships with other humans are part of the essential and intrinsic makeup of that human being. Although there are humans who do not actualize this aspect of their humanity to any great extent, that is to be viewed as a deficit in their lives. Their relative isolation should not be taken as the norm of full humanness.

Furthermore, when we are talking about obligations—about how people ought to act— the social aspect of human beings must be included in the account. It is not surprising, then, that each of these traditions has an important place for social obligations within its account of morality.

The core of the golden rule tradition is the principle that what is right (or wrong) for one person in a given situation is similarly right (or wrong) for any other person in an identical situation. Many philosophers call this the *principle of universality*. With regard to an action that has an impact on another person, for that action to be morally defensible, it must be the case that the actor would choose, and could reasonably choose, to be the "recipient" of an identical action by someone else under identical circumstances. In short, "Do unto others as you would have them do unto you."

The golden rule, developed into a more abstract and generalized rule of morality by the eighteenth century German philosopher Immanuel Kant, was held by him to be an unavoidable requirement of rationality itself. The alternative, he argued, was to live by contradictions. A contemporary version of this approach, developed by the Harvard philosopher John Rawls, urges that any social, legal, or economic regime that we choose to live under must be such that it would be chosen over alternative regimes by everyone who might live under it, even by those who might benefit the least. It must be reasonable for the latter to say, "This is the best social system of those that could really come into being under the present circumstances." Many contemporary social systems appear to fail this test miserably.

One implication of the golden rule tradition is that every human has an obligation to support only such social, political, legal, and economic structures as could reasonably be chosen (as the best structures actually available at the time) by everyone who has to live under them, even those in the least desirable social positions. This conclusion applies not only to the choice of a whole social system, but also to each rule and structure of social, political, legal, and economic life. One important social obligation implied by the golden rule tradition is that each of us must attend to the impact of such structures on *everyone in the community* whenever we select and support these structures, both directly through voting or other political action and indirectly through our acceptance and toleration of what happens to be produced by the political process and other processes of social change.

Moreover, as Rawls argues in detail, a social system constructed on this sort of golden rule principle will place a high premium on *equality*, both equality of civil and political liberty as well as equality of property and of access to the resources of which ordinary life depends. This is because many social structures that lead to unequal distributions of resources make the condition of the people on the bottom of the social ladder worse off. According to the golden rule principle, however, such inequalities will be moral only when they yield—by motivating some people to produce more and by implementing structures to distribute the results appropriately—a better situation for the people on the bottom as well as for everyone else. Consequently the Lockean prohibition against property being taken from some citizens by the government in order to secure or improve the well-being of others (except to fund the proper activities of government) is at odds with the golden rule tradition. Our obligation to take account of the impact of our institutions on everyone in the society will certainly require that, if there are enough resources to do so, we must direct our society's resources toward filling the basic needs of every citizen.

The implications of the Golden Rule tradition for social obligations on the part of health care practitioners are threefold. First, as in the Lockean version of libertarianism, all members of the community are obligated to obey and contribute their property to support properly conducted activities of government.

Second, in contrast to Lockean libertarianism, all members of the community are obligated to work for the restructuring of all or part of the social system insofar as it falls short of taking adequate account of the least well off within it. They have this obligation not by reason of having made commitments to these persons, or to the whole community in some sort of "social contract," but by reason of the character of sound moral reasoning, indeed of rationality itself.

Third, since every member of the community is obligated to work for a proper social system insofar as he or she has opportunity and since health care practitioners have greater influence than many other groups over the community's use of resources to meet people's health care needs, they are obligated to use their greater influence to assure that the least well off receive health care to the extent and in a manner consistent with golden rule principles. Health care practitioners are not obligated in this respect for any reason that does not apply to everyone else; all are obligated to work for a proper social system insofar as they have the opportunity. But because of health care practitioners generally greater influence in medical matters, they are, if not "more obligated," ordinarily obligated to do more.

Utilitarianism

Another tradition, the utilitarian or value-maximizing tradition, also is concerned with taking account of everyone in the society. Although the term *utilitarian* is used in many ways, some even derogatory, it refers historically to the tradition that holds that an action is morally obligatory if it is the one (of all available alternatives) that maximizes the realization of value in the lives of those affected. Thus, when my actions are expected to affect others, it is incumbent on me to weigh the positive values and also the pain, loss, and disvalue that my actions may bring about for each of the persons affected—myself and everyone else. What I ought to do is the available action that will bring about the greatest net value. Like the golden rule tradition, the utilitarian tradition claims there is a "socialness" of obligation in every action that might affect someone else.

The best known defenders of the utilitarian or value-maximizing tradition have argued strongly for representative government as the most effective means of securing the social, political, legal, and economic structures that would maximize values for a given society. Our fundamental obligation to attend to the effects of our actions on everyone entails that we are obligated to obey and support proper activities of government and to work for the restructuring of the whole social system or any of its parts that fail to bring about the greatest net value, among alternatives available at the time, for everyone who is affected. In this respect, the implications of the utilitarian tradition are much like those of the golden rule tradition. Especially in the contemporary versions of this tradition, great emphasis is placed on equality of civil and political liberties because of their crucial role in securing for everyone the best possible social system.

The utilitarian tradition explicitly acknowledges that the pains of some may have to be tragically accepted in particular situations in which the best realization of value for everyone affected makes them. But it is also concerned in a special way with the condition of persons whose needs are greatest or are least met in any given social situation. Most theorists in this tradition believe that the use of a given amount of resources to relieve pain and meet people's basic needs constitutes a greater realization of value than the use of the same measure of resources to produce positive benefits and pleasures for persons not in pain or persons whose basic needs are already met. So the Lockean prohibition against property being taken from some citizens by the government in order to secure or improve the well-being of others (except to fund the proper activities of government) is also rejected by the utilitarian tradition, unless in particular cases the "transfer costs," which must include the lost sense of security of those whose property is taken, come to outweigh the benefit of the transfer.

The Human Rights Tradition

Another tradition approaches moral obligations in terms of human rights. Every member of the human community is possessed of a fundamental worth or dignity that implies obligations on the part of everyone else to respect it. There are many different accounts of the rights that derive from this fundamental dignity or worth and many different accounts of the obligations which it entails. Some thinkers see these rights and obligations solely in terms of noninterference by others in the free choices and the freely chosen actions of others, in a manner that closely parallels the libertarian tradition. But many others claim that respect for human worth or dignity requires the acknowledgment not only of the civil and political rights that secure a person's ability to participate, at least to some extent, in a structure of representative government, but also of rights to the resources necessary to fill each person's basic needs. This second, more expansive human rights approach would hold for rights to basic nutrition, housing, and clothing, as well as basic health care, in any social situation with sufficient resources to provide for them. Like the golden rule and the utilitarian traditions, this version of the human rights tradition opposes libertarian constraints on government taking of property to secure or improve the well-being of other members of a society.

According to the human rights tradition, many of our most basic obligations to others derive not from any voluntary agreements we have made with them, but simply from their worth and dignity as fellow human beings. We may be able to fulfill some of these obligations to our fellow humans on a one-by-one basis. But many of them cannot be fulfilled without actions directed at changing the structures of human societies. Consequently, particularly in the more expansive version of the human rights tradition (as in the golden rule and the utilitarian traditions), everyone in the community has obligations, each according to his or her opportunity, to work for an appropriate social system, restructuring it in whole or in part insofar as it falls short.

The human rights, golden rule, and utilitarian traditions each have much more to say about the social obligations of humans generally (there are important variants of each of these approaches to morality that have not been considered here). But, as this brief summary has made clear, all three traditions can be seen to argue that we do have obligations to others over and above the obligations to specific individuals and groups that we voluntarily undertake and over and above the obligations stressed in Lockean libertarianism to obey and support appropriate actions of any government acting in the name of the majority. We have obligations in regard to the development, and if necessary the restructuring, of an appropriate system of social structures, and we have particular obligations in regard to meeting people's basic needs and rectifying the condition of those who are least benefited by the social system. (Each of these obligations is also frequently discussed as an obligation of *social justice*. But since the concept of justice is itself used in a variety of distinct ways, each of which requires thoughtful exposition and reflection, it has seemed simpler to focus here on the substance of these obligations and on the reasons proposed for them in the several traditions of moral reflection that have been discussed.)

If one of these three accounts of morality and social obligation is correct, then obviously health care practitioners have these social obligations, as do the rest of their fellow humans.

THE SOCIAL OBLIGATIONS OF HEALTH CARE PRACTITIONERS

We now need to ask if health care practitioners have any social obligations specifically due to their roles as health care practitioners. As was said at the outset, health care practitioners obviously have whatever obligations to specific individuals and groups that each has voluntarily undertaken. But again our question here is about social obligations, that is, obligations to others that are incumbent on health care practitioners for other reasons.

The key notion here is the notion of *profession*. Is it the case that in choosing to be health care professionals, people undertake obligations to others over and above their voluntary obligations to the specific individuals and groups, especially patients and colleagues, with whom they deal?

One view of the professional in health care takes health care practice to be no different in principle from the activity of any producer selling his or her wares in the marketplace. The health care practitioner has a product to sell and makes mutually agreed upon arrangements with any interested purchasers. Beyond the fundamental obligation not to coerce, cheat, or defraud purchasers (i.e., the producer must respect the liberty of others in the marketplace), the health care practitioner has no obligations to patients or anyone else other than the obligations he or she voluntarily undertakes with specific individuals or groups. Let us call this the ''commercial picture'' of health care practice.

In contrast with this picture is the ''normative picture'' of the health care professions. In the normative picture, the health care practitioner has joined a group of persons who have made, both individually and collectively, a set of commitments to the community at large. They have undertaken certain obligations, not by means of commitments to specific individuals or groups, but by means of a commitment to the whole larger community whom they, as a group of experts, serve. We shall survey these obligations in a moment, but first we need to describe in more detail the general circumstances surrounding the relationships between the health care professions and the larger community and between health care professionals and their patients.

The most characteristic feature of a profession is its expertise in a matter of great importance to the community at large. Moreover, the kind of expertise that we associate with a profession is also unavoidably exclusive. It involves knowledge and experience sufficiently esoteric that neither one can be gained effectively except under the direction of someone who is already an expert in the field. Consequently only the experts are in a position to recognize if another practitioner is expert or not and only they can give a timely judgement (i.e., before irreparable damage has been done) of the quality of a particular instance of professional practice.

Since the larger community is dependent upon such experts for effective health care, which it values greatly, it is in the community's interest, both individually and collectively, to place health care decisions to a significant extent into the hands of these experts. But to do so is to grant a great deal of power to the experts. Nevertheless the community does this, not only granting to health care professionals a great deal of decision-making power over people's well-being, but entrusting to these professionals the task of supervising how this power is used.

Compare the power granted to the health care professionals with, for example, the power granted to politicians in government. The community grants to politicians power over people's well-being without fully trusting the politicians to use it well or to supervise the exercise of such power. Instead the community supports a complex and inefficient system of checks and balances within government, periodic elections, a nosey free press, and other structures to maintain close supervision on the politicians' performance. But for health care professionals, no such close scrutiny or persistent distrust is maintained.

How then does the community at large assure itself that so much power will not be abused by health care professionals? The answer is by instituting health care *professionals* (as professions are understood in the normative picture). Each profession and each individual professional is committed to using this power according to norms mutually acceptable to the community and the expert group, norms that assure the community that the experts will use the power in such a way as to secure the well-being of the people whom they serve.

According to this normative picture of the health care professions, then, each health care practitioner clearly has important social obligations. We can describe these obligations briefly under seven headings: (1) expertise, (2) individual and collective control of practice, (3) relationship to clients, (4) central values, (5) impact on cultural values, (6) distribution of care, and (7) limits of professional obligation.

Expertise. The original reason for granting special decision-making power to health care professionals is their expertise. Obviously one important social obligation of a health care practitioner, then, is to maintain and improve his or her expertise and to work effectively to maintain and improve the expertise of other members of the profession and of the profession as a whole.

Individual and Collective Control. Because of the importance of health care to the community, and because of the necessarily exclusive character of the expertise needed to provide such care effectively, the community grants to the profession as a group—and individual patients grant to individual members of the profession—an amazing degree of unsupervised control over details of their work. For their part, the members of the health care professions are obligated by their commitments as professionals to use this power, not primarily for their own aggrandizement, but for the well-being of their patients. In the same way, the power given the profession as a whole—in its task of training and certifying new practitioners, in its relations with other groups, and in its management of its own internal affairs—must be used not just to benefit the members, but primarily to benefit their patients.

Relationship to Clients. There are many models of the proper relationship of a professional to patients and other clients. Of these, some place clients in the position of passive receivers of assistance, without any significant voice in matters that profoundly affect their lives and well-being. Others place the practitioner simply at the service of the patient's or client's ends. Others strongly affirm the moral status of patient and practitioner alike. Health care professionals are obligated to choose thoughtfully from among these models and to work to establish a proper relationship between themselves and their patients in daily practice.

Central Values. Every professional group ascribes to certain ranked values and uses them to resolve complex issues of priorities within the setting of actual practice. Each of the health care professions is obligated to identify thoughtfully the central values of their specific form of practice, and health care professionals are obligated to guide their professional practice in accord with these values.

Among the values proposed as central for the health care professions are life i.e., continued biological life; health, both as the experience of well-being and as conformity to physiological and statistical norms; relief of pain and discomfort; maximal functioning, relative both to the capacities of the species and to the capacities of the individual; autonomous decision making by the patient whenever possible; advocacy of the patients' values to the greatest extent possible, especially whenever the patient is not competent; maintenance of the profession's preferred patterns of practice; aesthetic considerations; and understanding, self-care, and health maintenance by the patient.

Impact on Cultural Values. Many professionals, by reason of the authority of their expertise in the eyes of the larger community and by reason of the importance of the benefits their practice secures for the larger community, have an impact on the larger community beyond securing these benefits. The impact particularly affects the community's collective priorities regarding certain means helpful in achieving the benefits which the professions' practice secures. Thus, for example, the emphasis within contemporary medicine on crisis intervention and cure and the relative lack of emphasis, until very recently, on health education, health maintenance, and prevention have over the years produced a comparable set of priorities regarding health care in the minds of large segments of the public. The members of the health care professions have an obligation to be sensitive to this broader, "cultural" impact on the larger community and to direct it thoughtfully insofar as it is in their power, both individually and collectively.

Distribution of Care. The broad social, economic, and legal structures that largely determine how resources (both health care and other kinds of resources) are distributed within the society and within the health care system itself ought ideally to be guided by general principles of social obligation like those discussed in the first part of this chapter. Health care practitioners' particular obligations in the application of such general principles, based on their generally greater influence on questions of health care distribution, have already been mentioned. In addition, many health care practitioners make decisions within care settings that also impact on the distribution of health care resources (although less profoundly). Do the health care profession's or the health care professionals' commitments to the larger community include a commitment to support a particular principle or pattern of distribution?

Many members of the health professions would argue that health professionals' commitments have nothing to say about the ethics of distributing resources. Mark Siegler has argued, however, that every physician is committed, by reason of his or her profession, to respond to patients' health care needs in proportion to need and therefore to also work for systems of distribution that make sufficient resources available to physicians so that they can fulfill this commitment. The question is a difficult one. But at least we can say that each health care practitioner is obligated to examine his or her professional conscience carefully in order to determine if the commitment that is the basis of his or her professional obligations has any implications specifically in regard to the distribution of health care resources.

Limits of Professional Obligation. Besides these important categories of social obligation—which derive from the health care practitioner's commitment as a professional if the normative picture of professions is accepted—it is important to note that any coherent account of professions will entail that there are limits to professional obligation. There are areas of a health care professional's life that are not subject to the norms of professional life. There are conflicts between professional obligations that cannot be resolved from within the norms of the profession. There are flaws in each profession and consequent obligations to work to rectify them rather than to blindly follow them. There may be complicated reservations in a health care practitioner's affiliation with a profession known to be flawed in significant ways. There may well be times when a practitioner's obligation as a professional is clear-cut, but he or she recognizes a more fundamental obligation, grounded in a more fundamental rule of morality, which overrides it—the professional equivalent of conscientious refusal or civil disobedience.

Every category mentioned in this part of the chapter presents a set of possible social obligations that the health care practitioner ought to examine carefully. Professionals' views about the nature of professions and about the specific obligations that flow from professions will differ. But the possibility that the health care practitioner's professional commitment gives rise to a significant class of social obligations cannot be lightly set aside.

CONFLICT OF OBLIGATIONS

It seems that when obligations conflict, those grounded in more fundamental and more broadly based moral principles ought take precedence over those grounded solely in our chosen commitments, unless special considerations grounded themselves in more fundamental, broadly based principles should indicate otherwise. Consequently, if conflicts between social obligations arise, those grounded in the fundamental principles sketched in the section "General Social Obligations" would take precedence over principles grounded in a person's commitment to a profession, with the exception just noted. Similarly, obligations of both these kinds would take precedence over obligations based on a person's particular voluntary commitments to specific individuals or groups, with the same exception. Consider the following case.

Case Example

You are a cardiologist practicing at University Hospital and also sit on its transplantation committee. You have a patient, Michael Plumner, a 45-year-old male who is afflicted with amyloidosis. The disease has focused its effects, for reasons unknown, on Plumner's heart. Several weeks ago you had to hospitalize him because of his deteriorating heart function, which now resembles that of a victim of advanced cardiomyopathy. His only hope of survival is a heart transplant, a procedure that is available at University Hospital. Plumner is now in the category of "most urgent" organ recipients for heart, along with two patients suffering from cardiomyopathy.

You and Plumner have had many conversations about his disease. He has indicated how he wishes his care to be handled in many respects. Among other things, he has asked you to promise him that, in event of his death, you will remind his family firmly of his wish to give his body to medical researchers studying amyloidosis; and you have so promised. He has also offered you a large financial bonus if you would use your position on the hospital's transplantation committee, which selects recipients of transplant organs, to make sure that the first available heart with a favorable tissue match will be given to him. How does the ranking of social obligations just proposed apply to your obligations in this situation?

First, consider your promise to Plumner. Obligations based on fundamental principles of morality and obligations based on professional commitment are to take precedence over obligations based on a person's particular voluntary commitments to specific individuals. But neither of the former sets of obligations would seem to conflict with your speaking firmly to Plumner's family about the disposition of his body. In addition, neither set of obligations would seem to *require* such action on your part (as it might if Plumner's disease was highly contagious and research on it was much more urgently needed). Therefore, if Plumner's family resisted offering his body for research, you might—if you had not made a promise to him about it—justifiably refrain from pressuring them. But given your voluntary commitment to Plumner to do so, you would be obligated in this case to speak forcefully to them about it.

What about Plumner's proposal that you use your position and influence to secure him the next available organ in return for a sizeable financial reward? If you had voluntarily agreed to such an arrangement, would you be obligated to carry it out? By the same token, is this a kind of arrangement to which you could morally commit yourself? The answer to these questions seems quite clearly to be no. The reasons are twofold. First, it seems clear that the obligations that a physician undertakes as a member of the medical profession preclude acting as an advocate for a patient specifically for financial gain rather than on the basis of the relationship between patient and professional.

Second, the moral criteria that should be used in determining the distribution of scarce life-saving resources, including organs for transplant, should be determined on the basis of fundamental moral principles, not by whatever particular business arrangements happen to be made between individuals. For both reasons, it would be morally unjustifiable for a physician to make a commitment like that proposed by Plumner, and it would also be immoral for a physician who made such an agreement to carry it out. The priority here is again that obligations founded on the commitment to a profession or on fundamental principles of morality should take precedence over obligations based solely on voluntary agreements with specific individuals.

Finally, having assumed that you would not agree to Plumner's proposal, let us consider how you should act when Plumner's case comes before the transplantation committee. Let us suppose that among the many professional obligations that you would have toward a patient is a genuine obligation to act as the patient's advocate within the complex bureaucracy of the health care system. Since you sit on the transplantation committee, you are involved in the decision as to whether Plumner or one of the other two equally urgent patients should receive the next donor heart (assuming equally successful tissue matches).

May you prefer Plumner to the others on the basis of your professional obligation to act as your patient's advocate within the system?

If it is true that the criteria that should be used in allocating scarce life-saving resources should be determined on the basis of fundamental moral principles, then unless these principles proved to be neutral between Plumner and the other patients under consideration, you would be obligated to set aside your advocacy of Plumner, as his physician, while you played your role in the deliberations of the transplantation committee. This is because obligations grounded in fundamental moral principles are to take precedence over obligations grounded in professional commitment (or so it has been proposed).

This case is only one example of how the various obligations examined above should be ranked. It would take many cases to examine carefully the comparative moral importance of all the elements of social obligation that have been discussed. In addition, the proposed manner of ranking social obligations will remain largely abstract until each health care practitioner has reflected carefully on the foundations of social obligation sketched in the first section above and determined to his or her satisfaction that one of them, some consistent combination of them, or some other foundation is the correct basis of social morality. The practitioner will also need to identify the commercial picture, the normative picture, or some other portrayal of professions and professional obligation as the most accurate representation of professional commitment.

At that point, the thoughtful reader will be able to identify his or her most important social obligations as a health care practitioner and to carry on the enterprise, undoubtedly already begun, of living up to them. The aim of this chapter has not been to resolve the question of which of these views is correct, but to explain a variety of positions and categories to facilitate the reader's thoughtful reflection.

BIBLIOGRAPHY

Libertarianism

Engelhardt, H. Tristram. *The Foundations of Bioethics*. Oxford: Oxford University Press, 1986.

Locke, John. *Two Treatises of Government*. 1690.

Machan, Tibor, ed. *The Libertarian Reader*. Totowa, N.J.: Rowman & Allenheld, 1982.

The Golden Rule Tradition

Daniels, Norman. *Just Health Care*. New York: Cambridge University Press, 1985.

Kant, Immanuel. *Foundations of the Metaphysics of Morals*, trans. Lewis Beck White (New York: Bobbs-Merrill, 1959).

Murphy, Jeffrey. *Kant: The Philosopher of Right*. New York: Macmillan, 1970.

Rawls, John. *A Theory of Justice*. Cambridge, Mass.: Belknap Press of Harvard University Press, 1971.

The Utilitarian or Value-Maximizing Tradition

Bentham, Jeremy. *Introduction to the Principles of Morals and Legislation*. 1789.

Mill, John Stuart. *Utilitarianism*. 1863.

President's Commission for the Study of Ethical Problems in Medicine and Biomedical and Behavioral Research. *Securing Access to Health Care*. Washington, D.C.: GPO, 1983.

The Human Rights Tradition

Ramsey, Paul. *The Patient as Person*. New Haven, Conn.: Yale University Press, 1970.

Shue, Henry. *Basic Rights*. Princeton, N.J.: Princeton University Press, 1980.

Veatch, Robert. *A Theory of Medical Ethics*. New York: Basic Books, 1981.

Werhane, P., A. Gini, and D. Ozar, eds. *Philosophical Issues in Human Rights*. New York: Random House, 1985.

Professions and Professional Obligations

Bayles, Michael. *Professional Ethics*. Belmont, Calif.: Wadsworth, 1981.

Camenisch, Paul. *Grounding Professional Ethics in a Pluralistic Society*. New York: Haven, 1983.

Freidson, Eliot. *Profession of Medicine*. New York: Harper & Row, 1970.

Jonsen, Albert, Mark Siegler, and William Winslade. *Clinical Ethics*. New York: Macmillan, 1982.

Ozar, David. "Patients' Autonomy: Three Models of the Professional-Lay Relationship in Medicine." *Theoretical Medicine* 5 (1984): 61–68.

_____. "Social Ethics, The Philosophy of Medicine, and Professional Responsibility." *Theoretical Medicine* 6 (1985): 281–94.

_____. "The Demands of Profession and Their Limits." In *Professional Commitment: Issues and Ethics in Nursing*, edited by M. Smith and C. Quinn. Philadelphia: Saunders, 1987.

Pellegrino, Edmund and David Thomasma. *A Philosophical Basis of Medical Practice*. Oxford: Oxford University Press, 1981.

Siegler, Mark. "A Physician's Perspective on a Right to Health Care," *Journal of the American Medical Association* 244 (1980): 1591–96.

Starr, Paul. *The Social Transformation of American Medicine*. New York: Basic Books, 1982.

Chapter 24

Treatment Refusal for Economic Reasons

Paul J. Reitemeier and Howard Brody

Medicine, throughout its history, has never provided all patients with all the treatment they have either needed or wanted. In some cases of treatment refusal, economics played a role (this statement is a bald truism and merely asserts that health care has been a scarce resource relative to demand). In some such cases, treatment was not given because its provision required financial expenditures beyond the means of that particular patient. In other cases, a patient voluntarily requested that treatment not be given because of a judgment that the money could be better used by the family for other purposes; The physician who acquiesces in such a request merely displays respect for the patients' autonomous choice.

What has changed to make treatment refusal for economic reasons a discrete ethical issue? In those older cases, the economic consequences of treatment could be viewed as restricted to the patient, family, and perhaps the local community. Today, health care technology and its attendant costs make it reasonable to view the consequences of rising health care costs as national in scope. There is thus increasing justification to view the physician's duty to constrain costs as a matter of general social responsibility. Further, physicians and hospitals may have their own financial interests (through prospective payment systems) in reducing costs and thus, potentially, in underserving patients; thus the dangers of conflict of interest are added to other morally troublesome features of nontreatment.

The modern physician must be both financially realistic about the actual costs of treating patients and still strive to remain faithful to the precepts and principles he or she has inherited from the Hippocratic tradition. While we recognize that this is no easy balance to maintain, we feel it is possible to do so. In this chapter we offer several suggestions concerning how physicians may be able to do just that when costs and principles come into conflict.

We begin with three cases which illustrate the sorts of problems associated with treatment refusal for economic reasons, cases which physicians would not have faced 50 or even 25 years ago under the previous health care payment systems but which must be dealt with almost routinely today. We then discuss the two main obligations physicians face in treating patients: the Hippocratic obligation[1] and what has recently been termed the *gatekeeper obligation*. Most of the remainder of the chapter is devoted to a discussion of the relations between the concepts of quality of care and justice and how they both can be responsibly and effectively managed in medical practice. The chapter ends with several recommendations and suggestions for physicians to incorporate into their daily practice. We believe doing so will provide a hedge against inadequate or inefficient health care to the needy as well as against charges of abandonment or unethical callousness on the part of physicians.

CASE EXAMPLE OF TREATMENT REFUSAL

Case 1

A junior resident in internal medicine has completed the physical examination on a 45-year-old woman without noting any abnormalities. Following current guidelines on screening for breast cancer, he orders a screening mammogram. The senior resident with whom he confers notes, "This patient is on Medicaid. They won't pay for a screening mammogram."

"What do you do, then? Do you refuse to order mammograms on your patients who fit the screening criteria? They can hardly afford to pay for that sort of test themselves."

"Oh, I order them, all right; only I don't write down 'screening'. I write, 'question of lump,' or 'outer quadrant thickening'. Then they'll pay for them."

"But isn't that falsifying records?"

"You could call it that. But that sounds better to me than letting patients go without the care I think they need, or battling with an entrenched bureaucracy where I'm sure to lose."

Case 2

Dr. Justin has just spent an hour evaluating Mr. Hobbs, an 87-year-old man with multiple medical problems, in the emergency room. He complains to the emergency room nurse about his limited options.

"The family has had it—they've been trying to care for him at home while working full-time, and after several years of that, they're plain tired out. Locally, we don't have what they really need, which is respite care—a nonskilled nursing home bed we could put him in for several days to a week, just to let the family get a breather. They really don't want to put him in a nursing home for good, but if this keeps up they'll be driven to it."

"I think if I send Mr. Hobbs back home, he'll risk getting worse, mainly because of the family's reduced ability to care for his needs. And yet none of his medical problems is demonstrably worse than his baseline. I really don't have a diagnosis that will justify admission to an acute care hospital. The family is begging me to admit him for a couple of days of observation, and I'm sympathetic to their request. But if I admit Mr. Hobbs, the Medicare people may refuse to pay, and the utilization review people will be after me as soon as the chart is reviewed."

Case 3

"Who should I call to get this guy admitted?" Dr. Wilson asks the emergency department triage nurse. "He's got emphysema and bronchitis, and his blood gases are lousy. We can't send him out."

"Well, you can't get him admitted here, either. He has no insurance."

"What do you mean? He needs hospitalization."

"You haven't worked here very long, Doctor. This hospital is concerned about its financial stability, and they've told us we can't accept any patients without insurance. We'll have to ship him over to County—unless you can certify, for sure, that he's too unstable to be transported."

"Well, I can't exactly say he's that unstable. But I'd be worried about him all the same. The cross-town trip, plus the delay in their ER, certainly couldn't improve him any."

These three cases illustrate a longstanding but only recently recognized tension between the Hippocratic and the gatekeeper obligations. The former demands that health professionals do whatever is medically indicated for their patients; the latter obligates them to act responsibly in conserving scarce resources on behalf of society.

Recently, three categories of treatment refusal have received a great deal of attention: withholding of nutrition and hydration; cessation of treatment for the irreversibly comatose; and withholding of treatment from severely handicapped newborns. Economic reasons may coexist with other kinds of reasons for treatment refusal in all three categories, but there are enough unique features in each category to require that they be dealt with in other chapters of this volume. We will accordingly not address them directly here, although the principles and decision strategies we suggest apply to those categories as well.

GATEKEEPER AND HIPPOCRATIC OBLIGATIONS

The notion of the physician as gatekeeper is relatively new. It focuses on the physician as an agent of society charged with what the President's Commission on medical ethics has called "responsible stewardship."[2] Since the cost of medical care in the U.S. is steadily growing as a percentage of the gross national product while the measurable health benefits produced seem to be leveling off, the pressure has increased for some method of containing the cost spiral. Several proposed methods—notably the prospective payment or DRG system in hospitals and HMOs, PPOs, IPAs, and other forms of prepaid outpatient care—place some of the responsibility for containing costs directly on the physician's shoulders. The primary care physician is expected to "close the gate" and not let some patients have access to some forms of expensive treatment, even though there is a chance that the patient could derive some benefit from the treatment.

Many would claim that the gatekeeper role represents a premature and inappropriate response to economic pressure. Some observers argue that even though costs are rising, the total spent on health care in our wealthy country is still not so high that a true crisis could be said to exist.[3] Others insist that the personal physician must be spared the responsibility of making gatekeeper decisions and that we should respond by making more health resources available or by forcing nonphysician administrators to assume responsibility for denying care.[4] However, it should be noted that these suggestions ultimately only displace the problem without solving it. As an example, assume that we were suddenly able to perfect a totally implantable artificial heart. It is estimated that about 50,000 patients in the U.S. could benefit from this annually. However, the costs of the device plus the surgical implantation and aftercare could easily reach $150,000 to $200,000 per patient, for a total annual budget of between 7.5 and 10 billion dollars for this single medical treatment.

What policy choices are open? We might provide only a limited number of devices and make physicians the gatekeepers to weed out all but the neediest patients (or perhaps the ones who would show the most benefit). We might ration access to the devices by blanket administrative criteria (e.g., no one over age 55, or no one with any renal failure, etc.). This would spare physicians from most of the gatekeeper responsibility, but would probably also lead to arbitrary decisions such that some patients receiving the device might get less benefit than some denied the device would have gotten. We might provide the devices for everyone, and either cut those billions of dollars from other forms of health care (AIDS research? elective cosmetic surgery? prenatal care for poor women?) or else take money slated for some other societal need (Social Security? state parks? space exploration?) Or we might simply refuse to produce the device and knowingly allow 50,000 people per year die who might have been saved. This list of policy choices does not prove that the gatekeeper role for physicians is ethically superior to all alternatives. It does show that those alternatives which avoid placing the physician in the gatekeeper role have heavy price tags of their own.

The newly recognized gatekeeper role is commonly contrasted with the more traditional Hippocratic role, which requires the individual physician to do whatever will benefit the individual patient.[5] To most physicians and health workers, practicing good medicine *means* bringing all of one's knowledge, experience, and resources to bear on meeting the needs of each patient, worrying about the cost later if at all. But on further reflection, this "full service" approach has not actually characterized traditional medical practice. Fuchs has pointed out that physicians have always rationed medical care, starting with the allocation of their own limited time in varying amounts to patients with differing needs. Further, our society has always rationed care by ability to pay—which has led to our currently having an estimated 25–35 million uninsured or underinsured Americans.[6] The present need for rationing is simply the result of adding limited technical and economic resources to that always limited resource: the physician's working hours.

Thus the role of physician as gatekeeper is not new, but it has taken on a new dimension in the kinds of decisions it requires. These new decisions, which focus on the need to pay for medical care, create the sorts of dilemmas pictured in the three cases described above. The question of whether care should be provided when the flesh is willing but the wallet is weak has implications both for social policy and for the trust inherent in the physician-patient relationship.

QUALITY OF CARE AND JUSTICE

Detractors of the gatekeeper role allege that impoverished quality of care will be the first result of any constraint upon the physician's ability to deliver whatever treatment he or she feels is indicated for an individual patient. Allegations of too hasty discharge under the Medicare DRG system and long waiting lines for elective surgery under the National Health Service in the United Kingdom are frequently cited.

Most of us would say that we want two things: the highest possible quality of care and a just system in which all persons have reasonable access to that care. Unfortunately, further clarification of the concepts of justice and quality of care suggest that they are not easy to reconcile unless we are willing to reexamine what we mean by them.

Quality of care is threatened by physician-gatekeeper if we uncritically assume that quality care is equivalent to the *best* care available anywhere. But this is not the way good medical care is, or ever has been, defined. Not every patient receives what might be available at the Mayo Clinic, Johns Hopkins, or Stanford, and yet we do not conclude that they have been denied quality care.

Whether quality of care conflicts with justice depends in large part on the order in which we ask two pertinent questions. If we first ask, "What's the highest quality of care that our science and technology can provide?" and only later ask, "Is the money available to purchase the level of quality for all citizens in need?" we are likely to find that we have defined quality at too expensive a level to allow for an egalitarian distribution of those benefits to all citizens at an affordable price (as the implantable heart example showed). On the other hand, if we first ask, "How much total expenditure of resources is reasonable for health care in a country like ours?" and *then* ask, "How can those resources be distributed so as to allow the highest quality of health care for each citizen within that total budget?" there is no conflict between quality and justice. Historically, the U.S. has defined quality of care by the first approach. The second approach is feasible in a system like the United Kingdom's, where a total health budget is set by the government. U.S. policymakers have been unwilling to propose or implement such a system.

However, to complete this analysis, one needs a more detailed picture of what counts as justice in health care. For example, is it true that egalitarian standards are the relevant measure of a just system? That depends on what sort of a commodity health care is. If good health care is considered as comparable to, say, fine art, then clearly an egalitarian standard is inappropriate. If the highest quality of art is represented by, say, a Picasso, and only a few can afford to own a Picasso, this is not necessarily an unjust state of affairs. But this is not the conception of medical care that most of us hold. We generally assume that at least a basic level of health care is a primary good. This view generates the idea of there being an *entitlement* to basic health care, and it follows from this idea that unequal distribution of access to such basic care is unjust.[7]

Ultimately, what is to count as quality care and what is to count as a just or fair system of distributing care are not for health professionals alone to decide. Broadly based, well-informed, and sustained discussions in social and political arenas at many levels will be required. What sort of health care we will provide for whom—and how it will be paid—is not just a question of how the health professions will be practiced; it is also a question of what sort of society we wish to live in. It is our guess that any resolution to these questions which our society is likely to reach in the next 10 to 20 years will retain or even increase the tension between the gatekeeper and the Hippocratic obligations, not eliminate it.

PRACTICAL RESPONSIBILITIES FOR HEALTH PROFESSIONALS

The ultimate need for a societal consensus cannot serve as a moral cop-out for the health professional, however. Clarification concerning gatekeeper and Hippocratic obligations, quality of care, and justice cannot by itself resolve all problems, but it can point the way to some preliminary conclusions and guidelines.

An important first step is not to assume less discretionary authority than in fact exists. It's easy for a health worker to say, "I just work here; I don't make the rules." But virtually no hospital, HMO, or other institution is totally unresponsive to the requests or demands of professionals who have documented legitimate, unmet medical needs of patients. The Hippocratic obligation then requires the professional to serve as patient advocate in trying to secure the needed care.

Unfortunately, lack of familiarity with payment mechanisms may complicate the advocacy problem. It has been reported that physicians have said to patients, "I know you're still sick, but I have to discharge you because your DRG has expired." The DRG system never orders a hospital or physician to discharge a patient. It simply places a limit on what expenditures will be reimbursed for the total hospitalization. If the patient is quite sick and stays longer, the hospital may lose money on that patient. But since the DRG reimbursement is based on an average, not a maximum, it's quite likely that the hospital will make money on other patients to offset this loss. At any rate, physicians should not be railroaded by jittery hospital fiscal officers into abandoning the Hippocratic obligation entirely. Indeed, a recent California appellate court decision declared that third party payers can be held liable when their cost-containment decisions unreasonably override medical decisions concerning needed medical care. It also noted that physicians may be equally liable if they comply without protest with the payers' limitations on service.

Where reimbursement is in fact too low to allow the institution to function properly, then political pressure must be applied to change the reimbursement structure. This requires clear documentation of the problem. For example, inner city teaching hospitals caring for many sick patients have demonstrated that current DRG rates do not adequately cover their costs.[8] This is why the senior resident's solution in Case 1, over and above any deception involved, is ethically questionable, even though understandable. If health professionals try to serve as patient advocates by "working the system" instead of by openly confronting and documenting inequities and inadequacies, corrective reform will only be delayed.

Legal as well as ethical considerations support the adoption of a strong patient advocacy role, especially in situations like Case 3. Courts have held that a hospital which "dumps" nonpaying patients from the emergency room onto the county or charity hospital will be liable if the patients later suffer harm due to delay in treatment.[9] Some state legislatures have enacted laws to prevent this dumping.

Being a patient advocate involves being able to clearly identify which patient is likely to benefit from which treatment and how much the benefit will be. One way to reduce the tension between the gatekeeper and Hippocratic obligations is to get a better understanding of which treatments produce only marginal benefit.[10] When a treatment is clearly beneficial at only moderate cost, clearly the Hippocratic tradition demands that the physician provide it. When a treatment is futile and provides no benefit (whatever the cost), then the gatekeeper obligation requires doing without it. The Hippocratic obligation is not violated since no benefit is denied the patient. However, many of the most troublesome decisions involve treatments that provide only marginal benefit, that is, the degree of benefit is very slight, even though the cost is great. Common examples of marginal benefit include a CT scan for a patient who most likely has migraine headaches, but who may have a .5 to 1 percent chance of a mass lesion in the brain; or an extra day in the coronary care unit for a patient with an uncomplicated myocardial infarction who has already stayed three days without an arrhythmia. In such cases, the Hippocratic obligation does not disappear from the equation, but it seems quite reasonable to argue that the gatekeeper obligation may take precedence. The problem is that medical research has done a poor job of distinguishing these marginal benefits from more substantial (or cost-effective) benefits. The duty to do a better job in the future rests with the medical profession as a whole, not with the individual practitioner.

Still, while it could be helpful to have much more data, physicians are obligated to use the data that is available to provide responsible gatekeeping. One of the features that defines responsible gatekeeping is the presence of a review process; this ensures that decision makers can be held accountable for the way in which treatment decisions are made.[11] The public does not have a right to snoop concerning every treatment or nontreatment decision made by the professionals working in a hospital, HMO, or other institution. But the public does have a right to be reassured that these decisions are being made in a nonarbitrary way, with adequate medical data, and with an eye toward the moral obligations of the professionals and the institution—especially when the decisions that are being made include the refusal of treatment for primarily economic reasons. In addition to reassuring the public, this review process ought to include a mechanism for internal data gathering; the resulting data can then be shared with other similar institutions. This will both allow an ethical "check" on how decisions are made at various centers and begin to address the lack of good data on which treatments provide only marginal benefits.

What other conditions allow the gatekeeping obligation to be fulfilled with the least amount of interference with Hippocratic obligations? As our comments above have suggested, the task would be much easier if we had a fixed total health care budget within which both quality care and equal access to basic care could be defined.[12] This cannot presently be accomplished in the U.S. at the level of national policy. Individual health care institutions, however, especially HMOs, can do this at the local level. Further, it seems a wise provision to specify that the health professional should not profit *directly* from the refusal of treatment to an individual patient for economic reasons. In settings like HMOs, where the staff will be laid off if the HMO goes bankrupt, it is impossible to eliminate an indirect profit for adequate gatekeeping. But any sort of bonus, kickback, or profit-sharing scheme that allows Physician X to put money into his own pocket because he denied Patient Y access to care is destructive both of the Hippocratic obligation and of the trust that patients should be able to feel for their physicians.

CONCLUSIONS

It is an undeniable if unhappy fact that our current consumption of health care resources exceeds our ability either to distribute them equitably or to continue to afford them. Some restraints are clearly necessary, and ultimately a new national health policy must be framed to accommodate these limits. Meanwhile, individual health professionals can take several steps.

First, we must contribute to sound record keeping which allows tracking the actual costs and benefits for individual patients. The resulting records will serve both as a tool for patient advocacy and as the beginning of a national data collection that can lead to more efficient use of our resources. Second, we must temper our traditional impulse to do whatever can be done with the realization that, ultimately, unrestrained use of treatments of purely marginal benefit will interfere with our ability to bestow substantial benefits on other needy patients. Third, we must develop the courage to do battle with government agencies, institutional administrators, and third party payers, and we must insist that they respond to the clearly documented and reasonable medical needs of patients.

Treatment refusal for economic reasons is a new and emerging issue in medical ethics and the discussion above can provide only a rough outline of the areas where further investigation and analysis are needed. The issue lies at the intersection of such varied disciplines as medicine, philosophy, public policy, economics, sociology, and law. It is therefore essential that informed discussion occur in the appropriate public forums everywhere in the country.[13] Only with maximal representative public input can we assuredly move into the next century with a health care system which efficiently serves those in need and protects the ethical integrity of the professionals who work within it.

NOTES

1. Robert Veatch, *A Theory of Medical Ethics* (New York: Basic Books, 1981), 21–25.

2. President's Commission for the Study of Ethical Problems in Medicine and Biomedical and Behavioral Research, *Securing Access to Health Care,* vol. 1 (Washington, D.C.: GPO, 1983).

3. Edmund Pellegrino, "Rationing Health Care: The Ethics of Medical Gatekeeping," *Journal of Contemporary Health Law and Policy* 2 (1986):23–45.

4. Norman Levinsky, "The Doctor's Master," *New England Journal of Medicine* 311 (1984): 1573–75.

5. Robert Veatch, "DRGs and the Ethical Reallocation of Resources," *Hastings Center Report* 16, no. 3 (1986): 32–40.

6. Victor Fuchs, "The Rationing of Medical Care," *New England Journal of Medicine* 311 (1984): 1572–73.

7. Norman Daniels, *Just Health Care* (New York: Cambridge University Press, 1985).

8. William Schwartz, Joseph Newhouse, and Albert Williams, "Is the Teaching Hospital an Endangered Species?" *New England Journal Medicine* 313 (1985): 157–62.

9. William Curran, "Economic and Legal Considerations in Emergency Care," *New England Journal of Medicine* 312 (1985): 374–75.

10. Lester Thurow, "Learning to Say No," *New England Journal of Medicine* 311 (1984): 1569–72; Marcia Angell, "Cost Containment and the Physician," *Journal of the American Medical Association* 254 (1985): 1203–7.

11. Christine Cassel, "Doctors and Allocation Decisions: A New Role in the New Medicare," *Journal of Health Politics, Policy and Law* 10 (1985): 549–64.

12. Ibid.; Norman Daniels, "Why Saying No to Patients in the United States Is So Hard," *New England Journal of Medicine* 314 (1986): 1380–83.

13. Ralph Crawshaw et al., "Oregon Health Decisions: An Experiment with Informed Community Consent," *Journal of the American Medical Association* 254 (1985): 3213–16.

BIBLIOGRAPHY

Bayer, Ronald, Daniel Callahan, John Fletcher, Thomas Hodgson, Bruce Jennings, David Monsees, Steven Sieverts, and Robert Veatch, "The Care of the Terminally Ill: Morality and Economics." *New England Journal of Medicine* 309 (1983): 1490–94.

Brody, Howard. "Cost Containment as Professional Challenge." *Theoretical Medicine,* in press.

Daniels, Norman. *Just Health Care.* New York: Cambridge University Press, 1981.

Menzel, Paul. *Medical Costs, Moral Choices.* New Haven, Conn.: Yale University Press, 1983.

Pellegrino, Edmund D. "Hospitals as Moral Agents." In *Humanism and the Physician.* Knoxville: University of Tennessee Press, 1979).

Shelp, Earl E., ed. *Justice and Health Care.* Boston: D. Reidel, 1981.

Chapter 25

Changes Affecting Health Care: Two Possible Scenarios

Charles H. White

SCENARIO I: THINGS GET WORSE BEFORE THEY GET BETTER*

What changes will affect health and hospital care between now and the year 2000? It is possible to construct at least two plausible scenarios—each involving changes having dramatic effects on patients and providers alike, changes caused and controlled by factors not in the grip of doctors and hospitals. The world economic picture, the U.S. economy, demographics, and the mood of the electorate—all of these will have much more impact than health provider behavior. Hospitals themselves will not cause any of these broad-scale social developments and hospitals will not alleviate their bad effects. We will call the first scenario "Things Get Worse before They Get Better." In this scenario, the economy remains essentially stagnant and the share of GNP devoted to health care is reduced. We will call the other scenario "Things Get Better before They Get Worse." In this scenario, the economy improves and the share of GNP devoted to health care increases.

In the first scenario, cost containment remains the guiding principle during the remainder of the 1980s and through the 1990s. Public policy and health politics are dictated more than ever by the largest segment of the U.S. population—the baby boom generation that now to a great extent composes the middle class.[1]

Relatively young and with much greater education than their parents, this middle-aged and middle class group primarily value family concerns. They are more sophisticated about consumer products and more skeptical about the value of major health care expenditures, such as survey and invasive procedures, unless there is clear evidence that longevity will be increased and quality of life will not be threatened.

They are skeptical about politics because they were the campus radicals of the 1960s, watched Watergate in the 1970s, and have been confronted with the defense contracting scandals of the 1980s. Both sophistication and skepticism lead them to view provider recommendations as simply professional points of view rather than as unchallengeable expert mandates.

In this scenario, the U.S. economy averages 2–3 percent real growth per year until 2000, with an accompanying annual inflation rate of 4 percent.[2] The U.S. continues to experience

*Source: Adapted from *Strategic Planning Assumption for Hospitals, 1985–87* and *1986–88* by C.H. White and S. Lewis, with permission of California Hospital Association, © 1985 and 1986.

a "baby bust" that reduces the supply of entry level workers. Competition among baby boomers for mid-level positions dampens incomes in what would otherwise be their peak consumption years, depressing demand for big-ticket items such as autos and new housing. International competition remains tight, world consumers find U.S. goods too expensive, and foreign loans are not repaid. World commodity and energy prices remain low, major smokestack industries continue to decline, and foreign competition and labor-saving technology reduce both the numbers and influence of unions, which results in relatively modest new wage awards.[3]

The business climate remains competitive, government is concerned with budget deficits, and capital for renovation, remodeling, or upgrading is somewhat available but difficult to amortize. Interest rates remain fairly constant but the middle-aged class consumers are trapped in their debtor position, paying off 30-year mortgages on simple family homes and paying installments for cars, clothes, etc. Their prime concerns are family needs (house, education and child care, careers) and establishing professional and community roles and personal financial position. Local concerns predominate (parks, recreation, job safety, the environment, police and fire protection). One major goal is keeping government spending constant. Getting ahead does occur, but only gradually and over a spread of years.

During the period of the first scenario, health concerns are minimal, involving primarily preventive care and routine childhood illnesses. One dramatic change over previous generations is the inability and unwillingness of baby boomers to care for elderly patients in their own homes. When the issue is between college for kids or care for parents, the parents will generally lose out. A phenomenon of this era is the family with 90-year-old retired grandparents needing financial help from their 65-year-old children, with all of them hoping for assistance from their descendants—a baby boom, middle-aged middle class professional couple who themselves have children ranging from early elementary school to college age.

Social Security will present a push-pull dilemma for baby boomers. They are aware that the system cannot survive as presently constituted and will not be adequate when they arrive at retirement age; yet being cash poor, they are unwilling and unable to pay additional taxes to expand or increase the program. As the new century arrives, however, many in the baby boom generation will focus on their approaching retirement, move from a debtor to saver position, and begin to worry about public policy issues concerning health care for themselves, long-term care for the elderly, and a viable Social Security system. But that comes later.

In this scenario, government cannot escape its vicious cycle of stagnation and deficit. Consumers unable to break free of financial constraints resist any major expansion of governmental activities. Neither defense nor social programs can grow. The GNP for health declines from 11 to 9 percent, "no new taxes" is the overwhelming national consensus, with the family-related issues of education, child care, and safety protection dominating.

As social program funding drops, means testing for benefits eligibility will increase, as will copayments and deductibles. Health insurance becomes taxable and first-dollar coverage is unavailable. Direct control on physicians' fees, caps on liability claims and lawyers' contingency fees, elimination of joint and several liability, shrinking of the liability insurance industry—all of these result from stubborn pressure on profits. Business concerns control health policy, and employers continue to push for managed systems and fixed prices on health care. Foreign competition is intense, import controls are imposed but do not effect a cure, and new technology is not able to be adopted across the board; these problems lead to continued patterns of "the rich get richer and the poor get poorer," with annual profit averaging only 2 percent.

Business is preoccupied with keeping health benefit costs as low as possible,[4] stimulating interest in delivering employee groups to prepaid capitation systems for a fixed price—the more managed, the better. Employers want workers to pay more upfront costs. They also want to closely monitor the cost patterns of individual providers, and to store up considerable information on care and outcomes to help consumers make more efficient choices.

Trust is placed in "gatekeeper" dominated systems to reduce the utilization of subspecialty services. A gatekeeper's function is to minimize the cost of the medical care delivered to the patient by seeing that only essential care is available. But what is essential is determined by the gatekeeper; this reduces both the *supply* of care by other providers and the effective *demand* for care by patients. If the patient really wants more care, then he or she must go outside the system and pay for it out-of-pocket.

There are incentives for changing the first allegiance from the patient's needs, wishes, or welfare to other goals. Under fee-for-service, the patient can fire a physician—and physicians know it. They are conscious of the need to please patients. In a capital or gatekeeper system, the incentives are to please the payer; there is greater financial discipline, sometimes supported by bonuses to physicians to order fewer tests, use fewer referral specialists, and have lower rates of hospitalization.

Funding for medical research is not a high priority and the previous faith in the benefits of technology wears thin.[5] Levels of education and availability of consumer product information creates more careful buyers. The formerly high level of trust in physicians is reduced to the levels of other professionals—educators, clergy, judges, the military.

In this scenario, there is a pronounced change in attitudes about the right of people to refuse use of extreme and costly measures to prolong life. Demands will increase for better information about costs and the relationship between extension and quality of life. A consensus will build in many communities, and patients, families, doctors, and the clergy will agree that individuals have a right to refuse heroic measures to prolong life. Consumers will favor allowing patients the right to die when faced with incurable diseases or coma. Medical practice is then forced to adapt, focusing on early detection, prevention, and functional remedies in both research and care and shifting away from heroic measures in the last days and months of life.

Down the road, it becomes clear that direct governmental controls such as DRGs work reasonably well in the short run, temporarily stemming the tide of automatic cost increases and pressuring both providers and consumers to work within the system to justify increases.[6] But such controls eventually become political, substituting bureaucratic maneuvering for market systems. This demonstrates once again that regulations either distort, run counter to, or ignore legislative intent. Eventually, cost-control systems begin to concentrate on the wrong things, retard innovation, are carried on by newly formed constituencies, destroy much needed but unprofitable products (e.g., hospitals serving the indigent), and gradually erode ethical standards. Implementers down the line always have trouble doing what was intended for them to do because of the difficulty of keeping competent staff and because of the changes in the political agenda each time a new governor is elected.

In the first scenario, new information technology is essential—more so than new medical technology—to allow a wider variety of nonphysicians to monitor patients. Inpatient care, discharge planning, and postacute care require improved payment mechanisms, administration of systems, patient scheduling, accuracy and comprehensiveness of records, and coordination of diagnosis and treatment. The balance of information-gathering activities will shift from providers to administrators, businesses, government, and fiscal intermediaries, who will collect and analyze data on care and cost outcomes in disparate geographical and institutional settings.

Some of the kinds of care most likely to be affected (perhaps curtailed) in a cost-containment scenario are included below.

- Services that depend on dedicated capital equipment and highly specialized staff will be cut far more than services that can be provided by regular hospital personnel and ordinary drugs and supplies.

- When economically unfeasible, specialized services will be cut, and physicians, hospitals, and patients will need to make appropriate adjustments.

- Decisions on more routine services will require individual physicians to deny individual care to specific patients—an especially difficult task.

- Arcane services for which the need is not clearly evident to patients will be curtailed more readily than services for which the need is clear and inescapable.

- Services for the elderly are more likely to be curtailed than services for children or young adults, though even treatment for children will be curtailed more readily if the cost per patient is very high.

- If an artificial heart is developed (at an estimated cost of $100,000 per patient), the fact that heart disease is the most frequent cause of death would force a budget-constrained system to ration its use quite ruthlessly.

- The higher the quality of life after successful treatment, the smaller will be the reduction of care under budget limits.

- There is no problem when the expected incremental benefit of medical care exceeds its incremental cost, but all developed nations will try to alter the behavior of providers and patients so that expenditures are curtailed on care that is worth *less* than it costs.

- Some behaviors can be foreseen with reasonable confidence. Providers are likely to seek ways of escaping the constraints; patients, of obtaining the care they might otherwise be denied.

- If financial limits prevent the provision of some beneficial care, certain patients and treatments will probably fare better than others. Demand will be fully met in some cases, but in others, constraints on expenditures will reduce either quality or quantity, or both.

- Limits on hospital expenditures will end some activities that yield no medical benefit but consume resources. If only these were eliminated, imposing the limits would be painless. However, it is naive to think that medical spending can be reduced by eliminating waste and inefficiencies, because an increase in wastefulness is not responsible for the rapid growth in hospital spending.

- Any appreciable restraint on expenditures will be accomplished only by denying medical benefits. Long-term cost containment will require hard choices about who gets what—in short, rationing.

- How budget constraints are imposed will determine how much the income of individual physicians is affected and, thus, the level and degree of intrahospital conflict that will ensue. Those physicians who perform procedures involving substantial use of hospital resources are likely to be affected significantly by almost every payment methodology adopted. By contrast, physicians who perform procedures involving little capital equipment or personnel should be affected least.

Slight Constraints, Slight Effects[7]

- In the early stage of slowing growth of hospital expenditures, few changes occur in actual medical practices. Hospitals curtail purchases and replacement of equipment, economize on heating and lighting, delay replacement of linen, reduce quality of food, and defer maintenance.
- Some hospitals run deficits, dip into endowment funds, fill nursing and other staff vacancies at slower rates, and increase workloads, with accompanying loss of staff morale but increased productivity.
- With slight constraints, admission and treatment policies are largely unaffected. Doctors might wait a bit longer for lab reports; patients, a bit longer for x-rays.
- Important services such as surgery and intensive care are fully staffed. Small changes in quality might occur, such as less film per x-ray, but these would be invisible to patients.
- Slight budget limits squeeze out pure waste and reduce a few amenities for patients and staff—the savings are slight.
- In short, mild budget limits only subject hospitals to cost disciplines that competitive businesses routinely face but that hospitals and physicians were sheltered from by reimbursement based on costs and charges.

Severe Limits, Severe Effects[8]

- As budget constraints become more severe, the days to easy adjustment end. Decisions have to be made on what services are to be available to whom, and since public expectations in the U.S. are so high, these restrictions are perceived as painful.
- As constraints increase, the effect on patient care becomes greater, because few options remain for reducing expenditures without appreciably changing patterns of medical practice. Diagnostic radiology and lab tests are among the most likely choices for reductions. Benefits lost with these reductions are probably small; the potential savings are large.
- The introduction of costly new treatments and diagnostic procedures is slowed, occurring only when, or even after, their effectiveness is clearly demonstrated.
- Physicians and hospitals are forced to redefine what care constitutes standard medical practice and what care exceeds that standard. Acute illness and traumatic injuries continue to be diagnosed and treated with the best each hospital has to offer, so long as the victim has even a small chance to recover and achieve a normal life.
- Most illnesses of children and young adults continue to be treated aggressively, but serious ethical and legal questions arise in treating the badly impaired and unborn.

Treatment of cancer probably continues to command nearly all the resources required to provide whatever benefit is available.

- Terminal care, on the other hand, is much reduced. Severe limits mean less consumption of goods and services for terminal care than for other medical care. Less intensive care and limitations on other specialized technologies curtail the provision of aggressive care for dying patients.

- Physicians in the U.S. realize that such aggressive treatment of many terminally ill patients is often pointless, but feel they cannot do less because of pressure from the patient's family, fear of malpractice suits, and threats of intervention by the courts on behalf of the patient.

- In a world of resource constraints, the rules inevitably change. Using resources on the terminally ill means death, disability, and pain for non–terminally ill patients denied care. When resources are too few to take care of all, care is provided to those who stand to benefit the most. This becomes the new ethic under the resource limits imposed by budget constraints.

- In general, budget limits slow the introduction of new therapies more than in the absence of constraints; therapies already in use are less affected.

- The total cost of a program is important in determining whether a new technology is introduced and how widely it is made available.

- Another way to save resources would be by cutting the number of hospital admissions and by developing waiting lists for those needing elective surgery, but it is hard to imagine such queues in the U.S. without private sector safety valves for those who have the means to pay and who would not tolerate delay.

Changes in Medical Practice

- Budget limits would gradually cause accepted standards of practice to change. Good medicine would call for fewer tests when the gain in information is slight and for less surgery and less use of costly drugs when the advantage of expensive over inexpensive therapies is small. Thus, U.S. doctors would build into their practice a sense of the relation between the costs of care and the value of benefits from it.

- Doctors would weigh not only the medical aspects of diagnosis and treatment, but the personal characteristics of each patient: age, underlying health, family responsibilities, and the patient's chance of recovering sufficiently to resume a normal life. This would indeed be a far-reaching change in attitude for many American doctors.

- Physicians would then have redefined what care is ''appropriate.'' Such rationalization is probably essential to the morale of the physician who finds that it is not Congress, not rate-setting agencies, not the insurance companies, but he or she alone who must say no to the patient.

- The task of saying no will become increasingly difficult as constraints become tighter. Care most easily denied is that dependent on costly capital equipment. Without technology, the care cannot be provided.

- If staffing is limited, volume of service will necessarily be restricted to the service which providers can give in the time available. In this case, providers are spared the psychologically insupportable burden of denying care because it is too expensive. Rather, they are given the role of allocating existing capacity to the patients who will benefit most from care.

- Services that do not require specialized technology or providers are hard to ration. Controlling expenditures on drugs, blood, and other expendable supplies will pose one of the most difficult problems in severely containing costs.

Patient Responses[9]

- As budget constraints become tight, patients would seek safety valves that allow them to obtain care they would otherwise be denied. Because patients may, in general, visit any physician, opportunities for doctor-shopping and for cajoling, browbeating, or bribing doctors to provide ''full'' care might increasingly be taken advantage of.
- Consequently, aggressive and affluent patients would probably obtain superior care and resources would tend to flow toward therapies about which patients are well-informed and for which they recognize the need.

Getting Care Outside the System

- Besides putting more pressure on the physicians, patients are likely to try to seek care outside the severely constrained hospital system.
- As constraints became more severe, a central question would be whether care could be obtained from providers not subject to budget limits. Could there be a system *outside* the system? Money can always buy everything.
- Budget limits would have meaning only if additional costs or disincentives were imposed on people who chose to purchase services from unregulated providers.
- Eventually, how large that cost or penalty should be would become as critical an issue as the level of the budget limit. Thus, Medicare patients would move back into the private sector.
- The same methods used to control flow of resources to the regulated system, including tax systems, licensing, and limits on reimbursement through public or private payers, could be used to discourage other providers. Each approach thus creates a price difference, explicit or black market, between regulated and unregulated providers.
- Each approach would also create political, administrative, and economic problems of its own, stemming from the desire of people to buy insurance to protect themselves from the risk that a given kind of care may be too expensive and from the fact that such insurance inevitably short-circuits the incentives of the regulated marketplace to balance costs against benefits.

Political Pressure

- Dissatisfied patients will appeal to their legislators. Media headlines and congressional mail will probably abound with horror stories about withholding or terminating care.

- To satisfy constituents, legislative staff will bring pressure on doctors and hospitals. Executive agencies of federal and state governments will inquire to see if fair decisions were reached. All of this will add to administrative complexity.
- Parents and families will turn to the media, which will highlight the effects of the budget shortfall by featuring heart-rending stories.
- Constituent pressure could become so widespread and intense that Congress might begin to mandate specific exceptions to the budget constraints.
- Heart disease, cancer, and stroke might be excluded from the limits, and the system of control would slowly become porous because of too many loopholes.
- Finally, slowly growing public pressure would build up in favor of larger investments in health care than the severely limited budgets permitted—and another era of expansion would begin.

The unresolved access issue would be the key to ending any general cost-containment policy. The number of people with no coverage or inadequate coverage would gradually increase from the current 10 percent to nearer 20 percent of the population, including temporarily unemployed people, part-time workers, recently divorced spouses and their children, increasing numbers of unmarried partners and their children, and increasing numbers of low-income workers in small businesses (the underemployed). As the governmental funding crunch continues year after year, this uncovered population's access to health care—access previously provided by county or teaching hospitals or clinics—will be reduced, and they will suffer the indignities of long lines, busy telephones, extensive delays, and spotty geographic coverage.

Less first-dollar coverage will cause consumers to become more hesitant to use routine services and especially hesitant to choose more expensive initial procedures. Employer-sponsored plans act as barriers to certain providers or certain services, payment plans like the DRG plan provide limited money per episode, and some patients receive less treatment than their condition might warrant.

As the cost-containment spiral circles ever downward, there is increased "tiering" of the health care system, care becomes more sporadic as most insurance rules grow more strict, and access to long-term care continues to be problematic.

Serious political tensions in the health care system will manifest themselves as a result of access problems disturbing the public. There will be a growing concern about the lack of progress in medical research, the decreasing pace of innovation, the lack of physicians entering research, and the difficulties with medical education.

However, the cost-containment movement that began in the early 1980s did succeed in reversing the trend toward major increases in cost rates that occurred during the preceding decade.[10] Quality of care and access for most people—those middle-aged and middle class—remains essentially uncompromised, even though people on the margins suffer some dislocations. The consensus of the public is that the health care system served them pretty well when they needed to concentrate on other things. But will it serve the baby boom generation when they become aged in the twenty-first century? Is there enough capacity and enough quality and quantity? Is there enough supply to meet the inevitable demand?

SCENARIO II: THINGS GET BETTER BEFORE THEY GET WORSE

What changes will affect health and hospital care between now and the year 2000? The introduction to the first scenario pointed to the controlling influence on health policy, health politics, and health care financing of some larger social forces. With a different set of assumptions about the world and national environment, the second scenario predicts that "things get better before they get worse" and in many details presents a very different picture.

In the second scenario, the cost-containment enthusiasm of the early and middle 1980s subsides as the economy improves. The historic growth pattern of the health care delivery system resumes its upward path after what appears historically to have been a temporary glitch from DRGs, Medi-Cal contracts, and a short-lived boom in HMOs and PPOs.

The driving force is the overwhelming pressure to provide a wider range of health services to an aging population. Although not nearly as numerous as the middle-aged baby boom generation, the aged hold the balance of political power and are very eager to use that leverage.[11] While the baby boomers are more concerned with family and career matters, the aged discover access problems and threats of denials of service in the erstwhile cost-containment philosophies and practices. Fortunately for them, the stimulated economy will allow growth in the health care system to resume.

Clear-cut distinctions emerge between the wants and needs of population subgroups. The effects of diet, exercise, health care, less smoking, pollution cleanup, and environmental safety produce a large group of the "young old" (65–75).[12] Still largely employed, the young old need health benefit plans that offer acute care services, transplants, and rehabilitation not based on means testing. They want coverage that looks very much like the commercial indemnity or Blues plans of the 1970s (i.e., before Blue Cross lost its tax-exempt status).

The "middle old" (75–85) include some workers; they want acute care services as well as long-term care, home care, and rehabilitation. Their needs become more sharply focused as the realization grows that their children do not want to care for aging parents—and cannot afford to. An improved economy based on growing productivity, higher oil and energy costs, and the rebuilding of the infrastructure also brings renewed inflation and a shortage of housing (and hence a shortage of space at home for parents).

Expanded numbers of the very old (over 85) create special demands for elderly housing, including both custodial care and life care projects.[13] As the market improves, pension and retirement systems are worth more; thus more seniors will qualify as income increases. The fastest growing subgroup of the aged consists of those over 100, and there is a resulting need for assisted-living units.

As the retirement center market expands, three segments appear. At the low-end are older, nonprofit government subsidy centers targeted at low-income residents living on Social Security and limited retirement income. Designed as apartment complexes, these centers offer no services and very few were built in the late 1980s and beyond.

In the middle segment are facilities offered both by nonprofit agencies and by private developers. The facilities stress independent living but provide a full range of services (short of full-time nursing care). Services typically include meals, transportation, social and recreational activites, and security.

High-end projects are built increasingly in the late 1980s and through the 1990s to meet the needs and wants of upscale retirees with large pensions, investment income, and the fruits of IRAs. Although there are fewer high-end projects than middle segment projects, they offer larger residencies, more services, and a more luxurious setting—of course, at greater cost.

But these institutions provide a different kind of care. Skepticism about medical technology—its uses and benefits in general and heroic medicine in particular—are still prevalent with regard to care for the terminally ill. With increased federal and private funding for research (some support coming from increased profits in the investor-owned hospital sector), progress is made in early diagnosis and detection of a wide variety of diseases. Greater attention and public support of mental illness reduces the number of homeless people, with an attendant reduction in morbidity, mortality, and uncompensated care.

Progress does not produce cures, necessarily, but does show measurable benefits that are clear and well understood by the public. Pressure builds to make interventions more available as the public accepts them. The elderly are particularly attracted to interventions aimed at chronic or debilitating illnesses (arthritis, Alzheimer's disease).

The number of community organizations and their assistance to the chronically ill increase after DRGs force more of the acutely ill elderly not to be treated in hospitals. The middle aged elect to support systems to care for elderly relatives rather than support heroic medical intervention. Subspecialty medicine continues its decline relative to its peak in the early 1980s. Public funds are poured into expanding the range of chronic and rehabilitation services. Acute care hospitals, improved by undergoing the shock therapy of competitive market economies, are more trim and efficient. Unnecessary costs were eliminated. Surplus beds remain out of the system and historical trends toward full-service hospitals are reversed.

The hospice movement continues to grow, because there are still many illnesses where the limits of medical science are obvious to the public and the bioethical attitudes that arose in the 1980s remain in force.

One difference now is that the elderly are increasingly from professional rather than blue collar or farm backgrounds. Their education levels become closer to those of the middle aged with the passage of time. Many of them supported (and some may have participated in) the social movements of the 1960s and 1970s. They strongly support product liability, have learned to use the legal system for solving problems, and have maintained limits on liability claims and lawyers' fees. Individually they are more consumer oriented; collectively they constitute the single most formidable political force, because their leaders can produce large blocks of votes on key issues, much as union bosses did in earlier generations.

Unions themselves become more of an anachronism. They have decreased numbers and power, because multinational industries continue to diversify and reduce plant size. The long-announced service economy arrives, with less need or opportunity for organizing collective-bargaining units.

This development comes just when there is a larger number of aging workers. Providing health benefits even in a booming economy becomes more difficult for the private sector, for Medicare is denied to workers over 65 and the Social Security threshold age moves toward 72. Growth in labor force participation among those over 60 poses a higher risk for those businesses that self-insured in the mid-1980s, particularly when the risk group is small. Fewer young people enter the labor market as the country grows increasingly older. Since self-insurance reserves are not deductible business expenses and health insurance benefits are taxed, putting together package offers to attract and retain scarce top new talent is increasingly difficult.

Regional effects appear that are caused by the demographic patterns of the nation, and these in turn affect national companies. Northeastern states have greater numbers of the resident working elderly, forcing employers to restore health benefits that were cut back or copaid during the cost-containment years. Higher proportions of younger workers in the western states enable business to offer other take-home or cost-shared benefits. The net result is pressure to standardize benefits across the country, by including reversing trends of self-insurance (as in the East) and by adding benefits. With changes largely forced through by older workers (although without union help), health care plans offer more and cost more.

Business has not completely forgotten its hard-learned lessons from the cost-containment years, and it continues to monitor health care delivery, maintain profiles of providers, and keeps its faith in review systems as the secret of success in restraining utilization. It still wants managed systems and fixed prices whenever available and imposes structural controls, such as bulk purchasing of services. But the continued aging of the labor force (which increases the volume of care), easier access to care, and the adoption of technology all have the same effect—cost increases.

Principal movement occurs after the 1992 election, shifting emphasis firmly toward a new growth cycle and stamping out sympathy for cost-containment. DRG systems, after endless tinkering and adjustments to fit transient political agendas, become totally discredited: too complex, too unwieldy, too unfair, too unpopular. In the end they lose all support. Business responds to a tight labor market at the lower end of the wage scale; highly paid older workers want better health care coverage; hospitals complain that physicians were never subjected to DRG punishment; physicians complain that reduced incomes from pressures on ancillary services have changed medical practice; governments have tried to patch the system with band-aid approaches; private sector insurers have enjoyed several years without cost shifting and forget how much they disliked it. Everyone wants more: more access to more high-quality health care at a more reasonable personal cost. And if it requires more tax money to pay for it, then that is acceptable in 1992.

The public's agenda is now very clear, but the federal government's dilemma is growing increasingly acute. Although the President promised in her campaign that Medicare would be reviewed and access would be increased, it is clear that a crisis will recur after the turn of the century when the baby boom generation passes retirement age. The President must figure out a way to offer a federal health system that will work in the short and medium term to hold off political pressure from seniors and fulfill political commitments to them, but will also anticipate the need to control massive expenditures when the time comes. Costs of health care are increasing rapidly enough even without the additional volume expected by 2010, when the baby boom generation reaches age 65.[14] A control mechanism seems inevitable to government planners, who devise a new proposed policy called "cost containment." However, the policy continues to remain unacceptable in the 1990s.

As the system becomes less constrained, it can accept increases in benefits, and services can be offered to the unsponsored and the underinsured. Medicare combines a more generous voucher system with stop-loss provisions of catastrophic insurance. As the liability crisis that occurred between 1975 and 1985 becomes history, the insurance industry has more flexibility, but both private and public payers want control of postacute care, better discharge planning, and continuity. Insurance (and tax benefits) for long-term care and rehabilitation are provided and health benefits show lesser rates of taxation. Regional and state differences again appear, with eastern states continuing their cross-subsidization, western states continuing with price competition (reflecting their younger population), and

Sunbelt retirement states slipping further into public-only support—the worst of both worlds for providers, with no private cost sharing or ability to bargain for rates.

Still, these developments are based on four major assumptions that underlie expanded growth in volume and cost:

1. The economy remains strong after a brief but inevitable recession in late 1980s that aggravates all the negative effects of DRGs, cost outliers, and cost containment.
2. Strong political support by seniors, especially in the East and Midwest, controls elections. Aged voters in Sunbelt states support the idea of expansion in health care, but will not share as much because of the inability of their states to participate in the costs.
3. Those middle-aged and middle class prefer to pay increased taxes to care for aging parents; they are unwilling to take care of parents in their homes and are too financially committed to stop working or pay long-term care bills. And they are beginning to look forward to their need for increased health care and want to ensure that some kind of appropriate system is in place.
4. Hope springs eternal, and enough progress in medical technology has been achieved to offer the promise of more advances if more research funding is made available.

The economy cooperates—real growth creates real gain for households, business, and government. Inflation stays low enough (as a partial result of recession), the balance of trade improves, international tensions ease enough for some repayment of international loans, and the U.S. deficit becomes manageable. Negotiations by the U.S. and U.S.S.R. on arms control are productive enough that tension eases somewhat. Both superpowers realize that arms escalation of the early 1980s is too expensive and extracts too great a cost in domestic restraint. Although American consumers favor fiscal conservatism, there is still a willingness to spend for those things people want most. As affluence increases, it becomes clear that health care is one of those things.

As the flow of medical technology increases again (with the release from cost containment), a wide range of diagnosis and treatment improvements appear. The shift of diagnostic functions to physicians' offices and the home, spurred on by DRGs, becomes permanent. Steady improvement creates benefits that do not reduce, but also do not substantially increase, costs. Progress in cancer therapy and AIDS detection (but not immunization) fuels public demand for access to highly publicized technologies.

Other technologies that ameliorate (at high cost) but do not cure include those for diagnosis of coronary artery disease, dietary links to arteriosclerosis, Alzheimer's disease, and management of patients in drug therapy. Public realization of destructive effects of substance abuse, developments in fertility diagnosis and therapy, microsurgery, and neonatal care open a wide range of new possibilities in enhancing reproduction and sustaining low–birth weight infants. As progress is made in providing better birth control information to teenagers, better prenatal care reduces the number of premature or defective infants, greatly reducing the number of expensive cases and liability claims. Ob/Gyn physicians enter practice in greater numbers, creating greater access and availability of care as the birth rate begins to climb again among the "baby bust" generation now becoming middle-aged and middle class.

In this scenario, there are no strong brakes being applied to increases in health care spending. Each sector, acting in its own best interest, does not yet see the danger signals, although the President and some economists are aware of them. They begin to plan for future spending crises while trying to balance the short-run political interests of the 1990s. Business, government, and consumers push for increases in both supply and demand. The decline during the mid-1980s in health spending proves to have been an aberration. Sympathy for alternative delivery systems was motivated by economic constraints, but this sympathy is now reduced. Pluralistic responses of competition (HMOs, PPOs, contracting, discounting) continue to co-exist with regulation (DRGs, fixed price payments), but fee-for-service plans make a comeback. Delegation of authority and funding responsibility to the states continues, resulting in very different Medicaid-type programs (depending on state attitudes and wealth). No matter what happens, a nationalized system like the British have is not perceived by the American public as a viable or desirable alternative.

By the year 2000, few people see any problems of access to the health care delivery system. All but the most serious care has been shifted to outpatient settings, and many new and exciting diagnostic and therapeutic modalities are being used in physicians' offices and ambulatory settings.

Hospital buildings have been adapted to a wide range of uses, with remodeling or renovation costs paid mostly by philanthropy. DRG plans removed operating funds as a capital source, loss of tax-exempt bond funding removed further traditional source, and most not-for-profit hospitals found it advisable to become publicly traded. Additional court rulings placed in doubt the tax-exempt status of many hospitals for not offering uncompensated care during the depths of the cost-containment period. When the economy revived, there seemed to be no reason to depart from investor-owned status.

Outpatient technology is cheap and effective, mental health care is benefited by breakthroughs in diagnosis and therapy, and custodial support for the elderly is included in third party payment. All of these are welcome to providers and patients. All help increases costs. There are no remaining controls on technology, and providers begin to duplicate costly facilities and services to compete for patients. Clinically inappropriate but available technologies are often used. After declaring a physician shortage in 1965 and a surplus in 1985, the federal government repeats history and declares a shortage in 2005 to begin gearing up for the baby boom generation.

Incentive structures change once again to favor treatment rather than prevention. Expanded use of technologies are seen not to yield relatively significant improvement in health status. The realization occurs that costs and expenditures, both absolutely and proportionally, are growing rapidly—and before the real increase in the elderly population has begun to take place.

In Scenario I, short-run cost containment gets worse, constrains the system, creates access problems, and results in a political backlash demanding new expansion. In Scenario II, the more favorable short-run environment eventually leads to the same excesses that caused cost containment in the first place. Neither is complete nor is there a happy ending—only the exchange of one set of problems for another.

NOTES

1. Institute for the Future, *Looking Ahead at American Health Care* (Menlo Park, Calif.: Institute for the Future, 1986), 4. The author is particularly indebted to the conceptual framework used in this book.

2. Charles H. White and Stephen Lewis, *Strategic Planning Assumptions for Hospitals, 1986–88* (Sacramento, Calif.: California Hospital Association, 1986), 6–7.

3. Charles H. White and Stephen Lewis, *Strategic Planning Assumptions for Hospitals, 1985–87* (Sacramento, Calif.: California Hospital Association, 1985), 1–3.

4. Institute for the Future, *Looking Ahead*, 13.

5. Ibid., 14.

6. Charles H. White, "Smaller Carrot, Bigger Stick," *Western Journal of Medicine* 145 (1986): 535.

7. White and Lewis, *Strategic Planning Assumptions for Hospitals, 1985–87*, 55.

8. Henry J. Aaron and William B. Schwartz, *The Painful Prescription—Rationing Hospital Care* (Washington, D.C.: Brookings Institution, 1985), 123.

9. Ibid., 129.

10. Charles H. White and Larkin E. Morse, *Hospital Fact Book: 1985,* 10th ed. (Sacramento, Calif.: California Hospital Association, 1985), 8.

11. Institute for the Future, *Looking Ahead*, 23.

12. Ibid.

13. White and Lewis, *Strategic Planning Assumptions for Hospitals, 1986–88,* 42.

14. Ibid.

Chapter 26

The Preferential Option for the Poor and Health Care in the United States

Laurence J. O'Connell

The "preferential option for the poor" has emerged from a frankly theological discussion that is very much colored by its origins in the Third World. The distinctiveness of its religious roots and cultural context may perhaps limit its direct applicability to the public debate over health care in the United States. But despite its potential limitations, the preferential option for the poor may appeal to some as a forceful analogy, if not an authoritative norm. Since the concept itself is similar to theories currently advanced by some American ethicists (e.g., John Rawls's principle of fair equality of opportunity), the preferential option for the poor may prove quite suggestive.[1]

Why, however, would a concept associated with poverty and misery among the marginalized and exploited masses of Latin America find currency in the debate concerning health care in the United States? The answer to this unsettling question lies in the changing nature of health care in this country.

HEALTH CARE IN THE UNITED STATES

The health care system in the United States is in the midst of a revolution that is transforming its very nature. There is a definite shift away from the traditional view of health care as a social good that is exempt from market forces and towards a view that health care is an economic commodity subject to the influence of supply, demand, and price. Concepts like *cost containment, competition, consumer attitudes,* and *capitation arrangements* presently shape the discussion of health care in the United States.

It would be difficult to deny that today health care is largely driven and shaped by economic considerations. Consequently, the participants in the U.S. health system—providers, consumers, payers, and policy makers—have begun to relate to one another and to health care in ways that reflect the prominence of economic considerations. For example, many hospitals are offering a wide array of new, economically profitable services to provide sources of income, maintain their share of the so-called hospital market, and meet competition from physician groups and entrepreneurs. Physicians, in an effort to guard their own economic interests in a competitive environment, have begun to carve out market niches by providing a variety of specialty services. And large American corporations are increasingly aggressive in their demands for cut-rate health care services, while at the same time the

306

federal government is focusing on limiting its financial outlays and is continuing to distance itself from the notion that government should ensure equal access to health care for all. Undeniably, health care has moved into the marketplace.

The Accessibility of Health Care

The general movement towards a view of health care as an economic commodity has a serious negative affect on access to basic health care. In a marketplace environment where health care is bought and sold, Americans depend upon health insurance as the principal means of access to the health care system. Given the fact that the availability of adequate health insurance is usually linked to a person's employment status, many people lack the means to obtain basic health care.

When people lose their jobs, even temporarily, they lose access to health care. Some unemployed or newly re-employed people who lack health insurance and are seriously ill or have family members with chronic medical conditions are able to buy only poor coverage at a high price. Many others are unable to buy health insurance at all. They must spend all their savings on medical care, become impoverished, and then rely on the government for publicly provided care. But that care is not always available. Various studies show that the major public programs that underwrite health benefits do little to meet even the basic health care needs of a significant number of Americans—more than 50 million according to one reliable report.[2]

There is supposedly a health care safety net in the United States which ensures access to health care. Perhaps there was something like a net in the past, but today the commercialization of hospitals and medical practice, the preoccupation of business and government with controlling health care costs, and stubbornly high unemployment are unravelling that net.[3]

The current market-oriented approach to the financing, distribution, and quality of health care indiscriminately compromises the health of millions of Americans as well as the continued viability of many institutions whose sponsors view health care as a social good rather than an economic opportunity. Health care is still widely available in the United States but that availability, and certainly the quality and extent of care, is usually linked to an individual's ability to pay or an institution's willingness to adopt the strategies and practices of the marketplace.

An American Irony

The transformation of health care in the U.S. has led Uwe E. Reinhardt to comment that "The United States currently finds itself in a situation that would be comical were it not so tragic."[4] In the so-called land of limitless opportunity many are deprived.

> Suffering fellow citizens are being denied health care resources of which we have too many! Almost daily, our newspapers bombard us with stories about the physician glut and the surplus of hospital beds. . . . And yet we read of a three-year-old comatose girl being denied access to a nearby hospital simply because the child's parents are poor and do not have health insurance.[5]

This kind of "denial of urgently needed health services to poor patients within sight of idle resources is a uniquely American phenomenon," according to Reinhardt. It simply would not happen elsewhere. "It is inconceivable, for example, that a Canadian, French, German, or Dutch three-year-old comatose child would ever be denied nearby available health care simply because that child is poor. . . . Sadly, it can be said that it happens 'only in America.'"[6]

Now what about the preferential option for the poor? Perhaps this Third World concept might indeed shed some light on the socioeconomic and political environment of health care in the U.S. today, an environment "not receptive to addressing the health needs of the poor and the near poor."[7] It is ironic but nonetheless true that this affluent nation, with its substantial resources, exhibits a third-rate attitude towards the poor, particularly in the area of health care.

THE PREFERENTIAL OPTION FOR THE POOR

A preliminary description of the concept itself, as well as some objections to it, will suggest possible lines of connection between the preferential option for the poor and the issue of health care in the U.S. Since in this context we are emphasizing the suggestive power and analogical force of the preferential option, we shall concentrate on the substantive features of the concept rather than its biblical and theological background and development.

The phrase *preferential option for the poor* has excited a good deal of controversy since 1978, when it first became widely used. Resistance to the term and what it implies is motivated by a variety of factors, some rooted in ideological repugnance, others based upon simple misunderstandings. "Some of the resistance comes from the reluctance of privileged groups—and those who serve them—to give up their unfair privileges."[8] The status quo is fine. The poor will always be with us. That's life. This type of selfish cynicism, though, is probably not the most prevalent source of passive resistance and occasional active public dissent.

The use of the term *preferential option* has also evoked strong negative reactions from those who have misunderstood the basic intent behind its use. Some critics view the adoption of an "option for the poor" as more or less equivalent to embracing the Marxist "class option" that encourages violent revolution. Although one could hardly deny that the concept could plausibly be developed along these lines, it would be a mistake to understand the preferential option itself as an invitation to violent revolution.[9]

Another source of resistance resides in a failure on the part of some to appreciate the difference between personal and structural injustice. "They think of [the preferential option for the poor] in purely interpersonal terms as a rejection of wealthy people; they fail to realize that it is directed towards developing a society that is structurally just."[10] In an effort to counter an exclusivist interpretation of the preferential option, some of its proponents have spoken of "a preferential but not exclusive option for the poor."[11] There is no intention to be exclusive.

> But the poor are given preference and special care because their need is greater. "Fair shares for all" leads to justice only if everybody already has a fairly equal share. Where some are already victims of injustice it only reinforces the

inequality. Therefore social justice does not require that we give equal shares of our time and resources to everybody. What it requires is that we work for some kind of balance in society. The better off groups already have adequate resources; to opt for the poor is to aim to rectify the balance.[12]

Thus, the preferential option for the poor is not inherently classist. It constitutes a call to all classes to cooperate in building a just society by attempting to overcome gross disparities between persons and nations in terms of power, education, and opportunities as well as income. Finally, the preferential option should not be viewed as a romanticization of the poor or their poverty. The idea that one finds an excess of goodness, beauty, or simplicity among the poor is as dangerous as it is naive. There is nothing inherently beautiful about material poverty. Good and evil know no social boundaries.

An Option for Social Change

Positively speaking, the preferential option for the poor implies a commitment to the revision of social structures. There is an ever increasing concentration of wealth in the world. The preferential option calls for breaking up this concentration and the development of a spirit of solidarity, both within and among nations. Redesigned economic structures must be put in place that guarantee each person in a society a reasonable share of certain basic or primary social goods.

It is an unfortunate fact that "new structures will not come about through the internal dynamics of the economic system alone."[13] Pressure must be applied. Concerted action is necessary "to achieve this renewal through meaningful political change and broader participation in political decision-making."[14] In short, then, the preferential option for the poor involves a political commitment to structural change that flows from the conviction that "the more fortunate should renounce some of their rights so as to place their goods more generously at the service of others."[15]

An Option for Personal Commitment

The preferential option for the poor entails more than a generalized commitment to social change; it demands personal choices. Recognizing the preferential respect due to the poor and the special situation they have in society calls for an individual response in at least three areas of personal life: judgment, advocacy, and evaluation.

Judgment. Individuals committed to the preferential option for the poor must make a concerted effort to integrate the perspective of the economically disadvantaged and the materially deprived into their judgments. There must be "an effort to appreciate the perspective from which the poor view political and economic decisions, public and private policies, personal and institutional attitudes, and individual and corporate events."[16] It should be stressed here that this does not imply that the perspective of the poor has a unique claim on the truth, "but that it is the one frequently ignored or neglected or relegated to a subordinate position when important judgments are made."[17]

Advocacy. Forming judgments, however, is not enough to change fundamentally flawed social structures and societal attitudes that oppress and exploit the poor. The preferential option for the poor is an insistent call to action. "It is not enough to recall principles, state intentions, point to crying injustices and utter prophetic denunciations; these words will lack real weight unless they are accompanied for each individual by a livelier awareness of personal responsibility and by effective action."[18] Thus, to opt for the poor is to opt for personal intervention.

Solidarity. But even a commitment to act is not enough; it must be *engaged* action. An authentic preferential option for the poor calls for intimate involvement with the poor themselves, a personal solidarity with those who are themselves economically and materially disadvantaged. Paternalism and condescension are a constant threat to the integrity of the preferential option, since "people who are used to exercising power over others can be easily tempted to continue to do so at the same time as they commit themselves to working for social justice."[19]

This kind of personal solidarity is very difficult to attain and it is not possible for everyone; but, in principle at least, it is part of the radical demand for personal commitment associated with the preferential option for the poor.

The Preferential Option and the National Debate on Health Care

As mentioned above, the distinctiveness of its religious (Judeo-Christian) and cultural (Third World) origins may limit the applicability of the preferential option for the poor to the public debate over health care in the United States. Despite its otherworldly inspiration, both theologically and culturally, the concept itself is clearly compatible with other perspectives on the problem of poverty and structural injustice. It is solidly rooted in common human experience and, therefore, applicable analogically, if not absolutely.

An analogy is, by definition, somewhat the same as and yet different from the thing to which it is analogous. For example, the four seasons (spring, summer, fall, and winter) may be viewed as an analogy for the course of human life (birth, childhood, young adulthood, and old age). Human poverty, structural injustice, and oppression, although they are found in different places at different times, will always exhibit certain features that are somewhat the same. There are clear analogies owing to the fact that all forms of poverty and social injustice take shape within the same fabric of human experience.

The experience of poverty generates responses from a variety of perspectives (e.g., philosophical, sociological, theological, etc.) that, although different, often share common elements. For instance, as already mentioned, the preferential option for the poor displays striking similarities to certain features of the philosopher John Rawls's principle of fair equality of opportunity. In this theory, Rawls justifies unequal (preferential) treatment for many classes of persons (e.g., the handicapped and materially disadvantaged) on the grounds that they cannot be held personally responsible for the conditions that prevent them from obtaining a reasonable share of certain basic or primary social goods.

Rawls's theory, then, is genuinely analogous—somewhat the same, yet different in many details—to the preferential option for the poor. The two approaches, one religiously inspired and the other philosophically grounded, share some common ground. Thus, they can be considered in tandem; they mutually reinforce and illuminate each other, even if indirectly by way of analogy.

Furthermore, their compatibility, and even mutual reinforcement, makes an important point: Secular and religious perspectives, although sometimes quite different in many details, are not always mutually exclusive. They are often complementary viewpoints that are fundamentally related. Therefore, secular perspectives can and do play a role in religious inquiry, while religious perspectives can and do support secular understanding of certain issues.

It follows, then, that the preferential option for the poor may have something to contribute, even if only by way of analogy, to the secular debate on health care for the poor in the United States today. In fact, it is the contention of this chapter that the preferential option for the poor does possess significant suggestive power with regard to this debate. It should be viewed merely as a suggestive analogy, however, not as an authoritative norm.

THE PLIGHT OF THE POOR

The preferential option for the poor has become a powerful summary and symbol of the plight of the poor everywhere, not just in Latin America. Anyone even vaguely familiar with the state of affairs in U.S. health care as outlined above will recognize its relevance. The number of poor people without adequate health insurance has recently increased, and newspapers, television, and radio frequently carry stories about uninsured poor persons unable to obtain necessary or timely care.

There does not seem to be any room in the health care marketplace for the poor, who are increasingly reduced to the status of "health care beggars" receiving care in an "unpredictable fashion, as an act of *noblesse oblige* on the part of some kindly provider."[20] Uwe Reinhardt has put his finger on one of the prime causes of this miserable state of affairs: "The nation's manifest impotence in this area reflects an inability to agree on the ethical precepts to govern the production and distribution of health care."[21]

The plight of the poor in the U.S., especially their limited access to health care, is clearly in need of ethical analysis. The personal and social perspectives highlighted in the preferential option can help focus some of the ethical concerns in question. For example, the preferential option lends support to a principle embraced by many thinkers, whether they be religious conservatives or secular liberals: A society has an obligation to care for its poor. As Samuel Johnson said, "A decent provision for the poor is the true test of civilization."[22]

It is important to note, though, that the preferential option can do more than lend support to a general principle. The substantive content of the preferential option can also suggest specific areas that might be considered in analyzing the situation of the poor. For example, the emphasis that the preferential option places on the revision of social structures as the central vehicle for achieving a decent provision for the poor suggests that the ethical precepts we develop to govern the production and distribution of health care must be social as well as personal in character. Changing one's personal perspective is good, and indeed may be the necessary prerequisite to a changed societal perspective. But without social change very little will be done to improve the lot of the poor, particularly in regard to health care.

Of course, this is not to minimize the importance of personal commitment. In fact, the preferential option is quite instructive with reference to the kind of personal commitment needed to achieve a decent provision for the poor. While the degree and form of personal commitment will vary from person to person, the preferential option does highlight certain areas for consideration by those who wish to develop a personal commitment. As we have already seen, judgment, advocacy, and solidarity are aspects of the preferential option that are relevant to personal commitment to the poor. In making judgments regarding indigent care and related issues, committed health care professionals should make a concerted effort to understand and incorporate the perspective from which the poor view political and economic policies, institutional attitudes, etc. Moreover, anyone personally committed to decent levels of health care for the poor should seriously consider moving beyond stating principles and intentions and pointing to crying injustices. To opt for the poor is to opt for advocacy through effective action and concrete decisions aimed at ameliorating the physical and emotional suffering of the poor.

Commitment to the poor through personal *advocacy* is not, of course, the preserve of religiously inspired persons. This type of commitment is surely to be found among solid secularists. Yet a careful analysis of advocacy within the context of the preferential option for the poor may serve to reinforce and even further illuminate the ethical sensibilities of committed humanists with regard to their commitment to health care for the poor.

Finally, the notion of *solidarity* as understood in the preferential option reminds us that personal commitment can be taken to heroic levels. Someone like Albert Schweitzer or Mother Theresa of Calcutta—one a humanist, the other a religious—exhibits what a total commitment to the health care needs of the poor might entail. Both have given themselves fully. Again, the substance of a particular aspect of the preferential option suggests lines of development for anyone interested in exploring the ethical context of health care in the U.S. today.

CONCLUSION

Many more areas where the preferential option for the poor is relevant to the current state of health care in the U.S. could be described. But, this would go beyond the introductory character of this chapter, which is meant as an invitation to those who might find the preferential option interesting. If the invitation leads to further exploration and the concept is adopted as a genuinely suggestive analogy, the effort to relate a frankly religious theme to a civic debate will have been worthwhile.

NOTES

1. J. Rawls, *A Theory of Justice* (Cambridge, Mass.: Belknap Press of Harvard University Press, 1971), 87.

2. "U.S. Health Care Faulted in Senate," *New York Times,* January 13, 1987, p. 1.

3. J. Feder, J. Hadley, and R. Mullner, "Falling through the Cracks: Poverty, Insurance Coverage, and Hospital Care for the Poor," *Milbank Memorial Fund Quarterly* 62 (1984): 544–66.

4. U.E. Reinhardt, "An American Paradox," *Health Progress* 67, no. 9 (1986): 43.

5. Ibid., 42.

6. Ibid., 42.

7. Catholic Health Association of the United States, *No Room in the Marketplace: The Health Care of the Poor,* final report of the Task Force on Health Care of the Poor (St. Louis, Mo.: Catholic Health Association of the United States, 1986), 50.

8. D. Dorr, *Spirituality and Justice* (Maryknoll, N.Y.: Orbis Books, 1984), 78.

9. D. Dorr, *Option for the Poor.* (Maryknoll, N.Y.: Orbis Books, 1983), 146–47.

10. Dorr, *Spirituality and Justice,* 78.

11. Dorr, *Option for the Poor,* 311, n. 19.

12. Dorr, *Spirituality and Justice,* 78–79.

13. D.M. Byers and J.T. Pawlikowski, eds., *Justice in the Marketplace* (Washington, D.C.: United States Catholic Conference, 1985), 201.

14. Ibid.

15. Ibid., 235.

16. P.J. Henriot, "Service of the Poor," *Justice and Healthcare* (St. Louis, Mo.: Catholic Health Association of the United States, 1984), 19.

17. Ibid.

18. Byers and Pawlikowski, *Justice in the Marketplace,* 244.

19. Dorr, *Spirituality and Justice,* 82.

20. Reinhardt, "An American Paradox," 42.

21. M. Novak, "The Option for the Poor: Clarifications," *St. Louis University Public Law Review* 5 (1986): 307.

22. Ibid.

BIBLIOGRAPHY

Byers, D.M., and J.T. Pawlikowski, eds. *Justice in the Marketplace.* Washington, D.C.: U.S. Catholic Conference, 1985. This volume brings together the Church's teaching over the past century on economic matters. The first section presents, in whole or in excerpt, all the major messages on economics that have emerged from the Vatican since Leo XIII's *Rerum Novarum,* the first social encyclical. The second section presents the much less extensive comments the United States Catholic bishops have made on economic issues, starting with the 1919 *Program of Social Reconstruction* and ending with *The Economy: Human Dimensions in 1975.*

Catholic Health Association of the United States. *No Room in the Marketplace: The Health Care of the Poor.* St. Louis, Mo.: Catholic Health Association of the United States, 1986. This excellent report represents the work of the Catholic Health Association's Task Force on the Health Care of the Poor. It identifies the health care poor, describes the problems they face in obtaining adequate health care services, traces causes of these problems, emphasizes the necessity and urgency of addressing them, and recommends several possible remedies.

Dorr, D. *Option for the Poor.* Maryknoll, N.Y.: Orbis Books, 1983. Dorr offers a clear description of the preferential option for the poor.

Feder, J., J. Hadley, and R. Mullner, "Falling through the Cracks: Poverty, Insurance Coverage, and Hospital Care for the Poor." *Milbank Memorial Fund Quarterly* 62 (1984): 544–66. An excellent description of the intricate relationship among the elements of poverty, health insurance, and access to health care in the United States.

Health Progress 67, nos. 9–10. These two issues of the official journal of the Catholic Health Association of the United States contain a symposium on health care of the poor. The preferential option for the poor is considered in several of the papers.

Novak, N. "The Option for the Poor: Clarifications." *St. Louis University Public Law Review* 5 (1986): 309–328. Novak discusses the preferential option for the poor within the context of his negative critique of the American bishops' pastoral letter on the U.S. economy.

Part V

Accountability and Responsibility

Chapter 27

Patients' Rights

William J. Ellos

A highly durable document in the history of the development of questions concerning patient's rights is the American Hospital Association's "A Patient's Bill of Rights." The basic right proposed is the right to considerate and respectful care. There is also the right to enough information to be able to give truly informed consent. The patient has the right to refuse treatment and also the right to privacy and confidentiality. There must be reasonable access to medical services and reasonable continuity of care.

The language of rights is itself a relatively new development in the long history of ethics. Its first clear appearance is during the Renaissance. Until then, the term *right* (and foreign equivalents) referred to the moral action or object itself. Something was right if a right ethical action was performed in the situation. *Right* might refer either to the action itself or to some aspect of the object of activity which had been rectified or made right by the right action.[1] An obvious example of this approach is in the area of medicine. If you have something wrong with you, there is a chance that the physician can make it right; by the right action of the physician what is medically wrong with you is made right. This use of the term *right* tends to blur the distinction between actions and objects. It fits a world view much more interested in the structure of objective reality than the world view that has since arisen, which is more concerned with creative personal involvement in various aspects of reality.

Our current notions of rights are founded on the notion that every one of us has a certain faculty or power. When we exercise this faculty or power, we are exercising our rights. But for every right there may well be a correlative duty. Both rights and duties play out their function by influencing real situations. As a result, a contemporary attempt to deal with the question of patients' rights might use any of three different approaches.

One approach concentrates on questions concerning the powers of patients to exercise their rights. This approach will very strongly stress the role played in rights talk by certain understood or clearly stated contractual arrangements which we have with each other.

A second approach to rights stresses the duties incumbent on other people to ensure that our rights are indeed respected and not violated. The focus here would be more on the physician than on the patient. It is a focus, however, which stresses the welfare of the latter rather than the former. In this way it concentrates more on the rights of the patient.

A third type of ethics, which harks back to a certain extent to the older, pre-Renaissance point of view, locates rights in how human nature is structured. We experience ourselves to be structured biologically, psychologically, and socially. Insofar as we are in harmony with these three ways of being structured, we are properly exercising our rights.

SOCIAL CONTRACT THEORIES OF RIGHTS

The Renaissance and the Reformation caused the destruction of the hierarchical medieval world view. Most important for our discussion is the change that occurred in the social and political situation. Rather than trying to locate human rights in some sort of harmonious relationship to nature, philosophers approached the question of human interaction in new ways. The importance of nature became greatly reduced. While momentarily leaving aside this notion of ethics as a harmonious interaction with nature's biological and social rhythms, we should not lose sight of this approach, as it will reappear in a more highly nuanced and practical form in our later consideration of the role and place for a virtue ethic in establishing the rights of physicians and patients.

The first of the new theorists who still exercise an influence on ethics is Thomas Hobbes (1588–1679). He maintains that by nature we have certain powers or rights which we can exercise practically at will. A human being is an individual with powers. A power is a right.[2] Since each individual has these powers, conflict of rights is inevitable. The human situation is one of constant struggle and strife. Resolution of this struggle is brought about by the forming of basic social contracts to prevent us from exercising the most basic power we have: the power to kill. Other parts of the social contract are agreed to because of the abiding fear and distrust we have for each other. Life is nasty, brutish, and short.

While Hobbes's version of the social contract was originally drafted to meet and explain social and political tensions, aspects of it remain remarkably applicable in the medical arena. Physicians do have the power of life and death. Patients are increasingly afraid of this power, especially in the problematic cases of termination of life. Tragically, in the wake of the malpractice crisis, massive distrust of the medical profession is emerging. The whole tone of ''A Patient's Bill of Rights'' is defensive. Legal litigation is inescapably Hobbesian. Is there any alternative?

John Locke (1632–1704), in the generation after Hobbes, also went beyond the harmony of nature, but in a different direction. This direction is much more in line with the view of rights more generally accepted today. Locke maintains, as does Hobbes, that the basis of rights is power. But the basic power, according to Locke, is not the power to kill. It is the power which we possess by virtue of owning and controlling private property.[3] This view introduced a third component into the rights scheme. Rights are based, not on direct relationships of person to person, but on indirect relations of persons to things. A considerable amount of the acerbity is taken out of the social contract. The view also places a certain distance between the individuals who claim and exercise rights. A great deal of the discussion in health care rights today rests securely on a Lockean base.

One of the functions of health care insurance in this country is to make certain that patients' rights are protected in the situations of catastrophic health care need. Rights are secured by the purchase of the appropriate amount of coverage. Problematic in this approach is that individuals have different degrees of purchasing power. Is it correct to assume that the richer person will be entitled to more rights, the poorer to less? A pure undiluted capitalism would tend to answer yes. Private carrier insurance companies tend strongly to echo that answer. Is it true that the wealthier physician who buys more malpractice insurance will, in this system of social contract, have the right to practice medicine in a more unimpeded way than his less well-off colleague? The answer would seem again to be yes.

A possible corrective to this approach might be found in the contemporary Hobbesian theory of Robert Nozick. Here the claim is made that an individual has a very strong entitlement to exercise rights over what has been acquired either by personal effort or by transfer of rights. There is, however, a powerful constraint on these rights, namely, that one cannot aggressively override the rights of another where there is a conflict.[4] A wealthy physician who can afford to and does purchase an inordinate amount of insurance just might be disrupting the rights of less wealthy colleagues, who would not be able to compete as well for patients. A patient who is able to buy a great deal of insurance might be securing a rather high level of physician service, a level denied patients who do not have such borrowing power.

An apparent problem in the practice of patients' rights is that the rights of the skillful physician, nurse, or other health care provider are much looked after, unlike the rights of the dependent patient. This very problem, however, has also served as a spur to the patient to become more conversant with details of the practice of medicine. Widespread publicity surrounding certain key questions in medicine and medical ethics—such as termination of life, truth telling, confidentiality, and informed consent—has alerted the public to a number of details on these questions. Acquired knowledge about these matters does allow for greater exercise of rights by patients. It is now also not unusual to encounter patients who, once they become ill, investigate in considerable detail their medical situation; in doing so they confer upon themselves many rights. The exercise of these rights is not confined to major medical decisions but increasingly involves such matters as the prescription of lower-priced generic drugs or the duration or frequency of therapy. Education is becoming recognized as the key to the exercise of rights.

This approach to the securing of rights through education suggests a quite different kind of social contract. There is a historical basis for this kind of contract in the writings of Jean-Jacques Rousseau (1712–1778). Such a social contract is based, not on fear, but on a presupposition of trust and cooperation.[5] It would appear that the context in which patients exercise rights involves trust and cooperation and is quite different from the context presupposed in Hobbesian theories. As much as patients are concerned at this time with the more threatening aspects of medicine, there remains a strong inclination toward trust and confidence in health care providers. Yet even in this context, certain features common to all rights must be carefully considered.

Even though the context of a social contract (as posited by Rousseau) may appear pleasant, it should not be treated too lightly. A cocktail party would not be a good example of such a context. This is because the trusting relationship involves very serious obligations. Choices and decisions have important and far-reaching consequences. We must also be able to specify just who has what rights. In the complex world of technological health care, this is by no means an easy task. Many of the health care technical professionals are never seen by the patient, yet many of them exercise rights over such key aspects of the patient's situation as confidentiality or access to treatment. It is impossible to be involved in a trusting relationship if you do not know who to trust. It seems that anonymity ought to be removed from health care as much as possible. Moreover, the precise roles of various members of the health care team should be made known to the patient. One ought to know what are the roles, responsibilities, and names of the attending physician, residents, and nurses.

Since the patient is in the more threatened situation, there is a need to protect patient rights. Nonetheless, the patient is also in control of the situation. While just the opposite often seems to be the case, yet the patient is only under the paternalistic care of the physician (except in specialized cases) by personal choice and delegation of authority. The patient may choose in the course of treatment not to exercise certain rights. Good clinical practice will as much as possible provide options to the patient. This may be as complex as the choice of a course of therapy or as simple as the possibility of taking a longer or a shorter walk down the hospital corridor. It is essential that the patient be given the opportunity not only of saying yes, but also of saying no.

A libertarian view of ethics rather strongly stresses both the honoring of positive rights and the importance of negative rights. Here the fundamental moral rule is to respect other people's liberty. It would be of the utmost importance never to interfere with the actions of a competent adult just to bring about better consequences. Clearly physicians face a danger here. This view would demand that the patient, in as much as possible, be a party to medical decision making on all levels. Further, the view does allow for and even encourages interference with the actions of someone who is interfering with someone else. The patient might very well be the individual interfered with. Strong action against a physician or other health care provider would then be called for. Hopefully the result of these actions and counteractions would be a growing voluntary agreement among all parties. Since the obligation not to interfere with the rights of another applies to noninterference with the body of another person and also to noninterference with the person's mind and property, care in the practice of medicine must be taken not to disturb the patient mentally or financially without the patient's clear consent.[6]

The most striking social contract theory since Hobbes and Rousseau is the one proposed by the contemporary American philosopher John Rawls. The Rawlsian scheme provides a model for the American ideal of equality for all. A somewhat imaginative mechanism is suggested for understanding the model. Suppose that we were all in a situation of complete equality. No single person would have any advantage over another person. All would have the same abilities, the same disabilities, the same prospects. Any movement out of this situation would involve probable disruption. In order to minimize as much as possible the disruption and resultant inequality, two principles would have to be followed. We should try to ensure equal liberty for all as best we can, even with regard to activities disruptive of this liberty. We should also look to the needs of the least advantaged. This second principle would serve as a strong and constant check on abuse of the first principle.[7]

Rawls's view has important consequences in the area of patients' rights. The ills in society clearly are suffered by the least advantaged. Physical disadvantage generates psychological, social, and financial disadvantage. The rights of patients must be vigorously protected so as to enable a return to the situation of equality inasmuch as this is possible. A specific adaptation of the Rawlsian method for the practice of medicine is proposed by Robert Veatch.[8] Veatch sees the social contract as a three-level model. Understanding the three levels will help in understanding how medicine does or should operate in this country.

The first level is simply a selection of what kinds of ethical principles should be involved in setting up a social contract. The selection follows Rawlsian principles. This is rather like the first aspect of the Rawls model, in that the stress is on equality for all. At the second level there is a tacit but very real contract between the medical profession and society at large. The health care providers are in a position of privilege and respect. They have a stringent obligation to look after patients. Patients have a compelling right to their services. The professional-patient contract must be marked at all points by the principle of equal liberty for all. This equal liberty will be fostered by a constant care for the least advantaged. The rights of the least advantaged will be emphasized. Finally, there is the third level contract between the health care provider and the patient. The patient hopefully will feel secure knowing that the provider places a high premium on removing not only the physiological disadvantages to the patient, but also the psychological, social, and financial disadvantages.

Lawyers enter the social contract at the third level. They present themselves as advocates of patients who are in a disadvantaged position. Often they truly are advocates. In these cases, a lawyer can be a strong defender of patient's rights and help to rebuild the three-level contract from the ground up. The situation is, however, open to abuse. The lawyer is in a position to exploit the need of the patient for the sake of personal financial gain. When this occurs, the second-level contract between the legal profession and the patient is subverted. The principles of equality of the first level of the social contract also are infringed, since the goal of the legal activity is not equality for all but personal gain for the lawyer.

Patients' rights, in the light of Rawls's and Veatch's models, currently seem quite secure at the grass-roots level but not very secure at the level of the relation of the professions of law and medicine to society. It is imperative that both law and medicine improve their posture of commitment to equality for all by aiding the disadvantaged. Unless this is done, the reliance on the one-to-one professional-patient or professional-client relationship will continue to subvert the credibility of the two professions. Professionals must operate within a healthy professional context. Continued going-it-alone will bring about a crisis of confidence in the organized professions and the system will become so complex that equity will not be attained. This is already the case with malpractice. A few individuals with the stamina, financial means, and access to the proper professionals enjoy a high degree of health and legal care, but at the expense of the majority of the population who do not. Patient and client rights are strongly secured for a few, but denied to most. Equality disappears, even as an ideal.

There is a remedy.

A free society of equals holds that law comes from the consent of the governed. H.L.A. Hart has developed a way of showing how the governed control the laws. Some changes in the present legal regulation of law and medicine are now necessary in order to rectify their relation to society. Since appropriate changes cannot be expected from within the professions, those now finding themselves governed by these professions will have to take action.

Hart views the legal system as being made up of primary and secondary rules or laws. Primary rules basically make up the main body of the law; secondary rules give the power of enforcement. There are three problems with primary rules which make enforcement problematic. The rules are (1) uncertain, (2) static, and (3) inefficient. But for each primary rule problem there is a secondary rule remedy. Rules of recognition clarify uncertainty; rules of amendment and repeal bring about change; rules of adjudication render law more efficient. The general public has more control over rules of recognition than over the other rules. There are three requirements for rules of recognition. The rules (and laws) must be internally consistent with each other, they must have a consistent external effect, and they must be accepted by the general public.[9]

Governmental laws and rules, as well as regulations internal to the health care and legal professions, are not now generally thought to be effective. Thus there is not a perceived consistency in the laws. Both governmental and professional regulation of the legal and medical professions need reform. Often these two types of regulation go hand in hand, as do the workings of state licensing boards for physicians and lawyers. Those of us receiving the services of these professions have been securing our rights, not because the legal system and the professions have provided clear and efficient regulations, but by not accepting the laws and regulations. The rising tide of malpractice suits in medicine and the entertaining of trivial and nuisance suits by the legal profession are indicators of this nonacceptance.

Since the control of the law is in our hands, it is imperative that we elect and support public officials in both the legal sphere and the professions who will bring about the reform of laws and regulations. This will ensure that the laws and rules form a consistent and effective tool for regulation of the professions. Once this is achieved, confidence in the professions will be restored and then enhanced. A secure base for patients' rights will be established in two ways. In the normal course of events, rights will be taken somewhat for granted, as the professions will be precisely regulated in ways to ensure these rights. In problematic cases, clear and efficient sources of redress will be available.

PROFESSIONAL DUTIES AS THE SOURCE OF RIGHTS

As problematic as the role of the professions has been, it may still be looked upon as the ultimate source of patients' rights. A medical profession with a strong sense of duty to its clients (patients) would be most concerned to maximize patients' rights, and any sort of self-regulation would necessarily have as its primary aim the securing of these rights. The emphasis on the duties that the profession has to secure these rights moves us into a discussion of a different approach to ethics.

The founder of this duty-based approach to ethics is Immanuel Kant (1724–1804). He actually developed a simple and a complex form of duty ethics, both of which are often employed by physicians. In the simple form, duties are recognized because each of us has a built-in moral sense that tells us what we ought to do. We respond to a strong feeling of ought.[10] Some call this *conscience*. Physicians who resent and reject medical ethicists often appeal to this inner sense. Not infrequently they claim that they developed it at their mother's knee. There is no need for advice or elaboration.

Patients' rights are put in peril by such a physician. The source of ethics is taken to be the inner moral sense of the physician, and the patient is left out of the account. This sort of a physician is also quite uncritical in the exercise of judgment and may even be hostile to suggestions. Yet there are times when intuitive ethic might be the only or best thing. Relying on one's best ethical intuitions in a case where immediate action is vital might be the best way of trying to ensure a patients' rights. But it would not be good policy to use emergency situations to establish general ethical rules.

Kant developed a number of ways of formulating rules which would spell out the duties urged upon us by our inner moral sense. One of these formulations continues to play a major role in medical ethics. It states that we are never to treat another human being merely as a means to an end.[11] Health care professionals are in a position where it is easy to do this, because the patients in their care are in a state of need and dependency. It is easy to see them as elements (means to an end) in one's professional advancement and not objects of concern for their own sake. Given the pressures of case load and the pressures from hospital administration, it is impossible not to manipulate patients, at least to some extent, and not to use them in some way as a means to an end (i.e., rather than simply curing or caring for them). Even the requirement of a fee is in some sense a manipulation.

The Oxford philosopher W.D. Ross developed some more specific rules to govern professional behavior, rules which give rise to what he termed *prima facie duties*.[12] The first of these rules entails a quite predictable curb on professional power. It requires that there be an absolute respect for patient autonomy. This has the effect of securing patient rights, because it compels a physician to ensure the patient's informed consent. The physician must inform the patient of the types of procedures which will be employed and the attendant risks, especially the risk of death or serious physical or mental harm. The probable length and difficulty of recuperation should be presented, as should the chances of success. Costs— physical, psychological, and financial—should be indicated. Alternative procedures should be outlined and assessed. In short, an attempt should be made to allow a patient to exercise as much freedom of choice as possible.

A second duty outlined by Ross is the duty of beneficence. This requires the physician always to act in the best interests of the patient. This is also often called *paternalism,* or in a more nonsexist form, *parentalism.* There are two types of paternalism. Weak paternalism allows intervention only in cases where the patient is already physically, psychologically, or socially impaired. Strong paternalism allows intervention with individuals who are not experiencing impairment.

The ethical conflict between patient autonomy and physician beneficence is mirrored in three landmark legal decisions in this area. In *Canterbury v. Spence,* the court leaned more in favor of autonomy. It set a precedent that what should be done in a problematic medical situation is what a reasonable person would do.[13] The physician would have to make sure that adequate disclosure of information is given so that a reasonable decision could be made. *ZeBarth v. Swedish Hospital Medical Center* reflects a more paternalistic approach. It was decided that a physician is required to disclose to a patient what a reasonably prudent physician in the medical community would disclose.[14] While both of these cases specifically have to do with questions of truth telling, the presuppositions of autonomy in the one case and beneficence in the other are quite clear.

The legal ruling in *Tarasoff v. Regents of the University of California* requires the breaking of confidentiality when there is foreseeable harm to an individual.[15] This reflects a somewhat curious blend of paternalism and autonomy. It requires a very paternalistic action in order to safeguard patient autonomy.

Recent articles in the *Archives of Internal Medicine* and the *Journal of the American Medical Association* have pointed out the weakness of trying to base clinical ethical decisions primarily on autonomy or beneficence. They call for a return to a more pragmatic ethics which will more directly reflect the experience of the physician in the actual practice of medicine.[16]

THE STRUCTURE OF MEDICAL PRACTICE AS THE SOURCE OF RIGHTS

While physicians in the actual practice of medicine are not unconcerned with patient rights, this cannot be the central focus of their activity. The malpractice crisis has perhaps tended to make physicians much more aware of these matters. The practice of defensive medicine which has developed has probably not made for better medical care nor advanced patients' rights. Legal and ethical reform is needed in order to permit physicians to do what they do best—practice medicine.

Medical practice (except for psychiatry) primarily involves the cure and care of the body. The body itself has a certain structure which is both anatomical and biological. Surgeons correct anatomical anomalies and physicians biological ones. The body itself has a remarkable number of built-in curing and maintenance mechanisms. Knowledge of the structure and working of these mechanisms is vital to the practice of medicine. But the body also becomes injured, ill, and eventually dies. There are structures and mechanisms for this as well. The basic reason why medicine today is held in such esteem is the respect rightly given to the virtuosic skills needed in order to care for and cure the injured and the sick. One set of talents is needed for acquiring the requisite scientific knowledge. The application of scientific data to individual cases requires quite another set of talents. There must be an ability to determine what will be most useful at a given time and to what degree.

This combination of scientific skills and precisely honed common sense requires an all-consuming activity. The more the physician can develop this combination the better the chance of curing or otherwise aiding patients. The caring aspect of the physician's work also helps to ensure patients' rights, because the patient has not only biological bodily elements, but also psychological, social, and cultural elements.

The basic ground rules of a culture are seen most clearly in its legal system. In most cultures, the laws tend to be very general. They set the ultimate parameters of human activity. Violation of these parameters is subject to some sort of punishment or fine. But important as they are, such minimal guidelines cannot fully delineate or even fully reflect a given culture. The physician, as a rich cultural figure, must not be taken to be too closely allied to the legal system. More complexity, more nuance, and more compassion should be expected. Even individuals holding both an M.D. and J.D. are more revered and respected because of the former degree.

Psychological and social needs are also tended to by the ethic of rights and duties which we have been exploring. The range here of human activity is more extensive, but the abstract nature of these ethical systems often does not allow them to be effectively applied in complex cases. There is a growing appreciation and respect for the role of the doctorally trained (Ph.D.) medical ethicist, but a patient would still much rather take the help and advice of a physician.

Habitual medical virtues are needed in the physician's demanding work, i.e., doing precise diagnosis and prognosis. Technical knowledge and skills in the various areas of medicine must become part of the physician's blood and bone. These skills must be worked and reworked in the process of constantly updating medical knowledge and continuing to apply it effectively. A virtuous and habitual practice of the biological aspect of medicine demands always going the extra mile.

The physician must have the capacity and the developed skills to understand something of the patient's experience of illness. There must be the ability and willingness to enter in some way into the situation so that the best outcome may occur. This suggests a whole list of virtues: persistence, courage, alertness, carefulness, resourcefulness, prudence, energy, strength, cool-headedness, and determination. Also needed are gentleness, humor, amiability, cheer, warmth, appreciativeness, and openness. Although the physician should not get too close to the case emotionally as to lose professional perspective and drain needed personal resources, emotional involvement does occur and indeed it is mandatory for a good outcome. A list of social virtues in medicine might include honesty, sincerity, truthfulness, loyalty, consistency, reliability, and dependability.[17]

The major problem with a ''virtue'' approach to medical practice is that the list of virtues seems arbitrary and endless. A neat and precise ethic citing duties and rights would be more clear, but it would not be nearly so workable. Medicine is a practical art with many loose ends. It works best when practical tools are put to practical use. There are no hard and fast rules as to what is best. If the best is being habitually done, a maximal, instead of a minimal, set of patients' rights are being protected and enhanced. Aiming at a minimal set will not produce more than the minimal, but aiming at a maximal set almost certainly will.

Certain patterns explicate the habitual practice of virtue in medicine. These patterns also best guarantee respect for patients' rights. Medical practice is a coherent and complex form of cooperative activity. This makes it inevitable that the rights of others be fully considered. Cooperation takes place at two levels, within and without the profession. Internal cooperation advances the practice. Here some improvement is needed, for medicine has not done a good enough job of internal policing and review. The more this is done, the more external activity towards the patient will take proper account of patients' rights.

Medicine is so closely allied to ethics because explanatory elements are also evaluative. What is known must always be put to good use. As a result, probably the most fundamental virtue is integrity. There must be a constant striving to be of maximum use. Again, this more strongly supports patients' rights.

Ronald Dworkin, along with H.L.A. Hart, has a current claim to pre-eminence in jurisprudence. He takes a virtue approach to law that is instructive for understanding the relation of law to ethics and to medicine. He assumes there are three key legal virtues.[18] Justice treats everyone equally. However, law, ethics, and medicine cannot actually do this. Fairness favors the majority opinion. In law, ethics, and medicine, the rights of the minority must always be defended. A constant, patient search for the meaningful inner patterns of the law will show how one part coheres with another in the healthy growth and application of law. The same is true for medicine. Law and medicine unfold rather like a narrative, especially a narrative written by a number of writers one after the other. A constant and tenacious focus on the narrative will bring greater and greater rewards to the readers. Patients are like these readers. What they get is more and more access to legal and medical care and more and more right to that care.

Three basic approaches to patients' rights have been presented: contractual arrangements that stress the power of the patient, professional duties, and the power of the physician. The complex structure of medical practice suggests pragmatic procedures. The richness of this pragmatic approach provides abundant resources for creative medical ethics.

NOTES

1. John Finnis, *Natural Law and Natural Rights* (Oxford: Clarendon Press, 1980), 206–7.

2. Thomas Hobbes, *Leviathan,* ed. Michael Oakeshott (New York: Collier, 1977), 103–5.

3. John Locke, *Second Treatise on Civil Government* (Chicago: Regnery, 1962), 21–22.

4. Robert Nozick, *Anarchy, State, and Utopia* (New York: Basic Books, 1974), 33–35.

5. Jean-Jacques Rousseau, *The Social Contract,* trans. Willmoore Kendall (Chicago: Regnery, 1954), 17–22.

6. David Ozar, ''Rights: What They Are and Where They Come From,'' in *Philosophical Issues in Human Rights,* ed. Patricia H. Werhane, A.R. Gini, and David T. Ozar (New York: Random House, 1986), 4–21.

7. John Rawls, *A Theory of Justice* (Cambridge, Mass.: Belknap Press of Harvard University Press, 1971), 60–61.

8. Robert Veatch, *A Theory of Medical Ethics* (New York: Basic Books, 1981), 108–38.

9. H.L.A. Hart, *The Concept of Law* (Oxford: Clarendon Press, 1961), 77–120.

10. Immanuel Kant, *Groundwork of the Metaphysic of Morals,* trans. H.J. Paton (New York: Harper, 1956), 65–68.

11. *Ibid.,* 95.

12. W.D. Ross, *The Right and the Good* (Oxford: Oxford University Press, 1930), 19 ff.

13. No. 22099, U.S. Court of Appeals, District of Columbia Circuit, May 19, 1972, 464 Federal Reporter, 2d Series, 772.

14. *American Law Reports* 52, 3rd series (1972), pp. 1069, 1075–78, 1080.

15. California Supreme Court, July 1, 1976. 131 California Reporter 14.

16. R.C. Sider and C.D. Clements, "The New Medical Ethics: A Second Opinion," *Archives of Internal Medicine* 145 (1985): 2169–71; C.D. Clements, and R.C. Sider, "Medical Ethics' Assault on Medical Values," *Journal of the American Medical Association* 250 (1983): 2011–15.

17. E.L. Pincoffs, "Definition of the Virtues," in *Virtue and Medicine: Explorations in the Character of Medicine,* ed. E.E. Shelp (Dordrecht, Holland: D. Reidel, 1985), 130.

18. Ronald Dworkin, *Law's Empire* (Cambridge, Mass.: Belknap Press of Harvard University Press, 1986), 177–78.

BIBLIOGRAPHY

Books

Dworkin, Ronald. *Taking Rights Seriously*. Cambridge, Mass.: Harvard University Press, 1978. A classic plea for equality in the area of rights. Everyone has a right to be treated equally, but not to equal treatment. That is, equals are to be treated equally; unequals should be given extra consideration to equalize their position.

Dworkin, Ronald. *Law's Empire*. Cambridge, Mass.: Belknap Press of Harvard University Press, 1986. A sustained argument for taking the virtue of integrity as a key to understanding the bases of rights.

Hart, H.L.A. *The Concept of Law*. Oxford: Clarendon Press, 1961. The basic text for the view that rights arise when differing levels of legal activities are generally accepted by the public.

Nozick, Robert. *Anarchy, State, and Utopia*. New York: Basic Books, 1974. The entitlement theory here developed holds that rights accrue to individuals who have in some way earned them or by a transfer of rights from others who have earned them.

Rawls, John. *A Theory of Justice*. Cambridge, Mass.: Belknap Press of Harvard University Press, 1971. Rawls's social contract theory of rights holds both that there should be equality for all and also that we should respond to the needs of the least advantaged.

Veatch, Robert. *A Theory of Medical Ethics*. New York: Basic Books, 1981. A detailed application of a basically Rawlsian theory to the specific complexities of medical practice.

Werhane, Patricia, A.R. Gini, and D. Ozar, eds. *Philosophical Issues in Human Rights*. New York: Random House, 1986. Besides an excellent introductory chapter outlining rights theory, there are chapters on rights to health care, life, and death.

Articles

American Hospital Association. "A Patient's Bill of Rights." Chicago: American Hospital Association, 1975. Standard and still controversial listing of 12 basic areas in which the patient is entitled to defense against the physician or hospital.

Annas, George J. "A Model Patients' Bill of Rights." *Civil Liberties Review* 1 (Fall 1974): 20–22. An expansion, in great detail, of patients' rights, including both legal and ethical rights.

Pellegrino, Edmund D. "The Virtuous Physician and the Ethics of Medicine." In *Virtue and Medicine: Explorations in the Character of Medicine,* edited by E.E. Shelp. Dordrecht, Holland: D. Reidel, 1985. A clear description of the structures of medical practice that through physician paternalism ensure autonomous patient rights.

Chapter 28

Protherapeutic Authoritarianism

Susan S. Braithwaite and David C. Thomasma

The ideal of routinely providing needed medical care has become so familiar that some would find moral fault with any omission of normally beneficial medical actions. The purpose of the present chapter is to argue that the right to treat cannot be assumed and that there should be no categorical presumption in favor of therapy except when therapy is compatible with the axiom of doing no harm and subserves the goals of medicine, which are to prevent untimely death, to relieve suffering, and to help people during their lifetime be unencumbered by physical ailments.[1] To support those claims, it is proposed that a rigidly protherapeutic stance is consonant neither with our artistic, philosophic, and medical tradition nor with the values of the majority of lay people, values which our artists and philosophers express. Furthermore, it is argued that protherapeutic authoritarianism, defined as advocacy or imposition of medical interventions by individuals whose personality, motives, and methods are authoritarian, not only exists but is directed toward other goals than the goals of medicine. When subserving authoritarian goals, protherapeuticism sometimes transgresses against humanity. By considering atrocities committed under other idealistic but authoritarian systems, one can infer that such "slippery slope" dangers are likelier to result from a protherapeutic policy than from a policy that requires justification for therapy.

Some authors on medicine in Nazi Germany[2] and on forgoing life-sustaining therapy in this country[3] implicitly suggest that selective nontreatment in the United States would lead to eventual tolerance of medical actions morally reminiscent of the "euthanasia" and genocide programs run by Nazi physicians. It will be argued here that instead the opposite conclusion can reasonably be drawn from a comparison of medical practices in the United States with those in Nazi Germany. The discussion to follow is motivated partly by a defensive reaction to criticism[4] of a previously stated position on anticruelty care,[5] in which an attempt was made to justify forgoing life-sustaining therapy for certain hopelessly injured incompetent patients.

The idea of protherapeutic authoritarianism partly arose from observations on medical authoritarianism dating to the initial encounters of one of the authors with academic medicine (in the late 1960s). The observations were of behavior so banal and so commonly remarked by fellow students that it is impossible to imagine anyone in the profession having escaped firsthand experience of it. Admittedly, there are pitfalls in describing a colleague or mentor as authoritarian. No doubt the attributes a physician imputes to medical power structures will be influenced by the temper of the times, by peer sentiment, and by his or her pre-existing attitudes about authority, notably those attitudes dating back to childhood. It is freely acknowledged that others might find the designation *authoritarian* inappropriate and might feel that in exerting its power the profession exercises legitimate authority.[6] Further-more, it is easy to imagine reasons why a physician who is not authoritarian might talk or write as if he or she is. We often do not know our colleagues very well; that an authoritarian style of expression exists can be asserted more safely than that a fundamentally authoritarian personality exists.

The 1980s have seen a burgeoning of lay interest in protecting the rights of the medically ill, especially the incompetent. The description of protherapeutic authoritarianism also arises from observations on the tone and content of recent legislative and legal actions undertaken by some physicians and nonphysicians and the tone of their rhetoric.

THE RIGHT TO TREAT CANNOT BE ASSUMED

Principles of personal liberty and autonomy are so well ingrained in our moral philoso-phy[7] that the issue of the "right to treat" arises mainly in connection with cases of altered mental status or incompetence. Modern literary tradition supports our philosophic tradition in criticizing usurpation of the competent patient's right to autonomy in making medical decisions. In Solzhenitsyn's *Cancer Ward,* the chapter "The Right to Treat" is ironically so captioned; the author compares the physician's supposed right to treat to other oppressive actions of his totalitarian society.[8] In Orwell's *Nineteen Eighty-Four*, the author explicitly posits through his character O'Brien that the fundamental operating factor throughout history has been humans' exertion of their will or power over other humans; the remainder of the book, though fiction, of course, demonstrates contemporary abuses of power and the germs therein of future degeneration of modern individualistic western society.[9]

Protection of the Incompetent

In protecting the rights of the incompetent patient, arguments of substituted judgment and best interests might apply to the question of the physician's right to treat. In regard to these yardsticks, the possibility arises that the physician, who must be restrained from exerting his or her will over competent patients, sometimes must be likewise restrained in the case of a helpless, incompetent patient. There is a risk that such interventions might not be in the best interests of the incompetent patient or that, in our substituted judgment, the physician's wishes would lead to undesirable actions. It is important to recall that Nazi atrocities began with "euthanasia" of nonJewish injured neonates and children. These actions by Nazi physicians were undertaken without permission or knowledge of the families, who would probably have the best interests of the children at heart. Nevertheless, such actions were undertaken for supposedly idealistic motives, such as sparing societal resources, putting injured children out of their misery, and curing society by excision of a gangrenous appendix.[10] Subordination of individual interests and rights to a larger cause characterizes authoritarian thinking.[11] Those Nazi physicians considered that benefiting society, not the individual, was the object of their profession. (See Chapter 23 on the social obligations of health care practitioners.)

Although we now would agree the physician has no claim to be able to decide to dispatch certain members of society, it also can be argued that the physician has no claim to be able to decide to intervene in other ways with respect to incompetent patients. Decisions to intervene, superficially motivated by idealism but not necessarily subserving the goals of medicine, sometimes result from peer coercion, a fear of peer reproach or legal action, the desire to develop a new treatment modality, the desire to expand a series for publication, the desire to support the physician's local image or reputation, or the desire simply to assert power and ideology. In claiming a right to treat, physicians or lay advocates for patients may even become adversaries of patients and families in the courts and through the media.[12] The most helpless patient has the greatest risk that a legal action will grant the physician a right to treat over the protestations of family. Interventions for the incompetent patient can produce great distress for the uncomprehending subject of therapy, and an understanding family is best able to predict and interpret the patient's subjective experience.[13]

To forgo therapy—i.e., to refrain from inappropriate exertion of the will—should not be described as *passive euthanasia,* a term which implies another inappropriate exertion of the will to cause the patient to die. The doctor has no right to will the death of a patient.

Families and patients need to be protected actively against physicians who urge the imposition of conventional medical therapy without consideration of whether the underlying condition of the incompetent patient can be benefited. Those interventions against the course of nature that do not provide clear benefit constitute a violation or an outrage against the person. (However, families and incompetent patients first and foremost need to be protected against social forces that might prevent appropriate interventions which could benefit the patient. Our traditional practice—to presume in favor of life—has provided excellent protection in this country in general.) Anticruelty care (forgoing disproportionate or life-sustaining treatment in certain defined cases of hopeless injury with known prognosis) has been advocated as protection of the incompetent, but concerns have been raised about possible abuses.[14] Rather than abandon anticruelty care for fear of abuse, the profession should find measures that protect against abuse (e.g., encouragement of patient expression of preference prior to becoming incompetent, encouragement of societal review on the definition of hopeless injury, and improvement of working conditions for residents).

Medical Authority in the Care of the Competent

The strongest lay complaints about authoritarian physicians come from the psychiatrically ill, emotionally stressed, or "worried well," who often seem to be deeply unhappy with interpersonal relations in other parts of their lives. Compared to other patients, they may require longer office visits precisely because, although their complaints have not been supported by investigation, they still are presented for resolution, often with stronger expressions of anger or depression than occur with the physically ill. Physicians resent the delays in their schedules which such patients cause for other patients, feel uncomfortable with these patients' wishes to involve the physicians in entangling emotional relationships, and sometimes terminate interchanges with a brusqueness (perhaps even expressing dogmatism) that is perceived as insensitive and authoritarian. These physician reactions do not reflect true authoritarianism, and education could help them improve their responses.[15]

Patients with physical illness of intermediate severity (illness requiring elective treatment but not immediately life threatening or attended by much physical discomfort) tend to display intermediate attitudes toward authority, often seeking to consider options and get second opinions. It is the most seriously ill, legally competent patients who, weakened and fearful, most readily embrace authority and paternalistic guidance, and therefore they are at most risk of potential authoritarian abuses. After balanced presentation of the facts, such patients finally ask, "Well, what do *you* advise?" Because their competence in fact is partially impaired by illness,[16] to help these patients make the best decision for their own well-being, physicians often give them firm advice, confidently delivered. One caveat is that a physician's personal flair may carry more weight than the physician's judgment, which a patient is unable to evaluate. Another caveat is that a patient's capacity to judge his or her best interests may be less impaired than the physician supposes or indicates; a physician's expressed confidence that a patient is incapacitated may reflect insecurity arising from his or her personal limitations or from lack of consensus within the professional community.[17] A third caveat is that a patient might seize upon the advice of a doctor who offers therapy of the most invasive or radical type, even when the benefit is known to be slight or risks disproportionate. The lay person knows that great pains require great risks but that the profession must be treated to represent the quality and likelihood of those gains and risks. As an example, the anticipated quality of life for the patient with cancer of the tail of the pancreas is unspeakable and the potential benefits of radiation or chemotherapy are doubtful or brief. Yet many patients, not hearing these facts in so many words, accept therapy. The same physicians who would refuse to treat with laetrile still offer other therapies only marginally more beneficial, saying, "You have to give the patient hope." Our strongest objections should be to those doubtful treatments that are radical, invasive, risky, or uncomfortable, such as inappropriate surgery. Here one must exempt legitimate medical research, for if the benefits and risks are truly under study, both the consenting informed patient and the society might benefit from the patient's participation.

The greatest reason this problem resists solution is the problem of definition and recognition of inappropriate treatment or motivation. Granting the competent patient's desperate and helpless complicity in occasionally making inappropriate decisions, the responsibility for solutions would nonetheless seem to lie within the profession and society. The patient's alternatives, both conventional therapies and investigational therapies, should be described accurately and without dogmatic expression of preference, except where justified by the facts. Force of personality should be used with care in persuading patients to take a given course of action. Means of maintaining hope without use of dramatic or state-of-the-art therapies need to be learned by physicians.[18] When it is found that physicians are imposing weakly indicated treatments merely to implement decisions of the larger community (or on the basis of its values), then the reasons for pressing such inappropriate therapies need to be subjected to discourse and corrections need to be made.

THE SLIPPERY SLOPE

The issue whether there is a slippery slope must be addressed in any discussion of decisions to offer or forgo life-sustaining therapy or therapy arguably beneficial. When an action or omission is morally justified at one end of a spectrum of cases and unjustified at the other end, it can be difficult to know where to draw the line. While biomedical research using freely consenting competent adults is justified and using unwilling minor prisoners is not, the morality of biomedical research upon a minor who might benefit is open to debate.

When some apply a treatment because of the will to power (career advancement, subjugation of the patient, sadism), a danger exists that others (from intimidation, custom, or brutalization of sentiment) will allow the treatment to be applied with increasing flexibility, until the treatment is applied habitually and freely in circumstances in which its use is indefensible.

It should be emphasized that one classic case of a slippery slope (Nazi "euthanasia" and "research" programs) began with programs having a protherapeutic policy, not a policy of forgoing therapy. Lifton traced the roots of devaluation of life to writings that antedated the ascendancy of the Nazis to power. Distinguished members of the medical profession began with enforced sterilization programs and followed with covert "euthanasia" programs for medically injured children and the mentally ill, who were registered, corralled, and killed before the systematic extermination of Jews began. Rationalizations for those actions offered by the promulgators are catalogued in Lifton's book, and they include the sparing of resources and the purification of the genetic pool. On another level, the killings can be explained by individual authoritarianism, exertion of power (will, control), and frank sadism. But even these explanations do not adequately account for the psychology of the "doubling" described by Lifton or the Nazi zeal to seek, find, and destroy.[19] As Bettleheim asserts, we have resisted understanding for fear we might have to forgive.[20] No doubt some physician participants grew up with anger caused by authoritarian parenting, helplessness, a need to take action, a need to belong, and a need for strong community and strong values. Some were also coerced. Thus a severely distressed society seems to have been a precondition for the slippery slope phenomenon in Nazi Germany.

In considering present day slippery slope dangers, an analysis of motivation may help predict the likelihood that any policy, if applied, would lead to beneficial results or to a progression of abuses. The bottom line in any analysis must be, not the motivation, but the morality of the resultant actions. Nevertheless, actions are influenced by the motivation of those who do them and by the temper of the society in which the policy is promulgated.

Tests of Motivation for Recognizing the Slippery Slope Danger

The example of Nazi Germany readily provides ideas for tests by which the slippery slope danger might be recognized. Tests include, but are not limited to, questions about the following nine risk factors, the first seven concerning individual patient decisions and the last two concerning the societal context:

1. Overconcern with Societal Resources: Does the care giver argue that society would be better off without the recipient of care? That societal resources should be expended elsewhere?

2. Self-interest: Does the proposed therapy or omission of therapy financially benefit some cause or person other than the patient?

3. Perceived Superiority: Does the care giver express disgust for the recipient of care? Superiority?[21] Judgmental attitudes toward the patient's morality, habits, age, intelligence, physical features, nationality, race, sexual orientation, employment, addictions, or overall worth?

4. Zeal: Does the care giver express pleasure, alacrity, or rationalized zeal at the prospect of aggressive intervention or passive euthanasia?
5. Sadomasochism: Does the proposed action or omission satisfy sadomasochistic impulses in the perpetrator or in the society?
6. Disregard for the Individual: Does the care giver or the law of the society neglect previously expressed wishes, the best interests, or the maximal comforts of the patient? Forget his individuality? Argue in terms of applicable ideals and abstractions?
7. Disregard for the Family: Does the care giver or the society show integrity in explaining the case to the patient or the family? Respect the opinion of the guardian?
8. Absence of Institutionalized Societal and Professional Ethical Safeguards: Do professional education, professional self-surveillance, and the political, legal, religious, and social forces of the community support the individual physician in the goals of nonmaleficence and beneficence, educating the physician in the value of life and individual worth? Provide rewards for carrying out the goals (properly defined) and only the goals of medicine? Provide negative incentives for improper behavior? Foster respect, honesty, and mutual trust between physicians and their patients?
9. Authoritarianism outside of the Medical Context: Unrelated to the patient, does the care giver or the larger society express a strong need to subjugate, a need to be subjugated, a need to belong, or a need to fill a void with strong values? Manifest xenophobia, racism, or alienation from the larger world?

MEDICAL AUTHORITARIANISM AND ITS PERPETRATORS

Motivations extraneous to concern for patient welfare have resulted in medical injustices in this country. The Tuskegee Syphilis Study of nontreatment of syphillis was allowed to continue among southern Blacks after the introduction of penicillin, an immoral act of commission as research and of omission as therapy.[22] Headlines daily remind us of the per capita expenditure for AIDS patients, as if to gratify a public appetite for rationalizations that might be used to deprive homosexuals of their rights to medical care. The motivations such as the will to power or even sadism are known to occur in medicine, affecting not only doctors but also paramedical and nonmedical persons concerned with medical issues. They are comparable to the sadomasochistic motivation that led to the Nazi atrocities.[23]

Literature in the English language hints at the authoritarian capacity of physicians and nurses. Since literature generally treats themes of justice and personal interactions with more interest than themes of sickness and health, it is not surprising that doctors are presented as flawed autocrats. In *The Elephant Man,* Merrick, a patient of Treves, helps the physician discover his controlling nature. Treves reverses roles with his patient by the end of the play, ceasing to be domineering and arrogant and acquiring self-knowledge and feelings of respect, love, and sorrow.[24] Bernard Shaw is much more direct in charging doctors with frank sadism.[25] Big Nurse, in Kesey's *One Flew over the Cuckoo's Nest,* ironically captures the authoritarian character in the person of a woman.[26] In the case of the handicapped or incompetent, a care giver reveals authoritarian motivation if he or she nurtures the handicap but neglects or suppresses potential strengths.[27] Literature also shows us that a minority of lay parents reject societal assistance or seize upon the care of a handicapped child as an outlet for masochistic tendencies, submerging their lives in that devotion. Nichols, in *Joe Egg,* asks a mother to realize the limitations of a child with severe cerebral palsy.[28] Arne Skouen, in the beautifully moving play *Ballerina,* asks the mother to help an autistic child "be all that she can be."[29] Both playwrights, perhaps guiltily, seem to contrast maternal caring favorably to paternal cynicism or rationality, but both also challenge the healthiness of maternal self-effacement and question whether it serves the needs of family or child.

Fromm equates the authoritarian personality with a sadomasochistic tendency in a person basically psychologically normal.[30] In a physician, a fine thread of authoritarianism may be laced through an otherwise admirable personality. The attribute can be observed in the power struggles that occur within academic medicine or group practices,[31] in professional neutralization of bureaucratic authority,[32] in degrading treatment of subordinates, and in the overvaluation of status ("my career") at the expense of family, personal, and patient welfare. The physician frequently resists efforts by the patient to gain control or understanding of the treatment, dismissing questions as neurotic, not because they are viewed as a challenge to his authority, but precisely because the patient is uncomprehending and ineffectual compared to the physician. This quality—scenting out weakness, then finding oneself goaded to destroy—is characteristically authoritarian.[33] The doctor's suppression of the offending questioner takes the form of irritability, contempt, or rejection.

Authoritarian attitudes about health care are by no means held only by physicians. Nursing personnel and lay people sometimes seem motivated by zealous adherence to a cause more than concern for the patient under discussion. Authoritarian nursing personnel challenging medical decisions from a position of ideology tend to come in groups of two or more, or with letters signed by several others supporting the same view. Normal people see strength in numbers or, having relatively little power, try to bolster their courage through affirmations by friends and colleagues. Nevertheless, the invocation by such group members of a larger ideology, affiliation, or organization is evidence that they partly are motivated by a need to belong.[34] Authoritarian personnel and lay people tend to be less capable of flexible discourse or complex reasoning on the subject of their vigilantism—and more susceptible to charismatic authority. Most importance, adherence to their beliefs provides secondary gains unrelated to the welfare of the particular patient of whom they have made a test case.

Dr. Koop recently attempted to establish "Baby Doe Squads" in certain federally supported hospitals for the purpose of posting warnings against discrimination toward handicapped infants and of providing toll-free hotlines for reporting abuses. These legislative plans, which failed, would have invited abstract depersonalized decision making.[35] Lay and professional people who have a tenuous relationship, if any, to a given case and who become protherapeutic advocates in a medical controversy will tend to be motivated more by ideology than by a knowledge of or moral reaction to the facts, and certainly in most (but not all) cases, their claim to have the welfare of the patient at heart should be considered less seriously than the claim of family and intimately involved care givers.[36] The authors feel both Baby Doe and Baby Jane Doe should have been treated and they recognize that parents or involved care givers may make mistakes. A prognosis for an injured infant is often difficult to make. For the protection of handicapped infants who might not have a hopeless injury, the authors favor the establishment of institutional infant care review boards or hospital ethics committees.

HOW THE GOALS OF AUTHORITARIAN THERAPY DIFFER FROM THE GOALS OF MEDICINE

Those who are militantly protherapeutic engage in power struggles over patient care with colleagues, superiors, subordinates, and the families of patients. But none of these groups are as helpless as the patients themselves. It is thus understandable that authoritarian physicians, nurses, and lay personnel focus upon injured children and incompetent patients as their principle targets, for they are weak and defenseless and can be controlled and even cruelly manipulated in the name of idealistic valuation of life. The perpetrators of such control then become a united elite.

Idealistic rationalization, of course, typifies authoritarian statements of motivation.[37] Discourse often is declamatory, abstract, and righteous. Concrete negative implications of proposed care are but lightly considered. Disproportionate therapies are advocated that might be controversial and only weakly indicated from a medical point of view. Together these characteristics suggest insufficient concern for the individual patient or recognition of the patient's personhood.

In subserving the needs of the authoritarian personality, protherapeutic authoritarianism often fails to subserve the goals of medicine. It does harm, it causes suffering, it perpetuates hopeless injuries, and it imposes cruel invasions upon the body of the sometimes incompetent and unconsenting patient. It fails to reduce encumberances, it interrupts timely death (even when that death might have come by course of nature), and it prolongs dying. Oddly, the political contingency most vocal in supporting wide application of life-sustaining therapy for injured children is also most opposed to legislation which might assist families and individuals attempting to live with the effects of such injuries. This indicates that a desire for punishment might underlie both postures: punishment of colleagues who would oppose futile or disproportionate therapies and punishment of families who face difficulty in caring for the handicapped.[38] Action for its own sake is a degenerated popular American theme, affecting the medical profession as well as the media. Protherapeutic authoritarianism should be viewed as aimless action, or as aggression having as its goal power itself.

Finally, the authoritarian need to dominate does not arise from strength but from psychologic weakness.[39] Out of beneficience toward others and concern for ourselves, we should resist allowing this kind of weakness to dominate policy making within our profession and our society.

SUMMARY

The decision to forgo potentially beneficial therapy never can be taken lightly, but incompetent patients and some competent patients are at risk of being subjugated to cruel and futile treatments in the name of beneficence and under pressure from protherapeutic authoritarianism, the goals of which are not the same as the goals of medicine. Some readers will feel this description exaggerates a problem that occurs in full only in a minority of protherapeutic decisions. But by stating the extreme position it is hoped to facilitate recognition of the commoner situation, in which an admixture of motivations leads to a therapeutic plan having both advantages and disadvantages. Other readers may so quickly recognize the problem herein described that it will seem unnecessary to have developed the idea of protherapeutic authoritarianism beyond naming it and identifying it as a failing of our time.

NOTES

1. S. Braithwaite and D.C. Thomasma, "New Guidelines on Foregoing Life-Sustaining Treatment in Incompetent Patients: An Anti-Cruelty Policy," *Annals of Internal Medicine* 104 (1986): 711–15.

2. R.J. Lifton, *The Nazi Doctors* (New York: Basic Books, 1986). The author deliberately refuses to expand upon a comparison of American medicine to the Holocaust, but he does state on pp. 45–46 that "anyone trained in American medicine has personal experience of doctors, nurses, and medical attendants colluding in the death of patients, usually children, who have been extremely impaired physically and mentally. . . ." At the end of the book, the focus briefly shifts to the possibility of a nuclear holocaust.

3. See E.J. Kleinman, "Foregoing Life-Sustaining Treatment," *Annals of Internal Medicine* 105 (1986): 307. Kleinman uses such language as "dangerous assumption," "hubris," desensitization of staff," and "officially sanctioned 'anti-cruelty policy'" in his succinct argument. Using such language to refer to a sequence of events that in Nazi Germany led to an officially sanctioned "euthanasia" policy subliminally reminds the reader to be on guard against the moral dangers of other officially sanctioned policies that might lead to a slippery slope.

4. Ibid; J. La Puma, Letter to the Editor, *Annals of Internal Medicine* 105 (1986): 469.

5. Braithwaite and Thomasma, "Foregoing Life-Sustaining Treatment in Incompetent Patients."

6. For a discussion of the problem of authority in medicine, see S.M. Hauerwas, "Authority and the Profession of Medicine," in *Responsibility in Health Care,* ed. G. Agich (Dordrect, Holland: D. Reidel, 1982), 83–104; R. Veatch, "Medical Authority and Professional Medical Authority: The Nature of Authority in Medicine for Decisions by Lay Persons and Professionals," *Ibid.,* 127–37.

7. See J.S. Mill, *On Liberty,* ed. E. Rapaport (Indianapolis, Inc.: Hackett, 1978). "But the strongest of all the arguments against the interference of the public with purely personal conduct is that, when it does interfere, the odds are that it interferes wrongly and in the wrong place" (81). See also T.L. Beauchamp and J.F. Childress, *Principles of Biomedical Ethics,* 2d ed. (New York: Oxford University Press, 1983), 59–105.

8. See also the chapter "Transfusion of Blood," in A. Solzhenitsyn, *Cancer Ward* (New York: Bantam Books, 1969) in which Kostoglotov accepts life-saving ministrations from Vega. By the end of the noval, Solzhenitsyn's hero emerges with a guarded sense of affirmation, alive but irreversibly altered, both strengthened and impaired by exile, imprisonment, disease, and medicine.

9. In the words of O'Brien, torturing Winston, later wielding a hypodermic, "The Party seeks power entirely for its own sake . . . the individual is only a cell . . . slavery is freedom. Alone—free—the human being is always defeated . . . if he can merge himself in the Party so that he is the party, then he is all-powerful and immortal . . . power is power over human beings. (G. Orwell, *Nineteen Eighty-Four* [New York, New American Library, 1984], 217–18).

10. See Lifton, *Nazi Doctors.*

11. "There is the wish to submit to an overwhelmingly strong power, to annihilate the self, besides the wish to have power over helpless beings. This masochistic side of the Nazi ideology and practice is most obvious with respect to the masses. Sacrificing the individual and reducing it to a bit of dust, to an atom, implies, according to Hitler, the renunciation of the right to assert one's individual opinion, interests, and happiness" (E. Fromm, *Escape from Freedom* [New York: Avon Books, 1966], 257–58).

12. "The wife of a comatose firefighter has cited a new "right to die" policy approved by the Massachusetts Medical Society . . . the fate of Paul Brophy, 48 years old, who lapsed into a coma in March 1983 after suffering a rupture of an aneurysm in his brain, had been turned over to Probate Judge David H. Kopelman" (*New York Times, September 6, 1985, p. 10). See also *New York Times,* September 19, 1985, p. 24, on the case of Dr. Howard Shapiro. A judge in Akron "directed a verdict in favor of a doctor who was being sued on the grounds that he had improperly refused to disconnect life-support systems on a 70-year-old terminally ill woman. . . . Mrs. Leach suffered from amyotrophic lateral sclerosis, or Lou Gehrig's disease." See also *New York Times,* April 24, 1986, p. 22. "Elizabeth Bouvia, a quadriplegic, was finally freed of the nasal tube through which she'd been fed . . . a state appeals court has ruled her way, unanimously. . . . Having removed the nasal tube, however, the doctors also wanted to remove the catheter in her chest through which she receives a steady infusion of morphine. Probably addicted by now, she construes the removal as punitive; the hospital says it just wants to detoxify her."

13. Even in the absence of verbalization, subjective distress and wishes (an unreasoning form of autonomous expression) can be displayed by some incompetent patients. See R.W. Momeyer, "Medical Decisions concerning Noncompetent Patients," *Theoretical Medicine* 4 (1983): 275–90. Momeyer discusses the case of Joseph Saikewicz, a profoundly retarded man who at age 67 was found to have leukemia: "It was widely felt that Mr. Saikewicz would further suffer pain and anxiety from his incomprehension of the treatment procedures and side effects he would undergo with chemotherapy. He would also be a singularly uncooperative patient and require physical constraint for the twelve to twenty-four hours during administration of chemotherapy or transfusions" (p. 281). Momeyer later argues, outside the immediate context of the Saikewicz case, that "where an entirely substituted judgement must be made, this ought to be done by one who knows best and cares most about the interests of the non-competent patient, an intimacy born of a long relationship. Ordinarily this would be a family member or group, the closer and more intimate the relationship the better. The duty of consultation and caring on the part of medical personnel is great here, but not so great as to warrant wresting decision-making authority out of the hands of the family. Only irresponsible or incompetent choices will warrant this, and only then can courts become involved" (pp. 287–88).

14. See Braithwaite and Thomasma, "Foregoing Life-Sustaining Treatment in Incompetent Patients"; Kleinman, "Foregoing Life-Sustaining Treatment"; and La Puma, Letter to the Editor. Sometimes treatments for hopelessly injured incompetent patients serve to perpetrate an injury of nature without potential for benefit to the patient's hopeless injury. Such treatments nevertheless cost the patient suffering and are accomplished by invasions of the body to which he or she has not consented, the harm of which is disproportionate to benefit.

15. N. Kessel, "Reassurance," *Lancet* 1 (1979): 1128–33.

16. J. Bergsma and D. Thomasma, *Health Care: Its Psychosocial Dimension* (Pittsburgh: Duquesne University Press, 1982).

17. See the Iphigenia case in J. Katz, *The Silent World of Doctor and Patient* (New York: Macmillan, 1984), in which a surgeon, having planned a mastectomy, nearly withholds information about the alternative possibility of lumpectomy with radiation from a young bride (p. 90).

18. J.E. Dunphy, "On Caring for the Patient with Cancer," *New England Journal of Medicine* 295 (1977): 313–19.

19. "It felt strange and uncomfortable to hold out even minimal empathy . . . for participants in a project so murderous. . . . For once a man performs an evil deed he has become part of that deed, and the deed part of him. That deed has probably required some doubling with the formation of an evil self. . . . And while . . . all of us are fallible human beings potentially capable of such evil deeds, we must also underscore the distinction between potential and actual evil" (Lifton, *Nazi Doctors*, 501–2).

20. "Dr. Lifton comes dangerously close to the attitude expressed in the French saying, "tout comprendre c'est tout pardonner," an idea I cannot subscribe to where ruthless and callous murders are concerned. . . . I shied away from trying to understand the psychology of the SS—because of the ever-present danger that understanding fully may come close to forgiving" (Bruno Bettleheim, "Their Specialty Was Murder," *New York Times Book Review*, October 5, 1986, p. 62).

21. "Differences, whether of sex or race, [to the authoritarian] are necessarily signs of superiority or inferiority" (Fromm, *Escape from Freedom*, 196).

22. A.M. Brandt, "Racism and Research: The Case of the Tuskegee Syphilis Study," *Hastings Center Report* 8 (December 1978): 21–29.

23. "All the different forms of sadism which we can observe go back to one essential impulse, namely, to have complete mastery over another person, to make of him a helpless object of our will, to become the absolute ruler over him, to become his God, to do with him as one pleases" (Fromm, *Escape from Freedom*, 178–79).

24. Merrick says, with respect to women, "Is it okay to see them naked if you cut them up afterwards?" (B. Pomerance, *The Elephant Man* [New York: Grove Press, 1979], 56).

25. "Why not perform a careful series of experiments on persons under the influence of voluptuous ecstasy, so as to ascertain its physiological symptoms? Then perform a second series on persons engaged in mathematical work or machine designing, so as to ascertain the symptoms of cold scientific activity? Then note the symptoms of a vivisector performing a cruel experiment; and compare them with the voluptuary symptoms and the mathematical symptoms?" (G.B. Shaw, Preface, *The Doctor's Dilemma* [Baltimore, Md.: Penguin Books, 1954], 46).

26. K. Kesey, *One Flew over the Cuckoo's Nest* (New York: Penguin Books, 1976).

27. "We paid far too much attention to the defects of our patients . . . and far too little to what was intact or preserved" (O. Sacks, *The Man Who Mistook his Wife for a Hat* [New York: Summit Books, 1986], 174).

28. P. Nichols, *Joe Egg* (New York: Grove Press, 1978).

29. An unpublished translation from the Norwegian was graciously provided by the North Light Repertory Co., Evanston, Ill.

30. ''Since the term 'sado-masochistic' is associated with ideas of perversion and neurosis, I prefer to speak instead of the sado-masochistic character, especially when not the neurotic but the normal person is meant, as the *authoritarian character*. This terminology is justifiable because the sado-masochistic person is always characterized by his attitude toward authority. He admires authority and tends to submit to it, but at the same time he wants to be an authority himself and have others submit to him'' (Fromm, *Escape from Freedom,* 186).

31. ''Such persons might fight against one set of authorities, especially if they are disappointed by its lack of power, and at the same time or later on submit to another set of authorities which through greater power or greater promises seems to fulfill their masochistic longings'' (Fromm, *Escape from Freedom,* 186).

32. See E. Freidson, *Doctoring Together: A Study of Professional Social Control* (New York: Elsevier Scientific Publishing Co., 1975). In the chapter ''The Neutralization of Formal Authority,'' Freidson states, ''The subordinates of the medical group, the working physicians, were inclined to concede legitimacy to the exercise of administrative authority in only extremely limited areas of their work . . . the physicians resisted the use of formal authority on the part of administrative officials . . . the dominant source of rules by which one evaluated performances lay in the collegium rather than in the administration (pp. 118–19). Nevertheless, Freidson found the collegium itself to be inadequate at self-discipline.

33. ''The very sight of a powerless person makes him want to attack, dominate, humiliate him. Whereas a different kind of character is appalled by the idea of attacking one who is helpless, the authoritarian character feels the more aroused the more helpless his object has become'' (Fromm, *Escape from Freedom,* 191).

34. ''The annihilation of the individual self and the attempt to overcome thereby the unbearable feeling of powerlessness are only one side of the masochistic strivings. The other side is the attempt to become a part of a bigger and more powerful whole outside of oneself, to submerge and participate in it. This power can be a person, an institution, God, the nation, conscience, or a psychic compulsion'' (Fromm, *Escape from Freedom,* 177).

35. Margaret M. Heckler, Secretary of Health and Human Services, v. American Hospital Association, et al., in the Supreme Court of the United States, October Term, 1985, No. 84-1529.

36. Note the actions of pro-life advocates in cases like *Paul Brophy v. New England Sinai Hospital* or the handicapped rights groups who picketed outside Elizabeth Bouvia's hospital room. See R. Steinbrook and B. Lo, ''The Case of Elizabeth Bouvia: Starvation, Suicide, or Problem Patient?'' *Archives of Internal Medicine* 146 (1986): 61.

37. ''A person can be entirely dominated by his sadistic strivings and consciously believe that he is motivated only by his sense of duty'' (Fromm, Escape from Freedom, 185). Also: ''Sadistic tendencies for obvious reasons are usually less conscious and more rationalized than the socially more harmless masochistic trends. Often they are entirely covered up by reaction formations of overgoodness or overconcern for others. Some of the most frequent rationalizations are the following: 'I rule over you because I know what is best for you, and in your own interest you should follow me without opposition''' (pp. 165–66). The quoted rationalization frequently is directed to competent patients and the competent families of incompetent patients. Many female patients feel such a rationalization is applied prejudicially by male physicians in dealing with women.

38. N. Fost states, ''There is a curious contradiction in the government's insistence that the handicapped be treated similarly to others while the funds necessary to accomplish that are being drastically reduced'' (N. Fost, ''Putting Hospitals on Notice,'' *Hastings Center Report* 12 [August 1982]: 5–8).

39. ''*The lust for power is not rooted in strength but in weakness*. . . . It is the desperate attempt to gain secondary strength where genuine strength is lacking'' (Fromm, *Escape from Freedom,* 184).

Chapter 29

What To Do with the Incompetent Doctor

Gene Cleaver

Who says it is not nice to be critical of someone? We doctors are taught to think critically about our patients, to leave no stone unturned, to answer every question possible, to permit no discrepancies. We are taught the critical skills of language, history taking, and observation and how to use mathematics, physics, chemistry, and physical examination. *Critical*, after all, means careful analysis and faultfinding. It suggests sudden changes and precision, as in critical angles, constants, and pressures. Being critical involves much more than showing disapproval. We critique our consultants, our staff, and our families with the best of intentions—to set them straight. Then we wonder why we are unpopular with those who do not fit our molds.

In a few cases, patients, after dissenting, have suddenly come around to our view, and we hold that up as the ideal every time we disagree with anybody. We tend to avoid issues in any relationship which we know in advance will be difficult, but the idea of telling another doctor, someone who tends to think the way we do, to change—what a challenge!

The solution to this problem involves several assumptions: (1) that few physicians readily recognize early states of substance abuse and other psychiatric and organic dysfunctions; (2) that the victims of such disease usually cannot recognize their own involvement, whether or not they are physicians or other paramedical personnel; and (3) that if they do notice, they may assume a posture of helplessness or indifference.

Making these assumptions and then reflecting on what we are doing professionally can lead to new directions of thought: (1) that to help a disabled physician out of a dysfunctional trap is a good thing; (2) that benefit will accrue to both physicians (the helper and the helped); and (3) that the patients of both physicians will be better served.

What to call this chapter? Some wanted it titled ''What to Do with the Bad Doctor.'' How about ''The Disabled or Distressed Doctor''? Would you accept ''Impaired, Inexperienced, Overaggressive, or Egocentric''? Maybe ''Doctors Nobody Knows What To Do With''? Whatever words we find, it is an uncommon physician who does not shrink from involvement with such a person. The majority of health professionals may feel immobilized when it comes to taking responsibility for doing something about serious errors in the practice of another.

In discussing the issues, physician-to-physician contact is stressed, although much of the commentary is applicable to other relationships, such as those between physicians and nurses, administrators, and other paramedical personnel.

338

IMPAIRED DOCTORS

How to define impaired doctors? Their problem, as we recognize it, revolves around their misperception of their limits. One definition, then, is that an impaired doctor has a loss of judgment affecting many aspects of his or her life (including medical practice); this loss of judgment is most often due to aging, emotional disorder, or substance abuse. As the discussion proceeds on the origin, recognition, and treatment of these impairments, it will be switched liberally. While there are differences among the disabilities,[1] the emphasis will be on their unifying characteristics. More questions will be asked than answered.

Many Americans take psychoactive drugs, that is, substances which have an effect on mood or behavior. Among these are alcohol, tobacco, caffeine, and related compounds. Abuse of a substance can be defined as taking enough of it to seriously interfere with one's health, economy, social functioning, or professional functioning. The last of these, however, is nearly always affected late in the process of abuse. One's colleagues often do not perceive the abuse unless they are skillful in recognizing the early behavioral signs.

Yet we know intellectually that our ranks are imperfect and that we must do the cleanup. We acknowledge that if we fail to do so, others who are ill-equipped for the job will grudgingly take it over—and likely perform it poorly and punitively. But how should we do it? Who has prepared us for this? For whom and what are we looking?

The purpose of this chapter is to outline why physicians should try to recognize impaired colleagues and help them. In addition, suggestions will be given as to how to do this. There is a wealth of commentary on this subject.[2] Our principal interest here is in the process of taking care of a colleague trapped in a dangerous practice. Trying to help such a colleague will encourage growth in the physician making the attempt. The capacity for such involvement may not have been nurtured in a professional's early education, medical training, or subsequent practice. A doctor's willingness to attempt such involvement will pay off in the doctor's practice and in other aspects of his or her life.

Let doctors so involved recall that their revulsion to malpractice comes from the standards they have for themselves. Their standards are the result of self-criticism, of correction of their own weaknesses. They must note their own substance use and must critique their own behavior. They review their knowledge of substance abuse and understand that it is a disease; hence, they refrain from moral judgment. They never forget the dignity and rights of the individual, which prevents misperceiving the physician-patient as repulsive. They feel a kinship based on having had similar aspirations and having worked just as hard. They accept that common origin does not dictate uniform outcome. As they watch their own stress responses, they recognize that some do not know how to respond gracefully. They recall the loneliness and the fear of disapproval inherent in the preparation for and the practice of medicine. They recognize that the impaired physician must pay any price to avoid confrontation.

Observing their relationship to their disabled colleagues lends doctors humility and understanding. It can also imbue them with a sense of duty to do some rescuing in a way no other profession can—by really understanding helplessness and immobility. The way out for the victims is to be given the help they will not and cannot seek.

Competent doctors must recognize their own limits when confronted with an impaired doctor, just as they do in their own practice. For example, an orthopedist who is inexperienced in ''alcohol intervention'' would not want to confront a suspected physician in the halls. But the orthopedist can learn to recognize one, just as he or she can recognize alcoholism in the emergency room—and make an appropriate referral in both situations. For doctors to declare themselves competent to function only within their specialty is for them to abandon their social recognition as a physician, and to abandon their patient-colleague as well. If a doctor refers for cancer, heart failure, bloody diarrhea, and psychosis, then of course that doctor is competent to refer behavioral disorders. There may be ignorance of the signs and distaste for delving into things not readily quantifiable and excisable, but these hurdles can be overcome by postgraduate education.[3]

KINDS OF INCOMPETENCE

Impairment comes in many guises, but both professional and behavioral incompetence can generally be recognized. Incompetence may be the result of youth, with excellent training but inadequate life experience. It can be the insidious product of age, with Alzheimer's disease taking its toll, often in combination with other illnesses causing specific organic brain syndromes. Commonly it is associated with alcohol abuse and, to a lesser extent, with illicit use of prescription or street drugs. Incompetence may slowly grow due to neglected continuing education, but it is seldom due to poor intelligence. Doctors are subject to the usual pathologic psychiatric diagnoses and to behavioral disorders. Acute situational reactions may take some doctors out of service briefly. Chronic emotional lability from any cause may make a doctor impossible to work with, and patients may begin to shrink from the doctor's rudeness.[4] Some doctors are sociopaths, some greedy prescription writers or drug dealers, and a rare few are bogus or frankly evil.

In any case, the physician immersed in such a syndrome will not admit it and seek help. He or she cannot. An alcoholic who has behavioral changes and sleep disorder can no more recognize the problem and seek help than can a patient with a two centimeter cancer who does not know self-examination. In fact, such an individual may become highly skillful at diverting attention and explaining away any telltale traits.

Scope of the Problem

"If he would just straighten himself out," we may hear. The chances are that neither an incompetent doctor nor the doctor's colleagues were trained to effectively recognize depression, substance abuse, or the other impairments mentioned. Even if they do see it, they may, out of fear, come up with rationalizations for not looking. For instance, the otolaryngologist may be very perceptive at recognizing leukoplakia, pharyngeal cancer, and other disorders related to smoking in a physician-patient. The otolaryngologist may be perfectly willing to ask about smoking habits, but might never question personal or family use of alcohol. When the specialist does think of asking, he or she may fear the patient's anger or humiliation and keep silence. The result of this phenomenon is gross underdiagnosis of impairment, especially alcoholism.[5] Failure of alcoholism to appear on the hospital chart may also be due to the patient's prominence in the community or a desire to protect an old family friend.

The very nature of impairment makes measuring the number of impaired physicians difficult. All specialties are adversely affected by the various personality disorders and substance abuse.[6] Overall dependence of the doctor and medical student on drugs has apparently not changed much for decades,[7] although doctors under 40 years old have more often smoked marijuana and used cocaine. Drug dependency at some time has affected 3 percent of that population. Estimates as high as 10 percent are probably not correct. Articles vary regarding whether surgeons, psychiatrists, obstetricians, or primary care practitioners are at greatest or least risk. All agree that any of us is at some risk, particularly those involved in primary care.[8]

Nonaddicted physicians frequently receive some form of counseling or psychotherapy and presumably many more could use it—perhaps half—during their careers.[9] Possibly a doctor's stress reaction to a patient is dependent on how much difficulty the doctor has escaping the obvious signs and symptoms of "emotional overlay."[10] That is to say, the day-to-day practice of medicine probably allows greater exposure to the feeling and situational causes of disease. This kind of work by a practitioner not in touch with his or her own feelings is liable to be stressful.

PHYSICIANS AND THEIR CHARACTERISTICS

Before talking about what to do with impaired physicians, what should we understand about unimpaired physicians? What kind of families do they come from? Why do they want to be good physicians? What are their expectations early in their training and once out in practice? What happens to their families in the face of this burdensome stewardship of goodness? We must understand ourselves as well as possible before undertaking such a major and unfamiliar project as changing our brother's or sister's life. To wander into what we know will be hostile emotional territory without the weapons of directness and a personal philosophy is to court disaster. We must not intervene casually.

When we get angry at unskilled medical professionals, it is worth some effort to understand that most frequently good ones (us) differ from bad ones (them) only in degree. If they do not keep up their education, we should question our own efforts. If they are abrupt with their patients and unprofessional, we should question our own behavior. If they give the nurse an inappropriately brusque answer in the middle of the night instead of examining the patient, perhaps we have done the same. In other words, maybe "they" are "us." After all they are (or were) as bright and had the same sorts of families. They had similar education, went through the same selection process and training by their elders, and presumably have endured many of the same life stresses.

American society may be slowly changing, but it has traditionally been a "doing" society, with little reward for "being" or "feeling." Much has been made of our continent as a refuge for ne'er-do-wells, escaped convicts and outcasts, and rigid religious sects. Whether this national heritage left as a legacy distrust of pain, fear of extreme emotions, and a tendency to withdraw from conflict is anybody's guess. What does seem clear is that some doctors are poorly trained from the start to handle emotional issues.

Accept for a moment that early childhood attitudes persist in a physician's life until modified by deliberate study or life experience.[11] Typical family disruptions which were found to contribute to physician addiction included active alcoholism or mental illness in a parent and divorce. These were important when found in conjunction with a distant relationship with the father and a mother who was rigid, dominating, perfectionistic, puritanical, or impersonal.[12] In short, the very physicians who obtained status in their childhood by service to others and sacrifice of their own feelings are likely to operate the same way in their professional careers.[13] Those physicians at greatest risk for disabling themselves with drugs in adulthood are those who saw drug abuse in their original families.

There are about 100 physician suicides a year in the United States.[14] Perhaps many of these stem from a family system which inhibits personal and emotional growth, leading to a career choice (and for that matter a life style) which follows suit. For doctors who experienced the extremes of early childhood polarity of this sort, some of the requirements of being a physician are nearly intolerable. We "normals" may wonder how many of these characteristics we have the potential to develop. Hints appear from time to time. Perhaps we are all ill-equipped for enduring weeks and years of emotionally draining problems and for engaging in the awesome task of trying to help members of society stop paying for their emotional mistakes with their bodies. But *are* we so ill-equipped? At least we are the one faction of society that wants to meet the maelstrom of human demands for health care.

The social graces we are all taught, together with our basic assumption that patients need and want us, leads to much of our pleasure at work. We can even tolerate a certain amount of noncompliance with our regimes as long as the relationships are pleasant and we feel basically in command of the regimes. And this is true of other relationships as well. Trouble brews when a peer, such as a colleague or spouse, threatens our sense of control. They can do this more effectively than a patient. We may pay any price to avoid such a threat, even if avoidance leads to silly degrees of nonconfrontation. Examples of this abound in each of our professional lives: abiding by the three Ds of successful management—delegate, dump, and defer; using a third party, such as a nurse, secretary, or committee, to communicate with a doctor instead of communicating directly; and circumverbigerting, i.e., writing in the passive voice in medical abstracts and not using subjects to start sentences. Internists are particularly susceptible to abibliophobia. (Abibliophobia is the fear of being caught without references. Someone so caught would have to put forward his or her own opinion.)

The human condition appears to be such that all children have perceived a lack of love to some degree, perhaps more than they can readily recall as adults. Moreover, survival in the impaired family of origin required self-sacrifice, self-esteem through meeting the demands of others, and denial of personal feelings. This sounds suspiciously like the functioning of many of our "normal" colleagues, and at times ourselves. One may see an irresistible desire for perfection, unrealistic practice standards, and disappointment from the practice. The strain on the family supporting such a physician—a family which is expected to take care of the doctor rather than vice versa—may stem from these roots. "The diligent, self-sacrificing physician who surrenders a personal life to patients wins respect from his colleagues, first in residency, later in private practice."[15] But what about the family of such a diligent servant?

Addicted physicians are loners for whom confidentiality is of the utmost importance. One will not find them in a group in the back room shooting up together. They are almost phobic about seeking help and are usually forced into a treatment program only by job jeopardy, family insistence, the influence of their personal physicians and friends, or legal pressure.

Stress is the usual scapegoat for the doctor's behavior. There is no doubt that hurry sickness, time consciousness, and the weight of practice obligations can be allowed to become overwhelming. These may be foisted on the individual by peers, who have the same expectations of themselves, or by hospital or office personnel. Some doctors act as if they are the constant victims of their patients. They have crossed over the line from stress (seeing the world the way it is and responding appropriately) to distress (responding to the world in a self-destructive manner).

In a treatment program for addicted physicians, 72 percent could give histories of clearly negative childhood emotional factors, and this number included all those less than 40 years old. Thirty-six percent of those over 40 were also in this group, while the balance were affected by an organic brain syndrome. Forty percent came from poor and lower middle class families and experienced overstress in relationship to a substantially higher income and a position of prestige. There was a correlation between these factors (together with parental deprivation) and a tendency toward addiction.

One of the most thoroughly ingrained principles is that physicians should never repeat the errors of colleagues. They accomplish this by doing their own complete history and physical—hopefully one-half page or more longer than the last doctor's—and by reordering all lab work not done in the last three days. This is not just defensive medicine thrust on us by an unfeeling legal system. It is what we did long before the need for defensive medicine. After medical school, time constraints foster cutting corners and the development of intuition. Physicians may then err through using unthinking intuition. Thus there exists a constant pull between the extremes of rigid thoroughness and sloppiness.

The near absence of practitioner role models in university programs means that the great majority of residents enter primary care practice with only a vague concept of what they will encounter. It is likely that for some of them career decisions are attempts to evade stressful or unpleasant experiences in medical school or residency rather than made on the basis of recent examinations of practice in the various specialties.

"My mother didn't send me to school to be a psychiatrist." As physicians grow professionally, they see relationships of mind and body that were not taught and have not yet been scientifically validated, but that they know to be true. They learn to endure the discomfort of intervention into others' lives even though they are not well trained to do so. Perhaps medical societies, which now have scientific advisory committees, will eventually become balanced by adding emotional advisory committees.

As it is, there are plenty of emotional issues confronted by any M.D. which are not likely to be answered by existing seminars. "If only I'm good enough (or smart enough or learn enough or grow up enough), I can expect a comfortable life free from conflict." This seems to be a universal misconception.

Poverty consciousness still affects many of us: "How can I take from the poor?" "How dare I look rich?"

Daily grief must be listened to and perceived without a self-destructive reaction, yet without shutting down constructive emotion. Even good doctors may perform badly during the communication breakdown often found in a family of a dying patient.[16]

One's own family must not be neglected, regardless of the expectations of colleagues and patients or fears of having a "never quite enough" practice. "Am I sure my spouse knows that he or she is more important than the practice?"

"Do I give medical care with strings attached (I'll care for you if you'll love me), or do I give care unilaterally and accept payment as payment in full?"

"If I must turn in a colleague, do I really expect painlessness?"

"Must I heal myself? Yes I must. Any sign of weakness—asking for help—is unacceptable."

The amazing thing is that few of us are very crazy and that fewer still handle stress so badly that it seriously alters our practice. If we can understand the difficulties of medical practice, is it humane to allow our colleagues to sink? Do we owe them an intervention before that occurs?

HELPING AN IMPAIRED PHYSICIAN

Enabling

What stands in the way of many helpers before they finally decide to help their own? It is called *enabling*. Enabling is providing the means, opportunity, power, or authority to do something. In the case of substance abuse, it is behavior by an abuser's associates that encourages the abuser not to change. Examples of enabling: ''He is our colleague; we can't do that to him.'' ''She has to make a living too.'' ''What an awful thing to do to her family.'' ''Everyone makes mistakes, and besides it's not my job.'' Making the problem of enabling more difficult is that ''the substance abusing or emotionally disordered physician is viewed as someone who is weak-willed, self-indulgent, or has somehow brought impairment on himself by his own imprudence.''[17]

Reasons like these come up in the course of considering what to do. The California experience with discipline has lead to avoidance of restrictions on an impaired physician's license,[18] as is the case in most programs in other states. Thus, a majority who have a correctable disability continue to practice! Of course, the prognosis is worst for those with irreversible organic brain syndromes and for those who drop out of treatment programs (enforced follow-up of clients for two to four years is required).

Nevertheless, knowledge of the lack of restrictions may not help to break through the conspiracy of silence formed by an impaired physician's peers.[19] They too like drink and approve of others who drink. They may be incapable of spotting the evidence and thus ''enable'' the alcoholic-impaired physician by seeming to give tacit approval for his or her ways. Even if they are aware, many physicians will assume the impaired physician has to ''hit bottom first.'' Finally, there is the aspect of seeing themselves in that physician. ''There but for the grace of God go I. How can I be cruel to him?''

There is a difference of opinion about whether small hospitals allow disabled physicians to avoid terminating a practice longer—or recognize them sooner—than more anonymous big city hospitals. Both can occur in small hospitals although whether their protection helps the doctor or hurts the patient must depend on the individuals in each situation.

I practice in a 33-bed, rural facility. A few years ago a staff physician had a stroke. He was prominent in local affairs and well liked by his peers. The hospital medical staff promptly passed a regulation requiring each of its members to be physically fit enough to assure competence in practice. The afflicted doctor was far from offended by this, and he welcomed the opportunity to demonstrate his recovery. I doubt his reaction would be universal, but in this case a tentative or apologetic staff posture could have altered the doctor's attitude.

Awareness: The Symptoms and Signs

Behavioral signs of impairment in a physician will occur long before end stage cirrhosis or blatant organic brain syndrome. The signs and symptoms are as variable as there are personalities in the world, but they are recognizable. There is a body of knowledge with which every physician should be acquainted and which can only be given cursory attention here. Look for a physician who withdraws from friends and colleagues, retreats from hospital practice, abruptly loses interest in continuing medical education, or undertakes reckless financial ventures.[20] Be alert for wide mood swings, numerous job changes, or deterioration in personal appearance. There may be "placebo" ordering of electrocardiograms and lab work. The physician may walk away from crises. The physician may have many personal somatic complaints, yet not acknowledge the seriousness of a patient's illness. Be alert to what the janitors, parking lot attendants, and especially hospital administrators, quality assurance professionals, and risk managers say. They will know of trouble long before our colleagues do. An observer who needs approval from his peers could interpret signs of impairment—turning away, reckless practice, emotional outbursts—as a personal affront. A caring but clear approach to the problem will thus be inhibited until the observer can overcome his or her initial reaction and recognize pain.

At the time we could be of greatest help to our colleagues, little tissue destruction is to be found. There may be signs or symptoms of heavy smoking, but this is less common these days. A variety of gut-related disorders may be present, such as signs and symptoms compatible with esophagitis, peptic acid disease, or irritable colon. Central nervous system disorders, particularly sleep disturbance, are common, often before behavioral abnormalities can be found.

The laboratory investigation of the alcoholic is often neglected. Not just a blood alcohol level, but intermittent hyperglycemia, hyperuricemia, and hypertriglyceridemia are frequent tipoffs. A mean corpuscular volume on an automated CBC of 96 cubic microns, which is less than the often reported upper edge of normal (98 to 100 cubic microns), can be a red flag. Red cell morphology abnormalities may be noted.

Decision Making

Now comes the time to do something. How is it possible to come to terms with such a major choice? "It is worthwhile remembering that peer review is an expression of a profession's standards—and standing—and it is out there for all to see."[21]

Moreover, to initiate change in a distressed colleague is an opportunity of enormous importance in the personal growth of the physician thrust into such a position. It may come to the physician because of membership on an ethics committee, because the physician is the second surgeon, or simply because the physician is a friend or a casual but acutely observant acquaintance. The growth potential comes from the process of doing something as much as from the result. The reporting physician must act to fulfill his or her own highest ideals.

Physicians may choose to report indirectly and anonymously through committees or medical staff officers. Even this may be too much for some. Though they may be the earliest to spot an impaired doctor, they may prefer to hope that continuing medical education will eventually do the trick, or that the state will come to require postgraduate retesting, or that, if it gets bad enough, somebody else will report. We have already seen why such rationalizations may be irresistible to physicians.

They also may fear the legal liability involved in reporting.[22] Efforts to legally protect peer review have left a small risk of liability. However, there looms beside it the fact that not reporting is an act of negligence, a very serious one if harm to a patient ensues.

Reporting physicians must expect denial and hostility at the time of intervention, no matter how compassionately it may be done. If this prevents them from proceeding, they must expect a judicial solution and ask whether their failure to act constitutes compassion and healing. Self-governing of the medical staff is required by law, and medical professional organizations would have it no other way.[23] Each physician must regularly evaluate him- or herself, as well as colleagues. If physicians fail to do so and harm is done, hospital medical staff can be sued as an unincorporated association. Moreover, the hospital itself must ensure that effective peer review is in operation.

Action

For the inexperienced physician observing another's disability, intervention is a growing up process with a predictable set of responses: not noticing; then looking the other way anxiously; finally silence due to ignorance of the signs or pessimism or fear for one's personal safety. Equally "enabling" responses are muttering ineffectively to others in the halls (where ancillary staff who have no business in these affairs can overhear distorting fragments of information or at least perceive an air of tension) and giving damaging and impulsive responses based on inadequate awareness (e.g., acting tentatively, permissively, or judgmentally).

Before any action is taken, a reporting physician should consider carefully making a referral and a high-quality intervention (e.g., a skilled, caring, nonpunitive confrontation), which hopefully will assist the physician in trouble. In addition, there should be education and information sharing for the physician, the family, and colleagues.[24] Exactly what action the medical staff takes depends on the problem, but it will be confidential and within the limits of the law. Physicians are entitled to due process when staff privileges are threatened. Accredited hospitals provide for this.

Physicians with Alzheimer's disease and other irreversible cognitive disabilities must be kindly and firmly stopped from practice, although a few might be allowed to carry on for a while under strict supervision. Some problems, such as an acute situational reaction or an excessive emotional outburst, can be handled by an informed friend or a discussion with the chief of staff. Drug and alcohol issues are probably best handled by a team headed by an individual skilled in such interventions.

After pertinent data has been collected and the disabled physician interviewed, he or she may be found *not* to have acted in a manner which threatened patient welfare, nor to be likely to so act in the future. On the other hand, the physician may be judged to have acted irresponsibly or to pose a future threat. If so, the next contact should be personal. If there is no response, a letter should be sent. If a hearing before a peer review committee is required through local due process procedures, sometimes attorneys may be allowed to be present (in an advisory capacity only), but this is rare. The emphasis has been and still is on doctor-to-doctor solutions.[25]

If the physician is found to be receptive to advice, the physician's progress will be monitored periodically by an appropriate component of the medical staff. If the physician denies illness or impairment, is hostile to intervention, and refuses any advice, then referral must be made to the appropriate staff committee with regard to the physician's privileges and to a competent treatment source. In many states an additional referral to the state licensing board may be required by law. State boards governing the quality of medical arts are anxious to value and protect the life and work of the doctor,[26] in no small part due to medical societies around the nation which have wrestled with these issues.[27]

Substance-abusing physicians have a lifelong, relapsing illness and require long-term follow-up. The California Physicians' Diversion Program is so named because its candidates are diverted from disciplinary action and so avoid loss of license. Because 57 percent of the physicians have been through a program already, their rehabilitation must be well supported. They must demonstrate two years of sobriety as well as a change in lifestyle. Only then can monitoring be discontinued, generally in two to five years. Until that time, the physicians are required to attend two Alcoholics Anonymous meetings and two other "board" meetings a week, to allow urine specimens to be taken, and to have a personal practice monitor on the hospital staff. There is thus a far greater than 60 percent success rate.[28]

It is certainly not simple to treat a doctor. Physician addicts share many characteristics with the general addict population: their capacity for rationalization, simulation, vacillation, subterfuge, and prevarication is infinite."[29] The therapeutic process is aided if physicians under treatment take time for themselves, whether forced or not, and try to increase the quantity and quality of their communication with others, especially those trying to help them. It should come as no surprise, that play and exercise are of great benefit.

The prognosis in the case of alcoholism is excellent. It exceeds 60 to 80 percent in treatment programs. The prognosis is less favorable in narcotics addiction, but success in any program depends on whether the doctor can be kept in it for long-term follow-up.

Some critics decry the efforts put into fighting substance abuse, because relapse is so frequent. They overlook the results from programs with teeth, such as the one in California. Even in the Alcoholics Anonymous program, where discipline is individual and relapse is expected, the number of "cures," in the sense of long-term sobriety, is impressive. In what other discipline of medicine or surgery is the rate of success as high in regard to a life-threatening disease?

It may be that prevention is best, with doctors speaking with one another about emotional issues in a reflective manner. Most often this is done one to one in a hospital or clinic. It may occur at medical staff or county medical society meetings from time to time. More conferences in various specialties are beginning to bring behavioral and emotional topics into the spotlight.

If one feels impatient and finds oneself shuffling about and looking out the door during such discussions, it is appropriate to ask why. Having overcome such a reaction, one may wish further insight and training. There is a question whether "healthy" physicians long in practice are educable in matters so foreign to their training as substance abuse. The answer is yes. Some medical schools have always attempted to teach the subject with varying success. Other educational programs are now available.[30]

Doctors should talk to recovering alcoholic doctors as a way of getting more information. They can go to an Alcoholics Anonymous meeting if they have never been to one, or to an Alanon meeting or a meeting of a similar organization. Just as members of a team within the healing arts must respect their own limits, so must they recognize the competence of others. Just as they forgive their own limitations, so must they accept the limitations of colleagues and paraprofessionals. They should receive criticism gratefully (perhaps after an initial shock) and answer thoughtfully. If criticism is given angrily, the person giving it is afraid of something; that fear must be recognized and respected by the receiver. If not, the receiver will reciprocate in anger, which at best feels good only for the moment.

CONCLUSION

The reader has probably noticed a similarity between the preparation proposed for the doctor who must intervene and the recipient's subsequent therapeutic process. First, discipline is needed to stop and look at automatic behavior and make it conscious. This education process requires that the loner break down the isolation within the profession and accept help. Later, choices appear and change becomes possible. What was feared is now experienced with a sense of relief and welcome.

So, if one is asked what to do about an incompetent doctor, the answer is to treat him or her like a human being one did not know well enough. If one liked the doctor before the incompetence was discovered, one still may. If one did not, one may come to do so after helping and really getting to know the doctor. Reporting helps the physician escape punishment as well as protects the physician's patients.

Confrontation means acknowledging and understanding a problem and then following with effective action. What action depends on one's skills, but whether and when to act is governed by one's oath. In this disease, like many others, there is an effective intervention, but it requires a truly personal healing involvement, both for the impaired physician and for oneself.

NOTES

1. K. Shuckit, *Drug and Alcohol Abuse*, 2d ed. (New York: Plenum Publications, 1984).

2. American Medical Association, *Bibliography on the Impaired Physician* (Chicago: American Medical Association, 1982).

3. California Medical Association, Chemical Dependency Education Program, P.O. Box 7690, San Francisco, CA 94120-7690.

4. J.E. Horsley "Now a Temper Tantrum Can Cost You Your Privileges," *Medical Economics,* May 12, 1986, pp. 77–79.

5. W.E. McAuliffe, et al., "Psychoactive Drug Use among Practicing Physicians and Medical Students," *New England Journal of Medicine* 315 (1986): 805–10.

6. R.P. Johnson and J.C. Connelly, "Addicted Physicians: A Closer Look," *Journal of the American Medical Association* 245 (1981): 256.

7. "The Impaired Physician," *LACMA Physician,* January 21, 1980, pp. 31–39; J.M. Brewster, "Prevalence of Alcohol and Other Drug Problems among Physicians," *Journal of the American Medical Association* 255 (1986): 1913–20.

8. Johnson and Connelly, "Addicted Physicians."

9. J.D. McCue "The Effects of Stress on Physicians and Their Medical Practice," *New England Journal of Medicine* 306 (1982): 461.

10. "Emotional overlay" is a popular term meaning "I think he's showing emotion—how juvenile, trite, misleading, injudicious, or inappropriate," and is a synonym of "crock." Its use tends to decline with the advancing clinical skills of the practitioner.

11. In fact, life experience tends to reinforce what a person does best, that is to say, the person's strongest traits, both positive and negative. These have been protective at some time in the person's life. The person may deliberately change the degree or the kind of "bad" reactions, but if life stresses are severe enough, he or she is apt to revert to the old patterns.

12. Johnson and Connelly, "Addicted Physicians." The sex of the studied physicians and dentists is not detailed—one assumes they were largely male. Highlights of the California Bureau of Medical Quality Assurance Activities for July–August 1986 shows the Diversion Program for Impaired Physicians to contain a ratio of 189 males to 15 females.

13. C. Black, *It Will Never Happen To Me! Children of Alcoholics as Youngsters—Adolescents—Adults* (Denver, Colo.: M.A.C. Printing and Publications Division, 1982).

14. J.A. Newsom and J.N. Chappel, "The Impaired Physician: What the Family Physician Should Know," *Seminars in Family Medicine* 1 (1980): 311–19.

15. McCue, "Effects of Stress."

16. Ibid.

17. Newsom and Chappel, "Impaired Physician."

18. A.C. Gualtieri, J.P. Cosentino, and J.S. Becker, "The California Experience with a Diversion Program for Impaired Physicians," *Journal of the American Medical Association* 249 (1983): 226–29.

19. A. Spickard and F.T. Billings, "Alcoholism in a Medical School Faculty," *New England Journal of Medicine* 305 (1981): 1646–48.

20. G.D. Talbott and E.B. Benson, "Impaired Physicians: The Dilemma of Identification," *Postgraduate Medicine* 68, no. 6 (1980): 56–63.

21. M.S.W. Watts, "Editors Forum on Physician Peer Review," *Internist*, July 1986.

22. P. Peck, "How Should the Professional Deal With Incompetent Doctors?" *Physician's Management,* September 1986: 154–78.

23. California Medical Association, *What You Need to Know about Impairment in Physicians* (San Francisco: California Medical Association, n.d.). This packet of materials covers a range of related subjects and can be obtained from CMA, P.O. Box 7690, San Francisco, CA 94120-7690.

24. J.N. Chappel, "Physician Attitudes Toward Distressed Colleagues," *Western Journal of Medicine* 134 (1981): 175–80; D.M. Baughan, "Crisis Precipitation in Alcoholism," *Western Journal of Medicine* 145 (1986): 680–81.

25. C. Pelton, Administrator Physicians Diversion Program, Bureau of Medical Quality Assurance, State of California, personal communication, September 1, 1986.

26. California Medical Association, *What You Need to Know;* R.E. Herrington, et al., "Treating Substance-Use Disorders among Physicians," *Journal of the American Medical Association* 247 (1986): 2253–57.

27. American Medical Association, *Bibliography.*

28. Herrington et al., "Treating Substance-Use Disorders." For information on the origins of formal help for physicians (programs in California and Georgia), see California Medical Association, *What You Need to Know;* S.A. Skillicorn, "Peer Group Committee Tackles Physician Behavior Problems," *Hospital Medical Staff*, July 1981: 2–6.

29. Johnson and Connelly, "Addicted Physicians."

30. California Medical Association, Chemical Dependency Education Program, supra n. 3.

Chapter 30

The Physician as an Entrepreneur

Harold L. Jensen

Entrepreneur: one who organizes, manages, and assumes the risks of a business or enterprise.

Entrepreneurism is part and parcel of the practice of medicine in America. One of the strong lures of the practice of medicine has been the high degree of self-determination that has characterized this profession. One could treat where, when, and how one wished. One set one's own fees, treated whomever one wished, and distributed free care as the circumstances dictated. The physician was, in short, the boss.

It is often asserted that medical practice has recently become commercial, entrepreneurial. It has not, because it has always been so.

COMMERCIALIZATION

Then why the outcry, this air of discovery and mild outrage, about what is clearly a time-hallowed practice? A moment's reflection shows us that the limits of promoting a physician's practice or promoting special skills (real or imagined) has been sharply circumscribed in the past. The limits were labeled "ethical," and it was the mark of a professional to observe those boundaries prescribed by the profession for its members. An errant physician-advertiser not only would run the risk of formal ostracization by his peers, but would also be shunned by the public, who understood that "good" doctors did not advertise.

This newly perceived commercialization reflects a weakening of the self-imposed restraints of the profession. This erosion arises from three sources. First is the extension of antitrust applications to the profession, treating medicine as a business. If physicians were to act together to restrict the business activities of another physician, no matter how professionally repugnant those activities might be, the Federal Trade Commission could intervene. Suits tried in a federal jurisdiction with the potential of large awards and triple damages are a danger few can ignore.

Second, the economic base of medical practice is marked by increased numbers of patients but proportionately decreased funding. While the economic pie is not increasing, the numbers of physicians are. This competition for fewer available dollars has the effect of weakening traditional ethical restraints on the individual practitioner. This is especially true

350

for the newer physicians, who face unusual difficulty in establishing a practice in a competitive environment, who are often burdened by the debt acquired with their education, and who have had little, if any, time to become familiar with and accept the traditional professional mores.

Finally, economic innovations in payment for medical services have been developed which reward the physician for doing *less* for the patient. Despite the obvious ethical distortion, these financial incentives have swamped doubts and forced acquiescence, quickly becoming accepted medical practice.

New Restraints

Medicine's position of autocracy, protected by law and custom, existed through the 1940s. Little by little the impact of specialization and regulation has eroded the self-determinism enjoyed by physicians. They now must demonstrate proficiency to perform certain clinical activities; submit to certifying and licensing restrictions; review and in turn submit to being reviewed by other physicians to maintain admitting privileges in a hospital; adhere to rules set by the government and a variety of other payers concerning how much to charge and how to submit charges; and suffer unilateral decisions by payers as to what portion and how soon the charges will be paid.

If, as an independent contractor, a physician decides the conditions are unacceptable, he or she is offered a "Hobson's choice": One can conform or get out of the program. If the physician opts out of a major program, such as Medicare or Blue Shield, the decision might result in the loss of half of the physician's income. Should the rules of medical practice in a hospital become too onerous, the physician can resign. However, hospitals are capital-intensive, technologically advanced, specialist-swarming, skilled nursing centers that are essential for the care of the seriously ill. They are indispensable for the modern practice of medicine.

Clearly, a choice that has such unacceptable options is no choice at all. The physicians adapt because they must. They adapt grumblingly. They adapt remembering the freedom they once had. They adapt with anger over being penalized for following the (expensive) former rules of cost-plus reimbursement.

Conflicts in Public Perception

There are some unresolved conflicts in how legislators view health care. In an era of competition and deregulation, the profession is regulated as if it were a public utility. The current Medicare freeze is not the first time medicine has been given unequal treatment by the government, nor even the first freeze of fees (the first occurred under President Nixon). The third party payers have a schizophrenic message. Health care practitioners are urged to be competitive, but the regulatory apron strings are firmly tied. The payers urge them to give the lowest possible rates and reduced services for their customers, but the same payers see no need to spare expense if their coronary arteries occlude or if their child sickens. The same distorted expectations give physicians no relief from medical liability suits which hold them to a fault-free standard while simultaneously stripping them of the financial resources required to practice the defensive medicine needed in a litiginous environment.

During the past several decades there has been ongoing pressure to make health care available to all. For a time, health care was described as a right, and whether those who needed such services could pay was not given consideration. Most western nations long ago defined health care as a right of citizenship. In this country, national health service legislation was proposed before World War I. It nearly became law as part of the Social Security Act of 1935; it was a major plank in the Democratic party's campaign for the 1948 election; it was developed for the aged in the Medicare program of 1965. This was the highwater mark for the concept in this country. It has occasionally but briefly surfaced since then, and failed to gain acceptance by increasing margins.

In part, this failure of acceptance has been attributed to linking the concept of national health insurance to socialism and the perjorative phrase "socialized medicine." This expression was repugnant to those who held the concept of the free enterprise system as integral to America. If health care was just another commodity, like bread and beer, and no more a right than any other goods or services, then it follows that the government ought not to violate the rights of physicians in an otherwise free society. Further, physicians have zealously guarded their autonomy and steadfastly fought government intervention in their professional affairs. In this vein it is interesting to note that the greatest of the entitlement programs (Medicare statute, Social Security Act, Section 1801) begin not with a bold assertion of the entitlement, but rather apologetically with the disavowal that any bureaucrat would "exercise any control over the practice of medicine." These government documents appear to have the truthworthiness of an Indian treaty.

John Naisbitt, of *Megatrends* fame, tells us that "the transition times between economies are the times when entrepreneurship blooms. We are now in such a period."[1] It also appears that we are trading in the poor soil of regulation-fettered entitlement for the rich loam of free enterprise. Entrepreneurial medical practices should flourish. However, there are forces at work, especially in the province of hospital care, which inhibit any rampant commercialism.

Limits on Commercialism

Not the least of these forces limiting commercialism in health care is the implied contract that exists between patients and physicians. Patients offer their trust and payment to physicians, who in turn fulfill their end of the bargain by offering their best efforts to meet the patients' needs. This contractual relationship has become distorted by the intervention of third party payers, who act as business agents, negotiate conditions under which treatment can take place, and bargain for discounts from the usual fees. But despite this jarring note, there is still the traditional special trust given by the public and the special sense of responsibility borne by the doctor and reinforced by law. Both the trust and the sense of responsibility are based on the premise that the medical profession has a unique competence and is committed to use its competence in the care of the ill.

Another impediment deterring the expansion of entrepreneurism into exploitation has been the prospective payment (or pricing) system. This system was designed to curtail the expensive habits of diagnosis and treatment as practiced by the physician, whose pen accounts for as much as 80 percent of costly hospital care. Under this plan, the hospital *must* be able to curtail expenditures per patient, and any significant control requires the cooperation of the medical staff.[2] Nonetheless, physicians have an overriding ethical and legal responsibility to do the best they can to assure that patients receive all necessary care. If a physician faces a serious conflict arising from a long-standing allegiance to a hospital (which the physician needs in order to treat more seriously ill patients), then a significant tension is created. One might say that the duty to the patients is of paramount concern. The issues of failure of reimbursement and curtailment of service lie in other hands—let the hospitals look out for themselves! Moreover, the physician under Medicare is still paid under a fee-for-service schedule. Therefore, ignoring the plight of the hospital and possible abuses of the Medicare system is to a physician's advantage.[3]

The reality of the situation is that the federal regulations are written so that a hospital cannot look out for itself. A hospital is penalized if the actions of the physician are deemed inappropriate. It is obvious that the physician has a duty not only to today's patients but to future patients as well. Those future patients will be poorly served if there is no hospital conveniently located or only one so depleted of expensive technologic resources that care is impaired.[4] The opportunities for manipulating direct patient care are restricted by ethical considerations that are more than simply old habits.

AN UNEASY PEACE

Despite the new strains inflicted by the government's pervasive prospective pricing system, there is an uneasy alliance, a bond, between physician and hospital. The care of the seriously ill patient requires cooperation between the two. There was a time when the hospital was clearly the doctor's workshop and the lines of control were defined. It was the duty of the hospital's board to run a hotel-like operation and secure the necessary capital. Physicians were in charge of medical care, and no challenge was thinkable.

A shift in these roles has been powered by forces tangential to medical care. A series of legal opinions has made the hospital responsible for the care rendered within its confines. The increasing presence of high technology in medical care, with its necessary hospital-based physicians and technicians, has put the hospital in charge of economic decisions about what capital expenditures they will make, and this has medical care consequences.[5] Formerly, medical staffs were fairly compact and stable. They had sufficient leverage through threatened boycott to control key aspects of medical care and preserve entrepreneurial positions within the hospital. Now, medical staffs are larger and less cohesive, with larger specialist subgroups with their own agendas. The medical staffs are less able to act as units. Further, if a medical staff acted to restrict admissions or jointly followed policies that would economically harm a hospital, charges of collusion and restraint of trade would result.

Despite the devisive forces that wrench apart these partners in health care, the mission remains the same. Physicians are charged to do whatever they must for the welfare of their patients, and this means at times the problems of the hospital must be ignored as secondary to the immediate problems of a given patient. Yet there is a recognition of the obligation to the patients of tomorrow. It is this tenacious adherence to duty that blunts any serious move toward having a completely deregulated, profit-driven health care system.[6]

Free Enterprise

The traditional discussion of free enterprise in medicine has always been the harmonic counterpoint of physician autonomy. After decades of mobilizing public and legislative opinion against entitlement programs that threatened physician autonomy, physicians find that they have been outflanked by movements of unappreciated strength, namely, competition, physician surplus, and the corporate practice of medicine. They have found that free enterprise extends to competition by large corporations, which are often well capitalized, well organized, and profit-driven. There have been those who welcome this competition and the appearance of efficiency that corporate medicine has introduced into the health care arena. There are those who say loudly that American medicine is an outdated cottage industry which is getting the treatment it needs—a good dose of "no nonsense" management to boil the fat out of the system. The corporate goal in medicine concerns the bottom line. There should be no surprise that corporations desire profit and that they view health care as only incidental to that end.

There is some revulsion when a concern for the bottom line and net profit is coupled to health care. It is somehow foreign to physicians who through training have come to truly believe they are *the* patients' advocates. Part of the confusion in the minds of practitioners arises from the realization that neither physicians nor hospitals can provide care to all who need it, because neither has the money (nor cost-shifting capacity) to do so.[7] There is the view—and legislation that supports it—that "medicine is a business like any other." This may seem true from a fiscal point of view, but when we consider the corollary—that health care practitioners are freed from any special ethical obligations—the view is clearly seen to be false. By training, by tradition, by law, and by public trust, an ethical duty binds the physician to a course of behavior that is decidedly unbusinesslike. The traditional medical ethic based on patient need is heavy baggage indeed for the medical entrepreneur.

The reverse side of that coin is that quality of care is integral to such enterprises available to physicians. The seamy side of sharp business practice, where quality is abandoned for profit, is combated in business by establishing brands that are of a known quality. Brands will not be necessary in medicine if physicians, with their curiously quaint ethics, maintain control of medical care.

The current vogue is to differentiate medical care into product lines that enable payers to establish selective pricing.[8] There are basic goals of health care: to save lives; to maintain the quality of life; to preserve health; and to restore health. Any attempt to develop a comprehensive set of product lines (or DRGs) must confront the fact that most serious medical problems involve multiple organs and that the subject of treatment for an illness (i.e., a human being) is an intricate physiologic entity capable of infinite and unpredictable variability. It really doesn't much matter if the patient or the payer has only allotted so much care for that illness (product line, DRG), the problem requires the resources *necessary,* forseen or not.

The vagaries of competition and the free market may control the price of a product, but medical care is a service. Fire protection and police protection are services. When a fire occurs, the resources aren't limited. Whatever is needed to fight the fire is used. Negotiating for the lowest bidder among competing fire companies invites underequipped companies with burst hoses and slow trucks.

Joint Venturing

Physicians who try to protect or increase their income with satellite offices, home services, increased office hours, free services to patients, and other more or less imaginative marketing innovations are putting themselves at some risk in the hope of a reward. The joint venture is a newer phenomenon with higher visibility. Here a practitioner, in concert with others (often a hospital), pools capital to achieve some gain. This capital may be in the form of money or other assets, and although the goal may be profit from providing a product or service of any kind, such activities are usually in medically related fields.[9]

The conflict inherent in joint ventures which deal with medical services has a different twist. Here an unethical physician might garner extra income, not from recommending that which is not needed, but from not recommending that which *is* needed. There is insulation for such a physician from patient criticism, as patients might never realize what potentially beneficial options they may have been denied.[10]

Many services provided to hospitalized patients do not require hospitalization. There is an increasing tendency by hospitals and others to unbundle the services traditionally provided by a hospital. The most profitable become available as outpatient and home care services, thus reducing hospital utilization while providing in many cases equivalent services at a lower cost and in more convenient settings. Even before the advent of prospective pricing and DRGs, this trend had begun; under pressure from current federal and commercial payment practices, it has accelerated. Ambulatory care centers, outpatient clinics, outpatient diagnostic centers, and a variety of home care medical services are thriving in every part of the country. Physicians, seeking to protect income from increasing competitive pressures, are becoming more involved in these ventures as owners, partners, or investors.

Although technologic changes in medical care are swiftly adopted and ever outpace the ability of society to pay, most of medicine, in terms of patterns of care and response to social change, has traditionally evolved with glacial speed. This has now been dramatically altered. Change in medical care in the past three years has occurred with revolutionary, rather than evolutionary, speed.[11]

REMAINING QUESTIONS

The results are not yet in on how successful joint ventures will be. However, the concept has raised disturbing questions about the medical profession. Physicians have been given the role (by law and custom) of patient advocate. They are to see that patients receive all necessary care. Furthermore, the conscience of the profession, the Judicial Council of the American Medical Association, states, "If a conflict develops between the physician's financial interest and the physician's responsibility to the patient, the conflict must be resolved to the patient's benefit."[12]

Under the current prospective pricing system of Medicare, the hospital benefits if services to the patient are reduced. As physicians still receive fee-for-service reimbursement for patient care in the hospital, there is a rough balance of interests. Even though the physician may be pressured directly by the hospital and indirectly by the government, the economic motive bolsters his role as advocate. In joint ventures with the hospital (or others), the economic incentive to provide all necessary care is diminished by pitting the economic incentives of both parties against the interests of the patient. Furthermore, it is clear that HMOs where there is risk-sharing between physicians and the HMO and a bonus from resources allocated but not spent are essentially joint ventures. In these ventures, the economic incentives are allied against the patient. It is the strong tradition among physicians of service and ethical behavior that has, so far, prevented exploitation. [13]

How long will this professional ethic of patient advocacy survive in a system in turmoil which rewards competitive innovation. How long will it survive when the profession is being told that it is a business and must act like a business, or when excess capacity— represented by physician surplus and empty hospital beds—threatens more than the bottom line, even making survival problematic? Can medical ethics outlast this onslaught by medical economics?

Often physician participants in a joint venture demand that their compensation from the venture be disproportionate to their actual investment in the enterprise. It seems reasonable to them that their rewards be contingent in some manner on the numbers of patients that they bring to the enterprise. However, many states have "fraud and abuse" statutes expressly forbidding this kind of compensation. [14]

An example might be cited of a hospital in partnership with physicians that required that they exclusively make referrals to it. An agreement might be made that a portion of the benefit received by the physicians was intended as an inducement to encourage such referrals. Medicare fraud and abuse statutes are so broadly drafted that any benefit contingent upon patient or service volume might qualify as a violation—a violation classified as a felony.

Even more subtle examples exist in those ventures involving a hospital and a group of physicians in a surgicenter. If the distributions to the physicians from the venture are increased after the break-even point is reached, if perhaps they are again increased after particular levels of utilization are realized, and if the physician members have the ability to refer patients to the surgicenter, then the compensation arrangement provides the physicians with a "kickback" for the increased referrals. The payment is indirect and not on a per-patient basis, but the fraud and abuse statutes specifically exclude indirect compensation. These can reflect many subtleties labeled leases, service agreements, and the like.

Our health care system has always provided strong financial incentives to physicians. Under fee-for-service practice, there is an incentive to deliver more care than is necessary. This has been countered by peer pressure and the tendency of physicians to conform to the norm, which is partly a result of their integrity and their sense of what is morally right. [15]

CONCLUSION

The management of costs by the management of health care delivery has become a major policy in the 1980s. The process of cost reduction is guided by competition and by financial incentives to encourage both physicians and hospitals to achieve greater efficiency. The concern lies not with the increased efficiency, but with the threatened tradeoff of quality. When all facets of health care costs are considered, savings have not yet been demonstrated. At issue is what effect these attempts at efficiency are having on the quality of care of the patient. If we cannot eliminate the financial incentives that threaten quality, then we must find ways to define the acceptable level of quality in health care so that limits and directions can be imposed on managed health care and financial incentives before patients are harmed. [16]

The growth in importance of the health care sector—it is the second largest market in the economy—has caused a flood of capital and a proliferation of profit-making entities. There is a longstanding tradition that makes the participation of doctors in such enterprises open to question. Light may be thrown on this issue by posing an important question. Is it better for nonmedical entrepreneurs interested only in the bottom line to be directing such projects or should physicians with appropriate medical background and interest be involved to set the needed standards of quality?[17]

The American health care system has always been entrepreneurial and is becoming increasingly so for many reasons. Some incentives will turn out to be effective and desirable in remodeling health care into a leaner and more efficient process. Others will be demonstrated to be undesirable or dangerous. The touchstone must be quality of care, and the physician and the hospital are the natural agents to protect their patients from insensitive economic imperatives.

NOTES

1. J. Naisbitt, *Megatrends* (New York: Warner Books, 1982), 16.

2. A.B. Cohen and L.J. Millenson, "Growing Partnerships Instead of Growing Apart," *Health Management Quarterly* (May–June 1986): 23–24. 101 (1984): 129–37.

3. J. Morone, "The Unruly Rise of Medical Capitalism," *Hastings Center Report* 15, no. 4 (August 1985): 28–31.

4. E. Friedman, "Because Someone Has to Be Responsible: Duty and Dilemma for the American Hospital," in *Making Choices: Ethics Issues for Health Care Professionals* (Chicago: American Hospital Publishing, Inc., 1986), 79–84.

5. E. Ginzberg, "Sounding Board: The Destabilization of Health Care," *New England Journal of Medicine* 315, no. 12 (September 1986); 757–60.

6. Ad Hoc Committee on Medical Ethics, American College of Physicians "American College of Physicians Manual," *Annals of Internal Medicine* 101 (1984): 129–37.

7. B.H. Gray and W.J. McNerney, Institute of Medicine Study, "Special Report: For-Profit Enterprise in Health Care," *New England Journal of Medicine* 314, no. 23 (June 1986): 1523–28.

8. S. Russell, "Unbundling Hospitals," *Venture* 7 (October 1985): 68–75.

9. K. Kaufman, M. Hall, and D. Higgins, "Joint Ventures in Health Care: What to Do before You Do the Deal," *Health Care Financial Management* 40, no. 7 (July 1986): 66–74.

10. A. Relman, "Dealing with Conflicts of Interest," *New England Journal of Medicine* 313, no. 12 (September 1985): 759–51.

11. Naisbitt, *Megatrends*.

12. American Medical Association, Judicial Council Opinions.

13. Ginzberg, "Destabilization of Health Care."

14. G. Richards, "How Do Joint Ventures Affect Relations with Physicians," *Hospitals*, 58, no. 23 (December 1984): 68–74.

15. R.H. Egdahl and C.H. Taft, "Sounding Board: Financial Incentives to Physicians," *New England Journal of Medicine* 315, no. 1 (July 1986): 59–61.

16. A. Relman, "Cost Control and Doctor's Ethics," *Issues in Science and Technology*, Winter 1985: 103–11.

17. J. Morone, "The Unruly Rise of Medical Capitalism."

Chapter 31

The Ethics of Health Professional Strikes

David C. Thomasma and R. Morrison Hurley

Striking is, as Dorothy D. Nayer describes it, an exercise of "just, lawful, and ethical rights to withhold or withdraw labor in order to gain concessions from employers." [1] Before the widespread institutionalization and consequent bureaucratization of health care, it would have been unthinkable that health professionals would strike. A second factor in Western countries that influences the propensity to strike is the degree to which health professionals have become public employees. The right to strike has not always been clear, especially for the latter group. In addition, the ethical propriety of any strike by those who provide services essential to life is still highly contested, despite recognition of workers' rights.

Our object is to examine as fully as possible the arguments about the ethics of health professional strikes. We do this in order to develop a policy for strikes by health professionals, a policy lacking in Lalonde's report regarding health care in Canada. [2] It would be fair to criticize that report in this regard, because the reality of health professional strikes had already emerged when the report was drafted in 1974. There had been three important strikes in Canada alone. As a consequence, one finds nothing in the report about strikes under the heading "Problems in the Organization and Delivery of Health Care" (p. 26), where one might expect such a discussion. Instead the report focuses on its theme of relating lifestyle and environmental factors to personal health.

Collective bargaining is clearly here to stay in England, Ireland, America, Canada, Australia, and Scandanavia, not to mention a host of other countries. [3] Our comments apply to all health professionals in these countries. For example, practicing physicians struck in Saskatchewan in 1962 and in other parts of Canada and the United States in the early 1970s. On May 1, 1980, almost half of Ireland's nurses struck for 17 days. [4] On July 19, 1981, one million health professionals in England went on strike, severely crippling 250,000 hospitals there. [5] In the United States, a 1974 amendment to the Taft-Hartley Act governing labor rights extended collective bargaining to 3,500 not-for-profit hospitals. The American Nursing Association in 1950 had adopted a typical stance among professionals at that time—a no-strike policy in favor of good faith bargaining. But by 1968 this policy was revoked. Without the threat of a withdrawal of labor, employers are not seen as forced to bargain in good faith and often will not do so. [6] This is true even where both parties are held to binding arbitration, as is the case with most public employees.

Thus, health professional strikes present to society (including health professionals themselves) problems arising from the altruism inherent in the profession the need for personal development, and patient care needs, especially needs for essential services. In our analysis, we shall first examine some of the major strikes in various countries, focusing on their causes and the reasons given for them in order to discover any commonalities. Second, we shall examine ethical arguments regarding strikes, presenting some of our own as well. Finally, we shall make some policy proposals with respect to strikes. Throughout this chapter, the term *medicine* should be taken to refer to that discipline shared by all health professionals. The term *medical* shall be the adjective. In this way we can shorten the cumbersome *health professional* to *medical*, and yet include all health professionals in the discussion.

STRIKES AND THEIR REASONS

Province of Saskatchewan, 1962

A particularly bitter strike occurred in the Province of Saskatchewan in 1962. It was the first of its kind in North America. Offices were completely closed for the 24 days of the strike, although there was a provision for emergency care. Some physicians left the province permanently. The reason for the strike was the imposition of control by the government over physicians and over what patients they could see. Saskatchewan was the first province to adopt socialized medicine along the lines of the model employed in England. Fears about the long-term consequences of this change predominated, especially with regard to quality-of-care decisions physicians felt they must be able to make. In retrospect, many of the fears of these early days were groundless. Governmental intervention soon developed in the other provinces and similar physician fears led to organized opposition, including withdrawal-of-service action in some.

Province of Quebec, Spring 1970

While both French- and English-speaking residents struck against the government (through hospitals) in this six-week strike, the reasons differed somewhat. The English-speaking residents wanted decent living conditions, better hours, and better pay for patient care. Because many of the French-speaking residents could moonlight, their pay problems were not as severe. However, they felt their educational experiences were inferior to those obtained in the "English" hospitals. During the strike, a work-to-rule mode (i.e., 8 A.M. to 5 P.M. daily) was adopted. Residents were publicly designated as "student" doctors. Of interest is the fact that the residents derived much support from the Association of General Practitioners but little from the Association of Specialists, many of whom themselves would be on strike later that same year.

Concerns in this strike were like those in many. They basically boiled down to this: Was the strike really worth possible danger to patients and to the reputations of medical practitioners?

Province of Quebec, Autumn 1970

A second strike—by practicing specialists themselves rather than residents—took place in Quebec. This strike was clearly about power. The physicians wanted to maintain the freedom of patients to choose a physician and the freedom of physicians to choose whom to accept as a patient. The pivotal issue was similar to that raised a decade earlier in the Saskatchewan strike. Would government completely control the practice of medicine because they bought the services of physicians? Some physicians were also concerned about the price to be paid for these services. In the United States, exactly parallel concerns are currently being raised about the role of third party payers in controlling medical practice (state Medicaid reimbursement plans and insurance company plans to hold down costs).

The 1970 strike was precipitously ended without resolution because of the events of the "October Crisis," during which the War Measures Act was invoked and civil liberties were suspended throughout Canada, particularly in Quebec. A separatist organization, the F.L.Q. (Front for the Liberation of Quebec), had provoked an armed uprising, requiring the presence of federal troops and the imposition of martial law. In the midst of this chaos, it would have been unprofessional to continue the strike.

In any strike similar to this one, serious questions may be raised about the seeming lack of altruism of the kind most persons expect from health professionals as well as about the legitimacy of the desire for a decent income and for control over one's practice. For example, most medical schools vigorously promote the view that patients' needs must come before items on one's personal agenda. Nonetheless, it has also been proposed that control over one's practice (where to practice, how much to charge, what patients to accept) is a matter of justice and not just of personal preference. In the U.S., R.S. Sade has indeed argued that persons have no rights to health care precisely because they would violate the right of health care professionals to control the conditions of their own labor.[7] Even within a national health model, then, the right to control labor conditions is of major importance and needs to be taken into account.

New York City, 1975

From 1958 until 1975, the Committee of Interns and Residents (CIR) in New York and New Jersey grew to 6,300 members, all of whom sought by their membership to improve their status in teaching hospitals. A four-day strike by 3,000 of them against New York City in 1975 was the most massive in U.S. history to that date. It involved 21 hospitals. The American Medical Association endorsed the action, something it has not done since. The CIR protested 110-hour workweeks, 50-hour shifts, poor pay, and out-of-title work.

As a result of the action, many other interns and residents were able to negotiate better conditions. A national union was formed (PNHA), whch faltered in the late 1970s but is now gaining momentum again, this time trying to organize house staff at voluntary rather than community-owned hospitals. According to union spokespersons, the famous Cedars-Sinai ruling in 1976, in which the National Labor Relations Board ruled that house staff at private, not-for-profit hospitals, were students rather than employees, actually only ruled that house staff at these hospitals do not fall under the National Labor Relations Act. We will discuss the ramifications of this ruling later in the text.

In 1981, the CIR organized a weeklong strike in New York which began on St. Patrick's Day. The goal of this strike was to gain better patient conditions (or, put differently, to gain a more prominent voice in patient care decisions).

As Steven Peacock, a King's County Pediatric resident, put it, "We're asking for a right to safeguard our patients and to take part in the process of defining standards of patient care."[8] In New York City this altruistic stance remains possible. One of the St. Patrick's Day disputes had to do with the fact that there was only one intensive care nurse per ten patients at Harlem Hospital—a ludicrous figure. Nevertheless, the CIR lost this strike, even though the union protested unnecessary deaths of poor patients due to terrible conditions. The defeat was largely due to laws prohibiting public employees from striking and a city administration little inclined to make changes in a recession. In the end, the patients suffered the most.

Chicago, 1975

The house staff struck at Cook County Hospital late in 1975. The issues were much the same as those in New York City—poor patient care facilities, terrible hours, poor pay, and little recognition of professional status and achievements, especially with regard to the running of the hospital. This strike seems to have drawn more national attention than the New York strike.

In December 1975, the interns and residents business section of the American Medical Association recommended that the AMA take several forms of direct action in strikes by house staff. Although the House of Delegates rejected this on grounds that such disputes were local rather than national AMA actions, it did affirm its stance, noted under the New York discussion, that interns and residents were employees and therefore had a right to strike. The principle announced for this position, more radical than usual for the AMA, was the June 1975 declaration that a physician has an "inalienable right . . . to decide for himself the circumstances under which he can or cannot continue his practice."[9] This principle could easily be derived from the right to work and to control the conditions of employment mentioned above.

United Kingdom, 1975–76

Also late in 1975, and for the first time in the history of the National Health Service, junior hospital doctors (residents) in England took industrial action. Of all the 1975 strikes, this one was the most complex. It is difficult, therefore, to settle on any one reason for the strike. First, there was an increasing dissatisfaction with pay in relation to long hours, despite extra duty allowances given for hours worked over 80. Residents did not have the right to determine the hours to be worked, nor was their salary really related to hours worked.

The industrial action took place around four specific events: a new contract and its provisions for a 40-hour workweek, the latter being hotly contested by practicing physicians (to September 1975); the setting of salaries covered in the new contract (September–November 1975); an independent audit of costs and new leadership in the negotiating committee (November 1975–March 1976); and, finally, new concerns and more industrial action (April 1976–October 1976).

At the heart of the disputes during this strike was the notion of a "unit of medical time." Residents were to be issued contracts for a certain number of units, above which they would receive supplements for extra duty. The rate of supplement was different for being on-duty and for being on-call (at home, but required to come to the hospital if called). In return for a more professional model of payment, however, many residents were to make less money than under the system then in place. Continued dispute about overtime pay led to recommendations for an industrial action in which only emergencies would be covered by a 40-hour flexible workweek. (We would call this a slowdown rather than a stoppage.)

The ethics of this strike was questioned even more than those in New York, Chicago, and Washington. Resident salaries had actually increased relative to those of other health professionals in the United Kingdom, but residents tended to compare their wages unfavorably with what doctors in other countries earned. Many academics and physicians, as well as the *British Medical Journal* and *Lancet*, opposed the strike as unprofessional, publicly alienating, and clinically dangerous. The public supported the juniors on the long hours, but it was much more cautious about the pay dispute. In the end, it is hard to say what the juniors gained by striking instead of disputing the terms of their contract.[10]

New York City, July 1976

A small incident occurred in New York in 1976 which highlights expectations by the public and the courts about physician conduct during strikes. Drs. Gold and Fisher, part-time preceptors at a family practice clinic run by Montefiore Hospital and Medical Center, without notice to the hospital walked out and joined the picket line of unionized employees at the clinic, although they were not union members themselves. On the picket line, they identified themselves as doctors and advised patients to get treatment elsewhere. From that time on, their requests to have admitting privileges and, later, full-time positions were unduly delayed, because of their activity during the strike. The official complaint leveled against them by the hospital administrators was that they had abandoned patients. Both the National Labor Relations Board and the United States Court of Appeals, Second Circuit, to whom the hospital appealed, judged that the physicians did not lose the protection of the National Labor Relations Act when they went on strike, even without notice. Hence they could not suffer retaliation by the hospital and were to be given positions, with remuneration for the delay.

However, the court came down sharply on the efforts of Drs. Gold and Fisher to discourage patients from entering the clinic. The court judged that their misconduct in this regard went far beyond their right to strike and to offer fair persuasion and honest appeals to the public. Instead, they used their authority as trusted physicians to aim "at eliciting a submissive, unreasoned, misinformed reaction from those whose cooperation they sought."[11] The point to be pressed is that people are inclined to listen uncritically to those whom they trust. Thus they are inclined to believe physicians, because of their position. Physicians, although they are free to take sides in issues such as strikes, must exercise special care to be truthful and balanced.

Nursing Strikes, 1979–82

Starting in 1979 (the winter of discontent), nurses and other nonphysician health workers started going on strike. Public employees, including nurses, went on strike in England in 1979. In 1980, half of Ireland's nurses went on strike. In 1981, one million health workers went on strike in England. Job actions were taken by nurses against individual hospitals in Scandanavia, Australia, the U.S., and Canada. In the media, horror stories abounded. Striking staff were labeled murderers and killers. In some cases, emergencies were not covered and patients died.

Perhaps because nurses are more directly responsible for the minute-to-minute care of patients, many who belonged to unions were nonetheless reluctant to strike. We would think that the attitude of English midwives was common. The Royal College of Midwives (RCM) argued that no one pressures one to become a midwife. Once one does, then certain rights one acquires are accompanied by equally serious responsibilities. Thus, the RCM did not endorse strikes during this period, because it held midwives have a legal duty to provide care to patients, even though they also have an undeniable right to strike. The RCM left it up to each member to decide his or her own level of commitment in the absence of any guidance about which value might override the other.[12]

Among nurses who did strike, dissention still occurred. In Sweden, a poll of nurses who went on strike was conducted after the action's resolution. About a thousand respondents answered. Sixty percent felt it was right to strike, 14 percent disagreed, 23 percent had no opinion or could not decide; 9.8 percent of the respondents on a separate question thought they could have obtained the same results without a strike.[13] A group of National Health Service nurses argued against resisters to strikes by claiming that there is a distinction between patient inconvenience (the purpose of a strike) and patient danger. In their view, the former may be put at risk in favor of improvements to the whole health care system, improvements such as higher morale and increased staffing levels. Emergency cover must be provided, of course, but other ancillary services during strikes by support personnel should not be supplied by nurses. The latter is a form of emotional blackmail of nurses, ''because we have kind hearts and consciences.''[14]

Conditions creating increased pressure to strike include greater control by the public over health care, increased unionization of health workers, changes in educational patterns of nurses and ancillary staff requiring greater team decision making, nonpay conditions of employment, burnout, and tighter fiscal restraint in matters of health care. As Jack Wilson said of the role of nurses when standards of care are decreased by bureaucratic decisions or cost-cutting measures, ''Surely in such circumstances, nurses have a moral right and, for that matter, obligation to bear witness to the situation if they are to fulfill their time-honored custodian relationship with their patients.''[15]

Less altruistic are the usual reasons for striking. In New York City, 2,200 registered nurses went on a short strike (one to five days) on February 1, 1980. The strike was long in coming. It began in May 1979 when negotiations for a new contract started. At issue were non-nursing functions forced on nurses, mandatory overtime, work schedules, and pay. Management was seen as uninterested in negotiating, especially about the non-nursing function issue.

After this strike was resolved through an improved contract, nurses identified the real issues under the rubric ''delivering high-quality care.'' It was not possible to deliver it when "we were angry, frustrated, disappointed, exhausted, and fearful about the future of the nursing profession." [16] Behind the anger and frustration was the recognition that management did not see nurses as *equals* in the delivery of care and that there was a male-female domination game and an authority-worker game being played during the dispute. Finally, the nurses felt rewarded by the gains in the strike because it was organized by nurses and for nurses—to obtain what nurses wanted, not what doctors, administrators, or legislators told them their role ought to be.

The feeling that strikes have to do with personal recognition more than any other matter (e.g., time to shampoo a patient's hair or other personal nursing choices) was echoed by Diana Hanson, a staff nurse who had been on strike in Oregon. She said: "I am a nurse by choice and I deserve respect. While I must take orders from physicians, supervisors, patients, management, and others, I am me and I won't be walked on . . . I will not be forced into a situation that dictates that I give poor patient care under poor working conditions for poor wages and benefits. I am not substandard in any way, nor is my care." [17]

When asked whether it is ethical for nurses to strike for these reasons, Thelma Schorr, editor of *The American Journal of Nursing*, answered, "Yes, I think it's ethical. In fact, when working conditions throughout this country are enervating superb nurses (16-hour shifts and the like), driving many of them away from the bedside and some out of nursing altogether, I think it's unethical not to take action to improve those conditions." [18]

Some Pros and Cons

All health professional strikes have certain themes in common. Like all essential service employees, health professionals must grapple with the duties of care that their profession enjoins on them and that restrict their right to control their work environment. Second, as greater and greater political control of health care economics occurs in every nation, more and more health professionals will experience a conflict arising from being forced to lower standards of care while trying to fulfill their duties toward present and future patients, including the duty to maintain high professional standards and the duty to preserve the kind of decision making that allows professional discretion. [19] As the nonpay rewards of the profession shrink (recognition, freedom, participation in patient care and policy decisions), the "poor" pay and long hours will appear less and less attractive. As a consequence, poor pay often becomes the focus of discontent that is largely caused by more profound issues of patient care.

Thus, though individual strikes may have different immediate causes, the strikes have in common a concern for the following:

- standards of care
- the role of professionals in national and local health organizations (which are often quite bureaucratic)
- the future of their professional freedom and their patients' freedom
- better pay (commensurate with the level of responsibility)

Given the risk of public disapproval, irretrievable isolation of staff from management, [20] or alienation from more conservative national academies (e.g., the Royal College of

Physicians and Surgeons, the Canadian Medical Association, or the American Medical Association), health professionals learn by striking that it does pay to be well-behaved.[21] They learn that it is possible to take effective action against hospitals without harming patients.[22] Hence, health professionals have no specific obligations to employers except those under a contract. But they do have special obligations to clients. As a consequence, professionals' withdrawal of services must always ultimately be based on altruism, i.e., intervening on behalf of patients to improve services or their conditions.

Questionable motives in this regard are desires to obtain better pay, time-off, a more comfortable lifestyle, or a better education. The question is therefore still germane: Is it ethical for health professionals to strike? We have considered a number of strikes which dealt with poor conditions for patient care, a number primarily concerning pay disputes, and a number concerning the control of medical practice by government or insurance carriers. The first kind of strike appears to be more ethically justified than the latter two kinds. Is this true? Is is true, as Schorr opined, that preserving the profession from burnout is an ethical justification for striking? These questions lead to the next section of this chapter.

THE ETHICS OF HEALTH PROFESSIONAL STRIKES

The discussion of the ethics of health professional strikes must be set against two backgrounds. The first is social; the second is institutional. In the first, there is a clash between greater educational requirements for house staff and nurses and a shrinking of the role of professional judgment through public and economic controls over health care. In the second, the traditional health professional–patient role has been subsumed by institutions and third party payers, since so much of our health care is delivered by hospitals and clinics. In place of the traditional relationship there is a new one, the hospital-patient relationship, with its attendant duties and norms.[23] House staff and nurses are employees of these institutions and, while under contract, are obliged to carry out the duties of the hospital toward patients. They are part of a corporate enterprise. The clash in the institutional backdrop occurs between perceived individual obligations to present and future patients and employee corporate obligations to maintain care now. Attempts to argue for better pay and working conditions under these circumstances usually falter.

As we have seen in the previous section, there are really only two ethical arguments advanced in favor of strikes. The first is the classic utilitarian argument: Even though we may inconvenience current patients, perhaps even harm them, more patients will benefit through this strike in the long run. The burden of proof is then on the strikers to demonstrate how future patients will benefit and that these benefits will be sufficient to balance the risk to current patients. Even though physicians and nurses are uncomfortable with this argument, because it violates contractual agreements with individual patients, when conditions become deplorable enough, the strikers have been able to gain some degree of public support for their actions. Perhaps there is an implicit recognition by all parties of a suspension of contractual obligations in all but emergency cases.

A second argument is sometimes offered. This argument is more sophisticated, because it recognizes that the care which is often the focus of a strike is offered by institutions. In this argument, patients are defined as all of those who demand care as a right in the community, either because they have been accepted as patients or potentially would be or because their rights are established in a national health care service law. On this view, persons who may not need immediate care or not even be admitted to the hospital may still be counted as patients of the hospital. Hence some patients are not sacrificed to utility. Rather, the house staff, physicians, and nurses are merely choosing from among their contractual obligations to these patients, since they cannot fulfill all the obligations at once.

The validity of this argument depends on whether a hospital is analogous to a private physician, who treats some patients on any given day but counts many others not needing immediate care as his or her patients. Hardly anyone would try to justify a private practice physician's neglect of patients scheduled for attention in favor of care for those the physicians counts as patients but in less need. By analogy, house staff could not violate the ethical principle of triage either—that more attention should be given to those more in immediate need. Hence this second argument, while deftly skirting some problems of the utilitarian argument, seems weaker than it. Much greater justification would be needed to ignore those needs of patients entering a hospital than the presumably more preventive needs of patients on the calendar for a visit to their private physician.

Harry Colfer, a physician at the University of Michigan, argues that strikes are a right. As such, he further argues, a limited strike is morally permissible. His argument is based on responsibility and obligation. Physicians have a responsibility to patients and to the hospital. If these are not met, legal recourse is possible by both patients and the hospital. The physician could be sued or fired. The patient has responsibilities, too. They are to the physician and hospital. To the hospital, the patients are obliged to pay the bill and to cooperate in the care they decide upon. But what about the hospital's obligation? What recourse is open if the hospital does not meet its obligations to the patients or to the house staff and nurses? If all dialogue breaks down, all attempts to negotiate, then a strike must be used as a recourse to gain satisfaction for neglect of the patients or neglect of the human needs (here we improve his argument a bit) of house staff and nurses.

Colfer dismisses the utilitarian argument for employing a strike as follows: "It cannot be considered correct to weigh the value of a current patient's welfare against that of some hypothetical future patient. Such reasoning dehumanizes the present patient: it turns him into a statistic or an unwitting subject to an experiment."[24] Colfer holds that any strike against hospitals, in order to be effective, leads to an unavoidable side effect: The failure of physicians to meet their obligations to patients. This is morally unacceptable.

His argument for a limited strike is therefore based on nonutilitarian grounds. While Colfer acknowledges the debt of physicians to society, even to those not their own patients, he also argues that patients have responsibilities to physicians and to society. First, they must act reasonably by curtailing claims to have the right to consume all resources of the health care system even when detrimental to other patients. Second, they cannot demand so much from physicians and nurses that these health care practitioners are inhumanely burdened. Third, patients are members of society at large and have social and political responsibilities.

It follows, according to Colfer, that claims made on the system vary with the seriousness of the illness. An acute illness must be cared for, because the patient cannot carry out other duties, including social ones, until healed. By contrast, for nonacute complaints or even nonserious but chronic complaints, physicians have no immediate obligations. They need not accept for treatment patients with these problems. The patients may also be free enough of acute disorder to exercise their social duties by not drawing too much from current resources and by demanding an end to conditions that dehumanize patients and health care professionals.

We might call Colfer's argument an argument from obligation. Because there is no absolute obligation of physicians to every patient, a limited strike is possible. His argument depends on two claims: first, that neglecting the good of current patients for the good of future ones or for physician job improvement is unethical; second, that patients have no absolute claim on care unless they are seriously ill. The argument is an advance on the usual utilitarian argument used to justify strikes because it introduces the distinction between acute illness and nonacute. In effect, Colfer claims that one cannot risk lives by striking, but one can inconvenience patients who have no right to treatment (because their sickness does not require immediate attention).

Colfer's line of reasoning is flawed, however. First, it is not always the case that utilitarian considerations do not justify a given practice. In fact, it is precisely during serious social calamities that we risk the lives of some who may not survive for the sake of those who have a better chance by attending to patients in the latter category first. This was done at Hiroshima after the bomb destroyed much of the city. Burn victims and those with radiation sickness were neglected in favor of those who might survive. It must be admitted, however, that in normal circumstances we do not always perceive the nature of the emergency and the probabilities of the outcomes as clearly.

The ethics of triage, while shocking under normal circumstances, is understood to apply under emergency circumstances. Therefore, it does not follow that strikes are unethical if based on utilitarian grounds, *provided a sufficient emergency exists*. This proviso is often what is at issue in a strike. Certainly better pay for doctors and nurses would be insufficient grounds to permit us to neglect the dying. But if the economic stress on the hospital is of sufficient import that the quality of care for those who may survive is in jeopardy, could not a strike be called in which the acutely ill were neglected in favor of treating those who will survive?

This question is posed rhetorically to show that neither can one dismiss the utilitarian argument out of hand nor can one accept the inconvenience principle, as Colfer does, without opening oneself to a reverse play—inconveniencing the dying for some supposed social good. Admittedly, at first blush Colfer's argument seems to escape the problem of gaining advances in health care at the expense of patients, but actually all he has done is to claim that these advances can be pursued at the expense only of those not acutely ill, because they have no absolute right to health care. In the end, it is hard to see how this limited strike position differs from a moderate form of the utilitarian position.

Peter Railton looks at the impasse created by arguments like Colfer's. As a philosopher, he is interested in the way rights bring about certain ends. About the clash of the right to strike versus a right to health care, he says:

> At this point, talk about absolute rights or utter sanctity of life becomes unhelpful. For which course of action better respects rights or the sanctity of life? Striking, at a definite cost of some suffering (or worse) to patients? Or not striking, at a definite cost of some suffering (or worse) to present and future patients, owing to the perpetuation of inadequate conditions?[25]

Railton points out that general talk about duties (e.g., "The doctors have a duty towards patients") does nothing to resolve the issue, because both horns of the dilemma are expressed in terms of duties toward patients. On the one hand, there is an immediate duty towards current patients; on the other hand, there is a duty to patients not one's own (other persons in the hospital) and toward future patients.

By considering rights as means toward certain ends rather than as inscribed in a natural law, Railton is able to argue that it is morally permissible to strike if the end to be brought about (better quality care) is the same as or complementary to having a "right to health care." It is regrettable that in order to bring about certain rights, similar rights must be violated, but such is often the nature of practical moral dilemmas.

To the objection of deontologists that his end-means schema leaves open the possibility of permitting everything, Railton has two answers. First, the injunction to respect rights, which is presented as a moral principle inconsistent with his view, is itself not as much a moral principle as a schema, in which the particulars must be filled in. Second, the goal of a strike is to satisfy human needs and interests, and not only are specific actions permissible, such as a responsible strike, but others are impermissible, such as abandoning patients. Thus two important human needs are obtained by striking: eliminating exploitation of health professionals as they try to provide health care needs and implementing to the fullest extent possible the right to decent health care for all.

While we find Railton's position particularly helpful, it nevertheless has three limitations. First, it assumes that the goal of a strike is to defend the right of present and future patients to decent health care. However, as indicated in the first section, this end is often not primary. Instead, better pay and working conditions are primary. Second, Railton does not explain completely enough when the end would not justify certain means. Finally, related to the second point, he does not provide sufficient social theory to establish any criteria by which we could decide what means are justified and what means are not.

With respect to all three of these limitations, the following considerations are in order. A professional must be able to measure the reasons for a strike against an explicit statement expressing the profession's attempt to meet a social need. Because a "service strike" differs from an industrial action, the reasons must be clear and the explicit professional statement must be carefully honed. A service institution such as a hospital is not involved in a product or in setting profit-making goals. In an industrial strike, direct pressure is placed on the owners of a business. In a health service strike, the pressure is applied to patients who need the services. Hence, "the effectiveness of service strikes is limited from the start," as Eugene Lauer notes.[26] This is because the strikers are genuinely concerned about the patients' well-being and must place limits on the inconvenience and harm caused.

Further, management has not usually invested money in the enterprise. Often management sympathizes but is powerless to act, because it does not determine the budget. This is especially true in a socialized medicine system. Thus, the reasons for a strike must be overwhelming regarding poor health conditions to justify harming innocent patients caught in the system. Lauer concludes that neither strikes nor binding arbitration are useful means for resolving service disputes; this is because of the personal and human dynamics of the relationship between providers and patients.

Once sufficient reasons have been developed, however, a moral judgment must be made. As Bleich notes, the primary moral consideration ought to be that members of a profession do assume personal obligations based on talent, training, responsibilities, and public trust. He argues that these specific obligations make all strikes unethical.[27] That the premise does not adequately support the conclusion can be seen from the use of a similar premise in the nursing literature. For example, Copeland rightly argues,

Nurses have no special obligation to their employers; they do, however, assume a moral responsibility toward their clients when entering the profession. They cannot deny clients their nursing needs. According to this perspective, nurses who strike are intervening on behalf of clients to demand better facilities, better salaries to attract and hold sufficient numbers of qualified nurses, and a clearer mandate governing nursing care.[28]

Copeland concludes that the decision to withdraw care must be based on each individual's conscience and must always be motivated by a desire to improve social conditions. The code for nurses upon which these judgments are based states that "the nurse participates in the profession's efforts to establish and maintain conditions of employment conducive to high quality nursing care."[29]

With these elaborations, we are able to see why Bleich's premise does not support the conclusion that strikes are unethical. First, obligations and duties to patients include patients not our own and future patients.[30] Second, as Veatch argued in a companion piece, the principle of justice as fairness identifies those less well-off as having a right to special attention. Duties toward present patients can therefore be waived in favor of duties toward less well-off future patients. Duties toward present patients can therefore be waived in favor of future patients who will be less well-off if conditions continue.[31] In fact, waiving duties can be an expression of justice, a point Veatch develops further in his more recent work.[32] Third, when one enters a profession, one also assumes additional obligations not only to patients, but also to professional standards in service to those patients. When hospitals, for whatever reason, do not live up to their ethical duties, the professional is obliged to confront this failure. A strike can be a means of making that confrontation forceful. Finally, there is the principle of humanization of one's labor, which is cited by Veatch. It is important to recognize that professionals have needs as persons not necessarily satisfied by altruistic sacrifice on behalf of those they serve. They have interests other than just serving patients, and these interests can be legitimately pursued. Presumably, a strike might be justified if the sole intent was to pursue these interests, provided the innocent did not suffer.

These arguments expand Railton's reasoning in precisely the necessary areas. An explicit professional statement can be used to judge the merits of reasons for a strike. The reasons may include interests other than care for patients (e.g., increased pay or leisure), but the strike must primarily aim at improving social conditions for those less well-off if putting current patients at risk is to be justified. Since hospitals more closely resemble service organizations than industrial ones, professionals should sort through the reasons offered, recognizing that their only real "handle" on a hospital (or health service) is to disclose to the public the failure of the hospital to meet its obligations to patients. Thus conditions must be clearly subpar to create any real possibility of an effective strike and to justify putting innocent people at risk.

In particular, a strike must serve the humanitarian goals of social institutions, neither neglecting them for economic ends ("We cannot afford decent health care for all") nor identifying them with impossible goals ("We must meet all the health care needs of all people"). The entrance of the state or the hospital or the insurance company, as Lord Smith of Marlow has pointed out, is not incompatible with the doctor-patient relation, but it can raise dangers, not the least of which is state or insurance control of clinical decisions.[33] This would certainly be a just cause for striking if other confrontation methods proved ineffective, precisely on grounds of the ineluctible bond between doctor and patient. Nonetheless, one cannot have it both ways. If this bond is so fiercely to be defended, one cannot abandon some patients in favor of others, thus causing the innocent to suffer for the good of others.

Despite all that we have written thus far, and the arguments we have considered, the ethical problem for some physicians will still remain. Thus Lowell E. Bellin, a professor of public health at Columbia, takes exception to the arguments of his colleague Samuel Wolfe, of the same department. In Bellin's view, the motivation of the striker, whether "good" (read, "altruistic") or "bad" (read, "to maintain control of power or fees"), has little to do with the outcome, whether a necessary abandonment of a patient on a respirator or of an ambulatory patient seeking a diagnosis of troubling signs. He asserts, "The strike may be appropriate as a last ditch weapon in the automobile plant or the steel mill. It has no civilized place in institutions that care for ailing human beings."[34] Wolfe's response questions whether *abandonment* actually occurs in strikes. He also wonders out loud if the abandonment, if it does occur (few or no data exist on strike impacts), may be the result of state, federal, or local government cutbacks rather than health professional action. He further holds that action against bureaucracies is required to reduce laws and decisions that deny access to needed care. In this way strikes may preserve or advance civil and human rights.[35]

If we accept the basic argument of Railton, modified by our subsequent discussion, then we may hold that when the right to care conflicts with a right to control the conditions of the workplace, a strike is a moral means of last resort for professionals, provided patients are not abandoned. If this abandonment occurs because of social policy or economic cutbacks, we may protest—indeed, must do so—on grounds of enlightened social policy, since meeting health needs is a matter of both justice and gift. Despite the overall strength of this position, at least two additional conditions are needed before a strike is justified.

The first of these is the presence of appalling medical or social conditions sufficient to justify putting current patients at risk, even if only at risk for inconvenience. The strength of justification must match the strength of objections to strikes. Gerald Dworkin's objection is classically expressed regarding the professional medical obligation, "It is . . . the more surprising that a profession which sets so much store on the ethical obligations towards individual patients can contemplate disregarding such standards when a wider, less personally identifiable group is at risk. The difference is one of degree not of kind and the patients who are affected do not appreciate any distinction."[36]

The answer to this objection requires attention to the principle of justice as fairness and to the double-bind dilemma—a professional is responsible for more than just his or her current patients. It would be difficult, however, to claim that the age-old, singular focus on obligations to individual patients can be easily dismissed in favor of nonaltruistic causes for striking, such as better pay and more vacations.

The second factor which must come into play for strikes to have merit is a better theory of the social obligations of health professionals. Dworkin argues that society suffers from an anomic disease with respect for law, and moral order is on the decline. Once senior physicians struck, why could not juniors? Once juniors struck, why not nurses? Once nurses struck, why not other health professionals and supporting staff. Dworkin proposes that health professionals, because of the Hippocratic tradition, are good candidates for setting a moral example by not striking. Even though there may be strong disagreement and confrontation, "there is yet no case for civil disobedience or abdication of fundamental professional standards."[37]

Dworkin's argument that to strike is to set a bad example rests on a view of medicine lacking a social awareness. Even though to obtain some set of conditions by collective bargaining, unionizing, or even striking is not equivalent to establishing that these conditions are social goods, there is no real dichotomy between professionalization and either the search for social improvement or unionization. Norman Daniels argues convincingly that, while it is true that trade unions have narrowly concentrated on bread-and-butter issues, this narrow focus is not essential to the concept of a collective: "Introducing broader social concerns into the goals of unionizing, however difficult, does not contradict the purpose and function of unionism. It only strengthens it."[38] What must also be changed, however, is the Hippocratic notion that a physician is autonomous, possesses the right to decide whom to treat, and is free from interference of nonphysicians and free to decide what course of treatment to follow without regard to economic constraints, social policy, or institutional values. In particular, using fee-for-service as the basis for health care delivery and marketplace distribution must be looked at critically, as it has been in many advanced nations.

We currently lack a general theory of medicine as a social enterprise, although Pellegrino and Thomasma attempted to construct one based on patient and class vulnerability,[39] and Veatch's works (already cited) make a similar attempt based on a theory of contractual exchange. Though the social basis of medicine is not yet fully understood, its main elements—particularly as it pertains to the end of providing ever more decent health care—have been identified. These elements can function as a standard which permits some means, such as strikes, but rules out others, such as abandoning patients.

With respect to the three basic causes of strikes, we pose three ethical responses. If the purpose of a strike is to gain better pay or benefits, these legitimate concerns do not justify putting patients at any risk or even any inconvenience. If the purpose of a strike is to bring about better conditions and thus benefit present and future patients, then it is ethical to place some patients at an inconvenience, provided emergencies are always covered. These first two reasons for striking and their ethical consequences are suggestive of the well-developed analyses regarding placing research subjects at risk. Greater risks to patients can be tolerated when greater possible therapeutic benefits are expected. For nontherapeutic issues (e.g., better pay), no patients can be put at risk without their consent.

A third cause for striking, as we have seen, is third party intrusion into the doctor-patient relation, whether that third party is the government or a private insurance carrier. We suggest that it is also ethical to strike over quality-of-care issues intimately linked to the interference problem. Physicians, in this instance, must speak for all patients, even those who are not under their immediate care, and try to solve the serious problems in national resource allocation. These problems are matters of just distribution of resources, especially resources to enhance the quality of human life. It is extremely important for medicine and for all patients that a two-tiered system of care (one for the rich and one for the poor) not be introduced through high-sounding economic policies. In this case, we consider the situation to be enough of an emergency that utilitarian considerations alone might justify a strike.

To summarize, our conclusion is that strikes are not only ethical, but sometimes required in order to bring about necessary social benefits. We present a proposed policy in the following section.

POLICY PROPOSAL

The following proposal would establish the right of health care workers to strike and the conditions under which it would be ethical to do so. (Legal aspects are not directly discussed.)

The goal of all social policy ought to be to create an ideological framework which encourages rather than discourages altruistic actions on the part of those affected by the policy.[40] This is especially true in the regulation of practices, those communal actions undertaken under norms or standards of perfection for conduct.[41] In such cases, the norms are rather explicitly spelled out. In medicine, the traditional norms of beneficence (acting for the good of another), nonmalfeasance (doing no harm), and respect for persons (treating each person as a class instance of the human race) are upheld as both ideals and expectations today.[42]

Altruism is therefore part of the ideology of medicine, and altruistic actions ought to be encouraged by social policy. However, altruism is at risk when health professionals intend to take industrial action. To encourage altruism, we suggest the motives and the timing of health professional strikes should be in accord with the following recommendations.

1. Service workers such as health professionals must be able to demonstrate to the public at large and to three impartial labor court judges that their social obligations are at issue in a proposed strike. These social obligations are based on both the ethical and practice standards of their profession, i.e., the primary motive for striking is to gain important advances for the quality of patient care in the institution or service area in which they are employed.

2. The health professionals must be able to demonstrate that a plan for the care of current patients and emergency patients will ensure that no patient is abandoned. (The three impartial judges in a labor court must certify that the plan is meritorious.)

3. A ten-day notice of intent to strike is to be implemented. This requirement ensures that time to implement the nonabandonment plan exists and that the hospital, government, or national health service may prepare objections and have these heard.

4. All other avenues must have been explored, because of the seriousness of the bond between health professionals and patients.

5. The ends sought by the strike are to be made explicit and publicly promulgated. In this way they can be subject to public scrutiny and discussion.

6. A desire to improve salary and/or benefits or to maintain certain professional prerogatives are to be judged insufficient in social merit to put innocent patients at risk of inconvenience or harm in a strike, although these objectives are decent and can be pursued through other avenues.

7. Finally, necessary volunteer care by the striking health professionals in capacities corresponding to their skills is to be encouraged as a means to rectify any bad example the strike may possibly set. Since this policy ethically justifies strikes by recognizing that medicine is often delivered in institutions run by bureaucracies, there should be no necessity for civil disobedience. (If this policy is legalized, there *will be no necessity* for civil disobedience.)

NOTES

1. Dorothy D. Nayer, "Unification: Bringing Nursing Service and Nursing Education Together," *American Journal of Nursing* 80 (1980): 1110–1.

2. Marc Lalonde, *A New Perspective on the Health of Canadians* (Ottawa, Canada: 1981). Lalonde is the Minister of National Health and Welfare of Canada.

3. Kristina Lindgren, "Konfliktutvardering visar: det var riktigt att strejka," *Vardfacket*, August 27, 1981, pp. 32–34.

4. "Taking Action," *Nursing Times,* June 19, 1980, p. 1078.

5. "Health Strike Hits Great Britain," *Chicago Tribune,* July 20, 1982, p. 3.

6. Mary Copeland, "To Strike. . . . or Not to Strike . . . ?" *NSNA Imprint* 5 (December 1980): 22.

7. Robert S. Sade, "Medical Care as a Right: A Refutation," *New England Journal of Medicine* 285 (1971): 1288.

8. Phyllis Gapen, "New York's Big, Brash Union," *New Physician* 30 (April 1981): 14–18.

9. Hugh H. Hussey, "Strikes by Physicians," editorial, *Journal of the American Medical Association* 235 (1976): 756.

10. Susan Treloar, "The Junior Hospital Doctors' Pay Dispute 1975–1976: An Analysis of Events, Issues and Conflicts," *Journal of Social Policy* 10 (1981): 1–30.

11. William A. Regan, "Physicians Required to Act Responsibly in Labor Dispute," *Hospital Progress* 62 (October 1981): 68–69.

12. Margaret Hardie, "The Right to Strike," *Nursing Mirror,* September 27, 1979, p. 18.

13. Lindgren, "Konfliktutvardering visar."

14. Radical Nurses Group, "Dispelling the Myths," *Nursing Times* January 13, 1982, pp. 50–51.

15. Jack Wilson, "The Delicate Question of Industrial Action for Professional Duty," *The Australian Nurses Journal* 9 (December 1980): 22.

16. Ruth Korn, Nurses United: One Staff's Decision to Strike. *American Journal of Nursing* 12 (1980): 2218–21.

17. Diana J. Hanson, "Why Are We on Strike?" *American Journal of Nursing* 5 (1980): 954–55.

18. Thelma Schorr, "Speaking of Ethical Behavior," *American Journal of Nursing* 80 (1980): 421.

19. Edmund D. Pellegrino and David C. Thomasma, *A Philosophical Basis of Medical Practice* (New York: Oxford University Press, 1981).

20. P.M. Stearns, "Making a Decision on Organizing," *Journal American Operating Room Nurse* June 31, 1980, p. 1211.

21. Cherill Hicks, "What Would You Do in Our Shoes?" *Nursing Times,* November 25, 1981, p. 2041.

22. "Taking Action," 1078.

23. David C. Thomasma, "Hospital's Ethical Responsibilities as Technology Grow," *Hospital Progress* 63 (December 1982): 74–79.

24. Harry Colfer, "On the Physician's Right to Strike," in *Ethics, Humanism, and Medicine,* ed. Mark Basson (New York: Alan R. Liss, 1980), 305.

25. Peter Railton, "Health Care Personnel and the Right to Strike: A Social Perspective," in *Ethics, Humanism, and Medicine,* 295.

26. Eugene Lauer, "Service Workers Strikes: A New Moral Dilemma," *Hospital Progress* 63 (March 1982): 48–51, 62.

27. David Bleich, "Commentary," in *Cases in Bioethics,* ed. C. Levine and R. Veatch (Hastings-on-Hudson, N.Y.: Hastings Center, 1982), 94–95.

28. Copeland, "To Strike," 65.

29. American Nurses' Association, *Code for Nurses* (Kansas City, Mo.: American Nurses' Association, 1976).

30. David C. Thomasma and Andrew Griffin, "The Social Responsibility of Pediatricians," unpublished.

31. Robert Veatch, "Interns and Residents on Strike: Commentary," in *Cases in Bioethics,* 93–94.

32. Robert Veatch, *A Theory of Medical Ethics* (New York: Basic Books, 1981), 324–330.

33. Rt. Hon. The Lord Smith of Marlow, "The Medical and Dental Professions and the State: An Uneasy Partnership," Bradlaw Oration, 1979, *Annals of the Royal College of Surgeons of England* 62 (1980): 259–70.

34. Lowell Bellin, "Strikes by Health Workers: Another View," Letters to the Editor, *American Journal of Public Health* 69 (1979): 1066.

35. Samuel Wolfe, "Author's Response," Letters to the Editor, *American Journal of Public Health* 69 (1979): 1066–67.

36. Gerald Dworkin, "Strikes and the National Health Service: Some Legal and Ethical Issues," *Journal of Medical Ethics* 3 (1977): 76–82.

37. Ibid., 81.

38. Norman Daniels, "On the Picket Line: Are Doctor's Strikes Ethical?" *Hastings Center Report* 8 (February 1978): 25–26.

39. Pellegrino and Thomasma, *A Philosophical Basis*, chap. 8 ff.

40. Robert L. Shelton, "The Gift Relationship as Basis for Health Care Delivery," abstracted in *AAR Abstracts* (Minneapolis: Scholars Press, 1982), 130. Abstracts are of Annual Meeting Program, New York, December 19–22, 1982.

41. Alasdair MacIntyre, *Beyond Virtue* (Notre Dame, Ind.: University of Notre Dame Press, 1982).

42. David C. Thomasma and Edmund D. Pellegrino, "Philosophy of Medicine as Source for Medical Ethics," *Metamedicine* 2 (1981): 5–11.

Part VI

Institutional and National Issues

Chapter 32

Quality Assurance, Risk Management, and Ethical Issues

John F. Monagle

Assuring patients quality of care and managing procedures or risks often involves issues of medical ethics (Figure 32-1). Quality of care has not been well defined in the literature. It has at least two important components that involve medical ethics.

Objective Component: (a) the evaluation of the competence of health care professionals and their social attitude to patients as individuals (ethical concerns, values, and issues are involved); (b) the evaluation of hospital management related to administrative and medical operational systems to assure their effectiveness and efficiency.

Subjective Component: the documentation of, and any subsequent appropriate action in response to, the *perception* of patients as to the effectiveness and efficiency of the treatment or procedures recommended or ordered for them by health care professionals and the reasonableness and affordability of the individual and collective cost of their health care. Ethical concerns, values, and issues are also involved in the subjective component.

Many health care professionals do not understand the interrelation among quality assurance (QA), risk management (RM), and ethical issues (EI). Even some quality assurance coordinators and health care risk managers are unaware of the similarities and differences between quality assurance and risk management. Furthermore, most professionals view quality assurance and risk management as necessary defensive and protective measures, but fail to discern the ethical issues often involved in both.

One purpose of this chapter is to distinguish quality assurance and risk management, which has not yet been adequately done in the health care literature.[1] The second purpose is to explain how quality assurance, risk management, and ethical issues are related and to encourage all hospitals and health care groups to include ethical fundamental review criteria (FRC) in their comprehensive quality assurance programs. Ethical fundamental review criteria are tests or standards for use in making an ethical judgment about an action, i.e., whether it is ethically acceptable or unacceptable. Specifiers are used to more fully define and refine ethical fundamental review criteria. (See Appendix 32-A.)

QUALITY ASSURANCE AND RISK MANAGEMENT: DISTINCT BUT NOT SEPARATE

The activities of quality assurance and risk management are important for the protection, recovery, and well-being of patients as well as for the financial survival of health care

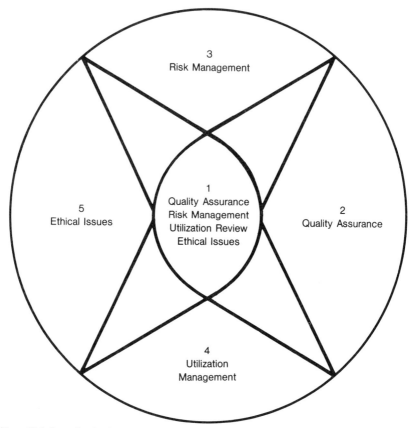

Figure 32-1 Comprehensive Quality Assurance. *Source:* Courtesy of American Institute of Medical Ethics, Davis, California, © 1987.

institutions and professionals. Both kinds of activities utilize information from the same sources (Figure 32-2) and are equally important. Moreover, risk management and quality assurance employ the same methodology or process: identification of risks and problems; monitoring; tracking; trending; summarizing by individual, by department, and hospital-wide; corrective action; and evaluation of effectiveness of correction. However, risk management includes considerations of self-insuring acceptable risks and transferring to insurance carriers those risks that are determined to be *above* the risk aversion level that the hospital or health care professional wishes to assume. As to information sources and methodology or process, they are not separate, but they are distinct. The distinction is one of focus (Figure 32-3).

Concerned Focus

Risk Management is focused on financial liability awareness and is defined as the science of identifying, monitoring, tracking, trending, summarizing, evaluating, correcting and

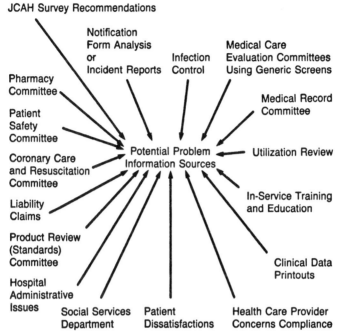

Figure 32-2 Potential Problem Information Sources. *Source:* Reprinted from *Risk Management: A Guide for Health Care Professionals* by J.F. Monagle, p. 89, Aspen Publishers, Inc., © 1985.

ensuring against risks that could cause financial loss. Such events as loss of life, surgical error, misdiagnosis, unexpected outcomes of treatment, and birth-related injuries are quality of care as well as risk management issues (Figure 32-1).[2]

All risk management concerns are, in the larger sense, quality assurance concerns. However, not all quality assurance concerns are risk management concerns. This is another basis for the distinction between them. The focus of quality assurance, while exercising most of the same assessment process as risk management (Figure 32-3), is the elimination or reduction of patient care problems through corrective action in order to enhance the quality of patient care.

Protection of the patient by enhancement of the quality of care delivered is distinct from the protection of the financial assets of the hospital or the health care professional. Ultimately, the *focuses* meet in the concept of protection; therefore, they are distinct but not separate. Protection through elimination or reduction of problems and risks is the ultimate purpose of both quality assurance and risk management.

Integration of Risk Management through Quality Assurance

Recently, the Joint Commission on Accreditation of Hospitals (JCAH) mandated the integration of risk management through revised quality assurance standards.[3] Although the Commission failed to distinguish adequately between quality assurance and risk manage-

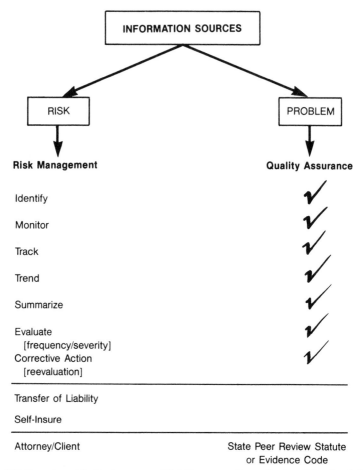

Figure 32-3 Comparison of Quality Assurance and Risk Management. *Source:* Courtesy of American Institute of Medical Ethics, Davis, California, © 1988.

ment, it mandated that they not be separated. An operational linkage relation between the two must be designed and implemented, as well as a process to identify and correct problems and risks. The premise is that a comprehensive quality assurance program includes risk management.

Just as in the past JCAH overlooked or refused to recognize risk management, so now it fails to realize or to accept the necessity for the inclusion of ethical issues in a *comprehensive* quality assurance plan.

THE INTERRELATIONSHIP OF QUALITY ASSURANCE, RISK MANAGEMENT, AND ETHICAL ISSUES

When health care professionals come together as an interdisciplinary health care team to discern, evaluate, and correct problems and risks involving ethical issues, they form a protective society. They come together "to do *ethics*."[4] Ethics is that part of philosophy which deals with the norms and principles which govern society. Ethics, which deals with the conduct of a society, can be distinguished from morality, which guides the individual in the personal conduct of life. Health care teams, hospitals, extended care facilities, and professional organizations such as HMOs and PPOs are a few of the groups and organizations which consciously or unconsciously conduct business and provide their services in an "ethical atmosphere." To engage in unexamined ethical conduct is not acceptable. Over time, unexamined conduct often results in the chaotic and divisive implementation of the moral norms of the most powerful, the most persuasive, or the most political member of a health care team or institution.

Quality assurance and risk management, by their very process and by their goal of problem solving through identification and corrective action, can be helpful in establishing the ethical norms and principles which should guide health care professionals and in raising the level of their sensitivity to the ethical problems which are in need of corrective action.

Computerized Ethical Fundamental Review Criteria (FRC)

Fortunately there is now available a methodology to increase sensitivity to and awareness of ethical issues. Not only are there medical fundamental review criteria (FRC), but now also *ethical* fundamental review criteria. (See Appendix 32-A.) The ethical FRC contain additional specifiers to define more specifically the ethical issues.

Until recently no microcomputerized system has offered to formally relate ethical concerns and issues through ethical FRC to the traditional medical FRC. There is microcomputer software[5] available that integrates ethical issues by means of ethical fundamental review criteria and specifiers into the data of medical quality assurance and risk management problems and risks. Customized comparative analysis can be produced that relate persons, places, and things with medical quality assurance, risk management, and ethical issues.

Much of the effort of quality assessment (or assurance) and risk management has been concerned with the quantitative minimum requirements for licensing and accreditation by national and regional regulatory agencies. The initial effort is praiseworthy when we consider that quality assurance and risk management standards are minimal. Broad ethical standards are established which must be implemented and followed. Licensing and accreditation standards do reflect basic principles and norms for guiding institutions and professional groups in their treatment and procedures related to the professional care to which all patients are entitled. But not enough *ethically* has been said or done for patients when they become copartners with a health care team in the recovery of their health and well-being.

Where in the past have the patients' rights, human values, and other ethical issues been seen as FRC fully specified to meet the wholistic needs of patients? Each institution and professional group needs to consciously select and prioritize the ethical issues and human values that will be protected and enhanced while patients are in their care.

Providing medical care that takes into account and respects patient rights, prioritized human values, and ethical concerns is not impossible. Hospitals under religious auspices include these quality assurance and risk management endeavors in their philosophy and mission statements, and hopefully their daily practice reflects this fact.

Such wholistic care is the responsibility of all health care professionals and institutions, not just those under religious auspices. *All* groups are capable of delineating the necessary ethical elements of wholistic care and can introduce these elements by way of ethical FRC into a formalized, computerized program (Figure 32-4). These should be essential elements of a *comprehensive* quality assurance program.

The neglect of these concerns can lead to patient dissatisfaction and, in too many instances, can become an emotional issue that generates anger and frustration among patients and staff. Neglect may lead to hospital and staff liability situations.[6] However, the fact that the neglect of ethical concerns in quality assurance and risk management may result in court action is not the principal concern of hospitals and health care professionals. Concern for the whole patient is fundamental to the philosophy of all who render health care.

Quality assurance, risk management, and ethical issues demand the conscious endeavor of hospitals and health care professionals to include in the management of patient care the assurance that their public conduct reflects the shared human values and rights of the individual patients whom they serve.

Because health care professions and institutions have their origin in a rich historical past of human caring for those who suffer, they are based on and tend to exhibit altruistic compassion for the whole person. Having only *minimum* standards of professional and ethical conduct have never been ideal for rendering care to patients who are copartners in their own health care.

One cannot find in the JCAH quality assurance or risk management standards any formal statements or specific guidelines for the concerns of the *whole* patient—physical, emotional, mental, and spiritual. Medical care and FRC related to patient care have been mainly in the *quantitative* arena. Little is said about the values, beliefs, and ethical concerns of patients, concerns which contribute so much to their health and well-being.

We cannot separate ethical issues from quality assurance and risk management concerns, because these ethical issues are the core of many quality assurance and risk management problems and dilemmas. The presence of these ethical issues makes the solution to the problems hard to attain.

As listed in the ethical FRC and specifiers, the issues cover the entire lifetime of an individual patient—from conception through death. Included are the ethical issues involved in genetic control as well as amniocentesis related to counseling or abortion. Many hospitals today are focusing on the use of surrogate mothers or other alternative reproduction techniques. Do such techniques violate ethical values or religious beliefs?[7] There are no easy decisions regarding sperm, ova, or zygote banking or their use, storage, or destruction. No one is certain when to treat or cease to treat defective newborns. Guidelines are difficult to implement.

What are the ethical FRC for expensive, media-attractive operations for Baby Does, Baby Faes, Baby Jesses? Is there discrimination based on racial, religious, or financial background? Have these issues been fully probed, reported, documented, computerized, and the data manipulated to expose hidden motives for refusal to treat? (See Figure 32-4.) Have practical and ethical protocols been developed before or after the fact?

Has the hospital or professional group done any computerized demographic studies related to high-risk community areas for child, spouse, or elder abuse and initiated corrective action through counseling and education? What are the hospital's prioritized and documented values?

1. *Medical FRC*
   (for Patient Occurrences)
2. *Medical FRC Specifiers*
3. *Ethical FRC*
   (for Ethical Issues — EI)
   Plus
4. *Ethical FRC Specifiers*
   Computerized for Customized
   Analysis of QA/RM/UR/EI

Patient Management Analysis for Action

1. Medical FRC: Description of Adverse Patient
   Occurrences (Problems and Risks)
2. Medical Specifiers: To More Fully Define and Refine
   Medical FRC
3. Ethical FRC: Description of Ethical Issues
   (A to Z: Abandonment of Patient of Zygote Banking)
4. Ethical Specifiers To Define and Refine Ethical FRC

Figure 32-4 Computerized Medical and Ethical Fundamental Review Criteria (FRC). *Source:* Courtesy of American Institute of Medical Ethics, Davis, California, © 1988.

How does a hospital monitor, track, trend, and take corrective actions for teenage pregnancies? Do we listen to adolescents, to their concerns and complaints, and take the quality of their emotional, mental, and spiritual health into consideration when they present themselves for help with chronic diseases? Are these concerns recorded, documented, and resolved?

How do we deal with the ethical issues related to heroin addiction, homosexuality, and AIDS? Are there human issues of sex therapy that we ignore or patients' human and religious values that are dismissed as irrelevant in the care of end stage renal dialysis, blood transfusions, and clinical trials of experimental drugs on the terminal oncology patient? What guidelines and human value considerations are in effect if an Elizabeth Bouvia insists that she has a right to assisted suicide in an institution even though she is not terminal? Is this considered to be a quality assurance, risk management, or ethical issue concern?

What ethical guidelines and FRC have been established to avoid diverting, dumping, or transferring the patient who has only Medicaid or no insurance at all? What decisions have been made from a viewpoint combining quality assurance, risk management, ethical concerns, and community involvement about whether to discontinue leading "revenue losers," such as a burn unit, ob/gyn services, or neonatal intensive care? Does the hospital have a comprehensive quality assurance plan for the withdrawal of nutrition or hydration for the patient in a persistent vegetative or comatose state? Does the hospital or professional group have a stated position on active euthanasia and professional involvement? (See Chapter 35 on the patient's choice of care.)

All these questions are screaming for attention. As ethical issues, they must be defined and refined through ethical FRC and specifiers. They must be monitored, tracked, trended, summarized, and evaluated in terms of precise patient management analysis. In short, qualitative concerns like these must be partially quantified in order to follow and evaluate efforts to resolve them. Ethically educated health care teams will then be better positioned to develop corrective actions.

CONCLUSION

All of the ethical issues mentioned above, as well as future ethical questions, need to be formally addressed in a systemized manner by utilizing ethical FRC and specifiers in order to generate a patient management analysis that may show the need for corrective action. These ethical issues and concerns are not esoteric and of interest only to academic ethicists. They are of public concern and society rightfully demands that they be responded to. All of us, especially health care professionals and health care facilities, have the *duty* to respond.

NOTES

1. John F. Monagle, *Risk Management: A Guide for Health Care Professionals* (Rockville, Md.: Aspen, 1985). This book is an initial endeavor to distinguish between quality assurance and risk management. Utilization review management (as part of Figure 32-1) will not be treated directly in Chapter 32. Many of the utilization review issues are similar to those of risk management.

2. Risk management documentation may be protected from discovery under a state's attorney or client privilege. Quality assurance documentation may be protected under a state's evidence code or peer review statute.

3. Joint Commission on Accreditation of Hospitals, *Risk Management through Quality Assurance,* 1986 Seminar Series Resource Book (Chicago: Joint Commission on Accreditation of Hospitals, 1986). This workbook is not paginated, but see the contents under Tab 3.

4. See Chapter 33, "Roles, Memberships, and Structures of Hospital Ethics Committees."

5. *The Patient Care Monitoring System* (PCMS), Cantor & Company, 9348 Civic Center Drive, Beverly Hills, CA 90210.

6. John F. Monagle, "A Question of Ethics or Murder," *CHA Insight,* April 13, 1984; see also Chapter 33, n. 1.

7. Richard Lacayo, "Whose Child Is This?" *Time,* January 19, 1987, pp. 56–58.

BIBLIOGRAPHY

Quality Assurance

Batalden, M.D., B. Paul, and Paul J. O'Connor. *Quality Assurance in Ambulatory Care.* Rockville, Md.: Aspen, 1980.

Journal of Nursing Quality Assurance. This journal is published quarterly by Aspen Publishers, Inc., Rockville, Md.

Meisenheimer, Claire Gavin, ed. *Quality Assurance: A Complete Guide to Effective Programs.* Rockville, Md.: Aspen, 1985.

Schroeder, Patricia S., and Regina M. Maibusch. *Nursing Quality Assurance: A Unit-based Approach.* Rockville, Md.: Aspen Publishers, Inc., 1984.

Risk Management

American Hospital Association. *The Incident: Implementing a Hospitalwide Risk Management Program.* Chicago: American Hospital Association, 1977.

American Hospital Association. *Risk Management Demonstration Projects.* Chicago: American Hospital Association, 1977. Tape recording no. 4565.

Cleverley, William O., ed. "Cost Containment." Part 2. *Topics in Health Care Financing* 3, no. 4 (1977).

Federation of American Hospitals, Inc. *Risk Management Manual: A Guide to Safety, Loss Control, and Malpractice Prevention for Hospitals.* Little Rock, Ark.: Federation of American Hospitals, 1977.

McGovern, Bernard J. "Risk Management." Parts 1, 2. *Topics in Health Care Financing,* 9 nos. 3, 4 (1983).

Maryland Hospital Education Institute. *Controlling Hospital Liability: A Systems Approach.* Chicago: American Hospital Association, 1976.

Mehr, Robert I., and Bob A. Hedges. *Risk Management: Concepts and Applications.* Homewood, Ill.: Richard D. Irwin, Inc., 1974.

Monagle, John F. *Risk Management: A Guide for Health Care Professionals.* Rockville, Md.: Aspen, 1985.

Morse, George P., and Robert F. Morse II. *Protecting the Health Care Facility: A System of Loss Prevention Management Effective for All Industry.* Baltimore: Williams & Wilkins, 1974.

National Safety Council and American Hospital Association. *Safety Guide for Health Care Institutions.* Chicago, National Safety Council and American Hospital Association, 1972.

Pena, Jesus J., Alden N. Haffner, Bernard Rosen, and Donald W. Light. *Hospital Quality Assurance: Risk Management and Program Evaluation.* Rockville, Md.: Aspen, 1983.

Richards, Edward P., III, and Katherine C. Ruthbun. *Medical Risk Management: Preventive Legal Strategies for Health Care Providers.* Rockville, Md.: Aspen, 1983.

Ethical Issues

Beauchamp, Tom L., and Laurence B. McCullough. *Medical Ethics: The Moral Responsibilities of Physicians.* Englewood Cliffs, N.J.: Prentice-Hall, 1984.

Bergsma, Jurrit and David C. Thomasma. *Health Care: Its Psychosocial Dimensions.* Pittsburgh, Pa.: Duquesne University Press, 1982.

Jonsen, Albert R., Mark Siegler, and William J. Winslade. *Clinical Ethics: A Practical Approach to Ethical Decisions in Clinical Medicine.* New York: Macmillan, 1982.

Pellegrino, Edmund D., and David C. Thomasma. *A Philosophical Basis of Medical Practice.* New York: Oxford University Press, 1981.

Appendix 32-A

Computerized Ethical Fundamental Review Criteria and Specifiers*

(CODE)	ETHICAL FUNDAMENTAL REVIEW CRITERIA	SPECIFIERS
( )	ABANDONMENT	Hospital Physician Nurse Therapist
( )	ABORTIFACIENT	IUD Morning after pill
( )	ABORTION	Therapeutic Nontherapeutic Spontaneous Life/health of mother Minor Request/demand Voluntary Court order Self-induced
( )	ABUSE	Child Spouse Parent Elder Reported
( )	ACUPUNCTURE	Authorized Unauthorized Request Denial
( )	ADDICTION	Drug Alcohol
( )	ADVOCATE	Patient representative Legal Durable power of attorney Patient appointed Family appointed

*Source: Courtesy of American Institute of Medical Ethics, Davis, California. © 1988.

| | *ETHICAL FUNDAMENTAL* | |
(CODE)	*REVIEW CRITERIA*	*SPECIFIERS*
( )	AIDS	Discrimination
		Isolation
		Inappropriate procedure/
		treatment
( )	AMNIOCENTESIS	Abortion to follow
		Genetic counseling
		Sex determination
		Spontaneous abortion
		Experimental
( )	ANATOMICAL GIFT	Requested
		Patient consent/family
		refusal
		Transfer of gift
( )	ANIMAL EXPERIMENTATION	Abuse
		Inappropriate
		Unauthorized
		Excessive pain
( )	ARTIFICIAL INSEMINATION	AIH (Husband)
		AID (Donor)
		Contaminated semen
		Defective semen
		Complaint
		Unsuccessful
		Inappropriate
		Lesbian
		Aids
( )	AUTONOMY	Breach of privacy
		Complaint
( )	AUTOPSY	Unnecessary
		Unauthorized
		Omitted
		Disposal of cadaver/parts
		Religious objection
( )	BEHAVIOR CONTROL	Medicinal sedation
		Physical restraints
		Voluntary
		Involuntary
( )	BLOOD	AIDS
		Banking
		Complaint
		Contamination
		Mismatch (transfusion)

(CODE)		*ETHICAL FUNDAMENTAL* *REVIEW CRITERIA*	*SPECIFIERS*
(	)		Mistyping (corrected) Religious objection
(	)	CARDIOPULMONARY RESUSCITATION	Omitted Contrary to physician/family request Physician verbal order Physician written order
(	)	COMMITMENT	Court order Inappropriate Involuntary Voluntary
(	)	COMMUNITY	Allocation of resources Lack of awareness Lack of involvement Need for education/ consultation
(	)	COMPETENCY	Lack of (minor) Lack of (adult) Legal guardian of person
(	)	COMPLIANCE	Refusal Unsatisfactory
(	)	CONFIDENTIALITY	Breach (verbal) Complaint Evidence code/statute Federal (drug/alcohol) Peer review Quality assurance Statistical identifiers Subpoena Unauthorized information
(	)	CONSULTATION (COUNSELING)	Against wish of patient Contrary to practice/policy Inadequate Inappropriate Not requested Unnecessary
(	)	CONTINUITY OF CARE	Denied Discharge without plan of management Given verbally only Inadequate

(CODE)		ETHICAL FUNDAMENTAL REVIEW CRITERIA	SPECIFIERS
			Not established
			Not documented
(	)	CONTRACEPTION	Against parental desire
			Contrary to policy
			Defective device
			Lack of policy
			Minor
			Referral
			Removal of defective device
			Side effects
(	)	COST	Care denied
			Complaint/error
			DRG/outlier
			Excessive charge (hospital)
			Excessive fee (M.D.)
			Medicaid (insufficient)
			Medicare (insufficient)
			MIA (insufficient)
			No insurance
			Refusal to pay
(	)	DEATH	Clinical judgment (not documented properly)
			Complaint (family)
			Criteria inadequate
			Criteria omitted
			Lack of confirmatory consultation
			Lack of family awareness/ timely notification/ counseling
			Lack of policy/standard
(	)	DEFECTS (INFANT)	Birth process
			Decision not to treat
			Decision to treat
			Drug/alcohol abuse (parent)
			Genetic
			Pediatric
			Perinatal
			Placenta pathology
			Prenatal
(	)	DIRECTIVES	Challenge
			Ethical
			No policy/guidelines

(CODE)	ETHICAL FUNDAMENTAL REVIEW CRITERIA	SPECIFIERS
		Policy change
		Policy formulation
		Religious
		Violation
( )	DISCRIMINATION	Genetic
		Racial
		Religious
		Socioeconomic
( )	DIVERSION (DUMPING)	Active labor transfer
		DRG/outlier
		Drug/alcohol (clinic refusal to treat)
		ER refusal
		Involuntary transfer
		Medicaid
		No insurance
		PRO refusal
		Unstabilized transfer
		UR notice
( )	DRUG	Abuse
		Contraindicated
		Experimental
		Labeling error
		Missing
		Not prescribed
		Possession of
		Selling/pushing
		Theft
		Unauthorized
( )	ETHICS COMMITTEE	Access to
		Advice
		Authorization
		Availability
		Confidentiality
		Consultation
		Decision
		Issue
		Mandate
		Policy
( )	EUTHANASIA	Active
		Allowing
		Involuntary
		Refraining

(CODE)	ETHICAL FUNDAMENTAL REVIEW CRITERIA	SPECIFIERS
		Voluntary
		Withdrawal (hydration)
		Withdrawal (nutrition)
		Withdrawal (respirator)
( )	EXPERIMENTATION (HUMAN)	Unauthorized
		Not reviewed (IRB)
( )	FAITH HEALING	Inappropriate
		Involuntary
		No policy
		Requested
		Unauthorized
		Voluntary
( )	GENETICS	Counseling
		Diagnosis
		Racial
		Religious
		Screening
		Therapy
( )	HEALING PRAYER	Inappropriate
		Involuntary
		No policy
		Requested
		Unauthorized
		Voluntary
( )	HOMOSEXUALITY	Complaint
		Discrimination
		Refusal to treat
( )	INCEST	Parent
		Reported
		Sibling
( )	INFORMED CONSENT	Incompetent adult
		Minor
		Not documented
		Not given
		Not understood
( )	IN VITRO FERTILIZATION	AIDS
		Conceptus (disposal)
		Conceptus (use)
		Contamination
		Donor
		Surrogate

(CODE)		ETHICAL FUNDAMENTAL REVIEW CRITERIA	SPECIFIERS
(	)	LIVING WILL	Directive
			Legal
(	)	MALPRACTICE	Battery
			Complaint/threat
			Negligence
			Suit
(	)	MEANS	Disproportionate
			Extraordinary
			Ordinary
			Proportionate
(	)	NOISE POLLUTION	Decibel levels
(	)	NOSOCOMIAL INFECTION	Policy violation
			No policy
			Transferred manually
			Lack of hygiene
(	)	OUTLIER (DRG)	MIA
			Medicaid
			Medicare
			No insurance
			Premature discharge
			Transfer
			UR/PRO
(	)	OVA BANKING	Ownership
			Contract
			Surrogate
			Donor
			Cryopreservation
			Disposal
(	)	PASTORAL CARE	Denied to
			Not given to
			Refused by patient
(	)	PEER REVIEW	Alcohol
			Drug
			Incompetent
			Education
			Privileges
			Malpractice Suits
(	)	POLICY (ETHICAL)	Inadequate
			Inappropriate
			Not clear
			Not established

(CODE)		*ETHICAL FUNDAMENTAL* *REVIEW CRITERIA*	*SPECIFIERS*
			Review/evaluation
			Revision
(	)	PROPERTY	Loss
			Theft
(	)	PSYCHOSURGERY	Involuntary
			Unnecessary
			Voluntary
(	)	QUALITY ASSESSMENT/ ASSURANCE	Complaint about care
			Frequency
			Lack of identification of problem
			Lack of policy
			Lack of standard/criteria
			Need for effective corrective action
			Severity
(	)	QUALITY OF LIFE	DNR
			Irreversible/terminal
			Irreversible/terminal/coma
			Level of care
			No code
			Request not to treat
			Request to treat
			Unacceptable to patient
(	)	RAPE (See ABUSE)	
(	)	REFUSAL BY PATIENT	Medication
			Procedure
			Treatment
(	)	RELIGION	Complaint
			Discrimination
			Family objection
			Patient refusal to consent
			Refusal to treat
(	)	RESEARCH	Experimental drug
			Fetal
			Involuntary
			Terminally Ill
			Unauthorized
			Voluntary
(	)	RESOURCES	Allocation
			Community awareness
			Community decision
			Community education

(CODE)		*ETHICAL FUNDAMENTAL REVIEW CRITERIA*	*SPECIFIERS*
(	)	RIGHTS	Assertion of Denial of Patient Staff Visitor Volunteer
(	)	RISKS (See MEANS)	
(	)	SEX THERAPY	Confidentiality Counseling Inappropriate Incompetent adult Invasion of privacy Minor Sexual contact
(	)	SMOKING	Active Complaint Passive Policy inadequate Restricted area
(	)	SPERM (See IN VITRO FERTILIZATION)	AIDS Banking Collection Contamination Disposal of Donation (AID) Donation (AIH) In vitro fertilization Sperm preservation Surrogate
(	)	STERILIZATION	Court order Hysterectomy Incompetent adult Involuntary Minor Tubal ligation Vasectomy Voluntary
(	)	SUICIDE	Assisted Attempted Completed Request assistance Verbal threat of

(CODE)	ETHICAL FUNDAMENTAL REVIEW CRITERIA	SPECIFIERS
( )	SURGERY	Frequency Unnecessary Questionable
( )	SURROGATE	Breach of contract Complaint Medical cost and fee Medical cost only Suit
( )	TOXIC WASTE	Air pollution Complaint Disposal Hazard No policy Regulations Side effects Water pollution
( )	TRANSSEXUAL	Procedure Refuse to treat Treatment
( )	TRANSFER (See DIVERSION, DUMPING)	
( )	TRUTH TELLING	Deception Experiment (double-blind) Intentional omission Lack of Misleading Partial
( )	VALUES	Personal Family Societal
( )	VENEREAL DISEASE	Reported Unreported
( )	VIOLENCE (See ABUSE)	
( )	ZYGOTE BANKING	Donor(s) Ownership Surrogate Contract Cryopreservation Disposal

Chapter 33

Hospital Ethics Committees: Roles, Membership, and Structure

David C. Thomasma and John F. Monagle

It has become commonplace for technological growth to outstrip society's methods of dealing with it.* Nowhere is this more true than in medical care. Life-saving equipment and techniques at times work only to preserve a semblance of life. These tragic results are becoming increasingly common. Physicians, when unable to predict what treatment will achieve in an individual case, must apply the best treatment available in emergency situations.

But after a patient is stabilized, the prognosis often becomes clear, and the patient's family and physician may have to confront several difficult questions: Is it ethical to discontinue treatment? Is it ethical to continue? Having to make hard decisions is becoming more frequent, producing in recent years a number of highly publicized, emotionally charged court actions over the ethical approach to withdrawal of treatment.

When two southern California physicians agreed with the patient's family to remove life-support systems, including medical feeding and hydration, from a hopelessly brain-damaged patient, they were accused of murder, although the charges were eventually dismissed.[1] Baby Doe cases are proliferating, with some families and physicians deciding to treat and others refusing to treat children born with serious birth defects. What is society's ethical position? Is there any consensus toward resolution?

BASIC ROLES OF THE ETHICS COMMITTEE**

The idea that ethics committees can form a consensus toward resolution and assist in bioethical decision making has now become widespread. Enough has been written about the ideal scope of such committees to allow their intended roles to be summarized as follows:

Source: The following material is reprinted from *CHA Insight*, Vol. 8, No. 26, pp. 1–4, with permission of California Hospital Association, © June 1984.

**Source*: The following material is adapted from *Quality Review Bulletin*, Vol. 11, No. 7, pp. 204–208, with permission of Joint Commission on Accreditation of Hospitals, © July 1985.

†*Source*: The following material is adapted from *CHA Insight*, Vol. 8, No. 26, pp. 1–4, with permission of California Hospital Association, © June 1984.

††*Source*: The following material is reprinted from *Quality Review Bulletin*, Vol. 11, No. 7, pp. 204–208, with permission of Joint Commission on Accreditation of Hospitals, © July 1985.

- *Education*: educating hospital staff about issues in ethical decision making and about how to use the hospital ethics committee[2]
- *Mutidisciplinary Discussion*: providing a locus for interdisciplinary participation in value classification and prioritization leading to conflict resolution[3]
- *Resource Allocation*: recommending in-hospital allocation policies to maintain quality of care in the face of cost-containment measures.[4]
- *Institutional Commitments*: expressing the spirit of the hospital regarding its stated mission, philosophy, image, and identity (most often applicable to religious or private hospitals)[5]
- *Policy Formulation*: developing policies and guidelines regarding ethical issues
- *Consultation*: assisting attending physicians regarding difficult decisions

Education

Even if a hospital ethics committee cannot function, because of its large membership, as the ethical decision maker nor directly in a consulting or policy-formulating capacity, nevertheless it can become the backbone of an institution's effort to educate its staff about ethics, ethical principles, and ethical issues. Initially, what is needed is a process for conducting interdisciplinary discussions about specific ethical issues. Later, as the issues become more clearly defined, a process should be established whereby ideas and guidelines about specific hospital policies can be directed to the hospital's ethical policy subcommittees for their consideration and for policy formulation. In this way, although it may function mainly to recommend guideline policies for further review and formulation, nevertheless the hospital ethics committee remains deeply involved in ethical issues and is never cut off from the clashes of fundamental values experienced by clinical staff and administration.

But what kind of activities are appropriate? Many hospital staff members are interested in discussing ethical issues but feel their training in ethics to be inadequate. They may also see formal education in ethics as too esoteric and remote from real-life problems. Given this common intimidation about ethics education, it is best to concentrate on case discussions in the context of a formal plan and under the leadership of an educator or medical ethicist. Most university medical centers employ such professionals,[6] as do many other hospitals and hospital systems.[7] Also, as existing hospital ethics committees have discovered, the faculty of nearby colleges may include professionals interested in discussing ethical problems in health care.

A necessary activity for the hospital ethics committee is to provide bioethical education for patients, their families, and the larger community in order to promote an understanding of ethical problems and an awareness of the desire and responsibility of physicians and hospitals to respond in an ethical manner. Hospital ethics committees, given the specific charge to analyze the community's ethical concerns, issues, and dilemmas and the authority to develop (through ethical policy subcommittees) policies for the care of severely handicapped infants and terminally ill patients, can be a source of great help to families and physicians directly involved in difficult decisions. Properly structured, an ethics committee can thereby demonstrate the hospital's and the medical staff's commitment to protecting patients' rights and community values.

INTERDISCIPLINARY MEMBERS

An interdisciplinary approach both to the makeup of hospital ethics committees and to proposed ethics discussions in hospitals is essential for several reasons. Ethical dilemmas are not confined to the physician-patient relationship alone; they can occur in regard to many other health care professionals, institutional demands, and social factors. The increased specialization of health care demands "defragmentation" of staff during attempts to resolve ethical issues. Communication across disciplines regarding difficult emotional issues (often involved in ethically complex cases) tends to minimize disruptions that could damage health care delivery.

For example, when a patient's wife and children request that the father be taken off a respirator, does the request represent the wishes of the father or of the family? Sometimes the nurses or the significant attending nurse know the answer better than the attending physicians, who in many hospital situations may not know the family well. In such cases, a sound decision cannot be reached without involving the nursing staff (or the significant nurse) and other relatives who know the patient's lifestyle, desires, and requests.

A second consideration is the effect the decision will have on the care givers. Staff members often form emotional bonds with patients, especially when the patient is so helpless as to need ventilator support. A physician's order to "wean" the patient off the respirator when this action may result in death requires at the very least some discussion with the attending nurses and respiratory specialists who have been providing the care (see the section "Consultation: Ethics Advisory Groups" later in this chapter. Nurses often ask hospital ethicists to approach physicians about such determinations—not in a spirit of rebellion, but with a simple request that the decision be discussed with them. Any attempt to avoid such interdisciplinary discussion at the specific case level not only ignores the emotional dimensions of ethical issues but also causes new ethical issues to arise for those who must carry out the orders. As one nurse stated privately years ago, the most fundamental ethical issue for nurses concerns the expectations that they will remain silent and "get used to" being excluded from the decision making process.

Multidisciplinary discussion does not merely address the emotional aspects of ethical issues; it is required by the inherently multidisciplinary nature of the ethical dilemmas that occur today. The federal government is directly involved in promulgating guidelines on research and on the care of defective newborns. State authorities are involved in executing prospective payment policies that may cause some persons not to receive the care they need. Insurance companies are involved, especially through preferred provider organizations (PPOs) and health maintenance organizations (HMOs), since they reward physicians who keep their patients away from expensive care. Hospital administrators are involved in determining who will receive expensive care that will not be reimbursed. And, of course, physicians and consultants are involved in day-to-day decisions to which they bring legal, moral, and professional standards. It becomes impossible to resolve some clinical ethical problems without considering the involvement of all these many participants.

Resource Allocation

One of the least discussed of the possible functions of a hospital ethics committee is assisting the hospital governing body to develop policies for resource allocation.[8] As the trend toward cost containment continues, more difficult allocation issues will arise in every institution. For example, can the hospital ethically limit the number of certain types of expensive cases it accepts should reimbursement fail to meet its actual costs? Should certain services no longer be offered at the hospital? Has the community been represented in these decisions?

A study at Rush–Presbyterian–St. Luke's Medical Center in Chicago revealed the loss of approximately $20,000 per elderly patient receiving care in an intensive care unit, despite reimbursement under Medicare's prospective payment system. The researchers expressed a concern that if costs cannot be recovered elsewhere, critical care for the aged will dwindle and patients will not receive the quality of care to which they have become accustomed.[9] Their concern rests on a profound ethical principle of medicine: Physicians must act in the best interests of their patients, no matter the cost. Fortunately, at Rush as elsewhere, costs for some services have been recovered through reimbursement for other more cost-effective services. But this momentary respite from hard choices is just that—momentary. The national plan, of course, is to equalize the payment for each procedure throughout the country. When this is fully accomplished, cost shifting will no longer be possible and resource allocation decisions will become all the more difficult.

The luxury of individual cases for which payments can be received will almost completely cease, replaced by the hardship of no longer being able to provide expensive services for which little or no payment will be received. Cost will become an essential ingredient in the ethical decisions regarding allocation of scarce resources unless the necessary finances are made available. The claim to necessary but expensive health care is to be weighed in the balance (of resource allocation).

As outside entities establish even greater control over reimbursement for specific diseases, each institution will face a major ethical question: How can cost containment and institutional survival be balanced with quality of care? If it is the responsibility of a hospital to fulfill its stated mission, philosophy, identity, and image, then particular judgments regarding allocation should be appropriate discussion matter for relevant administrators, staff, and community members. Each hospital employee ostensibly commits himself or herself to the aims of the institution, and individual determinations and actions should further these aims. When the achievement of these aims is in jeopardy, a consensus should be sought on how to maintain the best possible balance of values. This balance can then be conveyed to the community that the hospital serves. The hospital ethics committee can be central to this effort to renew and communicate the hospital's aims and the community's values and choices.

Institutional Commitment

The hospital ethics committee can begin to develop (or, in private and religious facilities, continue to develop) an ethical tradition for the hospital. By recommending policies—after consideration by the ethical policy subcommittees—on such issues as the care of newborns, cardiopulmonary resuscitation, DNR orders, resource allocation, and procedures that will not be performed, the ethics committee itself in effect becomes the conscience of the institution, linking the institutional philosophy with practical judgments about how to proceed in the best interests of the patient and the larger community.

Because of the extraordinary pressures currently brought to bear on hospitals as social institutions, they face the same kind of crisis regarding goals that universities faced in the 1960s. The social good traditionally offered—the highest quality of care—is called into question not only by "bureaucratic parsimony"[10] but also by alternative forms of delivery ranging from HMOs to surgical, emergency, and ambulatory care centers. Hospitals are responding to the challenge by altering their character, becoming less social institutions than businesses. Departments become product lines and services become ciphers in computer printouts of cost analyses.

However, one fact which often becomes lost in the jumble, remains essential: Hospitals provide a good that people cannot obtain on their own using their own resources.[11] This good is not like most consumer products, which in some sense are luxuries. To reduce it to mathematical or economic analysis alone is to diminish its vast importance.

To preserve its aims in the thicket of economics and bureaucracy, the hospital must have at its disposal a realistic but firm vision of its nature and purpose. Siegler has suggested that if we are to ration health care, perhaps we should begin by withholding it from the wealthy and articulate and giving it to the poor and downtrodden.[12] Less dramatically, a hospital ethics committee might suggest a policy that would involve donating several hours a week to care for the poor. Further, it might consider practical measures to foster cooperation among competing hospitals so that needed care can be provided to all who seek it. Philanthropy, charitable giving, marketing, and fund raising must be encouraged to ensure survival. Diversified business endeavors should be explored and implemented.

Policy Formulation: Ethical Policy Subcommittees[13]

Every hospital governing body has the duty to ensure that the institution reflects the mission and philosophy stated in its charter and developed in its traditions.[14] Staff turnover and a natural tendency, especially in institutions, for ideals to decay over time make it desirable to establish perdurable policies regarding ethical decision making. In effect, such policies are a form of prescriptive or directive ethics.

Yet one of the most astonishing features of hospitals to outsiders is precisely the lack of such directive ethics. Although most hospitals have numerous policies directing health care practice within their walls, few have attempted, until recently, to establish ethics guidelines. Religious hospitals have long had "mission and philosophy" committees, which have offered guidelines about procedures such as abortion and elective sterilization. Many other hospitals have developed guidelines for "Do Not Resuscitate" (DNR) orders as well. Apart from these exceptions, however, little attention has been given to policies regarding the significant ethical problems that challenge daily practice in the hospital, e.g., stopping certain forms of therapy for terminally ill patients, interprofessional conflicts, informed consent, and decision making for incompetent patients.

Resistance to policies governing such ethical problems stems from several sources. Inertia is certainly one; distractions and the pressures of time are two others. Some people think decisions by committee do not represent a sufficient advancement over individual decisions to warrant the effort. Still others are concerned that guidelines about care will adversely affect physician-patient relationships. Resistance also almost certainly results from the wrongheaded philosophy of medicine that views the one-on-one relationship of the physician and patient as sacred and exempt from outside interference.[15] Evidence exists that traditional Hippocratic ethics has been welded to an entrepreneurial concept of health care.[16] In a traditional fee-for-service system, emphasis on the almost "sacred" quality of the physician-patient relationship is not entirely altruistic. Keeping other interests out of the relationship could be seen, at least in part, as a protectionist rather than beneficent action. Traditional ethics and entrepreneurship can be decoupled without damage to the important ethical dimensions of the physician-patient relationship.

The hospital ethics committee's preliminary work serves as a starting point for more detailed analysis by ethical policy subcommittees appointed to study and recommend policy on specific areas of ethical uncertainty. The subcommittees, composed of physicians, some members of the hospital's ethics committee, and other health professionals with expertise in the subject area, forward the results of their analyses to the hospital ethics committee, which then can send them on to the appropriate authority for adoption as hospital policy.

Consultation: Ethics Advisory Groups†

These hospital policies are then available as guidance for ethics advisory groups, which are formed ad hoc when a specific case involving ethical issues arises. At this level there is direct involvement of the attending physician and the patient and/or family.

The composition and membership of an ethics advisory group might include the following:

- attending physician
- patient and/or family members
- significant nurse in the case
- clergy or bioethicist
- physician or other member of the ethical policy subcommittee of the subject area

In cases where there seem to be unresolved civil or criminal liabilities, an attorney for the hospital should be included. In certain cases, upon request of the patient or family, the attorney for the patient may also be invited to participate.

Perhaps the most important and most problematic role of the ethics advisory group is consultation.** Should the consultation on cases be, strictly speaking, an offering of advice to the physician or, alternatively, an actual decision making process? Physicians often resist interpolations of decision making bodies between themselves and their patients.[17] In part, this resistance stems from the view that the physician-patient relationship is the moral center of medicine.[18] But it may also derive from a failure to recognize that medical ethics is no longer the private domain of physicians, if it ever was. The issues almost always involve public perceptions, social and political presuppositions, legal standards, and ethical traditions.[19]

It is not yet clear which of the two options should predominate. At present the group should function at least as an advisory body. Successful optional consultation by the ethics advisory group requires support from the board members, administrators, and medical executive committee, along with continuing educational activities for the staff. Since ethically and legally society has placed the burden of medical decisions on the attending physician, the final treatment decision remains with the physician and the patient or family.

For the first time a hospital's bioethics committee (High Desert Hospital, Lancaster, California, operated by the Department of Health Services, County of Los Angeles) has been named in a malpractice suit. The plaintiff is Elizabeth Bouvia. Her attorney is Richard S. Scott. Elizabeth Bouvia, 30 years old, has suffered since birth from cerebral palsy and is a spastic quadraplegic, immobile and entirely dependent upon others. She alleges that a nasogastric tube for forced feeding was inserted, against her will and without her consent, on January 16, 1986. On April 16, 1986, the Court of Appeal, Second Appellate District, Division Two, ordered the tube removed. In an amended complaint filed on July 23, 1986, in the Superior Court of the State of California for the County of Los Angeles, Elizabeth Bouvia named the hospital's bioethics committee and individual members as defendants. (Case No. C583828). Bouvia's attending physicians were free to disregard the advice of the bioethics committee. The physicians are legally responsible for the actions taken, not the bioethics committee. The suit against the bioethics committee and the individual members should not chill or intimidate members of bioethics committees who act in good faith in the interest of the patient. Bioethics committees reduce, not increase legal exposure.

Ethics Committees: Membership†

The membership of hospital ethics committees should represent a broad range of value perspectives, professional expertise, and community representation. The committee should include[20]

- Medical staff, including staff from specialty areas such as obstetrics, neurosurgery, neurology, nephrology, oncology, psychiatry, etc.
- Nursing staff, such as the director of nursing, operating room supervising nurse, emergency department supervising nurse, etc.
- An administrator—a high-level qualified administrative person who is interested in ethical issues, sensitive to medical staff responsibilities, patient and employee rights, and community concerns.
- A social services representative—a person knowledgeable about what the hospital, as well as the larger community, can provide in the way of care for patients.
- Clergy or bioethicists. Having at least one such person is essential for the multidisciplinary discussions. Candidates should have training not only in moral theology, but also in the formal discipline of philosophical ethics in order to present the ethical theories and principles that can be applied to the individual case. Some clergy do not have these credentials. Although they can bring important and essential insight to the committee, it cannot replace the formal discipline in ethics that is also needed.
- A member of the hospital board. Since the hospital board represents the community, the person selected should be knowledgeable about the larger community's concerns as to the kinds of medical procedures and treatments that are needed in the demographic area which the hospital serves. And since all of the hospital's services are ultimately the responsibility of the hospital board, the governing body representative should

participate in and have knowledge of the hospital ethics committee's discussions and decisions.

STRUCTURES: THREE MODELS*

There are at least three possible structures for an ethics committee, each determined by what part of the hospital has authority over its operations. The three organizational diagrams presented in Figure 33–1 show an ethics committee as a committee of the hospital's governing board, as a committee reporting to the hospital's chief executive officer, and as a committee responsible to the hospital medical staff executive committee.

Each structure has its advantages and disadvantages. The committee's structure and membership, its authority and responsibility, its charge and scope of activity, and its limits of purpose and authority should be clearly defined according to the particular needs of each hospital.

Under the governing board model, the ethics committee uncovers, discusses, and clarifies ethical concerns or problems and, in consultation with the medical staff executive committee and the hospital administration, forms an ethical policy subcommittee to analyze the available information on the subject.

The subcommittee's policy recommendations are reviewed by the ethics committee and forwarded for adoption by the governing board as hospital policy. When a case involving those issues arises, those policies serve as guidelines to ethics advisory groups formed to help the family and physician understand the ethical choices involved. The flow of information and development of hospital policies is similar in the other two models, but in those models the hospital's administration or the medical staff executive committee has more or less direct authority for final review and approval of the policies.

One of the differences between the governing board, administration, and medical staff organizational models is in the level of public disclosure each affords. Because the ethics committee's primary focus is on patients' rights and hospital and community education in bioethical issues, it may not be advisable to seek the protection from discovery in legal action that state law gives deliberations of medical staff quality care review committees.[21]

To the extent that the discussions and recommendations about or solutions to ethical concerns, issues, and dilemmas are shared openly, the medical staff's and the institution's assumption of ethical responsibility for policies and actions will be visible and recognized. Furthermore, if a hospital's ethical practices are challenged through civil or criminal suit, summary documentation of the ethics committee's proceedings may well serve as a defense for the physicians and the hospital.

Under the medical staff organizational model, the ethics committee may seek protection from discovery for the records and proceedings of its ethical policy subcommittees, since these report to the ethics committee of the medical staff. Likewise, protection from discovery may be sought for the ethics advisory groups under either the medical staff or governing board organizational models. The governing board structure may be the most amenable to openness of information, discussion, and recommendations, while at the same time protecting records and proceedings related to individual case discussions of the ethics advisory groups.

The administration model, while unable to seek protection from discovery under quality assurance confidentiality statutes, may be more responsive to management control of cost

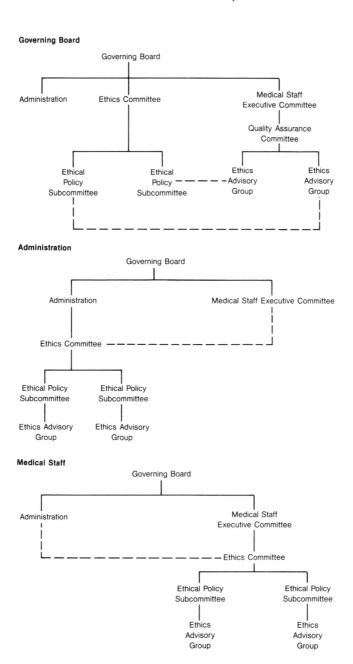

Figure 33-1 Three Hospital Ethics Committee Structures. *Source:* Reprinted from *CHA Insight*, Vol. 8, No. 20, p. 3, with permission of California Hospital Association, © 1984.

effectiveness and to evaluating risk management and professional liability implications of hospital ethical policies. The medical staff model, while fully protected from disclosure of discussions, has to guard against domination by physicians and lack of interaction with the community.

CONCLUSION††

To retain the ethical dimension of health care delivery, hospitals interested in ethics committees can select from the roles discussed in this chapter. The needs of each institution are different, as is its capacity to establish such committees firmly. Some of the roles are more problematic than others. In many hospitals, several of the roles are already carried out by other committees—allocation decisions by the quality assurance committee, institutional commitments by the mission and philosophy committee, and so on. However, none of the functions will be successfully integrated within the hospital unless the ethics committee is part of an educational effort that involves both the primary disciplines responsible for patient care and the personnel responsible for hospital governance.

Ethical issues are not going to diminish in frequency or complexity.* The individual treatment dilemmas raised by new technology are difficult enough. But even more agonizing dilemmas are just beginning to surface, with the introduction of PPOs, HMOs, DRGs and the other responses to limited resources.

In *Securing Access to Health Care*,[22] the President's Commission for the Study of Ethical Problems in Medicine and Biomedical and Behavioral Research concluded that society is obligated to provide "equitable" access to "adequate" health care.[23] But as new technology redefines what care is "adequate," its cost restricts access to its benefits. The inequity of limited access—first to the poor, but eventually to everyone—may become society's thorniest bioethical dilemma, one that will necessitate more hospitals to establish ethics committees.

NOTES

1. 47 Cal. App. 3d 1006 (1983). See John F. Monagle, "A Question of Ethics or Murder," *CHA Insight* April 13, 1984, pp. 1–4.

2. A.R. Fleischman and T.H. Murray, "Ethics Committees for Infants Doe?" *Hastings Center Report* 13 (December 1983): 5–9; J.A. Robertson, "Ethics Committees in Hospitals: Alternative Structures and Responsibilities," *Quality Review Bulletin* 10 (January 1984): 6–10; R.J. Rooney, "Ethics from the Bottom Up: A Participative Approach to Health Care Ethics," *Bioethics Reporter* 3 (1984): 970.

3. J. Curtis, "Multidisciplinary Input on Institutional Ethics Committees: A Nursing Perspective," *Quality Review Bulletin* 10 (July 1984): 199–208; D. Ozar, "The Challenge of Multiple Professional Perspectives in Institutional Ethics Committees," *Bioethics Reporter* 1 (1984): 153.

4. A. Griffin and D. Thomasma, "Health Care Distribution and Hospital Impartial Panels," *Bioethics Reporter* 1 (1984): 124.

5. B. Bader, "Medical Moral Committees: Guarding Values in an Ambivalent Society," *Hospital Progress* 63 (October 1982): 80; E. Lisson, "Active Medical Morals Committee: Valuable Resource for Health Care," *Hospital Progress* 63 (October 1982): 36.

6. T.K. McElhenny and E.D. Pellegrino, *Teaching Ethics, the Humanities, and Human Values in Medical Schools: A Ten-Year Overview* (Washington, D.C.: Institute on Human Values in Medicine, Society for Health and Human Values, 1981).

7. M.M. McDonnell, "Holy Cross Health System: Medical Ethics Program," *Bioethics Reporter* 3 (1984): 960; G. Graber, "One Philosopher's History in His Work with Hospital Ethics Committees," *Bioethics Reporter* 3 (1984): 956.

8. Griffin and Thomasma, "Health Care Distribution."

9. P.W. Butler, R.C. Bone, and P. Field, "Technology under Medicare Diagnosis-Related Group Prospective Payment: Implications for Medical Intensive Care," *Chest* 87 (February 1985): 229–34.

10. M. Siegler, "Should Age Be a Criterion in Health Care? *Hastings Center Report* 14 (October 1984): 24–27.

11. D. Ozar, "Justice and a Universal Right to Basic Health Care, *Soc. Sci. Med. (Ethics)* 15 F (March 1981): 135–41.

12. Siegler, "Should Age Be a Criterion in Health Care?"

13. John F. Monagle, "Blueprints for Hospital Ethics Committees," *CHA Insight*, June 26, 1984.

14. D. Thomasma, "Hospitals' Ethical Responsibilities As Technology, Regulation Grow," *Hospital Progress* 63 (December 1982): 74–79.

15. D. Ozar, "Social Ethics in the Philosophy of Medicine, and Professional Responsibility," *Theoretical Medicine.*

16. W.B. Schwartz and H.J. Aaron, "Rationing Hospital Care: Lessons from Britain," *New England Journal of Medicine* 310 (1984): 52–56.

17. Robertson, "Ethics Committees in Hospitals."

18. E.D. Pellegrino and D.C. Thomasma, *A Philosophical Basis of Medical Practice* (New York: Oxford University Press, 1981).

19. D. Thomasma, "Medical Ethics Committees Find New Roles," *Quality Assurance–Risk Management Bulletin* 5 (January–February 1985): 1–3; D. Callahan, "Shattuck Lecture: Contemporary Biomedical Ethic," *New England Journal of Medicine* 302 (1980): 1228–33.

20. Monagle, "Blueprints."

21. Forty-five states protect medical staff committee records under the state's evidence code or peer review statute.

22. President's Commission for the Study of Ethical Problems in Medicine and Biomedical and Behavioral Research, *Securing Access to Health Care*, vol. 1 (Washington, D.C.: GPO, 1983). For a review of its conclusions, see Allen Toon, "Equitable Access to Adequate Care," *CHA Insight*, October 19, 1983, p. 9.

23. Bader, "Medical Moral Committees."

BIBLIOGRAPHY

American Hospital Association, *Hospital Committees on Biomedical Ethics*. Chicago: American Hospital Association, 1984.

Craig, Robert P., *Ethics Committees: A Practical Approach*. St. Louis, Mo.: The Catholic Health Association, 1986.

Chinn, P.L. *Ethical Issues in Nursing*. Rockville, Md.: Aspen, 1986.

Hosford, B. *Bioethics Committees*. Rockville, Md.: Aspen, 1986.

Chapter 34

Legal Liability and Clinical Ethics Consultations: Practical and Philosophical Considerations

Donnie J. Self and Joy D. Skeel

Legal liability is not new to clinical medicine. Volumes have been written about it from virtually every perspective. Indeed, a literature search readily shows that literally thousands of articles have been written about legal liability in medicine. Some works addressing the legal aspects of clinical ethics have begun to appear in print, such as those of Wolf and Robertson.[1] These works, however, address general issues, such as the relationship of institutional ethics committees to the courts, whether ethics committee opinions should be mandatory or optional, and what the function of an ethics committee should be (e.g., should it serve a gatekeeping function in determining whether a given case goes to court). But these works do not explicitly address the potential legal liability of individual persons involved in clinical ethics consultations, which in fact has been almost completely ignored in the literature.

Recent exceptions to this include the work of Areen and Robertson.[2] Areen has argued that while the field is too recent for many precedents to have been set by court cases, clearly the potential exists for individual ethicists to be legally liable when conducting clinical ethics consultations. She notes that at this point it is difficult to draw generalities, because the legal implications depend upon the nature of the consultation and the circumstances under which it occurred. But the vulnerability of the ethicist is certainly increased if he or she does not recognize, respect, and make clear to others the limits of his or her expertise. For example, an ethicist might increase vulnerability by discussing court decisions with physicians without emphasizing that what is being provided is not legal interpretation or legal advice but only examples of applied ethics.

One recent study found that approximately 50 percent of the respondents who acknowledged that they do clinical ethics consultations do not have professional liability insurance coverage for their clinical activities and that approximately 75 percent of the respondents said they have very little or no concern about the potential risk of legal liability action against them.[3] Some people would commend their courage for not letting concerns for legal liability interfere with their providing a helpful service, while others would condemn their foolishness for exposing themselves to such enormous potential risk. Although some hospital ethics committees have now been named in suits, to our knowledge no ethicist has ever fallen victim to the risk or been sued individually for his or her clinical ethics consultation activities.[4]

CAUSES FOR INDIFFERENCE

The relative indifference to the potential risks by persons doing clinical ethics consults can be explained in several ways. First, clinical ethics consultation is a relatively new field and those participating in it have not previously had to be concerned about professional liability coverage in their work. For example, a recent study has shown that of the people doing clinical ethics consultations in this country, approximately half have a theological background and approximately half have a philosophical background.[5] In their roles as clergy or university professors, most of these professionals give little thought to the need for protecting themselves from legal liability in their work. Seldom do professors get sued for delivering poor lectures or giving a poor education to their students. Similarly, seldom do clergy get sued for delivering poor sermons or giving poor pastoral care to their parishioners. Until recently, few people have gone into clinical ethics as their first job. Therefore, they are not accustomed to thinking in terms of professional liability. Former hospital chaplains may be more aware of the risks, since they have spent time in the hospital setting and are familiar with the concern of other health professionals in this area. But generally clinical ethicists as independent contractors are used to performing a helping function, and since they are "doing good," it seldom occurs to them that someone might sue them for it. This assumption may be a little naive or unsophisticated, but it probably accounts for most of the apathy and indifference on the part of clinical ethicists toward professional liability coverage.

A second explanation is that the indifference is only apparent; the clinical ethicists may in fact have thought carefully about the problem and have concluded that the risks are so remote and the probabilities so small that there is simply no need for concern over professional liability. We would like to think that this explanation is correct, but in all honesty we do not believe that it is. For one thing, many clinical ethicists do not know the necessary conditions in tort law that constitute malpractice.

However, there may be an explanation for the indifference. In clinical ethics consultations the occurrence of the necessary and sufficient conditions for incurring legal liability may never be present—indeed theoretically cannot be. There are four necessary conditions for establishing that medical malpractice (by an ethicist) has occurred: (1) a duty must be owed to the patient by the ethicist, (2) the ethicist's performance must fall below the standards of the profession, (3) harm must actually occur to the patient, and (4) the ethicist must have caused the harm to the patient. Theoretically, all four of these conditions for malpractice must occur together, and a detailed analysis might show that circumstances never permit this.

The first condition for there being a duty owed to the patient raises questions about the nature, structure, and function of ethics consultations. Is the duty of the ethicist to the patient or to the physician who cares for the patient? Who is the patient or client of the clinical ethicist? Certainly arguments could be made for either the patient or the physician being the focus of the ethicist's work. There are various interpretations of the structure and function of ethics consultations. But if the traditional understanding of consultations in the medical setting is applied to ethics consultations, then clearly the client or recipient of the efforts of a clinical ethicist is the physician. The law, according to Areen, would view the ethicist as an advisor to the treating physician rather than as an advisor to the patient.[6] Indeed she notes that in ethics consultations there is a curious reversal, as if the physician becomes the patient and the ethicist becomes the expert. Thus when physicians ask for the ethicist's opinion, it is analogous to the patient's asking for the physician's opinion. However, if the traditional understanding of consultations in the medical setting is accepted and the analogy continued, then just as physicians sometimes sue consultant medical specialists for bad advice, similarly physicians may start suing consultant clinical ethicists for bad advice. There may be legitimate concern about the legal liability of the clinical ethicist regardless of whether the patient or the physician is the object of the clinical ethicist's efforts.

In addition to a duty being owed to the patient or client, the ethicist's performance must fall below the standards of the profession in order for malpractice to occur. This may be the salvation of clinical ethicists—at least for the time being. This is because currently there are no standards to fall below. It would be relatively easy to get "expert witnesses" who would argue on the opposite sides of almost any bioethical issue. Clinical ethics as a discipline or profession is very loosely organized, with no entry and exit qualifications, no generally accepted educational requirements, and no board certification. Perhaps this will change as ethics consultations for difficult and controversial cases become more common and requirements begin to constitute a national standard of practice in most hospitals. National standards for hospital ethics committees are developing rapidly and perhaps national standards for individual clinical ethics consultations will soon follow. Similarly, there are increasingly frequent discussions at various levels within the clinical ethics profession regarding explicit certification, educational requirements, and professional standards for conducting clinical ethics consultations.

CAUSES FOR CONCERN

One of the causes for concern over legal liability in clinical ethics is the generally increasing litigious atmosphere of society and the heavy emphasis on rights of all kinds, including patient rights, civil rights, women's rights, gay rights, and animal rights. Currently anyone can get sued for anything by anybody. News reports frequently relate stories about physicians being sued by their patients, lawyers being sued by their clients, teachers being sued by their students, parents being sued by their children, and churches being sued by their members. Currently, there is a different attitude toward litigation than used to exist. Formerly, leaders of the community, especially those who had higher education levels and positions of authority (e.g., physicians, lawyers, ministers, and teachers), were respected and trusted to such an extent that they were sued only as a result of gross violations of professionalism. But there has been a significant change in social attitudes in recent years, so that now when anything is not completely satisfactory, the response that comes to mind first (rather than last) is "Sue for whatever you can get." Medicine provides a good example of this change in societal attitudes toward professionals, and persons providing clinical ethics consultations need to take this change seriously.

There is a widely held misconception that many malpractice claims are frivolous and based on greed. But in 1984, Dr. Richard Wilbur, executive vice president of the Council of Medical Specialty Societies, reported that a review of 72,000 malpractice claims found that only 5 percent of monetary awards involved frivolous claims.[7] The remainder were legitimate claims. Similarly, it was found that of 2,500 patients admitted to tertiary care institutions for surgery, 36 percent of the charts indicated that a preventable error had occurred, with 1 percent resulting in death and 3 percent resulting in major complications.

Finally, Dr. Wilbur noted that a California study found that only 10 percent of the cases with probable legal liability had claims filed. These studies suggest there are so many cases involving legitimate liability that if they all went to court, no form of insurance could cover them all. The present court structure could not handle them all just because of the sheer volume.

Perhaps paying more attention to the quality of the physician-patient relationship may be the most efficient and effective way to prevent legal action in those instances when preventable error occurs. Physicians need to stop doing the things that get them sued and start doing more of the things that keep them from getting sued when an error does occur, since errors will occur from time to time. While one may not be able to prevent all errors, one can for the most part prevent being sued when an error occurs.

Practicing defensive medicine is not being suggested or advocated. Indeed, defensive medicine has significantly contributed to the enormous rise in the cost of health care. Some estimates, including those of the AMA, indicate that defensive medicine increases medical costs by 25–50 percent.[8] Rather than practicing defensive medicine, physicians need to take the offensive and create an atmosphere in which the patient-physician relationship can be less adversarial than it has become in the past decade and can return to the fiduciary relationship of earlier times. This fiduciary relationship need not be paternalistic in nature. A patient wants the physician to look out for his or her best interests through a fiduciary relationship. Patients sue physicians out of anger, resentment, hurt, and a feeling of violation of trust. People do not often sue friends or those whom they care for or those who they believe care for them.

In the past, a patient could assume that whatever the physician did was in the patient's best interest, i.e., there was trust implicit in the relationship. Patients no longer make that assumption; the trust is not there. Now when patients are discharged from the hospital, they do not know whether they have been discharged in their own medical best interest or in the hospital's best interest because the money allocated for their medical care by the current DRG system has run out.

As a result of the increasing litigious atmosphere and changing social attitudes, malpractice suits in medicine have sky-rocketed. Often the litigious attitude is expressed in the form of a threat to sue, even though the aggrieved person has no intention of carrying out the threat. Sometimes just the threat achieves what is sought by the patient, in the form of an out-of-court settlement. But these threats are much more than just a nuisance. They consume enormous amounts of time, energy, and resources, which is partly why they are sometimes successful. A settlement is made to avoid costly litigation and damages.

The reasonableness of this approach was increased significantly as a result of the case of *Scott v. United States*.[9] In that case, a baby was born severely damaged, and the plaintiff's mother alleged that physicians at Elmendorf Air Force Hospital in Alaska provided her with inadequate prenatal and postnatal care, besides performing unnecessary surgery on her late in pregnancy and doing improper monitoring during labor and delivery. According to the mother, all of these factors led to the child's having spastic quadriplegia, with no expectation that he would ever be able to walk or care for himself. The attorneys for both sides negotiated and agreed to a $3.6 million settlement out of court. However, the Justice Department overruled their defense attorney's efforts and took the case to trial in an attempt to get a lower award—whereupon the plaintiff was awarded $11.1 million in damages! Because of such a precedent, physicians, hospitals, and insurance companies have an added impetus to reach out-of-court settlements, even in circumstances in which they clearly believe they are in the right and without fault. Indeed, such circumstances create the dilemma of either paying a moderate loss when one knows that one has done nothing wrong or running the risk of paying an enormous loss when reason is overcome by emotion in the courtroom.

This leads to another concern about liability in clinical ethics, namely, the enormous size of awards in recent years. There have been hundreds of multimillion dollar awards or settlements for damages in malpractice cases, with several awards over $10 million. For example, in *Stutt v. Birdsong* an $11.5 million settlement was reached in Texas for improper administration of anesthesia; in *Cauwenberg v. St. Vincent Hospital* a $9.7 million settlement was reached in Wisconsin for failure to administer asthma medication on an emergency basis; in *Urcia v. Kaiser Foundation Hospitals* a $3.0 million settlement was reached in Hawaii for failure to diagnose an epidural hematoma. [10] These examples demonstrate that the risks of enormous rewards are widespread in all medical specialties throughout the entire country.

The medical specialty of obstetrics certainly has its share of risk, as shown by *McLeod v. Wellington*, where a $6.3 million jury award was granted in California for failure to recognize fetal distress. [11] In the cases cited here, there were actually multiple defendants named, as is usual. This being common practice and the risks being widespread throughout health care, it seems reasonable that there would be legitimate concern over the legal liability of clinical ethicists, who might be named in suits when consulting on difficult cases (cases whose controversialness would be indicated by the fact they required an ethics consultation).

Although the risk of legal liability in clinical ethics may be small, nevertheless the danger is real. There have been numerous counseling suits involving other nonphysician professionals, such as psychologists and ministers doing counseling or providing consultation services. [12] In *Nally v. Grace Community Church*, a couple brought a wrongful death suit against the church after their son, who had been counseled by the ministers, committed suicide. The claim was that negligence of the church prevented the son from seeking professional psychological counseling. There is currently a $35 million suit being brought against a hospital chaplain for allegedly giving bad advice. [13] There is no reason to think that clinical ethicists would be exempt from lawsuits in the future. Of course, some clinical ethics consultants do not claim to give advice, make recommendations, or make entries in patients' charts, but others acknowledge that these activities are part of their job and that they do them regularly. It seems that there is legitimate cause for concern by this latter group. This also raises some interesting conceptual and practical questions, which are not addressed here, about the nature, structure, and function of ethics consultations.

Lastly, an additional cause for concern over legal liability in clinical ethics, which is related to the increasingly litigious atmosphere in society, is the decrease in respect for authority generally in recent decades, particularly the lack of respect for any moral or ethical authority. This decline in respect is demonstrated by the campus unrest of the 1960s, the racial riots, the Vietnam war protests, the Watergate scandal, and the malpractice crisis. It is reflected in steadily falling public opinion polls measuring respect for various professionals traditionally associated with authority, including physicians.

This decrease in respect for authority has interesting and important philosophical underpinnings, including but not limited to the rise in popularity of ethical relativism. Ethical relativism has been gravely misunderstood in our society, often being confused with subjectivism. [14] Ethical relativism does not necessarily lead to a subjective theory of value, although its more popular version has done so. There are two ways values can be relative. Values can be relative to the person making the judgment, which necessarily leads to subjectivism. Or values can be relative to the circumstances, which leads to objectivism. Given exactly the same circumstances (or situation) at another time, the same values will again occur. However, modern culture has for the most part accepted the first interpretation, taking values to be relative to the person making a moral judgment. It also tends to accept the philosophical assumptions behind that interpretation. The lack of respect for authority is an indirect reflection of changes in the philosophical assumptions of society. What is philosophically problematic for a person is to a large extent a function of that person's assumptions, premises, and beliefs. Problems are set within a given philosophical framework or context. Philosophical perplexity about values and authority is generated by difficulties that have led philosophers to question the possibility of certain kinds of knowledge (such as moral knowledge) and the meaningfulness of certain apparently meaningful statements.

Philosophical assumptions and moral philosophy are certainly not irrelevant to daily life. It is through philosophical analysis that our culture has come to understand the structure of experience and the world. For example, it is by philosophically analyzing value experience, through an analysis of value language and of what can sensibly be said about such experience, that one comes to understand the value structure of the world. Similarly, it is by analyzing the value language in medicine that one comes to understand the value structure embedded in medicine. The change in the philosophical stance of our culture with respect to science that occurred from the thirteenth to the seventeenth century is an example of how changes in philosophical assumptions can influence daily life.[15] During this period, there was a subtle but significant shift in our concept of knowledge of reality. People ceased to be satisfied simply to seek their place in the order of things. No longer did an answer such as "Nature abhors a vacuum" serve as a sufficient explanation why the mercury came to a given level in Torricelli's barometer. People aggressively addressed the possibilities of controlling the environment instead of resignedly accepting fate.

Philosophical changes with respect to cultural assumptions and presuppositions generally occur over a long time, but that does not mean they are irrelevant. Sometimes they happen quickly. Almost within a generation the philosophical views of existentialism, such as views that persons have no essence (or essential properties) and choice determines right, affected the daily lives of millions, especially in regards to their respect for authority. So clearly philosophical analysis is relevant and important.

The decline in respect for authority which has resulted in a litigious atmosphere and more legal liability in medicine is a result of a tendency toward consistency with respect to both the philosophical assumptions and the thoughts and actions of people within the culture. The scientific naturalistic interpretation of the world so prevalent in modern Western culture has resulted in the systematic elimination of all that is not consistent with it, including the notion of any moral authority.

Value language has been taken to be philosophically problematic and in need of accounting for, because it differed from what was commonly accepted as the paradigm of meaningful language, namely, the descriptive-explanatory language of natural science. With the descriptive-explanatory approach of natural science taken as the paradigm, knowledge of reality has been taken to include only what is known through or grounded in sensory experience. As a result, value judgments and the notion of moral authority have seemed not justifiable. When a factual judgment was questioned, one could resort to the necessary sensory experiences to verify the claim and thereby justify the assertion. Such has not been thought to be the case with value judgments.

Philosophical tension arose because people claimed, believed, thought, and felt both that knowledge was to be obtained in the scientific way through sensory experience and that there was moral knowledge. When they came to feel an intellectual incompatibility between the two, in order to achieve consistency they tended to expunge their belief that there was such a thing as moral knowledge or that there was a rational epistemic procedure for getting such knowledge. But common moral experience and the language of ordinary moral discourse are permeated with claims of the objectivity of moral principles and judgments. People feel obligations impinging upon them and experience certain things as right and others as wrong. For example, one feels obligated to keep a promise unless overriding circumstances prevail, and one experiences child abuse or the needless infliction of pain upon the innocent as wrong.

But the epistemological theories popular in modern Western culture based on the paradigm of natural science allow only subjectivism in moral judgments. Thus there has arisen a tension, incompatibility, conflict, or inconsistency within modern culture, a conflict between our ways of experiencing and thinking about values and our epistemological beliefs. This incompatibility of subjectivity and objectivity has to be resolved. How this issue is resolved will have considerable influence both for value theory and behavior in daily life. Indeed, the resolution will have significant influence on the general respect for moral authority, the litigious atmosphere of society, and ultimately the incidence of malpractice litigation.

Since the turn of the century there has been a tremendous rise in the popularity of existentialism and the subjectivism of values which it represents. From this subjectivism arose the belief that there could be no logical disagreement in matters of moral values. The subjectivism of existentialism maintains that moral judgments are merely expressions of emotions, preferences, or decisions and do not make truth claims—and so cannot be true or false.

Existentialism explicates *right* and *good* in terms of freedom. It holds that with respect to basic life-constituting decisions, one is completely free to choose whatever lifestyle one pleases. No reason can be given for the choice; and the choice cannot be wrong, for choice at this level defines what is right. Decisions internal to a lifestyle can be right or wrong depending on whether they are consistent with the life-constituting choices. But these higher-level choices cannot be right or wrong, for nothing could count for or against such judgments. The internal decisions which are judged to be wrong are explained as bad faith. The person was not fully aware of his or her freedom or did not have the courage to act upon the freedom. Self-deceit was therefore chosen as camouflage. The decline in respect for authority and the general unrest of the past decades has been simply an acting out of the philosophical assumptions of our culture. In medicine these changes have been exemplified in the last couple of decades by the enormous increase in concern over patient autonomy, informed consent, patients' rights, and the corresponding decrease in the acceptance of paternalism as appropriate in medicine.

CONCLUSION AND RECOMMENDATIONS

Currently if a malpractice suit were brought against a clinical ethicist for his or her professional activities, it is highly unlikely that the suit would be successful. But that may change rapidly. There is no easy solution either in clinical medicine or clinical ethics to the professional liability problem. Placing caps on awards, creating no-fault or patient compensation funds, establishing review panels to screen out frivolous claims, and so forth may help, but all that is like putting a band-aid on cancer. Nothing less than a change in social attitudes about the appropriate roles of physicians and the functions of the health care delivery system and in the realistic and unrealistic expectations about what medicine can accomplish will ultimately solve the problem. Nothing less than changes in the philosophical assumptions of society will suffice. While the task will be difficult, physicians are in the best position to influence these changes and indeed may be the only group who can bring them about. Philosophers and theologians may share the burden, because of their responsibility to analyze and influence the philosophical assumptions of the culture. But it will require swimming upstream and reversing all forms of professional paternalism and the trend toward commercialization of health care. If the patient is abandoned to the business model, physicians will deserve the scorn they will get.

In spite of there presently being only a small risk, everyone doing clinical ethics consultation should be covered with professional liability insurance. The risk is small but unnecessary. Generally, if the clinical ethicist is an employee of a hospital, the hospital's professional liability policy usually will cover the ethicist for defense and damages (to the limit of the policy). However, if the ethicist charges a consultation fee or works outside his or her place of employment, then the ethicist is considered an independent contractor and usually will not be covered by the hospital policy. Also, if sued, the ethicist without liability coverage must hire a defense attorney, even though the final settlement or court decision does not result in financial damages. It may be difficult to obtain professional liability coverage for the clinical ethicist who is an independent contractor. Nevertheless, securing such coverage will result in personal and professional comfort in a litigious society.

NOTES

1. Susan M. Wolf, ''Ethics Committees in the Courts,'' *Hastings Center Report* 16 (June 1986): 12–15; John A. Robertson, ''Ethics Committees in Hospitals: Alternative Structures and Responsibilities,'' *Quality Review Bulletin* 10 (January 1984): 6–10.

2. Judith Areen, ''Legal Implications of Ethics Consultation,'' in *Ethics Consultations in Health Care*, ed. John Fletcher (Ann Arbor, Mich.: Health Administration Press, in press); John A. Robertson, ''Clinical Medical Ethics and the Law: The Rights and Duties of Ethics Consultants,'' ibid.

3. Donnie J. Self and Joy D. Skeel, ''Clinical Ethics and Legal Liability,'' unpublished.

4. Dianne Craig-Clark, ''Bouvia Names Ethics Committee Members in Malpractice Suit,'' *Medical Ethics Advisor* 2 (December 1986): 153–55.

5. Joy D. Skeel and Donnie J. Self, ''An Emprical Study of the Roles of Medical Ethicists in the Clinical Setting,'' unpublished.

6. Areen, ''Legal Implications of Ethics Consultation.''

7. ''Malpractice Crisis Said to Need Medical Solutions,'' *Skin and Allergy News*, August 1984:14.

8. American Medical Association, *Professional Liability in the 1980's* (Chicago: American Medical Association, 1985).

9. ''Spastic Quadriplegia Resulting from Unnecessary Surgery on Mother Late in Pregnancy,'' *Medical Malpractice Verdicts, Settlements and Experts* 2 (August 1986): 21–22.

10. ''Failure to Examine Records Prior to Administration of Anesthesia,'' *Medical Malpractice Verdicts, Settlements and Experts* 2 (August 1986): 3–4; ''Failure to Order Asthma Medication on Emergency Basis,'' *Medical Malpractice Verdicts, Settlements and Experts* 2 (August 1986): 17; ''Failure to Diagnose Epidural Hematoma,'' *Medical Liability Reporter* 8 (August 1986): 921–22.

11. "Delivery Turned Over to Physician Who Had Not Practiced Obstetrics Full Time Since 1971," *Medical Malpractice Verdicts, Settlements and Experts* 2 (August 1986): 22.

12. Claudia J. Postell, "Clergy Malpractice: An Emerging Field of Law," *Trial* 21 (December 1985): 91–93; "Suing Clergymen for Malpractice," *Time*, January 12, 1981, p. 75.

13. Max Maguire, personal communication, December 1986.

14. Donnie J. Self, "Methodological Considerations for Medical Ethics," *Science, Medicine and Man* 1 (1974): 201.

15. E.M. Adams, "The Academic Revolution," *Modern Age* 13 (Summer 1969): 270–76.

Chapter 35

The Patient's Choice of Care: Suggested Hospital Policies

Jack C. Siebe

Physicians, administrators, and medical ethicists want to do what's best for the critically ill or dying patient. But each one's interpretation of what's best leads to criticism by the others, creating a terrible situation for the patient.

The physician sees the traditional medical prerogatives weakened by administrative and ethical intrusion. Yet health law, economic considerations, and patients' rights modify paternalistic medical practice patterns.

The administrator sees the medical ethicist and physician interfering with hospital operational decisions and thereby adversely affecting economic planning. But someone must defend patients' rights and the doctor-patient relationship, even though such issues may not be cost effective.

The medical ethicist speculates that it would be better if pure logic and humanistic behavior governed the principles of patient care. However, the physician, the patient, and hospital administrator are bound together by the issues of self-concern, mutual trust, and a fiduciary relationship serving the interest of all parties.

Despite the conflicting opinions of what's best for a critically ill or dying patient, one fact emerges. What's best should be decided by that patient and expressed as a choice of care statement. Thus, every hospital should have a policy regarding a patient's right to choose or to refuse treatment. Since many states have passed living will legislation, a relevant patient's choice of care policy is mandatory. But whether or not the patient's choice of care statement is in the form of a living will (as legislated by some states), it is basically a declaration of the patient's intent and should be given great weight by the physician and the hospital.

The physician and his patient should not allow a crisis situation to arise. They should agree about how to resolve medical ethical problems, making important treatment decisions early in the hospital stay.[1] Moving this decision-making process forward in time facilitates full and open discussion of the issues, involves the patient and the patient's family, and reduces the risk of future misunderstanding. Unnecessary and unwanted treatment can be avoided, patient discomfort can be reduced, and money can be saved.

There is some logic in asking for a choice of care statement during the admission process. It's just one more routine, but it sets the stage for future conversation.

It is important that a physician review a patient's choice of care statement, as it is related to the patient's condition and available treatment options. Possible risks and hoped-for outcomes should be explored fully. This discourse can be prologue to a written living will if the choice of care statement is formulated in accordance with applicable state statutes.[2]

Subsequently, a physician should be very sensitive to the patient's need to talk further. When that patient asks ''Am I dying?'' the time may be near for conversation. The question, ''Am I going to die?'' signals an immediate need for discussion to take place: the patient senses death.

Appendix 39-A suggests a hospital policy blending a living will with a patient's choice of care statement. The policy allows any patient to make a *life prolonging procedures declaration*. This is a request that any and all procedures or tests be done to preserve life at all costs. Additionally, it supports a critically ill and deteriorating patient's choice of *supportive therapy*, e.g., forgoing cardiopulmonary resuscitation in the event of cardiopulmonary arrest. Similarly, it permits a patient who has reached a permanent irreversible vegetative state of life to select *terminal care orders* and forgo medical treatments which only prolong dying. Finally, it provides for the competent patient to specify *do not resuscitate*. This option limits treatment alternatives should the patient be faced with an acute life-threatening condition which meets the criteria for do not resuscitate.

Although the physician has a moral, if not a legal, obligation to discuss choice of care options with a patient, the physician may not be obligated to carry them out if the physician has strong objections, if the patient's choice of care statement is not a valid living will, or if the physician has reason to believe that the patient was not competent at the time of the declaration. However, if the living will is valid and the patient is competent, a physician must honor it or transfer the patient to a physician who will honor it.[3]

DEFAULT MODE

If there is no choice of care statement or the patient is not competent, the physician's safest course of action is to assume that the patient wants all available treatments to preserve life, unless it can be clearly documented otherwise. If this documentation involves the concept of substituted judgment, it injects legal issues into the decision-making process.

Substituted judgment is a matter of inferring what a patient would have wanted if the patient had made a valid choice of care statement. Any decision made for this patient should be based on any prior statements or expressed wishes that he or she may have made previously.[4]

If the substituted judgment concept is applied, a physician should attempt to ascertain the patient's intent by consulting with persons readily available, as suggested in Appendix 35-E. It is important to tell these people the nature of the patient's condition, the options and availability of treatments, and the risks and outcomes of these treatments. It is wise for a physician to recommend a level of care based on a desired outcome, which allows the family or other significant persons to decide for the patient by applying the patient's personal values to the present situation. Appropriate documentation of the discussion and the decision reached must be included in the patient's chart. Further, a corroborating medical opinion recorded in the chart is advisable in these instances.

Twenty years ago, the terms *ordinary* and *extraordinary* were used to characterize treatments. An ordinary treatment was not considered to be burdensome to a dying patient either spiritually, physically, emotionally, or economically. Conversely, extraordinary treatments were always considered to be burdensome to the patient.

Through years of usage, the meanings of the terms changed. Ordinary treatments came to mean required treatments. Extraordinary treatments came to mean unusual treatment modalities not really required; they were optional and served only to prolong dying. The confusion of terminology is understandable. Considering today's highly technical medical environment, what is *not* unusual, extraordinary, or burdensome in one way or another?

Recently, the courts and medical ethicists have come to favor the concept of proportionality in their discussions about treatments and their outcomes. Since the outcome of an action can be desirable or undesirable in proportion to the reason for taking that action, it follows that an action such as a treatment can be decided upon in proportion to the desired outcome.

The goal of proportionality of treatment is a clearly defined therapeutic endpoint which should produce the desired outcome without being burdensome either spiritually, physically, emotionally, or economically to the patient, the physician, or the hospital.

Treatments given to the critically ill or terminal patient should be proportional to the desired outcome and can be classified as obligatory or optional. Selected treatments which are not burdensome are considered to be *obligatory* for the physical and spiritual comfort of the patient. All other treatments, whether or not they are burdensome, are considered to be *optional*.

POLICY DISCUSSION

Appendix 35-B, C, and D suggest hospital policies which present practical applications of the proportionality concept of obligatory and optional treatments. In these policies, the proportionality of the action contemplated and the degree of the patient's illness are factors in determining the outcome.[5] Of necessity, they are criteria-based and suggest categories for obligatory and optional treatments.

For example, a critically ill patient in deteriorating health has elected to not be "coded" in the event of cardiopulmonary collapse. After a clear and open discussion with the patient, a physician may write supportive therapy orders, documenting the discussion, the patient's competence, and the deteriorating nature of the patient's illness. A written corroborating medical consultation is desirable.

The supportive therapy orders policy suggested by Appendix 35-B would obviate the need only for cardiopulmonary resuscitation procedures. Supportive therapy orders would not obviate the need to provide selected optional treatments, as well as obligatory treatments, to assure the critically ill and deteriorating patient's physical and spiritual comfort.

In the event that the process of deterioration progresses to the terminal stage of an illness, it may be more appropriate for a physician to discontinue supportive therapy orders, writing terminal care orders instead. Documentation of the patient's wishes in the matter, the patient's competence, the terminal nature of the illness, and corroborating medical consultation should be included in the patient's chart.

The *terminal care orders* suggested by Appendix 35-C preclude the use of all therapeutic or emergency procedures to maintain life functions. No "code" should be called or resuscitation instituted on a terminal patient while such orders are in effect. Terminal care orders imply that care can be given outside of intensive care units. Terminal care orders obviate the necessity of providing optional treatments which are not medically warranted and serve only to delay dying. Terminal care orders do not obviate the need for obligatory treatments which provide physical and spiritual comfort for the dying patient.

A patient does not need to be dying to select do not resuscitate as a choice of care. Any competent patient can choose to limit future treatment in the event that he or she becomes critically ill, deteriorates, and ultimately needs the criteria for do not resuscitate orders to be written. For example, a choice of do not resuscitate may be the "living will" of a healthy young adult who fears the consequence of massive head trauma (e.g., being brain dead but kept on a respirator). In another example, a chronically ill patient chooses do not resuscitate rather than undergo another aggressive resuscitation, followed by intubation, cannulation, catheterization, and tube feeding during many uncomfortable weeks of intensive unit care.

After discussing a do not resuscitate declaration with a patient, a physician should write such orders. Further, the physician should document the conversation, including the patient's understanding that when his or her condition meets the criteria, no cardiopulmonary resuscitation will be initiated while a written do not resuscitate order is in effect. A corroborating medical consultation should be recorded in the chart at the appropriate time.

Appendix 35-D suggests hospital policy for *do not resuscitate orders* and outlines the criteria for judging when such orders are appropriate. These orders may be written for patients who are in a critical care unit, and they do not obviate the need for critical care other than cardiopulmonary resuscitation. They do not obviate either the need for optional treatments that can be clearly documented as medically necessary or the need for those obligatory therapies that assure physical and spiritual comfort for the patient.

A physician should initially (and frequently thereafter) evaluate all written orders which limit medical care to assure that they are consistent with the patient's condition and desires. The pastoral care service and the nursing staff can be generally helpful in this concurrent review.

If a patient should unexpectedly improve or recover, a physician should fully inform the patient of the change of condition and provide an opportunity to amend the choice of care decision. Appendixes 35-B, C, and D suggest that if his patient is not physically or mentally capable of making a decision, a physician should consult with the family or other significant persons before writing any orders that limit medical care or changing them afterward.[6]

It is important for every hospital to have a policy concerned with limiting treatments and procedures that are not medically indicated and are burdensome to the dying patient, the physician, and the hospital. This policy should state that the patient's medical care will be proportional to the desired outcome for such care and does not violate the ethical and philosophical directives of the sponsoring organization. Appendix 35-E is a policy statement that satisfies these objectives.

The temptation to use the appended policies without revision is to be avoided. Each hospital and its medical staff is dynamically different and each should develop its own policies, using these suggested policies as prototypes.

It is important to remember that a policy states an authoritarian viewpoint. A policy is not a procedure: It specifies no method for implementation. Procedures to implement policies should be generated by the appropriate hospital administrative units in cooperation with the hospital medical staff.

It is further suggested that legal council review all policies and procedures to be certain that they do not violate applicable state law.

NOTES

1. Ronald L. Stephens, "Do Not Resuscitate Orders: Ensuring the Patient's Participation," *Journal of the American Medical Association* 255 (1986): 240–41.

2. American Hospital Association, Special Committee on Biomedical Ethics, *Values in Conflict: Resolving Ethical Issues in Hospital Care* (Chicago: American Hospital Association, 1985), 67–74.

3. B. Schoen-Sefert and James F. Childress, "How Much Should the Cancer Patient Know and Decide?" *Ca: A Journal for Clinicians*, March-April 1986: 92.

4. Catholic brother Charles Fox, aged 83, suffered hypoxia during surgery, which resulted in irreversible coma. His close friend, Father Eichner, petitioned the court to terminate Brother Fox's life-support systems based on his often expressed desire not to be so treated if such circumstances arose. The court found that it was proper to discontinue life support in these circumstances. In re Eichner, 52 N.Y. 2d 363, 420 N.E. 2d 64. (1981).

5. Schoen-Sefert and Childress, "How Much," 90.

6. R. Steinbrook and B. Lo, "Decision Making for Incompetent Patients by Designated Proxy: California's New Law," *New England Journal of Medicine* 310 (1984): 1598–1601.

REFERENCES

Bedell, S.E., and T.L. Delbanco. "Choices about Cardiopulmonary Resuscitation in the Hospital: When Do Physicians Talk with Patients?" *New England Journal of Medicine* 310 (1984): 1089–93.

Bedell, S.E., D. Pelle, P.L. Maker and P.D. Cleary. "Do Not Resuscitate Orders for Critically Ill Patients in the Hospital: How Are They Used and What Is Their Impact?" *Journal of the American Medical Association* 256 (1986): 233–37.

President's Commission for the Study of Ethical Problems in Medicine and Biomedical and Behavioral Research. *Deciding to Forego Life Sustaining Treatment.* Washington, D.C.: GPO, 1983.

————. *Making Health Care Decisions.* Vol. 1. Washington, D.C.: GPO, 1982.

Robertson, J.A. and American Civil Liberties Union. *Rights of the Critically Ill.* New York: Ballinger Publishing Company, 1983.

Veach, R.M. "Deciding against Resuscitation: Encouraging Signs and Potential Dangers." *Journal of the American Medical Association* 253 (1985): 77–78.

Younger, S.J., S. Lewandowski, D.K. McClish, B.W. Juknialis, C. Coulton, and E.T. Bartlett. "Do Not Resuscitate Orders: Incidence and Implications in a Medical Intensive Care Unit." *Journal of the American Medical Association* 253 (1985): 54–57.

Zimmerman, J.E., W.A. Knaus, S.M. Sharpe, A.S. Anderson, E.A. Draper, and D.P. Wagner. "The Use and Implication of Do Not Resuscitate Orders in the Intensive Care Unit." *Journal of The American Medical Association* 255 (1986): 351–56.

Appendix 35-A

Patient's Choice of Care

Policy

A uniform method will be followed in determining the hospitalized patient's choice of care in compliance with Indiana P.L. 176-1985.

Explanation

Competent adults have the right to control the decisions relating to their own medical care, including decisions to have life-prolonging medical, surgical, or emergency treatments or procedures implemented, withheld, or withdrawn. Health care providers are protected from civil or criminal liability if they withhold or withdraw such treatments or procedures from a patient who has refused them.

For every hospital admission, it is appropriate to determine what, if any, written or verbally expressed wishes a patient may have regarding his or her care in the hospital. To accomplish this, the competent patient will be asked about his or her choice of care at the time of hospital admission.

In the case of a minor patient or a patient incapable of making his or her own choice, the responsibility for choice rests with the person recognized as being morally and legally responsible for the patient, or in certain circumstances, with whomever is designated by the court to assume responsibility in this matter.

In all instances, the patient's expressed choice of care, as well as the communication requirements and objective criteria appropriate to the patient's choice of care, shall be complied with.

The attending physician has the obligation to tell the patient, family, and/or significant individuals, in language they can reasonably be expected to understand, about the nature of the patient's condition, the options for and availability of applicable treatment and care, possible risks, and hoped-for results from treatment.

If the patient makes a *life-prolonging procedures declaration* (i.e., a request that any and all therapies, treatments, procedures, or tests be done to preserve life at all costs), that course of action will be followed.

If the patient chooses supportive therapy, the *supportive therapy orders* policy will be implemented.

If the patient chooses terminal care, the *terminal care orders* policy will be implemented.

If the patient chooses do not resuscitate, the *do not resuscitate* policy will be implemented.

The *patient's choice of care statement* is to be treated as presumptive evidence of the patient's intent. Any choice of care statement is binding upon the physician but is not meant to require the physician to enter into a relationship against his or her will. The physician has an obligation to discuss choice of care options with the patient. The physician is not obligated to carry them out if the physician has strong objections.

When the physician refuses to honor a patient's choice of care statement, the physician must transfer the patient to a physician who will honor it unless (1) the patient's choice of care statement is not a valid living will, (2) the physician has a reason to believe that the patient was not competent at the time of the declaration, or (3) there is evidence that the patient no longer intends the declaration to be enforced.

If the patient is not competent or cannot communicate, the physician shall attempt to ascertain the patient's intent by consulting with those of the following persons who are reasonably available:

- a court-appointed guardian
- person(s) whom the patient has designated in writing to be responsible for his or her treatment decisions
- the patient's spouse
- a majority of the patient's adult children
- parents of the patient
- a majority of the patient's adult siblings
- a member of the clergy who has firsthand knowledge of the patient's intent

The patient's general condition should be assessed at the time of admission and frequently thereafter. If the patient unexpectedly improves or recovers, the physician should inform the competent patient of the change of condition and provide the patient with the opportunity to change the choice of care statement. When the patient is not competent or cannot communicate, the physician should attempt to ascertain the patient's intent, as aforementioned.

If the patient's condition should deteriorate significantly or if the patient's condition becomes terminal, the patient, the family, and/or aforementioned significant individuals have the right to know and to choose what will and will not be done for the patient, as appropriate.

A patient's choice of care statement is valid if it meets the following three criteria:

1. The patient must be 18 years of age and competent to make the declaration.
2. The declaration must be witnessed by two persons who have no interest in the patient's estate.
3. The declaration must be made part of the patient's medical care record.

The declaration has no effect if the patient is pregnant.

The patient's choice of care statement may be revoked in writing, verbally, by destruction of the document, or through any other kind of communication the patient makes with the physician that is duly witnessed.

Documentation Requirements

Admission Documentation

Documentation as to the existence of the patient's written statement concerning choice of treatment (or choice to forgo certain types of treatment) must be a part of the patient's medical record.

As a part of the admission procedure, the following questions will be asked of this patient and recorded.

- Do you have any written instructions for your physician concerning the type of care you wish to receive in this hospital? Yes _____ No _____
- If you have such instructions, would you please furnish the original or a copy for your hospital records? Yes _____ No _____

Physician Documentation

A statement must be recorded that the patient and/or family have been properly and adequately informed regarding the condition of the patient, the agreed upon treatment, and the party responsible for the decision.

A printed form (Exhibit 35-A-1) may be used. It is suitable for this statement when the questions are answered, with the form dated and signed by the physician.

Alternately, a written, dated, and signed progress note may be used if the same questions are asked and recorded.

Duration of the Patient's Choice of Care Statement

A properly written and witnessed choice of care statement will stand until changed by the competent adult patient. Any new declaration by the patient, communicated by any intelligible means and duly witnessed, can invalidate or amend any previous choice of care declaration. In the event the patient is not competent, any changes must be discussed with the nearest family relative, keeping in mind the primacy of any prior statements or previously expressed wishes of the patient.

Written and Verbal Orders Requirements

Reference is made to the appropriate written requirements of attendant policies:

- Supportive Therapy Orders
- Terminal Care Orders
- Do Not Resuscitate

Exhibit 35-A-1 Disclosure of Information Verification Form

---

1. The patient, the family, and significant other persons have been properly and adequately informed (to the extent possible) regarding the condition of the patient.
   Patient:
   Yes _____   No _____
   If not, why?

   Family:
   Yes _____   No _____
   If not, why?

2. The patient has written a statement concerning a positive choice of treatment (a negative choice to forgo certain treatments) and wishes to make or has already made that written statement part of the medical record.
   Yes _____   No _____
   If not, why?

3. The patient has a *living will* or a *patient's choice of care statement* which I have discussed with the patient.
   Yes _____   No _____

4. The patient is not competent or cannot communicate. The family or significant other persons have made a treatment decision, applying the concept of substituted judgment.
   Yes _____   No _____
   What decision?

5. The patient, family, or other significant persons wish to consult with the pastoral care service about the choice of care issue.
   Yes _____   No _____

_____   _____
Physician's Signature   Date

Communication Requirements

When appropriate, a patient's choice of care statement might be suggested by the physician to a patient who has not written such a document. The document must be formulated according to the directions as contained in Indiana P.L. 176-1985, Living Wills and Life-Prolonging Procedures Act, on file in the pastoral care office.

When a patient has made a choice of care statement, the physician must discuss the implications with the competent patient and the family. When the patient is not competent or cannot communicate, the physician shall attempt to ascertain the patient's intent by consulting with persons readily available, as aforementioned.

In the event that the patient is a minor (under 18), any changes need be discussed only with the minor's parent or legally appointed guardian. In the event of divorce of the minor's parents, the physician should discuss any changes with the parent who has been awarded custody. The parent(s) may decide if the minor should be told of any changes and who should tell him or her.

Reference is made to the communications requirements of the attendant policies.

Policies Referenced

- Limiting Medical Care
- Supportive Therapy Orders
- Terminal Care Orders
- Do Not Resuscitate

Appendix 35-B

Supportive Therapy Orders

Policy

A uniform method will be followed for the writing of supportive therapy orders.

Explanation

Under certain circumstances, it becomes appropriate to enter *supportive therapy orders* in a patient's medical record. The orders preclude the use of all therapeutic measures or emergency procedures to maintain life functions and indicate that there will not be a "code" called or initiated on a critically ill patient in deteriorating health while this written order is in effect.

In all such cases, appropriate documentation and communication requirements, as well as objective criteria for the determination of a critically ill patient in deteriorating health, shall be complied with.

Supportive therapy orders should be initially and frequently reviewed to ensure that they are consistent with the patient's condition and desires. The nursing staff and the pastoral care service can be generally helpful in the review process. If a patient unexpectedly improves or recovers, the physician should inform the competent patient of the change of condition and provide the patient with the opportunity to withdraw the request for supportive therapy orders.

If the patient is not competent or cannot communicate, the physician shall attempt to ascertain the patient's intent by consulting with those of the following persons who are reasonably available:

- a court-appointed guardian
- person(s) whom the patient has designated in writing to be responsible for his or her treatment decisions
- the patient's spouse
- a majority of the patient's adult children
- parents of the patient

- a majority of the patient's adult siblings
- a member of the clergy who has firsthand knowledge of the patient's intent

In the event that the deterioration process progresses to the terminal stage of illness, it is appropriate to discontinue supportive therapy orders, writing terminal care orders instead, with the competent patient's consent. If the patient is not competent or cannot communicate, the physician shall attempt to ascertain the patient's intent, as aforementioned.

Supportive therapy *does not obviate* the necessity of providing selected optional therapies and obligatory therapies to assure the critically ill and deteriorating patient's physical and spiritual comfort.

Selected optional therapies and procedures which can be considered to be medically beneficial include, but are not limited to, the following:

- diagnostic procedures of value
- airway maintenance and ventilator assisted respiration
- hyperalimentation and IV fluids p.r.n.
- oncologic medications and treatments
- dialysis
- blood and blood products

Obligatory therapies include, but are not limited to, the following:

- food and drink by mouth, if tolerated
- bodily cleanliness, including oral and eye care
- bodily repositioning
- maintenance of bodily warmth
- appropriate pain medication and treatments
- verbal and tactile communication
- spiritual and psychological care

Definitions

A patient who is critically ill and in deteriorating health is defined jointly by these criteria:

- The patient's condition has been determined to be irreversible and irreparable based upon ordinary medical standards as generally practiced and understood in this hospital and by this medical community.
- There are no known therapeutic measures or emergency treatments which offer reasonable expectation of reversing or curing the condition.
- The patient's condition has progressed beyond the existing knowledge to retard the patient's deterioration.

Supportive therapy is defined as the withholding of the optional therapeutic measure of cardiopulmonary resuscitation in the event of cardiopulmonary arrest in a critically ill and deteriorating patient.

Documentation Requirements

Written Orders

All supportive therapy orders must be written and signed by the physician on the physician's order sheet in the patient's medical record.

Writing this order on any other document (e.g., Kardex) will be in violation of policy.

Failure to write supportive therapy orders in the chart will result in appropriate optional therapeutic measures to sustain life being carried out, including cardiopulmonary resuscitation.

Improper terminology will be in violation of this policy (e.g., *no code, slow code, do not intubate*).

Verbal Orders

Verbal or telephone supportive therapy orders can be received only from a licensed physician and must be witnessed by two people, one of whom is a registered nurse. Each must individually hear the order and document it on the physician's order sheet in the medical record.

These verbal or telephone orders must be authenticated and countersigned by the medical staff member issuing the order within eighteen (18) hours after the receipt of such order.

Duration of Orders

Properly written (or properly signed) verbal orders will stand until changed by the physician.

The physician's order sheet will be stamped daily to read "supportive therapy orders in effect."

Physician Documentation

A progress note entry, attendant to the order itself, will be written which includes the following information:

- a short description of the patient's condition corroborating the supportive therapy orders
- reference to any consultations which corroborate the supportive therapy orders
- references to any discussions about the supportive therapy with the patient or his or her family

Communication Requirements

Any supportive therapy recommendations should be discussed with the patient or members of the family. The physician should realize that members of the patient's family do not necessarily have the right to impose their wishes or decisions about the patient's care upon either the patient or the physician.

In communicating with families, the physician and nurses shall consult with the pastoral care service. Pastoral care is a resource for help when difficulties arise in discussing the limiting of medical care.

If the patient is a competent adult, the recommendation limiting medical care need only be discussed with him or her. In the event that the patient is not competent or cannot communicate, the recommendation to limit medical care is to be discussed with the family or other significant persons, keeping in mind the primacy of any prior statements or previously expressed wishes of the patient.

In all cases, before writing orders which limit medical care in the chart of an adult patient who is not competent or who cannot communicate, the physician shall attempt to ascertain the patient's intent by consulting with those of the following persons who are reasonably available:

- a court-appointed guardian
- person(s) whom the patient has designated in writing to be responsible for his or her treatment decisions
- the patient's spouse
- a majority of the patient's adult children
- parents of the patient
- a majority of the patient's adult siblings
- a member of the clergy who has firsthand knowledge of the patient's intent

The physician should obtain their agreement before writing orders limiting medical care. If it is impossible to contact the family or others, and a reasonable effort has been made, the physician may rely on his or her own judgment in writing such orders. The physician should document the fact that the effort was made to contact the family or others.

In the event that the patient is a minor (under 18), the recommendation to limit medical care need be discussed only with the minor's parent(s) or legally appointed guardian. In the event of divorce of the minor's parents, the physician should discuss the recommendation with the parent awarded custody. The parent(s) should decide if the minor should be told and who should tell him or her.

Policies Referenced

- Limiting Medical Care
- Patient's Choice of Care
- Terminal Care Orders
- Do Not Resuscitate

Appendix 35-C

Terminal Care Orders

Policy

A uniform method will be followed for the writing of terminal care orders.

Explanation

Under certain circumstances, it becomes appropriate to enter *terminal care orders* in a patient's medical record. These orders preclude the use of all therapeutic measures or emergency procedures to maintain life functions and indicate that there will not be a "code" called or initiated on a terminally ill patient while this written order is in effect.

In all such cases, appropriate documentation and communication requirements, as well as objective criteria for the determination of a terminal illness, shall be complied with.

Terminal care orders should be initially and frequently reviewed to ensure that they are consistent with the patient's condition and desires. The nursing staff and the pastoral care service can be generally helpful in the review process. If a patient unexpectedly improves or recovers, the physician should inform the competent patient of the change of condition and provide the patient with the opportunity to withdraw the request for terminal care orders.

If the patient is not competent or cannot communicate, the physician shall attempt to ascertain the patient's intent by consulting with those of the following persons who are reasonably available:

- a court-appointed guardian
- person(s) whom the patient has designated in writing to be responsible for his or her treatment decisions
- the patient's spouse
- a majority of the patient's adult children
- parents of the patient
- a majority of the patient's adult siblings
- a member of the clergy who has firsthand knowledge of the patient's intent

Terminal care orders obviate the need for special unit care (e.g., I.C.U. or C.C.U.).

Terminal care orders obviate the necessity of providing optional therapeutic measures or emergency procedures which are not medically warranted and serve only to prolong the process of dying.

Such optional procedures include, but are not limited to, the following:

- cardiopulmonary resuscitation
- diagnostic procedures
- airway intubation and ventilator assisted respiration
- hyperalimentation and IV fluids p.r.n.
- oncologic medications and treatments
- dialysis
- blood and blood products

Terminal care orders do not obviate the need to provide obligatory therapies to assure the terminal patient physical and spiritual comfort. Such obligatory therapies include, but are not limited to, the following:

- food and drink by mouth if tolerated
- minimal parenteral sustenance or IV fluids to prevent hunger and thirst
- bodily cleanliness including oral and eye care
- bodily repositioning
- maintenance of bodily warmth
- appropriate pain medication and treatments
- airway suction
- oxygen when needed by face mask or nasal cannula
- verbal and tactile communication
- spiritual and psychological care

Definitions

A patient with a terminal illness is defined jointly by these criteria:

- The patient's condition is such that death is imminent, based upon ordinary medical standards as generally practiced and understood in this hospital and by this medical community.
- There are no known therapeutic measures or emergency treatments which offer reasonable expectation of remission or cure of the condition.
- There is no treatment which offers any reasonable alternative to certain death.
- There is no rational basis found in ordinary medical practice standards to render further or additional therapy or to undertake emergency procedures or new treatments.

Terminal care is defined as the withholding of optional therapeutic measures or emergency procedures which are not medically warranted and serve only to prolong dying.

Documentation Requirements

Written Orders

All terminal care orders must be written and signed by the physician on the physician's order sheet in the patient's medical record.

Writing this order on any other document (e.g., Kardex) will be in violation of policy.

Failure to write terminal care orders in the chart will result in appropriate optional therapeutic measures to sustain life being carried out, including cardiopulmonary resuscitation.

Improper terminology will be in violation of this policy (e.g., *no code, slow code, do not intubate*).

Verbal Orders

Verbal or telephone terminal care orders can be received only from a licensed physician and must be witnessed by two people, one of whom is a registered nurse. Each must individually hear the order and document it on the physician's order sheet in the medical record.

These verbal or telephone orders must be authenticated and countersigned by the medical staff member issuing the order within eighteen (18) hours after the receipt of such order.

Duration of Orders

Properly written (or properly signed) verbal orders will stand until changed by the physician.

The physician's order sheet will be stamped daily to read "terminal care orders in effect."

Physician Documentation

A progress note entry, attendant to the order itself, will be written which includes the following information:

- a short description of the patient's condition corroborating the terminal care orders
- reference to any consultations which corroborate the terminal care orders
- references to any discussions of the terminal care orders with the patient or his family

Communication Requirements

Any terminal care recommendations should be discussed with the patient or members of the family. The physician should realize that members of the patient's family do not necessarily have the right to impose their wishes or decisions about the patient's care upon either the patient or the physician.

In communicating with families, the physician and nurses shall consult with the pastoral care service. Pastoral care is a resource for help when difficulties arise in discussing the limiting of medical care.

If the patient is a competent adult, the recommendation limiting medical care need only be discussed with him or her. In the event that the patient is not competent or cannot communicate, the recommendation to limit medical care is to be discussed with the family or other significant persons, keeping in mind the primacy of any prior statements or wishes the patient may have expressed previously.

In all cases, before writing orders which limit medical care in the chart of an adult patient who is not competent or who cannot communicate, the physician shall attempt to ascertain the patient's intent by consulting with those of the following persons who are reasonably available:

- a court-appointed guardian
- person(s) whom the patient has designated in writing to be responsible for his or her treatment decisions
- the patient's spouse
- a majority of the patient's adult children
- parents of the patient
- a majority of the patient's adult siblings
- a member of the clergyman who has firsthand knowledge of the patient's intent

The physician should obtain their agreement before writing orders limiting medical care. If it is impossible to contact the family or others, and a reasonable effort has been made, the physician may rely on his or her own judgment in writing such orders. The physician should document the fact that the effort was made to contact the family or others.

In the event that the patient is a minor (under 18), the recommendation to limit medical care need be discussed only with the minor's parent(s) or legally appointed guardian. In the event of divorce of the minor's parents, the physician should discuss the recommendation with the parent awarded custody. The parent(s) should decide if the minor should be told and who should tell him or her.

Policies Referenced

- Limiting Medical Care
- Patient's Choice of Care
- Supportive Therapy Orders
- Do Not Resuscitate

Appendix 35-D

Do Not Resuscitate

Policy

A uniform method will be followed for the writing of do not resuscitate.

Explanation

Under certain circumstances, it becomes appropriate to enter *do not resuscitate* in a patient's medical record. This order precludes the use of all therapeutic measures or emergency procedures to maintain life functions and indicates that there will not be a "code" called or initiated on a terminally ill patient while this written order is in effect.

In all such cases, appropriate documentation and communication requirements, as well as objective criteria for the determination of a terminally ill patient for whom do not resuscitate is appropriate, shall be complied with.

Alternatives to do not resuscitate orders may be more appropriate:

- Supportive therapy orders may be written for the critically ill and deteriorating patient. The supportive therapy orders policy applies.

- Terminal care orders may be written for the patient whose illness has reached a terminal stage. The terminal care orders policy applies.

- The do not resuscitate order may be written in response to a competent patient's "living will." The patient's choice of care policy applies.

The do not resuscitate order should be initially and frequently reviewed to ensure that it is consistent with the patient's condition and desires. The nursing staff and the pastoral care service can be generally helpful in the review process. If a patient unexpectedly improves or recovers, the physician should inform the competent patient of the change of condition and provide the patient with the opportunity to withdraw the request for do not resuscitate.

If the patient is not competent or cannot communicate, the physician shall attempt to ascertain the patient's intent by consulting with those of the following persons who are reasonably available:

- a court-appointed guardian
- person(s) whom the patient has designated in writing to be responsible for his or her treatment decisions
- the patient's spouse
- a majority of the patient's adult children
- parents of the patient
- a majority of the patient's adult siblings
- a member of the clergy who has firsthand knowledge of the patient's intent

The do not resuscitate order obviates only the necessity of providing cardiopulmonary resuscitation and related emergency procedures which are incompatible with this order, i.e., those that serve only to prolong the process of dying.

The do not resuscitate order does not obviate the necessity of providing selected optional therapies to assure the critically ill patient comprehensive medical care which is not incompatible with the order.

Selected optional therapies which can be clearly documented as medically beneficial and are not incompatible with a do not resuscitate order include, but are not limited, to the following:

- diagnostic procedures
- airway maintenance and ventilator assisted respiration
- hyperalimentation and IV fluids p.r.n.
- oncologic medications and treatments
- dialysis
- blood and blood products

The do not resuscitate order does not obviate the need for critical unit care if it can be clearly documented that such care is medically beneficial.

The do not resuscitate order does not obviate the need to provide obligatory therapies to assure the critically ill patient physical and spiritual comfort. Such obligatory therapies include, but are not limited to, the following:

- food and drink by mouth, if tolerated
- minimal parenteral sustenance or IV fluids to prevent hunger and thirst
- bodily cleanliness, including oral and eye care
- bodily repositioning
- maintenance of bodily warmth
- appropriate pain medication and treatments
- airway suction
- oxygen when needed by face mask or nasal cannula
- verbal and tactile communication
- spiritual and psychological care

Definitions

A critically ill patient for whom do not resuscitate is appropriate is defined jointly by these criteria:

- The patient's condition is such that death is imminent, based upon ordinary medical standards as generally practiced and understood in this hospital and by this medical community.
- There are no known therapeutic measures or emergency treatments which offer reasonable expectation of remission or cure of the condition.
- There is no treatment which offers any reasonable alternative to certain death.
- There is no rational basis found in ordinary medical practice standards to render further or additional therapy or to undertake emergency procedures or new treatments.

Terminal care is defined as the withholding of optional therapeutic measures or emergency procedures which are not medically warranted and serve only to prolong dying.

Documentation Requirements

Written Orders

The do not resuscitate order must be written and signed by the physician on the physician's order sheet in the patient's medical record.

Writing this order on any other document (e.g., Kardex) will be in violation of policy.

Failure to write do not resuscitate orders in the chart will result in appropriate optional therapeutic measures to sustain life being carried out, including cardiopulmonary resuscitation.

Improper terminology will be in violation of this policy (e.g., *no code, slow code, do not intubate*).

Verbal Orders

A verbal or telephone do not resuscitate order can be received only from a licensed physician and must be witnessed by two people, one of whom is a registered nurse. Each must individually hear the order and document it on the physician's order sheet in the medical record.

This verbal or telephone order must be authenticated and countersigned by the medical staff member issuing the order within eighteen (18) hours after the receipt of such order.

Duration of Orders

Properly written (or properly signed) verbal orders will stand until changed by the physician.

The physician's order sheet will be stamped daily to read ''do not resuscitate in effect.''

Physician Documentation

A progress note entry, attendant to the order itself, will be written which includes the following information:

- a short description of the patient's condition corroborating the do not resuscitate order
- reference to any consultations which corroborate the do not resuscitate order
- discussions about the do not resuscitate order

Communication Requirements

Any do not resuscitate recommendations should be discussed with the patient or members of the family. The physician should realize that members of the patient's family do not necessarily have the right to impose their wishes or decisions about the patient's care upon either the patient or the physician.

In communicating with families, the physician and nurses shall consult with the pastoral care service. Pastoral care is a resource for help when difficulties arise in discussing the limiting of medical care.

If the patient is a competent adult, the recommendation limiting medical care need only be discussed with him or her. In the event that the patient is not competent or cannot communicate, the recommendation to limit medical care is to be discussed with the family or other significant persons, keeping in mind the primacy of any prior statements or previously expressed wishes of the patient.

In all cases, before writing orders which limit medical care in the chart of an adult patient who is not competent or who cannot communicate, the physician shall attempt to ascertain the patient's intent by consulting with those of the following persons who are reasonably available:

- a court-appointed guardian
- person(s) whom the patient has designated in writing to be responsible for his or her treatment decisions
- the patient's spouse
- a majority of the patient's adult children
- parents of the patient
- a majority of the patient's adult siblings
- a member of the clergy who has firsthand knowledge of the patient's intent

The physician should obtain their agreement before writing orders limiting medical care. If it is impossible to contact the family or others, and a reasonable effort has been made, the physician may rely on his or her own judgment in writing such orders. The physician should document the fact that the effort was made to contact the family or others.

In the event that the patient is a minor (under 18), the recommendation to limit medical care need only be discussed with the minor's parent(s) or legally appointed guardian. In the event of divorce of the minor's parents, the physician should discuss the recommendation with the parent awarded custody. The parent(s) should decide if the minor should be told and who should tell him or her.

Policies Referenced

- Limiting Medical Care
- Patient's Choice of Care
- Supportive Therapy Orders
- Terminal Care Orders

Limiting Medical Care

Policy

This policy states our position concerning limiting treatments and procedures that are not medically indicated and are burdensome to dying patients, their physicians, and this facility.

We hold human life in high regard. We are prepared to do that which is reasonable to sustain life in the belief that patients' medical care should be proportional to the desired outcome for such care, in accordance with patients' wishes, and not violate the ethical or philosophical position of physicians and our sponsoring organization. To that end, mentally competent patients should be made aware of their condition so that they may share in decisions about treatment options. When patients are not mentally competent or cannot communicate, people who are readily available and close to a patient should be consulted to determine what the patient would want, keeping in mind any prior statements or wishes the patient may have expressed previously.

When discussing the limitation of medical care, patients and health care providers may need emotional and spiritual support. If requested, pastoral counseling will be made available.

We believe that sometimes it is better to let a patient die than to prolong his suffering through the use of medical technology. It may be acceptable to withhold or withdraw cardiopulmonary resuscitation and forgo medical treatments that only prolong dying. Appropriate times to consider discontinuing treatment are:

- when the patient believes that treatment is burdensome and not beneficial
- when the patient has reached a permanent, irreversible state and therapy is determined to be ineffective and medically useless

We believe that we have a duty to treat every patient and to do no harm. No therapy will be initiated without the expectation that its medical advantages outweigh its burdens. Accordingly, when medical care or emergency treatments designed to prolong life are withdrawn or withheld, certain optional procedures that are not medically necessary may be omitted. These optional procedures include but are not limited to:

- critical unit care and cardiac monitoring
- intubation and assisted ventilation
- the administration of blood and blood products
- hyperalimentation
- dialysis
- the administration of antibiotics
- laboratory studies
- radiologic and other diagnostic imaging procedures

This facility will provide the patient with spiritual and physical comfort. Certain obligatory procedures will be provided that include but are not limited to:

- airway maintenance
- oxygen by face mask or nasal catheter
- food and drink by mouth if tolerated
- medication and treatment for pain
- maintenance of body warmth
- bodily repositioning
- bodily cleanliness (including oral and eye care)
- verbal and tactile communication
- spiritual and psychological care

IMPLEMENTATION REQUIREMENTS

In cooperation with medical staff, nursing staff, the pastoral care service, and the risk management department, the hospital's administration will generate procedures to implement the policies referenced in this master policy.

Before the procedures are promulgated they will be subject to review by the biomedical ethics committee, the medical staff executive committee, and the hospital governance.

To oversee these administrative procedures, the biomedical ethics committee will establish a review subcommittee, which will comprise members of the nursing staff, the medical staff, the pastoral care service, and the risk management department. Additionally, the biomedical ethics committee will offer consultation to the parties involved when conflict arises from carrying out written orders involving cardiopulmonary resuscitation and the limitation of treatment designed to prolong life.

Each of the hospital's unit managers will be responsible for routinely informing the nursing service, pastoral care service, risk management department, and medical director that orders to limit life-prolonging treatment were given. When conflict arises from such orders, managers will immediately notify nursing service, who will in turn notify the pastoral care service and the medical director. If the problem cannot be easily resolved at this level, the biomedical ethics committee will be invited to consult with the principals in the conflict.

Every new employee will be oriented to these policies and procedures upon hire. Current employees will be reoriented annually.

Policies Referenced

- Patient's Choice of Care
- Supportive Therapy Orders
- Terminal Care Orders
- Do Not Resuscitate

Chapter 36

Ethical Issues of the AIDS Epidemic

Nancy Milliken and Ruth Greenblatt

The ethical issues surrounding the acquired immunodeficiency syndrome (AIDS) epidemic have been prominent since the initial description of AIDS in homosexual men during 1981.[1] AIDS has provoked claims of holy retribution, biologic warfare, and social stigmatization; not unlike what has occurred historically with other sexually transmitted diseases, such as syphilis early in the 20th century. As in times of previous epidemics, conflicts between individual rights and societal imperatives come to the forefront as public health authorities grapple with methods of epidemic control.

In the years since 1981, the term AIDS has become a part of the language of health in the United States. While the meaning of AIDS as a new and uniformly fatal illness is generally understood, the subtle implications of the disease have a much larger range of appreciation. To retroviral oncologists, AIDS represents the proof of the existence of tumors and immune deficiency due to transmissible agents; to the lay media, AIDS is a story that generates a high degree of public interest; and to the public, AIDS may represent a family tragedy, a frightening phenomenon that children must be protected from, or the just ends to poorly understood lifestyles. For public health officials and those who deal with the issue of AIDS on a day-to-day basis, AIDS is a sexually transmitted and fatal disease, two qualities which help to determine the myriad sociological, legal, and ethical implications that surround the disease.

Despite the relatively rapid pace in the development of a scientific understanding of AIDS, lay misconceptions plague both medical experts and patients. As much a characteristic as any clinical manifestation of the disease, the rapid rate of change in AIDS information and technology often makes discussion of ethical issues moot within the time required for most publication or policy implementation. Policy and ethical considerations of AIDS must take into account potential development of new screening methods and treatment modalities.

AIDS: THE ENTITY

AIDS is a disease that cripples the cell-mediated immune system, often in previously healthy adults. Intensive scientific effort has resulted in identification of the etiologic agent, the human immunodeficiency virus or HIV (formerly known as human T-cell lymphotropic virus type III [HTLV-III], lymphadenopathy virus [LAV], and AIDS retrovirus [ARV]. Knowledge of the etiology of AIDS has led the way to methods for detection of individuals who have been exposed to HIV and has facilitated scientific investigation of the epidemiology and manifestations of HIV infection. It is now clear that HIV is a new virus and has been introduced to populations worldwide. Transmission of HIV and the incidence of AIDS is rapidly increasing, resulting in the most significant pandemic of the 20th century.

It is the biology of HIV itself that determines the nature of this epidemic, the outcome of the infection, and the prospects for treatment or for the development of an effective vaccine. Human behaviors, particularly sexual and drug use behaviors, determine the growth rate and proportions of the epidemic. HIV is a fragile virus, sensitive to mild heat, drying, and most disinfectants. HIV has a low rate of transmission, but is transmitted through a frequent event, sexual intercourse. Thus this relatively inefficient virus is transmitted often enough to establish epidemic conditions.[2]

HIV has been identified in blood and blood products, semen and cervical secretions, cerebrospinal fluid, and (in extremely low titers) tears and saliva. The target tissues of HIV are primarily the so-called T-helper lymphocytes, which are located throughout the body, and macrophages and cells within the central nervous system. This makes a cure of HIV infection through removal of any single tissue, for example through bone-marrow transplantation, impossible. The infection of cells with HIV results in one of three events: establishment of latency, cell breakdown and death, or cell fusion and death. Destruction of T-helper cells results in injury to the immune system, permitting the occurrence of the opportunistic infections and neoplasms that have come to be recognized as AIDS. Injury of the central nervous system or of the immune system is virtually irreversible and eventually results in death of the AIDS patient.

AIDS is the endpoint within the broad spectrum of manifestations of HIV infection; a spectrum of disease that may represent the natural course of disease in infected individuals. AIDS, the advanced stage of HIV infection has been uniformly fatal; the cumulative survival for more than 3 years is 12%. Death occurs within a mean of 12 months after diagnosis.[3] The frequent delay between diagnosis and death due to AIDS is reminiscent of cancer, a disease syndrome that also evokes great anxiety. The clinical course of AIDS is not predictable, but a great proportion of patients face a slow and at times agonizing deterioration marked by the relentless recurrence of opportunistic infections and neoplasias. The manifestations of AIDS include conditions that are disfiguring and easily recognized, such as Kaposi's sarcoma.

Clinical manifestations of infection with HIV range from asymptomatic to fulminant. The great majority of persons infected with HIV are asymptomatic at any given point in time; in fact most individuals infected with HIV are not aware of it. If a group of individuals with serum antibody to (and, therefore, infection with) HIV are followed over time, the proportion with symptoms characteristic of HIV infection progressively increases. Within the San Francisco health department hepatitis B study cohort, 76% of men who were infected with HIV for 7 years had symptomatic disease; 30% had AIDS, and 46% had an AIDS-related condition.[4]

Evidence of exposure to HIV via detection of serum antibody virtually always means active infection and infectiousness to others, unlike many other infections. For example, the presence of serum antibody to the mumps virus may indicate active infection, previous infection, or previous vaccination. In these last two cases, the virus itself can no longer be recovered, and the individual is not infectious. In contrast, HIV is a persistent infection, so that previous infection means current infection. HIV can be recovered by culture from more than 95% of individuals with serum antibody to the virus.[5] The exceptions are persons who have received antibody passively via the placenta or administration of γ-globulin; the presence of serum antibody in these individuals is transient.

When an individual is infected with HIV, infection is life long because the virus is able to establish latency. Latency means that the viral genes enter and mix with the genes of the human host making complete eradication from the host impossible even though viral replication is potentially suppressible by means of antiviral drug treatment. Because HIV infection is persistent and active, blood and genital secretions of persons with serum antibody to HIV are potentially infectious to others if the mode of exposure is permissive of transmission.

EPIDEMIOLOGY AND PROJECTIONS

AIDS has been reported on six continents and in various population groups throughout the world. On the whole, individuals with HIV infection have behaviors rather than demographic characteristics in common. For example, the AIDS epidemic among homosexual men in the United States has less to do with homosexual intercourse than with the tendency of some homosexual men to have large numbers of sexual partners. It is not the sexual contact between them that confers increased risk, but the number of partners and specific sexual practices. Likewise, among intravenous drug abusers, it is the practice of sharing injection devices rather than the injection of drugs that confers risk of HIV infection.

Depending on individual circumstances, a member of a so-called high-risk group may actually be less likely to become infected with HIV than a member of a low-risk group. For example, a man who has had strictly monogamous, homosexual relations for 10 years with a partner who has likewise been monogamous is less likely to develop AIDS than a heterosexual man who has had frequent sexual contact with a woman who used drugs via contaminated injection devices. HIV is transmitted under very specific conditions and with a relatively low frequency per risk event.[6] Nevertheless, transmission occurs frequently because activities that permit transmission occur frequently and are often compounded by multiplicity of partners and the lack of planning for the consequences of sexual encounters. High-risk behaviors are often spoken of as if these behaviors are in some way aberrant. The behavior most often associated with HIV transmission, however, is sexual intercourse, and this so-called high-risk behavior is practiced by the great majority of adults.

Of all AIDS cases, 66% have been reported in homosexual or bisexual men and 25% have occurred in parenteral drug abusers.[7] Virtually all reported AIDS cases have occurred among individuals who have had intimate contact with persons known or likely to be infected with HIV. This includes sexual intercourse partners of and children born to HIV-infected persons and recipients of HIV-contaminated materials via a parenteral route (blood transfusion or injection equipment shared with infected individuals).[8] Sexual intercourse, whether vaginal or anal, can transmit the virus, but it is estimated that the efficiency of HIV transmission is greater with anal than with vaginal intercourse.[9]

At this time, 29,000 cases of AIDS have been reported in the United States; 28,000 victims are adults. Of the adults, 93% are men, and 36% of these men are members of racial minority groups. Of women diagnosed with AIDS, 72% are non-white. Of all adult AIDS victims, 74% are homosexual or bisexual men; 17% of all cases comprise heterosexual IV drug users (15% of men and 51% of women); persons having heterosexual contact with AIDS patients or persons at high risk for AIDS make up 4% of cases (2% of men and 27% of women); and the remaining percentage of cases comprise recipients of contaminated blood products. For 3% of adults AIDS victims the mode of acquisition of HIV is not known.[10]

Of the 400 or so children (<13 years of age) with AIDS, 88% are less than 5 years of age and 79% are non-white, reflecting the occurrence of cases among women and a perinatal mode of transmission. Of children with AIDS, 79% have a parent or parents with AIDS or who are at high risk of developing AIDS.[11] Because drug use behavior, either on the part of women or their sexual partners, is closely linked with AIDS among women, drug use is also associated with a great proportion of pediatric AIDS cases. It is estimated that 40% to 60% of the children born to women who are infected with HIV are infected themselves.[12] HIV transmission via breast feeding has also been reported.[13] The remaining 21% of pediatric AIDS victims acquired the disease through blood component therapy.[14]

Increased fetal wastage among HIV-infected women has been described. HIV-infected infants frequently present with clinical manifestations including AIDS and ARC.[15] Parental illness and death may complicate the lives of infants born with HIV infection; abandonment of a sick child because of the death of a parent results in a societal dilemma in the need to provide housing and care for children stigmatized by a communicable disease.

In the next 5 years, AIDS will continue to grow in its impact on the health of the U.S. population. Although the number of AIDS cases has increased steadily since 1981, the time required for the cases to double has progressively lengthened, suggesting that the rate of increase in the epidemic is not exponential.[16] Projections of the total number of AIDS cases occurring in the United States by 1991 vary from 121,000 to 270,000.[17] Current information about the prognosis of asymptomatic but seropositive individuals suggests that a high proportion, if not all, will eventually have symptomatic disease (AIDS-related complex [ARC] or neurologic sequelae).[18]

AIDS is currently a major cause of loss of years of potential life among single men in the United States;[19] trends in the data reported AIDS cases suggest that the impact of AIDS will extend to other population groups. Heterosexual transmission is projected to account for 10% of cases in 1991.[20]

AIDS affects relatively young adults and children, frequently causing disability and medical conditions requiring hospitalization, expensive diagnostic procedures, and prolonged treatments. Furthermore, the poor and poorly educated, who have limited economic resources available to them, are at higher risk for AIDS than other groups in society. AIDS disables people during the time of peak work productivity and greatest childbearing. There is no way to assess the cost of lost hopes and dreams, but in terms of health care services, human suffering, and lost productivity the AIDS epidemic is and will continue to be increasingly costly.

The economic implications of the projected epidemic are staggering. In the United States during 1985, personal medical costs equaled $630 million; direct costs of research, screening programs, and education equaled $319 million; and indirect costs due to decreased productivity and years of potential life lost equaled $2.3 billion.[21] For 1991, personal medical costs are projected at $8.5 billion, direct costs from research are projected at $2.3 billion, and indirect costs are projected at $55.6 billion.[22] The economic burden produced by such costs can be overwhelming. For example, the city of San Francisco, which is recognized as a model for low-cost, local AIDS health services planning, has had to rely on volunteer support and charitable donations as well as local government contribution. These resources are limited, and the city now must seek increased state and federal support.[23]

ETHICAL QUESTIONS

The medical information presented above clearly documents that AIDS is a devastating disease potentially capable of killing all who become infected with HIV. The population at risk for this fatal disease is much larger than originally anticipated and is best described not by high-risk groups but by the practice of behaviors that confer risk. Furthermore, HIV infection has neither a known cure nor a preventive vaccine. It is these medical characteristics of HIV infection that largely define what type of ethical concerns, voiced by both health care providers and society as a whole, arise in its treatment.

Terminal Care Issues

As an ultimately fatal disease with expensive palliative treatment, AIDS presents medical dilemmas familiar to modern medicine. The care of AIDS patients requires sophisticated medical knowledge, complex technology, and emotional fortitude. As in the treatment of any terminal disease, AIDS raises questions about the appropriate use of technology[24] the implementation of resuscitation, the use of intensive care, the performance of certain surgical procedures, and the initiation or withdrawal of assisted ventilation or artificial nutrition. These dilemmas are perhaps exacerbated by the youth and vulnerability of AIDS patients, their difficult medical course, and the many emotions surrounding their disease. The questions that arise in the intensive care of AIDS patients, however, are not qualitatively different from those surrounding the care of any critically ill patient.

Duty to Treat

The existence of AIDS, a fatal infectious disease without a cure, brings forth questions of professional duty that have been quiescent for many years. The question being asked by individual providers and medical societies is simply: Do health care providers have a duty to care for patients if those patients may pose a significant risk to a provider's own health?

The recognition of AIDS has been accompanied by fear on the part of members of the medical community as well as others in our society. Professionals' fear of personal risk of infection has been expressed in many actions or inactions: refusal to perform surgery or other procedures such as bronchoscopy, which requires close intimate contact with the patient; refusal to accept the hepatitis B vaccine because it was obtained from blood possibly donated by homosexuals; and even the refusal to provide routine care for AIDS patients.[25] Often this fear has been based on the unknown, for initially there was little knowledge of the exact modes of transmission of this infectious disease or the actual risk to health care providers.

Adverse reactions of health care providers to AIDS patients have also been influenced by their negative attitudes toward these patients' sexual or drug use practices.[26] Many view these behaviors with attitudes ranging from a moral repugnance to a personal distaste. This has contributed to some providers' desire to avoid contact with AIDS patients.

Deliberations of the duty to care for AIDS patients must be influenced by the ethical obligation of health care providers to help those in need and to do so impartially. The history of medicine reveals gradual progress toward the goal of overcoming prejudice. From at least the 16th century, Western culture has recognized a clear obligation on the part of health care providers to treat persons in need regardless of their social status, political affiliation, or religious beliefs and regardless of whether they be enemy or friend.[27]

Although the goal of fairness in health care provision has yet to be fully implemented, this goal still exists. Health care providers must always be cautious when moral prejudices exist, that is, when morally irrelevant traits are confounded with reasons to deny service to those in need. Such prejudices need to be recognized by the individual care provider and not allowed to prevent service to those in need of skilled care. Health care providers must be cognizant that they can never avoid exposure to HIV by simply avoiding AIDS patients, homosexuals, or drug users. This is becoming increasingly true as HIV infection spreads into the heterosexual population. A much more effective method of avoiding HIV infection is to comply carefully with infection control guidelines with every patient in a manner appropriate to the field of practice.

The Good Samaritan Ethic is one that is endorsed by our culture. It asserts that there is a strong ethical obligation to assist an individual who is in danger or in need of help. The strength of this obligation is qualified by the circumstances of each situation. If an individual is incapable of providing effective aid, such as the non-swimmer in the case of a drowning person, clearly he or she is absolved from providing aid that would be futile and perhaps endanger his or her life.

On the other hand, those who have a superior expertise and have chosen a profession dedicated to providing aid have a strong obligation to do so in spite of the personal risk entailed. The community ethic is buttressed by their professional duty. This characterizes the situation of any health care provider who is working with an AIDS patient. While this professional duty is close to absolute, there may be circumstances in which this duty is qualified by the magnitude of the personal risk involved, the certainty that the risk is present, and the harm to the patient if the aid is not provided.

Occupational Risk

For health care workers, the potential to contract HIV in the workplace is a significant concern since HIV has been transmitted in a pattern similar to that of hepatitis B and syphilis, including via needle stick and other occupational exposures.[28] While transmission of HIV to health care providers has occurred, it has been on an exceedingly infrequent basis, much less frequently than either hepatitis B or syphilis.

HIV transmission in the workplace has been reported in nine instances; six involved needle stick or laceration injury, and the remaining three involved accidental skin or mucous membrane contact with infected body fluids.[29] The Centers for Disease Control's (CDC) infection control guidelines were not followed in two of these last instances. Only nine cases have been reported, and yet the total number of potential exposures that have occurred in the medical workplace are not known. This makes it difficult to calculate the risk of infection generated by any single potential exposure event. One study reported an incidence of seroconversion to HIV after needle stick of 0.3%.[30] Anecdotal reports point out potential modes of occupational transmission but tend to result in an over-appreciation of risk and may mislead in their assessment of the frequency of events they describe. Sporadic reports of seroconversion after minimal exposure will continue to accrue; however, it is clear that HIV is not easily or frequently transmitted in the medical occupational setting.[31]

In sum, given our current knowledge, there appears to be little risk to health care providers in participating in the routine care of HIV-infected patients. Furthermore, there are clearly defined ways to limit this risk even more through the observance of standard infection control procedures. Thus the health care provider's ethical duty to treat HIV-infected patients is not mitigated by the very small risk of infection accompanying routine medical care.[32]

Some providers refuse to care for AIDS patients on the grounds that they do not have the necessary level of training to treat the complications associated with the disease. Since AIDS is a new disease, however, the proportion of health care providers with specific training in the medical care of AIDS-related problems is small. In communities where AIDS is already a common medical problem, a serious shortage of medical providers for AIDS patients exists. While AIDS is a complex medical syndrome, most AIDS patients present with one of a small number of medical problems such as *Pneumocystis carinii* pneumonia, which may be treated by primary health care providers if they acquire the necessary skills through continuing medical education. This should be considered no different from the continuing education efforts undertaken to acquire new procedural and treatment skills made necessary by advances in technology, pharmacology, and the basic sciences. In the time of an epidemic such as AIDS, health care professionals have an obligation to obtain additional training that will enable them to serve their patients and to help halt the spread of the disease.[33] (Exhibit 36-1).

As HIV infection spreads to the general population, all providers must consider their patients at risk unless they have certain knowledge that there has been no exposure to the virus. Health care providers have a duty to be informed regarding the mechanisms of transmission of the HIV virus so that they can recognize which patients are at risk and can educate all their patients. Similarly, patients need to be aware of their individual risk of HIV infection and of ways in which they can modify personal behaviors that put themselves or others at increased risk. Therefore, health care providers must become comfortable with explicit discussions of sexuality and drug use. Thus, in addition to a duty to provide routine health care to an HIV-infected individual, health care providers have a duty to stay informed regarding HIV and to educate all patients regardless of their antibody status.[34] Failure to fulfill this obligation will result in a more rapid spread of this fatal disease.

Exhibit 36-1 Professional Duties in an Epidemic

To provide services consistent with skills
To obtain skills if needed by the patient population and if consistent with abilities
To provide accurate and up-to-date information
To promote the patient's best interests regardless of personal feelings toward the patient

STRATEGIES TO CURB THE SPREAD OF AIDS

The primary aim of any program to control the AIDS epidemic must be prevention, for there is no cure for AIDS, and it is not known whether the available treatment will be effective in reducing the transmission of HIV. Prevention of an infectious disease may be accomplished through elimination of susceptibility either via vaccination or prevention of transmission, which in the case of HIV means the alteration of behaviors that confer risk of infection. The only method for curbing the spread of HIV infection is the prevention of contact that permits transmission between infected and noninfected individuals.

The public health goal of preventing the spread of HIV infection is accepted. It is the means of accomplishing this goal that is hotly debated on the grounds of efficacy, ethics, and the law. Many approaches have been advocated, ranging from public education alone to mandatory mass screening with the subsequent isolation of HIV-positive individuals. Health care providers will play an important role in any program designed to prevent the spread of HIV infection. If the course chosen emphasizes education, health care providers will have the responsibility of providing part of this education or, at the very least, notifying those in need of education and referring them to the appropriate resources. If the alternate routes of mandatory testing, contact tracing, or isolation are chosen, health care providers will find themselves in the role of coercive agent enforcing the strategies designed to protect the public health. Thus all health care professionals have an interest in becoming informed and participating in this debate. The remainder of this chapter will concentrate on an ethical analysis of the proposed strategies involving mandatory mass screening programs.

An ethically acceptable public health strategy for dealing with the AIDS epidemic must meet several criteria: (1) the goals must be ethical; (2) the methods must be efficacious and appropriate to the stated goals; (3) implementation of the policy must avoid discrimination and be justly administered; (4) any harm to society or its members that may result from the proposed policies must be identified and clearly understood; (5) the balance between harms and benefits must weigh heavily toward benefit. A policy that meets these criteria would be ethical and likely to succeed.

MEANS OF DETECTION

To be effective, an HIV screening program must have an accurate means of detecting HIV infection. Accuracy is important to ensure a just and ethical administration of any program that is based on the positive identification of infected persons; this is essential if the policy includes sanctions against infected individuals. Detection of HIV infection can be accomplished through recovery of the virus by culture, identification of serum antibody, or clinical assessment employing a strict case definition such as the CDC's case definition of AIDS. Because culturing HIV is cumbersome and costly, it is used primarily as a research tool.

The case definition of AIDS is specific and all inclusive with regard to individuals with AIDS, but it does not identify those with asymptomatic HIV infection. Cases of AIDS reflect HIV infection of years long gone. The use of the AIDS case definition provides data on the minimal prevalence of HIV. Clinical assessment is not useful in establishing the presence of asymptomatic HIV infection and thus would miss many individuals who are capable of infecting others.

Identification of serum antibody to HIV is the most widely applied method for the detection of HIV infection. This method was developed for use in blood banking and has been used in all large screening programs such as those applied by the U.S. military and alternate test sites. The most widely used technique for the detection of serum antibody to HIV is the enzyme immunoassay (EIA frequently referred to as ELISA). This technique is highly specific and sensitive.[35] A high sensitivity means that few persons with HIV will be missed with this test; that is, there will be very few false negatives. A high specificity means that few persons testing positive will not have AIDS; that is, there will be few false positives. Because the antigens used in the first-generation EIAs were not completely pure, false positives did occur. The proportion of false positives per population tested is dependent on the prevalence of infection within that population. In other words, with this test there would be more false identifications in a population of individuals less likely to be truly infected.[36]

Western blot analysis, another technique for the detection of serum antibody, has been applied to HIV. This test is also highly sensitive but is more specific than the EIA, resulting in fewer false positives. Western blot analysis is primarily used as a confirmatory test because it is expensive and cumbersome. The likelihood of HIV infection in a person who tests positive in the EIA and Western blot analysis approaches certainty (unless the person has a history of passive transfer of serum antibody via recent birth or administration of γ-globulin). False positive Western blot results have been reported only rarely.[37] With both tests positive, laboratory error, such as a mislabeled specimen, may be more likely than true test error. The possibility of laboratory error has been addressed by some screening programs through the practice of obtaining and testing a second specimen from all persons who test positive initially.

New tests for serum antibody to HIV have recently been developed that may eliminate the need for Western blot confirmation[38] and therefore reduce the cost of screening. In addition, tests for serum HIV antigen are in development that would also be maximally specific for HIV infection. Use of antigen assays is expected to bring about development of a urine test that could potentially be used in the home.

With the available antibody tests described above, it is possible to identify with excellent accuracy, by medical standards, those individuals who are infected and thus infectious with the HIV virus. The proportion of false positives is increased, however, when the serum tests are applied to populations less likely to be infected, as would be the case if universal mass screening were to be undertaken. Inaccuracy or the generation of false positives is probable even if a detection test existed with 100% specificity because the human laboratory error can never be completely eliminated. Because administration of mass screening programs is cumbersome at best, increases in human error can be anticipated as a result of the increased demand on testing facilities.

In sum, while costly and imperfect, the technology for mass screening programs is currently available. The appropriate and productive response to the information to be gained from mass screening programs is not clear, however. Identification of HIV-infected and uninfected individuals through screening does not of itself prevent the spread of infection. A societal decision must be made as to whether and how the information gained can be ethically used to halt the spread of the AIDS epidemic. In evaluating proposals for mass screening programs, one must look closely at the benefits and detriments for society and for the individuals involved.

BENEFITS AND DETRIMENTS OF SCREENING

A potential societal benefit of large-scale HIV screening is that knowledge of HIV antibody status, when accompanied by individual counseling, may give added impetus for behavioral change. Infected individuals may feel an increased obligation to prevent transmission to others, and the uninfected may better perceive the risk to themselves of unsafe behaviors and reduce their exposure. The value of screening in producing these behavioral changes has been suggested.[39] Studies are contradictory, however, and it is likely that behavioral response to information regarding HIV infection would be highly varied, particularly if testing is unaccompanied by counseling.

While there is no cure to offer persons infected with HIV, there are several potential benefits for these individuals. One potential benefit of screening is that HIV-infected persons may take advantage of the early institution of therapy as it becomes available. At this time, clinical trials using antiviral agents such as azidothymidine (AZT) have shown efficacy in delaying AIDS-related mortality.[40] Early results also suggest that the benefit of antiviral therapy may be maximized by early institution, before destruction of the cellular immune system has advanced.[41] These findings require verification, and the potential for adverse outcomes of antiviral therapies has yet to be determined. It is fair to speculate that, as new treatments become available, the benefit that testing recipients receive from detection of asymptomatic HIV infection is likely to increase with time. To receive this benefit, those identified with HIV infection would have to receive adequate counseling as to the therapies available and be able to take advantage of what are often very costly treatments.

Awareness of HIV infection can promote beneficial behavior change. Theoretically, the continuation of high-risk behaviors among HIV-positive individuals may contribute to the progression of the disease. In addition, initial evidence suggests that pregnancy may accelerate the progression of HIV-related disease in the pregnant woman. Awareness of HIV infection can give asymptomatic individuals the opportunity to implement behaviors that will promote their health. It also can spare individuals from unwittingly transmitting HIV to their sexual partners or unborn children. These benefits are particularly applicable to asymptomatic individuals, especially heterosexuals who may not understand their risk of infection.

There are many serious potential detriments associated with identification for the HIV-positive individual. Profound emotional distress and depression can result from being told that one has an infection that may progress to a fatal disease and for which there is little or unavailable effective treatment. The expression of suicidal thoughts among those testing HIV-positive is not uncommon. Significant harm can be done to seropositive individuals if their antibody status is not treated with strict confidentiality. Disclosure of an HIV-positive result by testing centers can result in irrational rejection by colleagues, friends, and loved ones. Disclosure can also result in unwarranted and unjust loss of work, housing, and health and life insurance.

An overemphasis on screening can be criticized on the grounds that screening may provide false reassurance about one's sexual partners because it only reveals the uninfected person's status at one point in time and does not guarantee his or her future status. Also, because of the delay in antibody expression, a negative test result may be inaccurate in an individual who has been engaged in high-risk behavior.

Before any screening program is adopted, serious consideration must be given to the proposed use of the results. Will the information be anonymous or reported? If reported, to whom, and to what use will the information be put? If confidentiality is promised, how will it be assured? How will the potential benefits be maximized and the potential harms minimized for the individuals tested?

ETHICS OF SCREENING

Screening is often heralded as the means of halting the spread of AIDS. An ethical analysis of screening requires a separate consideration of methodology and goals. The health policy goal of preventing the spread of HIV infection is an ethical one; however, it is not always clear that what advocates of screening say in their stated goal is their only goal. With the current concentration of HIV infection among homosexuals and drug users, the information gained in the course of screening could be used unfairly against groups that already suffer from discrimination within our society. To disguise social approbation and sanction against certain groups as public health policy would be unethical[42] and unjust in our pluralistic society, which is committed to the protection of individual rights. An ethical screening program must not be used to further discrimination; it must be applied evenly to all appropriate populations and include provisions to prevent the misuse of the private and sensitive information obtained.

MANDATORY SCREENING AND ISOLATION

Mandatory screening has been advocated as a means of identifying HIV-infected persons for the purpose of isolating them to prevent transmission of the infection to others. An analysis of this policy reveals a number of practical and ethical problems with its intent and implementation.[43]

To administer a mandatory screening program with subsequent isolation of certain individuals in a just and effective fashion, all members of our society would have to be screened for HIV infection. This screening would need to be repeated at frequent periodic intervals to ensure that all new infections were detected. Careful evaluation and confirmation of each positive test would be necessary to minimize the possibility of false positive results because of the serious consequences to an individual who is being falsely identified as infectious. The sequelae of a false positive test would be unwarranted and unjust restrictions of an individual's personal liberty. Furthermore, in the setting of universal mass screening, frequent false positive results would be likely. The practical problems of setting up such a program are enormous and the costs prohibitive. Such amounts of money, it could be argued, would be more productively spent on creative, comprehensive public education or on scientific research for more effective treatments or a vaccine for HIV infection.

Even if all infected persons would be accurately and inexpensively identified, the population to be isolated would still need to be defined. It is important to understand that an HIV-positive individual is at high risk for infecting others only if he or she engages in high-risk behaviors. Because AIDS cannot be transmitted casually, an HIV-positive individual who does not donate blood, is not sexually active, and does not share drug injection devices cannot transmit AIDS to others.[44] To incarcerate such an individual would be as unjust as incarcerating at random an HIV-negative individual. To determine which HIV-infected individuals pose a danger to others would entail surveillance of their most personal behavior and an invasion of privacy unprecedented in this country. It is hard to envision an ethically acceptable or practical way in which this surveillance could be done.

Clearly, implementation of this policy would require an enormous invasion of privacy into the lives of many who are unlikely to transmit HIV as well as a tremendous restriction of the personal liberties of those to be isolated. The decision to implement such a program could only be warranted if there were a significant advantage of isolation over alternative voluntary testing and education programs in curbing the spread of HIV infection. The disruption of the fabric of our society represented by the loss of privacy and personal liberty for millions, which is inherent in the proposal of mandatory testing and isolation, cannot be ethically justified by the results anticipated.[45]

Finally, because HIV infection is not spread casually but only through shared sexual activities and contaminated injection devices (excluding perinatal and transfusion transmission), it can be considered a disease of consenting adults. Most individuals become infected with HIV when they engage in the known transmission behaviors. Therefore, it can be argued that isolation of infected persons is unnecessary and inappropriate for this infectious disease. Given the nature of the transmission, a much less restrictive and personally invasive intervention to stop the spread of HIV would be extensive public education about the transmission behaviors and the need to avoid them. The responsibility of avoiding infection would thus be placed on each individual in choosing to avoid these behaviors or to engage in sexual activity and drug use but implementing techniques to minimize the risk of infection. Any policy which can achieve the public health goal of limiting AIDS with less intrusion into the privacy and lives of its citizens is ethically preferable to a more restrictive policy.

REPORTING AND CONTACT TRACING

Voluntary behavior change is essential to reducing the transmission of HIV. All prevention strategies must be directed at encouraging individuals to participate in this difficult task. Public education has been used to inform all members of society about which behaviors will expose them to HIV and how they can minimize their risk. This program of education has been accompanied by voluntary testing programs by which individuals can determine whether or not they are infected. All programs provide confidentiality, and some provide anonymity.

It is hoped that individual knowledge of antibody status will increase responsible health behavior on the part of infected and uninfected individuals and thus prevent the spread of AIDS. Most organized testing programs stress pre- and post-test counseling to maximize the benefit from testing and to minimize its detriments. On-site counseling has been of particular value in assisting test recipients to accept and respond appropriately to the information provided by HIV testing. On-site counselors often provide advice about how individuals testing positive may approach others with information regarding HIV infection, thus increasing the likelihood that they will contact persons that they may have put at risk.

Contact tracing of HIV-positive individuals has been proposed as a way to improve on this voluntary system. Contact tracing is a method of following an infectious disease in which public health officials identify the exposed contacts of known infected individuals. They then attempt to curb further spread of the disease by informing and treating those contacts. Effective contact tracing requires the cooperation of the known infected person in supplying the names of his or her sexual or drug use partners.

Contact tracing involves an invasion into the personal and private lives of those individuals who are investigated and contacted. The information obtained could disclose the commission of a criminal offense; sodomy is a crime in half the states, and drug use is proscribed throughout the country. An individual identified as infected may thus be asked to incriminate himself or herself and others.[46] As with mandatory screening and isolation, contact tracing can only be justified if there is a clear health benefit.

It is important to understand that contact tracing among groups with a high prevalence of infection would not be useful. Contact tracing within large groups that approach saturation with the infection, such as the homosexual community in San Francisco, would be useless because it would lead the investigator to almost every member of the community. In addition, homosexual men and drug users can easily identify themselves as at risk if they engage in certain activities. All members of these communities should be informed of their risk by public education programs. This is a more effective and economical method of reaching these groups.

Contact tracing would be most beneficial in areas or populations where there is a low incidence of HIV infection and where the route of transmission is heterosexual. In such cases the contacts may be unaware of their exposure to the virus, and the information provided by a trained counselor would allow for behavior change that otherwise would not be considered necessary. For example, the wife of a bisexual man with HIV infection would discover her unexpected risk and could change her sexual practices or reproductive plans. It is important to remember that the contact tracing in this hypothetical case would only be possible with the cooperation of her bisexual husband.

Contact tracing is most beneficial in diseases where a cure can be offered to both the identified index case as well as the exposed contacts. There is increased justification for contact tracing when the capacity to prevent disease transmission is enhanced by the ability to cure an existing disease. With the availability of antibiotics to treat gonorrhea or syphilis, contact tracing for these diseases can be accompanied by treatment. Thus contact tracing for syphilis and gonorrhea protects the health of the contact and also prevents that person from transmitting the disease further. In HIV infection there is neither a cure to offer those infected nor a vaccination to offer those who are not yet infected. Thus the intervention resulting from contact tracing in HIV is identification of risk and education that may promote behavior change and the future possibility of effective treatment. For persons who are aware of their risk because of participation in behaviors clearly associated with risk, identification of the risk and the need for behavior change can be accomplished largely through public education programs and does not require the invasiveness of contact tracing.

For heterosexuals in what they believe are monogamous relationships, contact tracing would provide important information that could decrease the spread of HIV infection through sexual and perinatal transmission. While not documented, the number of heterosexuals without known risk behaviors who are exposed to HIV and thus would benefit from contact tracing is probably small at this time. Even if it were a significant number, contact tracing might not be justified because of the potential serious harm brought to individuals and public health programs due to the loss of confidentiality that occurs with contact tracing.

The decision to undertake contact tracing represents a sacrifice of the well-established ethical principle of preserving individual confidentiality within the health care provider-patient relationship. Patient confidentiality is at the foundation of the trust between patient and provider and is essential if individuals are to seek and benefit from medical care. The loss of guaranteed confidentiality with its attendant risks for HIV-infected individuals of social isolation and discrimination might prevent high-risk individuals from voluntarily participating in existing public health programs. "The probable outcome of statutorily mandated investigation of sexual contacts, therefore, is that individuals vulnerable to HIV infection would not come forward for testing, impeding epidemiologic and public education efforts; they would not seek counseling, care, and treatment in sexually transmitted disease . . . and drug dependency clinics, harming these vital public health programs; and they might even refrain from seeking therapeutic treatment for physical illness caused by HIV infection, creating human hardship."[47]

Notification of sexual partners or others who are at risk by virtue of shared activities is the ethical obligation of HIV-positive individuals. This notification provides those exposed with the opportunity to seek further medical diagnosis or treatment, as it becomes available, and to change sexual, reproductive, and drug use behavior to their benefit and to the benefit of their community. There is an especially strong obligation to notify those who have little reason to expect that they may have been exposed. This ethical obligation, however, cannot be ethically or effectively mandated by law.

CONCLUSION

The AIDS epidemic exists and grows within the context of our medical knowledge and our societal fears, prejudices, and mores. Within this context, notification of contacts and behavior change can best be encouraged and effected through public education and voluntary testing programs that provide confidentiality and counseling. Mandatory testing, reporting, and contact tracing cannot be ethically justified because of its inefficacy, impracticality, inability to administer without discrimination, and possibility of harm to the individuals tested. On the other hand, voluntary testing programs that guarantee confidentiality and provide counseling are a positive and ethical approach to the prevention of HIV transmission. Certainly there is a chance of inadvertant disclosure with its risks of social alienation and discrimination, but this is a risk that each individual can balance for himself or herself against the benefits of being tested when choosing to be tested.

Potentially, future medical and societal advances could shift the risk:benefit ratio of screening for individuals and the public and justify reporting, contact tracing, or mandatory testing programs (Exhibit 36-2). These advances might include development of effective treatment for HIV infection that would be accessible to all infected individuals, the development of a vaccine, increased guarantees of confidentiality, or the legislative protection of the rights of HIV-infected individuals. Until many of these advances have been realized, mandatory screening accompanied by reporting, contact tracing, or isolation cannot be ethically justified.

We can anticipate increased urgency for action as the AIDS epidemic inevitably progresses and affects more lives. There will be increasing demands on an already stressed health care system. As competition for limited resources soars, the societal conflict surrounding AIDS will become even more apparent. Conflict between providers and HIV infected patients could increase. Health care professionals have an obligation to remain informed regarding the treatment and transmission of HIV infection, to inform patients of their risk, and to remain actively involved in the care of HIV infected patients and in the

Exhibit 36-2 Factors that Influence Benefit from Screening

Increase benefit

- Guaranteed freedom from discrimination
- Sensitive and specific tests
- Effective treatment
- Effective counseling
- Guaranteed health care for those with positive tests
- Freedom to terminate pregnancy

Decrease benefit

- Mandatory disclosure
- Permitted loss of personal rights
- Insensitivity or nonspecificity of test
- Error within testing laboratory
- Lack of treatment
- Lack of counseling
- Potential for loss of health care
- Risk of isolation

---

prevention of the transmission of this disease. In their roles as professionals and citizens, health care providers must play responsible roles in ongoing policy debates, bringing a knowledge of both the medical and ethical consequences of the proposed health policies to the societal deliberations.

NOTES

1. Centers for Disease Control, "Pneumocystis Pneumonia—Los Angeles," *Morbidity and Mortality Weekly Report* 30 (1981): 250–52.

2. R.M. May and R.M. Anderson, "Transmission Dynamics of HIV Infection," *Nature* 326 (1987): 137–42.

3. W.M. Morgan and J.W. Curran, "Acquired Immunodeficiency Syndrome: Current and Future Trends," *Public Health Report* 101 (1986): 459–65.

4. N. Hessol et al., "The Natural History of Human Immunodeficiency Virus in a Cohort of Homosexual and Bisexual Men: A 7-year Prospective Study." Abstract M.3.1, presented at the Third International Conference on AIDS, Washington, DC, June 1–4, 1987.

5. L. Corey, personal communication.

6. M.A. Fischel et al., "Evaluation of Heterosexual Partners, Children, and Household Contacts of Adults with AIDS," *Journal of the American Medical Association* 257 (1987): 640–44.

7. Centers for Disease Control, "Current Trends: Update: Acquired Immunodeficiency Syndrome—United States," *Morbidity and Mortality Weekly Report* 35 (1986): 757–66.

8. Ibid.

9. N. Padian et al., "Male-to-Female Transmission of Human Immunodeficiency Virus." *Journal of the American Medical Association* 258 (1987): 788–90.

10. Centers for Disease Control, "Current Trends."

11. Ibid.

12. G.B. Scott et al., "Mothers of Infants with the Acquired Immunodeficiency Syndrome: Evidence for Both Symptomatic and Asymptomatic Carriers," *Journal of the American Medical Association* 253 (1985): 363–66. N. Cirau-Vigneron et al., "HIV Infection among High-Risk Pregnant Women (letter)," *Lancet* 1 (1986): 630.

13. P. Lepage et al., "Postnatal Transmission of HIV from Mother to Child." *Lancet* 2 (1987): 400. J.B. Zeigler et al., "Postnatal Transmission of AIDs-Associated Retrovirus from Mother to Infant," *Lancet* 1 (1987): 896–988.

14. Centers for Disease Control, "Current Trends."

15. S. Blanche et al., "Longitudinal Study of 18 Children with Perinatal LAV/HTLV III Infection: Attempt at Prognostic Evaluation," *Journal of Pediatrics* 109 (1986): 965–70.

16. Morgan and Curran, "Acquired Immunodeficiency Syndrome."

17. Morgan and Curran, "Acquired Immunodeficiency Syndrome." R. Brookmeyer and M.H. Gail, "Minimum Size of the Acquired Immunodeficiency Syndrome (AIDS) Epidemic in the United States," *Lancet* 2 (1986): 1320–22.

18. Hessol et al., "History of HIV." W. Lang et al., "In a Cohort of Seropositive Men Followed for 30 Months, Initial Leu 3A T-Lymphocyte Counts Predict Subsequent Declines in T-Cell Counts, Clinical Findings and AIDS," Paper presented at the Third International Conference on AIDS, Washington, DC, June 1–4, 1987.

19. J.W. Curran et al.: "The Epidemiology of AIDS: Current Status and Future Prospects," *Science* 29 (1985): 1352–57.

20. Morgan and Curran, "Acquired Immunodeficiency Syndrome."

21. A.A. Scitovsky and D.P. Rice, "Estimates of the Direct and Indirect Costs of Acquired Immunodeficiency Syndrome in the United States, 1985, 1986, and 1991." *Public Health Report* 102 (1987): 5–17.

22. W. Lang et al., "In a Cohort of Seropositive Men."

23. P.S. Arno, "The Nonprofit Sector's Response to the AIDS Epidemic: Community-Based Services in San Francisco," *American Journal of Public Health* 76 (1986): 1325–30.

24. R. Steinbrook et al., "Ethical Dilemmas in Caring for Patients with Acquired Immunodeficiency Syndrome," *Annals of Internal Medicine* 103 (1985): 787–90.

25. A.R. Jonsen, M. Cooke, and B.A. Koenig, "AIDS and Ethics," *Issues in Scientific Technology* 2 (1986): 56–65.

26. W.M.C. Mathews et al., "Physicians' Attitudes toward Homosexuality—Survey of a California County Medical Society," *Western Journal of Medicine* 144 (1986): 106–10.

27. A.R. Jonsen, "Ethics and AIDS," *Bulletin of the American College of Surgeons* 70 (1885): 16–18.

28. S.H. Weiss et al., "HTLV-III Infection among Health-Care Workers: Association with Needle-Stick Injuries." *Journal of the American Medical Association* 254 (1985): 2089–93.

29. Centers for Disease Control, "Update: Human Immunodeficiency Virus Infections in Health-Care Workers Exposed to Blood of Infected Patients," *Morbidity and Mortality Weekly Report* 36 (1987): 285–89.

30. R.F. Stricof and D.L. Morse, "HTLV-III/LAV Seroconversion Following a Deep Intramuscular Needlestick Injury," *New England Journal of Medicine* 314 (1986): 1115.

31. J.L. Gerberding et al., "Risk of Transmitting the Human Immunodeficiency Virus, Hepatitis B Virus, and Cytomegalovirus to Health-Care Workers Exposed to Patients with AIDS and AIDS-Related Conditions," *Journal of Infectious Diseases* 156 (1987): 1–8.

32. Health and Public Policy Committee, American College of Physicians; and the Infectious Diseases Society of America, "Position Paper on Acquired Immunodeficiency Syndrome," *Annals of Internal Medicine* 104 (1986): 575–81.

33. Ibid.

34. Ibid.

35. J.W. Ward et al., "Laboratory and Epidemiologic Evaluation of an Enzyme Immunoassay for Antibodies to HTLV-III." *Journal of the American Medical Association* 256 (1986): 357–61.

36. K.B. Meyer and S.G. Pauker, "Screening for HIV: Can We Afford the False Positive Rate?" *New England Journal of Medicine* 317 (1987): 238–41.

37. A.M. Courouce, J.Y. Muller, and D. Richard, "False-Positive Western Blot Reactions to Human Immunodeficiency Virus in Blood Donors," *Lancet* 2 (1986): 921–22.

38. D.S. Burke et al., "Diagnosis of Human Immunodeficiency Virus Infection by Immunoassay Using a Molecularly Cloned and Expressed Virus Envelope Polypeptide: Comparison to Western Blot on 2,707 Consecutive Serum Samples," *Annals of Internal Medicine* 106 (1987): 671–76.

39. L. McKusick, W. Horstman, and T.J. Coates, "AIDS and Sexual Behavior Reported by Gay Men in San Francisco," *American Journal of Public Health* 75 (1985): 493–96.

40. M.A. Fischl et al., "The Efficacy of Azidothymidine (AZT) in the Treatment of Patients with AIDS and AIDS-Related Complex: A Double-Blind, Placebo-Controlled Trial," *New England Journal of Medicine* 317 (1987): 185–91.

41. Ibid.

42. R. Bayer, C. Levine, and S.M. Wolf, "HIV Antibody Screening: An Ethical Framework for Evaluating Proposed Programs," *Journal of the American Medical Association* 256 (1986): 1768–74.

43. R. Machlin, "Predicting Dangerousness and the Public Health Response to AIDS," *Hastings Center Report* 16 (1986): 16–64. L. Gostin and W.J. Curran, "The Limits of Compulsion in Controlling AIDS," *Hastings Center Report* 16 (1986): 24–29. L. Gostin and W.H. Curran, "Public Health and the Law: Legal Control Measures for AIDS: Reporting Requirements, Surveillance, Quarantine, and the Regulation of Public Meeting Places," *American Journal of Public Health* 77 (1987): 214–18.

44. A. Berthier et al., "Transmissibility of Human Immunodeficiency Virus in Haemophiliac and Non-Haemophiliac Children Living in a Private School in France," *Lancet* 2 (1986): 598–601. J.M. Jason et al., "HTLV-III/LAV Antibody and Immune Status of Household Contacts and Sexual Partners of Persons with Hemophilia," *Journal of the American Medical Association* 255 (1986): 212–15.

45. Gostin and Curran, "Public Health and the Law," 214–18.

46. Ibid.

47. Ibid., 26.

Part VII

Principles and Method

Chapter 37

Basic Theories in Medical Ethics

Glenn C. Graber

MORAL DECISIONS

In straightforward situations, we all know right from wrong. Stealing, murder, and lying are morally *wrong*, and thus the right thing to do is to avoid these.

Other situations are less straightforward, and it is sometimes not easy to know the right thing to do. It is wrong to lie, but suppose you lived in Holland during the Nazi regime and knew the hiding place of Anne Frank and her family. If a Nazi storm trooper asked you whether you knew the whereabouts of any Jews, should you tell him the truth or should you lie? Stealing is wrong, but suppose money that you hold is destined for some evil purpose. To take extreme example, suppose you learn that the person who entrusted the money to you plans to use it to hire a "hit man" to assassinate Mother Theresa. Would it be wrong to steal the money if this is the only way to prevent the person from accomplishing this purpose?

Ethical theory has two tasks. (1) For those situations in which we already know what is right and what is wrong, it should help us explain why the one choice is right and the other wrong. (2) For those situations in which it is not obvious what is right and what is wrong, it should guide us to discover what is the right thing to do.

The first step we must take in developing an ethical theory is to distinguish different sorts of judgments which are made in connection with ethical issues.

ETHICAL JUDGMENTS

Evaluative Judgments

Evaluative judgments are concerned with what it is worthwhile or valuable to have or to do. For example, one might say, "That is a good car because it gets excellent gas mileage" (or "because it is comfortable to drive" or "because it looks pretty"). Again, one might say, "A career in medicine is worthwhile to pursue because you have the satisfaction of helping people" (or "because this sort of work is absorbing"). In more general terms, one might judge, "The only thing that really matters is how much pleasure you get out of life. Even if you learned all there was to know, your life would not be very satisfying unless you had lots of enjoyment from your knowledge."

All these are evaluative judgments. They state the goals which people set out to reach in their lives (e.g., what career to pursue), or they furnish the basis for choices which they make along the way (e.g., which car to buy). Some things are rated as valuable in themselves (intrinsic values), others are good because of what they lead to or produce (instrumental values). The latter are often the subject of technical judgments, e.g., "This is the best suture material to use for this surgical procedure because it will hold securely and not give trouble to the patient."

Judgments of Moral Obligation

Judgments of moral obligation are the sorts of judgments that first come to mind when one thinks of ethics. They concern the choice of the action to be performed or avoided in a given situation. One might say, "You have an obligation to write him a letter. He has written you several times, and you promised to reply if he wrote." Or one might say, "You should not spend that money. It does not belong to you." Or one might speak of "obligations," "rights," "the right thing to do," "what one ought to do" (or "ought not to do"), etc.

All these are obligation judgments. They embody insights about the proper choice and the basis of the choice of actions.

One set of obligation judgments are often singled out for special attention: claims of *rights*. Rights claims have some special features. For one thing, the demand for action falls, not on the person who *possesses* the right, but on the party or parties *against* whom the right is possessed. For example, if I have a right to be paid $5 by you on Friday (because I loaned $5 to you yesterday and you promised to pay me back on Friday), then the duty involved (i.e., to repay me) falls on you, although I am the one who possesses the right. However, in spite of these distinctive features, it is most plausible to treat rights as a subclass of obligation judgments since their focus is on the proper choice of actions to do or refrain from doing.

Character Judgments or Judgments of Moral Evaluation

These judgments concern evaluation of *persons* in their capacity as moral agents and express praise and blame for what they have done (or have failed to do). Evaluations of agents' motives and character are central to these judgments. One might say, "I think he is reprehensible for having done that." Or one might say, "I admire her for having the courage to do a thing like that." Notions of praise and blame, respect and condemnation, and good and bad motives (or reasons for acting) are central here.

Character judgments embody insights about the kind of person one ought to try to become, the kinds of motives one ought to try to develop, and the kind of character one ought to cultivate.

One way of showing the distinction between these different sorts of judgments is to recognize that a judgment could be made about a given issue at the same time as an opposite judgment of another sort. One might say, for example, that a certain action was the best thing you could do (evaluative judgment), perhaps it was even the right thing to do (obligation judgment), but it was *not* an admirable thing to do (character judgment).

Suppose, for example, that a scientist works hard for several years doing research on a dread disease and achieves a dramatic breakthrough. We would undoubtedly judge that this use of her energy and skill was the right thing to do. Furthermore, given the amount of suffering that will be relieved as a result of the breakthrough, it is probable that doing the research was the best thing she could have done with her time. But now suppose that we probe the scientist's motivations for undertaking this research. And suppose that we find out from talking to her that she did not care at all about the people whose lives were improved by her research, or even about the knowledge that was gained through it. Instead, we find that her sole reason for undertaking the research was *spite*—she knew a rival was working in this area and she wanted to "scoop" him in reaching results. If this was her sole motivation, we are not likely to admire the scientist for what she did, though it is still true that it was a right and good thing to do.

It is also possible to claim that a certain action was the right thing to do (obligation judgment) and an admirable thing to do (character judgment), but *not* the best thing to do (evaluative judgment). This might occur in regard to some of the tragic choices faced daily in medical care. A patient with a terminal illness requests to be kept alive as long as possible and the health providers comply. The suffering of the patient, family, friends, and care givers may lead one to say that it would have been best for all concerned if the patient had not lingered so long. However, to honor the patient's request in this matter seems to be the right thing to do, and the respect for the patient this embodies prompts admiration.

THEORIES OF MORAL OBLIGATION

Teleological Theories

Why is it wrong to tell a lie?

One sort of answer that is commonly given focuses on the *consequences* of the deed. The person to whom you lie may act on the basis of the misinformation and this may lead to harm to him- or herself and to others. A simple example: A child breaks her mother's favorite vase and falsely pins the blame on her brother. Her mother punishes him for it, which causes him pain (the more so since he cannot understand *why* he is being punished). Later, she learns the truth and experiences regret at what she has done (more pain). She then punishes her daughter all the more severely (still more pain), since she is angry for being made to feel guilty towards her son. We must also look at the long-term consequences. The daughter, like the boy who cried "wolf," will probably find people disbelieving other things she tells them in the future once they discover she has lied to them in the past. This is likely to be a source of frustration to her (still more pain). It perhaps will be a danger to others (still more pain) if what she has to tell them is important—as it was, finally, with the shepherd boy when a wolf actually appeared.

This sort of account of right and wrong is called a *consequentialist, goal-based*, or *teleological* theory. The latter term is derived from the Greek term for outcome or goal (*telos*) and the Greek term for theory (*logos*). We will look at this sort of account more fully in the next section.

For situations in which the right thing to do is unclear, teleological theories would have us choose the alternative that can be predicted to produce the most good and the least harm. In the example at the beginning of the chapter, it would be morally right to lie to the Nazi storm trooper—as long as you could be fairly certain that you would be successful in deceiving him and that you and your family would not be punished. By lying, you would save the lives of the Frank family; the only harm you would cause is to frustrate the zealous storm troopers in their search.

Deontological Theories

Some cases suggest a different explanation of the wrongness of lying. For example, informing patients that they have an untreatable fatal disease causes such anguish for everybody concerned that sometimes it clearly does more harm than good. And yet surely patients have a *right* to this information, even if the consequences of their being given it are predominantly negative. Instead of giving primacy to evaluative judgments, as teleologists do, justification for this sort of claim (i.e., that patients must be given such information) typically focuses directly on features of *duty*. Hence, theories which include this general sort of explanation are given the name *deontological*, derived from *deontos*, the Greek term for duty. A variety of duty-oriented elements may be focused upon. Some would speak in general of a ''right to know'' which is violated when someone is told a lie, as in the example above. Other deontologists would give primacy to the notion of ''respect for persons'' (or lack of it, ''disrespect'') embodied in the act. To tell a lie to a patient is to fail to respect the patient's capacity to deal with the information and to make decisions based upon it concerning his or her life. Similarly, to deceive a scientific rival about the progress of one's research is a personal affront, aside from any harm it might do by leading the rival astray in his or her research.

Thus, on this view, it is wrong for the child who broke the vase to tell her mother a lie about the event, even if she can arrange things so that her brother will not be punished and her mother will never find out the truth. No *harm* is done, yet the daughter has shown disrespect for her mother by the lie. If she really respected her mother as a person, she would tell her the truth and trust in her compassion and reasonableness not to make the punishment greater than she deserves. (Further, she should be willing to face *just* punishment.)

The foregoing has been a quick sketch of two general types of theories of moral obligation: teleological and deontological. The point was to communicate the ''flavor'' of each kind of theory. Now let us now look at some of the details of each.

UTILITARIANISM AND OTHER TELEOLOGICAL THEORIES

Teleologism: The Goal-Based Approach

On this view, the main task of the moral life is to produce as much good as we can through our actions, while at the same time avoiding or eliminating harm or bad to the extent possible.

More formally, the basic guiding principle of teleologism can be stated as follows.

The Principle of Teleologism: Of all the alternatives open to a given agent at a given time, the one he or she ought to perform is the one which produces the greatest balance of good over evil for the members of the moral reference group. If two or more alternatives are equally optimific (i.e., create an equivalent balance of good over evil or bad), then the agent ought to perform one or the other of these and it would be equally right to perform any of them.

There are at least three important questions which this guiding principle of teleologism leaves unanswered: Who is to be included in the moral reference group? What is to count as good and bad? Is the standard to be applied to specific actions one at a time, or can it be used to formulate rules or policies for actions of certain kinds?

The answers to these three questions are what distinguish different forms of teleological or goal-based theories. In the next several sections, we will be looking at some different answers which have been given to each of these questions.

The Moral Reference Group

Who counts, morally? Whose welfare do we, as moral agents, have a responsibility to promote? The answer to these questions determines the moral reference group.

A full spectrum of answers to these questions has been given in the history of Western philosophy and theology. At one extreme is the view known as *egoism*, which is that the only person towards whom each agent has any moral responsibility is himself or herself.

Intermediate positions limit membership of one's moral reference group to some identifiable set of individuals. For example, one form of *racism* is the view that only persons with a certain racial heritage count as members of the moral reference group. One form of *sexism* says the same about members of one gender. A form of *nationalism* counts only fellow citizens of one's nation as members of the moral reference group.

One group for whom claims of limited moral reference might perhaps be justified comprises *one's patients*. The act which establishes a professional-patient relationship might be sufficient to single out this group for special (or even exclusive) attention regarding welfare.

The doctrine of the moral reference group type which has been most widely held in Western thought does not close the circle as narrowly as sexism, etc. Known as *utilitarianism*, this view holds that the moral reference group includes *all* sentient beings.

Theories of Value

The second question left open by the guiding principle of teleologism deals with evaluative issues: What counts as good (and thus to be promoted) and what counts as bad (and thus to be avoided or minimized)? Without an answer to these questions, the teleological approach cannot give us guidance in particular choices we must make. We would not know what aspect of the consequences counts for and against the alternatives.

Suppose, for example, that you were invited to take part in a certain activity and were told only that it would have the effect of causing certain body tissues to increase in size and quantity. No reasonable judgment can be made about whether the activity is worth the effort until we know what tissue is being referred to and whether an enlargement would be valuable or disvaluable. Is it muscle tissue, so that the result would be a healthier, more robust appearance? If so, then it might be worthwhile to pursue. Is it brain tissue, so that the result would be increased intellect? Again, it might be worthwhile. On the other hand, it might be fatty deposits, so that the result would be an obese appearance. Or the tissue might be of a tumor, so that the result would be suffering and death. Obviously, the *value* of the consequences makes all the difference.

In general philosophical ethics, at least three different kinds of answers have been given to this question of what things have value.

Subjective Preference

Many people would contend that it is at once both futile and presumptuous to attempt to develop a general theory of value, because value judgments are totally subjective and individualistic.

The only sound alternative, then, would be to make subjective preference the standard of value and to orient teleological theories towards maximizing the satisfaction of preferences and minimizing their frustration. This is the approach that many contemporary economists, sociologists, and psychologists take in their analyses of values, especially as applied in social planning.

Hedonism

The theory of value most discussed in the history of Western philosophy is the view known as *hedonism*, which holds that the one and only thing intrinsically good is pleasure and the one and only thing intrinsically bad is pain.

This view may initially appear to be just as subjective as the preceding view, but in fact it is not. For example, a hedonist view provides a basis for criticizing some specific goals as mistaken. Individual preferences would, on this view, be regarded as involving *predictions* about what would bring the person pleasure (or avoid pain). Any such preference (or prediction) could be criticized as being incorrect.

The disvalue of pain is especially well recognized in the health care setting, where enormous efforts are directed at palliation. And the value of pleasurable states seems to require no defense. To experience them is to recognize them as worth pursuing.

It is notoriously difficult to establish objective standards for measuring these parameters. The measure that is especially difficult is intensity. It is difficult enough for one to compare different pains or pleasures of one's own with respect to intensity. (Is the pain of today more or less intense than the one I experienced yesterday?) The difficulty is even greater for interpersonal comparisons. (Is *my* pain of today more or less intense than *your* pain of yesterday?) Anyone who has ever worked with patients in pain knows how difficult it can be to judge the intensity of the pain. The health sciences have developed some descriptive terms that may help in classifying degrees of pain, but these are still far from precise.

Pluralism

Another possibility is suggested by standard criticisms of hedonism, i.e., that certain things (such as knowledge) are intrinsically good independent of their relation to pleasure or pain. Since theorists who take this approach almost always identify more than one such intrinsic good, the position is usually called *pluralism*.

Sir David Ross, for example, whose theory of obligation we shall examine later, maintains that at least four things are fundamental intrinsic goods:

- pleasure
- knowledge
- virtue
- justice

William Frankena offers a comprehensive list of things that have been claimed to be intrinsic goods:[1]

- life, consciousness, and activity
- health and strength
- pleasures and satisfactions of all or certain kinds
- happiness, beatitude, contentment, etc.
- truth
- knowledge and true opinion of various kinds, understanding, wisdom
- beauty, harmony, proportion in objects contemplated
- aesthetic experience
- morally good dispositions or virtues
- mutual affection, love, friendship, cooperation
- just distribution of goods and evils
- harmony and proportion in one's own life
- power and experiences of achievement
- self-expression
- freedom
- peace, security
- adventure and novelty
- good reputation, honor, esteem, etc.

Values in Medicine

Beauchamp and McCullough offer a listing of goods (and corresponding harms) especially relevant to the health care context (Table 37-1).[2]

The following list of goals of medical intervention is, in effect, a list of fundamental values in medicine.

1. Restoration of health.
2. The relief of symptoms (including physical distress and psychological suffering).
3. The restoration of function or maintenance of compromised function.
4. The saving or prolonging of life.

Table 37-1 Intrinsic Goods and Harms in the Health Care Setting

Goods	Harms
Health	Illness
Prevention, elimination, or control of disease (morbidity) and injury	Disease (morbidity) and injury
Relief from unnecessary pain and suffering	Unnecessary pain and suffering
Amelioration of handicapping conditions	Handicapping conditions
Prolonged life	Premature death

Source: Reprinted from *Medical Ethics: The Moral Responsibilities of Physicians* by T.L. Beauchamp and L.B. McCullough, p. 37, with permission of Prentice-Hall, Inc., © 1984.

5. The education and counseling of patients regarding their condition and its prognosis.
6. Avoiding harm to the patient in the course of care.[3]

At least one additional basic value that should be added to these is the intrinsic value of the professional-patient relationship. This sort of intimate, trust-filled, human-to-human tie is itself an important value above and beyond the beneficial results which may be achieved by means of it.[4]

Act versus Rule Approach

The third general question to be answered by a teleological or goal-based theory is whether the standard is to be applied to *individual concrete actions* or more generally to *policies* for action in all situations of a certain type. A policy or rule approach offers the advantage of promoting consistency of action, but at the expense of lack of sensitivity to the particularities of the situation at hand. An act approach is similar to the process of clinical reasoning and attempts to take into account all the details of the specific case. The cost of this is added complexity of decision making and the necessity to repeat the process with each new situation.

The characteristic flavor of teleological theories of moral obligation is that of an ethics of *production*. Once the fundamental values are determined, the task of ethical decision making is to predict what values and disvalues will be brought into being by the available alternatives. The choice that is likely to maximize good and minimize harm is the one to choose.

DEONTOLOGICAL THEORIES

This approach proposes a very different way of making moral decisions than the process we have just examined. Instead of weighing and balancing the values in the situation, a duty-based theory examines the situation for moral factors of a different order.

Kant's Deontological Theory

Immanuel Kant is often taken to be the paradigm deontologist. He maintains that it is absolutely and always wrong to treat persons "merely as a means and not at the same time as an end in themselves."[5] To treat someone as an end is to respect the ends or goals that the person has set for him- or herself. Thus, Kant maintains that we should never impose anything on a person against the person's will. We may even have a positive obligation to do what we can to help further the person's goals.

In other words, moral factors serve as "side constraints" on our goal-based calculations. They restrict our freedom, not only the freedom to serve our own interests, but also the freedom to attempt to maximize the balance of good over evil for others as well.

Absolute Duties

According to Kant and some other deontological theorists, moral factors or side constraints (at least certain of them) cannot be overridden by *any sort of consideration whatever*. This claim has a certain initial plausibility, for example, in connection with very serious moral principles such as the following:

- It is wrong to kill an innocent person.
- It is wrong to tell a lie.
- It is wrong to do physical harm to an innocent person.

Charles Fried expresses his view of the absolute or categorical character of these norms in the following passage:

> It is part of the idea that lying or murder are wrong, not just bad, that these are things you must not do—no matter what. They are not mere negatives that enter into a calculus to be outweighed by the good you might do or the greater harm you might avoid. Thus the norms which express deontological judgments—for example, Do not commit murder—may be said to be absolute. They do not say: "Avoid lying, other things being equal" but "Do not lie, period." This absoluteness is an expression of how deontological norms or judgments differ from those of consequentialism.[6]

Prima Facie Duties

One serious problem with the absolutist view is that moral rules may conflict with one another. If one holds that it is absolutely and always wrong to tell a lie and also to do physical harm to an innocent person, what is one to do if a situation arises in which the only way to *prevent* physical injury to an innocent person is through telling a lie, as in the Anne Frank case above?

One way of dealing with this sort of problem is to deny that moral rules are absolute. Instead, they may be taken to hold prima facie or "other things being equal." This means that nothing except another moral rule could override them. For example, I would not be justified in ignoring a moral duty because I found it inconvenient or because I did not want to do what was dictated. However, when two moral rules conflict with each other (such as in the example above, where the only way to avoid bringing physical injury to an innocent person is to tell a lie), then the weight or stringency of the conflicting rules must be determined and the weightier or more stringent rule must take precedence.

Ross's List of Prima Facie Duties

Sir David Ross sets out a list of seven fundamental *prima facie* duties:[7]

1. *Fidelity*: We ought to keep promises we have made.
2. *Reparation*: We ought to make restitution for wrongful acts we have done in the past.
3. *Gratitude*: We owe a debt to others who have benefited us in the past.
4. *Justice*: We ought to do what we can to ensure that pleasure or happiness are distributed in accordance with the merit of the persons concerned.
5. *Beneficence*: Whenever we can improve the condition of others with respect to virtue, intelligence, or pleasure, we ought to do so.
6. *Self-Improvement*: Whenever we can improve our own condition with respect to virtue or intelligence, we ought to do so.
7. *Nonmaleficence*: We ought not to do anything that would injure another.

This list incorporates some teleological elements (especially in the principle of beneficence), but it also includes some deontological side constraints. The act with the greatest weight of duty behind it is the final or "actual" duty.

Prima Facie Principles in Medical Ethics

The *Belmont Report* argues for regarding three principles as the basis of ethical decision making in medicine.[8]

1. respect for persons
2. beneficence
3. justice

Beauchamp and Childress present four basic principles:[9]

1. the principle of autonomy
2. the principle of nonmaleficence
3. the principle of beneficence
4. the principle of justice

The bulk of their highly regarded book is occupied with exploring the meaning of these principles and their application to medical decisions.

Howard Brody develops a method of ethical decision making that is quite different from a Rossian system.[10] However, much of his discussion of concrete issues in medical ethics is conducted by reference to four "fundamentals" of medical ethics which can be regarded as prima facie principles:

1. the doctor-patient relationship
2. informed consent
3. quality of life
4. determination of ethical participation

Robert M. Veatch develops his ethical theory with greater attention to the formal conditions of its justification than to substantive principles per se.[11] In his view, what is most important about a theory of obligation is that it can be justified as the set of principles which would be agreed to in a (hypothetical) situation of a social contract or (as he prefers to call it) a "covenant." However, as a part of his Draft Medical Ethical Covenant, he sets out the following substantive principles (for which I have supplied the names):

1. *Principle of Fidelity*: We acknowledge the moral necessity of keeping promises and commitments to one another, including the commitment of this covenant.
2. *Principle of Autonomy*: We acknowledge the moral necessity of treating one another as autonomous members of the moral community free to make choices that do not violate other basic ethical requirements.
3. *Principle of Honesty*: We acknowledge the moral necessity of dealing honestly with one another.
4. *Principle of Respect for Life*: We acknowledge the moral necessity of avoiding actively and knowingly the taking of morally protected life.
5. *Principle of Justice and Equality*: We acknowledge the moral necessity of striving for equality in individual welfare and equality in the right of access to health care necessary to provide an opportunity for health equal insofar as possible to the health of others.
6. *Principle of Respect for Persons*: We acknowledge the moral importance of producing good for one another and treating one another with respect, dignity, and compassion insofar as this is compatible with the other basic principles to which we are bound.

Beauchamp and McCullough speak, not of principles as fundamental, but of models which specify goals or values and derivative obligations and virtues, as well as fundamental obligations.[12] In particular, they stress the contrasts between the beneficence and the autonomy models:

Model of Beneficence—*Basic Moral Principle*: The principle of beneficence is the sole fundamental principle. It requires the physician to promote goods for patients, as medicine sees those goods, and to avoid harms, as medicine sees those harms.[13]

Model of Autonomy—*Basic Moral Principle*: The principle of respect for autonomy is the sole fundamental principle. It requires the physician to respect the patient's autonomous decisions and actions regarding medical care.[14]

Jonsen, Siegler, and Winslade develop their ethical theory in terms of four "categories" or "considerations" of obligation, here listed in priority order:[15]

1. patient preference
2. medical indications
3. quality of life
4. external factors

THEORIES OF CHARACTER

Another focus in ethical theory besides what things it would be good to achieve through action (evaluative judgments) or what one ought to do (moral obligation judgments) is what sort of person one ought to strive to become. This focus may be an important supplement to the other two, with attention paid to motives and patterns of action as well as to the "externals" of action. This is the approach suggested by Beauchamp and Childress in Table 37-2, which indicates the virtues that correspond to the principles listed above.[16]

Other authors argue that virtues can/or should be the primary focus of the moral life. For example, Gregory Pence develops an ethical theory in which moral virtues form the core of the moral life.

> Certain core virtues are always necessary for any decent society—the cardinal virtues of courage, justice, temperance, and *phronesis*. I would also add friendship (from Aristotle) and honesty and love (from Christianity) . . . physicians need additional virtues, such as humility (the opposite of arrogance), compassion, and respect for good science (integrity).[17]

Table 37-2 Principles, Rules, Actions and Corresponding Virtues

Fundamental Principles	Primary Virtues
Autonomy	Respect for Autonomy
Nonmaleficence	Nonmalevolence
Beneficence	Benevolence
Justice	Justice or Fairness

Derivative Rules	Secondary Virtues
Veracity	Truthfulness
Confidentiality	Confidentialness
Privacy	Respect for Privacy
Fidelity	Faithfulness

Ideal Actions	Ideal Virtues
Forgiveness	Forgiveness
Beneficence (high risk)	Benevolence (high risk)
Acting mercifully	Mercy
Giving generously	Generosity

Source: Adapted from *Philosophical Ethics: An Introduction to Moral Philosophy* by T.L. Beauchamp, p. 165, with permission of McGraw-Hill Book Company, © 1982.

CONCLUSION

We have examined the several aspects of ethical theorizing and have sketched several different theories. The sketches can be most helpful if used to identify which of these ways of thinking about moral issues most closely matches the reader's own approach to moral decision making. Each theory can be applied to some problematic cases to see which yields the answers that seem most plausible. In this way, the reader can begin to determine which approach to use in his or her own critical thinking about moral issues.

NOTES

1. William K. Frankena, *Ethics*, 2d edition (Englewood Cliffs, N.J.: Prentice-Hall, 1973), 87–88.

2. Tom L. Beauchamp and Laurence B. McCullough, *Medical Ethics: The Moral Responsibilities of Physicians* (Englewood Cliffs, N.J.: Prentice-Hall, 1984), 37.

3. Albert R. Jonsen, Mark Siegler, and William J. Winslade, *Clinical Ethics: A Practical Approach to Ethical Decisions in Clinical Medicine* (New York: Macmillan, 1982), 13–14.

4. See Charles Fried on "the good of personal care," in *Medical Experimentation: Personal Integrity and Social Policy* (New York: American Elsevier, 1974), 67–78.

5. Immanuel Kant, *Foundations of the Metaphysics of Morals*, trans. Lewis White Beck (Indianapolis, Ind.: Bobbs-Merrill, 1959), 47.

6. Charles Fried, *Right and Wrong* (Cambridge, Mass.: Harvard University Press, 1978), 9–10.

7. W.D. Ross, *The Right and the Good* (Oxford: The Clarendon Press, 1930), 21–2.

8. National Commission for the Protection of Human Subjects of Biomedical and Behavioral Research, "Belmont Report—Ethical Principles and Guidelines for the Protection of Human Subjects of Research," *Federal Register* 44, no. 76, April 18, 1979, 23192–97.

9. Tom L. Beauchamp and James F. Childress, *Principles of Biomedical Ethics*, 2d ed. (New York: Oxford University Press, 1983).

10. Howard Brody, *Ethical Decisions in Medicine*, 2d ed. (Boston: Little, Brown, and Co., 1981).

11. Robert M. Veatch, *A Theory of Medical Ethics* (New York: Basic Books, 1981), 327–30.

12. Tom L. Beauchamp and Laurence B. McCullough, *Medical Ethics: The Moral Responsibilities of Physicians* (Englewood Cliffs, N.J.: Prentice-Hall, 1984).

13. Ibid., 40.

14. Ibid., 49.

15. Jonsen, Siegler, and Winslade, *Clinical Ethics,* 7.

16. Beauchamp and Childress, *Principles of Biomedical Ethics*, 265–66.

17. Gregory E. Pence, *Ethical Options in Medicine* (Oradell, N.J.: Medical Economics Company, 1980), 49–50.

BIBLIOGRAPHY

Beauchamp, Tom L., and James F. Childress. *Principles of Biomedical Ethics.* 2d ed. New York: Oxford University Press, 1983. The two authors, who hold different fundamental theories of ethics, approach issues on the basis of principles they can agree upon.

Childress, James F. *Who Should Decide?: Paternalism in Health Care.* New York: Oxford University Press, 1982.

The Encyclopedia of Bioethics. Warren T. Reich, editor-in-chief. New York: Macmillan and the Free Press, 1978. For the subject matter of this chapter, the following are the most relevant entries. Under "Ethics," see these subentries: "The Task of Ethics" by John Ladd; "Rules and Principles" by Wm. David Solomon; "Deontological Theories" by Kurt Baier; "Teleological Theories" by Kurt Baier; "Situation Ethics" by Joseph Fletcher; "Utilitarian Ethics" by R.M. Hare; "Theological Ethics" by Frederick S. Carney; "Objectivism in Ethics" by Bernard Gert; "Naturalism" by Carl Wellman; "Non-Descriptivism" by R.M. Hare; "Moral Reasoning" by Philippa Foot; "Relativism" by Carl Wellman. See also "Bioethics" by K. Danner Clouser; "Double Effect" by

William E. May; "Law and Morality" by Baruch A. Brody. Under "Life," see "Quality of Life" by Warren T. Reich. See also "Natural Law" by Eric D'Arcy; "Obligation and Supererogation" by Thomas J. Bole III and Millard Schumaker; "Paternalism" by Tom L. Beauchamp; "Patients' Rights Movement" by George J. Annas. Under "Religious Directives in Medical Ethics," see "Jewish Codes and Guidelines" by Isaac N. Trainin and Fred Rosner; "Roman Catholic Directives" by Bernard Haring; "Protestant Statements" by Thomas Sieger Derr. Under "Rights," see "Systematic Analysis" by Joel Feinberg; "Rights in Bioethics" by Ruth Macklin.

Fletcher, Joseph. *Morals and Medicine*. Boston: Beacon Press, 1954. A teleological approach to a variety of ethical issues in medicine. Fletcher is the author who coined the term "situation ethics" in an earlier book with that title.

Frankena, William K. *Ethics*, 2d ed. Englewood Cliffs, N.J.: Prentice-Hall, 1973. An excellent summary and analysis of the range of ethical theories.

Graber, Glenn C., Alfred D. Beasley, and John A. Eaddy. *Ethical Analysis of Clinical Medicine*. Baltimore, Md.: Urban, 1985.

Veatch, Robert M. *A Theory of Medical Ethics*. New York: Basic Books, 1981. A comprehensive approach to medical ethics from a deontological perspective.

Chapter 38

A Method of Ethical Decision Making

Edmund L. Erde

A person has a dilemma when, caring to do a good job, he or she believes that serious losses are at risk or gains at stake in a situation no matter what is done. In health care, moral dilemmas can arise in several ways. They can arise when determining what is permissible in trying to correct a patient's medical problem. They can arise when what is medically indicated conflicts with other loyalties, for example, concern about society's limited resources. Finally, they can arise when simultaneously doing what is indicated for a patient and attending to one's own personal well-being—one's health, income, and relations with partners or legal authorities. To resolve a dilemma, one must be clear about what is involved and have a method for generating options and choosing from among them. This chapter sketches such a method.

Although we do encounter tough cases about which it could be said there is no right answer, this is not restricted to ethics. The same is true of many kinds of practical problems. Diagnosing, investing, and deciding where to live are subject to this kind of uncertainty. Thus, we must take to heart Aristotle's warning not to seek answers that are more precise than a field of enquiry allows.[1] So perhaps the most this chapter can provide is a way of asking better questions, both about cases and about underlying ethical theories, concepts, rules, and principles.

The gist of the method is this. First, characterize the dilemma as fully as possible: Analyze it into its constituents by gathering all of the relevant facts and identifying the ideas and values in conflict.

Second, keeping the nature of morality in mind, discard those constituents that arise as a result of inclinations and prejudices.

Third, if the second step does not suffice to solve the problem, consider the fully characterized case in the light of the available moral theories. This should increase one's grasp of what is at issue in each option.

The method presupposes that moral decision making has a logic. To be sure, the logic is not as mechanical as, say, the rules of arithmetic. A moral decision has to be assembled more like a bridge than a chain. Assembling takes imagination. We should not expect the method to produce incontestable resolutions.

SOME KEY CONCEPTS AND THEIR BEARINGS ON DILEMMAS

To clarify the nature of one's dilemma (and reassess it frequently) the following notions can be most helpful: (1) welfare, (2) interests, (3) the moral status of the patient, and (4) social ties (which primarily involves reference to approaches to morality and to social roles). In elaborating these, I first discuss each concept and then explain its application.

Welfare

Welfare is the *general* condition enabling any relatively independent person of any age, in any era, culture, or circumstance to function well and happily. The separate elements of welfare are necessary for it to be realized. None alone is sufficient. Trying to specify its elements produces platitudes: "It is better to be alive, sane, pain-free (and comfortable in other ways), strong, healthy, whole (including having good hearing, sight, all limbs working, etc.), free, wealthy, attractive, well liked, and smart than the opposites." Fine-grained specifications like "It is better not to have blood pressure above 135 over 90" or "It is good to have investments in IBM" do not describe welfare. Rather they state markers, predictors, or indicators of it.

Medicine is the science that specifies the fine-grained markers of bodily welfare. It also concerns ways of bringing abnormal values into normal range and even defines tests of being alive and dead.

Application

Sometimes reminding oneself about the logic of the concept *welfare* will resolve problems by showing that an upsetting situation is a pseudodilemma. One may, for example, feel trapped in a dilemma because certain test values imply that an intervention is appropriate but other features of the situation speak against using it. If a patient's white count is high, typically one should try to determine the cause of infection and treat it. However, attempting to bring a value into line may not be required if the patient is fine or if other indicators of welfare are grim and cannot be corrected. Consider the sense of conflict that arises over the issue of feeding an anencephalic baby or adjusting the blood gases of someone about to die. To refrain in these situations is not to refrain from pursuing welfare. It is to refrain from pursuing a marker of welfare. Treating the marker when welfare is not expected to be served is "treating the numbers," not "treating the person."

Interests

Interests are variable, relative, and subjective values. They may appear arbitrary, in that those who hold them just subscribe to or adopt them.[2] In general, they appear as (1) ideals and goals (investments of meaningfulness, aspirations), (2) practical interests (a sense of the worth of various ingredients in a trade-off), and (3) dispositions (gut-level or experienced values, including preferences, prejudices, and tastes, which might be called one's "preset").

Interests can be fleeting or lifelong, common or unusual, legitimate or illegitimate (that an interest is illegitimate does not mean anyone may intervene to stop its pursuit). They make life worth living for the person who lives it. When understood in the richest way, interests are essential constituents of one's personality. We hold them (1) as individuals, (2) as members of groups (e.g., the professions), or (3) as products of socialization.[3]

Consider one possible distribution of interests regarding abortion (Table 38-1).

Application

Typically a person is interested in his own welfare. In a conflict situation, use the kind of grid shown in Table 38-1 to understand the sources of the positions of all concerned—patient, care givers, and others.

Regarding patients, use a grid to see what is at stake for an individual. Is it an ideal, a sense of the worth of risks, or a disposition? All have moral significance. For example, a demented patient's enjoyment of meals or visits from friends is a personal, gut-level interest that carries moral weight.

Regarding care givers, use a grid to identify prejudices. Have care givers been conditioned to act rather than wait? If so, they may be rushing a patient and take his or her delay as irrational and as creating a dilemma. Is anyone holding unachievably high goals as standards of success? Ageism may incline some to neglect an elderly patient. The grid can help identify what one should note about oneself and perhaps disclose as prejudices to patients or patients' spokespersons.[4]

A grid can show how a patient's decision to refrain from pursuing his or her own welfare may not be irrational. We should define *irrational* in such a way as to provide individuals maximum freedom to pursue interests.[5] Consider something irrational if and only if it is destructive and serves no interest.[6]

The Patient's Moral Status

Conceptions of the moral status of the patient structure dilemmas. Frequently the question is cast in terms of whether the patient should be considered a person or a human. The difference is momentous. Being human is being a member of a biological species.

Table 38-1 Interests regarding the Issue of Abortion.

	Personal	Professional	Social
Ideals, Goals, and Aspirations	Treasure life	Care for individual women	Prize big families
Practicality	Make money by performing them	Lay low on the issue; avoid mortality and morbidity	Respect self-determination
Gut-Level Dispositions (Preset)	Guilt, disgust	Detached concern	Repulsion

Being a person is having certain mental abilities, specifically those needed to process one's interests.

We see humans as makers (self-determiners) of much of their own lives. However, given that there is so much about human beings' welfare that they cannot know or, knowing, cannot manipulate on their own, we also see them as less than masters. Further, as creatures who slowly emerge from oblivion through interacting with others, humans develop ideas, ideals, feelings, and preferences. Sometimes these are driving passions. Not infrequently we find individuals who are rash and self-destructive.

Not all humans achieve personhood. And having once achieved it, no one retains it forever. That is the point behind the concept of *brain death*. It recognizes that the human part is still alive, i.e., alive in the biological sense (metabolizing). But it also recognizes that the person is dead—has permanently and irreversibly lost the power to experience, act, think, remember, and communicate.

Application

There seems to be a general assumption that we are most clearly immoral when we act against a person's welfare, especially without his or her permission.[7] Such actions we treat as the most criminal. The model of criminal law, however, is a misleading one for ethics. Many actions that fail to respect someone's ideals are not criminal but are clearly immoral.[8]

Taking all actions against someone's welfare to be morally wrong is an error. It is an error because an action contrary to welfare might conform to the person's expressed interests. Forcing conformity to the prescriptions of welfare inflicts moral wrong by treating persons as mere biologic entities and by giving no weight to their (other) interests. If we overcome the bias toward welfare, we are most likely to give recognition to a person's ideals. We generally think that to fail to respect a person's ideals is a serious wrong. Self-determination regarding one's ideals is central to the autonomy that is constituitive of personhood. Acting against a person's ideals can be construed as making a mockery of them. That is why the refusal of Jehovah's Witnesses to accept life-saving blood transfusions is so poignant. Thus, in deciding whether to override a patient's choice, one should know whether the choice is based on an ideal or a lesser value.

But a person's sense of what is practical can be just as worthy of respect, just as authentic as his or her ideals, and just as rational as those of care givers. Moreover, a person's preference may be very ingrained. A hospitalized patient's constipation might be disregarded because the teams co-managing him or her might be absorbed by their interest in the fine-grained aspects of the patient's welfare. But ignoring the patient's values and preferences is very disrespectful even if all of his or her ideals are acknowledged. This wrong can be characterized as treating a person (a rational individual with interests) as a human (a creature subject to assessment in regard to welfare alone).

The mirror image of this wrong is to treat humans as persons. Giving in to the unsafe preferences of young children or retarded, confused, intoxicated, or psychotic individuals *may* be wrong. I emphasize "may," because there seems to be a concept that negotiates the gap between personhood and mere humanhood. This is the concept of the *self*. Its nature is a vast topic. To put the point intuitively, note that there can be a self even in the case of individuals who may not yet have reached rational personhood or have declined from it due to dementia, intoxication, or mental illness. The enduring self has a sense of continuity with its past and future, a sense of having a story it is living.[9] Selves can suffer great harm if action is taken on behalf of their welfare when their values strongly dispose them another way.

A methodological advantage to using the concept of the self is that the concept person-hood, through its connection to rationality, sets a very high standard for humans. Further-more, personhood is probably associated with more prescriptive cultural assumptions than is the concept of the self. Personhood suggests individuality. But to talk of a patient as a self may allow ready recognition that the patient does not see his or her own individuality as central, but rather sees him- or herself as a member of a family or tribe. To talk of the self allows ready recognition of the patient's preset (perhaps ethnically derived) notions about the body and expectations about the doctor-patient relationship (expectations that may not involve informed consent or confidentiality). One way of looking at the matter is that a person is a *kind* of self—the kind for whom individuality and what attaches to it is central.

Some dilemmas arise because some patients—newborns, severely demented individuals, profoundly retarded individuals—are neither persons nor selves. Other patients are selves but not rational persons. Others are marginally able to weigh risks and benefits. They have values and think in ways that tempt care givers to consider them incompetent, perhaps partly because care givers are always welfare-oriented, while patients are not.

These variations have moral implications. To care for patients as humans inclines one to treat them as *objects* of value—their existence counts most. To care for them as persons inclines one to respects their zone of autonomous decision making (what care givers value is thus irrelevant). To care for patients as selves is to not transgress against their interests (such as the joy they get from having their hair combed). When the patient has no interests at all and is incapable of regaining the capacity to have them, moral respect for the patient can only be minimal. All of this helps show the contrast between the two rival approaches to morality which I turn to now: those that direct dilemma resolving.

Social Ties

Because we can affect one another's welfare and interests for good and ill, we benefit from social ties. Because we have the means to communicate, we can create such ties, including authority, roles, shared values, ideals, ideas, language, moral theory, science, myths, economic cooperation, and prejudices.

Not all of these are wonderful. As regards dilemmas, remember that some socially created expectations can be dangerous. For example, society has idealized the family. We should not expect people to be good to each other just because they share a family. Thus, we should not turn control of a patient's health care over to someone just because they are members of the same family. Other nonwonderful ties include social prejudices such as racism, ageism, and sexism. Social ties both help and cause havoc. In this chapter, roles and morality are the two most important ties that will be explored.

MORAL THEORIES

Moral theories come in three variants: (1) those emphasizing consequences, (2) those emphasizing compliance to rules, and (3) those emphasizing dispositions to behave (what used to be called *character*). Each variant provides insights but also runs into difficulties.

Consequentialism

The consequentialist approach (sometimes called *teleological* or *utilitarian*) has us focus on effects of actions in deciding a dilemma. The best decision is taken to be the one that produces the greatest happiness (or least unhappiness). The best way to understand this approach is to see it as welfare-centered. It also tends to engender paternalism. This is because humans are not perfectly rational and patients cannot foresee how they will react or adjust to their condition, whereas an experienced professional can make fairly accurate predictions.

Aside from the problems with paternalism, difficulties of consequentialism include questions about whose experiences should be taken into consideration (those of society?, care givers?, family members?). Also, how much weight should be accorded to each person? How shall the consequences be weighed? How far into the future should we project? How shall levels of certainty influence such judgments? (Many of these questions can only be answered by having made assumptions about the third approach to morality discussed below.)

Application

To take advantage of consequentialism's strengths, be willing to live with its implications. Imposing treatment over protestations becomes much more morally hazardous if those who impose it cannot re-create the state of the patient at the time of imposition; they tend to follow the patient's choice the second time around. Sometimes the re-creation is easy. Forcing continuation of dialysis for a time is not very morally risky, since it can be discontinued if the patient's predictions are correct. Sometimes, however, re-creating the state is difficult. For example, a patient who was forced onto a ventilator may come not to need it to live, but find his or her life unacceptable anyway. Those who were willing to force the patient onto the machine might now rectify the error at the expense of killing the patient. The logic of consequentialism seems to require it. Finally, sometimes re-creating the state is impossible. The bad consequences for a Jehovah's Witness from a forced blood transfusion cannot be undone. But these consequences should not be ignored. Perhaps they justify refraining from the transfusing.

Note, too, that different individuals live with the consequences differently. A physician might not be able to sleep a wink the night after performing elective sterilization for a young woman. Even so, that sleeplessness is slight in contrast with what the woman would suffer from an unwanted pregnancy.

Deontological Theories

The deontological approach to moral decision making has us focus on obligations and duties that are specified independently of consequences. The commanding duty is to respect persons. This does *not* mean that one should esteem or value persons. Rather it means that one should respect the person's rights and the boundaries within which the person can exercise self-rule (autonomy). Rights are entitlements to protection, courses of action, goods, and control over information.

Rights are taken to belong to persons not merely as matters of social convention. Rival justifications for them exist, but we need not choose among these for most purposes of method.[10] Rights are often the basis of claims persons can make against evildoers, such as those who compromise their welfare against their will (e.g., by raping or stabbing them), and do-gooders, such as those who want to force them to adopt a religion or remain fertile. Within the limits of equal protection for all, rights protect a person's control over the holding and pursuing of the person's interests (at the personal, professional, and social levels). They protect a person from other individuals and from the all-powerful state itself.

Many rights relevant to medical ethics are well known. They include rights to the truth about diagnosis and prognosis, to confidentiality, to helpful information about the risks and potential benefits of the various tests and interventions available, and to the opportunity to freely choose among such interventions. Less well known are rights to information about the hospital's quality of care or the professional competency of consultants.

That persons possess a sphere of decision making that no one is entitled to infringe is one of the principle insights of deontological theories. This acknowledges the moral equality of persons. However, deontological theories have several important problems. Who should get which rights? What should be done when rights conflict? How shall one handle a case in which respecting a right seems likely to produce an easily avoided disaster? How far does a right extend? Controversies over what constitutes a person and issues about duties to nonpersons also present complications. These problems suggest that among the social ties an authoritative source of answers will be needed. In an ethical society, someone (or some group) will have to voice stipulative answers on behalf of the people when logic fails.

Application

This approach to morality suggests a way to distinguish the bad, the sad and the wrong. *Bad* connotes negative consequences regarding welfare or interests. *Sad* connotes negative feelings. *Wrong* connotes actions that violate boundaries of moral conduct. Rights to privacy and to informed consent are boundaries.

The moral applications of this approach begin with an instruction. Do not cross a person's boundary without authorization from (1) the person, (2) society, when it produces the authorization in a fair and publicly accepted fashion, or (3) ourselves, when a reasonable understanding of what is explicitly authorized strongly implies that if there were a process for consulting it, a fair society would allow crossing the boundary in that kind of case.[11] Not getting one of these kinds of authorization and usurping autonomy on one's own is the height of presumptuousness. It presumes that one has authority over the most private sphere of a moral equal. But be aware that going to society for permission to override a right—that is, going to court—can lead to the stipulation of rules that undermine autonomy. Respecting autonomy in such cases may lead to a sad outcome but leave us free from the encumbrances of unwise legal decisions.

Although sometimes those who answer (courts or legislatures) do provide help (e.g. in stipulating *brain death*), sometimes their answer is disastrous. For example, the law's language and ideas regarding death and dying are terribly confusing and generate moral dilemmas. Desperate attempts have been made to retain the traditional repugnance to killing, to endorse letting die, and to declare withholding and withdrawing life-prolonging interventions to be acceptable equivalents.[12] Part of the error depends on ignoring the function of social roles, which is dealt with below. Note here that if one is in a role which makes one responsible for a patient, then action and omission are moral equivalents. They do not divide in such a way that letting die is permissible and killing is not.[13] They are both morally acceptable options in some cases and both unacceptable in others, depending on what the patient chooses.

Having recognized the muddle, one might still have a dilemma about acting morally versus complying with stipulations (especially when it is the law that is stipulating). But that is not a purely moral matter. It involves one's own practical interests. The moral dimension shifts to whether there is a moral way to refuse to comply with laws that draw illogical distinctions which force great injury. If one considers the general system moral (government by consent, due process of law, law subject to public review and alteration), then disobedience is most justified when one disagrees with a particular law (not just its application to a particular case) and violates it openly, seeking a public hearing in order to alter it. Approving of the system and the particular law but disregarding both in a given case without putting oneself on the line is very self-indulgent at best. It seems to happen often, especially in "no coding" patients without authorization from an appropriate source.

The Role of Character

Many dilemmas arise from conflicts between the two approaches to ethics described above. In short, there is a controversy over the nature of morality itself! The two approaches clash when, for example, care givers feel that telling a patient the truth will discourage the patient from accepting a "needed" intervention (at least on the physician's timetable) or when a patient declines all interventions. In cases like these, the exercise of the patient's rights is thought to conflict with the patient's pursuit of his or her welfare. So when, if at all, may care givers disregard rights?[14] Before answering, I shall discuss the third approach to morality. Perhaps it will be helpful, dissolving the sense there is a dilemma in many situations that otherwise beckon care givers to override patient's rights.

This approach focuses on character or integrity. It brings us back to the fact that roles are social ties. The point is that persons will reliably know and fulfill the duties attached to a specific role only if they themselves are defined by performing its fundamental actions well.

Roles establish expectations about behavior. There are, of course, many roles: sex roles, family roles, etc. Each role forms relationships with the complementary roles with which the role holders interact. These relationships create ill-defined strata in society, along with duties and rights for each holder.

Professionals have their places in the strata and among the relationships. Through licensing and through funding education and research, society directs what the institutions and practitioners may do. What they do relates to both society at large and to patients. Until recently, patients occupied what has been called "the sick role."[15] To enter it, one needs certification from an expert (professional) that one falls below certain norms of welfare determined by science. That is part of the professional's role. While in the sick role, patients may receive official benefits (insurance, prescriptions) and unofficial ones (attention from family members). A principal official benefit is being excused from ordinary responsibilities, but one is obliged to try to recover and leave the role.[16] Assisting in the patient's recovery in ways that untrained persons could not is another part of the professional's role. This requires patients to comply with the professional's advice.

Application

Under this approach to morality, physicians who take their role as complementary to the sick role should be conditioned to do the following: (1) certify honestly, and (2) do anything to get patients out of the sick role. Dilemmas frequently arise because such built-in imperatives conflict with patients' interests and rights to choose freely. Realizing that a conflict has arisen because original aspects of the social role have been transported inappropriately to new kinds of cases should be very helpful. For example, if society creates and sustains a role for acute and unexpected conditions from which patients could recover, the role may not fit those suffering from a horrible chronic disease. To force them to conform would be an error.

One problem with the character approach to morality is the rival formulations of a role. Often a formulation is too vague to help with a problem (e.g., "The physician is a teacher"). Or what sounded fine in the abstract may seem heartless, rigid, and morally wrong when we get to cases (e.g., "The physician fights disease").[17]

Many dilemmas arise from professionals' sense of their enterprise—the "proper ideals of the profession." If society creates and sustains medicine to prolong life and restore health, letting persons die will be difficult or impossible to accept. If the purpose is to provide an effective work force, caring for a dying or unemployable person will be very difficult. If the purpose is to reduce bodily suffering in ways consistent with patients' wishes, forcing treatment on patients will be nearly unthinkable.

The ideals define what could be called the profession's "ultimate logic," its reason for being. Ultimate logic contrasts with domestic logic—the practical structures of conduct. Many such practical structures are compromises with the physical and human environment, but they eventually become norms of behavior. For example, if a policy requires CPR on *all* patients suffering cardiac arrest, it may be a compromise to avoid the emotional difficulties involved in discussing death with patients, and it may also give rise to that great hypocrisy "the slow code." Having to economize leads to rooms in which "privacy" is "provided" by curtains. Compromises with limited salaries space, time to gather information, etc., do shape day-to-day functioning.

Subscribing to the correct ultimate logic is important. The correct ultimate logic will help avoid the inspired or conscientious wronging of others. And it will help avoid making a sham of the calling to which one is dedicated. Shamming occurs if one is driven to violate fundamentals of the profession because of commitments to incidentals, such as protecting a partnership instead of a patient.

Two rival ultimate logics for health care should be assessed.

One contends that medicine exists to foster welfare. The imperative in every case, then, is to bring tests, values, etc., into line with what is scientifically indicated unless welfare itself will not be served by doing so. The domestic logic of this encourages care givers to treat even when the prospects of success are extremely unlikely and even when patients decline treatment. It encourages a plan of tests that starts with the least invasive, even if that test is the least reliable and even if the patient would accept some risk to welfare for a faster diagnosis. It inclines care givers to get court orders if patients are acting against their own welfare.[18] Thus, how the ultimate logic is defined and, once defined, how efficiency and emotional frailty effect the domestic logic raises important moral questions.

The second ultimate logic contends that health care exists to help persons pursue those interests that involve their having a human body. This includes the persons' particular interests in their own welfare. To be sure, there must be stipulations about the bounds of permissible help. (One may not help a patient hurt another person; however, one may be obliged, owing to confidentiality, to allow such injury, for example, by not disclosing to a woman that her prospective husband is a homosexual.) The domestic logic of this view would include ways to discover and honor the preferences of patients, for example, through effective living wills, patient advocates, and revised ways of history taking (so that each patient's "value history" is documented).

The rivalry between the two ultimate logics is in the background of many dilemmas. How could there be professional dilemmas unless professionals have made assumptions about or commitments to the purpose of their profession? Without a goal, no sense of seriousness could attach to making a choice. This approach leads us to distinguish those who make good surgeons because they enjoy cutting and sewing from those who like to solve medical problems and are good at cutting and sewing.

The resolution to the conflict between ultimate logics appears to be in a third option. Assume that the role of care givers is to help selves with the problems arising from their bodily nature. This is consistent with the idea that medicine exists to help selves as valuable entities, and it gives care givers license to foster a patient's welfare. Consequences for that welfare would then be nearly decisive for medical decision making.[19]

Taking selves to be the object of medicine also incorporates insights from the view that directs us to help persons with the problems arising from the nature of the body. This offers several advantages. When appropriate, it acknowledges the self as a person with rights. Second, it avoids the presumptuousness of approaching individuals as though they are not persons, treating them as something of value rather than respecting their rights. Third, it suggests the moral necessity of helping patients toward personhood, for example, by teaching children to think about risks, benefits, confidentiality, etc.

THE METHOD

1. By means of the above concepts, state the dilemma as fully as possible.
2. Assess how much of it is driven by the personal and professional biases of the care givers (e.g., inclinations to foster patients' welfare, professionals' finances, etc.).
3. Eliminate all of the biases except those of the patient.
4. Consider the case and options in light of the ethical theories. Take the option most strongly indicated by that process. If two are very close, discuss the dilemma with several reasonable persons playing the devils advocate. If the issue still seems too close to call, flip a coin.

That's it—that's the method.

But before closing, I must elaborate a bit more, and then make some theoretical remarks on the nature and limits of method.

Medical Dilemmas and Decision Making

Competent Patients

In dealing with a competent patient, use respect for autonomy and the ultimate logic of helping persons with their interests. Remember the difference between sad and bad. If the patient is exercising a fundamental right—especially in ways that do not violate the rights of others—consider the right a moral trump (i.e., as decisive).[20] Resist paternalism and appeal to consequences unless (1) you are convincingly sure (and I do not see how one could be) that informing the patient will cause his becoming incompetent and you can find a trustworthy representative of the patient's interests; (2) the patient's ideals, practical interests, or notions about the quality of experience are known and the patient seems to be speaking inauthentically (this should not be just an excuse for professionals to have their way, and the evidence should be very compelling, since none of us is a mindreader); (3) the protesting patient is unwilling to give reasons and the care giver can undo what would be forced upon the patient; or (4) the protesting patient is basing his refusal on a completely and incontrovertibly false premise, not just playing a long shot.

Assuming that there is time, one should go to court to test one's judgment that society would accept overriding the right.[21] Be very careful about doing this, though. If the ultimate logic of medicine is to help persons, care givers should be very reluctant to create legal precedents that undermine the autonomy of persons.[22]

Short of being able to get to court, one should try to test one's thinking on someone functioning as an ethics consultant. This person should work in two stages. First, from as objective a presentation of the case as possible, the person should reach his or her own decision. Second, after being told the care givers' inclinations, the person should play the devil's advocate. And if one decides not to risk violating the law and being heard in court, perhaps one should agitate for reform.

Incompetent Patients

If the patient is not competent but had a self that might be restored, try to determine what the patient would have wanted in the situation. Comply with that, not with the preferences of others (the family, care givers, or hospital administrators). Living wills, official or unofficial guardians, or "value history" should help here.

If nothing about the patient's value history is known, use *welfare* broadly considered. If a self can be restored, try to restore it. Be sure social prejudices are not operating to dilute the pursuit of welfare. Having a guardian appointed is the ideal solution, and inconvenience to care givers is not morally relevant. What is relevant is how well the guardians would do their job. There is no requirement to comply with mere ritual.[23] One really is thrown back on custom here, except that one should minimize suffering.

Newborns

Regarding newborns, society's stipulations (e.g., through law) can have acceptable moral goals. Thus, society may wish to protect newborn babies for the symbolic value of doing so. However, those that will never even develop a self (much less personhood) can hardly serve that moral purpose. If society forces parents and care givers to sustain such newborns, society should pay all monetary costs. Humans lacking a self should receive attention regarding their welfare. Usually this means they should not suffer. But there is no direct moral duty to sustain them. Morally, parents ought to be free to decide whether and how to treat them.

Nondilemmatic Decision Making

Consider two kinds of cases. First, consider persons who endanger the welfare or interests of others. Can they so abuse their liberty that they alienate themselves from some of their rights to health care? Second, consider persons in serious situations beyond their control (indeed, even barely involving them) that may threaten the welfare and interests of many others. May we override the rights of such persons in trying to defeat the threat?

Above, rights were considered to be a moral trump. However, perhaps they should not always be decisive. It seems that persons are entitled to have their rights respected unless they have done or will do something so bad that they destroy their entitlement to the right or unless the world is such that complying is impossible. Rarely is a care giver able to decide on his or her own whether either of these situations obtains. Furthermore, one should have criteria to justify overriding rights or to justify claims that persons have alienated themselves from their rights. Be sure that overriding will not undermine the point of having the right in the first place or that a thoughtful, consistent, ethic would accept the override for all persons equally.

Using the misbehavior of others and the serious needs of third parties can sometimes result in justifying too much. If misdeeds or needs are taken vaguely, one might find any previous infraction by the patient or any shortage of resources sufficient to justify depriving individuals of their rights. Strong social safeguards are supposed to protect individuals from such abuse. Primary among these is the due process of law. It provides that governmental powers must be passed into law in an elaborate way that includes being open to public scrutiny. So, too, the exercise of power must be open to review. In law, individuals can ask for judicial review both of the rules that are being used against them and of the trials in which they are litigants. Ideally such due process should protect people from the overly zealous. There should be no less in health care.

Deonotological theories, as well as the role society has constructed for care givers, imply that it is not up to care givers to decide how to allocate resources. A care giver should not decide that using a workable treatment is wasteful because the patient does not contribute to society or because he or she offends care givers in some way. This does not mean that allocation cannot be controlled in some ways. But it does mean that the criteria or policies should not be set by a patient's care givers. The hospital door should not be a trap for uninformed patients. Policy must be publicly made and subject to revision, and the consequences of its applications must be subject to review.

The best examples of this are the laws requiring care givers to report certain conditions and situations to specific authorities. That such laws are "on the books" is a mark in favor of taking them as justifying certain exceptions to the right of confidentiality. But it is just a mark in favor. The right answer is murky. We do not know whether confidentiality should be an absolute right. If medicine is a social creation, perhaps society can experiment with varying approaches to problems, collect data, and see what is the best policy.[24] Society should be able to test what is best regarding child abuse or impairment and addiction.

Cases like these draw care givers away from the ideal of helping selves with the problems they have that are derived from possessing a human body. Singleness of purpose may be more than we can hope for. But surely if we remember the difference between a role binding professionals to patients deontologically and a role making one responsible for consequences, we will recognize the duty cannot be to prevent all sad and bad things. Absolute rights are not unthinkable.

CONCLUSION

It should be part of methodology—underlying ideas about how to devise a method—to acknowledge that if a situation poses a true moral dilemma, losses should be expected no matter which option is taken. Further, it should be part of methodology to recognize that one situation can embody different dilemmas for different parties. Patients, friends, family members, medical students, physician, nurses, and janitors will likely face different dilemmas in their roles. Perhaps each needs a different method for deciding. An analysis of welfare, interests, and social ties may help all of them. The role of rights should not be further in the background for some as opposed to others. Friends are not bound to the same duties and not limited by the same patients' rights as professionals.[25] The language of political morality is more applicable to strangers taking care of strangers.[26]

Regarding the method offered above, I expect many problems to emerge. Sometimes it implies that taking a situation as a dilemma is a mistake. Those who disagree will find the method shallow or worse. Sometimes the method implies that there are moral problems that practitioners fail to notice. To those who disagree with those allegations, the method might appear picky or worse. Sometimes it implies resolutions that individuals will find morally offensive. They will want to work through the justifications of the method (the methodology) to critique the method. For example, they will want to know how to recognize a principle invoked to justify a choice. I wish there were enough methodology to do them the honor, but space forbids anything more than the incidental attention that has been paid to it. The most I can say about this is that I have found the method useful in teaching and consultation.

Sometimes, no doubt, the method will not generate a resolution. We may feel then that we need both more method and more methodology. This, however, may be naive. In many fields, methods have led to the discovery of limits to and difficulties about themselves. This holds even in former paradigms of potentially complete and absolutely certain systems of knowledge, such as advanced mathematics or advanced physics. But this does not reduce the field of study or the problem solving to insignificance, subjectivity, or relativism. "There are no right answers" cannot be used in a flip way to dismiss either cases that can be compellingly resolved after hard analysis or cases that cannot be so resolved. Regarding the former, society has made progress in its method of deciding. Regarding the latter, there is a morally appropriate way of dealing with pure, true dilemmas: Share them as dilemmas with those involved. Face the fact that serious matters are at issue. Do not allow the secondary inference that there is no right anwer to detract from the seriousness of the situation.[27]

NOTES

1. Aristotle, *Nicomachean Ethics*. 2.2.1104a5–7.

2. This contrasts with the values specified in the previous section; they seem objective, universal, rational, etc.

3. A discussion of the particulars of (2) will be offered later. A discussion of (3) belongs in the next section. I omit it from the chapter in the hope that the meaning is evident enough. For a general discussion of values see Edmund L. Erde, "On Peeling, Slicing and Dicing an Onion: The Complexity of Taxonomies, Values and Medicine," *Theoretical Medicine* 4 (1983): 7–26.

4. This could be a threatening prescription. It bears on the issue of how few dilemmas are purely moral and absent of any self-serving considerations. It also requires one to know a patient's prejudices. "Poor quality of life" may represent one thing to young, healthy, energetic, resident physicians and another to older patients or in regard to the retarded. See John A. Robertson, "Dilemma in Danville," *Hastings Center Report* 11 (October 1981): 5–8.

5. Accordingly, the term *best interests* should be avoided. It is pretentious in implying some connection with noble interests. It is presumptuous in implying that some stranger is an expert about what should interest a person. *Welfare* is much less likely to mislead. But neither *best interests* nor *welfare* does the work necessary for moral communication with patients. Both are general terms with many individual ingredients. Furthermore, neither political science nor the science of medicine provides knowledge of an ideal type. The most they can do is inform about trends within populations. We live in a pluralistic world with few certainties about how one should live or define oneself.

6. See Charles M. Culver and Bernard Gert, *Philosophy in Medicine* (Oxford: Oxford University Press, 1982). Culver and Gert distinguish irrational ideas and desires from incompetence in a helpful way.

7. Entering competition is a form of risking one's welfare. Many forms of competition risk welfare in many ways. Some people thrill to the risk. There is nothing patently immoral about such competition. And though competitors do not consent to losing, they consent to risking loss.

8. To baptize a baby known not to be Christian but brought to an emergency ward with critical injuries is wrong, but not criminally wrong.

9. See Stanley Hauerwas, "Self as Story," in *Vision and Virtue: Essays in Christian Ethical Reflection* (Notre Dame Ind.: Fides Press, 1974).

10. But it is worth identifying them. One bases rights in the kind of beings we are—persons. Rights are options to which persons are entitled. They are social ties, both because they specify the moral grounds of peaceful coexistence among persons and because social cooperation is necessary for their realization. Another account bases rights in the value of allowing persons to look out for themselves given the shortcomings of existing social arrangements. Their approaches to the right to abortion will exemplify the differences between the two accounts of rights. The first approach acknowledges women's inviolate right to privacy and bodily self-determination. The second creates a right as an "out" in a society that stigmatizes illegitimate and adopted children, has not created or made accessible safe and effective contraception, and does not decently supplement the costs of raising children.

11. See Ronald Dworkin, *Taking Rights Seriously* (Cambridge, Mass.: Harvard University Press, 1977), especially chap. 7.

12. Two opinions of the Supreme Court of New Jersey are worth reading critically in this regard: In re Quinlan, 355 A 2d 647 (N.J. 1976) and In re Conroy, 98 N.J. 321 (1985). The process laid out in Conroy has been challenged as seriously flawed. However, some of the decision's analyses are excellent. The flaws probably arise from a concern to be politically tactful or a lack of courage by the justices to face pressure groups.

13. James Rachels, *The End of Life: Euthanasia and Morality* (New York: Oxford University Press, 1986).

14. Actually not many dilemmas arise from this sphere, for patients have been found to want more information than care givers tend to give them. (Many studies show this. See, for example, William M. Strull, Bernard Lo, and Charles Gerald, "Do Patients Want to Participate in Medical Decision Making?" *Journal of the American Medical Association* 252 [1984]: 2990–94.) Also, paperwork (i.e., the informed consent form, terrible as it is) is often taken as a substitute for true consent. Rarely is a patient told all that the moral (and legal) model requires. The moral model requires offering the patient all the options so that informed choosing occurs rather than mere consenting to the physician's choice. For example, consider that physicians' professional values may include them to offer the least risky test procedure of several available ones, even though it is least likely to yield useful information. However, the patient may, for personal reasons, wish not to climb the ladder of increasingly risky procedures, but take the riskiest one first to get answers as quickly as possible.

15. Talcott Parsons, *The Social System* (New York: The Free Press, 1951).

16. That compliance is built into the patient role is in part the triumph of medicine's power play over the last century and a half. Compare Jeffery L. Berlant, *Profession and Monopoly: A Study of Medicine in the United States and Great Britain* (Berkeley, Calif.: University of California Press, 1975) and Paul Starr, *The Social Transformation of American Medicine* (New York: Basic Books, 1982).

17. For an excellent discussion of some rival characterizations of the physician's role, see William F. May, *The Physician's Covenant: Images of the Healer in Medical Ethics* (Philadelphia: Westminster Press, 1983). Part of the reason that the character approach to morality does not work fully is that we are unavoidably in the grip of history. Perhaps society's reasons for sustaining an institution are different from the reasons for having created it or sustaining it in the past. Perhaps there were several values involved in creating or sustaining an institution, and some of them conflict from time to time. It is possible that we have brought forward and feel bound to ideals that are now out of date.

18. One problem with the account thus far, though, is that professionals who subscribe to this view seem to have evolved their own focus on bodily welfare and leave a great deal out that would seem to belong in. For example, if care givers were attuned to all aspects of bodily welfare, they would note and take action about such mundane

considerations as whether a patient is uncomfortably warm or cold or needs a hearing aid, eyeglasses and/or podiatric care, even though the patient is being seen for a completely different problem. This pattern of attending only to long-term welfare tends to cause neglect of the patient who is at the end of life and suffering a great deal.

19. They could not be completely decisive, because care givers might be tempted to certify about a patient's health in the way the patient prefers, and this could become quite dangerous, for example, if the patient is a pilot.

20. I cannot say exactly what makes a right fundamental. It is connected with rules that all should agree to live by—rules that respect moral equality. But consider the difference in invasiveness between forcing a parent to live with and take care of a child on the one hand and forcing a parent to contribute economically to the support of a child on the other. The first is reminiscent of slavery. The second is simply holding a person accountable. To force someone to accept a life-saving intervention because he or she has dependent children violates the fundamental rights of the parent. Children do not have a right to be raised by their biological parents.

21. Do not consider the time qualification lightly. Economics cannot side with those who want to deprive persons of their rights. We have to keep lawyers and courts available, astute, and fair.

22. According to this ethic, it is proper (but might be sad) to help someone—even someone who is not terminally ill—die. And awful as the case may be, we should not compromise the fundamental freedom of persons to determine what happens in their own private sphere of control. We should not invade that sphere, e.g., for the sake of a fetus or even the person a fetus may become. If a law were to be made prohibiting a woman carrying a fetus from endangering it, the law would be terribly invasive. Both deontological theories and the approach to character ethics that conforms to them produce morally binding social ties between care givers and patients which require care givers to allow many sad and harmful events to occur. They probably will not happen often. See George Annas, "Forced Cesareans: The Most Unkindest Cut," *Hastings Center Report* 12 (June 1982): 16–17, 45.

23. A few studies and analyses show how this has dilemmatic dimensions. See John W. Warren et al., "Informed Consent by Proxy: An Issue in Research with Elderly Patients," *New England Journal of Medicine* 315 (1986) 1124–28; also, the companion editorial by George J. Annas and Leonard Glantz, "Rules for Research in Nursing Homes," *Ibid*. Also see Grant H. Morris, "Conservatorship for the 'Gravely Disabled': California's Nondeclaration of Nonindependence," *San Diego Law Review* 15 (1978) 201–37, esp. 225–37.

24. Marx W. Wartofsky, "Medical Knowledge as a Social Product: Rights, Risks and Responsibilities," in *New Knowledge in the Biomedical Sciences*, ed. William B. Bondeson et al.

25. Edmund L. Erde and Anne H. Jones, "Diminished Capacity, Friendship, and Medical Paternalism: Two Case Studies from Fiction," *Theoretical Medicine* 4 (1983) 303–22.

26. Robert A. Burt, *Taking Care of Strangers: Rule of Law in Doctor-Patient Relations* (New York: The Free Press, 1979).

27. I would like to thank Professors Nancy Moore and Jay Yanoff for their help with early drafts of this chapter.

BIBLIOGRAPHY

Bedell, Susanna E., and Thomas L. Delbanco. "Choices about Cardiopulmonary Resuscitation in the Hospital." *New England Journal of Medicine* 310 (1984): 1089–93. This is worth reading to get a grasp of how poor is decision making and communicating regarding DNR status decisions. Almost three-quarters of the patients suffering an arrest did so unexpectedly. Physicians and residents had different ideas about who did not want to be code status. Only 30 per cent of the patients and half the patients' "families" were consulted about code status in advance. Fifteen percent of those receiving the code were alive a year later. A third of those would have refused the code and were still sorry to have been put through it. If the physicians were consequentialists, they do not have a record of which to be proud.

Brody, Howard. *Ethical Decisions in Medicine*. 2d ed. Boston: Little, Brown, and Co., 1981. An early attempt to put ethical theory into a decision-making format. Flow chart–like instructions are incorporated. The author is a physician and holds a Ph. D. in philosophy.

Buchanan, Allen. "Medical Paternalism." *Philosophy and Public Affairs* 7 (Summer 1978): 370–90. This is a masterful critique of paternalism, both when the patient is put in the child's role and when the family is. The argument is very reminiscent of some by John Stuart Mill, who is considered a consequentialist in the sense defined in this chapter. On this view, paternalism should be rejected, because only the person who is living a life can know what fits into it best when the choices are grim. The distinction between ordinary and extraordinary is convincingly rejected as nonsensical or question begging.

———"Medical Paternalism or Legal Imperialism: Not the Only Alternatives for Handling Saikewicz-type Cases." *American Journal of Law and Medicine* 5 (1979): 97–118. As the title suggests, this essay attempts to negotiate between two opposing positions on the role of the courts in deciding not to treat terminal conditions. The rival options were articulated by Charles Baron, a professor of law who favors legal oversight, and Arnold Relman, now editor of *The New England Journal of Medicine*, who recoils from the intrusiveness of the court. Buchanan suggests ethics committees as a way of getting the best of both sides. He does not explore well enough the shortcomings of these committees, but represents the public policy dilemma very well.

Childress, James F. *Who Should Decide?* (Oxford: Oxford University Press, 1982). This detailed analysis of paternalism and the issues surrounding it is very well written and well thought out. Many kinds of paternalism are distinguished. Paternalism of most sorts requires both minimizing harm to the patient and that the patient be mentally incapable of deciding. Cases are provided and referred to as the argument develops.

Clements, Colleen D. "Bioethical Essentialism and Scientific Population Thinking." *Perspectives in Biology and Medicine* 28 (Winter 1985): 188–207. This essay offers a powerful critique of attempts to devise a formal moral theory. The critique is based on the idea that just as science gave up ideal types and began to build its study on populations and variations, so too ethics should do the same. Clements does not even sketch how the scientific paradigm should be applied to ethics. Nevertheless, I believe I have used her view in writing this chapter, especially in stressing the role of the concept of *self* over any other notion of the patient. Perhaps her view could be furthered by combining my approach and that of Jonsen, Siegler, and Winslade, which is discussed below.

Clouser, K. Danner. "The Sanctity of Life: An Analysis of a Concept." *Annals of Internal Medicine* 78 (January 1973): 119–125.

Engelhardt, H.T., Jr. *The Foundations of Bioethics* (New York: Oxford University Press, 1986). This is an exploration of the fundamental concepts and principles in bioethics. Engelhardt is a thoroughgoing deontologist. He grants government very little authority in medical matters, and holds that competency establishes very strong rights. The book is very scholarly. The author holds both an M.D. and Ph.D. in philosophy.

Engelhardt, H.T., Jr. and Edmund L. Erde. "Philosophy of Medicine." In *A Guide to the Culture of Science, Technology, and Medicine*, edited by Paul T. Durbin, 2 vols. New York: The Free Press, 1982, 1984. This is a comprehensive review of both medical ethics and philosophical issues in medicine, such as the analysis of concepts of health and disease. The volume in which the cited chapter is contained provides a survey of the issues and literature in the history, sociology, and philosophy of science, technology, and health care. Extensive bibliographies accompany each chapter.

Jonsen, Albert, Mark Siegler, and William J. Winslade. *Clinical Ethics.* 2d ed. New York: Macmillian, 1986. This has been referred to as a "Merck Manual" for ethics. The authors are highly accomplished writers on ethics who are trained in philosophy, theological ethics, medicine, and law. They categorize medical conditions according to how the condition should direct moral thinking. Chronic conditions allow patients time to think, adjust, etc.; acute onset serious diseases or injuries may require more impulsive decisions. The method they offer adjusts to kinds of medical conditions.

McCullough, Laurence B. "Methodological Concerns in Bioethics." *Journal of Medicine and Philosophy* 11 (February 1986): 17–39. This is a very keen overview of the issues concerning theories or methodologies which could give rise to methods, public policies, and medical education.

The President's Commission for the Study of Ethical Problems in Medicine and Biomedical and Behavioral Research produced several volumes in its series of reports and appendixes which are relevant to this chapter. They are major public policy statements. One volume is *Deciding to Forego Life-Sustaining Treatment. Making Health Care Decisions* is a set of volumes. Volume 1 is the *Report*; volumes 2 and 3 include studies (e.g., on informed consent and on medical education) commissioned for preparing the report and materials submitted to the Commission. Readers should remember that the *Report* is the product of a political process.

Shelp, Earl E. *Virtue and Medicine: Explorations in the Character of Medicine.* Dordrecht, Holland: D. Reidel, 1985.

Veatch, Robert M. *A Theory of Medical Ethics.* New York: Basic Books, 1981. The author gives compelling arguments for why professions may not develop their own ethics independent of those whom they serve. He attempts to provide a three-way contrast among practitioners, patients, and society to justify governmental intervention into the doctor-patient relationship when, for example, doctors learn of dangers to third parties. This book is a classic, but see the critique by John Kultgen, "Veatch's New Foundation for Medical Ethics," *Journal of Medicine and Philosophy* 10 (November 1985): 339–69.

White, W.D. "Informed Consent: Ambiguity in Theory and Practice." *Journal of Health Politics, Policy and Law* 8 (Spring 1983): 99–119. This is one of the best criticisms of the legal doctrine of informed consent.

Glossary of Key Terms and Concepts

Aesthetic. Relating to or dealing with the beautiful.

Altruism. Unselfish regard for or devotion to the welfare of others.

Appeal. A complaint to an appellate court of an error committed by an inferior court, whose decision the appellate court is called upon to correct or reverse.

Appellate Court. A court having jurisdiction of appeal and review.

Arbitration. The investigation and settlement of a matter of contention between opposing parties, by persons or organizations chosen by the parties.

Aretaic Ethics. Ethics of the kind that places the primary emphasis on the character of moral agents. In aretaic ethics, primacy is given to the dispositions, motives, and intentions of the moral agent, instead of to the ends of action (as in consequentialism) or to the rules or principles of ethics (as in deontologism).

Assault. An intentional act that is designed to make the victim fearful and that produces reasonable apprehension of harm.

Assignment. Transfer of rights or property.

Attestation. An indication by a witness that the document of procedures required by law has been signed.

Battery. The touching of one person by another without permission.

Best Evidence Rule. A legal doctrine requiring primary evidence of a fact (such as an original document).

Bill. A draft of an act presented to a legislature, but not yet enacted.

Bona Fide. In good faith, openly, honestly, or innocently; without knowledge or intent of fraud.

Borrowed Servant. An employee temporarily under the control of another. The traditional example is that of a nurse employed by a hospital who is "borrowed" by a surgeon in the operating room. The temporary employer of the borrowed servant will be held responsible for the act of the borrowed servant under the doctrine of *respondeat superior*.

Case Law. Law established by judicial decisions.

Cause. That which produces or effects a result, even though unintended.

Cause of action. Fact(s) that establish or give rise to a right for judicial relief.

Certificate. An instrument accorded by an authority competent to confer the right to perform some act (used instead of license in some states).

Circumstantial Evidence. Facts that establish a condition or circumstances from which the principal fact is a possible conclusion.

Civil Law. The law of countries (e.g., Germany and France) that follow the Roman law system of jurisprudence, in which all law is enacted. It is also the portion of American law that does not deal with crimes.

Civil Rights. Rights of a nonpolitical kind, secured to citizens by the Thirteenth and Fourteenth Amendments to the Constitution of the United States or by various state or federal statutes.

Client and Patient. The *client* is the individual who gives consent for a procedure, as well as assumes financial responsibility for services rendered and negotiates the details of what is to be done. The *patient* is the individual upon whom the procedures are done. In human medicine dealing with conscious and mentally competent adults, the same person will fill both client and patient roles. In pediatrics, the child is the patient, whereas his or her parents are the clients.

Common Law. The legal traditions of England and the United States, where part of the law is developed by means of court decisions.

Compassion. People are said to be compassionate or to show compassion if they exhibit their mercy, pity, or empathetic consideration for the pain, suffering, or harmful deprivations of others. Compassion may thus be viewed as the obverse of cruelty. (See *Cruelty*.) Whereas sadistically cruel people enjoy the suffering they cause others and brutally cruel people are insensitive or indifferent to it, compassionate people neither enjoy nor are indifferent to the suffering they cause or that is caused by others. Because the feelings of pity or of mercy are morally appropriate or fitting, compassion has the status of a moral virtue, while cruelty, because it involves morally inappropriate or unfitting feelings, is a human vice.

To say that a person is compassionate is thus both to describe *and* praise that person, whereas we both describe and condemn people when we say they are cruel. Moreover, just as there is no guarantee that those who act "with good intentions" do what is right, so there is no guarantee that those who act compassionately do the right thing or that those who are cruel do what is wrong. The *virtue of the agent* (that is, whether the person who acts has a morally admirable character, motive, or intention) is to be distinguished from the *rightness of the act.* Good people can do what is wrong; evil people can do what is right.

Complaintant. One who applies to a court for legal redress.

Confidentiality. This is fundamentally an issue of who is to control the dissemination of certain information. In the pledge of confidentiality typically found in codes of professional ethics, the professional promises not to reveal information about a patient and/or client without consent. Ethical questions are acute when protecting the confidence of a client and/or patient resulting in general social harm or infringements of the rights of other parties.

Consent. A voluntary act by which one person agrees to allow someone else to do something. For medical liability purposes, consent should be in writing, with an explanation of the procedures to be performed.

Consequentialism. The name given to ethical theories that hold that moral right, wrong, and obligation depend solely on the value of the consequences (effects, results) of what we do. There are three major options, *Ethical egoism* states that moral right, wrong, and obligation depend solely on the value of the consequences for the agent, i.e., excluding everyone else. *Ethical altruism* states that moral right, wrong, and obligation depend on the value of the consequences for everyone except the agent. *Utilitarianism* states that moral right, wrong, and obligation depend solely on the value of the consequences for everyone, including both the agent (thereby denying ethical altruism) and everyone else (thereby denying ethical egoism). The opposite of consequentialism is deontologism. (See *Deontologism.*)

Contract. A promissory agreement between two or more persons that creates, modifies, or ends a legal relation; an agreement creating legal rights enforceable by action.

Contributory Negligence. Negligence on the part of a person claiming damages for injury from the negligence of another; it sometimes affects the awarding of damages, which can be reduced or even nullified.

Criminal Law. The division of the law dealing with crime and punishment.

Cruelty. Various kinds of cruelty are distinguishable. Sadistic cruelty occurs when people enjoy making others suffer, whereas brutal cruelty is present when people are insensitive to the suffering they cause others, failing to recognize it as suffering. Again, people are actively cruel when they inflict suffering on others and either enjoy this (active sadistic cruelty) or are insensitive or indifferent to the suffering they cause (active brutal cruelty), whereas people are passively cruel when, through their inaction or negligence, others suffer and they either enjoy this (passive sadistic cruelty) or are indifferent (passive brutal cruelty). A person who enjoys beating dogs or children, for example, exhibits active sadistic cruelty; parents or pet owners who are indifferent to the suffering they cause to those in their care, because they fail to provide them proper shelter or nourishment, display passive brutal cruelty. Irrespective of the form of cruelty (active, sadistic, etc.), to say that someone ''is cruel'' is to express a negative moral assessment of that person as a person by imputing either the presence in them of morally inappropriate feelings (namely, their pleasure in inflicting or allowing suffering) or the absence in them of morally appropriate feelings (namely, pity or mercy). To the extent that people are cruel, to that extent they fall short of an ideal of human excellence. (See *Compassion.*)

Deontologism. An ethical position which claims that it is possible for us to identify a right act or a justified moral rule in other ways than by considering the goodness or badness of the consequences. Whereas teleologists hold that right acts are those which have the best consequences, deontologists may identify right acts by appeals to such things as one of Kant's categorical imperatives (e.g., always act on that maxim which you could will to become a universal law), intuitions of self-evidence, rules of behavior chosen under conditions of rational choice, divine command, authoritative religious sources, etc.

Decision. The judgment or decree of a court.

Defamation. The injury of a person's reputation or character by willful and malicious statements made by a third person. Defamation includes both libel and slander.

Defendant. In a criminal case, the person accused of committing a crime. In a civil suit, party against whom suit is brought demanding that he or she pay the other party legal relief.

Deposition. A sworn statement made out of court, which may be admitted into evidence if it is impossible for a witness to attend in person.

Descriptive Ethics. The empirical activity of describing the values, normative practices, and processes of explaining and justifying values and norms in a given cultural, social, professional, or institutional setting. This activity is to be distinguished from theoretical or critical ethics, in which one attempts to determine what is most reasonable to do or be, instead of what simply is the case.

Egoism. See *Consequentialism.*

Emergency. A sudden unexpected occurrence or event causing a threat to life and health. The legal responsibilities of those involved in an emergency situation are measured according to the occurrence.

Equality. As an ethical notion, equality may be applied either to individuals or to their interests. In the latter case, respect for equality requires that similar interests be accorded similar value or importance, no matter whose interests they are—prince or pauper, black or white, male or female. If we are to judge interests equitably, we cannot place greater value or importance on the interest one individual has in avoiding pain, for example, than we place on the comparable interest of others, whoever they may be. When equality as an ethical idea is applied to individuals (as distinct from their interests), we are asked to view and treat all relevantly similar individuals as having equal value or worth in themselves, independently of their (or anyone else's) interests. In themselves, that is, men have a distinctive kind of value. But so do women. And both have this value equally. If viewed against either interpretation of equality, one can say that moral prejudice characteristically takes the form of viewing and treating equals as if they were unequal. Thus, for example, racism and sexism characteristically discount the value or importance of either the individuals or the interests of those who belong to a certain race or sex. Utilitarians hold that individuals are treated equally if (a) their interests are considered and if (b) equal interests are weighed equally. Nonutilitarian theories that feature moral rights argue that respect for equality requires something different from this. Since certain individuals have certain moral rights (e.g., the right to life), since their rights are equal, and since possession of moral rights are independent of anyone's interests, respect for equality requires counting and respecting equal rights equally, independently of who has what interests. (See *Moral Rights* and *Consequentialism.*)

Equity. Equal treatment in justice.

Ethics Grand Rounds. A teaching and learning technique for addressing ethical and value issues in which a concrete case is reviewed and discussed and the appropriate treatment decision is determined. Frequently, a case will have one presenter and one or more discussants before general participation is solicited. This technique can be effective with a large group.

Ethics. The pattern of values and norms that are assumed and ''taken for granted'' in a given cultural, professional, or institutional setting.

Expert Witness. One who has special training, experience, skills, and knowledge in a relevant area and who is allowed to offer an opinion as testimony in court.

Extrinsic value. That which is desirable or useful as a means to an end.

Good Samaritan Law. A legal doctrine designed to protect those who stop to render aid in an emergency.

Grand Jury. A jury called to determine whether there is sufficient evidence that a crime has been committed to justify bringing a case to trial. It is not the jury before which the case is tried to determine guilt or innocence.

Guardian ad Litem. A guardian assigned to act for one who is involved in a lawsuit and who cannot, for various reasons, legally act in his or her own behalf.

Harm or Injury. Any wrong or damage done to another, either to the person, to rights, or to property.

Hearsay Rule. A rule of evidence restricting the admissibility of evidence that is not the personal knowledge of the witness. Hearsay evidence is admissible only under strict rules.

Holographic Will. A will handwritten by the testator.

Homicide. The killing of one person by another.

Humane. Marked by compassion, sympathy, or consideration for other human beings.

Indictment. A formal written accusation of a crime brought by a prosecuting attorney against one charged with criminal conduct.

Informed Consent. According to the requirement of informed consent, no procedure can be performed until the patient or client (a) has been informed of the nature of the procedure, risks, alternatives, and the prognosis if the procedure is not done; (b) has been determined to be mentally competent to give or refuse consent; and (c) has given a free and willing consent to having the procedure done. This is a principle of law and general ethics, and is included as a provision in some professional codes of ethics.

Injunction. A court order requiring one to do or not to do a certain act.

In Loco Parentis. A legal doctrine that, under certain circumstances, the courts may assign a person to stand in the place of parents and possess the parents' legal rights, duties, and responsibilities toward a child.

Instruction. Direction given by the judge to the jury concerning the law applicable to the case or some aspect of it.

Interests. An interest is something that matters in some way to some conscious living being, such as desires, aspirations, wants, goals, needs, beliefs, intentions, objectives, preferences, etc.

Interrogatories. A list of questions sent from one party in a lawsuit to be answered by the other party.

Intestate. Said of one who dies without leaving a will.

Intrinsic Value and Disvalue. An intrinsic value is something which is good or desirable for its own sake, as an end in itself. An intrinsic disvalue is something which is bad or worth avoiding for its own sake. Many things have been thought to be intrinsic goods, such as pleasure, happiness, virtue, knowledge, truth, autonomy, civil liberty, creativity, love, friendship, self-realization, beauty, satisfaction of desires, etc. Many things have been thought to be intrinsic disvalues, such as pain, unhappiness, suffering, vice, ignorance, falsehood, constraint, stagnation, hatred, enmity, lack of self-realization, ugliness, lack of desires or interests, etc.

Joint and Several. A legal doctrine under which the plaintiff may sue one or more defendants separately or all together. If the plaintiff receives a judgment, that judgment may be collected from one or more defendants, at the option of the plaintiff.

Judge. An officer who guides court proceedings to ensure impartiality and enforces the rules of evidence. The trial judge determines the applicable law and states it to the jury. The appellate judge hears appeals and renders decisions concerning the correctness of actions of the trial judge, the law of the case, and the sufficiency of the evidence.

Jurisprudence. The philosophy or science of law on which a particular legal system is built.

Jury. A certain number of persons selected and sworn to hear the evidence and determine the facts in a case.

Liability. An obligation one has incurred or might incur through any act or failure to act.

License. A permit from the state allowing certain acts to be performed, usually for a specific period of time.

Litigation. A trial in court to determine legal issues, rights, and duties between the parties to the litigation.

Majority Opinion. The opinion of the majority of judges of a court (usually an appellate court) in which their version of the facts and the law, plus their decision regarding the particular case, are set forth and explained; this is the opinion that becomes part of the case law in the area.

Malfeasance. The doing of an act that a party ought not to have done at all or the unjust performance of some act that the party had no right to do or had contracted not to do.

Malice. Conduct intended by the defendant to cause injury to the plaintiff or conduct that is carried on by the defendant with a conscious disregard for the rights or safety of others.

Malpractice. Professional misconduct, improper discharge of professional duties, or failure to meet the standard of care of a professional, resulting in harm to another.

Mandatory. Said of a court order or statute that must be obeyed.

Mayhem. The crime of intentionally disfiguring or dismembering another.

Misdemeanor. An unlawful act of a less serious nature than a felony, usually punishable by fine or imprisonment for a period of less than one year.

Moral Obligation. An obligation is something one is required (on some basis or other) to do. In the case of a moral obligation, the basis of this "requiredness" is a moral principle. In some cases (but not necessarily in all), the moral obligation arises from a specific interaction with another moral agent (e.g., a promise); often in these cases, the obligation is said to be owed to that agent. (See *Moral Responsibility.*)

Moral Problems. Moral problems present a clash of competing rights, values, or goods. Professional technical analysis may be important to the solution of these problems, but ethical analysis is necessary as well.

Moral Responsibility. A responsibility for which one is held accountable. In a moral responsibility, the basis of accountability is a moral principle. Moral responsibility differs from moral obligation (defined above) in at least two ways. First, moral responsibility is less determinate and thus generally leaves room for individual discretion about what exactly to do. Thus I may have an obligation to be on time for dinner since I promised (which is quite specific), but we would speak of the responsibilities of parenthood in a much less determinate fashion. Second, although the person to whom we are responsible must be a moral agent (as is true of obligation), it is also natural to speak of being responsible for an individual—and this individual need not be himself or herself a moral agent.

Moral Rights. Moral rights, unlike legal rights are (a) universal, (b) equal, (c) inalienable, and (d) natural. To say they are universal means they are possessed by *all* relevantly similar individuals. If people in America have a moral right to life, for example, then so do people in England and Russia, Iceland, and Iran. And no one who has this moral right has it to any greater extent than any one else—which is what it means to say that moral rights are equal. As inalienable, moral rights are not transferable. People may give their life in defense of their country or honor but none can give their right to life to another. Moral rights are natural in the sense that they are not the product of human acts or institutions. We can no more create our moral rights than we can create the molecular structure of salt. In contrast, legal rights are not inalienable (e.g., we can transfer our right to an inheritance to someone else), are not universal (e.g., not all people have the legal right to vote), and are not always equal (e.g., blacks and women did not always have the equal right to vote in America). Since legal rights are created by human acts and institutions (legislation, the courts), they are not natural.

Negligence. Carelessness, failure to act as an ordinary prudent person, or action contrary to that of a reasonable person.

Next of Kin. Those persons who by the law of descent are adjudged the closest blood relatives of the decedent.

Non Compos Mentis. Not of sound mind; suffering from some form of mental defect.

Noncupative Will. Oral statement intended as a lawful will, made in anticipation of death.

Nonsuit. A term applied to a judgment against a plaintiff who is unable to prove his or her case (involuntary nonsuit) or who refuses or neglects to proceed to trial (voluntary nonsuit). A nonsuit terminates the action without an adjudication on the merits.

Obligations. Obligations are duties which follow from ethical principles, professional commitments, or contracts and covenants, binding the person to some specific ethical action.

Opinion of the Court. In an appellate court decision, the reason for the decision. One judge writes the opinion for the majority of the court. Judges who agree with the result, but for different reasons, may write concurring opinions to explain their reasons. Judges who disagree with the majority may write dissenting opinions.

Pain and Suffering. Pain in its broadest sense includes suffering and refers to any quality of feeling which is normally experienced as disagreeable or undesirable and which we normally wish to avoid for its own sake. In a narrower sense, however, pain and suffering may be distinguished as follows. *Pain* in the narrower sense refers to localized bodily disagreeable feelings such as those resulting from bodily lesions, infections, cuts, bruises, burns, cramps, broken bones, poisons, stings, etc. *Suffering*, by contrast, refers to such nonlocalized disagreeable feelings as are involved in depression, anxiety, uncertainty, guilt, shame, grief, boredom, sadness, fear, anger, terror, alienation, loneliness, etc.

Parens Patriae. The sovereign power of the state as a guardian over pesons under legal disability, such as minors and insane or incompetent persons.

Perjury. The willful giving of false testimony under oath.

Petitioner. One who requests, in a writing addressed to a court, some form of relief against another party, called the *respondent*.

Plaintiff. The party to a civil suit who brings the suit seeking damages or other legal relief.

Police Power. The power of the state to protect the health, safety, morals, and general welfare of the people.

Power of Attorney. A legal document authorizing one to act as the attorney or agent of another.

Precedent. An earlier decision of a court considered an example or authority for an identical or similar case arising later on a similar question of law.

Prima Facie. So far as can be judged from the first disclosure; on the first appearance. A prima facie case is presented when all the necessary elements of a valid cause of action are alleged to exist. The actual existence of such elements is then subject to proof and defense at trials.

Privileged Communication. Statement made to an attorney, physician, spouse, or anyone else in a position of trust. Because of the confidential nature of such information, the law protects it from being revealed, even in court, without the consent of the person who made the statement. However, the law provides an exemption from liability for disclosing information when there is a higher duty to speak, such as statutory reporting requirements.

Probate. The judicial proceeding that determines the existence and validity of a will.

Probate Court. Court with jurisdiction over wills. Its powers range from deciding the validity of a will to distributing property.

Professional. A professional is a person who has made a specific commitment to meet a need and has received certification by a largely self-regulating body to which he or she belongs, confirming public expectations of training and skill to meet that need.

Professional Ethics. A set of ethical principles generated by a group of professionals and designed specifically to govern their professional practices. Controversy arises when principles of professional ethics appear to claim immunity on behalf of professionals from general ethical obligations, e.g., when a doctrine of therapeutic privileges is invoked to justify deception.

Professional Role Model. One who exemplifies in his or her professional activities the technical skills, value sensitivities, and personal qualities representative of the highest ideals of the profession.

Proxy Consent. Voluntary informed consent given on behalf of another who is for some reason incapable of giving it for himself or herself.

Quality of Life. A measure of the value of an individual's life *from the point of view of that individual*. This is to be distinguished from the value of the individual's life to others or to society at large. For example, a man who is quadriplegic may not be able to function as a productive member of society (and thus be a net burden from the societal perspective), but he may find life in this state quite meaningful and thus rate his quality of life satisfactory.

Regulatory Agency. An arm of the government that enforces legislation regulating an act or activity in a particular area, e.g., the federal Food and Drug Administration.

Respondent. The person who argues against a petition on appeal, generally the person who prevailed in the lower court; the appellee.

Reversed. Made void. A judgment of a trial court may be reversed by an appellate court for error or irregularity.

Right of Service. The delivery of a summons and complaint to the person named, either in person or by some other means, such as through the mail.

Rights. Rights are specific legal, moral, and/or social claims predicated of living things which bind others in their conduct towards the holder of these claims. In short, rights are claims on another's obligation. In general, moral rights are inalienable or established to ensure respect for the life or dignity of another living being.

Standard of Care. Those acts performed or omitted that an ordinary prudent person would have performed or omitted. It is a measure against which a defendant's conduct is compared.

Stare Decisis. Let the decision stand; the legal principle indicating that courts should apply previous decisions to subsequent cases involving similar facts and questions.

State Statute. A declaration of the legislative branch of government having the force of law; statutory law.

Statute of Limitations. A legal limit on the time allowed for filing suit in civil matters, usually measured from the time of the wrong or from the time that a reasonable person would have discovered the wrong.

Subpoena. A court order requiring one to appear in court to give testimony.

Subpoena Duces Tecum. A subpoena that commands a person to come to court and to produce whatever documents are named in the order.

Subrogation. Substitution of one person for another in reference to a lawful claim or right.

Suit. Court proceeding in which one person seeks damages or other legal remedies from another. The term is not usually used in criminal cases.

Testimony. Oral statement of a witness given under oath at a trial.

Thanatology. The study of various aspects of death as these relate to the dying patient and the significant individuals in his or her environment.

Tort. A civil wrong. Torts may be intentional or unintentional.

Trial Court. The court in which evidence is presented by a judge or jury for a decision.

Uniform Act. A model act created by a nonlegal body in the hope that it will be enacted in all states to achieve uniformity in the area of the law with which the act is concerned.

Utilitarianism. See *Consequentialism.*

Value. Any object or quality that is found to be desirable or worthwhile. In contrast, a disvalue is something *undesirable* and a nonvalue is something neutral with respect to value. It is important to distinguish two ''species'' of value. When an object or quality is judged to be good because it brings about, or helps to bring about, some future state of affairs which itself is judged to be desirable, then it is said to have *instrumental* or *extrinsic value.* When something is judged to be good in and of itself, independent of its consequences, it is said to have *intrinsic value.* A similar distinction can be made with respect to disvalue.

Verdict. The final declaration of a jury's finding or act, signed by the jury foreman and presented to the court.

Waiver. The intentional relinquishing of a right, such as allowing another person to testify to information that would ordinarily be protected as a privileged communication.

Index